Susan

THE AMERICAN HORTICULTURAL SOCIETY
Flower Finder

by Jacqueline Hériteau
and
André Viette
with The American Horticultural Society Staff and Consultants

to Susan

Happy Gardening!

André Viette

A Stonesong Press Book

Simon and Schuster

New York   London   Toronto   Sydney   Tokyo   Singapore

SIMON AND SCHUSTER
Simon & Schuster Building
Rockefeller Center
1230 Avenue of the Americas
New York, New York 10020

Copyright © 1992 by Jacqueline Hériteau
and The Stonesong Press, Inc.

THE AMERICAN HORTICULTURAL SOCIETY FLOWER FINDER
was developed and produced by The Stonesong Press, Inc.

Interior Design by Michaelis/Carpelis Design Associates, Inc.
Typesetting by Trufont in the United States of America
Printed and bound by Oceanic Graphic Printing in Hong Kong

10 9 8 7 6 5 4 3 2 1

Library of Congress Cataloging-in-Publication Data

Hériteau, Jacqueline.
    The American Horticultural Society flower finder / by
Jacqueline Hériteau ; with the American Horticultural Society
staff and consultants and Andre Viette.
        p.   cm.
    "A Stonesong Press book."
    Includes index.
    ISBN 0-671-72345-6
    1. Flowers—Identification.
    2. Flower gardening—United States.
    I. American Horticultural Society.   II. Title.
    SB406.93.U6H47   1992   91-27554
    635.9—dc20   CIP

Matthew 6: 28, 29

. . . Consider the lilies of the field, how they grow . . .
And yet I say unto you, that even Solomon in all his glory
was not arrayed like one of these.

ACKNOWLEDGMENTS

The purpose of this book is to help you find the flowers that will make the garden you want a reality. I developed this book in much the same way as my *National Arboretum Book of Outstanding Garden Plants*. I asked an outstanding horticultural institution to identify the nation's top "flower finders," award-winning and nationally recognized horticulturists and gardeners who know which are the truly *best*—the best of the best—flowers for each type of garden. Then I wrote about the flowers they recommended. This book deals only with flowering border plants (herbaceous flowers), no flowering shrubs or trees. I have, however, included the foliage plants, herbs, and vegetables that are wonderful with flowers. A shrub or two crept in—fuchsias, for instance—justified in my mind by the fact that we tend to group them with the container and border flowers.

As with the National Arboretum book, we used three criteria to choose the best of the best flowers: flowers that have the most lasting beauty, the greatest pest and disease resistance, and the lowest maintenance needs. My philosophy is that the use of outstanding plants makes gardening easy, and environmental pollution through spraying and excessive fertilization unnecessary.

I went to Frank Robinson, the director of the American Horticultural Society, with my concept for a book. Frank's response was that a good flower finder would have saved his new neighbors a lot of grief. That summer, they had planted one batch of luscious garden center flowers after another, but they just never grew together to form the tapestry of color that is a good garden. Frank set my proposal before the AHS Board of Directors. The members of the Board of Directors of the Society welcomed the project as a new way to reach out to the home gardener.

I wish to express heartfelt thanks to my chief consultant, Andre Viette. I can't say too much in praise of this wonderfully knowledgeable, efficient, sunny, energetic, and generous man who met my dreadful deadlines. Andre is one of those remarkable people whose contributions to their profession require the stamina of a whirling dervish, the patience of an angel, and the generosity of a saint. His life is rooted in and nourished by flowers. The Andre Viette Farm & Nursery near Fishersville, Virginia, one of the oldest privately owned nurseries of herbaceous perennials in the East, was started by Andre's father. With his wife Claire, their son Mark, and the staff, Andre supplies Wayside Gardens and other major plant retailers as well as home gardeners from a stock of over 3,000 varieties of perennials. He holds degrees in biology and floriculture (Cornell University), and every year teaches ten different horticulture courses at Blue Ridge Community College. Andre also conducts a radio gardening program for WSVA in Harrisonburg. He has won many professional awards. Andre serves on the Advisory Council of the U.S. National Arboretum, and on the AHS Board of Directors, is a director of the Lewis Ginter Botanical Garden, and presently serves as president of the 1200 member Perennial Plant Association.

It was Andre, with an assist from Frank Robinson, who undertook the huge job of identifying the 70 or so outstanding flower finders I wanted and, one by one, enlisted them as sources for the project. He also edited my entire text, checked every flower list, and passed it on to the source for further editing with, when necessary, his recommendations. The AHS supporters who chose the flowers for my lists are a wonderful group to work with because, like Andre, they genuinely enjoy growing flowers and helping others to do it.

In addition to all the editing, Andre contributed many of the photos in the book from his personal collection of over 30,000 slides. Andre also checked all the other slides and their 450 captions. With Mark Viette, Andre provided three important flower finder lists—poppies, phlox, and the list of flowers for the seashore and other sandy places. That particular list is the outcome of test plantings of 459 varieties of plants grown by the Viettes over a five-year period both at the shore and 600 feet from the ocean—a measure of the depth of knowledge our flower finder sources have brought to the project.

I am very grateful to Claire Viette, who took my hundreds of phone calls, and to Mark Viette and staffer Bonnie for hours and days of photo research and other assistance.

My thanks also to the U.S. National Arboretum for providing the USDA Plant Hardiness Map on page 286 of this book. The hardiness zones I have given for each plant are keyed to this map. They indicate the temperature range in which each plant is generally most successful.

In preparing to write this book, I studied issues of *American Horticulture* magazine covering the last 10 years, and wish to thank Pat Connaughton and the staff of the AHS for their help in this, and my friend June Steward and daughter Holly Hunter. My deepest gratitude is to my husband, Earl Hubbard, for his unfailing encouragement, his wise counsel, and his patience with years of deadlines.

My thanks also to Anne Halpin, garden editor extraordinaire, James Gullickson, a thorough copy editor, Sylvan Michaelis, a meticulous designer, and Teresa Mamone Colavito, who turned my word processing into a typesetter's gift.

The pool of talented gardeners from which the flower finder recommendations were drawn is very broad and glittering. I am truly in awe of the knowledge each one has of his/her area of flower culture. For their great contribution to the book I thank each one.

Jacqueline Hériteau
Washington, D.C.

Fast-growing annual, Love-in-a-mist, *Nigella damascena*. See List 72, To Dry for Winter Bouquets. (Viette)

CONTENTS

. . . .
Miniature pumpkins and morning glories share a rustic trellis in a garden combining strawberries, lettuces, tomatoes, and other food plants with flowers—among them, marigolds, geraniums and, in shady places, impatiens. See List 78, Flowers with Vegetables. (Creasy)

Chapter Three: ANNUALS—
THE ONCE-ONLY FLOWERS 119

Chapter Four: WORKHORSES
OF THE GARDEN 155

SPECIAL PERFORMANCE FLOWERS

FOLIAGE PLANTS FOR CONTRAST

FOREWORD

This book fulfills a dream of the American Horticultural Society—to see the brightest horticultural minds in America come together in a reference book on herbaceous flowers and garden plants of unique value to gardeners. It also is the first AHS compendium of the "best" flowers. By "best" we mean beautiful flowers that thrive with a minimum of pesticides, irrigation, and maintenance.

The Society is grateful to Jacqueline Hériteau for the high standards she set as author. We particularly thank André Viette and the seventy outstanding horticultural experts who donated their time and knowledge to benefit the AHS and American gardeners everywhere. Their generosity will long be appreciated.

On behalf of the Board of Directors, I extend a cordial invitation to all home gardeners to join the thousands of AHS members dedicated to beautifying and preserving our planet. Our commitment is to keep adults and children aware of the importance of plants in every aspect of our lives. Join us.

The Society's monthly publications, educational programs, lectures, symposia, and special events are headquartered at historic River Farm in Virginia, surrounded by flower gardens and collections donated by major American plant societies. This 27-acre garden park on the banks of the Potomac River once belonged to George Washington and was purchased for the Society through the generosity of the Enid A. Haupt Charitable Trust—it is a lovely place to welcome members.

A wealth of outstanding American resources has made this book possible. You have the best of the best guiding you along, and we are very pleased to have had the opportunity to bring it to you.

For membership and other information:
American Horticultural Society
7931 East Boulevard Drive
Alexandria, VA 22308
1-800-777-7931

Frank L. Robinson
Executive Director
American Horticultural Society

Sure star of the wild meadow garden in summer is lavender lythrum. It thrives almost anywhere—in good garden soil, dry soil, boggy soil, even in standing water. See List 15, Summer Perennials for Sun, List 59, Wet, Boggy Soils, and List 57, Seashore and Sandy Soils. (Viette)

SOURCES

The experts who contributed to the plant lists in this book are credited at the end of each list, but here I wish to thank them all individually for their generous assistance.

John Mason Allgood, a horticulturist and the contributor of the daylilies list, grows over 3,500 daylily cultivars in his garden in Walterboro, South Carolina. Some of his daylily introductions have won international awards. He has been editor of *Daylily Journal* and other publications.

Suzanne Frutig Bales, director, W. Atlee Burpee & Co., is a garden designer, author, and photographer noted for her interest in long-season beauty and native plants. She contributed the marigolds, petunias, and zinnias list.

George C. Ball, Jr., president of the FlowerSeed Group, George J. Ball, Inc., and current president of the American Horticultural Society, contributed the begonias, impatiens, and salvias lists.

Dr. David J. Beattie, associate professor of ornamental horticulture at the Pennsylvania State University, recommended asters and astilbes. Dr. Beattie runs a wholesale nursery specializing in *Astilbe*, and has published more than 100 scientific and popular articles and textbook chapters on horticulture.

Kurt Bluemel, the founder and president of Kurt Bluemel, Inc. Landscape Design-Construction and Nurseries, helped introduce ornamental grasses to this country in the 1960s. He grows over 500 varieties, follows extensive testing programs for new varieties and cultivars, and searches out wild grasses in America, Europe, and Africa. He supplied the list of ornamental grasses for the flower garden. His assistant, Janet Draper, helped with editing.

M. Kent Brinkley, ASLA, a landscape architect and the Garden Historian for Colonial Williamsburg, assisted with introductory notes for the historic garden list.

William Brumback, of the New England Wild Flower Society's Garden in the Woods, Framingham, Massachusetts, contributed the fern, wildflower, and woodland garden lists. Garden in the Woods researches and preserves native plants by demonstrating and teaching their horticultural value.

Dr. H. Marc Cathey, director of the U.S. National Arboretum, and my mentor and friend, spent nearly three decades at the USDA's Agricultural Research Center in Beltsville, Maryland. He was a major source of information on culture and planting, and supplied names of flowers for children to grow.

LuAnn K. Craighton, an interpretive naturalist with the Education Department of Callaway Gardens, Pine Mountain, Georgia, manages the

Callaway ornithology program. She provided the list of flowers that attract butterflies and hummingbirds.

Rosalind Creasy, a landscape designer and author, is closely associated with the concept of edible landscaping and is famous for the remarkable beauty of her West Coast flower gardens. She provided the list of flowers that combine beautifully with food plants.

Dr. A.A. DeHertogh, professor of horticultural science at North Carolina State University, has conducted research on flower bulbs for 25 years. He assisted with the bulbs lists, particularly tulips and bulbs for the South.

Woodrow F. Dick, Jr., provided the AAN Nursery Crops Coding-System in the Index for the American Association of Nurserymen.

Michael Dodge, a horticulturist with White Flower Farm, Litchfield, Connecticut, assisted with begonias.

Dr. Theodore R. Dudley, a research botanist and internationally recognized plant scientist on the staff of the U.S. National Arboretum, assisted with nomenclature. Dr. Dudley is botanical consultant for numerous organizations and general editor for Dioscorides Press.

Rudy Favretti, ASLA, Professor Emeritus, Landscape Architecture, University of Connecticut, and a practicing landscape architect and historian, provided plant names for the historic garden list.

J. Barry Ferguson, a botanist, horticulturist, author, and award-winning and internationally known floral designer, gave us the names of plants whose foliage gives form and texture to the flower garden. He also recommended flowers for the cutting garden and to dry for winter.

Viki Ferreniea, a horticulturist and the assistant horticultural director for Wayside Gardens, has held horticultural and curatorial positions at a number of institutions, including the New York Botanical Garden and the New England Wild Flower Society's Garden in the Woods. She recommended flowers for the list of perennials for the South, primroses, violets, pansies, and annuals for shade and for fall.

Ryan Gainey, the foremost designer of cottage gardens, a horticulturist, and co-owner of retail centers for garden and party design in Atlanta, is known for classic garden designs. He contributed information on garden planning and design, and the plant list for cottage gardens.

Margaret Gitts, a horticulturist, breeder, and owner with Nick Gitts of Swan Island Dahlias, Canby, Oregon, the largest dahlia nursery in America, provided the list of dahlias.

Charles H. Goodwin, a talented amateur gardener, has since 1974 devoted his time to a search for the perfect annual. He has conducted trials of 900 types of annuals in some 2,500 separate plantings in his garden in Sherrill, New York. He contributed the lists of annuals for the full sun, that self-sow, and to grow indoors.

Pamela Harper, a horticultural author, photographer, and lecturer, has gardened in England, Connecticut, Maryland, and Virginia. She contributed the list of campanulas.

Bunch-flowering tulip 'Georgette', bears several blooms on each stem. See List 12, Tulip. (Heath)

Brent Heath, a nurseryman, lecturer, and consultant, was the primary source of information for bulbs. He is a world authority on daffodils, and internationally known for the development of flowering bulbs. Brent and his wife Becky hybridize bulbs on the original Heath farm in Gloucester, Virginia.

Robert Hebb, a distinguished horticulturist and the director of the Lewis Ginter Botanic Garden in Richmond, Virginia, shared information on garden planning and design, and gave recommendations for the first five perennials lists.

Michael Kartuz, of Kartuz Greenhouses in Vista, California, assisted with begonias.

Roy G. Klehm, a horticulturist, peony breeder, and nurseryman, is past president and director emeritus of The American Peony Society and owner of Klehm Nursery in South Barrington, Illinois. He has introduced numerous peonies to the market and recommended peonies for this book.

Anne S. Lowe, president, Historic Iris Preservation Society and editor of *Roots: Journal of the Historic Iris Preservation Society*, and Michael B. Lowe, editor, *Reblooming Iris Recorder,* contributed to the iris list.

Clarence E. Mahan, an iris hybridizer, the owner of The Iris Pond Nursery and president of the Society for Japanese Irises, also contributed to the iris list.

Byron Martin, of Logee's Greenhouses in Danielson, Connecticut, assisted with begonias.

Laura Coogle Martin, a biologist, naturalist, journalist, and author of several important books on wildflowers, developed the list of plants for the meadow garden.

Elvin McDonald, director of Special Projects for the Brooklyn Botanic Garden, and an author and columnist, assisted with begonias.

Frederick and MaryAnn McGourty, owners of Hillside Nursery in Norfolk, Connecticut, specialize in uncommon perennials and garden design. Both well-known authors, educators, and consultants, they contributed the lists of plants for hot, dry conditions and boggy soils as well as the list of rare and choice plants.

Everett L. Miller, a landscape designer, source director for Live Oak Gardens in Louisiana, and former director of Longwood Gardens, provided information on garden planning and design, as well as the lists of exotic bulbs, and perennials for indoors.

Lynden B. Miller, a distinguished garden designer, holder of the National Landscape Design Award, director of New York's Central Park Conservatory Garden, and garden designer for the New York Botanical Garden, contributed information on garden planning and design, and the list of plants interesting in winter.

Nickolas Nickou, M.D., is an amateur gardener whose two thirty-year-old rock gardens have benefited from collecting trips to many parts of the world. He supplied names of easy alpine plants and flowers for the rock garden list.

Wolfgang Oehme and James van Sweden, Washington, D.C., landscape architects whose names are closely associated with some of the most famous grass gardens in this country, assisted with the list of ornamental grasses.

Ed R. Rasmussen is founder of The Fragrant Path, a nursery specializing in seeds for perfumed flowers, P.O. Box 328, Fort Calhoun, Nebraska. He was the author's second consultant on the list for fragrant flowers.

Rayford Clayton Reddel is an author and the founder and co-owner of Garden Valley Ranch, Petaluma, California, a nursery devoted exclusively to fragrant plants and roses. He recommended the fragrant flowers.

Tom Robertson served as the author's computer consultant.

Osamu Shimizu, a botanist, horticulturist, and internationally known landscape designer, was trained in landscape design in Japan. He prepared the list of plants for Japanese gardens.

Dr. Steven Still, professor of horticulture, Ohio State University, an author, photographer, and executive secretary of the Perennial Plant Association, contributed lists of plants to use as edgers, climbers, ground covers, and for colorful foliage.

Alex Summers, a retired professional gardener, founded The American Hosta Society and served as its president for ten years. More than 1,000 hosta species and cultivars thrive in his four-acre garden. He contributed the list of hostas.

Donna M. Swansen, president of the National Association of Professional Landscape Designers, provided information on garden planning and design.

Barbara C. Vaughan and the Old Dominion Chrysanthemum Society of Falls Church, Virginia, a chapter of the National Chrysanthemum Society, provided the list of mums.

Andre Viette was a major source of information on culture and planting, and the primary consultant for the general text on perennials. He also recommended the plants for seashore and sandy soil.

Mark Viette, a third-generation horticulturist and general manager of the Andre Viette Farm and Nursery in Fishersville, Virginia, supplied the lists of phloxes and poppies.

Julius Wadekamper, M.A., past president of the North American Lily Society and a trustee for the Society's Research Trust, is the founder of Borbeleta Gardens, Faribault, Minnesota, specializing in lilies and irises. He has introduced several distinguished lilies into culture, and serves on the board of directors of several important plant societies. He prepared the list of lilies.

Janet Walker, an author and the curator of the National Herb Garden at the U.S. National Arboretum, provided the lists of herbs.

Linda Yang, a well-known author and columnist for the "Home" section of *The New York Times* since 1979, supplied the recommendations for bulbs that succeed in containers, flowers for urban conditions, and plants for container gardens. She is the author of *The City Gardener's Handbook: From Balcony to Backyard* (Random House).

Among many distinguished works I consulted in writing the text were: *Herbaceous Perennial Plants* by Allan M. Armitage (Varsity Press, Inc., Athens, Ga.); *Perennials for American Gardens* by Ruth Rogers Clausen and Nicolas H. Ekstrom (Random House, Inc., New York, N.Y.); *Gardening with Perennials* by Joseph Hudak (Timber Press, Portland, Ore.); *The American Horticultural Society Encyclopedia of Garden Plants* (Macmillan, New York, N.Y.: A Dorling Kindersley Book); *Wyman's Gardening Encyclopedia* (Macmillan), and books on specialized garden subjects written or recommended by the plant finders named here. Botanical and common names conform to *Hortus Third*, prepared by the L.H. Bailey Hortorium, Cornell University. For easier reading, you will find in the plant lists in this book that genus, species, and variety names are set in boldface roman type rather than italics.

The codes assigned to species in the Index are from the Nursery Crops Coding System of the American Association of Nurserymen. Include the code when buying plants to make sure the plant you buy is the one you want—not an unproven look-alike.

Photography

My thanks to the following amateur and professional photographers who took the time and made the effort to ransack their slide collections and libraries for just the right pictures to illustrate their own and other lists.

All-America Selections
American Horticultural Society
Suzanne Frutig Bales
George J. Ball Seed Company
Dr. David J. Beattie
W. Atlee Burpee & Co.
Callaway Gardens
Colonial Williamsburg
LuAnne K. Craighton, Callaway Gardens
Rosalind Creasy
Dr. A.A. DeHertogh
Denham Seed Co.
Viki Ferreniea
John M. Frease
Margaret Gitts, Swan Island Dahlias
Charles H. Goodwin
Pamela Harper
Brent Heath

Roy G. Klehm
Longwood Gardens
Anne and Michael Lowe
Elvin McDonald
Lynden B. Miller
Netherlands Flower Bulb Information Center, Sally Ferguson
Erik Neuman
New England Wild Flower Society
Nickolas Nickou, M.D.
Oehme, van Sweden & Associates, Inc.
Pan American Seeds, Meredith Shank, and Photo Librarian Lisa Segroves
Holly Shimizu
Osamu Shimizu
Dr. Steven Still
Stokes Seed Co.
James van Sweden
Andre Viette
Julius Wadekamper
Wayside Gardens and Geo. W. Park Seed Co.
Williamsburg Restoration
Tom Woodham for Ryan Gainey
Linda Yang

PART ONE:

Getting To Know Your Garden

FLOWERS—THE PLAN

The best designers say their intention is to plan a garden that looks as though God just dropped the flowers there. But gardens that delight and endure aren't accidents and they are never really finished—thank heavens! The hard part is to learn enough about flowers so that you can choose groups that come into bloom in waves of color from early spring to late fall—and are interesting in winter. Happily, the flower finders who contributed to this book have named the best for you. Their recommendations for every garden purpose are set out in the 78 lists that follow.

To plan a flower garden you don't need a degree in design. You need a dream. So take a rocking chair out to your garden and sit with the flower finders in your lap. Together you will dream up a wonderful flowering sequence for spring, for summer and for fall, and decide what to do about winter. An artist who is now a leading garden designer has color for that fourth season all worked out—see list 49.

Sequence of Bloom

The flower finder lists are divided into five chapters. Each chapter begins with a general introduction to the group. The first three chapters organize the flowering sequences of the flowers for you: Chapter One—Bulbs; Chapter Two—Perennials; Chapter Three—Annuals. The first lists in each chapter deal with timing: 1. Early Spring, Specialty Bulbs. The other lists in each section deal with plants for special purposes: for containers, for naturalizing, for growing indoors, and so on. And because some bulb flowers and perennials are less adapted to no-frost regions, there are special lists for the South. It's wonderfully comforting to know these flowers are the best "doers," stamped with an expert's approval. The last lists in Chapters One, Two, and Three are devoted to the major bulbs, annuals, and perennials.

Before you buy or plant, make a rough drawing showing flower beds with the positions, names, and colors of the major perennials on lists 20 to 30. The big perennials are the heart and soul of the garden and they come back next year. The fall asters, big silky peonies, oriental poppies, feathery astilbes, and essential phloxes will be taller than the bulb flowers in summer, but in spring groups of bulbs can easily come up among them.

In estate gardens tulips and even daffodils often have beds of their own. After the bulbs fade out these are given to annuals such as marigolds and petunias. In a home landscape the big bulbs are effective grouped in planting pockets—minigardens by the steps, the garage wall, in an angle of the fence. But they also work out beautifully as part of a mixed flower bed.

The annuals are planted in late spring, summer, and early fall as quick color to fill empty or dull spaces. In the garden's early years annuals usually are already blooming when they are bought—on irresistible impulse. Maybe you can stop yourself from impulse buying at the supermarket by shopping after a meal, but I've never been able to resist impatiens, marigolds, ageratum, or snapdragons just waiting to fill containers and baskets—so able to complete the summer garden and hide my failures. I find I add a few annuals every couple of weeks well into midsummer. And when the garden dies out in fall, in go the showy ornamental brassicas and mums which I grow as annuals and discard in winter. Washington, D.C., heat being what it is—antithetical to pansies and primroses—I grow these as cool-season annuals, too. They thrive under the fringe tree and the flowering plums, the dogwood and weeping cherry. In good years they live through winter and summer heat as well.

Color Combinations

Big flower borders are made up of modules—combinations of flowers and foliage plants that make a pleasing pattern—repeated.

Now, about color. In any bed 4 feet long and up, a flower here and a flower there—a scrap of red here and a scrap there—have no impact. Set out enough plants of each flower and color to make a strong statement. "Enough" in a 4-foot area means you should plant three or four each of plants the size of geraniums or Dusty-millers. In a window box or in a narrow ribbon of edging one of each might be enough. By autumn the annuals especially flame up and bush out.

You can strengthen a color chord by repeating it in other nearby flowers.

White binds and harmonizes the colors. It can be a white flower—Baby's-breath, impatiens—or a silver-white foliage plant such as the perennial artemisias or the annual quick-fill Dusty-miller. Plant lots of fragrant white or pale yellow flowers in gardens seen at night.

Baby's-breath, by the way, is one of the best "fillers." A filler is an airy, bushy plant used to contrast with strong architectural plants—like Scotch Thistle—and bring the other plants into harmony. But many flowering plants have dainty leaves, and adding fillers isn't often necessary.

Bright yellow in the garden is like sunshine. Andre Viette loves it in the spring garden and designer Ryan Gainey dares to combine bright yellow yarrow with pink roses. Most colors work wonderfully together if the plant combination includes interesting texture and structure. In designing your own garden, dare everything at least once.

....

An exuberant example of the romantic cottage garden. Irises, foxgloves, larkspur, lamb's-ears and roses bloom above the rising foliage of next season's flowers. This is the home garden of Ryan Gainey, of Atlanta, Georgia, famous for his cottage garden designs. (Woodham)

Sometimes I find I must mix the colors in the garden rather than in my head. If a group of colors doesn't have the desired effect, try adding a strong color to the group. Just one or two red or cherry impatiens, garnet mums, hot pink petunias, or clear orange calendulas can pick a color scheme right up. If you find the garden has too much strong color, add white flowers to tone down the colors.

Another approach is to make a garden of shades of a single color. White gardens and blue gardens are much loved, if not easy to keep up all season. But it is simple enough to put together three or four plants of one color that will bloom together for a brief time. Blue softens the greens of the garden and heightens reds, pinks, and lavenders. But many blue flowers without pink or pink-lavender nearby can fade into the greens; the blue-lavender of irises and pansies, however, has enough pink in it to stand alone.

Form, Structure, Texture

The first 42 flower finder lists in this book make planning for colorful flowers in all four seasons easy. They're like having expert flower finders on the other end of the telephone recommending plants. But flowers aren't the only source of garden color. Learning to know and use showy foliage plants such as caladium and coleus, and silvery white artemisia and Dusty-miller gives you more versatility when designing your garden. Chapter Four is an introduction to the many uses of foliage in the flower garden. In addition to color, foliage plants are used to bring in contrasts in form, structure, and texture. Nature mixes forms and textures in her gardens as well as colors—and so must we or the garden seems boring and somehow not quite right.

A basic rule of garden design—and you'll follow it instinctively—is to combine contrasting flower structures. The basic structures are obvious: spires and spikes, loose racemes, feathery panicles; think of snapdragons and astilbes. There are also flat-topped corymbs, umbels, cymes, and flowerheads; think of yarrow and Queen-Anne's-lace. (I tend to call all these flowerheads because they aren't always easy to tell apart.)

It is also important to think about flower forms. There are daisy-faced forms, bell-like, usually pendent forms (Lily-of-the-valley, for instance), upward-facing funnel forms, globes (such as ornamental onions), and salverform types of which nicotiana is an example. Play with contrasting forms and structures this year and in future years until you find groups that you just love. That's what designing is, an exploration of your own concepts of beauty.

When you are making flower choices, take into account what your flower finder says about the form and texture of the foliage. Is the leaf shape a real asset? Will the foliage last after blooming is over? Good foliage makes an excellent filler all season long—aquilegia and irises are two of the best. It is an error to plant together ten or fifteen flowers that all have half-inch oval leaves. You need big leaves, small leaves, spiky leaves, leaves that are very rough and very smooth, and very dull and very shiny. Plant herbs for their foliage, too. The major foliage plants—hostas, ferns, and ornamental grasses—have as much beauty as flowers once you learn to see it.

Chapter Four also offers selections of flowers and foliage plants that solve site problems—bare stone walls, cold, heat, drought, wet, sand, city pollution. And others that add a little spit and polish. Use the flowering

Yellow, the sunshine color, combines well with others when there's lots of green around. Ryan Gainey's daring combination pairs pink roses and achillea 'Coronation Gold'. (Woodham)

edgers to create ribbons of color to separate the garden from the lawn and lead the eye to, or away from, objects. Use ground covers to transform bare spots under trees. Use flowering climbers to soften harsh outlines and hide architectural mistakes. Fill weedy corners with wild flowers that will displace the weeds and some morning surprise you with unexpected bouquets.

Classical Garden Designs

The last flower finder lists in Chapter Five offer a sampler of classical garden themes—flowers for rock gardens, herbs, cutting flowers, fragrance flowers, drying flowers, flowers to grow with vegetables. They also introduce a few of the traditional garden concepts and collectors' themes—the historic garden, the woodland garden, the fragrance garden, and so on.

You will learn a lot about gardens and yourself by studying the differences between the classical cottage garden and the Japanese garden—two dominant designs that are polar opposites. Plant-finder Ryan Gainey's cottage garden in Atlanta, like the meadow garden, represents nature captured and rioting in explosions of romantic color and contrasting form. Conversely, in a Japanese garden the plant combinations never shout or amplify. Water is always a presence, though not necessarily there in person. No bold, brash colors are introduced. A cottage garden appeals to the senses. A Japanese garden invites the spirit.

To these dominant themes we can add one that recently has stepped into nearly all designs—the New American Garden. It's a neo-prairie whose signature is ornamental grasses. Even garden designers who have no intention of imitating a prairie are using grasses for their marvelous linear quality, their movement and sound, and ease of culture. Kurt Bluemel's ornamental grass recommendations for home gardens are given in list 53. Use tall types as laborsaving espaliers against blank walls—they turn golden and wonderful in winter. Use the smaller types as hummocks and clumps to soften corners, medium sizes as contrast to the ubiquitous oval leaves of the flowers.

Take All the Time in the World

Spend lazy hours in your rocker and get this book really dog-eared. In gardening the process—not the product—is the point. The flowers, foliage, and stems, the birds and butterflies and worms—all these are sustained by forces well beyond our control. Gardens are expressions of an invisible truth. The experience is substantially lessened unless we submit to it.

Planning from a garden rocking chair can restore the five senses to their proper sharpness. Hearing once more discerns the crickets, bees in the monarda, birds tattling on the cat hiding in the thicket.

Vision sharpens to note the barely perceptible leaf droop that means plants need water now. We perceive what is almost beyond perception, a ridge where a tulip presses toward the sun from the dark, wet winter of the soil.

And the sense of smell, what a primeval alarm system! Let the garden teach you to smell the earth, to know by the smell of raw wood chips that it's raining in distant hills. You will learn to sniff the coming of snow so you can save the last of the basil; draw deeply on the hot noon scent of mint and lavender and summer savory.

Indulge your senses of taste and touch, too. Taste the mint tips, smaller than a seed, plucked to garnish raspberries and cream. Taste the chives. Touch the silken petals of crinkled poppies. Caress the furry, moist lamb's-ears. Pinch the snapdragons between finger and thumb and see the miniature lion's maw roar. Stroke fuzzy flowers like ageratum and astilbes.

Go barefoot into the garden. Feel between your toes the difference between cool, moist, soft earth in which very small, amazingly strong roots can grow—and the hard-packed dirt to which only a French marigold can bring life.

Garden design is an art of the heart and hands and knees, seasons and time—not at all a science—and there's no hurry.

Make It Sing:
Make a plan for a garden that sings.
It should make you feel better in some way
for having been there.
If it doesn't raise you up,
if it doesn't give your soul a lift,
it has missed the point.

Key to Good Design:
Think of the garden as a group
of colors, textures, and forms —
a collage, a painting
you keep changing and perfecting.

Keep It Healthy and Easy:
Use only outstanding plants—that
makes gardening easier and
environmental pollution unnecessary.

Gainey combines three lavender-blue flowers of contrasting heights and textures to make a strong, exciting color statement: pansies, forget-me-nots, irises. (Woodham)

GROWING FLOWERS

My first flower garden was composed of perennials—irises, tuberoses (yes, tuberoses), and violets among them—inherited from the north Vermont farmer who sold us the house. The only thing in the world it needed was admiration. This encouraged me to fill a steep, boulder-strewn hollow with dirt and call it a rock garden. In spring I planted flowers and discovered the importance of knowing the names of plants you bed with. My flowers were beautifully illustrated, had romantic names, and/or came with lush foliage in flats from the supermarket. By August stringy 2-foot blue flax were waving at the foot of the rockery while drooping petunias crawled around at the top, lost in a forest of salvias. The next year great patches were barren—I didn't know that annuals don't come back. And since no one had mentioned the bulbs that should have been planted the previous fall, my slope was bare, oozy mud until May.

Simply put, the herbaceous flowers perform in ways that have given rise to three major categories: bulbs, perennials, and annuals. In addition, each flower has individual quirks and needs and established attributes—color, height, bloom season, and so on.

Plants are identified by a system of Latin nomenclature originated by the Swedish botanist Linnaeus. A plant's first name is the genus to which it belongs and is given in Latin—*Phlox*, for instance. (Groups of similar species make up a genus.) Next comes either the name of the species—*Phlox drummondii*, Annual Phlox—or its variety name. Varieties that nature created have Latin names—*nana*, for instance. Varieties selected or developed by horticulturists are given names in the language of the country of origin, such as 'Miss Lingard'.

'Miss Lingard', an established perennial cultivated variety ("cultivar") of the genus *Phlox*, is a mildew-resistant beauty. Cultivars are bred for performance as well as beauty. (Viette)

To be legitimate, a cultivated variety name must be published with a description in agreement with the *International Code of Nomenclature of Cultivated Plants*. A cultivar name appears in Roman type, enclosed in single quotes, like this—'Miss Lingard'—unless it is preceded by the words "cultivated variety." In that case the single quotes are dropped and the name appears as the cultivated variety Miss Lingard. Species and varieties may vary in color, be perennial or annual, bloom early or late, be tall or low. Variations on all these themes have been created for the most desirable flowers.

There is no such thing as an accurate common name for a plant. Common names are different all over the world and are not much help in locating plants. Even where a language is shared, as in the U.S. and Canada, common names change from region to region. Those given in this book are from *Hortus Third*, a major reference work compiled by the staff of Cornell University's L.H. Bailey Hortorium. Most of the names are

---

Cultivar: Cultivars are plants courtesy of gardeners, not nature. They are developed, selected variations and hybrids—deliberate crosses. For example, **Iris sibirica** variety **alba** occurs in and originated in the wild—in natural habitats. But **Iris sibirica** 'Cathey's Perfection' was selected by gardeners from plants under cultivation. 'Cathey's Perfection' is a cultivated variety, or cultivar.

In botanical literature the word "variety" is reserved for variants of a species *that occur in the wild or natural habitat*. It should not be used instead of, or confused with, "cultivated variety"—which has been shortened to "cultivar"—indicating a variant developed in cultivation.

In this informal border the color of the summer perennials, dainty yellow coreopsis and pink and rose achillea, is enhanced by annuals in complementary shades—golden-toned marigolds and red and maroon verbenas. (Viette)

Hybrids: Hybrids are crosses between plant species or genera. Sometimes a hybrid is attributed to one species and sometimes to another. An example is **Colchicum** 'Waterlily', a hybrid between **C. speciosum** and **C. autumnale**. In some works it is listed as a cultivar of **C. autumnale**, elsewhere as a cultivar of **C. speciosum**. It also is correctly written **C. speciosum** × **autumnale** 'Waterlily'—information that is useful to advanced gardeners and plant lovers.

Peony 'Krinkled White' is a magnificent example of one of the longest-lived perennials. Although perennials come back in the spring, to stay in top form most require attention every four or five years. (Klehm)

British antiques included for their charm—for example, Love-in-a-mist and Wild Fennel for *Nigella damascena*. Nothing makes a taxonomist angrier than a new common name, and it is far easier to order exactly the plants and seeds you want if you know their correct botanical names.

Giving the correct name is a way of asking for that plant's attributes and performance. The more exact you can be about the name, the more likely you are to get a plant that does what you hope it will do. *Phlox* 'Miss Lingard' describes a mildew-resistant, perennial phlox that never reverts from its pristine white to magenta (a bad habit some phloxes have). If the nursery doesn't carry 'Miss Lingard', it will know exactly what to offer as a substitute.

You will notice pronunciations for the genus names of the flowers on the lists in this book. They usually follow authoritative gardening literature. They are scripted in the clear and simple style initiated in Ralph Bailey's 16-volume *The Good Housekeeping Illustrated Encyclopedia of Gardening*, unfortunately now out of print.

The Three Groups of Flowers

The flowers of hardy bulbs are the first to appear in spring. Some beautiful summer and fall flowers also grow from bulbs. Bulbs are especially useful because they can be counted on to bloom a few months after planting, in sun or shade. In good conditions many come back year after year. A true bulb is onionlike: the foliage usually is grassy and the flower stems branch little or not at all. Daffodils and tulips are typical.

Perennialize, naturalize: The two words are not synonymous. The tulips in List 12 usually perennialize—they come back for four years or more. But they don't really become wild plants. *Naturalize* applies to a garden plant that becomes a wildflower of the region. The Annual Phlox has naturalized on the Outer Banks of North Carolina and may be thought of as a wildflower.

The root forms called rhizomes, tubers and corms are a little different from true bulbs, but gardeners generally think of them as "bulbs." I have included all these swollen root forms in the Bulbs section of this book.

The spring-flowering bulbs are planted the fall before they bloom. Summer-flowering bulbs are planted in spring. Fall-flowering bulbs are planted in summer.

Perennials take longer to bloom after planting than bulbs; a few perennials flower the first year, most the second year, after they are planted. Perennials anchor the border because they come back. Many go on for four or five years and a few—peonies, for instance—for decades. The rootstock of a perennial can be described as a fibrous knot crowned by a leafy rosette, and those parts of the plant develop the first season after the seed is sown. Most perennials will continue if they are dug, divided, and replanted every four or five years.

Grouped with perennials in this book are short-lived flowers called biennials. They bloom the second year, set seed, and die. An exceptional few biennials bloom in summer or fall the first year from seed started early indoors. They are grouped with annuals.

Perennials may be started from seed in the garden or indoors early, or purchased as seedlings in spring or late summer and early fall. To avoid false expectations, ask the nursery when your container perennials will bloom—this season or next. Often you can find seed for plants that are hard to find as seedlings or divisions.

Annuals are the pop-up, one-season-only flowers. They develop quickly from seed and most of them—marigolds, for instance—flower within a month or two. The roots live just one season. Often grouped with annuals are perennials usually treated as annuals because they cannot withstand

---

Volunteer, self-sow: Many popular annuals and some biennials and perennials reseed themselves—self-sow—and develop the next season. Petunias and four-o'clocks are typical. Often they mature later than the seedlings set out for the season's show, and I welcome the fresh color in late summer and fall. If they don't fit the needs of the garden, remove them as weeds.

---

the cold (or heat) of the region and bloom the first year from seed sown early indoors. These plants are referred to as tender perennials, and I have included them in the Annuals section of the book. Some annuals self-sow and may seem perennial, but they are annuals nonetheless, completing their entire life cycle in a single growing season.

Many gardeners prefer to start annuals early indoors from seed and set them out after the ground warms, but many more buy flats of seedlings in spring and late spring.

Climate

Choose flowers that will thrive in your climate. A palm might look beautiful in Alaska but the palm will need considerable help to survive. Plants able to withstand some degree of frost are called hardy. Some tender perennials that can't survive icy winters will contradict the norms by thriving where there is a permanent winter blanket of snow. The tuberoses in my Zone 3 Vermont garden are an example. They die here in Washington, D.C., four zones further south, where there's little snow. But you can't count on anomalies. In gardening, the only thing you can count on is that some other gardener out there has had experiences that contradict everything that has happened in everyone else's garden. All my best reference books contradict each other—his or her plants grow taller, or shorter, bloom in pink rather than lavender, prefer sun not shade, tolerate wet not drought, and on and on. Gardening is an art, not a science!

The USDA Plant Hardiness Map published by the U.S. National Arboretum and reprinted in this book assigns numbers from 1 to 11 to the climate zones in North America. The zones indicate the average annual minimum temperatures. Much of southern Canada and some of the northern U.S. are in Zone 3, where winters drop to $-40°$ and $-30°$ F. Learn your hardiness zone and stay with plants identified as surviving cold within the zone's annual lows.

The zones assigned to each plant in this book indicate the coldest and warmest regions in which the plant is known to do well, zones related to the USDA map. Be aware that cities are often $5°$ to $10°$ F hotter than the countryside. Take advantage of opportunities created by microclimates in your yard.

Microclimates can be defined as places in a landscape that are warmer or cooler than the prevailing local temperatures. Walls, corners, reflective surfaces (especially white surfaces or windows that act as mirrors), windbreaks, and the shelter afforded by a large tree or evergreen shrubs raise surrounding temperatures in both winter and summer. Shade, a northern exposure, or the proximity of running water generally lower temperatures. A winter or summer mulch will buffer temperature extremes.

Please note that the zones given in this book pertain only to the plants covered in this book. Where zone numbers are listed with a genus name, it means those zones are appropriate for all the species covered in that entry, but not necessarily for all species in that genus.

> **Humidity:** It has been observed that increased humidity and mist help plants survive cold. The observation was made in a study in which temperature charts were used on rhododendrons. Plants that survived the cold in the maritime West Coast were devastated by the same degree of cold on the East Coast. But in areas of high heat, humid days can devastate poorly drained plants.

The weather along the West Coast of the U.S. is considered to be quite a bit like that of the West Coast of England. Our West Coast weather comes from off the water which is warmed by the Japanese Stream, as the English coast is warmed by the Gulf Stream. Many plants that do well on our West Coast also do well in England. Mediterranean plants generally do very well in southern California and the Southwest, which is hot and dry like their homeland.

East Coast weather is more like the weather in China and Japan, and many oriental plants do well in this part of the country. Prevailing winds blow from west to east, and for the East Coast, as for China and Japan, they come from inland. Land weather is considered more severe than water-based weather, which is tempered by the slowness with which water temperatures change.

Establishing a Flower Bed

A successful flower bed produces stocky sturdy plants covered with long-lasting flowers and handsome, healthy foliage. Transplants take hold quickly and plants stand up to adverse weather. Watering every ten days will be sufficient to keep things going in most seasons. And the plants will be so hardy few will be lost to pests or diseases.

Site and Light

The first step in starting a new garden is to site the bed. The minimum light for plants that call for full sun is 6 hours and more is better. With less sun the plants will flop over and won't flower nearly as well as they can. If your garden has less than 6 hours of direct sun a day, choose plants for semi-sun or partial shade. These plants are beauties—in shade, impatiens glows all summer and by fall is a little bush covered with blooms. Astilbes and aquilegia, ferns, ageratum, and begonias—there's no shortage of plants for shade. The ideal light in every case is morning sun

Double Late tulip 'Angelique', an exquisite example of the beauty of man-made flowers. (Heath)

and in the South after-four sun. Noon sun is the hottest.

Light shade, or semi-sun, is defined in this book as 4 to 6 hours of direct sun daily. Shade and deep shade are defined as only two hours of direct sun a day, or dappled sun all day.

The key to success in sun or shade is fertile, fluffy soil that is well drained and rich in humus (almost completely decomposed organic materials, such as fallen leaves or animal manures). Preparing soil is definitely not the easy part of gardening, but it only has to be done once if it is well done. A raised-bed garden is recommended as a way to achieve instant good drainage and improved soil. The steps are essentially the same as for the preparation of a new ground-level bed, but additional topsoil is added.

Fall is the best time to prepare a new bed and there are many ways to lay it out. The ground should be relatively level. If there's a steep slope, consider shaping it into shallow terraces. The easiest bed to work is a strip or an island that gives access to the plants without walking into it. When you walk on soil, you crush the spaces needed to hold air and water.

Bed and Soil

Lay out the bed with markers, or outline it with a garden hose. Shape it with lazy S's and gentle, sweeping curves, even if its basic form is a square or a rectangle.

Here is Andre Viette's recipe for soil preparation:

1. Get rid of the weeds. Water the outlined bed, then treat the entire area with a weed killer such as Roundup. Seven days later, water again, repeat the treatment, and allow it to rest another seven days.

2. Create a raised bed (berm, island bed) by bringing in enough topsoil to bring the level up 12 to 15 inches about the ground. Look for imported soil that is first-rate and weed-free.

3. Next, improve the soil with additives. To know which additives, determine the pH reaction of the soil. PH refers to the relative acidity or alkalinity of soil and that governs the availability of nutrients in it. U.S. Agricultural Extension Services at state universities test pH for a modest fee. But it is best to buy a soil testing kit because you'll use it often. One that is reliably accurate and easy to use is the Standard Kit pH 5.0 to 7.2 available from Cornell Nutrient Analysis Laboratories, 804 Radfield Hall, Cornell University, Ithaca, NY 14853.

Optimum soil pH for the widest range of flowers—and many vegetables—is slightly acid, in the 5.5 to 6.5 range. Except for areas where limestone is prevalent, most garden soil in America is in this range. This pH is also suited to most plants I describe as acid-loving.

If your soil pH is above 6.5, apply water-soluble sulfur or iron. If the pH is below 5.5, spread finely ground limestone or hydrated lime. Ask your garden center or nursery for product recommendations for your area and apply the materials at the prescribed rates. Don't be generous! Till the correctives in along with the next ingredients recommended.

4. Spread an all-purpose fertilizer at recommended rates (see below). For a bed being prepared in fall for spring planting, choose Osmocote eight- or twelve-month slow-release formulations—twelve will take you through summer.

5. For clay soils spread on gypsum at the rate of 50 pounds per 1000 square feet. If the soil is very heavy clay, add gypsum at the rate of 100 pounds per 1000 square feet.

6. In addition, spread on phosphorus, which is essential for good root growth. The rate for all soils is 50 pounds per 1000 square feet. There are three sources: superphosphate, now being marketed as triple superphosphate; rock phosphate; and bonemeal. Bear in mind that rock phosphate releases its nutrients very slowly, and bonemeal adds calcium, which injures Japanese iris and acid-loving plants.

7. Cover the bed with 2 to 4 inches of humus—decomposed bark, compost, leaf mold (partially decomposed leaves), sphagnum peat moss (dried, compressed sphagnum), black peat humus (composted peat), decomposed animal manures, or composted sewage sludge that is dry and odorless. Seaweed is wonderful where it is available. Use any one of these or a combination. There are many other suitable sources of organic material.

8. Rent a rear-tine rotary tiller and churn all of the above into the soil.

9. The bed should now be as soft as chocolate pudding (Andre's phrase.) When you are ready to plant, rake the bed smooth and discard any rocks, tough lumps, and bumps. Soil preparation in this manner is excellent for bulbs and annuals as well as perennials.

Watering

After planting, water with a sprinkler that lays down 1 to 2 inches in five to twelve hours—the equivalent of gentle rain. Set a coffee tin under the sprinkler to register the rate.

Strength through stress: A little stress slows growth enough to make very sturdy plants. Leaves in the garden are not supposed to be as lush as the lettuce in the supermarket. Plants fresh out of the nursery are somewhat overgrown and tender enough to turn to mush in open air without water. But continuing the practices that made them lush—constant watering, constant fertilizing—results in crowded, weak plants more vulnerable to pests and diseases.

Ideally, there will be a couple of hours of gentle rain every ten days to two weeks. If not, set the sprinkler to put down 1 to 2 inches in the early morning before the sun is on the garden. There is nothing wrong with overhead watering provided the foliage remains dry between waterings, and the garden gets a good inch or two—but only every ten days to two weeks. Healthy plants growing in well-prepared soil can go without water for a time. But when the thermometer hits 100° F at noon, or in high winds, you may have to water more often. If they begin to wilt, water! Research has shown that drought causes plant starches to change to sugars that insects may find tastier.

Watering during the day lowers leaf temperatures and reduces stress. It cools the garden environment and the foliage on hot days. Evening watering is good, too. The foliage gets wet from the dew anyway. Avoid watering at midday, when the most moisture will be lost by evaporation.

Automatic underground watering systems are recommended for flowering beds only if the water rate and timing are adjusted for flowers.

Container Soils

Good garden soil is the basis of successful container gardens. For baskets, mix in almost half as much perlite as soil. For tubs and big planters, mix in a third as much perlite. Mix water-holding gels in the growing medium for baskets and small pots. These starch based super-absorbents help keep the medium moist. They come in grains and sticks, and can hold from 200 to 5,300 times their own weight in water. Mix gel grains into the soil very thoroughly or they will clump together into globs like jellyfish. Even with gel additives, containers require watering daily in hot weather.

Replace all the soil in baskets and small planters every year. Established perennials in big tubs and planters benefit from an annual addition of an inch or two of humus and fresh top soil. Scratch it into the surface along with fertilizer in late winter.

Planting

Plant in soil that is damp but not wet. Rake the bed smooth, removing large stones and clumps. Sow large seeds at a depth equal to the diameter of the seed. Broadcast small seeds over the soil surface and tamp them firmly into place. I do it with my hands because I love the feel of good dirt—it's silky, soft as cat fur, and cool.

For seedlings, container plants, and root divisions, open a generous hole. Before putting a container-grown plant into the soil, loosen roots binding the soil ball. When planting bare-root plants, dip the roots in a bucket of water that contains a light dose of houseplant fertilizer. Set the plant upright in the hole. If you do not plan to install a permanent mulch, set the crown at ground level. If you plan a permanent mulch, plant a little high—otherwise, with mulch on top, the roots will end up too far underground. That can kill.

When the plant is in the hole at the proper level, fill the hole with soil and firm the plant into place with your hands. Water the plant gently but thoroughly.

> **Dig deep:** Plants do better everywhere when they're given plenty of well-prepared soil in which to spread out. Don't just doctor the hole; prepare the soil. And dig deep—18 inches for larger perennials, 12 inches for smaller ones. They develop rapidly over the whole area that has been freed up and will be much more productive.

Staking

Most plants can carry their own weight without bending all over the garden. But where there's not enough light, sun-lovers flop over. And old plants sometimes stretch when they need dividing. Staking isn't a permanent solution to either problem but will help for a season.

Sometimes there is just too much plant—as with lilies and delphiniums—to deal with height and weight without help. And windy locations can call for staking.

My preference is for a single discreet stake plunged a little to one side of the center of the clump, well hidden by stems and leaves. Use green wool or twist ties to draw each flopping branch upright and tie it loosely to the central stake.

Pinching, Pruning, Deadheading

Seedlings of *most* branching annuals and some perennials that put up a strong, central stem develop loads more flowering branches if 3 to 4

Well-prepared soil is the secret to the carefree success of this perennial border, where each spring tall bearded irises riot among the crimson and pink peonies. (Viette)

inches of the leaders (tops of the central or main stems) are pinched out. Pruning early invites new growth. The plants will be bushier and the foliage better looking.

In spring and summer, I deadhead the garden every day—pinching

---

Key to more flowers: The secret to greatly increased flowering in most *branching* annuals and some perennials that *put up a single central stem* ("leader"): pinch out the first 3 or 4 inches of the lead stem early—after blooming starts, deadhead (relentlessly). An example is snapdragons.

But—proceed with caution. The key words here are *branching* and *leader*. This does not benefit flowers rising from bulbs, corms, or rhizomes, or other plants without branching stems.

---

out spent flowers, especially in petunias, encourages new blossoms. Also, it's an excuse to get out there and see how they're doing without becoming entangled in a major project. Deadheading or shearing monthly throughout the flowering season encourages flowering and longevity.

Summer dormancy: In high heat, plants shut down. Don't prune—it is an incentive to growth and stresses the plant.

Coreopsis and daisies bloom in the tall grass of a flowering meadow at the American Horticultural Society—a garden that nourishes our friends, the worms, insects, and birds. (McDonald)

Pruning also may help plants suffering from mildew. Cut them back to the ground. (Diseased foliage goes into the garbage—not into compost.) Sometimes, the new foliage will come in clean.

Mulches—Permanent and Winter

After planting, put down 2 to 3 inches of an attractive, permanent mulch. Make sure it is no more than 3 inches deep. Its purpose is to keep roots cool and weeds down. Add about an inch annually to maintain the depth. Pine bark, hardwood bark, or West Coast fir bark, cedar bark, or cypress are recommended. Andre Viette prefers fine-grade hammer mill bark. You can also mulch with compost or leaf mold, but weeds and roots grow into it and it decomposes quickly.

In the plant lists that follow, winter mulches are recommended for some plants growing in southern gardens and for those in areas on the edge of their cold hardiness. The purpose of winter mulch is to keep the soil from heaving the plants as the ground freezes and thaws. The materials for winter mulches are different—airy marsh hay, salt hay from the shore, straw, or pine boughs. Tent over the plant so thinly that some of the plant and soil are visible through the mulch. Lay the mulch after the ground has frozen hard. Remove it when active growth begins in spring.

Weeds and Pests

Weeds aren't always ugly but they always take up water and soil nutrients. They come into their own in midsummer along with drought and high heat. A permanent mulch discourages weeds, but if the little green heads pop rake them away before they're an inch high. When they're 8 inches high, you'll need a hoe. The worst thing that can happen to a newly established garden is for weeds to flower and set seed there—or even nearby. They'll haunt you.

Don't pull big weeds from bone-dry soil during a drought—the upheaval of soil can cost moisture. Water the garden first, then pull the weeds.

Spraying

Be prepared to lose a few plants to hungry insects. Insects, bees, butterflies, and birds are a natural part of a garden's ecosystem. Always look for plants billed as pest- and disease-resistant. Don't repeat plantings that failed. Do as nature does—build on success.

I spray only for whitefly. If you must spray for pests, choose the least toxic spray and spot-treat only. Mass spraying is not environmentally sound. It destroys not only the problem but other parts of the ecosystem sustaining the garden.

Annual Fertilizing

There's great beauty in the fall and winter aspects of the garden—allow it to happen. Let healthy flowers develop at their own pace throughout the cold months. The ripened seedheads provide food for birds and landing strips for snowflakes. The fallen leaves and vegetative debris nourish other elements of the ecological cycle that keeps the garden wholesome. Then, in late winter—January and February in moderate regions, late March in the North—remove the annuals and cut back the foliage of perennials and ornamental grasses. Clear away weeds.

Don't compost any of this debris—dispose of it in the garbage.

In choosing a fertilizer, try to stay with natural "organics," which are slow-release fertilizers. The best organics are based on cocoa hulls, dehydrated manures of various animals, tankage, blood meal, cottonseed meal, or crab meal. They include lots of nutrients. Osmocote is a man-made, slow-release fertilizer that is also sold in eight- and twelve-month and in three- and four-month formulations. When a picker-upper is needed, light applications of a liquid organic fertilizer are recommended, such as seaweed or fish emulsion, or a water-soluble inorganic fertilizer.

An improved established bed needs a light fertilization only once a year—in early winter when all the plants are dormant. Dust the ground with a light application of a complete organic fertilizer. Before you do, recheck the pH and, if necessary, adjust it as before.

A new bed well supplied with gypsum and phosphate won't need more for two to four years. A bed established without gypsum and phosphate will

---

Hold the fertilizer: Underfertilizing is always better than overfertilizing. A heavy dose of all-purpose chemical fertilizer can burn tender rootlets and cause more harm than good.

---

benefit from a yearly winter dusting of both. Add everything at the same time and scratch it into the top layer of soil.

In sandy soils, additives and correctives disperse rather quickly, so make the applications lighter and more frequent.

Dividing, Transplanting

Dividing and replanting renews established perennials. Every four to five years is the usual time frame but there are exceptions. Cushion mums, for instance, should be divided every year. Plants that respond badly to transplanting are divided only when they show signs of deterioration, usually in spring before growth begins—*unless otherwise recommended*. Some flowers, such as poppies, are divided or planted after flowering, when the foliage has died down and dormancy has begun.

The optimum seasons for division and transplanting—or planting—are according to region and plant preference. In the North, early to mid- and late spring are recommended, depending on the winter hardiness of the flowers; in temperate regions, mid-fall is as popular as spring for most plants; in the South, winter.

Fibrous-rooted flowers transplant successfully at any season, including summer, providing the stems are cut back to 2 to 3 inches from the crown. The exceptions are taproot perennials, such as hollyhocks and platycodons. An antiwilt spray applied to foliage is helpful in maintaining moisture during transplanting.

I use a spading fork for digging up plants, but a spade or shovel is suitable. Shove the tines down deep under the crown, lift it, and shake off loose dirt. Study the crown to discover its natural lines of division. Most crowns show three to five divisions. Press firmly with your fork or spade to break the pieces apart. Discard the central portion of the old clump and replant the young outer shoots. Cut rhizomes and clumps with a large

single crown into sections that contain both an "eye" (bud) and a good set of roots.

To divide a plant with rooted runners or stolons, cut the connection between the new plants and the parent, then dig and replant the plantlets.

When transplanting or dividing growing plants, prune to help them to establish themselves quickly. Cut all branches back to within 2 or 3 inches of the crown.

Nurture Your Soil

In the wild, nature raises up the plants that flourish in the local climate, light, and soil. They are planted by birds and bees, butterflies, and wind, and they thrive despite stresses and within ecosystems that include pests and diseases. No one has to feed, water, prune, deadhead, or spray them.

Instead, they have the protection of a constantly renewed mulch that buffers climate excesses and regenerates the soil. Our topsoil was created by the erosion of rocks and the decomposition of organic matter, including leaves and other vegetation. Good garden soil needs constant renewal.

Autumn smells of damp woodlands and moss, fallen leaves and rustling harvests. It calls me out to gather leaves, every single leaf I can lay claim to. The fallen gold is real treasure. Leaf compost and leaf mold are the perfect cost-free soil conditioner, a larder for worms and the multitudinous life-forms that aerate and enrich the soil. Raking and bagging leaves bright as gold on a warm fall day with the sun on your back and the horizon rimmed with a blue mist—that very much is what gardening is all about. It's an annual farewell to the green and growing, the things that happen on the surface. In the next months the action will be mainly underground. And what action there is! Roots stretch out in the still warm, moist earth; the tough outer coat of the garden's self-sown seeds breaks down in the wet and cold; molds, insects, and worms are hard at it, chewing the leaves blanketing the pachysandra and lapping at the feet of the ornamental grasses.

Choose the day well—really be there.

Scientific composting is for gardeners looking for a hobby. I recommend the laissez-faire approach. First, chop dry leaves with a shredder. (If they're wet, you will be too.) For each 10-quart plastic bagful, I add to the hopper two cupfuls each of gypsum and organic fertilizer and as much green garden debris as is available. There are always some fresh weeds, and the ivies constantly need pruning.

Then, each bag is doused with a couple of quarts of warm water and I roll back the top so it stays open to the rain. I also punch a few holes around the bottom to encourage air circulation and drainage. By the following late summer here in D.C. about two-thirds is compost and a third leaf mold. In cooler regions it might take two or three years to convert.

I use a little compost to refresh my garden in summer, but most of it goes into the soil just before I start raking leaves in fall. I drag the bags out to the yard, and dump compost as far as it will stretch. Some of the leaf mold goes into the bottom of new planting holes and some is kept for use the following spring.

You see—from autumn to autumn, the soil, the worms, the insects, and all the flowers on the lists that follow are nourished by the grand system of which each is an essential part.

PART TWO:

The Flower Finder Lists

CHAPTER ONE:
Bulbs—Fast, Different Flowers

Like annuals, bulbs come into bloom quite soon after planting. And like perennials, some come back year after year. But the bulb "root" is unique. Onionlike in a true bulb, it has a papery cover called a "tunic," a pointed top, and a flattish bottom with a modest system of roots. Tulips are typical. Included here with true bulbs are tubers (swollen structures similar to a yam), rhizomes (elongated, segmented root structures), and corms (round, flattish structures).

In a mixed flower bed, the bulbs are planted after the perennials in groups spaced to come up between and through the perennial clumps. Those that bloom and fade in spring will be screened or replaced later by annuals. Planting seasons for various types of bulbs are given below.

There are twelve bulb lists in this section. The first three describe spring flowering bulbs and are organized according to flower size. To generalize very loosely, the first bloom of the year comes from small, hardy bulbs—winter aconite and snowdrops. The second flush of bloom comes from intermediate size bulbs—squills and oxalis. Many of the large bulbs flower last—the tall Darwin tulips, the big fritillaries. Actually, a few early tulips, daffodils, and irises bloom early, and some small bulbs bloom later—but simplifying the spring flowering sequence to small, medium, and large makes their flowering times easy to remember.

All the hardy bulbs are planted in fall and most need winter chilling to come into bloom. Only certain spring bulbs succeed without the chilling—see list 6, Best Bulbs for the South.

Another whole set of big, beautiful bulbs flower in summer and fall—the magnificent lilies and glamorous dahlias, the brilliant poppy anemones and elegant fall-flowering crocuses. Some of the most remarkable summer-flowering bulbs, the tropicals, are grown in the North as annuals—that is, they are planted in spring for summer bloom

and taken indoors for winter or discarded.

There are four major bulbs with lists of their own—daffodils, dahlias, lilies, and tulips. Their displays range from early to late but the big show is toward the end.

Most bulbs can be grown in containers.

Before buying bulbs, study the labels' projected height and bloom periods. Varieties that look very similar can behave very differently—spring and fall crocuses, for instance. Bigger bulbs produce bigger flowers. "Bargain" bulbs may be smaller—fine for perennializing, but not choice for specimen planting. Avoid bulbs with soft or mushy spots. Squeeze, and check for mold and bruises. A loose or torn tunic does not damage the bulb and may actually promote faster rooting.

Store bulbs-in-waiting for a planting date at between 45° and 55° F, never above 63° F. The refrigerator crisper or a cool garage or cellar are good storage places. But don't put apples together with bulbs in a crisper.

Spring and late winter bloomers: set these out the preceding fall before the first real frosts. In the northern U.S.—above the Mason-Dixon line—plant bulbs in September, October, or November. Farther south, plant them in October, November, or December. Bulbs planted toward the end of the planting season tend to bloom several weeks later and have shorter stems.

Summer bloomers: set these out in mid-spring.

Fall bloomers: set these out in midsummer. Some of these may not flower until the following fall.

Planting and Growing Bulbs

The farther south the garden, the more shade is acceptable. Bulbs that require full sun in New England will do better in partial shade in the hot South, and especially benefit from protection from the hot midday sun.

Bulbs must have very well-drained soil or they rot. Follow the suggestions in

Spring's first big color show is provided by a casual scattering of perennialized flowering bulbs—tall red tulips, creamy narcissus, and low blue muscari. Starry pink and lavender *Phlox subulata* carpet the background. (McDonald)

Tulips, the most formal of the flowering bulbs, combine with masses of pansies in a lavish spring display at the Lewis Ginter Botanic Garden, Richmond, VA. (Viette)

the section on Culture given for most plants in this book for improving soil. Most bulbs thrive in soil with a pH range between 6.0 and 7.0.

If you are planting large bulbs in individual holes in *unimproved* soil, mix a handful of Holland Bulb Booster 9-9-6 slow release fertilizer into the soil at the bottom of each hole. This fertilizer was formulated based on research conducted at North Carolina State University. When planting a large area of unimproved soil apply 4 pounds for each 100 square feet of surface soil.

Once the bulbs are established, they will perennialize more readily if they are fertilized in early spring, just as the tips break through the soil, at the rate of 4 pounds of 9-9-6 Holland Bulb Booster for each 100 square feet of surface soil. In unimproved soil, daffodils require more potash; use 5-10-20 slow release organic fertilizer instead.

Contrast creates interest—here the big daffodil 'Stainless' and the dainty *Leucojum* 'Gravetye Giant'. (Heath)

Where squirrels, voles, and other rodents are a severe problem, line the planting hole with small, sharp gravel, plant the bulbs, and add another inch of gravel before filling the hole with sand. Or, cover bulb plantings with hardware cloth or a close metal mesh, then anchor it with rocks.

Where no specific planting dimension is given, set small bulbs 1 or 2 inches apart, and large bulbs 2 to 3 inches apart. Place the bottom of the bulb at a depth that equals twice the bulb's height. As a rule of thumb, small bulbs are planted 3 to 5 inches deep, large bulbs 5 to 8 inches deep. In heavy soil the planting may be a little shallower; in light sandy soil, the planting may be a little deeper. If you err, err on the deeper end— when large bulbs are planted close to the surface they tend to start new bulbs and flower production suffers.

Plant true bulbs with the flat rump down, pointed tips up. The tops of the round flat corms are hard to distinguish from the bottom, so plant these on edge—the roots will head down, the foliage and flowers up. Set rhizomes and tubers so that the portions showing roots are on the bottom, the eyes on top.

Use a bulb planter (a small hand tool) to make digging individual holes for bulbs easier. To plant large lots of bulbs dig a bed between 3 and 5 inches deep (small bulbs) or 5 to 8 inches deep (large bulbs), prepare the soil, and rake it smooth. By the handful skim the bulbs out over it to create a casual drift. Set the bulbs upright where they

Crocus, one of the earliest and hardiest of the little bulbs. This is *Crocus chrysanthus*. (Netherlands Flowerbulb Information Center)

fell and cover them with prepared soil.

Most bulbs require ample moisture during the season of active growth, but they last longer if the soil is somewhat drier during the hot months.

For spring bulbs to flower the next year, the foliage must be allowed to yellow for eight to twelve weeks. Then cut it off to the base. This is a new view: letting the foliage die to the ground before removing it is still considered by many breeders to be the best way to enhance the next season's flowers. Deadheading—the removal of the stems of spent flowers down to the ground—is also important.

Be patient with the foliage of larger bulbs—tulips, daffodils, and hyacinths. Do not bend it over to finish ripening. That cuts off the light and oxygen needed to nourish next year's flowers. Rather, plan the garden so the developing leaves of companion and follow-on plants will rise and screen the ripening foliage.

In formal landscapes—complete with gardeners—the bulbs are lifted after flowering and either discarded (tulips) or replanted in fall. Some of the smallest bulbs do not come back but the large hardy bulbs recommended here will perennialize and return for several years. Under good conditions daffodils multiply indefinitely.

To harvest or reset bulbs, allow the foliage to partially yellow, then dig up the rootballs and set them to dry. Clean and store them in a cool place —45° to 55° F, never above 63° F—until time for fall planting. Or, heel the rootballs into an out-of-the-way spot in the garden and replant them in the fall before the growth starts.

1. EARLY SPRING, SPECIALTY BULBS

■ These small bulbs are planted in fall. Included are the very earliest flowers of the year and a few that come in mid-spring. The first dainty little blossoms appear when the witch hazels bloom mid-February through March. Some shine through the last snow. Winter aconite, snowdrops, *Iris reticulata,* and crocus species pop first. The ferny foliage of *Anemone blanda* comes up with them and continues showing off its daisylike flowers as other bulb blooms come and go. There are lots of whites and blues, some yellows, and, from the small species or botanical tulips, brilliant splashes of strong mixed colors.

To be effective, little bulbs must be planted in groups of at least 20, and 50 to 100 are better. They are a delight to come upon fronting a flower bed, under shrubs, in rock gardens, or edging woodland paths. In sunny, sheltered locations they come up earlier. Place a few near windows and entrances, where they can't be missed.

Some of these perennialize but many little bulbs need to be replanted annually—they're inexpensive. To flower well most species require an extended period of low temperatures and that makes them poor subjects for the Deep South. List 6 recommends bulbs that are successful in that region.

Follow-on and Companion plants: Good companions are *Anemone blanda,* winter-flowering pansies, early primroses, and sedum; muscari with red tulips and white daffodils; and miniature daffodils that come up through ground covers. Large, late bulbs are good followers for small, early bulbs. Set Single Late tulips 8 to 9 inches deep with crocuses on top, no more than 5 inches deep. Oriental poppies and daylilies are ideal follow-ons for bulbs.

The little bulbs are most effective planted in masses—blue and white muscari with yellow daffodils and red tulips just coming into flower. (McDonald)

ANEMONE (an-*nem*-on-ee) blanda

Greek Windflower   Zones 4-8

Excellent. This first and hardiest anemone has pretty, fernlike foliage up to 8 inches high, and is a perfect ground cover and companion plant for early tulips and miniature daffodils. It flowers right after *Iris reticulata,* one of the earliest bulbs, and remains while others come into bloom and fade away. The flowers are yellow-centered and daisylike, white, pink, or blue. 'White Splendour', 'Blue Shades', and 'Rosea' are recommended. Two larger anemones that flower in summer into fall are described later. The beautiful summer flowering *A. coronaria,* poppy anemone, is on list 4, Summer-into-fall Bulbs, and the tall *A. hupehensis* var. *japonica,* Japanese anemone, and hybrids are grouped with perennials that flower in summer and fall on list 17.

Culture: Soak the tubers 12 hours in tepid water before planting. In mid-fall plant the tubers on edge (it's hard to tell the top from the bottom) 2 to 3 inches deep, 4 to 5 inches apart, in sun or partial shade in rich, well-drained neutral soil. Maintain moisture. In Zones 4 and 5 mulch for winter. Once established, they perennialize.

CHIONODOXA (kye-oh-nod-*dox*-uh)
luciliae

Glory-of-the-snow   Zones 4-8

So early the flowers are called "snow glories." It bears long-lasting, 3- to 8-inch spikes of up-facing, starry flowers with white centers that stand above grassy leaves. In cool weather the blossoms can last three to four weeks. The colors are blue or pink and there are large-flowered forms—blue 'Gigantea' and 'Pink Giant'. Most attractive massed in groups of 50 to 100.

Culture: In the North plant in the sun; in hot climates protect from afternoon sun. Set out in early fall 5 inches deep, 1 to 2 inches apart in well-drained, sandy, humusy soil. Maintain moisture at the roots.

CROCUS (*kroh*-kus)

The late-winter and early spring crocuses flower with *Galanthus,* often through the last snowfall. Brightly colored little cup- or chalice-shaped flowers 4 to 6 inches high, may be white, pink, lavender, purple, yellow, or orange. Some have contrasting stripes or streaks. The grassy green leaves come up after the flowers and in some forms have a white or silver midrib. Thrive and perennialize even in lawns. They may be grown in large containers outdoors in Zones 7 and 8 and are sometimes forced into flower indoors. There are also fall flowering crocuses—see list 5, Fall and Winter Bulbs.

Culture: Most withstand air temperatures to −10° F. Set out in the fall in full or partial shade, pointed ends up, 3 to 4 inches deep, 2 inches apart in light, well-drained soil. Tolerant of variations in moisture.

C. chrysanthus cvs.   Zones 3-7/8

Among the very first to flower, this is a historic and favorite crocus that bears many stemless yellow, blue, or white blossoms with yellow anthers. Delightful in mixed colors including 'Blue Pearl', blue-purple; 'Cream Beauty', white with bright orange stamens; 'Dorothy', pale yellow-bronze; and 'E. P. Bowles', yellow.

C. tomasinianus 'Ruby Giant'   Zones 3-7/8

Weatherproof 'Ruby Giant' bears large, deep red-purple blossoms and is the most squirrel-proof of a squirrel-resistant species. 'Whitewell Purple' is silver-gray in bud and opens in full sun to show a cobalt-violet interior and yellow stigmas. Perennializes quickly. Often planted with *C. chrysanthus.*

C. vernus Dutch Crocus   Zones 3-7/8

A little later to flower, extra-large white, yellow, or purple crocuses 4 to 6 inches tall often striped or feathered, lovely in mixed colors. Introduced in 1765. 'Yellow Mammoth' is a giant yellow. 'Jeanne d'Arc' is pure white on a purple base with orange stigmata. 'Pickwick' is silvery white with lilac stripes. 'Remembrance' is violet with a silver gloss and flowers early with *Galanthus nivalis,* Snowdrop.

ERANTHIS (eer-*anth*-iss) species
Winter Aconite   Zones 3-7

Winter aconite flowers early with the snowdrops and crocus—sometimes carpeting sunny slopes with long-lasting, yellow flowers like buttercups 3 to 4 inches tall. It leafs out when the flowers go and disappears in late spring. Best massed in drifts or clumps in 50s and 100s under deciduous trees or along stream banks.

Very early little bulbs to plant where they can be seen—
by entrances and from windows:

TOP, LEFT *Anemone blanda*, ideal bulb companion.
(Heath)

TOP, RIGHT *Chionodoxa luciliae*, "snow glories", with
miniature daffodil 'Tete-a-tete'.
(Netherlands Flowerbulb Information Center)

ABOVE *Crocus* 'Remembrance'.
(Netherlands Flowerbulb Information Center)

RIGHT *Puschkinia*, the first bluebell. (McDonald)

Culture: In cool regions it perennializes quickly. Handle the tubers carefully—some will fail—and soak them for several hours before planting. Plant during fall in sun or semi-shade so the bottom of the bulb is 6 inches deep, 1 to 2 inches apart. Maintain moisture. Nice precedent to bulbs that flower later.

ERYTHRONIUM (her-ith-*roh*-nee-um) 'Pagoda'

Mountain Trout Lily, Dogtooth Violet   Zones 4-8
Better known as "dogtooth violet," it produces 2 leaves that have beautiful mahogany mottling and small, yellow-banded, plum-brown, lilylike nodding flowers 10 to 12 inches high. Choice little plant for woodsy places.

Culture: In cool regions it perennializes readily, especially in moist soils. Plant in very early fall in semi-shade 5 inches deep and 3 inches apart in soil that is slightly acid to neutral. Maintain moisture. Do not disturb the plantings.

GALANTHUS (gal-*anth*-us)   species

Snowdrop   Zones 3-8
All species are recommended. Often the first bulb to flower, it bears one delicate, pendent, bell-like white flower streaked emerald green on each slender stem above grassy leaves on plants 4 to 6 inches high. Delightful massed and perennialized in a lawn or along slopes. *G. nivalis* is offered by most nurseries. The rather similar *G. elwesii* has more tolerance of full sun. This is a good follow-on plant for *Eranthis,* the Winter Aconite.

Culture: Set out in early fall 4 inches deep, 1 to 2 inches apart, in moist, well-drained soil in sun or partial shade. Some afternoon shade is required in warm regions. Maintain moisture.

HYACINTHUS (hye-uh-*sinth*-us)
Multiflora 'Borah' and 'Snow White'

Hyacinth   Zones 3-8
Excellent. The familiar Dutch hyacinth in mid-spring produces only 1 or 2 chunky, 8- to 12-inch spikes of fragrant outfacing bells. Multiflora describes a hyacinth bulb that has been specially treated to bear several delicate flower spikes 8 inches tall. 'Borah', a blue, and 'Snow White' produce 5 or more flower stalks in the Multiflora manner. Lovely where delicacy is the objective.

Culture: Set out in fall in full or partial sun, 5 inches deep 2 inches apart in fertile, well-drained soil. Maintain moisture. The flowers last longer in semi-sun. Remove faded flowers at once.

IRIS (eye-riss)

Flag, Fleur-de-lys
The irises described are dwarf beardless types that rise from bulbs and flower in late winter and early spring. Short—3 to 5 inches tall—and pretty in containers, rock gardens, the front of flowering borders, or under shrubs. The colors are yellow, blue, white, lavender, purple, and burgundy. They go by quickly, so accompany the bulbs with plantings of *Anemone blanda,* early crocuses, and species or botanical tulips that will screen the empty spaces. The tall irises that flower in late spring develop from tuberous rhizomes; these are grouped in the perennials section and appear on list 25, *Iris.*

Culture: Plant in fall in full sun to partial shade 3 to 4 inches deep, 2 to 3 inches apart, in very well-drained soil. They need to be somewhat dry after flowering.

I. danfordiae   Zones 4-8
Bright yellow, sweetly fragrant iris with brown spots, only 4 inches tall. Space 2 inches apart and replant every few years.

I. histrioides 'Major'   Zones 4-8
The flower is blue with white spotted falls, 4 inches high. Plant 2 inches apart. One of the first to flower.

I. reticulata   Zones 4-8
This is the very first flower of the year, only 5 inches high. Among these beautiful irises are 'Harmony', a fragrant mid-blue, the best; 'Cantab', small, sky blue; 'J. S. Dijt', a fragrant, dark purple that usually repeats for several years; 'Violet Beauty', fragrant, purple-violet with an orange ridge; and 'Joyce', a fragrant sky blue with a bright yellow central ridge likely to repeat for a few years.

MUSCARI (muss-*kar*-eye)
Grape Hyacinth

Excellent as a mid-spring underplanting for shrubs and small trees, muscari is extraordinary perennialized in "rivers"—long drifts—of blue. The flowers, usually blue or white, are thickly clustered on stems 6 to 8 inches high. Some forms look like miniature hyacinths. Other types are sterile and the unopened buds cluster like tiny grapes on the stems. The leaves are grassy. Pretty at the edge of the lawn, as a carpet between larger bulbs and in bulb baskets or shallow pots, as underplanting for large white daffodils. There's a faint spice-and-grape fragrance, especially in *M. macrocarpum,* a rather rare yellow species.

Culture: Plant in late summer or very early autumn in full sun or partial shade 5 inches deep, 1 inch apart in well-drained, rich soil. Tolerates some drought, especially in summer.

M. armeniacum 'Blue Spike'   Zones 3-8
This popular cultivar is light blue and double. The species has long-lasting, intense blue flowers white-lined at the edges on 6- to 8-inch stems, and perennializes quickly. It is the muscari usually chosen for planting in "rivers." Excellent as a companion to the white daffodil 'Thalia' and pale yellow 'Hawera'.

M. botryoides var. Album   Zones 3-9
Delightful, just 6 to 8 inches tall in pure white, but not as vigorous as *M. armeniacum.*

M. comosum 'Plumosum' Feather Hyacinth
     Zones 6-8
Fluffy, double, mauve-lilac flowers on 6-inch stems. It flowers a little later than the other species here. Exquisite planted in groups of 30 about 3 to 4 inches apart. A historic plant seen in restoration gardens at Monticello and Mount Vernon.

M. latifolium   Zones 3-8
A species sought after for rock gardens but not often seen, with small, blue-purple flowers on 10- to 12-inch stems. It has just one large leaf, very distinctive and unusual.

NARCISSUS Daffodil. From southern Canada to
northern Florida and westward these symbols of spring raise gold, cream, or bicolored trumpets on straight 4- to 20-inch stems wherever flowers grow. They come in early, midseason and late types, are rodent-proof, perennialize easily, and are wonderful with *Anemone blanda.* Among the earliest to flower are the dainty 6- to 8-inch 'Little Beauty', white with a sulphur trumpet; 'Little Gem', to 4 inches, bright yellow with a yellow trumpet; and 'February Gold', to 12 inches, which bears large, gold-yellow petals with slightly darker trumpets. 'Jumblie', an especially good 6-inch pot plant, has 2 or 3 long-lasting flowers on each stem, golden petals, and a flanged orange-yellow cup. The species *N. obvallaris,* a beautifully proportioned 8-inch dwarf, flowers in winter or late winter and also is a superb container plant. Daffodils are long-lasting cut flowers, delightful in rock gardens and containers, and many are suited to forcing. Plant these small daffodil bulbs in early to mid-autumn, 5 to 8 inches deep, 2 to 3 inches apart in groups of 10 to 20. They require well-drained soil, full sun or partial shade. See list 9, Daffodil, for the many types of daffodils, their culture and seasons of bloom.

PUSCHKINIA (push-*kin*-ee-uh)   scilloides
(syn. *libanotica*)   Zones 3-7
Also known as striped squill, this is another early spring bulb. It is one of the first bluebells, a pale flower 4 inches high with a darker stripe and grassy foliage. Especially successful in sunny rock gardens, and charming perennialized in small drifts. There is a pure white form.

Culture: Plant the bulbs in full sun to partial shade, 3 to 5 inches deep, 2 inches apart in groups of 20 in well-drained sandy soil, acid to neutral.

SCILLA (sill-uh)
Squill

This is a beautiful little bluebell 4 to 6 inches tall that in early and mid-spring raises slender stems covered with little pendent, bell-like blossoms usually in blue. Perennialize under shrubs or trees and in lawns where the pretty, green grassy foliage will have time to ripen before mowing begins—it makes sheets of intense color. *Scilla campanulata,* which blooms in May, has been reclassified and presently is found either under *Endymion* or *Hyacinthoides non-scripta.*

Culture: Plant in early fall in full sun to partial shade 3 inches deep and 2 inches apart in well-worked, well-drained, slightly moist enriched soil. Maintain moisture.

S. siberica

Siberian Squill   Zones 3-8
Excellent. The species is also known as blue squill, and the color is a magnificent gentian-blue. It flowers a little later than the species below, mid- to late spring. There are white cultivars. 'Spring Beauty' is a superb blue with large blossoms.

S. tubergeniana   Zones 3-7
This little squill is pale blue to white on 4- to 6-inch stems and one of the earliest—it flowers with *Eranthis, Galanthus,* and *Iris reticulata.*

TULIPA (tew-lip-uh)
Tulip

These early species or botanical tulips are small, informal, but often showy flowers that brighten borders of mixed spring bulbs and are charming in groups of 3 to 6 by stones, steps, or along paths. The colors may be red, white, pink, yellow, purple, mauve, orange, gold, or green, and there are exciting bicolors.

Culture: Plant tulips in fall before the ground freezes—up to late October in Zones 2 to 4, October or November in Zones 5 to 8. Set these species out in full sun or partial shade 5 inches deep, 3 to 4 inches apart in deeply dug, well-drained, sandy soil enriched with compost and humus. Deadhead consistently. Another set of early tulips is given on list 2, Spring, Intermediate Bulbs, and its culture and the main discussion appears on list 12, Tulip.

T. pulchella   Zones 3-8
Look for early-early types. This species is typically 3½ inches tall with pointed purple-red petals, the lower outer segment tinged green with a green-black basal blotch. 'Humilis', earliest of all tulips, is an exquisite soft purple-pink, 4 to 6 inches tall, hardy in Zones 3 to 7. It bears 1 to 3 flowers per bulb. 'Violacea', 'Persian Pearl', and 'Black Heart' are handsome cultivars that flower a bit later.

T. saxatilis 'Lilac Wonder'   Zones 4-8
An early midseason tulip 8 to 10 inches tall, lilac-pink with a yellow center; fine, delicate, distinctly different.

T. tarda (syn. T. dasystemon)   Zones 4-8
Earlier than 'Lilac Wonder', a star-shaped, bunch-flowering tulip that bears up to 5 flowers per stem and is 3 to 5 inches tall. Dainty pointed petals have a yellow inner eye and broad white edge. Perennializes well.

T. turkistanica   Zones 4-8
This bunch-flowering tulip bears up to 12 blossoms on each stem. It grows 4 to 12 inches tall and flowers in early midseason, about the same time as *T. tarda*. The stems are hairy, the leaves gray-green and the blooms are star-shaped and creamy white with orange-yellow eyes and dark anthers.

SOURCE: BRENT HEATH IS A WORLD AUTHORITY ON DAFFODILS AND INTERNATIONALLY KNOWN FOR THE DEVELOPMENT OF FLOWERING BULBS. HE AND HIS WIFE BECKY HYBRIDIZE BULBS ON THE ORIGINAL HEATH BULB FARM IN GLOUCESTER, VIRGINIA.

2. SPRING, INTERMEDIATE BULBS

■ **The bulbs recommended here ring in spring's great flush of color—yellow early daffodils, sapphire scillas, luminous species tulips, dainty white leucojum—on stems 6 to 12 or 24 inches tall. They arrive with the flowering trees—plum, peach, cherry, and crabapple—and forsythia, in April and May for much of the country.**

All are planted in fall. They are most impressive grouped in 10s in flower borders and naturalized in drifts of 20 or more. Many perennialize if conditions are right. Deadheading and fertilization in fall or late winter help them to become established and maintain vigor.

Follow-on and Companion Plants: Attractive coming up through small-leafed ivy, vinca, and pachysandra, which then become their follow-on plants. The foliage of oriental poppies, daylilies, coreopsis, and other spring- and summer-blooming perennials, and bulbs that flower later is rising as the group here comes into bloom, so these plants are good choices for follow-on plants. Annuals are also recommended.

Another good companion is *Convallaria majalis* (Lily-of-the-valley). Sold by bulb growers although it is not a bulb, Lily-of-the-valley also flowers at this season. See list 70, The Fragrance Garden.

ALLIUM   neapolitanum
Daffodil Garlic, Flowering Onion. Pest-proof. This medium-sized uniquely fragrant ornamental onion flowers from mid- to late spring on a stem about 12 inches high. The flowerhead of white, star-shaped florets rises above long, thin, strapshaped leaves. It's a good cut flower. The variety *grandiflorum* is larger and more vigorous than the species, and is suited to forcing indoors. In cool regions grow it in containers and in late fall dry down and store the containers for winter in a cool place. Begin watering again as the days grow longer. For culture see list 3, Spring, Large-flowered Bulbs.

ENDYMION (en-dim-ee-on)   hispanicus
(syn. *Scilla campanulata*)
Spanish Bluebell, Spanish Jacinth,
Bell-flowered Squill   Zones 3-8
An excellent bluebell offered in the catalogs as "wood hyacinth." In late spring—May—it bears nodding bells in bright blue, white, or pink on graceful stems 8 to 12 inches tall. Lovely in mixed colors with ferns or late narcissus and tulips. Several of these bell-flowered plants are classed as scillas (see below and list 1); this one has been reclassified from *S. hispanica* to *E. hispanicus* and more recently to *Hyacinthoides non-scripta*.

Culture: Plant in fall in shade or partial shade 5 to 6 inches deep and 2 to 4 inches apart in rich, well-drained, sandy soil; maintain moisture. Perennializes easily even in rough grass and tolerates more shade than other bulbs.

Endymion hispanicus, the tall wood hyacinth, blooms toward late spring. Delightful naturalized under trees.
(Heath)

Small mid-spring bulb flowers, perfect for small spaces:
TOP Silver bells, *Ornithogalum nutans*, adds elegance and fragrance. (Heath)
ABOVE Clover-like foliage and dainty flowers of *Oxalis adenophylla*, popular companion plant for early bulbs. (Heath)
RIGHT Long-blooming *Ipheion uniflorum*, 'Wisley Blue', perennializes quickly in rock gardens and even between stepping stones. (McDonald)

FRITILLARIA meleagris

Checkered Lily, Snake's-head. Excellent. Pest-proof. Pretty for partly sunny woodlands, the species is 12 to 15 inches tall and in spring bears nodding checked and veined bells from deep brown to rose-lilac, wine, and white. 'Alba' is a creamy white cultivar without checkering, 8 to 12 inches tall. For culture, see list 3, Spring, Large-flowered Bulbs.

IPHEION (**if**-ee-yon) **uniflorum 'Wisley Blue'**

Spring Starflower   Zones 5/6-9

A dainty, deep violet-blue, star-shaped, upward-facing little blossom on a 3- to 5-inch stem. It flowers over a long period in mid-spring. When crushed the grassy leaves smell faintly of garlic.

Culture: Perennializes quickly in rock gardens, meadows, borders, even between flagstones, and is a good choice for lawns. In fall, plant in full sun or partial shade 5 inches deep and 2 inches apart in well-drained soil. Plant in a sheltered place in Zones 5 and 6.

IRIS (**eye**-riss)

Flag, Fleur-de-lys

These early irises are dwarf beardless types that come from bulbs and flower in late winter and early spring. The color range is yellow, blue, purple, white, and bronze. Irises that grow from rhizomes are grouped with perennials, as in garden catalogs, on list 25, Iris.

Culture: Plant in fall in full sun 5 inches deep and 3 to 4 inches apart in very well-drained soil.

I. bucharica   Zones 6-8

In mid-spring, 2 to 5 of these 3-inch fragrant flowers in white or golden yellow are borne on each 12- to 16-inch stem. They are easy to grow and good cut flowers. Typically, they last 3 to 4 weeks. Very good drainage is essential.

I. hollandica

Dutch Bulbous Iris   Zones 6/7-9

A large popular group to 20 inches tall, handsome in the flower bed, and lasting if they are cut while they are still tightly budded. They appear a little later than I. bucharica. Colors are deep and light blue, purple, yellow, white, and bicolors. Recommended are 'Purple Sensation', amethyst with orange markings; 'Angel Wings', yellow touched with orange; 'Royal Yellow', tall with 5-inch blooms; 'Blue Ideal', a very hardy, clear sky blue.

LEUCOJUM (lew-**koh**-jum) **aestivum**
'Gravetye Giant'

Giant Snowflake, Summer Snowflake   Zones 3-9

Excellent. Large, long-lasting, pendent, bell-shaped flowers, white with green markings, 2 to 8 on each 18-inch stem, flowers in spring to late spring on lush grassy plants 18 to 24 inches high. Squirrel-proof and delightful interplanted with tall daffodils and tulips.

Culture: Set the bulbs out in fall in full sun or partial shade 5 to 6 inches deep, 4 to 6 inches apart in well-drained, rich soil. Perennializes especially in moist soils but is versatile.

Elegant *Leucojum aestivum* 'Gravetye Giant' is squirrel-proof and handsome interplanted with taller, larger bulbs or on its own. (Viette)

NARCISSUS Daffodil. From southern Canada to northern Florida and westward, these symbols of spring raise gold, cream, or bicolored trumpets on straight 4- to 20-inch stems wherever flowers grow. These golden heralds of spring come in early (list 1), midseason, and late bloomers, and are a mainstay of the spring show. See list 9, Daffodil.

ORNITHOGALUM (or-nit-**thog**-al-um)

nutans   Zones 6-9

Excellent. Known also as silver bells. Fragrant, elegant, waxy, star-shaped flowers white inside, green-silver outside, rise in mid-spring in loose clusters on stems 8 to 12 inches tall above light green ribbon-like leaves. Nice in flower arrangements and attractive perennialized in drifts.

Culture: Perennializes quickly in well-drained soil that is moist during the growing season. Plant in fall in full sun or partial shade 5 inches deep, 3 inches apart.

OXALIS (**ox**-al-iss) **adenophylla**

Wood Sorrel, Lady's Sorrel   Zones 7-9

Excellent. A pretty little tuberous perennial whose lush, mounded bluish green, deeply divided cloverlike foliage is charming mixed in with and around spring bulbs and lasts beyond their flowering period. It bears dainty lilac-pink flowers with darker pink veins singly or in small clusters on stems about 3 inches tall that stand above the foliage.

Culture: Perennializes in mounds but doesn't spread. Plant the tubers in fall or early spring in full sun or partial shade 5 inches deep, 3 inches apart in well-drained, sandy, alkaline soil. Keep moist during growth. Mulch for winter in Zone 7.

SCILLA **campanulata**

see **Endymion hispanicus,** above.

SCILLA **siberica**

Siberian Squill

Excellent perennialized. This also is known as blue squill, and it is one of the bluebells. It flowers a little earlier than the similar *Endymion hispanicus*, mid- to late spring, but later than *Scilla tubergeniana* on list 1. It bears several delightful gentian blue flowers on 4- to 6-inch stems and there are white cultivars. 'Spring Beauty' is a superb blue with large flowers. See list 1, Early Spring, Specialty Bulbs.

TULIPA (**tew**-lip-uh)

Tulip

The excellent early tulips here are species or botanical types in varying heights, delicate forms and good shades of red, blue, white, yellow, purple, and bicolors. Charming in groups of 5 or 6 under shrubs, by steps, walls, and entrances, and striking planted in twos and threes in a small border. They flower in mid-spring, April and May. The tall tulips come in toward the end of this period and in June.

Culture: Plant tulips in fall before the ground freezes—up to late October in Zones 2 to 4, October or November in Zones 5 to 8. Set these species out in full sun or partial shade 8 inches deep 3 to 4 inches apart in deeply dug, well-drained, sandy soil enriched with compost and humus. Deadhead consistently. For more on culture, see list 12, Tulip.

T. batalinii   Zones 4-8

The species is a pale yellow early tulip about 7 inches tall, choice for rock gardens. 'Bronze Charmer' is yellow tinged with apricot, a little hardier than the species. 'Bright Gem' is creamy yellow-orange, 6 inches tall, and flowers in late midseason. Space these bulbs 2 inches apart.

T. linifolia   Zones 4-8

An early showstopper 4 to 12 inches tall with bright red petals and black-purple centers. The flowers open flat in sunlight.

T. praestans 'Fusilier'   Zones 4-8

Early, about 12 inches high, with 2 to 5 small, luminous, orange-red flowers per bulb and abundant foliage. It perennializes easily massed in beds. Nice packed in containers. Perfect with Forget-me-nots and blue *Anemone blanda*. It has been cultivated in Holland since the 1600s.

SOURCE: BRENT HEATH IS A WORLD AUTHORITY ON DAFFODILS AND INTERNATIONALLY KNOWN FOR THE DEVELOPMENT OF FLOWERING BULBS. HE AND HIS WIFE BECKY HYBRIDIZE BULBS ON THE ORIGINAL HEATH BULB FARM IN GLOUCESTER, VIRGINIA.

3. Spring, Large-Flowered Bulbs

■ These large bulbs are planted in fall and in mid- and late spring produce big, outstanding flowers on stalks 12 to 24 inches high or taller. In late spring the air is filled with fragrance and the azaleas are in flower. Fat oriental hyacinths open, and daffodils and tulips stage their main event followed by Crown Imperial fritillaries and the giant ornamental onions. For much of the land this climax of the spring flowers comes in May and the early part of June. In the cold areas of the U. S. and Canada it's late May and all of June.

The tallest of these bulb flowers are used with striking effect in groups of ten or fifteen at the center or back of large flower beds. Three to five hyacinths make a bright pastel clump and scent the air for days. They, and many among the large bulbs, will come back for two or four to five years if conditions are good. Deadheading and allowing the foliage time to ripen fully before removing it improve next year's performance.

Follow-on plants: Oriental poppies, peonies, and other major spring perennials; daylilies and perennial asters; marigolds; bearded and Siberian iris. A mixture of annual wildflowers is a choice follow-on. In shady places follow bulbs with impatiens; in sun, a companion planting of low-growing cucumbers, melons, and squash will shade the soil and help the big bulbs enjoy a cool, dryish summer. If bulbs are interplanted among the major perennials on the following lists, they become the follow-on plants.

ALLIUM (al-lee-um)
Ornamental Onion

The flowering onions are excellent pest-proof plants and several of the best bloom towards late spring. Purplish blue or white-pink flowerheads composed of many florets top leafless stalks and tufts of dark green strap-shaped foliage that gives off an onion scent when crushed. Those with perfectly round flowerheads are remarkably different from most flowers, striking accents in a mixed border and lasting, eye-catching cut flowers. Plant them where the foliage of other plants acts as a filler and takes over when the onion foliage dies. Some other useful alliums in this book are *A. thunbergii,* a fall flowering species, *A. senescens,* recommended for hot, dry conditions, and *A. schoenoprasm,* the grassy kitchen herb called chives.

Culture: Plant the bulbs in late fall in full sun or light shade 3 to 5 or 8 inches deep, 3 to 6 inches apart—according to size—in well-drained soil. Maintain moisture during growth, and later, keep average to dry.

A. aflatunense   Zones 3-7

This soaring, perfectly round purple Allium rises on a 2- to 3-foot stem in late spring and early summer. It is as remarkable as, but earlier than, the similar but very tall *A. giganteum,* below. Plant the bulbs 4 inches apart in groups of 10 for a dramatic effect. 'Lucy Ball', a magnificent intense purple, and 'Purple Sensation' are outstanding cultivars; plant these 5 inches deep.

Allium giganteum bloom is about 6 inches around on a stem 35 to 45 inches tall. Always dramatic, the giant onion is most effective used as here on the Viette farm, in groups of 6 or 8. (Viette)

RIGHT Fragrant hyacinth 'Carnegie' can be brought into bloom indoors. (Heath)
BELOW Foxtail lilies, *Eremurus stenophyllus*, create bright linear accents. (Harper)
BOTTOM Tall, stately, dramatic *Fritillaria imperialis*. (Viette)

A. caeruleum (syn. *azureum*) Zones 4-7
Also called Blue Globe onion, this azure Allium flowers in late spring on a 20-inch stem. It thrives even in dry, hot conditions and is a lasting cut or dried flower.

A. christophii (syn. *albopilosum*)
Stars-of-Persia Zones 3-7
Summer bloomer 10 to 20 inches tall with a huge, airy, round head 8 to 10 inches in diameter composed of 50 or more star-shaped, silvery purple florets. Will perennialize and is a very good cut or dried flower. Plant the bulbs 5 inches deep, 6 to 8 inches apart.

A. giganteum
Giant Onion Zones 3-7
A late-spring flower, this round, reddish purple flowerhead is about 6 inches in diameter and borne on a stem 35 to 45 inches tall. Groups of 6 or 8 make an outstanding show at the back of the border. 'Rosy Giant' is a pinkish mauve cultivar. Plant 8 inches deep, 4 inches apart. New and interesting used in fresh arrangements with branches of flowering trees such as dogwood and weeping cherry.

A. karataviense Zones 3-8
A spring to late spring bloomer and superior bedding plant. The fragrant, compact, round, lilac-pink flowers are 8 inches tall above clumps of broad, decorative, gray-purple leaves spotted with violet. Choice for rock gardens and it will perennialize. Space the bulbs 8 inches apart.

A. moly Lily Leek Zones 3-8
A summer bloomer also known as Golden Garlic. The flowerhead rises on a 12-inch stem above gray-green leaves and is made up of bright yellow star-shaped florets. Thrives when massed and perennialized in light shade. *Veronica latifolia* 'Crater Lake Blue' is a good companion.

A. neapolitanum
Daffodil Garlic, Flowering Onion Zones 7-10
Early flowerhead of white star-shaped florets on a stem 12 inches tall above long thin strap-shaped leaves. It is lasting as a cut flower. The variety *grandiflorum* is larger and more vigorous than the species. Plant in autumn for spring bloom or in spring for bloom in early summer.

A. nigrum (syn. *multibulbosum*) Zones 4-11
Comes in late spring, a 5-inch flowerhead composed of dozens of fresh green-centered white florets on a 30-inch stem.

A. schubertii Zones 4-11
An early summer bloomer 12 to 24 inches tall. Each large flowerhead is composed of 40 or more little pink or purple florets on stems of very unequal length. The effect is delightfully airy.

A. sphaerocephalum
Round-headed Garlic Zones 3-8
A late spring Allium known as Drumsticks. It produces small, round heads of densely packed, purplish red blooms on 20-inch stems. Eye-catching in flower arrangements and with Aurelian lilies.

A. tuberosum
Chinese Chives, Garlic Chives, Oriental Garlic
                                    Zones 3-8
In late summer spreading clusters of fragrant white flowers with a green midriff are borne on 18-inch stems. Handsome white seedheads follow in winter. Nice in dried arrangements.

EREMURUS (her-rem-*mew*-rus)
Desert Candle, King's Spear
Also known as the Foxtail lilies, the 2- to 4-foot-tall flower spike covered with little shallow-cupped florets rises in late spring or early summer. White, yellow, or pink flowers appear above a clump of strap-shaped basal leaves. Dramatic in groups of 7 to 10 in a mixed border. Lasting cut flowers.

Culture: In fall in a sunny sheltered spot at the back of the border spread each clump of tuberous roots in a planting hole 4 to 6 inches deep and 24 inches in diameter in light, well-drained, fertile soil. The foliage dies after the flower fades down—avoid disturbing the roots. Tolerant of drought.

E. himalaicus   Zones 4-7
An impressive 4-foot clump of foliage that is topped by a white flowering stalk 24 inches long that opens over a period of weeks. Protect with mulch in winter.

E. stenophyllus (syn. *bungei*)   Zones 4-7
This flowers later, a smaller foxtail with flowering spikes 2 to 4 feet high. The yellow or golden yellow flowers burn orange with maturity.

FRITILLARIA (frit-il-*lay*-ree-uh)
Fritillary
Unusual and eye-catching. The bulbs lift straight, stately stems topped by clusters of large, pendent bells under rather amazing tufts of narrow, pointed, upright leaves. Pest-proof, hardy, and easily perennialized. Very dramatic in groups of 10 or 20.

Culture: Handle the bulbs with care and do not allow them to dry out. Plant as soon as received in fall in rich, humusy, very well-drained but never dry soil that is nearly neutral. For outdoor planting, group the bulbs 12 inches apart. Set out in full sun in Zones 3 and 4, partial shade in warmer regions. Leave them to perennialize. Divide every three or four years.

F. imperialis Crown Imperial   Zones 3-8
One of the most ancient flowering bulbs in cultivation and very impressive when it blooms in late spring or early summer. The stems are 24 to 36 inches tall and from the top a cluster of 2- to 3-inch-long, brick red, purplish red, red, or yellow flowers hangs down beneath a tuft of pointed green leaves. Plant this species 8 inches deep, 12 inches apart. Remove the foliage after flowering. 'Aurora' has red-orange blooms and 'Maxima' has orange-red flowers. 'Lutea' is yellow.

F. meleagris Checkered Lily, Snake's-head
                                    Zones 3-8
A pretty fritillary 12 to 15 inches tall for partly sunny woodlands. In spring it bears nodding checked and veined bells colored deep brown to rose-lilac, wine or white. 'Alba' is a creamy white cultivar without checkering, 8 to 12 inches tall. Plant this species 6 inches deep and 2 to 3 inches apart.

GLADIOLUS × colvillei, Corn Flag, Sword Lily.
The long, tapering gladiolus stem studded with big bright blossoms is one of the most elegant and long-lasting summer flowers for cutting. The blossoms open starting at the bottom and in some forms look like perched butterflies. Flowers come in every color but blue, as well as many breathtaking bicolors. In early summer this small-flowered modern hybrid only 18 inches tall bears white, salmon-pink, red, and bicolored blossoms. See the discussion of gladiolus on list 64, The Cutting Garden.

HYACINTHUS (hye-uh-*sinth*-us) orientalis
Hyacinth, Dutch Hyacinth   Zones 4-8
Excellent. A beautiful very fragrant flower composed of starry, outfacing little bells clustered thickly on a straight spike 8 to 12 inches high. Generally, the whites are the most fragrant, then the pastels, but some deeply colored hyacinths have a powerful scent. For bedding, choose slightly smaller bulbs. They'll have outstanding blooms the first year and a looser cluster the second. For forcing indoors, choose the largest bulbs. 'Carnegie', a good forcer, is an elegant white; 'Violet Pearl' is a magnificent purple; 'Ostara' is deep blue; 'Anne Marie', another good forcer, is clear light pink. In containers, plant the bulbs in sets of 3 to 5; for flower beds, plant them in groups of 5 to 15.

Culture: Planting in partial shade can prolong flowering but in the North full sun is recommended. Plant in fall 8 inches deep, 3 to 4 inches apart in well-worked fertile loam with excellent drainage. Maintain moisture in spring. In the cooler reaches of its hardiness range the bulbs repeat at least 2 or 3 years if the stem is cut after flowering and the foliage is allowed to mature fully before it is removed. In the South the sudden onset of summer heat often prevents this.

NARCISSUS, Daffodil.
From southern Canada to northern Florida and westward these symbols of spring raise gold, cream or bicolored trumpets on straight 4- to 20-inch stems wherever flowers grow. These golden heralds of spring come in early (list 1), midseason, and late bloomers, and are a mainstay of the April and May show. See list 9, Daffodil.

TULIPA, Tulip.
Tulips are the garden's big showstoppers from late March to May and June, bred through centuries by the Dutch to create an extraordinary range of colors and forms. Hybrids that flower at midseason are bigger and more impressive than the early types on the preceding lists. They are described on list 12, Tulip.

SOURCE: BRENT HEATH IS A WORLD AUTHORITY ON DAFFODILS AND INTERNATIONALLY KNOWN FOR THE DEVELOPMENT OF FLOWERING BULBS. HE AND HIS WIFE BECKY HYBRIDIZE BULBS ON THE ORIGINAL HEATH BULB FARM IN GLOUCESTER, VIRGINIA.

4. SUMMER-INTO-FALL BULBS

■ **Summer-into-fall bulbs begin to flower after the nights warm up—in mid- or late June, according to climate. The majestic lilies (list 1) and tropicals like the Peacock orchid share the season with the brilliant poppy anemones, regal cannas, crocosmia and big gladiolus, and the lovely Summer Hyacinth, *Galtonia*. Many bloom on until mid-September. There are a few low-growing flowers here, such as *Zephyranthes*, the little Rain Lily, but most of the summer bulbs produce big plants with lots of flowers. They'll screen the dying foliage of the late spring bulbs and provide wonderful splashes of color just when the garden needs color most—in the hot, dry end of the season. Most flower from bulbs planted six to eight weeks before—a quick show of color which, in the tender types, is over before frost.**

Most of these bulbs thrive in containers, and whether in sun or shade, flower reliably the first year. The flowers are already set when the bulbs are planted. Taller types may flop over unless they have some sun, but lower-growing species will do well. To flower the second year, the foliage must have sun and time to ripen before it is removed. Otherwise, treat these as annuals and discard them after flowering.

In the flower border plant the big bulbs in groups of five or ten toward the center or rear. They need lots of space all around and will benefit from backing by some of the bigger foliage plants on lists 50 and 51.

Culture: Plan to replant the bulbs that don't tolerate northern frosts each year in mid-spring. In autumn lift, clean, and store them for winters indoors in a cool, dry, airy place. Exact storage conditions are recommended by suppliers. Summer bulbs hardy enough to be left in the ground in Zone 6 (−10° F winter lows) or Zone 7 (0° F winter lows) may be planted either in fall or spring. On the northern edges of their hardiness zones, protect them for winter with a light mulch.

Six hours of daily sunlight are necessary to bring most of the big bulbs to full flower the second season. Bulbs meant to perennialize benefit from deadheading and early-spring fertilizing.

Follow-on plants: The fall-flowering bulbs on list 5, Fall and Winter Bulbs, are good follow-on plants for the smaller bulbs here. So are most midsize and tall perennials that bloom in late summer and early fall, such as *Boltonia asteroides*, *Cleome basslerana*, Spider Flower, blue salvias, asters, and mums.

ACIDANTHERA (ass-id-*anth*-er-uh) bicolor
var. **murieliae**
Peacock Orchid   Zones 9-11
Tall—24 to 36 inches—beautiful, long-lasting, very fragrant summer flower superb for cutting, containers, and bedding. The stem grows from swordlike foliage and bears 4 to 6 or more gladiolus-like flowers that are creamy white blotched with purple-crimson. It also is called Abyssinian or fragrant gladiolus, and is a good follow-on plant for *Mertensia* and *Doronicum*.

Culture: In Zones 3 through 6 this is grown as an annual, planted each spring and lifted in fall. It may be hardy with a mulch in Zones 7 and 8. Plant in spring when the weather warms, in full sun 4 to 6 inches deep, 6 inches apart in fertile soil. Maintain root moisture.

Orange-scarlet crocosmia makes a good cutting flower and deserves feature treatment in the summer perennial border. (Viette)

ANEMONE (an-*nem*-on-ee) coronaria

Poppy Anemone   Zones 7-9

Few flowers give as much pleasure as this glowing florist's anemone that blooms in late spring or early summer. The blossom has a white-margined, black velvet heart surrounded by broad petals in wonderful colors—white, light and deep blue, violet, purple, pink, red, or mauve. The height is usually 8 to 10 inches. The most intense colors develop in the semi-double St. Brigid series—scarlet 'Hollandia' and purple-violet 'Royal Purple' are known for brilliance. The single-flowered De Caen series has the more subtle colors—violet-blue 'Mr. Volker', violet-rose 'Sylphide', and pure white 'The Bride'. A very different but charming and useful early anemone, *A. blanda*, is described on list 1. The elegant, tall, fall-flowering anemones are grouped with perennials, as in the catalogs, on list 17, Summer-into-fall Bloom.

Culture: In Zones 4 to 6 plant these in spring and in fall lift the tubers and store them indoors for winter. In Zones 7 to 9 plant in the fall. In a sunny or semi-sunny sheltered place set the tubers on edge 3 inches deep and 3 inches apart in somewhat neutral and well-drained soil. Maintain moisture. Provide winter mulch in Zone 7. The flowers come 3 to 4 months after planting and in warm regions will likely repeat with smaller blossoms for a few years.

BRODIAEA laxa

see below **Triteleia laxa** Grass Nut, Triplet Lily

CALADIUM, Elephant's-ear. Excellent. These

large, shield-shaped leaves colorful as flowers on slender stems 12 to 24 inches are called "dancing ladies" because they flutter in the wind. Superb bedding and pot plants, with translucent leaves. The fanciful leaf patterns are variations on combinations of pink, red, and/or white on green, and brighten partially shaded borders with reliable color in late spring, summer, and early fall. See list 51, Foliage for Color. They also can be grown indoors at high temperatures in a humid atmosphere with good light.

CAMASSIA (kam-*mass*-ee-uh) cusickii

Camass, Camas   Zones 4/5-7

In early summer, a 36-inch spike rises bearing a prodigious display of up to 300 long-lasting, star-shaped, light blue flowers. Best at the back of the border as the grassy foliage fades after flowering. Very successful in the wild or at the edge of a pond or bog. The bulb weighs half a pound. Other species have deep blue, white, or yellow flowers. This species is native to Oregon. The pale blue, smaller-flowered Eastern Camass, *C. scilloides,* also called Wild Hyacinth, Meadow Hyacinth, or Indigo Squill, is only 10 to 15 inches high and flowers earlier, in mid- to late spring.

Culture: Plant in fall in full sun or partial sun 6 to 8 inches deep and 4 to 6 inches apart in well-drained soil and maintain moisture. Prefers moist situations and does not like to be disturbed.

CANNA (*kan*-uh). The big, lush, often highly colored

leaves and exotic yellow, red, orange, apricot, or pink iris-like flowers provide dependable summer color and are a feature of massed municipal plantings. New hybrids from 1 to 7 feet tall are sized to suit small beds as well as public parks. They are handsome in groups, useful as a backdrop for a mixed border, and lovely in islands. The aquatic types make superb tall clumps, flower luxuriously, and are a mainstay of water gardens and wet places.

Culture: Plant the rhizomes in spring after danger of frost, in full sun or light shade in well-drained, fertile, humusy soil, and then maintain moisture. Set dwarf strains 5 inches deep and 12 inches apart; place large cannas 24 inches apart. Deadhead for continuous flowering.20 North of Zone 8, lift them in autumn before cold weather. Protect with mulch in Zone 8.

C. × generalis

Garden Canna   Zones 8-11

The name represents the many popular modern hybrid strains. For small gardens and containers, choose the 18-inch Seven Dwarfs strain. The taller Pfitzer's Dwarfs, 24 to 36 inches, are suited to the middle of a big border. A group called the Crozy, or French, cannas reach 3 to 4 feet and are magnificent in municipal plantings.

Summer bulb flowers with lasting blooms:
ABOVE Huge *Camassia cusickii* bears up to 300 flowers on each stem. (Heath)
LEFT Very fragrant *Acidanthera*, the peacock orchid—for cutting, containers, bedding. (Heath)
BELOW Pineapple flower, *Eucomis*, for bedding and containers.
(Netherlands Flowerbulb Information Center)

C. × hybrida
Water Canna   Zones 8-9

In moist sites and water gardens, these reach a stately 4 feet and bear large orange or reddish or yellow flowers. In water, set them out in early spring in containers up to 6 inches under the surface. Where there is frost, store the containers indoors for winter.

CROCOSMIA (kroh-*koz*-mee-uh). Rather like gladiolus, in late summer crocosmia sends up sword-shaped leaves followed by a slender, branching spike about 18 inches high of deep orange-scarlet flowers. Fine for cutting and attractive in small gardens.

Culture: Handle the corm as gladiolus and plant in spring in full sun to bright shade 3 inches deep, 6 inches apart in well-drained, light, sandy soil. Lift for winter in Zones 4 and 5; mulch for winter in Zones 6 and 7. Best with sustained moisture but the plant is versatile.

C. crocosmiiflora   Zones 6-10
Often sold as Montbretia. The starry blossoms are orange-red and flower over a long period. Quick to perennialize.

C. masoniorum (syn. *Tritronia masoniorum*)
'Lucifer'   Zones 6-11
Superb long-lasting red cultivar about 18 inches tall and an exceptional garden perennial, hardy without cover for at least the southern half of Zone 6.

DAHLIA, Dahlia. A major perennial and exhibition flower for late summer and early fall. It bears daisylike blossoms in luminous pastels, strong deep colors, and brilliant bicolors. There are two groups—the extraordinary hybrids grown from tubers whose flowers may be 10 to

12 inches across, and, lately, the modest bedding plants grown from seed and treated as annuals. Heights range from 12 to 18 inches to bushes 5 feet tall. Dahlias are among the best flowers for cutting. See list 10, Dahlia. List 33, Annuals for Fall, discusses growing dahlias from seed.

EUCOMIS (yew-*kom*-iss) **comosa**
Pineapple Flower   Zones 7-11
Fascinating, long-lasting 24- to 36-inch flower spike whose upper half in late summer is tufted with yellow-green blossoms crowned at the top with a green-yellow pineapple-like rosette of green leaves. The leaves can be spotted with purple on the underside. Showy grouped 3 to 5 in containers. Eye-catching in arrangements.

Culture: Plant in spring in full sun or light shade so the top is covered with 4 or 5 inches of rich well-drained soil and maintain moisture during active growth.

GALTONIA (gol-*toh*-nee-uh) **candicans**
Summer Hyacinth   Zones 6-11
Excellent. This South African bulb somewhat resembles a tall hyacinth, and in late summer bears spikes of slightly fragrant, green-tinged white flowers on stalks to 36 inches tall. The strap-shaped leaves are 2 inches wide and 3 to 4 feet long. Good for cutting and massed at the back of the border or grouped in large containers.

Culture: Where the climate allows permanent plantings, set out in fall or spring in full sun. Plant with 6 inches of soil over the tops, 6 to 8 inches apart in well-drained soil. Maintain moisture. Mulch through winter. The species *G. princeps* flowers earlier and is a good choice for container growing in cooler regions.

GLADIOLUS. In the North, this is one of the most elegant and long-lasting of the flowers for cutting; in north and central Florida it is grown as a bedding plant. Attractive swordlike foliage develops before the flower stem. The blossoms—in bicolors and every color but blue—are borne on tapering stems 18 to 36 inches long and open starting at the bottom. There are two major groups—the big 36-inch modern cultivars and the smaller 18-inch plants that flower in late spring and perennialize in warm climates. *G. byzantinus* is a violet-red species 18 to 20 inches tall, with narrow leaves. Hardy above −20° F. Recommended for restoration landscapes and historic collections. Gladiolus and culture are described on list 71, The Cutting Garden.

GLORIOSA (gloh-ree-*oh*-suh) **rothschildiana**
Gloriosa Lily, Glory Lily, Climbing Lily
                                            Zones 9-11
A small tendril-climbing vine to about 6 feet that in summer and fall bears yellow-based, crimson-edged, wavy-petaled flowers rather like lilies turning inside-out. The flowers are excellent for cutting. Groups of 5 to 10 grow into a magnificent screen.

Culture: In the North, set them out in containers and winter the pots indoors. In warm regions, grow them as perennials but in Zone 9, mulch for winter. In spring, plant the stoloniferous corms in full sun or semi-sun horizontally 2 inches deep in well-drained, acid to neutral soil and provide a mesh for climbing. If possible, keep the feet shaded and foliage in full sun. Maintain moisture. Potted up in January to March, they will flower summer through fall. By varying planting times, they can be brought into flower through several seasons.

HYMENOCALLIS (hye-men-oh-*kal*-iss)
narcissiflora (syn. *Ismene calathina*)
Basket Flower, Peruvian Daffodil   Zones 8-11
Excellent bedding plant with straplike leaves. In summer it raises a 36-inch, fleshy stalk that bears 2 to 5 exquisitely fragrant, lilylike white or yellow flowers with exotic curving petals. 'Sulphur Queen' is yellow banded with green. Group toward the back of the bed or in containers in sets of 3 to 5.

Culture: In the North, plant the bulbs out in late spring, lift them in early fall, and winter them indoors. Set the bulb so the neck tip is at the surface of the soil. In warm regions, plant in full or semi-sun 6 inches apart in well-drained, rich, moist soil. Maintain moisture. Flowers 10 days to several weeks after planting. In Florida it requires protection from full sun and is dried in winter.

LILIUM, Lily. Magnificent, major summer flower. A hybrid lily stalk 7-feet tall and spangled with 40 or 50 huge, elegant flowers is the garden's most commanding plant, but there are also medium and small lilies in all colors except blue. The little 12- to 20-inch Pixie series is delightful at the back of narrow borders. Lilies remain in flower 3 to 4 weeks and are very desirable and lasting cut flowers. Plant in groups of 4 to 6 at the back of the border, in a bed of their own, in the cutting garden, or in islands. See list 11, Lily.

NERINE **bowdenii.** For several weeks in late summer and fall this tender, bulbous, 15- to 18-inch plant bears exotic clusters of pink funnel-shaped flowers with wavy reflexed petals and long bright red stamens. Decorative and challenging, it is grown as a pot plant in the North. See list 7, Exotic Bulbs.

POLIANTHES (pol-ee-*anth*-eez) **tuberosa**
Tuberose   Zones 8-11
Source of commercial perfume, these dainty flowers are exquisitely scented of orange blossoms or hyacinths. The waxy white blossoms are borne July to fall in loose spikes on wandlike stems 18 to 36 inches tall. Stocky doubles such as the 24-inch-high 'The Pearl' are best for flower borders. Plant near porches or entrances where the heady scent can be enjoyed in the evening when it is most intense. 'Early Mexican' which flowers in early fall, is intensely fragrant and survives southern winters in the ground.

Culture: For pot culture in April crowd the tubers in 5-inch containers, tip at the soil surface, in rich, well-drained soil. Move the pots outdoors to flower. In the garden, plant after frosts in full sun in well-drained, humusy soil, in holes 3 to 4 inches deep. For a long season of fragrance, make weekly plantings in groups of 6 at the back of the border. Maintain soil moisture. Tuberoses planted deeply may survive cool climates that experience lots of snow cover, but generally they are lifted in fall and wintered indoors. In Zone 8 mulch for winter.

SPARAXIS (spuh-*rax*-iss) **tricolor**
Wandflower   Zones 7/8-11
The flower somewhat resembles the iris-like tritonia, below. In late spring and summer the stem rises from a broad, basal fan of leaves about 12 inches tall and bears several bright, often bicolored, funnel-shaped flowers in orange, maroon, white, yellow, copper, red, or cherry red with a dramatic flash of black. Good cutting flower. In cooler regions plant 10 to 12 corms to a container.

Culture: In fall or spring plant in full sun with an inch of soil over the tops, spaced 2 inches apart in well-drained sandy loam. Maintain moisture during growth and allow to dry and bake when flowering ends. Mulch for winter in Zones 7 and 8.

TRITELEIA (trye-*tell*-lee-uh) **laxa**
(syn. *Brodiaea laxa*)
Grass Nut, Triplet Lily   Zones 5-10
Excellent American native that blossoms in early summer, bridging the gap between the bulbs and the perennials. Tall, eye-catching in meadows, woodland gardens, and containers, the upward-facing, funnel-shaped violet-purple, blue, or white flowers grow in loose clusters on stems up to 24 inches high. A superior bedding plant for the Southwest where it perennializes and is a lasting cut flower. 'Queen Fabiola', the best cultivar, has intense blue-mauve flowers larger than the species.

Culture: In the fall plant the corms in full sun 5 inches deep and 3 inches apart in soil that is very well-drained, especially in regions of heavy summer rains. Maintain moisture during the growing season but allow to become somewhat dry in summer. Mulch for winter in Zones 5 and 6.

TRITONIA (trye-*toh*-nee-uh) **crocata**
                                          Zones 6/7-11
Excellent. In spring or early summer tritonias bear trumpet-shaped blossoms in salmon, coral, peach, pink, orange, or creamy yellow on 24-inch stems above sword-shaped leaves. They are at least as beautiful as gladiolus and last well when cut. This *Crocosmia* relative often is sold as montbretia or Saffron Tritonia. Handsome planted 12 or more in an 8-inch container. The variety *miniata* is smaller and red-flowered.

Culture: In the North the corms are lifted and wintered indoors, but they perennialize in warmer regions, especially California. In fall or spring, set out in full sun with 1 inch of soil over the tops in well-drained, sandy loam. Maintain even moisture during the growing season. Mulch for winter in Zones 6 and 7.

ZANTEDESCHIA (zan-ted-*desh*-ee-uh)
Calla Lily
An excellent early summer flower. The familiar form (*Z. aethiopica*) is a heavily textured, creamy white lily 2 to 4 feet tall that looks as though it has been swirled onto the top of its round, stately stem. The smaller, colorful hybrids from New Zealand are suited to home gardens. The flowers also may be pink, lavender, or yellow and rise above large, textured, heart-shaped leaves. It often is grown in cutting gardens in warm regions.

Culture: North of Zone 8, pot tubers 2 inches deep, one to a 5- or 6-inch container or three- to a 12-inch pot in March or April, and move outdoors when the weather warms; when flowering ends, dry, lift, and store the tubers at 50° F to 60° F. In the South, during fall or spring, plant in holes 4 inches deep and 1 inch apart in well-drained soil that contains lots of peat moss. Maintain moisture evenly until flowering ends. Prefers full sun in the North, partial sun in the South.

Z. albamaculata
Spotted Calla, Black-throated Calla Zones 8-11
The flower of this species is trumpet-shaped with a purple blotch at the base. The stems reach a height of 12 to 18 inches. It is somewhat hardier than others.

Z. elliottiana
Golden Calla, Yellow Calla   Zones 9-11
This is the loveliest species, dark sulphur yellow flowers 6 inches or more on 24-inch stems above bright green leaves.

Z. rehmannii   Zones 9-11
Pink, shorter than the yellow above, with flowers that show just topping the leaves. It goes dormant right after flowering.

ZEPHYRANTHES (zeff-er-*anth*-eez)
Zephyr Lily, Rain Lily, Fairy Lily
Excellent late summer color. When there's plenty of moisture present the grassy tufts, 9 to 15 inches high, are covered with crocus-like flowers 2 to 3 inches across in pink, purple, yellow, white, orange, or rose-red. In frost-free climates it is a lawn substitute and seashore ground cover.

Culture: In regions with temperatures below 25° F, grow these in containers wintered indoors, 10 or 12 to a 6-inch pot. During growth even moisture is essential, but allow a dry spell after flowering. In early spring in the North, fall in the South, plant in full sun 1 inch under sandy loam with 2 inches between bulbs.

Z. × ajax   Zones 6-9
A light yellow that flowers summer and autumn and in warm regions keeps its leaves all winter.

Z. candida
Autumn Zephyr Lily   Zones 6-9
This is the hardiest species. In summer and autumn it bears a white flower about the same height as the leaves, sometimes blushed pink on the outside. In frost-free areas narrow, stiff leaves up to 12 inches high appear in late summer and last until spring.

Z. grandiflora   Zones 9-11
Bears rose-red flowers larger than other species on stems to 15 inches tall. Flowers in late spring and summer and is very popular.

Z. rosea   Zones 9-11
The leaves are spreading and flat, and the blossoms are rose-red, about an inch long, and appear in fall. Grows to 12 inches tall.

TOP Brilliant, eye-catching flowers of *Sparaxis tricolor*, a choice container plant. (Harper)
ABOVE *Triteleia laxa*, excellent native whose blooming bridges the gap between spring bulbs and early summer perennials. (Heath)
LEFT Exquisite black-throated calla, *Zantedeschia albamaculata*, a rather hardy calla lilly. (Viette)

SOURCE: BRENT HEATH IS A WORLD AUTHORITY ON DAFFODILS AND INTERNATIONALLY KNOWN FOR THE DEVELOPMENT OF FLOWERING BULBS. HE AND HIS WIFE BECKY HYBRIDIZE BULBS ON THE ORIGINAL HEATH BULB FARM IN GLOUCESTER, VIRGINIA.

5. FALL AND WINTER BULBS

■ These are planted in summer and they are the last flowers of the year—some so late it's practically next spring before they appear. The fall bloomers are especially appealing. The tender lavenders of colchicum and the fall crocuses in the midst of autumn's assertive reds, russets, and golds is always a surprise. I've seen tall, delicate-seeming Japanese anemones in full flower tossing in northern Connecticut's fall winds without losing a petal. In the South the hardy Amaryllis is an essential element of the fall garden, and it perennializes.

The vulnerability of fall flowers is an illusion. In the cool, moist air of autumn the wax begonias and geraniums brighten and stretch. The flowers last longer than in summer, especially when sheltered from storms by a stone wall or a big rock, a shrub or the high canopy of a tree, or the angled corner of a building. In their hardiness zones, most bulbs described here will perennialize.

The flowering season for fall and winter bulbs varies according to climate. At the northern end, Zone 6 and above, these bulbs bloom toward the end of winter, with the thawing of the snow. But in Zone 7 and south where there is no snow cover, they flower in December and January and even earlier. My palest daffodils insist on flowering here in Washington, D.C., in November. Exceptions are the fall crocus and hardy *Amaryllis belladona* which flower only in fall or early winter.

Plant large bulbs in sets of three to five; small bulbs such as the crocuses look best in groups of at least 20, or 50 to 100.

Companion and Follow-on Plants: Asters and cushion mums are good companions. In the North, all the autumn color the garden can hold is provided by sugar maples and sumacs. Farther south, the hollies color up at this season and 'Autumn Joy' sedum turns from jade green to pink, then coral, and finally russet. Many ornamental grasses mature now, lifting light-catching inflorescences to the breeze. To maintain an interesting winter garden it often is enough to let be the browning structures of summer flowers—eventually they'll bind sculptures of snow. The early spring bulbs, the garden's new beginning, are the ultimate follow-on plants for fall flowering bulbs.

Planted in summer, these bulbs bloom through fall and some till winter: LEFT *Crocus speciosus*, an easy perennializer, often holds its flowers until hard frosts. (Heath) BELOW Hardy amaryllis, *Lycoris squamigira*, in full bloom at the U.S. Botanic Garden in Washington, D.C. (Viette)

AMARYLLIS (am-ar-*rill*-iss) belladona
(syn. *Brunsvigia rosea*)
Belladonna Lily, Cape Belladonna, Naked-lady Lily   Zones 7-11

Excellent. A magnificent, fragrant flower 24 to 36 inches tall resembling the big Amaryllis, *Hippeastrum*, which is grown indoors in the North. In the South it perennializes and is an essential element of the fall garden. Long blue-green leaves develop in spring and after they subside, in late summer and autumn, a tall stem rises, bearing 2 to 4 fragrant rose-pink blossoms. Plant it with mums or hosta to mask the naked stem. 'Hathor' has huge flowerheads.

Culture: In early summer set the bulbs in full sun or semi-shade 12 inches apart with the tops just under the surface of well-drained, slightly acid soil, pH 6.0 to 6.5. Benefits from somewhat dry soil in summer. Divide just as or when flowering and before new growth begins. Protect with mulch for winter in Zones 7 and 8. In colder regions, grow this in a pot and winter it indoors.

LEFT The marbled foliage of baby cyclamen lasts until spring and makes a handsome background for the bulbs. (Harper)
BELOW Autumn crocus, *Colchicum autumnale*, comes back year after year. (Heath)
BOTTOM Winter daffodil, *Sternbergia lutea*, lovely with fall crocus, should be grown more. (McDonald)

ARUM (ay-rum) italicum 'Pictum'
Italian Arum   Zones 6-11

Grown for the big, 24-inch-tall, arrow-shaped, very decorative white-marbled leaves that emerge when everything else is fading away in fall and persist all winter. In early spring, greenish yellow flowers rather like a narrow Calla Lily rise, followed by a bunch of attractive red berries that persists through summer. It is a good pot plant, and leaves and flowers are interesting in flower arrangements. Group in sets of 5 to 10 in containers in the North, in beds in Zone 6 and southward.

Culture: Plant the tubers in full or semi-sun in late summer or early fall 2 inches deep, 6 inches apart, in groups of 5 or 10 in well-drained, humusy soil. Maintain moisture, especially during growth and flowering.

COLCHICUM (kol-chik-um) autumnale
Autumn Crocus, Meadow Saffron, Mysteria,
Wonder Bulb   Zones 4-9

Excellent perennialized. Like a big crocus 4 to 8 inches tall in shades of amethyst, purple, rose, violet, mauve, pink, and white, it flowers with the coming of cool weather and is followed by large, glossy, persistent leaves. Best planted in drifts of at least 20 in the rock garden, or turning a corner of a woodland path, or in a big container near an entrance. 'Waterlily' is a romantic, large, lilac-pink with many-petalled double flowers that last for weeks; the early 'The Giant' is a showy lavender-pink, with white at the base; 'Album' which flowers later, is a luminous white.

Culture: Plant in late summer or early fall for fall bloom. Set the corms out in full or semi-sun 3 inches deep and 4 to 6 inches apart. Maintain moisture. Mulch for winter in Zone 4. Perennializes when conditions are right, but not in frost-free areas. The corms often will flower in a saucer without soil or water near a window.

CROCUS (*kroh*-kus)
Excellent. The fall crocuses flower in early and mid-fall, with small, elegant, cup-shaped blooms 4 to 6 inches high in rose, pink, blue, violet, and yellow. The grassy leaves streaked with white or silver rise in spring, then die down in summer. In warm regions a thoughtful choice of species can have crocuses flowering from September through April. Charming by rock outcroppings, in rock gardens, by rock walls and steps, at the wood's edge or in the border. Spring flowering species are discussed on list 1, Early Spring, Specialty Bulbs.

   Culture: Plant in August or September. They may flower later the same fall. Set out in full sun or partial shade, pointed end up, 3 to 4 inches deep and 2 inches apart in light, well-drained, rather sandy soil. Most successful if they dry out a bit in summer after the foliage goes, but they are tolerant of variations in moisture. Crocuses perennialize quickly, and some are good pot plants.

C. kotschyanus (syn. *C. zonatus*)   Zones 5-9
Excellent. The 4- to 6-inch-high, rose-lilac flower rises earlier than the popular *S. speciosus* below and has a white or deep yellow throat and usually two yellow spots at the base. There is a lovely white form, 'Albus.'

C. sativus Saffron Crocus   Zones 6-9
Excellent. This is the crocus whose red stigmas, when dried, become saffron. The 3- to 6-inch-high flowers are large, purple with deep purple veins, and have bloodred pistils that hang beyond the petals.

C. speciosus   Zones 5-9
Excellent. One of the showiest, easiest, earliest types, and it can stay in bloom until hard frosts. The flowers are about 4 inches high, light lavender-blue with bright orange stigmas. A superb bulb for perennializing, it tolerates more moisture than *C. sativus* and a wide range of soil conditions.

C. tomasinianus 'Barr's Purple'   Zones 3-7
A lavender-blue crocus that most often appears in early spring but also may flower in fall. Excellent for perennializing. The leaves come with the flowers in this species.

CYCLAMEN neapolitanum (syn. *hederifolium*), Baby Cyclamen. Excellent. It forms a clump of beautiful marbled leaves that raises slender silky stems bearing exotic pendent flowers with reflexed petals. This species is usually grown for its foliage—ivy-shaped leaves well-marbled with white. The flowers appear first, borne on 4-inch stems in late summer and autumn, white to rose-pink with a deep carmine blotch. Where it can be grown outdoors, cyclamen flowers in fall and sporadically, depending on weather, into spring. See list 7, Exotic Bulbs.

ERANTHIS hyemalis, Winter Aconite, is a little plant 3 to 4 inches tall that bears a long-lasting golden blossom in late winter, but sometimes as early as January. Charming as a carpeting for sunny slopes. See list 1, Early Spring, Specialty Bulbs.

GALANTHUS nivalis, Snowdrop, is one of the earliest of the little bulbs. It bears delicate, pendent, bell-like white flowers streaked with emerald green, in January or as late as March, according to climate. See list 1, Early Spring, Specialty Bulbs.

LYCORIS (lye-*kor*-iss) **squamigera**
Magic Lily, Resurrection Lily   Zones 5-8
Excellent. This is also known as autumn lycoris and hardy amaryllis. Straplike leaves rise in spring, die down, then in late summer or early fall tall stems appear bearing 4 to 7 fragrant, exotic, airy, trumpet-shaped, rose-pink flowers fringed with amethyst blue. About 24 inches tall. The Spider Lily, or Red Spider Lily, *L. radiata*, is recommended for The Japanese Garden, list 61.

   Culture: Plant the bulb in August in sun or partial shade 5 inches deep in well-drained, rich, humusy soil where it can remain undisturbed. Mulch for winter. Perennializes readily but needs to be in a bed that dries out a little in summer. Divide after foliage dies down in spring. Avoid transplanting.

NARCISSUS, Daffodil. The three daffodils here are among the earliest to flower—or the latest—depending on climate. In warm regions they appear in late fall or winter; in the cooler reaches of their hardiness zones, they flower in late winter or very early spring. The two small species are suited to rock gardens and container growing and all three may be forced into indoor bloom. *N. asturiensis* grows to 4 inches high and bears nodding flowers in two shades of yellow, like a miniature 'King Alfred'. *N. obvallaris* (the Tenby daffodil) is excellent for pots, a very early long-lasting daffodil about 8 inches tall with a golden yellow trumpet. Perfect for perennializing in grass. Prefers loamy soil. *N.* 'Grand Soleil d'Or', 14 inches tall, is a glorious, fragrant orange and golden flower with many florets, like the Paper-white, a good forcing daffodil. In Zones 8 and 9 it is grown in the garden, where it flowers in autumn or early winter. For culture see list 9, Daffodil. See list 1 for the very early spring daffodils.

STERNBERGIA (stern-*berj*-ee-uh) **lutea**
Winter Daffodil, Lily-of-the-field   Zones 6-11
Four or 5 of these bright yellow, crocuslike blossoms rise from each bulb after the long strap-shaped leaves die in summer, and then flower on until frost on plants 6 to 8 inches tall. Nice with *Colchicum autumnale*, Autumn Crocus.

   Culture: In early fall plant the bulbs in full sun 4 to 6 inches apart with 1 inch of soil over the tops in dry, very well-drained, rather heavy soil. In Zones 6 and 7, mulch for winter. Perennializes easily in a warm, sheltered place.

SOURCE: BRENT HEATH IS ONE OF THE WORLD AUTHORITIES ON DAFFODILS AND INTERNATIONALLY KNOWN FOR THE DEVELOPMENT OF FLOWERING BULBS. HE AND HIS WIFE BECKY HYBRIDIZE BULBS ON THE ORIGINAL HEATH BULB FARM IN GLOUCESTER, VIRGINIA.

6. BEST BULBS FOR THE SOUTH

■ **Many bulbs, especially spring-flowering bulbs, require a period of chilling. The bulbs recommended here for mild climates—approximately Zones 8 through 11—were chosen based on extensive recent observations of their performance in *warm* regions. They not only tolerate the South's gentle winters and extended periods of over 80° F in summer, but they are the best and *easiest* bulbs that do so.**

   Two sets of plants are suggested. The first set describes bulbs that are planted in fall, the second those that are planted in spring. The list of secondary plants given for each set describes bulbs which are *not easiest* in the average home garden—not as useful or not quite as foolproof—but which are good nonetheless.

   Culture: Winters are variable in Zone 8, so a protective cold-season mulch is suggested for plants whose hardiness is marginal there. Mound organic materials—ground leaves, composted garden debris, or peat moss—2 or 3 inches deep around the base of the plant. In hot, dry areas a summer mulch helps keep the roots cool. It is easier for bulbs to survive high heat if the moisture level is right. Good soil drainage is essential and a substantial humus content helps to sustain even moisture.

   Be aware that winter in a dry part of Zone 8—Texas, for instance—is quite different from winter in Zone 8 on the moist coast of the Pacific Northwest.

   The farther south the garden, the less the sun is necessary for top performance. Bulbs that thrive in full sun or light shade in New England will do better in partial sun or semi-shade in the hot South. Sudden summer heat shuts down plant production just as next season's flowers are forming.

BEST AND *EASIEST BULBS* FOR THE *SOUTH—* *FALL PLANTED*

HIPPEASTRUM, Amaryllis, Barbados Lily. The tall, bare 24- to 36-inch flowering stalk of the biggest hybrids is topped by a cluster of 4 to 6 extraordinary 6-inch-long, outward-facing, trumpet-shaped flowers that may be white, pink, red, orange, salmon, or striped. Strap-shaped leaves come up later. Where plants are hardy—Zones 8 to 11—smaller hybrids are grown outdoors with a winter mulch. For culture, see list 7, Exotic Bulbs.

IRIS, Flag, Fleur-de-lys. The familiar late-spring irises develop from tuberous rhizomes and are among the finest of all garden perennials. They are described on list 18, Perennials for the South, and are sold by perennial nurseries. The small irises that grow from bulbous roots and bloom very early are described with the spring bulbs—lists 1 and 2. *I.* × *germanica* and the Japanese and Siberian irises are among types recommended for the South. See also list 25, *Iris.*

Hippeastrum, the amaryllis that blooms indoors in winter in the North, anchors a turnaround in the warm South, where it perennialized. The species is the better "doer" —a term used in the nursery industry to indicate top performers. (de Hertogh)

LEUCOJUM, Snowflake. Large, long-lasting, pendent, bell-shaped flowers, white with green markings, 2 to 8 on each 18- to 24-inch stem, appear in spring to late spring on lush, grassy plants. Three species are successful in the South: *L. aestivum*, Giant Snowflake, Summer Snowflake, which flowers in mid- to late spring, has 18-inch flowering stems on a plant 18 to 24 inches tall; *L. autumnale*, smaller, somewhat difficult to establish, has pink-flushed flowers in late summer or early fall on stems 4 to 6 or 8 inches tall, with thin leaves that remain till summer—hardy Zone 6 with mulch, and Zones 7 though 9; *L. vernum* is an intermediate size, 9 to 12 inches tall, that flowers before the Giant Snowflake, with 1 or 2 bells per stem. See list 2, Spring, Intermediate Bulbs, for culture.

LILIUM, Lily. Blooms in late spring, summer, and fall; plants grow to 7 feet tall. The modern hybrids are garden aristocrats, serving as magnificent and lasting cut flowers whose fragrance can scent a home and garden as no other flower can. However, success is not sure below Zone 8. Asiatic and Oriental hybrids usually will do best in warm regions. See list 11, Lily.

MUSCARI armeniacum, Grape Hyacinth. Long-lasting, intense blue flowers, white-lined at the edges, cluster thickly on 6- to 8-inch stems with grassy foliage. Excellent as a mid-spring underplanting for shrubs and small trees, muscari is extraordinary perennialized in long drifts ("rivers") of blue. See list 1, Early Spring, Specialty Bulbs.

NARCISSUS hybrids, Daffodil. Southward, Paper-white Narcissus succeeds along with other Tazettas, especially Poetaz or Polyanthus. The bulbs need little or no chilling and some are suited to the very warm South. There's a cluster of 4 to 15 small flowers (known as 17 Sisters) on each stem, usually with short cups. They are excellent perennializers, the best daffodils for forcing and choice in beds. Some especially recommended are 'February Gold', 'Geranium', 'Jumblie', 'Salome', 'Tahiti', 'Tete-a-tete', and 'Unsurpassable'. See list 9, Daffodil.

BEST BUT NOT EASIEST— FALL PLANTED

These bulbs do well in the South but generally are not as useful or as easy to grow as those described above.

ALLIUM species cowanii, neapolitanum, unifolium, schubertii. Flowering ornamental onions that bloom in mid- to late spring. Several species are discussed on list 3, Spring, Large-flowered Bulbs.

ANEMONE coronaria, De Caen and St. Brigid series. Magnificent anemones in spectacular colors for late spring and early summer. See list 4, Summer-into-fall Bulbs.

DIETES. It is a little like a very dainty tall iris and thrives on the dry West Coast, but is not available everywhere at this time.

ENDYMION hispanicus (syn. *Scilla campanulata*), Spanish Bluebell, Spanish Jacinth, Bell-flowered Squill. A pretty little bluebell, or squill, that blooms in spring. See list 2, Spring, Intermediate Bulbs.

FREESIA Tall, delicate flower included for its haunting fragrance, but it is challenging to grow. In southern gardens hybrids do well for a time, but usually succumb to viruses and Fusarium. The handsome new cultivated varieties are generally fragrant. Usually grown in containers. See list 8, Bulbs for Containers.

GLADIOLUS byzantinus, see list 71, The Cutting Garden. Also suitable is the 24-inch-tall *G. tristis*, which has creamy white-yellow flowers, often striped purple, that are fragrant in the evening.

IPHEION uniflorum, Spring Starflower. A dainty, deep violet-blue, star-shaped, upward-facing little blossom on a 3- to 5-inch stem in mid-spring. See list 2, Spring, Intermediate Bulbs.

IXIA Daisylike flowers with rather stiff pointed petals on long, wiry stems—lasting when cut. Thrives in long, cool winters.

LYCORIS species aurea, radiata, squamigera, Magic Lily, Resurrection Lily. The latter is discussed on list 5, Fall and Winter Bulbs. These are exotics whose flowers look like spidery lilies.

OXALIS species bowiei, hirta, maritiana (corymbosa), purpurea (variabilis), regnellii, versicolor. Full mounds of decorative clover-shaped leaves and dainty little flowers—a charming filler for spring bulbs. A spring-flowering species is discussed on list 2, Spring, Intermediate Bulbs.

RANUNCULUS (ran-*nun*-kew-lus) Buttercup, Crowfoot.

These delightful cultivated buttercups have cup-shaped blossoms in brilliant shades that flower on upright stems over a long period in late spring and early summer. The leaves are quite ornamental and differ according to species—some resemble the print of a crow's claw. Two types are recommended, the big full-petaled Persian Buttercup and a more delicate species for rock gardens. All cultivars should perform well where winters are long and cool. This is not one of the easiest bulbs for the South, but it is included here because its beauty attracts so much attention.

Culture: Not always reliable but worth an effort, especially in regions with long, cool, rainy winters and dry summers, such as those in California and up the coast towards Seattle. Generally hardy in Zones 8 and 9 with winter mulch. Elsewhere they are planted in spring and lifted in fall. Started plants are offered in the same season as pansies, for late fall or early spring planting. Or, sow seeds: where there is frost sow the seeds in early spring; farther south, sow the seeds in autumn. Prefers full sun, very well-drained rich soil, and sustained moisture.

R. asiaticus Persian Buttercup, Persian Ranunculus   Zones 8-9/10

The hybrids may resemble single, brilliant, black-centered poppies or, in strains such as the Telecote or Bloomingdale, very small double peonies. The colors range through shades of yellow, gold, orange, red, pink-rose, and white, and there are picotee types. Attractive, much-divided foliage.

R. gramineus   Zones 6-8

Fairly easy to grow and recommended for rock gardens, a very pleasant plant with long-lasting, blue-green, grassy leaves. The brilliant yellow, cup-shaped flowers appear in late spring and early summer. Height is 15 to 20 inches.

SPARAXIS Cultivars and hybrids do well enough where winters are long and cool. See list 4, Summer-into-fall Bulbs.

TRITELEIA laxa (syn. *Brodiaea laxa*) 'Queen Fabiola', a tall native plant with upward-facing, funnel-shaped, blue-mauve flowers in loose clusters on stems to 24 inches high. Blooms in early summer. See list 4, Summer-into-fall Bulbs.

TULIPA. See list 12, Tulip. Species tulips that succeed in climate Zone 8 include: *T. batalinii,* a small, pale yellow early tulip about 7 inches tall, choice for rock gardens; and *T. clusiana,* a dainty, eye-catching flower called Lady Tulip, is pink and white with a deep purple base, about 12 inches high. It tends to perennialize on the dry West Coast. So do *T. saxatalis,* an early midseason tulip 8 to 10 inches tall, lilac-pink with a yellow center—lovely, delicate, distinctly different—and *T. sylvestris,* a yellow tulip that spreads rapidly.

Successful as annuals on the dry West Coast are *T. praestans* 'Fusilier', an early bulb about 12 inches high, with 2 to 5 small, luminous orange-red flowers per bulb

Three beauties for warm regions:
TOP *Belamcanda chinensis.* (McDonald)
LEFT *Crinum.* (de Hertogh)
ABOVE *Watsonia.* (de Hertogh)

Tulips for warm regions:
ABOVE Greigii 'Plaisir'.
(Netherlands Flowerbulb Information Center)
RIGHT *Tulipa chrysantha*. (Heath)
BELOW *Tulipa tarda*.
(Netherlands Flowerbulb Information Center)

and abundant foliage, and *T. tarda* (syn. *T. dasystemon*), which flowers earlier than 'Lilac Wonder' (see list 1, Early Spring, Specialty Bulbs), a star-shaped, bunch-flowering tulip with up to 5 flowers on each 3- to 5-inch stem. The dainty, pointed petals have a yellow inner eye and broad white edge. *T. chrysantha*, which resembles the Lady Tulip and may be an 8-inch-high variety of it, also succeeds as an annual on the dry West Coast.

In Zones 9 and 10, tulips should be grown as annuals and pre-cooled before planting in December. Cultivated varieties of Single Late, Darwin, Triumph, Lily-flowering or Fringed tulips generally perform better than the species. A few proven highly adapted to Zone 8 are 'Golden Parade', 'KeizersKroon' ('Grand Duc'), 'Parade', 'Plaisir', and 'Queen of the Night'. There are many more.

T. turkestanica, a graceful, creamy white, star-shaped species with a touch of yellow-orange at the base on an 8-inch stem, is a historic tulip that succeeds in the South.

WATSONIA, Bugle Lily, 'Malvern', 'Mrs. Ballards White', 'Rubra'—these are gladiolus-like hybrids that flower in late spring for several weeks. Hardy with a winter mulch in Zone 8, without in Zones 9 through 11.

BEST AND EASIEST BULBS FOR THE SOUTH— SPRING PLANTED

ACHIMENES, Monkey-faced Pansy, Orchid Pansy, Japanese Pansy, Cupid's-bower, Mother's-tears, Widow's-tears, Nut Orchid, Magic Flower, Kimono Plant.   Zones 10-11
These smallish plants from the American tropics have drooping or upright branches 12 to 24 inches long that grow from a scaly rhizome which looks like a tiny pine cone. Summer to fall the plants bear many small, gloxinialike flowers that are blue, white, violet, cerise, pink, salmon, or yellow. Primarily a container plant, drooping types are excellent basket plants, prettiest when grouped 12 to a large container. See list 7, Exotic Bulbs.

AGAPANTHUS. During the late spring to early fall, a dense cluster of wonderful blue, white, or pink funnel-shaped flowers appears on a 36-inch to 5-foot stalk that stands well above a handsome mound of strap-shaped leaves. It makes a wonderful show lining embankments or featured in island beds. It is also highly regarded as a tub plant for terraces, steps, patios, or near outdoor pools. Great with hedge-size marigolds. See list 7, Exotic Bulbs.

BELAMCANDA (bel-am-*kan*-duh) **chinensis**
Blackberry Lily, Leopard Flower   Zones 6-11
The plant is rather like a 24-inch to 4-foot iris in foliage, with 3 to 12 showy 1- by 2-inch bright orange blossoms sprinkled with red spots thick as a leopard's. The flowers develop in July and August and are followed by pods that split to reveal shiny black seeds. Attractive in dried arrangements. Good container plant.

Culture: Easy, almost foolproof for most of the country. Set out rhizomes in full sun or light shade in well-drained, rich, sandy soil. May also be grown from seed. Mulch for winter in Zones 6 and 7.

CALADIUM, Elephant's-ear. Excellent for shade and partial shade. These large, shield-shaped leaves colorful as flowers, on slender stems 12 to 24 inches tall, are called "dancing ladies" because they flutter in the wind. Superb bedding and pot plants, with translucent leaves bearing fanciful patterns in varying combinations of pink, red, and/or white on green, they brighten late spring, summer, or early fall borders with color often more reliably than flowers. In the South, set out tubers in spring when daytime temperatures reach 70° F. Caladiums also can be grown indoors at high temperatures in a humid atmosphere with good light. See list 51, Foliage for Color.

CANNA. The big, lush, often highly colored leaves and exotic yellow, red, orange, apricot, or pink irislike flowers provide dependable summer color and are a feature of massed municipal plantings. New hybrids are sized to suit small beds as well as public parks—they range from 1 foot to 7 feet tall. Cannas are handsome in groups, useful as a backdrop for a mixed border and in islands. The aquatic types make superb tall clumps, flower luxuriously, and are a mainstay of water gardens and wet places. See list 4, Summer-into-fall Bulbs.

COLOCASIA (kol-oh-*kay*-see-uh) **esculenta**
(syn. *antiquorum* var. **esculenta**)
Taro, Kalo, Dasheen, Eddo   Zones 8-11
This is a huge, water-loving foliage plant 3 to 6 feet tall, grown for its 24-inch-long velvety green leaves, which are shaped like an elongated heart or an elephant's ear. Exotic and tropical in appearance, and evergreen in frost-free areas. The flowers are insignificant. The tubers are a food source in the Tropics.
    Culture: In Zones 5 through 8 the tubers are started indoors like caladiums or tuberous begonias, planted out in summer, and lifted before winter. Set in full or partial sun 36 inches apart under 3 inches of moist, rich, acid to neutral soil in up to 12 inches of water. Constant plentiful moisture is essential. Protect with mulch in Zone 9.

CRINUM (*krye*-num) **moorei**
Crinum Lily, Spider Lily   Zones 8-11
The genus resembles the amaryllis, *Hippeastrum*. This species is large, with clusters of beautiful 4-inch, long-tubed, funnel-shaped, rose-red flowers topping a tall, bare flower stalk that grows from the neck of a big bulb. The neck may be as much as 18 inches high. There are white and red cultivars. The strap-shaped leaves can be 3 inches across and 36 inches long. Imposing accent plant in large beds or islands and, above all, a great container plant.
    Culture: Hardy in Zones 8 and 9, and perhaps 7 with a winter mulch. Plant 5 to 6 inches deep, 12 inches apart, in well-drained, well-fertilized soil. Allow to dry down after flowering and for winter. North of its hardiness zone, lift and store indoors. For container growing, crowd as amaryllis in a pot barely 2 inches larger in diameter than the bulb. Avoid dividing.

GLADIOLUS × **hortulanus**. The long, tapering gladiolus stem studded with big, bright blossoms is one of the most elegant and long-lasting summer flowers for cutting. The blossoms open starting at the bottom and in some forms look like perched butterflies. This name covers the hundreds of big modern hybrids borne on tapering stems to 36 inches tall and grown as annuals in the North. Large-flowered types may be 4 to 7 inches across; butterfly-flowered types with striking throat markings are smaller. There are many bicolors and every color but blue. See list 71, The Cutting Garden.

NERINE bowdenii. For several weeks in late summer and fall, this tender, bulbous plant up to 15 inches tall bears exotic clusters of flowers that are pink marked with deeper pink, funnel-shaped with wavy reflexed petals. They are followed by strap-shaped leaves. See list 7, Exotic Bulbs.

POLIANTHES **tuberosa**, Tuberose. Source of commercial perfume, these dainty flowers are exquisitely scented of orange blossoms or hyacinths. Waxy and white, they are borne from July to fall in loose spikes on wandlike stems 18 inches to 36 inches tall. Stocky doubles such as the 24-inch-high 'The Pearl' are best for flower borders. Plant near porches or entrances where the heady scent can be enjoyed, especially in the evening when it is most intense. See list 4, Summer-into-fall Bulbs.

BEST BUT NOT EASIEST— SPRING PLANTED

ACIDANTHERA bicolor var. **murieliae**, Peacock Orchid. Tall, beautiful, long-lasting, very fragrant gladiolus-like flower for cutting, containers, and bedding. See list 4, Summer-into-fall Bulbs.

ALSTROEMERIA, Lily-of-the-Incas, Peruvian Lily. A favorite cut flower, 12 to 18 inches tall, with upright clusters of blossoms rather like azalea florets, 2 inches long, daintily etched or blotched with black and often bicolored—in pink, rosy salmon, red, mauve, lavender, cream, or white. See list 71, The Cutting Garden.

AMARYLLIS belladonna (syn. *Brunsvigia rosea*), Belladonna Lily, Naked Ladies. A handsome, fragrant flower 24 to 36 inches tall resembling the big-flowered Amaryllis, *Hippeastrum*, found on list 7, Exotic Bulbs.

BABIANA stricta is 12 inches high with clusters of 5 or 6 cup-shaped flowers in shades of blue, lavender, creamy white, and some crimson. Thrives on the dry West Coast and should be hardy with a mulch in Zone 8 and without mulch in Zones 9 through 11.

BLETILLA striata. An exquisite and easy member of the orchid family that puts up 24-inch spikes topped by several small lavender or white orchid blossoms. Blooms over a 2-week period in late spring. Good on the West Coast.

CLIVIA miniata, Kaffir Lily. Sword-shaped evergreen leaves that spread into a fan topped in spring (indoors) or summer (outdoors) by one or two 24-inch-tall, very showy flowers in brilliant orange-red, salmon, or white. See list 7, Exotic Bulbs.

CROCOSMIA. Quite easy to grow, and rather like gladiolus, the sword-shaped leaves are followed in late summer by a slender, branching stem of deep orange-scarlet flowers about 18 inches high. Fine for cutting and attractive in small gardens. See list 4, Summer-into-fall Bulbs.

DAHLIA. Those grown today are hybrids and they do well in Zone 8 in the Southeast and West Coast. There is an extensive range of good cultivars. See list 10, Dahlia.

EUCOMIS comosa, Pineapple Flower. Fascinating, long-lasting, 24- to 36-inch flower spike whose upper half in late summer is tufted with yellow-green blossoms crowned with a green-yellow, pineapple-like rosette of leaves. See list 4, Summer-into-fall Bulbs.

GALTONIA candicans, Summer Hyacinth. This South African bulb somewhat resembles a tall hyacinth and in late summer bears spikes of slightly fragrant, green-tinged white flowers on stalks up to 36 inches tall. The strap-shaped leaves are 2 inches wide and 3 to 4 feet long. See list 4, Summer-into-fall Bulbs.

GLORIOSA rothschildiana, Gloriosa Lily, Glory Lily, Climbing Lily. A small, tendril-climbing vine up to about 6 feet in length that in summer and fall bears yellow-based, crimson-edged, wavy-petaled flowers rather like lilies turning inside-out. See list 4, Summer-into-fall Bulbs.

HYMENOCALLIS narcissiflora (syn. *Ismene calathina*), Basket Flower, Peruvian Daffodil. Excellent bedding plant with strap-shaped leaves. In summer it raises a 36-inch fleshy stalk that bears 2 to 5 exquisitely fragrant, lilylike white or yellow flowers that have exotic curving petals. See list 4, Summer-into-fall Bulbs.

SPREKELIA formosissima, Jacobean Lily, St. James's Lily, Aztec Li y, Orchid Amaryllis. This relative of the amaryllis has a flower like a waxy, exotic, fire-red orchid. Rather brief flowering period. Hardy with a mulch for winter Zone 8, hardy without mulch in Zones 9 through 11.

ZEPHYRANTHES, Zephyr Lily, Rain Lily, Fairy Lily. When there's plenty of moisture the grassy tufts 9 to 15 inches high are covered with crocus-like flowers 2 to 3 inches across in pink, purple, yellow, white, orange, or rose-red. In frost-free climates it is a lawn substitute and a seashore ground cover. See list 4, Summer-into-fall Bulbs.

SOURCE: DR. A. A. DE HERTOGH IS PROFESSOR OF HORTICULTURAL SCIENCE AT NORTH CAROLINA STATE UNIVERSITY. FOR 25 YEARS HE HAS CONDUCTED RESEARCH ON FLOWER BULBS. HE IS THE AUTHOR OF THE HOLLAND BULB FORCER'S GUIDE AND THE HOLLAND BULB GARDEN GUIDE.

7. EXOTIC BULBS

■ Here are a handful of exotic bulbs that flourish outdoors in frost-free areas—usually in winter. In cool regions they are grown in containers that winter indoors. The fritillaries are a little different—quite hardy in our gardens but they also can be brought into bloom indoors as are tulips and daffodils. Most of these plants are from Africa, for example *Agapanthus*, the Lily-of-the-Nile, and *Clivia miniata*, the Kaffir Lily. They are as dramatic as the familiar amaryllis and no harder to grow.

Culture: Most of the recommended bulbs require sustained moisture when developing, but want less water after flowering and a period of dormancy in somewhat dry soil before the next flowering. Summering outdoors in full sun or partial shade encourages good growth and better flowering the following winter. When flowers fade, remove the stalks to their base.

ACHIMENES (ak-*kim*-in-eez)

Monkey-faced Pansy, Orchid Pansy, Japanese Pansy, Cupid's-bower, Mother's-tears, Widow's-tears, Nut Orchid, Magic Flower, Kimono Plant.

Zones 10-11

These smallish plants from the American tropics have drooping or upright branches 12 to 24 inches long that flower generously through summer to fall. The scaly rhizome looks like a tiny pine cone and bears gloxinialike flowers that may be blue, white, violet, cerise, pink, salmon, or yellow. Used primarily as a basket (drooping) and container plant, and best 12 to a large container, the upright forms are also planted in the garden.

Culture: Indoors, achimenes prefers warmth and full sun or artificial light, and it must have humidity during the day. Outdoors, it summers well in semishade and usually is brought indoors for winter. Plant the rhizomes in late winter or early spring 1 inch apart, 1 inch deep, in well-drained, porous soil with generous proportions of organic matter, either peat or leaf mold. Maintain moisture. Pinch out the tips of new 3- to 4-inch shoots to encourage bushiness and more flowers. Indoor plants can be moved outdoors when night temperatures reach 60° F. As flowering ends, let the plants dry down for dormancy and store indoors at between 60° and 70° F. The rhizomes will be ready for replanting during late winter.

A. andrieuxii looks like an African violet and has violet flowers. The blossoms of *A. cettoana* are violet to blue in color. *A. longiflora* has blue flowers appearing in July and August. A number of good cultivars are offered, including the variety *alba*, which is white.

AGAPANTHUS (ag-a-*panth*-us) africanus

African Lily, Blue Agapanthus, Lily-of-the-Nile

Zones 7-11

An imposing flower from southeast Africa whose cultivars are hybrids and will do well in beds in warm regions. In late spring to early fall a dense cluster of beautiful blue, white, or pink funnel-shaped flowers appears on a 3- to 5-foot stalk that stands well above a mound of strap-shaped leaves. It is highly regarded as a tub plant for terraces, steps, patios, or near outdoor pools. Great with hedge-size marigolds. 'Alba' is a white cultivar.

Exotic bulbs that flourish outdoors in frost-free areas
and bloom indoors in the North:
FACING PAGE Lily-of-the-Nile, *Agapanthus africanus,*
blooms late spring to early fall. (McDonald)
ABOVE The Kaffir Lily, *Clivia*, flowers indoors in spring.
(Viette)
ABOVE, RIGHT *Veltheimia viridifolia,* blooms in winter.
(McDonald)
RIGHT *Nerine bowdenii* flowers for several weeks in late
summer and fall. (Harper)

Cyclamen persicum, Persian cyclamen, is used as follow-on ground cover for spring bulbs in the warm South.
(McDonald)

Culture: In spring plant the rhizomes 12 inches apart with tops 1 inch below the surface in well-drained, deep, fertile, loamy soil, and maintain even moisture. Full sun to light shade is suitable. Allow the plants 4 or 5 years to become crowded before dividing. In the North, grow them in containers and winter them indoors on the dry side in good light with temperatures around 53° F, gradually increasing light and warmth in March and April.

CLIVIA (*klye*-vee-uh) **miniata**
Kaffir Lily   Zones 9-10
From South Africa. Good-looking plants to 24 inches high with a fan of sword-shaped evergreen leaves topped in spring (indoors) or summer (outdoors) by big long-lasting, showy, amaryllis-like flowerheads in brilliant orange-red or salmon. 'Aurea' is a clear yellow variety. *C. × cyrtanthiflora* is a brilliant orange species whose flowerheads are composed of fewer, larger florets—see list 8, Bulbs for Containers.

Culture: In mild climates clivia survives a little frost in the garden with a mulch. In cool regions, it is planted in fall to flower indoors in spring and may reflower outdoors later. Start the fleshy roots in shade or partial shade, set just beneath the surface of rich soil that includes a superphosphate, moss, or compost leaf mold and a fair amount of sand for aeration. Maintain moisture. A quarterly feeding of 10-6-4 keeps the plants healthy and green. Night temperatures of 50° F and days at about 65° F are ideal. Potbound plants seem to produce more flowers, but plantings will need dividing every 4 or 5 years.

CYCLAMEN (*sik*-lam-en)
Persian Violet
These clumps of beautifully marbled leaves raise graceful stems 4 to 8 inches high that bear small pendent flowers with exotic reflexed petals. The flowers appear first, in late summer and autumn—they may be white, pink, or carmine and there are bicolors with a deep carmine blotch.

The big-flowered florist's cyclamen blooms indoors in winter and spring in bright light but not direct sun, and is sold as a potted plant. Where it can be grown outdoors, hardy cyclamen flowers in fall and sporadically, depending on weather, into spring. Nice follow-on ground cover for spring bulbs.

Culture: Plant with the flat side down in the garden in July under 2 to 3 inches of topsoil and allow room to spread. Garden cyclamens do best in partial to full shade in well-drained soil. Prefers night temperatures of 50° F and requires even moisture. Avoid planting where nematodes are a problem.

C. europaceum (syn. *purpurascens*) Zones 5-11
Garden cyclamen with kidney-shaped leaves that are white on top, purple beneath, and 4- to 6-inch-tall, fragrant, bright carmine flowers during late summer and fall. There are pink cultivars.

C. ibericum (syn. *coum* subsp. *caucasicum*)
                                                  Zones 6-11
Fragrant garden cyclamen for late spring flowering, the flowers are white or carmine and the leaves are round and green. Delightful in rock gardens or bright woodlands. Plant 1 inch below the soil surface in September.

C. neapolitanum (syn. *hederifolium*)
Baby Cyclamen   Zones 5-9
Hardy garden cyclamen grown for the ivy-shaped, marbled-white leaves. In late summer and autumn the flowers—white to rose-pink with a deep carmine blotch—are born on 4-inch stems. Plant in the garden in July under 2 to 3 inches of topsoil and allow room to spread.

C. persicum Persian Cyclamen   Zones 9-11
The hybrids are the florist's large cyclamen with large blooms in white, pink, rose, salmon, or bicolors, on 8- to 12-inch stems. The leaves are heart-shaped moss-green and mottled white. Sold as a potted plant, it thrives in cool, humid rooms, 60° to 65° F daytime, 40° to 50° F at night. In summer withhold water until the leaves die back, then repot and maintain barely damp in a shady place until new growth begins.

FRITILLARIA, Fritillary.
Native to North Temperate regions, these hardy bulbs flower in our gardens in spring, bearing nodding red, white, yellow, or purple flowers under amazing tufts of narrow, pointed, upright leaves. They make unusual houseplants. The first two recommended are garden types and readily available—the others are less common but worth looking for. Allow potted types to dry down a little when blooming ends and when the tops die, repot or transplant outdoors. *F. imperialis,* Crown Imperial, is 24 to 36 inches tall, and the flowers are brick red, yellow, red, or purplish red. 'Aurora' has red-orange blooms. 'Lutea' has yellow flowers. 'Maxima' has orange-red flowers. Remove the foliage after flowering. *F. meleagris,* Checkered Lily, Snake's-head, is small and dainty (9 to 10 inches high) with checkered pinkish purple or white flowers. Remove foliage only after it has yellowed. *F. pudica,* Yellow Fritillary, which is hardy in Zones 2 to 8, is a tiny, narrow-leaved fritillary. It's yellow flowers which are sometimes tinged red, are borne on stems 3 to 8 inches high. It prefers humusy soil and flourishes in the Northwest. *F. recurva,* Scarlet Fritillary, hardy in Zones 6-9, is a tall plant with pink to red flowers that have turned-back edges on stems 18 to 30 inches high. It thrives in the Northwest and is one of the rarest in cultivation. See list 3, Spring, Large-flowered Bulbs.

HIPPEASTRUM (hip-pee-*ast*-rum) **cultivars**
Amaryllis, Barbados Lily   Zones 9-11
The bare, round 24- to 36-inch flowering stalk of the biggest is topped by a cluster of 4 to 6 extraordinary 6-inch outward-facing, trumpet-shaped flowers. The color may be white, pink, red, orange, salmon, or striped. Strap-shaped leaves rise up later. The largest bulbs produce as many as 3 stalks in a season. For indoor blooms the bulbs are potted in fall and flower once in winter or spring. 'Picotee' is a lovely white edged with red. Where they are hardy—Zones 8 to 11—smaller hybrids are grown outdoors with a winter mulch. See also the hardy *Amaryllis belladonna,* Belladonna Lily, Naked Ladies, recommended on list 5, Fall and Winter Bulbs.

Culture: For indoor winter bloom, in fall plant the huge bulb so that a third of it is above the soil, in a pot not more than 2 inches larger than the bulb. Place it in sunlight and keep the soil moist, not wet. During blooming, move to indirect light and remove the stalk when flowering ends. Summer the pot outdoors in bright shade. At the end of August, dry it down indoors at about 50° F for 8 to 10 weeks, or until you see signs of growth. Repot and moisten for a new round of blooming. Offsets can be cut away and potted up, but if the bulb and its offset are transferred intact to a larger pot the result will be a tremendous show.

In mild areas, smaller hybrids are grown outdoors with a winter mulch in Zones 7 through 9 and without mulch in Zones 9 to 11. Plant them in the fall in semi-sun with the base about 8 inches deep, 12 inches apart just under the surface of well-drained, slightly acid soil (pH 6.0 to 6.5). During growth water regularly and fertilize two or three times a month. After foliage fades in spring and summer allow a somewhat dry rest period.

NERINE (nee-**rye**-nee)

In late summer and fall for several weeks this tender, bulbous plant 15 to 18 inches tall bears exotic clusters of red, rose, scarlet, pink, mauve, or white funnel-shaped flowers with wavy reflexed petals and long, bright red stamens. They are followed by strap-shaped leaves.

Culture: Challenging. It flowers reliably when the roots are confined to a pot, but must not be watered after potting until the flower stalk appears. Repotting is done after several years. Plant in August alone or grouped 3 or 4 in a clay pot. Requires porous, loamy soil mixed with coarse sand and dried cow manure. Indoors, grow nerine in a sunny window in nighttime temperatures of 50° F. Plant in the garden in spring, either in sun or light shade, and in Zone 8 mulch for winter. During growth, provide plenty of water but keep the bulb very dry during dormancy.

N. bowdenii   Zones 8-11

Tall—to 15 inches—clusters of flowers that are pink marked with a deeper pink. A plant called "magnifica" has larger flowers.

N. curvifolia   Zones 8-11

Has curved, glaucous leaves and scarlet blooms on slender stalks about 18 inches high. *N. c.* var. *fothergillii* is larger and more floriferous.

N. filifolia   Zones 8-11

A smaller species, to 10 inches tall, this has red flowers.

N. sarniensis Guernsey Lily   Zones 9-11

Has fuller, bright red, iridescent flowerheads and then produces narrow, light green leaves. Hybrids are offered in pink, salmon, red, scarlet, mauve, white, and bicolors.

VELTHEIMIA (velth-**eye**-mee-uh)

From South Africa. This winter-blooming bulb produces a plant of great beauty 12 to 18 inches tall. The leaves are strap-shaped, often undulating and bright green. Its red, white, or yellow drooping flowers are borne in a dense raceme at the top of a bare stalk. It is grown indoors as a potted plant or outdoors in frost-free areas where it is handled much like *Hippeastrum*, Amaryllis, above.

Culture: Best with night temperatures at 50° F and day temperatures of 65° F or higher. Keep dry during summer dormancy and resume watering and fertilizing at the first sign of growth in early winter.

V. capensis   Zones 10-11

The flowers are red or pale pink with greenish tips, and the leaves are especially undulating.

V. viridifolia   Zones 10-11

Has about 12 glossy green leaves, and the flower spikes are light purplish pink and appear in late winter.

SOURCE: EVERETT L. MILLER, LANDSCAPE DESIGNER, SOURCE DIRECTOR TO LIVE OAK GARDENS, LOUISIANA, FORMER DIRECTOR OF LONGWOOD GARDENS, IS COAUTHOR OF VOLUMES 1 AND 2 OF THE AMERICAN GARDEN GUIDEBOOK.

8. BULBS FOR CONTAINERS

■ **Containers display flowering bulbs beautifully. In spring, a lilliputian drift of blue muscari and miniature daffodils is especially appealing under small trees and shrubs in a big planter. And the tall, exotic, lily-flowered tulips combine marvelously with ornamental grasses that take over as the tulips go by— which is rather quickly. In summer, a few lilies in a big tub or a planter full of dancing caladiums can brighten the most prosaic porch.**

Two kinds of bulbs are recommended here: frost-tender types such as caladiums, which are set out in spring and come indoors for winter, and hardy bulbs. Good quality hardy bulbs—tulips, daffodils, hyacinth, and squill—bloom the first spring in sun or shade, a guaranteed show even in poor light. The flowers are already set when you plant the bulbs in fall. For places receiving two hours or less of direct sun a day, choose low-growing bulbs; taller types may flop over without some sun. Bulbs in shade are often treated as annuals and discarded after blooming. The space may then be replanted with summer annuals.

Bulbs intended as permanent plantings do require sun—it's needed to ripen the foliage and set next year's flowers.

In containers, plant big bulbs in groups of five to seven, smaller bulbs in groups of at least ten.

For more ideas see list 4, Summer-into-fall Bulbs— these, too, are reliable bloomers the first year, either in sun or shade.

Culture: Spring and summer flowering bulbs thrive in well-drained, well-fertilized soil in large containers. The hardy species need a generous buffer of soil to insulate them from frost, and require some soil moisture through fall and winter. In Zones 6 and 7 a safe minimum container size is 14 to 16 inches in all dimensions. In colder zones this minimum size should be increased. In warmer zones, it can be somewhat reduced.

Spring-flowering bulbs are planted in fall, summer-flowering bulbs in spring. Many can also be forced to bloom early indoors—hyacinths, daffodils, and tulips among them—provided they are purchased prechilled or given at least six weeks in their pots in the refrigerator. For forcing, crowd the bulbs into shallow pots called bulb pans.

Follow-on and Companion Plants: Any of the annuals. *Lavandula,* Lavender; *Mentha spicata,* Spearmint; *Origanum majorana,* Sweet Marjoram, Annual Marjoram; *Petunia* × *hybrida, Thymus* × *citriodorus* 'Aureus', Golden Lemon Thyme; *Vinca minor,* Periwinkle; and *Catharanthus roseus,* Rose Periwinkle, Madagascar Periwinkle.

AGAPANTHUS. During the late spring to early fall, a dense cluster of wonderful blue, white, or pink funnel-shaped flowers appears on a 36-inch to 5-foot stalk well above a handsome mound of strap-shaped leaves. This is a specimen plant for large, outdoor containers. 'Peter Pan', a 15-inch dwarf, is suited to small planters. Winter indoors in areas of frost. For culture, see list 7, Exotic Bulbs.

ALLIUM neapolitanum, Daffodil Garlic, Flowering Onion. This early ornamental onion flowers from mid-spring to late spring on stems about 12 inches high. The flowerhead of the white, star-shaped florets rises above long, thin, strap-shaped leaves. It's a good cut flower. Plant outdoors in autumn for spring bloom or in spring for bloom in early summer. For culture, see list 3, Spring, Large-flowered Bulbs.

CALADIUM, Elephant's-ears. These large, shield-shaped leaves colorful as flowers dance on slender stems— and so are called "dancing ladies." Superb container plants for outdoors, with translucent leaves bearing fanciful patterns in varying combinations of pink, red, and/or white on green. These can be forced to bloom indoors. See list 51, Foliage for Color.

CHIONODOXA luciliae, Glory-of-the-snow. So early, the flowers are called "snow glories," the long-lasting, 3- to 8-inch spikes of upward-facing starry flowers with white centers rise above grassy leaves. In cold weather they can last three to four weeks. The colors are blue or pink and there are large-flowered forms—blue 'Gigantea' and 'Pink Giant'. Plant outdoors in autumn in generously sized containers in well-drained soil. Add water if there is little winter rain or snow. Another attractive species for containers is *C. sardensis;* the flowers are darker blue and more loosely arranged on the stem. See list 1, Early Spring, Specialty Bulbs.

CLIVIA × cyrtanthiflora. This kaffir lily is evergreen, with deep green, sword-shaped leaves topped by a 24-inch stem bearing 5-inch flowerheads in brilliant orange. It can take a little frost. In cool regions it blooms indoors in spring or early summer, and may rebloom outdoors later. Best when potbound. Plant it in fall in peaty soil and keep it moist and fertilized. After flowering, allow it to dry slightly. See also list 7, Exotic Bulbs.

CROCUS. The late winter-early spring crocuses flower with *Galanthus,* often through the last snowfall. The brightly colored little cup- or chalice-shaped flowers are 4 to 6 inches high, and they may be white, pink, lavender, purple, yellow, or orange. Some have contrasting stripes or streaks. The grassy green leaves come up after the flowers and in some forms have a white or silver midrib. They may be grown in large outdoor containers in Zones 7 to 8 and are sometimes forced indoors. Recommended for forcing are 'Remembrance', lavender; 'Victor Hugo', lavender; 'Pickwick', striped; 'Joan of Arc' and 'Peter Pan', white; and 'Large Yellow'. For culture, see list 1, Early Spring, Specialty Bulbs.

FREESIA (free-zee-uh) × hybrida   Zone 9

The small, funnel-shaped flowers are extraordinarily fragrant. Eight flowers are usually borne on each slender, 18-inch stem. Its colors are subtle combinations of red, orange, yellow, white, or pink. Modern doubles are as fragrant as the singles. Freesia can be forced indoors or planted outdoors in sheltered boxes and planters. Staking may be necessary.

TOP, LEFT Hyacinths and cineraria in containers with pansies and forsythia in garden writer Linda Yang's Manhattan yard. (Yang)

ABOVE 'Tete-a-tete' miniature daffodils bloom in a basket. (Heath)

LEFT Persian cyclamen and ivy basket thrive as pot plants in cool, humid rooms, 60° to 65° F. daytimes, 40° to 50° F. nights. (American Horticultural Society)

FACING PAGE The fragrant freesias can be forced into bloom indoors or planted outdoors in sheltered boxes and planters. (McDonald)

Culture: Plant between October and December. For forcing indoors, set 10 or 12 corms about 2 inches deep in 8-inch pots in well-drained, somewhat acid soil. Placed under a bright light in a cool room, they flower in 12 to 14 weeks. Water after planting, and not again until the bulblike corms sprout. After flowering, allow the foliage to ripen and dry; if you have room, store in a cool, dry place for reuse, or discard and begin again next year with fresh bulbs.

GALTONIA candicans, Summer Hyacinth. Excellent. This South African bulb somewhat resembles a tall hyacinth and in late summer bears spikes of slightly fragrant, green-tinged white flowers on stalks up to 36 inches tall. The strap-shaped leaves are 2 inches wide and 3 to 4 feet long. A superb cut flower. Lovely massed in large containers in full sun or some shade, and usually treated as an annual and discarded after blooming. The species *G. princeps* flowers earlier and is a good choice for container-growing in cooler regions. See list 4, Summer-into-fall Bulbs.

HYACINTHUS orientalis, Hyacinth, Dutch Hyacinth. A beautiful, very fragrant flower composed of starry, outward-facing bells thickly clustered on a sturdy spike 8 to 12 inches high. Generally, whites are the most fragrant, then pastels, but some deeply colored hyacinths also have a powerful scent. For forcing indoors, choose the largest bulbs.

Among good forcers are 'Amsterdam', red; 'Anna Marie', pink; 'Carnegie', white; 'Delft Blue'; 'L'Innocence', white; 'Ostara', light blue with a stripe; and 'Pink Pearl', dark pink. For indoors, set them 3 to a 6-inch pot—in planters, in groups of 3 or 5. For culture, see list 3, Spring, Large-flowered Bulbs.

LILIUM, Lily. Lilies come in every color except blue and remain in flower for 3 to 4 weeks beginning in June in most areas. They are superb cut flowers and many are remarkably fragrant. The 7-foot lilies are suited only to large gardens, but medium and small lilies do very well in deep tubs and planters. The little 12- to 20-inch Pixie series lilies are delightful at the back of large planters. In big tubs, plant midsize lilies in groups of 3 to 5. For culture and recommended cultivars, see list 11, Lily.

MUSCARI, Grape Hyacinth. The flowers, usually blue or white, are thickly clustered on stems to 6 to 8 inches high. Some forms look like miniature hyacinths. Other types are sterile and the unopened buds look like tiny grapes. The leaves are grassy. Pretty when planted in big boxes, especially as the underplanting for large white daffodils and in bulb pans. Recommended for containers are the very early, 8-inch-tall *M. azureum*, which bears dense spikes of bright blue florets, and the white 'Album'. See list 1, Early Spring, Specialty Bulbs.

NARCISSUS, Daffodil. Daffodils, especially miniature cultivars, thrive in large containers outdoors and many are successfully forced into early bloom indoors. Some do both—the charming little yellow 'Tete-a-tete', for instance, and the fragrant 15-inch 'Cragford'. 'Cragford' has beautiful creamy white overlapping petals and a bright orange-red cup, needs no chilling, and is a good choice for southern gardens.

Most easily forced for indoor flowering is the early-blooming, cold-tender *Tazetta* called Paper-white. It bears small, short-cupped blossoms in clusters of 4 or 8 on each stem, with a strong fragrance that fills the house. Paper-whites may be forced into flower buried to two-thirds their height in a shallow bowl half-filled with pebbles, or in a regular pot with soil. List 9, Daffodil, indicates many other cultivars for forcing.

The species *N. obvallaris*, a beautifully proportioned 8-inch dwarf, flowers in winter or late winter outdoors and is a superb container plant.

SCILLA siberica, Siberian Squill. Beautiful little bluebell 4 to 6 inches tall with grassy foliage topped in mid- to late spring by dainty flowering stems of gentian blue blossoms. Similar, but later to bloom, is *Endymion hispanicus* (syn. *Scilla campanulata*), Spanish Bluebell, Spanish Jacinth, Bell-flowered Squill. See list 1, Early Spring, Specialty Bulbs.

TULIPA, Tulip. The brilliant cup-shaped tulips on their round, jade green stems are the garden's big showstoppers from late March to May. They have been bred through the centuries by the Dutch to produce an extraordinary range of colors and forms. Recommended for outdoor containers are Single Late and Double Late, Lily-flowered, and Parrot tulips. Culture and cultivars are given on list 12, Tulip.

SOURCE: LINDA YANG, GARDEN COLUMNIST FOR THE HOME SECTION OF *THE NEW YORK TIMES*, TILLS HER OWN CITY PLOT IN MANHATTAN. SHE IS THE AUTHOR OF *THE CITY GARDENER'S HANDBOOK: FROM BALCONY TO BACKYARD* (RANDOM HOUSE).

9. DAFFODIL (NARCISSUS)

■ From southern Canada to northern Florida and westward wherever flowers grow, these symbols of spring raise gold, cream, or bicolored trumpets on straight 4- to 20-inch stems. By choosing bulbs that come up early, midseason, and late, you can have daffodils from late winter until early summer. And in warm climates, a few will flower (whether you want them to or not) before Christmas. The larger types are breathtaking perennialized in woods, fronting evergreens, edging meadows, and along the banks of ponds and streams. The miniatures are exquisite in rock gardens, containers, in the shelter of boulders, and tucked into sunny nooks and crannies. Quite a few are fragrant.

Daffodils perennialize readily and are safe from squirrels and other rodents because they are poisonous to them. With time, the flowers may grow smaller, but they will be more numerous and eventually make lovely stands of gold. They are most effective planted in irregular drifts of ten, twenty, or more, and are best of all massed where they can perennialize.

Cut daffodils are long-lasting. A note of caution: before combining just-cut daffodils with tulips, place the daffodil stems in water overnight to detoxify them.

Daffodils especially suited to forcing into early bloom indoors are so noted below; the most popular are the paper-whites—Division 8—and the miniatures.

Follow-on and Companion Plants: Large perennials such as daylilies and annuals such as marigolds are ideal follow-on plants for daffodils growing in full sun; hostas, astilbes, and asters for those in semi-sun. They will come up through ground covers such as ivy, myrtle, and pachysandra, which then act as their follow-on. Early daffodils are superb combined with dense plantings of low-growing white *Anemone blanda* and crocus, ringed with blue muscari, pansies, and scilla, or with early species tulips. Yellow and white daffodils are pretty together.

NARCISSUS (nar-*siss*-us)
Daffodil   Zones 3-9

The names daffodil, narcissus, and jonquil cause confusion. *Narcissus* is the botanical name and the common name daffodil may be used in its place. Jonquils are a specific type of *Narcissus*, usually late bloomers that bear a cluster of fragrant flowers on each stem; they are related to the species *N. jonquilla*. All daffodils are classed in divisions (see below) published by the American Daffodil Society and the Royal Horticultural Society, but they usually are offered commercially by name. The class tells how the flower will perform, so it is helpful information.

Culture: Most daffodils succeed in well-drained soils from Zones 3 to 9, but not all are hardy *everywhere*. Most, but not all, require a low temperature period to flower and they thrive in climates that experience frost. A few of the handful that succeed without low temperatures appear below—note that these are not hardy.

Set daffodils out in early or mid-autumn, in slightly acid soil. Good drainage is essential. Plant large bulbs 8 inches deep and 3 to 6 inches apart; small bulbs 3 to 5 inches deep and 1 to 3 inches apart. Add a handful of 5-10-20 slow-release fertilizer as top dressing after planting. To encourage spreading and sustain the beauty of

TOP Large Cup 'Accent', a sun-proof pink. (Heath)
ABOVE Classical trumpet daffodil 'Unsurpassable'.
(Netherlands Flowerbulb Information Center)
RIGHT Double-flowered 'Tahiti'. (Netherlands Flowerbulb Information Center)

perennialized bulbs, fertilize at the rate of 4 pounds for each 100 square feet each fall, and again in early spring as the shoot tips show through the soil.

Daffodils thrive in full sun or partial shade. After the flowers have faded, allow them to remain undisturbed until the foliage begins to yellow, at least 12 weeks after flowering. Then cut the foliage back close to the soil, if you wish. This is a new view; letting the foliage die to the ground before removing it is still considered by many growers the way to best enhance next season's flowers. Binding daffodil foliage over to tidy the garden while the leaves ripen is discouraged; binding cuts off light and oxygen needed to nourish the next year's flowers.

The time to divide or harvest bulbs is immediately before the foliage has died. Replant them at once, or store them in well ventilated trays at 50° F to 80° F, never above 90° F. If necessary, they may be stored for several months.

The plants named here were chosen because they perennialize easily and are among the strongest garden plants in their groups. They are outstanding cultivars and named plants, but there are many others in each division.

DIVISION 1, TRUMPETS

This is the classical daffodil form, a very large, showy flower that appears early to midseason and is excellent for bedding, forcing, and cutting. One blossom develops on each stem and the trumpet is as long as, or longer than, the petals. The average height is 16 to 20 inches.

'Arctic Gold', 12 to 16 inches, buttercup yellow, show-quality flowers. Early midseason.

'Lunar Sea', to 18 inches, yellow with a white trumpet. Midseason.

'Spellbinder', 16 to 18 inches, reverse-bicolor with yellow petals surrounding a greenish, sulphur yellow trumpet. A choice bulb for landscaping. Midseason.

'Unsurpassable', 18 to 22 inches, giant canary yellow flower with a golden yellow trumpet. Early midseason.

TRUMPET MINIATURES

'Little Beauty', 4 to 6 inches, bicolor trumpet in two shades of yellow. Excellent for forcing. Very early.

'Little Gem', 4 to 6 inches, upward facing flowers in golden shade of yellow. One of the earliest of all daffodils. Excellent for forcing.

DIVISION 2, LARGE CUPS

This is the most popular division. There's one flower to a stem and the length of the cup is more than one-third, but less than equal to, the length of the petals. The average height is 12 to 20 inches. Midseason.

'Accent', 14 to 16 inches, white petals and a salmon-pink cup. The best sun-proof pink. Midseason.

'Ceylon', 14 to 16 inches, yellow with an orange cup. One of the longest-lasting in bloom. Early midseason.

'Salome', 16 to 18 inches, white petals perfectly frame an almost trumpet-length coral-pink cup rimmed with gold. Show winner, and best all-purpose pink. Late midseason.

'St. Patrick's Day', 16 to 18 inches, primrose yellow with a large, flat, white cup. Midseason.

DIVISION 3, SMALL CUPS

'Barrett Browning', 12 to 16 inches, white petals, brick red cup. One of the earliest predominantly white daffodils. Superb naturalizer.

DIVISION 4, DOUBLES

Excellent. Tall, 14 to 16 inches, with one or more double flowers on each stem. Instead of cups or trumpets, the blooms are filled with petals, roselike, very showy, good for bedding and cut flowers. Midseason to late.

'Sir Winston Churchill', to 15 inches, a fragrant white with white and orange in the doubled cup and 3 to 5 blooms on each stem. Late.

'Tahiti', to 15 inches, sulphur yellow with gold-yellow and vermilion segments and a strong stem. Superb display plant. Late midseason.

DIVISION 5, TRIANDRUS HYBRIDS

Excellent. Zones 4 to 9. These small daffodils are multi-flowered, bearing several small, graceful, fuchsialike, pendent blooms on each stem. The petals are turned back, sometimes twisted, and often have a delicious fruity fragrance. Good perennializers and rock garden plants. Average height is 10 to 14 inches. Spanish bluebells (*Endymion*) are perfect in combination or companion plantings with late and midseason types.

'Hawera', 6 to 8 inches, miniature, with dainty, pendent, lemon yellow flowers. Vigorous in the rock garden and for forcing, bedding, and perennializing. Late.

'Ice Wings', to 13 inches or more, fragrant ivory white, one of the best perennializers. Early midseason.

'Petrel', 12 to 14 inches, fragrant, the short cup and petals are white and each stem bears 3 to 6 drooping flowers with reflexed petals. Good edger in part shade. Late midseason.

DIVISION 6, CYCLAMINEUS HYBRIDS

Excellent. Hardy only in Zones 6 to 9. Exotic, sprightly little flowers characterized by a usually drooping single bloom with a long, narrow cup and petals that curve back like those of a cyclamen. Some are among the first to flower, most are good perennializers and choice for rock gardens. Average height is 7 to 10 inches. Space bulbs 2 to 5 inches apart.

'February Gold', to 12 inches, large gold-yellow petals with slightly darker trumpets. Long-lasting flowers excellent for cutting and a good perennializer. Very early.

'Jack Snipe', to 8 inches, ivory white reflexed petals with clear lemon yellow cups. Spreads quickly. Midseason.

'Jetfire', to 12 inches, yellow petals with an orange-red cup. Early midseason.

'Jumblie', to 6 inches, golden petals and a flanged orange-yellow cup. It bears 2 or 3 long-lasting flowers on each stem and is an especially good pot plant. Sister to the popular 'Tete-a-tete'. Early midseason.

'Quince', to 5 inches, soft yellow with 2 to 3 blooms per stem. Perfect for rock gardens. Midseason.

'Tete-a-tete', to 6 inches, 1 to 3 exquisite little golden yellow

and orange flowers on each stem. Good forcing bulb for small pots. Very popular. Early. (Reclassified into the new Division 12, Miniatures.)

'Winged Victory', to 16 inches, white petals with a yellow cup. It is the largest of the group. Early midseason.

DIVISION 7, JONQUILLA HYBRIDS

Excellent. Multiflowered, with clusters of 2 to 6, usually very sweetly fragrant, yellow flowers on each stem, most with a short cup. This division likes hot but not humid summers. The average height is 12 to 15 inches but there are dwarfs and full-size plants. Midseason.

'Baby Moon', to 6 inches, pale gold-yellow. A free flowering, spicily fragrant miniature. Plant near rocks, foundation or scree in full sun. Late midseason. A selection from the species *N. jonquilla*.

'Quail', to 14 inches, yellow. Multiflowered and extremely vigorous. Midseason.

'Suzy', to 15 inches, gold-yellow with a bright orange cup. There are 3 to 4 fragrant, long-lasting flowers on each stem. Midseason.

'Trevithian', to 16 inches, pale primose yellow flowers with broadly overlapping petals and a wide, shallow crown. There are 2 or 3 large blossoms on each stem and they have a powerful, sweet fragrance. This is an old favorite and one of the best perennializers. Early midseason.

DIVISION 8, TAZETTAS

Also known as Poetaz and Polyanthus daffodils, these delightful flowers hold a historic place in our gardens and have an exquisite, musky fragrance. There's a cluster of 4 to 8 or even 15 small flowers on each stem, usually with short cups (known as 17 Sisters). They are excellent perennializers, the best daffodils for forcing and choice in flower beds. They need little or no chilling; some are suited to the very warm South. The perfumed paper-whites, the most popular daffodil for forcing, belong to this group.

'Avalanche', to 16 inches, white with a yellow cup. It is recommended for historic plantings and restoration gardens. Hardy in Zones 5 to 9. Good perennializer south of New England. Midseason.

'Cragford', to 15 inches, beautiful creamy white, overlapping petals and a bright orange-red cup. An excellent plant, it has a musky fragrance, is a good forcer, and needs no chilling for southern gardens or forcing. Hardy in Zones 6 to 11. Early midseason.

'Geranium', to 15 inches, crisp white petals around frilled orange cups. It bears 4 to 7 musk-scented flowers on each stem and is an excellent perennializer. Hardy in Zones 5 to 9. Late midseason.

DIVISION 9, POETICUS

Cultivars of the Pheasant's-eye daffodil, *N. poeticus* var. *recurvus* (see below). Another old-time favorite featured in historic gardens, this is one of the latest to bloom. They are long-lasting, spicily fragrant, excellent perennializers in Zones 4 to 8. Each stem bears a single flower with white petals and a short yellow cup that has a wavy, red-edged border. Average height is 16 to 18 inches.

'Actaea', to 16 inches. The whitest of all narcissus petals

TOP, LEFT Historic Tazetta 'Avalanche'. (Heath)
TOP, RIGHT Poeticus, 'Actaea', for lawns. (Heath)
LEFT 'Brandaris', big border daffodil. (Heath)
ABOVE 'Suzy', a jonquilla, fragrant, multiflowered. (Heath)

Plant (and divide) dahlias after danger of frost is past and the wetness has left the earth—when the lilacs bloom. Provide an open, sunny location or a good western exposure. Sun for half a day or more is essential.

Dahlias do best in soil improved as described in the section on Growing Flowers—very light and well-drained, and humusy enough to hold moisture with readily available nutrients. Provide a rich diet in late spring with a slow-release, low-nitrogen fertilizer that will make nutrients available through early fall.

Set the tubers 18 to 24 inches apart, according to the plant's mature size. Prepare sturdy stakes tall enough to support the upper third of the mature plant—18 inches to 4 feet. For each tuber, scoop a hole 6 to 8 inches deep and punch a stake deep into the soil 2 inches away. Set the tuber flat with the eye portion nearest the stake. Cover the tuber with 2 to 3 inches of soil. Do not water until a shoot appears about 4 weeks later. Then add a few inches more soil, and water; repeat the procedure at intervals as the plant grows until the hole is filled. Dahlias require water once a week but must never soak in water. When the stem is 12 inches tall, tie it to its stake. Tie on other branches as the plant matures.

After flowering begins, deadhead to keep flowers coming.

Dig dahlia tubers for storing after the yellowing tops die back and after the first killing frost. Cut away the foliage. Use a spading fork to lift the crown. Wash off the dirt. Allow the tubers to dry out of direct sun for a day or so. Label them with an indelible pencil for identification. Store them in cedar chips, vermiculite, sand, or peat moss in a cool, dry area 40° to 45° F. If the tubers get too dry they shrivel, but if they get too wet they rot, and they mustn't freeze. After the eyes have begun to sprout in spring, cut the tubers from the crown. To be good, a tuber must have at least one eye.

SHOW DAHLIAS FROM TUBERS

These produce magnificent flowers on shrublike plants grown from tubers. For bedding choose compact growers. Dahlias best for cutting have good, sturdy stems. Plants that are choice for training for exhibition are noted.

INCURVED CACTUS

The petals are rolled to their full length with tips of the petals curved toward the center of the flower.
'Nutley Sunrise', 8-inch or bigger flower, 36-inch bush, burnt orange with a perfect incurved form.
'Orchid Lace', 6-inch flowers, exquisite white edged with lavender; recommended for arrangements. Very vigorous 5-foot bush.
'Romance', 3-inch miniature flowers, pink with cream centers; very firm texture, long lasting when cut; 4-foot bush.

SEMICACTUS

The petals are flat at the base with less than half of the petals rolled or quilled.
'Andrie's Orange', 4-inch, soft orange, miniature flower; one of the nicest for cutting; 5-foot bush.

'Bella Bimba', 7-inch flowers in apricot-pink that cover the 4½-foot bush; early.
'Happy Face', magnificent 7-inch exhibition and garden flowers in bright yellow; neat 4½-foot bush; early-blooming.
'Hee Haugh', 6-inch flowers, exhibition quality gold-orange to almost beige with a glowing heart and light mauve undertones on the reverse; bush is 4½ feet.
'Little Lamb', miniature with 2½- to 3-inch flowers, dainty and pure white on a sturdy stem, choice for weddings. Bush grows 4 feet tall.
'Miss Rose Fletcher', 6-inch flowers in delicate shell pink; leading cut flower. Bush is 4 feet.
'Nicky K', 6-inch flower in bright red with lacinated petal tips; free-flowering, reliable, easy to grow. Bush is 4½-feet.
'Pari Taha Sunrise', very showy 5-inch flowers are bright yellow tipped with red; excellent cut flower on 4½-foot bush.
'Show and Tell', 9- to 10-inch flowers, red tipped with yellow on good stems. Bush is 4 feet tall. Exhibition quality; late.
'Surprise', 10- to 12-inch giant exhibition flowers in a soft peach with pink near the center and yellow at the base; bush is 4 feet tall.
'Tanjoh', 4-inch flowers, very showy white tipped with deep fuchsia; great little all-around dahlia. Bush is 4 feet tall.

STRAIGHT CACTUS

The petals are rolled for half their length, and are straight or nearly straight.
'Mary Evelyn', 5-inch flowers, bright red, on excellent stems. Bush is 3½ feet.

FORMAL DECORATIVE

The petals are flat and placed evenly and regularly over the face of the flower.
'A La Mode', 6- to 7-inch flowers, unusual shade of lush apricot-orange deeply tipped with white; profuse bloomer. Bush is 4 feet.
'Alabaster', 8- to 9-inch flowers, beautiful pure white on stems good for cutting and exhibition; sturdy 5-foot bush; late.
'Camano Choice', 5-inch flowers, outstanding, exhibition-quality, light lavender blooms on strong stems. Bush is 4½ feet tall.
'Duet', 8-inch flowers, dark red tipped with white; very strong stems. Bush is 3½ feet tall; late.
'Edna C', 8- to 10-inch, ball-shaped flower, primrose yellow petals cup back. Bush is 4 feet; late.
'Gerry Hoek', 5-inch flowers, wonderful shade of deep shell pink with gold base in a waterlily form. Good cut flower. Bush is 4 feet.
'Kidd's Climax', lovely 8- to 10 inch flowers, cream shaded to soft yellow blended with heliotrope; an award winner. Bush is 36 inches tall.
'Lady Linda', 5-inch, exhibition-quality flowers, light yellow blending to gold in the center. Bush is 4½ feet tall.
'Margaret Duross', 10- to 12-inch exhibition flowers; vibrant, deep golden orange on strong, canelike stems. Bush is 5 feet; late.

'Patches', 7- to 8-inch flowers, a maze of fuchsia randomly tipped with white or marked in fuchsia-purple with white tips. Bush is 4½ feet.
'Red Garnet', 4-inch miniature flowers, velvety dark red; good cut flower. Bush is 5½ high; early.
'Reedley', 5-inch flowers in water lily form; clear orange and long-lasting when cut. Bush is 4 feet tall.
'Sassy', 3-inch miniature flowers; bright salmon-pink with a lavender blush, iridescent quality; outstanding for cutting and exhibition. Bush is 4 feet tall.

INFORMAL DECORATIVE

Generally flat petals, sometimes rolled slightly at the tips but with the petals arranged regularly over the face of the flower.
'Envy', 11-inch flowers, rich red; exhibition quality. Bush is 3½ to 4 feet tall; late.
'Gay Princess', 5- to 6-inch flowers, pink with a light cream center; long-lasting when cut. Bush is 4½ feet; early.
'Gitts Respect', huge 9½-inch flowers, Oriental red with yellow-bronze tips. Bush grows to 3½ feet.
'Matchmaker', 4-inch flowers, creamy white just edged with fuchsia; very showy in the garden. Bush is 6 inches tall.
'Sherwood's Peach', 12-inch flowers, golden peach on a very leafy, 5-foot bush. An old favorite; late.
'Tartan', exceptional bicolor with 7- to 8-inch flowers, rich velvety maroon petals edged and tipped with white; an award winner. Bush height is 5 feet.
'Walter Hardisty', 11-inch flowers, snowy white; award winner with good stems and foliage. Bush is 4 feet; late.

POM PON

Fully double, almost round flowers 2 inches across or less, with tightly quilled petals.
'Amber Queen', 2-inch flowers, golden amber and bronze. Bush is 4 feet; very early.
'Betty Ann', 1½-inch flowers, deep pink; prolific bloomer; good for cutting. Bush is 3½ feet; very early.
'Czar Willo', very full little 1½-inch flowers, showy red-purple; good stems on exhibition-quality flowers. Bush is 3 feet tall.
'Yellow Gem', 1½-inch flowers, yellow, popular for cutting. Bush is 3½ feet.
'Zonnengoud', 1½-inch flowers, beautiful fall gold; good for cutting and exhibition. Bush is 4 feet tall.

SINGLE

A single row of flat petals surrounding a central disk.
'Bonnie Esperance', miniature 1-inch flowers, old-fashioned pink surrounding a golden center. Bush is 12 to 14 inches; early.

COLLARETTE

One row of flat or slightly cupped peals surrounding a central disk. There is an inner set of generally multiple petaloids forming an irregular collar around the disk.
'Cherubino', 4-inch, perfectly formed flowers, white with a white collar around a yellow center. Bush is 4 feet tall.

'Cottontail', 4-inch flowers, dark maroon with a white collar; wiry stems. Bush is 4½ feet; early.

'Mickey', excellent 4½-inch flower, dark velvet red with a yellow collar; long-lasting when cut. Lush, neat, 3½-foot bush. Highly praised for bedding and cutting.

'Needles', 4-inch outer petals in ivory-yellow lightly dotted and streaked with rosy wine red surround a golden heart; unusual and striking. Bush height is 4 feet.

'Yellow Bird', 4-inch flowers with large crisp and very pretty curled petals surrounding a matched heart. Bush is 4 feet tall.

BALL

Fully double flowers, ball-shaped or slightly flattened at the face; the ray florets are blunt, rounded, or indented. Involute for most of their length, fully involute for about one-half of their length, and normally displayed in the spiral arrangement.

'Brookside Snowball', 4-inch flowers, pure white, perfect exhibition-quality ball held erect on strong stems. Bush is 4 feet; late.

'Nettie', 2½-inch miniature flowers, real ball form in soft yellow on strong stems; good for exhibition and cutting. Bush height is 3½ feet.

'Rothsay Superb', 2½-inch miniature flowers, lasting red; for cutting and exhibition. Bush is 3½ feet.

MINIATURE NOVELTY

'Japanese Bishop', 3-inch flower, blazing orange-red with a yellow-edged, sooty black center against dark foliage; rather like a Red Anemone. The most popular dahlia for bedding and arrangements. Bush height is 36 inches .

BEDDING DAHLIAS FROM SEED

D. × hybrida Unwin Hybrids

These tender perennials are small and useful for bedding and massing. They grow easily from seed or seedlings, form tidy, small bushes 12 to 36 inches high, and bloom from midsummer until frost. The colors from seed are unpredictable and usually sold in mixed combinations. They usually are discarded at the end of the season. Nice in low containers. The flowers are short-stemmed and generally not first-rate for cutting.

Culture: Plant in late spring for late summer and early autumn flowers. Garden centers offer container-grown seedlings, but plants are easily raised from seed sown indoors 6 to 8 weeks before the weather warms. Provide full sun and moist, fertile soil. Generally more successful in moderate climates than in warm regions. Recommended is the Rigoletto Mix, bushy 12-inch-tall dahlias with double and semidouble flowers 2½ inches across in yellow, red, orange, pink, and white—all colors except blue.

SOURCE: MARGARET GITTS, A HORTICULTURIST AND BREEDER, IS OWNER OF SWAN ISLAND DAHLIAS, CANBY, OREGON, ONE OF THE WORLD'S LARGEST DAHLIA GROWERS.

11. LILY (LILIUM)

■ **A hybrid lily stalk 7-feet tall, spangled with 40 or 50 huge, elegant trumpet-shaped flowers is the garden's most commanding plant. Some lily blooms face upward, others outward, and some are pendent. The big lilies are for collectors, but there are medium and small lilies in every color except blue for every garden purpose. The little 12- to 20-inch Pixie series are delightful at the back of narrow and low borders. For tubs or flower beds, plant midsize lilies in groups of three to five. For big borders, mass 6-footers at the back in sets of 10 to 15.**

Lilies remain in flower for three to four weeks, beginning in most areas in June. The three major categories—Asiatics, Trumpets, and Orientals—bloom in that order, but their flowering periods overlap somewhat since there are late Asiatics and early Trumpets and Orientals. The bloom times described here include early, midseason, and late designations where appropriate. By thoughtful selection you can have lilies flowering from late spring until frost. The cut flowers are highly desirable but must be taken with next year's blooms in mind, as discussed below.

The plants recommended here are found at garden centers and in mail order catalogs and nurseries specializing in lilies. They are the most outstanding growers, tolerant of disease, and excellent subjects for the home garden. They thrive in some parts of southern Canada and all parts of the U.S., but are not sure growers below Zone 8.

Follow-on Plants and Companion Plants: To screen the legginess of lilies, use *Salvia sclarea* or blue salvias, hostas, and Baby's-breath. To follow-on: *Anemone hupehensis* var. *japonica,* Japanese Anemone; *Boltonia asteroides;* big chrysanthemums; *Cleome hasslerana; Helenium autumnale.*

LILIUM (*lil*-ee-um)
Lily   Zones 4-8

There are approximately 100 species of lily, all native to the northern hemisphere. The Royal Horticultural Society and the North American Lily Society officially classify lilies in nine divisions, but they are grouped here in the categories offered in most nursery catalogs. A few of the beautiful species lilies are described on list 70, The Fragrance Garden.

The plants popular today are hybrids of lilies from other lands. Native American lilies and their hybrids have been brought into culture, but for the most part are difficult to find and to grow. The North American Lily Society at the American Horticultural Society can help to locate these and other hard-to-find lilies.

The lilies described as tetraploids are very desirable. They have greater hardiness and thicker petals than others and offer the newest color combinations. This is a new direction for breeding and it is expected to produce superb hybrids.

Culture: Lilies don't go on forever in one location. They're heavy feeders and need a new location every three or four years, one rich in trace elements as well as regular nutrients. They also require perfect drainage and somewhat acid soil that includes a mix of sand for drainage, humus to hold moisture, and loam. The exceptions to this rule are the Martagons and the species *L. candidum,* which thrives in alkaline soils loaded with calcium and wood ashes. But do not plant the other lilies in recently or heavily limed soils. Work the soil to 24 inches to ensure

good drainage, especially in clay. The bulbs can tolerate a dry period after flowering to ripen the bulbs.

Lilies do best in full sun where temperatures remain under 90° F, but need protection from noon and afternoon sun in hotter regions. Four to six hours of full sun, plus partial sun the rest of the day, is the rule of thumb. Pastel shades are more successful in partial shade. All lilies enjoy cool feet. A mulch or ground cover such as alyssum, petunias, or short marigolds does that job beautifully.

While a lily in full bloom adapts to transplanting, to plant a bulb with a shoot over 2 inches long in spring is sure death. These big bulbs usually are shipped in damp peat moss and should be kept there until planted. Each bulb produces one big flowering stem.

Plant, move, or divide lilies in the fall. Add a handful of bone meal to each hole and set the bulb about 6 inches deep with 2 to 4 inches of soil—depending on size—on top. Plant the bulbs 12 to 18 inches apart. The tallest benefit from shelter from sweeps of wind.

As they wither, remove dead blooms at their point of attachment to the stalk, but don't cut the stalk itself. They produce chlorophyll and contribute to the size of next season's bulb. When lily stalks are cut before the foliage has ripened, the plant suffers. If one-third of the stem is cut, the bulb will be two-thirds of its normal size the following year. When the last bloom is gone the stalk can be cut to just above the leaves. When all the leaves are yellow, the stalk may be cut to the ground, or left to mark the bulb's location.

EARLY, ASIATIC HYBRIDS
Zones 3-8

Flowering in June and early July, some earlier, these lilies offer the greatest variety of colors, are the most colorful, and are widely grown as garden plants and for cut flowers. They come in every color but blue, including bicolors and the patterns called brush marks, in which the familiar lily spots are replaced by solid colors painted or blotched on the petals.

The blooms of the Asiatic lilies may be flat, reflexed, or trumpet-shaped, face up, or out, or down with exotically recurved petals. Some, like 'Maureen', have 7- to 8-inch wide flowers and others, like 'Corsage', have small, dainty flowers 1½ inches across. Heights range from the early blooming 12- to 20-inch Pixie Series in red, yellow, and orange (great for potting, edging, perennializing), to giants 7 feet tall. Examples are 'Nutmegger', canary yellow with brown spots and known to bear 54 flowers, and 'Prawn Tiger', shrimp pink with narrow twisted petals.

The blooming season for Asiatics is early but variable. Some flower in late May and early June, but the best known are hybrids derived from *L. leichtlinii* var. *Maximowiczii* and *L. lancifolium* that bloom toward mid-July. Among late-blooming Asiatics are such outstanding cultivars as 'Orange Monarch' and 'Nutmegger'.

Some of the greatest Asiatic lilies grow in Oregon, Washington, and California, among them crosses of *L. cernuum, L. davidii, L. leichtlinii* var. *Maximowiczii, L. pumilum, L. concolor, L. lancifolium,* the European species *L. bulbiferum,* and some others. These are the most disease resistant and cold-hardiest lilies, hardy to −40° and −50° F, surviving winters as far north as Parkside, Saskatchewan, Canada, some 90 miles north of Saskatoon.

TOP, LEFT *Lilium concolor*, one of the species behind the superior modern hybrids. (Wadekamper)

TOP, RIGHT 'Nepera' has the waxy petals typical of the Martagon strain, a June bloomer with a powerful scent. (Wadekamper)

LEFT Flared form of fragrant 'Thunderbolt' is typical of the Trumpet Lily. (Wadekamper)

ABOVE 'Dandy Lion' is an Asiatic Hybrid, one of the hundreds of new lilies in this popular group that flowers in June and July—some earlier. (Wadekamper)

Asiatic lilies grow well on any soil type and prefer a pH of 5.8 to 6.8. The modern cultivars, now 7 to 8 generations removed from the original species and containing 3, 4, or 5 species in their ancestry, are easy to grow.

WHITE
'Matterhorn', 24 inches. Early midseason. Upward-facing.
'Mont Blanc', 24 inches. Midseason. Upward-facing.
'Morning Mist', 28 inches. Midseason. Upward-facing.
'Peaceful', 28 inches. Late midseason. Upward-facing.
'Snow Lark', 28 inches. Midseason. Outward-facing.
'Sterling Star', 40 inches. Midseason. Upward-facing.

CREAM
'Connecticut Beauty', 28 inches. Midseason. Upward-facing.
'Connecticut Star', 28 inches. Late. Upward-facing.
'Dawn Star', 24 inches. Late midseason. Outward-facing.
'Honey Cream, 32 inches. Early. Outward-facing.
'Honey Wind', 32 inches. Early. Outward-facing.
'Trade Winds', 36 inches. Late midseason. Upward-facing.

BUFF, TAN
'Ambrosia', 28 inches. Midseason. Outward-facing.
'Chinook', 36 inches. Late midseason. Upward-facing.
'Maple Cream', 30 inches. Midseason. Outward-facing.
'Sally', 38 inches. Late. Downward-facing.

YELLOW
'Connecticut King', 30 inches. Midseason. Upward-facing.
'Dandy Lion', 30 inches. Midseason. Outward-facing.
'Gold Lode', 36 inches. Upward-facing.
'Haydee', 32 inches. Early. Upward-facing.
'Indian Brave', 36 inches. Late midseason. Upward-facing.
'Lime Ice', 38 inches. Late midseason. Upward-facing.

ORANGE
'August Gold', 36 inches. Late. Outward-facing.
'Jolandra', 34 inches. Midseason. Upward-facing.
'Jolly Miller', 22 inches. Early. Upward-facing.
'Kismet', 36 inches. Midseason. Upward-facing.
'Rusty', 12 inches. Early. Upward-facing.
'Space Age', 42 inches. Midseason. Upward-facing.

PINK
'Corsica', 36 inches. Early midseason. Outward-facing.
'Gypsy', 42 inches. Midseason. Upward-facing.
'Malta', 32 inches. Early midseason. Upward-facing.
'Pink Tiger', 36 inches. Late. Downward-facing.
'Unique', 34 inches. Midseason. Upward-facing.

RED
'Chippewa Star', 36 inches. Early. Downward-facing.
'Mildred', 32 inches. Late midseason. Nonfading. Outward-facing.
'Miss Alice', 36 inches. Late midseason. Outward-facing.
'Red King', 30 inches. Early midseason. Upward-facing.
'Red Velvet', 36 inches. Late midseason. Outward-facing.
'Rhodos', 34 inches. Midseason. Upward-facing.
'Schellenbaum', 48 inches. Midseason. Downward-facing.

LEFT Fragrant trumpet lily 'Golden Temple' comes into bloom in mid- to late summer. (Wadekamper)

BELOW A rubrum lily, beautiful cultivar of the late-blooming species *L. speciosum*. Once grown in quantity for cut flowers, the species has been overshadowed by improved hybrids but is a fine plant. (Viette)

BICOLORS, BRUSH MARKS

'Electric', 36 inches. Pink and orange bicolor. Early mid-season. Upward-facing.

'Grand Cru', 36 inches. Red and orange bicolor. Mid-season. Upward-facing.

'Tamara', 32 inches. Cream and pink bicolor. Early. Upward-facing.

'Delta', 36 inches. Orange and tan brush marks. Mid-season. Upward-facing.

'Hot Fudge'. White with chocolate-crimson brush mark. Midseason. Upward-facing.

'Willowwood', 36 inches. Yellow and oxblood. Midseason. Upward-facing.

EARLY, MARTAGON LILIES
Zones 3-8

The Martagon lilies are 5- to 6-foot hybrids of species native to eastern Europe and the Caucasian and Ural mountain areas and China. A common name for them is Turk's-cap lilies, for they look like a special form of turban. The flowers are small and mostly pendent, thick-leaved, and waxy, and the leaves grow in whorls around the stems. They emerge very early and usually bloom in June. The scent is powerful and not to everyone's taste.

The color range is wide, derived from four principal species—*L. martagon* varieties *album* and *cattaniae*, white and deep purple respectively; *L. tsingtauense*, bright orange; and *L. hansonii*, light yellow-orange.

The Martagons like partial sun, perennialize easily, and can be left for many years without moving. In nature they tend to grow in limestone areas. A pH of 6.8 to 7.2 is preferable, but our Source reports that they succeed at pH 6.2, a more acid soil.

Martagons may not be easy to find. Ambergate Gardens, 8015 Krey Avenue, Waconia, MN 55387, specializes in Martagons, and they are also found at B&D Lilies and a few other nurseries. Some of the best-known hybrids are:

'Claude Shride', 5 feet, deep purplish red. Early.

'Nepera', 36 inches tall, rusty orange. Early.

Terrace City Hybrids, to 6 feet, from gold to pink. Early.

MIDSEASON, TRUMPET and AURELIAN HYBRIDS
Zones 5/6-8

Flowering in mid-July to mid-August, these are vigorous plants with up to 12 large, trumpet-shaped blooms on a stem. They can grow to 8 feet but usually are 5 to 6 feet tall. The color range is white, gold, and pink. Height depends a great deal on cultural conditions.

The trumpet lilies grow well anywhere if the drainage is good, and they like a crumbly soil. They are disease resistant and cold hardy to −10° or −15° F. One disadvantage is that their new shoots are very susceptible to late spring frosts. If they do freeze back the bulb will remain dormant until the following year.

A cross between a Trumpet and the species *L. henryi* resulted in a group known as Aurelian lilies, each 8 to 10 inches across, fragrant and good for cutting. These prefer partial shade but tolerate full sun, and are hardy in the warm reaches of Zone 3. The colors range from creamy white through gold to apricot.

FLARING TRUMPETS

'Gold Eagle', 5 to 6 feet, golden yellow, very fragrant. Midseason.

'Thunderbolt', 4 to 5 feet, apricot, flaring trumpet tinged green outside. Fragrant. Late.

'White Henryi', 6 feet, lovely white flowers with yellow spotted centers. Fragrant. Virus resistant. Midseason.

TRUMPET-SHAPED FLOWERS

'Anaconda', 38 inches, apricot. Fragrant. Late.

'Black Dragon', 5 to 7 feet, white with a purple reverse, intensely fragrant, up to 20 blooms on each stem. Early and midseason.

'Damson', 32 inches, rich maroon. Fragrant. Midseason.

'Golden Temple', 36 inches, yellow with a dark reverse. Fragrant. Midseason.

'Lady Ann', 36 inches, white with gold center. Fragrant. Midseason.

MIDSEASON, EASTER LILIES
Zones 6-8

L. longiflorum, **Trumpet Lily, White Trumpet Lily**
The fragrant Easter lily. In the garden, these grow between 12 and 36 inches tall, bear one to six outward-facing flowers, and bloom in mid-July and early August. Those that have been potted and forced into bloom for Easter transplant outdoors well enough. Cut the whole plant back after blooming is over and plant it in a sunny spot in ordinary soil. Usually it will send up a new shoot that will bloom again in August or September. In warm climates, Zones 6 to 7, it will persist and come up year after year.

'Ace', 24 inches, white, nonfragrant. Usually forced for Easter.

'Nellie White', 28 inches, white. Fragrant. Usually forced for Easter.

'Longistar', a new and hardy hybrid between *L. longiflorum* and the Asiatic lily 'Sterling Star', is hardy in Zone 4, and is expected to become a bridge to new hardier forms. It is not fragrant.

LATE, ORIENTAL LILIES
Zones 4-8

In bloom from late July into September, the flowers are highly fragrant, spectacular—up to 10 inches in diameter—and either bowl-shaped, flat-faced, or have sharply recurved petals. There usually are 8 to 10 flowers on stems 28 to 38 inches tall. 'Star Gazer', developed by the famous lily breeder Leslie Woodriff, made a sensational entry into the lily world with its upward-facing red flowers edged with white and will be the forebear of many hybrids with this characteristic. These lilies were developed from four Japanese species—*L. speciosum, L. rubellum, L. auratum,* and *L. japonicum*—and are the last to bloom.

The color range goes from white to pink to red. Some cultivars derived from the Gold-banded lily, *L. auratum* var. *platyphyllum,* have yellow bands in the center of the petals.

The Orientals used to be regarded as the least hardy and most difficult of plants. Hardiness is not a problem if the soil is sufficiently acidic and well drained. They require a pH of 5.2 to 6.2 and will grow well with azaleas. They have withstood our Source's Minnesota winters down to −40° F with only a 5- to 6-inch covering of straw, and also thrive on the West Coast. These are the best lilies for warm regions, where they tend to come up early and require protection from late spring frosts.

WHITE

'American Eagle', 36 inches, white with lavender spots. Fragrant. Early.

'Casa Blanca', 34 inches, pure white with wide petals. Midseason.

'Everest', 38 inches, white with spots. Late.

'Imperial Silver' strain, 6 feet, huge white flowers with maroon spots. Fragrant. Midseason.

'Star Gazer', 18 to 24 inches, upward-facing red flowers edged with white. This is a small, unusually early (June) Oriental, good for the middle border and pots.

PINK

'Allura', 32 inches. Midseason.

'Blushing Pink', 4 to 5 feet, unspotted, with a wonderful fragrance. Early to midseason.

'Journey's End', 36 inches, rose with a red band. Very fragrant. Midseason.

'Rosario', 32 inches. Midseason.

RED

'Black Beauty', 6 to 7 feet, 4- to 5-inch wide recurved red flowers with a green star center, cold-hardy, and late to bloom. A healthy triploid* developed by Leslie Woodriff, it is one of the most persistent and long-lasting lily hybrids known today and the first named to the Lily Hall of Fame.

'Jamboree', 30 inches. Midseason.

'Imperial Crimson', 36 inches. Midseason.

'Sequoia', 32 inches. Late.

---

* A triploid has three sets of chromosomes, a diploid two, and a tetraploid four. Chromosomes carry the inherited characteristics—so the more chromosomes, the more desirable characteristics can be added to a plant. Tetraploids are just coming in and there's much interest in their potential.

SOURCE: JULIUS WADEKAMPER, PAST PRESIDENT OF THE NORTH AMERICAN LILY SOCIETY AND A TRUSTEE FOR THE SOCIETY'S RESEARCH TRUST, HOLDS AN M.A. IN HORTICULTURE. HE IS THE FOUNDER OF BORBELETA GARDENS, FARIBAULT, MINNESOTA, SPECIALIZING IN LILIES AND IRISES, AND HAS INTRODUCED SEVERAL DISTINGUISHED LILIES INTO CULTURE.

12. TULIP (TULIPA)

■ The brilliant cup-shaped tulips on their round, jade green stems are the garden's big showstoppers from late March through May. They have been bred for centuries by the Dutch to produce an extraordinary range of colors and forms. Their first appearance of the season is in the very early little species (called botanical tulips in the trade) described on list 1, Early Spring, Specialty Bulbs. They're interesting, bright, perky, and informal.

The tulips recommended here are big cultivars that flower in midseason or later. Most familiar are the 24-inch, long-lasting, classical Darwin Hybrid tulips so often massed by the regimented hundreds in formal beds in city parks and estate gardens. In small gardens, grouped by tens and twelves, they are quite beautiful at the back of the border, especially with a few late daffodils and muscari as companion plants.

The many forms tulips have been given are a delight to explore. Some are so dramatic that a cluster of three to five makes the season unforgettable. In the exquisite lily-flowered tulip the cup is elongated to a vase shape; in another group the cup is feathered and colorful as a parrot. There are full-petaled tulips (double late) as luscious as a double peony, fringed, ruffled, streaked, and multiflowered tulips—tulips that glow in every imaginable color and combination including near black (which is wonderful with white.)

The tulips on the first list below are superb flowers able to come back under most conditions for at least four years. A few are fragrant. There are many other outstanding performers in each category.

The fantastic tulips on the small list at the end of this section are not likely to come back a second year and are challenging to grow. But every season a few should be tucked into corners that will show off their exotic colors and forms.

Follow-on and Companion Plants: Combine early tulips with small bulbs in complementary colors, for instance *Anemone blanda*, miniature daffodils, and late crocuses. Plant early and late tulips together for a long season. In spots where the spring sun will be followed by the shade of leafed-out trees, plant primroses, bleeding-hearts, and astilbes. The big annuals are fine followers and provide screening for ripening tulip foliage; *Antirrhinum majus* (snapdragon), *Pelargonium × hortorum* (geranium), big marigolds, and zinnias are all possibilities.

TULIPA   (tew-lip-uh)
Tulip

Tulips flourish in the long cold winters, wet springs, and dry summers of their native Asia Minor. They are best suited to our Zones 3 to 7. A number of hybrids and a few species tulips are successful in warmer regions—see list 6; Best Bulbs for the South. A number of the tulips named here, along with *T. batalinii* and *T. clusiana*, perform well in Zone 8. On the dry West Coast, *T. clusiana*, *T. saxatilis*, and *T. sylvestris* tend to perennialize while *T. praestans*, *T. tarda*, and *T. chrysantha* are used as annuals and replanted every year. Some of these are recommended on lists 1 and 2.

Culture: Plant tulips in fall before the ground freezes—up to late October in Zones 2 to 4, October or November in Zones 5 to 8. Results past mid-December are poor. Store bulbs until planting time in an airy container at temperatures of 45° F to 55° F, never above 70° F. A refrigerator at the right temperature is suitable.

FACING PAGE Spring's biggest show is staged by the tulips. (Frease)

TOP, RIGHT Fosterana 'Juan', largest early tulip. (Heath)

BELOW 'Ancilla', a very early Kaufmania, perfect for rock gardens. (Heath)

BOTTOM, RIGHT 'Parade', has the classical tulip form of the stately mid-season Darwins. (Heath)

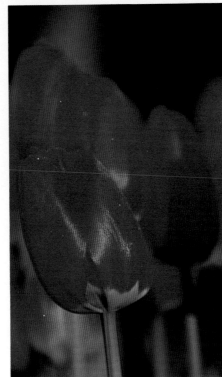

In Zones 9 and 10, all tulips should be considered annuals and only precooled bulbs planted. Few flower without a cold period of about 8 to 10 weeks before planting in December. Cultivars of Single Late, Darwin, Triump, Lily-flowered and Fringed tulips generally perform best.

Set large tulips 4 to 6 inches apart and 8 inches deep; small bulbs 3 to 4 inches apart and 4 to 5 inches deep. Deeper planting can be successful but is not recommend below 10 inches.

Tulips need only 6 hours of sun daily to perform well, preferably 6 hours of morning and afternoon sun. Midday sun is too intense and too hot. Ideal soil for tulips is slightly acid, *well-drained,* deeply dug, and enriched with compost and humus. Work a handful of bulb booster into each hole before planting.

To help tulips repeat, cut spent blooms to the ground after flowering, and in the fall add a cupful of bulb booster for every 10 square feet of perennialized tulips. Fertilize yearly in early spring just after the shoots have emerged from the ground, six to eight weeks before bloom time. Place a handful of small, sharp-edged gravel around each bulb where wild furry things rob the beds.

The order of presentation here introduces the general order of bloom.

EARLY TULIPS

KAUFMANNIANA WATER-LILY TULIP   Zones 3-7

Excellent. One of the earliest tulips to flower, in March and April, it has long, pointed petals that open out flat to reveal interiors in colors that are different and often contrasting. Height is 4 to 8 inches. The stems are short and the leaves often are mottled or striped. Perennializes in northern regions. Perfect for rock gardens.

'Ancilla', bright pink, white, yellow, and deep pink with green leaves; looks a little like a water lily.

FOSTERANA   Zones 3-7

Early, medium tall tulips in luminous colors. Height is 10 to 20 inches. This is the largest of the early bloomers. Some have truly immense petals and the foliage often is mottled or striped. There are interesting elongated forms. Nice with daffodils.

'Juan', 12 to 14 inches, luminous deep orange with a yellow base and long-lasting, decorative purple-mottled leaves.

'Purissima', to 12 inches, a stately pure white tulip with long-lasting flowers. Good perennializer.

GREIGII   Zones 3-7

This type flowers a bit later—in April. They are low-growing tulips, 8 to 10 inches, that open out wide in the sun and are prized for their decorative, broad leaves, which are streaked or mottled with purple. A good choice for the front of the border.

'Oriental Splendour', to 14 inches and taller than most Greigii, with carmine yellow flowers. The foliage is striped almost solid purple and remains attractive after the blossoms go. Good perennializer.

'United States', just 8 inches high, orange with yellowish edges, early and vigorous. Very showy.

TOP, LEFT Lily-flowered 'Ballerina', great in grass gardens. (Heath)

TOP, RIGHT Long-lasting Triumph hybrid, 'New Design'. (Heath)

ABOVE 'Lilac Wonder' *T. saxatilis*, here with forget-me-nots. (McDonald)

FAR RIGHT 'Estelle Rynveld', one of the extraordinary Parrots. (Netherlands Flowerbulb Information Center)

RIGHT Lush peony-flowered tulip, 'Mount Tacoma', beautiful with blue irises. (Netherlands Flowerbulb Information Center)

EARLY HYBRIDS

SINGLE EARLY   Zones 3-8

Excellent midsized, often fragrant, single tulips in the classical tulip shape, 10 to 14 inches high. They flower in April to early May, two weeks before the Single Late tulips (formerly classified as Cottage Tulips and Darwin Tulips). Superb cut flowers, long lasting, and fragrant. Good forcing bulbs.

'KeizersKroon' ('Grand Duc'), 12 to 14 inches tall, red and yellow. This is a historic tulip registered in 1750, recommended for restoration gardens and antique collections.

DOUBLE EARLY   Zones 3-7

Excellent. Long-lasting, softly colored double tulips that flower towards late April on stems averaging 8 to 12 inches. Choice for bedding, forcing, and cutting.

'Monte Carlo', to 16 inches, lemon yellow with a deep gold interior and a few red streaks. A good perennializer.

MIDSEASON HYBRIDS

TRIUMPH   Zones 3-7

Midseason tulips flower between Single Early tulips and the late bloomers—mid-May in most regions. They are handsome set in front of the taller midseason Darwin Hybrids. These are substantial flowers on strong, medium tall stems—usually 12 to 16 inches.

'New Design', to 14 inches, pretty pink with an unusual stripe on the foliage. Long lasting.

DARWIN HYBRIDS   Zones 3-7

These flower in April to mid-May, are about 12 to 24 inches tall and are the stately, classical tulips seen in municipal and estate plantings. Hybrids are better than the ordinary Darwins and more easily perennialized. Large-flowered, brilliantly colored, long lasting and magnificent combined with Fosteranas and Single Early tulips.

'Big Chief', to 20 inches. Each stem bears very large, two-toned crimson flowers. Will repeat.

'Golden Parade', to 24 inches, pale buttercup yellow, almost perennial in cool climates.

'Ivory Flordale', to 24 inches, ivory-white spotted red, immense in size.

'Oxford Elite', to 24 inches, red and orange-yellow.

'Gordon Cooper', to 24 inches, bright magenta.

'Parade', to 24 inches, splendid fire-truck red, one of the best, very large and strong.

'Pink Impression', to 20 inches, pink on a very strong stem. Long lasting.

LATE SEASON HYBRIDS

SINGLE LATE   Zones 3-8

This group flowers two weeks after the Single Early group—mid- to late May—and includes tulips formerly classed as Darwins and Cottage Tulips. Height to 20 inches. Excellent in flower beds.

'Maureen', to 20 inches, a creamy white sport of the very popular plant below and a great repeat bloomer. Long-lasting flowers.

'Mrs. John T. Scheepers', to 20 inches, bright yellow, a graceful, perfect tulip and one of the best to perennialize. Exceptional.

LILY-FLOWERED   Zones 4-7

Excellent. The group flowers in May. They are arresting designer favorites, elegant, long-waisted or vase-shaped, with pointed, reflexed, lilylike petals on slender stems. Long-lasting cut flowers. Perfect choice with contemporary buildings and low ornamental grasses.

'Mariette', 14 to 16 inches, pure pink.

'West Point', 14 to 16 inches, perfectly formed primrose yellow flowers on graceful stems, striking in groups of 10.

FRINGED   Zones 4-8

Excellent and long lasting. Known as Orchid-flowering and Crispa tulips, they resemble Parrot Tulips below and are usually about 20 inches tall. The top edges of the petals are fringed, some are frosted, and some combine both for a fantastic effect. Flower with the Single Lates.

'Burgundy Lace', to 20 inches, glowing red with a cerise interior and ivory center. Especially successful perennializer.

PARROT   Zones 4-8

Informal tulips about 20 inches tall that open widely and have frilled and curled edges and many surprising and brilliant color combinations. They flower in mid- and late May.

'Estella Rynveld', to 20 inches, streaked red and white and has extraordinarily attractive frilled petals.

'Flaming Parrot', to 20 inches, red and yellow. This is the best and tends to perennialize well.

DOUBLE LATE (PEONY-FLOWERED)   Zones 3-8

Excellent plants and magnificent flowers. They are similar to the Double Early, but tall, to 18 and 24 inches, and look like real peonies. Wonderful planted in groups of 4 or 5 with tall blue irises in a long border. They flower toward the end of spring, before the peonies.

'Angelique', 12 to 14 inches, soft pink, one of the loveliest.

'Mount Tacoma', to 14 inches, a beautiful white, unusual in this class.

BUNCH-FLOWERING   Zones 4-7

Excellent. Tall tulips with 4 to 5 large, cup-shaped flowers on each stem. The colors generally are brilliant. This is not an official classification, but rather a collection of cultivated varieties that have the multiflowering characteristic.

'Georgette', to 20 inches tall, rich, buttery yellow with edges just brushed with red, 3 to 5 flowers per stem.

'Modern Style', to 20 inches, flamed rose-purple on a white ground, 3 to 5 flowers per stem.

CHALLENGING, FANTASTIC TULIPS

The names that follow belong to various tulip divisions and flowering periods. They are all tulips to be in awe of—stars chosen for their beauty alone, and not as likely to perennialize as the tulips described above. They are presented here more or less in the order of their flowering season.

GREIGII   Zones 3-7

'Red Reflection', to 14 inches, a glowing deep scarlet, exquisitely marbled, with extremely large flowers for a Greigii. This is an early botanical tulip.

SINGLE EARLY   Zones 3-8

'Apricot Beauty', to 16 inches, apricot pink and rosy salmon combination, one of the most popular tulips. It is suitable for bedding and forcing. It flowers in April and May.

TRIUMPH   Zones 3-7

'Arabian Mystery', 14 to 16 inches, violet with a fine, clear white edge. Very sturdy. Mid-May.

'Baronesse', to 16 inches, a very desirable pastel pink with a broad, white edge to the petals. The white edge is a bit feathered. Midseason.

BUNCH-FLOWERING TRIUMPH   Zones 3-7

'White Bouquet', to 16 inches, pink-white with 3 to 5 flowers per stem—one big bloom and 3 or 4 little ones around it. Very attractive and unusual. Midseason.

DARWIN HYBRID   Zones 3-7

'Bienvenue', 20 to 24 inches, elegantly large, canary yellow bloom that has flames of rose rising through it. Early midseason.

'Ivory Floradale', 18 to 24 inches, ivory white with a hint of red veination and a good strong stem. This is one of the best and largest of all the tulips and an excellent repeat bloomer. Early midseason.

SINGLE LATE   Zones 3-8

'Imannuella', 20 to 24 inches, soft lemon yellow, a big tulip, kin to the wonderful 'Mrs. John T. Scheepers' and having some of that tulip's strength. Excellent for the South. Perennializes.

'Queen of the Night', to 16 inches, purple-black. The deep color is interesting combined with various other colors— soft pinks and white, for instance. Rather late midseason.

'Sister Francoise', 20 to 24 inches, ivory white with sulphur yellow flames coming up through the white. Excellent for the South.

LILY-FLOWERED   Zones 4-7

'Ballerina', 18 to 20 inches, intense orange. Midseason to late.

PARROT   Zones 4-7

'Rococo', to 20 inches, two colors of red in combination, a carmine and a fire red, exceptionally cut and fringed. Midseason.

SOURCE: BRENT HEATH IS A WORLD AUTHORITY ON DAFFODILS AND INTERNATIONALLY KNOWN FOR THE DEVELOPMENT OF FLOWERING BULBS. HE AND HIS WIFE BECKY HYBRIDIZE BULBS ON THE ORIGINAL HEATH BULB FARM IN GLOUCESTER, VIRGINIA.

CHAPTER TWO:
Perennials—The Come-Back Flowers

Perennials give the garden continuity and structure. They are the first plants chosen for a mixed flower bed and should be planned with lots of room all around for groups of bulbs—15 to 24 inches apart for small to moderate sizes, 28 to 30 inches for big plants, and 36 inches for peonies. The bulbs go in next, and in late spring or early summer the annuals are set out to enhance color and fill in for fading spring bulb foliage.

The plants recommended on lists 13 through 17 describe a progression of bloom from mid-spring through late fall for a garden in either sun or shade. The plants were chosen for lasting bloom, disease resistance and low maintenance. Among the most useful as cornerstones for a first garden are: *Sedum* 'Autumn Joy', for foliage all year and glowing flowers in autumn; *Aquilega, Dicentra,* and *Geranium,* for exquisite spring flowers and dainty foliage; and *Perovskia,* tall, very structural blue background plants for late spring and early summer. *Achillea, Coreopsis, Rudbeckia,* and *Hibiscus* provide lasting summer color. *Cimicifuga* and the brilliant poppy anemones are also recommended for summer. Japanese anemones are wonderful in late summer and fall. Also try the unique winter perennial, *Helleborus,* a "rose" that blooms in snow. The species and

variations of all these plants are recommended on many lists and are the pool of perennials from which garden designers frequently draw, along with the 11 major perennials on lists 20 through 30: *Aster, Astilbe, Campanula, Chrysanthemum,* Daylily *(Hemerocallis), Iris,* Peony *(Paeonia), Phlox,* Poppy *(Papaver),* Primrose *(Primula),* and Pansy and Violet *(Viola).*

Perennials are the cornerstone of herbaceous flower gardens because they come back—but they don't all come back forever. To put in perennial plantings that won't disappoint you, you need to understand their seasons of bloom.

While a few perennials bloom the first year from seed, most come into flower only the second year. Perennial seedlings in packs will not bloom the first year, but container-grown and bare-root perennials usually will bloom the first year.

To stay in top form, many perennials must be divided and replanted every four or five years. A few come back for decades—anemone hybrids, cimicifuga, dicentra, some geraniums, helleborus, hibiscus, hostas, and perovskia, for example. But not asters, astilbe, some irises, and phloxes. Peonies are probably the longest lived, surviving for a century or more. At the other end of scale, cushion mums should be divided every spring to remain beautiful.

Can you make a perennial more perennial? Yes, by starting it off in the improved garden soil described in the section on Growing Flowers, earlier in this book.

Plants labeled "tender perennials" don't survive frost, so they're grown as annuals. I knew snapdragons as annuals in my Connecticut gardens—but here in Washington, D.C., they repeat well, and elsewhere they perennialize (but are woody).

The short-lived biennials are grouped with perennials in this chapter. Set out one year, a biennial flowers the next year, then dies. An example is cheiranthus, the beautifully scented lemony orange-red English wallflower. A few biennials appear to be perennial because they sow seeds that flower the next year. Some hardy perennials are also short-lived. Pansies, for instance, act like biennials and often need replanting every year.

FACING PAGE In late summer in the lavender perennial garden at River Farm, *Clematis jackmanii,* larkspur, and roses take over. (American Horticultural Society)
ABOVE 'Ruby Giant' star Japanese iris. (Viette)

Sold as *Oenothera speciosa* 'Rosea', this willowy, enduring American native blooms profusely in spring. The leaves are flecked with red. (Viette)

Choosing for North and South

Perennials come into flower early, midseason, or late within their period of bloom. For the cool regions, early bloomers are the best choices. The North has four distinct seasons and flowers bloom in three of them. The warm South has two seasons—winter, which melds into late spring, which in turn vanishes into hot summer, and now and then there are erratic cool snaps. Yet northern and southern gardens share many of the same perennials. Flowers come into bloom earlier and all in a heap in the South rather than in the set stages familiar to the temperate zones. Asters which bloom in August, September, and early October in the North wait until July, August, and September to bloom in the South. They don't necessarily last longer, either. Heat shuts down a bloom period just as cold does. Daylilies flower in late May in Florida, June 5 in South Carolina, July 10 in Virginia, later on Long Island, and later yet in Maine and Canada.

Winter can play havoc with early perennials in the South because there is no snow cover to protect them from the cold. Farther north, 9 inches or more of snow will keep the ground from freezing, though the air temperature might be 20° F. In unprotected southern gardens a warm spell can set early bloomers growing, then a cold spell will freeze them back. Winter mulches and late-flowering species are recommended precautions.

Planting Perennials

Perennials grow from fibrous rootstock developed from seeds or from root or crown divisions. The crown is the upper portion of the rootstock from which stems grow.

You can sow perennial seeds indoors in flats four to six weeks before transplanting time—in late winter, after all danger of frost is past. Transplant about two weeks after the average date of your last spring frost. The healthiest temperatures for seedlings are between 65° and 70° F. While annuals may germinate within 20 days, seeds for perennials may germinate slowly over a long period, even if a few seedlings pop up at once. Keep seeded flats moist for two or even three months to give all the seeds a chance to sprout.

Hardy perennials also are started successfully outdoors from seed. Sow the seeds in spring two weeks after the last frost date—or in summer or fall, up to two months before the first frost date. When fall sowing is recommended, it indicates those seeds will benefit from the action of frost. When directions call for planting "fresh" seeds, sow the seeds as soon as they are gathered, whatever the season; to germinate, these particular seeds need the months and weather ahead.

A few perennials and some biennials come into flower the first season after sowing, but that's unusual.

For spring planting, some perennials—astilbes, for instance—are shipped "bare root" (with the dormant rootstock protected with a packing medium). These probably will flower the second season. Follow the planting instructions enclosed in the package.

The best route to getting top-quality perennials is to buy them as container plants. The finest forms of perennials—big flowers, long-lasting flowering period, best color—do not come true from seed. (Annuals are different.) Containerized plants are sold in spring, summer, and early fall. Some are root or crown divisions (see Growing Flowers) that flower the first year. Others are cuttings that will flower the following year. Ask when the plants will bloom.

Always loosen the roots of container-grown plants before planting.

Maintaining Perennials

How do you know when a perennial needs dividing? The stems become crowded and leggy, and there are fewer and smaller blooms.

The general rule is to divide spring-flowering perennials a month before the ground freezes in the fall, or before new growth begins in early spring. Divide autumn-flowering perennials, such as chrysanthemums, in the spring before growth begins. The special times for division of a few finicky flowers are noted in the lists—poppies, for instance, can only be divided or transplanted successfully after flowering when the foliage has died down. See also Growing Flowers.

The information given about light in Growing Flowers, under Establishing a Flower Bed, applies to perennials. In hot climates less light is needed and protection from noon sun is welcome. Perennials that do best in full sun in New England will prefer partial sun or bright shade in the hot South. Perennials that want light shade in the South can manage in direct sun in the North.

The perennials recommended on lists 13 through 17 are not fussy about soil as long as it is well-drained and reasonably fertile. All herbaceous flowers, except for bog plants, list 59, call for soil that is well drained. Most perennials thrive in soil with a pH range between 5.5 to 6.5.

The best time to clean up the flower garden for winter in Zones 4 to 7 is late

Small, durable 'Champagne Bubbles', an iceland poppy, *Papaver nudicaule*, perennialized with crimson pyrethrum—painted daisies. (McDonald)

December and January, before the bulbs start up. Before raking through perennials such as lilies, cut back the stems and foliage. Don't pull them up—cut them off, otherwise you may make holes in the bulbs, and that can lead to rot.

See Growing Flowers for information on soil preparation and watering.

13. SPRING PERENNIALS FOR SUN

■ Here are the flowers to plant for that first wave of perennial color toward mid-spring. The blossoms open above foliage that already is screening the fading bulb flowers. There's candytuft like snow banked against Christmas-green leaves, and quilled aquilegia nodding above foliage as dainty as Maidenhair ferns. The satiny peony globes come into bloom from stems that soar upward as quickly as Jack's beanstalk, then irises open out like orchids. Finally the silky, sooty hearted poppies and majestic lilies lead the way to summer. You can plant some of these in early spring but most of them will have gone into the ground the summer or fall before.

Nothing in a garden is static. Spring color fades, then it's time for the garden to start the next show. Part of the summer display will come from spring-flowering perennials that left foliage behind to lend texture and interest all summer—aquilegias, astilbes, and irises, for instance. All around them the space is filling with the developing clumps of perennials and biennials that will flower in summer and fall, and were planted last spring or the year before. Often, the greatest difficulty presented by an established bed of spring perennials is finding space for the exotic summer and fall bulbs you should make up your mind to try. Meanwhile, an irresistible flood of annuals already in bloom is building at garden centers—temptation alley for gardeners.

The flowers see to it that you do find space for them, somehow.

Follow-on Plants: For season-long foliage, plant silvery *Senecio cineraria* 'Silver Dust' (Dusty-miller) and *Teucrium chamaedrys*, Germander. Good flowering edgers include evergreen cottage pinks, blue ageratum, pink wax begonias, fragrant *Lobularia maritima*, Sweet Alyssum, and *Gypsophila repens*, the creeping Baby's-breath. Tall plants include *Aruncus dioicus*, Goatsbeard, *Macleaya cordata* (syn. *Bocconia cordata)*, Plume Poppy, Tree Celandine, and ornamental grasses. Add lavender, mints, or oregano for fragrance. Annuals to follow spring perennials include petunias and geraniums (*Pelargonium.*)

AMSONIA (am-*soh*-nee-uh)
Tabernaemontana
Bluestar   Zones 3-9
Slow-growing, easy-care native perennial that forms clumps 12 to 36 inches tall and for several weeks in late spring bears drooping or upright clusters of persistent, small, truly blue flowers. Pods follow the flowers and are attractive in flower arrangements. The willowlike foliage sways with every breeze, remains green and lush all season, and turns a striking yellow-gold in fall.

Culture: Pruning after flowers fade helps maintain the beauty of the foliage. Some gardeners cut it back twice in a season, after flowering. Divide, plant 30 inches apart, or sow seed in early spring in ordinary garden soil well supplied with humus. Best in semi-sun or shade, but it can take half a day of direct sun. Water weekly during dry spells. Fertilize in early winter.

AQUILEGIA (ak-wil-*leej*-ee-uh)   Columbine
One of the most exquisite spring and early summer plants for foliage as well as flowers. The delicate, intricate nodding or upright blossoms end in spurs usually in two shades and are displayed against fresh blue-green scalloped foliage on plants 12 to 36 inches tall. They are borne over many weeks in mid- to late spring. Cut back the foliage when it begins to spoil—it usually returns and remains a low filler for the rest of the season. Modern hybrids offer a wide range of heights and colors, including bicolors—white, yellow, blue, rusty pinks, lavenders, purples, and reddish orange. There are hybrids with lovely big spurs ('Spring Song',) double-flowered strains, and charming dwarfs for the rock garden. The wild-garden elegance of the old-fashioned *A. vulgaris*, European Crowfoot, Garden Columbine, is preferred for cutting and cottage gardens. Aquilegias are best planted in groups of at least 3 to 5, but be wary: they self-sow and turn up here and there.

Species best for shade are discussed on lists 14, Spring Perennials for Shade, and 66, The Rock Garden.

Culture: Fresh seed sown in late spring or early summer produces flowers the following year. For first year bloom set out root divisions 12 to 15 inches apart in well-drained, humusy, moist soil in early spring. Established plants are tolerant of drought and many self-sow lavishly. Aquilegias succeed in sun in mild regions and prefer some shade in warm regions.

A. × hybrida   Zones 3-9
These are the best and most popular. They are spring-blooming hybrids 18 to 36 inches tall in various colors, with either long or short spurs. Recommended as best are 'Crimson Star', to 30 inches, crimson and white; and McKana's Giants strain, 18 to 36 inches, very large flowers in lovely pastels.

Also recommended: 'Copper Queen', the Dragonfly Hybrids, 'Langdon's Rainbow', and the Mrs. Scott Elliott strain, a long-established group; 'Rose Queen', 'Spring Song', whose spurs may be up to 3 inches long, and 'Snow Queen'.

A. flabellata 'Nana'   Zones 3-9
Spring bloomer that succeeds in partial shade, especially in the South. Short plants 6 to 8 inches tall with large, gracefully hooked spurs on nodding blue and white blossoms. 'Nana Alba' blooms a little earlier, displaying an exquisite white-on-white flower. Easy-to-grow plants that self-sow and are recommended for rock gardens.

A. longissima 'Maxistar'   Zones 3-8
Early summer bloomer, 18 to 24 inches tall, that bears very large, very long-spurred blue flowers. The plants may need replanting every 2 or 3 years.

ARMERIA (arm-*meer*-ee-uh)
Thrift, Sea Pink
Sturdy little evergreen plants that in spring form neat, dense mounds of grassy leaves and bear attractive globe-shaped flowers held well above the foliage. Used especially in rock and wall gardens and as edgings. Attractive container plants.

Culture: Set out root divisions in fall or early spring or sow seed during early spring in full sun in light, gritty, well-drained soil. Requires shades from afternoon sun in the South.

A. maritima   Zones 4-8
This is the best. Tufts 6 to 12 inches high are covered with tight heads of pink, mauve, lilac, or white flowers. Extremely tolerant of salt and coastal conditions. Recommended are 'Alba', 5 inches tall, and creamy white; 'Dusseldorf's Pride', 6 to 8 inches tall, pink to carmine; and 'Vindictive', 6 inches tall, with bright rosy red flowers. Flowers in late spring in almost any soil or exposure.

A. plantaginea (syns. *pseudarmeria, cephalates*)   Zones 4-9
Also excellent, with wider leaves and smaller flowerheads in summer. 'Bee's Ruby', with spectacular cerise flowers on 18-inch stems, is recommended.

BAPTISIA (bap-*tiz*-ee-uh)   australis
Blue False Indigo, Plains False Indigo, Wild Blue Indigo   Zones 3-8
A tall, vigorous plant that produces masses of pretty gray-green foliage in spring, followed in early summer by spikes of pealike indigo blue flowers used in arrangements, as are the black seedpods that develop later and are interesting in winter. Mature height, 3 to 4 feet.

Culture: Requires staking in partial shade and grows best in a sunny location. Fresh seeds sprout easily in early spring but the simplest way is to plant root divisions 24 inches apart in pairs in well-drained, humusy, somewhat acid soil. Moisture should be average to dry.

BERGENIA (ber-*jee*-nee-uh)   cordifolia
Zones 3-8
Also called heartleaf bergenia and pig squeak, this vigorous plant 12 to 16 or 18 inches high bears graceful spires of dark pink flowers in mid-spring. It is prized in particular for its clumps of glossy, leathery evergreen leaves which turn bronze in winter sun. There's a white-flowered variety and a tall, purple-toned 'Purpurea' that grows up to 20 inches, with dark pink blossoms and leaves that turn burgundy in cold. It is not invasive and is most effective in groups.

The very best are 'Abendglut' ('Evening Glow'), 9 inches tall, with crimson-purple flowers; 'Morgenrote' ('Morning Red'), 8 to 12 inches tall, carmine red; and 'Silberlicht' ('Silver Light'), 12 inches tall, whose pink-tinged white flowers have red centers.

Also first rate is *B. c.* 'Perfecta', which has purplish leaves and rosy red flowers that stand well above the foliage.

Culture: In moist, well-drained soil in cool regions, *B. cordifolia* tolerates full sun, but partial shade is better for the South. Grows easily from seed or root divisions planted in early spring near streams or pools, or in flowering borders or rock gardens in well-drained soil with lots of humusy organic matter added. Tolerates drought.

CAMPANULA, Bellflower. These gossamer cups
of blue, lavender, white, or sometimes pink are called bellflowers, but in some of the small forms the flowers are more like stars spangled on a canopy of green. From a few inches to a few feet tall, they have an airy, dancing grace. The flowering period can be 2 or even 3 months in late spring or early summer and into fall. Erect types are often showy enough for use in mixed flower borders, but collectors—seekers of charm rather than glamor—delight in more subtle species. There are low mounds for

Among the prettiest and most enduring perennials:
LEFT *Armeria*, a very small pink that thrives in sandy soils and by the sea. (Viette)
BOTTOM, LEFT Cranesbill, the true *Geranium*, 'Johnson's Blue'. (Viette)
BELOW *Aquilegia caerulea*, important ancestor of the long-spurred modern hybrid columbines. (Viette)

rock gardens and creepers that flourish in, around, and through dry stone walls, tall sorts for cottage gardens, and a few for alpine gardens. Many are good cutting flowers. On the whole, they're long lasting and many species multiply and naturalize. See list 22, *Campanula*.

DICTAMUS (dik-*tam*-nus) albus
Dittany, Fraxinella, Gas Plant, Burning Bush
Zones 3-8

Outstanding, long-lived, upright perennial foliage and flowering plant that grows up to 3 feet tall with dark green, lemon-scented leaves which reputedly give off a gas. The foliage is topped by tall, handsome sprays of fragrant, starry white flowers in late spring or early summer. It is slow to establish, but the foliage is attractive all season long and the plants eventually form handsome clumps. Seeds as well as leaves are lemon-scented and both can cause rashes and allergic reactions. 'Purpurea' has mauve-pink flowers with darker veins.

Culture: Transplants badly so sow seeds where they are to flower or, best of all, purchase two-year-old plants. Does best where nights are cool. Set out with lots of space to spread in full sun or partial shade, in well-drained, rich, moist soil. It tolerates some drought in good conditions.

DORONICUM (doh-*ron*-ik-um)
Leopard's-bane
Zone 4-7

The daisylike yellow flowers brighten the spring garden and are showy and long-lasting above bright green, large-leaved foliage mounds. Excellent with bulbs and nice as a cut flower.

Culture: Easily grown. Set out container plants or root divisions in spring in sun or light shade (South), in rich, humusy, deeply dug soil with sustained moisture. Divide every 2 or 3 years before flowering.

D. 'Miss Mason'
Neat in the border and can be used as edging. Two-inch flowers appear early on plants 12 to 24 inches tall above a spreading mound of glossy leaves that tend to persist until frost. Cut back after flowering to encourage more blooms. 'Spring Beauty' is earlier and a double.

Plant these for foliage that is decorative before and after flowering:

ABOVE 'Red Wings' *Geum quellyon*'s lasting spring blooms are followed by fluffy seedheads. (Viette)

RIGHT Early foliage of showy blue false indigo, *Baptisia australis*. (Viette)

FAR RIGHT 'Rube', a rosy-purple cultivar of the gas plant, *Dictamus albums*, outstanding upright perennial with fragrant flowers. (Viette)

D. plantagineum 'Harpur Crewe'

A big, coarsely handsome plant for the back of the border. Mature height is to 5 feet and the 4-inch flowers are borne generously through late spring.

GERANIUM (jer-**ray**-nee-um)
Cranesbill

Excellent. Don't confuse this with *Pelargonium*, whose common name is geranium. These plants—4 to 24 inches tall—are mat- or clump-forming herbaceous perennials; some are suitable for sunny beds or borders, others for ground covers for woodland and rock gardens. In spring and early summer, and often again in fall when the weather cools a little, this "true" geranium produces small, saucerlike, five-petaled pastel pink, mauve, purplish, magenta, violet, cerise, red, blue, or white flowers abundantly on wandlike stems above dainty, deeply divided foliage. Their common name refers to the beaklike fruit that follows. For geraniums that do well in the South or in some shade, see lists 18 and 14. See also the recommendations on list 66, The Rock Garden and 48, Wildflowers to Naturalize.

Culture: The best performance in northern gardens comes from plants given full sun; in Zone 8 and south, provide protection from the afternoon sun. Geraniums thrive in well-drained, humusy, evenly moist soil of modest fertility. Water during droughts. Plant root divisions or seeds (results from seeds are not predictable). Transplant or root in early spring or fall. Set plants 18 to 24 inches apart. The following are especially recommended:

G. 'Johnson's Blue' Zones 4-8

The clear violet-blue flowers are 1½ to 2 inches across on 15- to 18-inch stems. They set little seed, flower for a long time, and do quite well in the South.

G. macrorrhizum Zones 3-9

The best geranium for ground cover. It produces dense, weed-smothering, noninvasive clumps 12 inches or taller. Quite drought resistant even in warm climates, it produces beautifully textured, rounded, divided leaves. Magenta flowers are borne in spring. In the hot summers of Zone 8 it grows best in partial shade, but elsewhere it benefits from the sun.

G. sanguineum var. prostratum

(syn. *lancastriense*) Zones 3-8

(Usually sold as 'Lancastriense' or 'Prostratum'.) One of the best perennials—a nearly indestructible, exceptionally tough plant, 6 to 12 inches tall, easy to grow and long-blooming with magenta-pink flowers that have darker veins. Attractive spreading foliage forms a mound and in fall turns crimson or maroon. Good everywhere, including cool and hot climates, the seashore, in sun (best) or shade. The bright magenta species is a good choice for cottage gardens and spreads rapidly in fertile soils. Among the superb varieties are 'Album', a pure white, and 'New Hampshire', a deep reddish pink, both 12 inches tall. Space the plants 12 inches apart.

Some other geraniums of note:

G. endressii 'Wargrave Pink' Zones 3-9

Low-growing, to 12 inches, and excellent at the front of the border or as a small patch of ground color. One of the few geraniums available for summer bloom—midsummer in cool areas, early summer in hot regions—it bears a profusion of clear, bright pink flowers.

G. himalayense (syn. *grandiflorum*) Zones 4-8

Although it gets a bit floopy from its dense growth, this is a wonderful plant to combine with peonies, bearded irise, and columbines. The large violet-blue flowers have darker veins and a reddish center. The foliage turns orange and red in fall. Height is 10 to 15 inches.

G. × magnificum Zones 4-8

For fall foliage, a sterile hybrid 24 inches tall that has been cultivated for over a century; in late spring and early summer it bears dark-veined violet-blue flowers. Fall foliage is rich orange-scarlet. Needs division every 2 or 3 years.

GEUM (**jee**-um) **quellyon 'Red Wings'**

Avens Zones 5-7

Excellent. This cultivar is the best in its rather limited hardiness range. Bright, showy, five-petaled, intense red-orange flowers a little like small poppies with golden centers are borne on tall slender stems. They bloom for a long period in spring and are followed by fluffy seedheads. The low-growing leaves are attractive. Heat destroys the plants.

Culture: Requires some shade in the warmer reaches of its hardiness zones, as well as constant moisture. Plant fresh seed in late spring for next season's bloom, or set out divisions during spring or fall in full sun, in well-drained, deeply worked garden soil.

IBERIS **sempervirens**, Edging Candytuft. Low-growing, spreading, clump-forming, narrow-leaved plant with attractive foliage on semiwoody stems, 6 to 12 inches high with a 24-inch spread. In early to mid-spring it is blanketed with dense heads of white flowers. Thrives without care in full or semi-sun and somewhat acid soil. Recommended are 'Autumn Beauty', 8 inches tall, which flowers in spring and reblooms in fall; 'Alexander's White', 8 to 10 inches tall, a very dense, floriferous plant; 'Little Gem', 5 to 8 inches tall, a charming, rare plant; and 'Snowflake', 8 to 10 inches tall, a late-blooming plant with large leaves and flowers. There's also an annual species and smaller forms. See list 43, Flowers for Edging.

IRIS, Flag, Fleur-de-lys, are almost indispensable. First come the very early, low-growing bulbous irises discussed on lists 1 and 2. The stars of spring and early summer in the flowering border are the rhizomatous irises—tall bearded and Siberians—with extraordinary blossoms that can be 8 and 10 inches across. In colors that cover most of the rainbow, the iris show usually lasts 3 to 5 weeks, but by careful selection can run from spring to fall. For watery places, there are the magnificent 5-foot *I. pseudacorus* and its relatives. For rock gardens and naturalizing there are charming little species and miniatures with foliagelike grass and dainty little flowers. For cultivars see list 25, Iris.

PAPAVER **orientale** cultivars, Oriental Poppy. These are the stars of the poppy family, big crinkled-silk blossoms 5 to 8 and 10 inches across that unfold in spring and early summer in vibrant reds, exquisite pinks, oranges, whites, and combinations, usually with a dark or sooty center. The petals of some are splotched at the base in a contrasting color, usually black, and others have contrasting edges. The deeply cut foliage dies in late summer but reappears in fall and is evergreen or semievergreen in winter. For culture and recommended cultivars see list 28, Poppy.

PAEONIA, Peony. The big, satiny peonies that bloom in spring are unmatched for showy beauty and ease of culture, particularly in colder regions. And they're the first of the very big flowers to bloom—in April and May, according to region, species, and weather. The great globes of crinkled silk with an unmistakable fragrance come in creamy whites, pinks, blush pinks, brilliant yellows, corals, and crimsons. Some reds are so rich they're nearly purple. For beginning gardeners, peonies are among the most bountiful of all the important perennials, and make superb cut flowers as well. Both herbaceous and woody tree forms are discussed on list 26, Peony.

TRADESCANTIA (trad-es-**skant**-ee-uh)
× **andersoniana** cultivars
Spiderwort Zones 4-9

The spiderworts are excellent invaders for wild patches, forming dense clumps 24 to 36 inches tall with long, thin leaves on joined stems (that root too readily) familiar to owners of the related Wandering Jew houseplants. In late spring and early summer clusters of small, bright, flat, three-petaled flowers are borne—deep blue in the species, and purple, pink, rose, or white. Some recommended cultivars are: 'Blue Stone', lavender-blue; 'Innocence', white; 'Osprey', white with a blue center, 'Purple Dome', purple; 'Red Cloud', dark magenta or pink; and 'Snow-cap', white.

Culture: Very easy to grow in full sun or partial shade. Sow seeds, or set out rooted plants in spring or summer in ordinary garden soil, moist or dry. Uproot unwanted volunteers at once—it tends to spread relentlessly.

VERONICA **latifolia 'Crater Lake Blue'**
(syn. *teucrium*) Zones 3-8

The cultivar is the finest of the veronicas, 12 to 15 inches high. For several weeks in mid- and late spring it puts up flowering spires densely packed with gentian blue flowers. Next best is the smaller *V. gentianoides*, a mat-forming species approximately 6 inches or taller that in spring lifts loose racemes of flowers that are pale blue, almost white, with darker veins. Tolerant of moisture, but must not be allowed to dry out. The species *V. spicata*, which blooms in summer, is larger. For culture, see list 66, The Rock Garden.

SOURCE: ROBERT HEBB, A HORTICULTURIST, IS DIRECTOR OF THE LEWIS GINTER BOTANIC GARDEN IN RICHMOND, VIRGINA, AND WAS FORMERLY WITH THE ARNOLD ARBORETUM, LONGWOOD GARDENS, THE NEW YORK BOTANICAL GARDEN, AND OTHER DISTINGUISHED ARBORETA.

14. SPRING PERENNIALS FOR SHADE

■ A few of the very earliest perennials to flower are shade-loving plants. For example, there's the hellebore called Christmas Rose. It's not showy, but its earliness draws you out to see what's going on—push dry leaves aside to find it down there, catch a whiff of that good, moist earth smell, bring in a branch or two of an early-blooming shrub or tree for forcing. It makes you want to be part of everything growing. And its flowers are long lasting, so you go back outdoors often. Another fairly early favorite is the old-fashioned bleeding-heart. *Dicentra spectabilis*, whose heart is as pink and perfectly shaped as a Valentine. In a moist, semishaded spot the very attractive foliage lasts for many months.

It's a fact that several of the interesting spring flowers thrive only in shade. The prettiest blue of all— *Lobelia erinus*—is a little plant for semishade thats usually grown as an annual. So, even if you already have a satisfying sunny border that flowers in spring, the season will be far more interesting if you add a lightly shaded bed for some of the plants listed here. Plant bulb flowers among them—they bloom the first year in sun or shade.

The most important rule to remember: in cool regions, plants can stand more direct sun than in hot regions. Plants growing in improved, moist, but well-drained soil (see Growing Flowers) can stand more direct sun than those growing in hot, dry, sandy soil.

There can be too much of a good thing. One symptom of too much shade is that plants flop forward— and they don't bloom as generously as they should.

Follow-on Plants: A good ground cover *Lamium maculatum*, Spotted Dead Nettle. Flowering edgers and fillers include wax begonias, impatiens; New Guinea Impatiens; *Lobelia erinus*, and *Nicotiana*. Try white *Catharanthus roseus*, Rose Periwinkle, or Madagascar Periwinkle, for the middle of the border. Other good follow-on plants are *Caladium*, **Elephant's-ear**, hostas, ferns, and Lily-of-the-valley.

AQUILEGIA canadensis, Wild Columbine, Meeting-houses, Honeysuckle. Hardy but delicate pink and yellow or orange-red flowers with long spurs that bloom in early spring above ferny bluish green foliage. They reach 12 inches and are charming in a semishaded corner of the flower bed and ideal for rock gardens. This species succeeds in Zones 3 to 9. Other aquilegias for shade appear on list 66, The Rock Garden. For culture, see list 13, Spring Perennials for Sun; the species there prefer some shade only in warm regions.

BRUNNERA macrophylla (syn. *Anchusa myosotidiflora*), Siberian Bugloss. A deciduous ground cover that includes a long-lasting—up to 6 weeks— spring display of dainty flowers of a true blue like Forget-me-nots. Plants have 12-inch-high, deep green, round, bold foliage that remains fresh all season. Easily perennialized, adaptable in most of the country, and a good choice for large spaces. For culture see list 44, Flowering Ground Covers.

Creeping carpets of *Phlox divaricata*. The starry little blooms enhance any corner of the garden and, in a good situation, will spread for years. (Viette)

CORYDALIS lutea. Excellent exotic plant for wall crevices and cracks in walkways. For weeks in mid-spring, wiry stems bearing 6- to 8-inch spikes of soft yellow spurred flowers about 12 inches tall are held above ferny, light blue-green foliage. For culture see list 45, Rock Walls and Crevices.

DICENTRA (dye-**sent**-ruh) Excellent. The bleeding-hearts so named for the shape of their pink blossoms, are hardy, old-fashioned, delightful favorites for spring and early summer bloom in bright shade. Pretty pink, white, or red heart-shaped flowers dangle from gracefully arching stems above very attractive lacy foliage. Their height ranges 9 to 24 inches. Mass planting among ferns, hostas, and Solomon's-seal is very effective, and a good idea if the foliage dies to the ground in summer as happens with the beautiful *D. spectabilis*. Delightful in shady gardens, with wildflowers, and in rock gardens.

Culture: Bright shade is the best exposure. In cool areas where soil moisture is retained evenly, some exposure to full sun is acceptable. The best time for planting is during active growth in early spring. The bleeding-hearts require rich, moist, humusy soil in the pH range of 5.0 to 6.0.

D. eximia Turkey Corn, Staggerweed, Wild Bleeding-heart   Zones 2/3-9
The attractive foliage remains if moisture is maintained. It is a plumed, or fringed, bleeding-heart, with rosy pink flowers in arching sprays on stems 12 to 18 inches long above mounds of ferny blue-green foliage 12 inches wide. Blooms heavily from mid-spring to early summer. Even if it goes dormant, there usually is a new flush of bloom during cool weather. Plant or divide in late summer or early spring. Space plants 15 inches apart. Recommended is 'Luxuriant', a free-flowering hybrid that bears cherry red flowers on upright stalks that adapts to semishaded southern gardens and succeeds in the full sun north of Washington, D.C.; 'Alba', with sumptuous pure white flowers; and 'Adrian Bloom', with ruby red flowers. 'Bountiful' is a nice light pink.

D. spectabilis Bleeding-heart   Zones 3-9
Also known as live forever, this old-fashioned perennial is the most beautiful and longest-lived, a true aristocrat, but the foliage tends to die out where summers are hot. Plants grow to 36 inches across and bear up to 20 or more arching racemes decked with pendulous pink hearts in May. Do not water in dormancy. Established plants resent being disturbed, but can be divided with care in early spring. 'Alba', a beautiful pure white flower, is not quite as vigorous as the species. Space plants 36 inches apart.

EPIMEDIUM (ep-im-*meed*-ee-um)

Spring-flowering plants for shady places and rock gardens, grown for the clumps of long, beautiful, semievergreen or evergreen, heart-shaped leaves that turn reddish or gold in the cold of spring and/or autumn. Exotic little flowers rather like columbines, some long-spurred, are borne in clusters on slim, gracefully arching stems. The plants succeed in the competitive zone under trees. Choice ground covers, lasting once established.

Culture: In early spring plant root divisions in moist but well-drained, acid-range soil to which a great deal of peat moss has been added. Prefers light to full shade but tolerates full sun if soil moisture is maintained during summer. Avoid drought. Slow to establish so set out the plants no more than 12 inches apart. Clip back in spring to expose new growth and enhance the floral display.

E. grandiflorum   Zones 5-8

About 10 inches tall, it bears up to 12 large, long-spurred, pale pink flowers on each stem and has beigy brown foliage in spring. Beautiful foliage accent. Best are 'Rose Queen', which has scarlet leaves and pinky rose flowers with long spurs, and 'White Queen', whose flowers are white-silver above the scarlet leaves.

E. pinnatum (syn. *colchicum*)   Zones 5-8

Handsome brownish foliage, 10 to 12 inches high, and a flowering stem that bears up to two dozen short-spurred yellow flowers.

E. × rubrum (syn. *alpinum* var. **rubrum**)   Zones 4-8

Dainty, durable, and 6 to 12 inches high, in late spring it bears graceful sprays of irregular bicolored flowers, red with yellow. The leaves turn bronzy red at the onset of cold weather.

E. × versicolor 'Sulphureum'   Zones 5-9

Excellent foliage accent and ground cover 12 inches high with small, airy clusters of delicate yellow flowers with long rosy spurs. Evergreen in the South.

E. × youngianum   Zones 5-9

Smaller, with narrow bronze leaves in cold weather; turns a fresh green when the delicate, airy flower clusters appear in late spring. 'Roseum' has lilac flowers, and 'Niveum' is a late-blooming white. Height is 6 to 12 inches.

HELLEBORUS (hel-leb-*bor*-rus)   Hellebore

Evergreen plants 12 to 18 inches high with distinctive, shining, leathery, deeply divided foliage that remains interesting in winter. The flowers—which appear in December, January, or early spring according to the climate—are the finest of any winter and late winter herbaceous perennial. The rounded, nodding, roselike flowers in white-green and pink—actually 5 petal-like sepals—are also rather leathery for added resistance to bad weather, and persist for 2 to 3 months. Undisturbed, beautiful colonies form and self-sow. Plant near well-used paths, or where they can been seen from a window. Mixed plantings of two or more species stretch out the blooming period and provide a fascinating textural contrast.

TOP *Aquilegia canadensis*, wild columbine, adds charm to a shaded corner. (Viette)
CENTER Durable Lenten rose, *Helleborus orientalis*, blooms very early in gardens from Maine to Georgia. (Viette)
RIGHT The fine foliage of *Epimedium × versicolor*, 'Sulphureum', makes it a good ground cover. (Viette)

Culture: Set out root divisions in early spring in damp, humusy, nearly neutral soil. Consistent light shade is best, but in cool climates exposure to morning sun is suitable if moisture is sustained. Fertilize in late winter and remove old foliage before the new appears. Established clumps are relatively drought tolerant. Divide in late spring or early summer only if essential and instead increase by means of small offsets taken from younger growth in the periphery of the crown. Good contrast for *Skimmia*.

H. foetidus   Zones 5/4-9

Only second best but its narrow, divided, shiny leaves make this an elegant foliage plant. Reaches a height of 18 to 24 inches. Panicles of drooping, bell-like, pale apple green flowers edged with red appear as early as January in Zone 7 and in early April in Zone 5. Self-sows and eventually forms a large, bold clump. A common name is stinking hellebore, given for the musky smell close to the blossoms. Set plants 24 inches apart.

H. niger Christmas Rose   Zones 3-8

Third best, though it is the most famous species. The pure porcelain white sepals surround a central tuft of yellow stamens. Not as vigorous as the Lenten Rose, it reaches a height of 12 to 18 inches. The flowering is genetically controlled, so only particularly early-flowering forms bloom during the Christmas season even in Zone 7 and south. Most plants bloom in January and February in mild regions, and farther north will bloom in the snow during the lengthening days of early spring. Plant these in fall, 15 inches apart. The best variety is *macranthus* (syn. *altifolius*), which is freer flowering and more vigorous than the species; it blooms in February in the South. Very hardy and rather difficult to get started.

H. orientalis Lenten Rose   Zones 3-9

Best of all the hellebores and easier to grow than the species above, it thrives in gardens from Maine to Georgia, producing loads of 2- to 4-inch saucer-shaped flowers, white through pink to maroon—speckled, mottled, or streaked with various color configurations. In Zone 5, the common name describes the bloom time. In Zone 7 and below, it can flower in February. The 12- to 18-inch-tall plants are slow-growing but quite vigorous, and in time form clumps nearly 36 inches wide. Self-sows after a few years and develops into an excellent ground cover for light shade. Set 24 inches apart.

GERANIUM   maculatum

Wild Geranium, Wild Cranesbill, Spotted
Cranesbill, Alumroot   Zones 5-9

Don't confuse this 18- to 24-inch-high native with the *Pelargonium* whose common name is geranium. In spring this "true" geranium produces small, saucerlike, flattish pale to deep pink flowers spaced over loose plants. Its dainty, deeply divided leaves color tan and red in fall. Good choice for the South. 'Album' is white. Excellent in woodland gardens and rock gardens. Prefers bright shade. Geraniums for sunny situations are given along with culture on list 13, Spring Perennials for Sun.

Many of the spring flowers that prefer shade are exceptionally beautiful. ABOVE The lovely foliage of old-fashioned bleeding-heart, *Dicentra spectabilis*, lasts all summer in cool regions. (Viette) RIGHT Greek valerian, *Polemonium caeruleum*, forms large upright mounds and in May bears showy flower clusters. (Viette)

IRIS cristata cvs., Crested Iris. Best in partial shade, a creeping native dwarf 6 to 10 inches high, very appealing perennialized on rocky wooded slopes, in rock gardens, and light woodlands—especially in the South where it blooms in late April to late May. In the North it blooms in early May to early June in light shade. The lavender-blue, 4-inch-wide flowers have narrow falls with a central white or yellow ridge. In summer, the shiny, arching foliage may die back. Soon after flowering, the plants grow vigorously, spreading in all directions. Divide every four years, just before growth begins. Deteriorates when crowded. Prefers somewhat acid soil, pH 4.5 to 5.5. Recommended are 'Alba', white with a yellow blotch, best in woodlands; 'Shenandoah Sky', a light lavender-blue; and 'Summer Storm', a deep blue. For culture, see list 25, Iris.

MERTENSIA virginica, Virginia Bluebells, Virginia Cowslip, Roanoke-bells. Early spring flower up to 24 inches tall with nodding sprays of pink buds that open into bell-shaped, violet-blue blossoms. Fresh, pale green foliage disappears during summer. Nice with *Aquilegia*, Columbine, and *Dicentra*, bleeding-heart. For culture see list 48, Wildflowers to Naturalize.

PHLOX. Treasured for their spring color, the little creeping phloxes spill mats of lavender-blue, purple, pink, or white florets over sunny or shady slopes, rock gardens, and masonry walls. Their foliage remains as a ground cover through summer.

P. divaricata Wild Sweet William, Blue Phlox, develops low-growing leafy mats that bear iris-scented, soft lavender-blue flowers 9 to 15 inches tall, from April to June. 'Fuller's White', 14 inches tall, covers itself with sparkling white flowers. The subspecies *Laphamii* has large, rich, blue-violet flowers. *P. × chattahoochee* is 12 inches tall and 18 inches across, lavender-blue with a striking purple-red eye. Suitable for Zones 5 to 9. When flowering ends, cut it back to encourage growth.

P. stolonifera, Creeping Phlox. For semishade or shade, 5 to 12 inches tall, this is a superb mat-forming ground cover. Some are evergreen in warm winters. The flowers, purple or violet with a lilylike scent, are borne in dense clusters from mid- to late spring. May bloom again intermittently. Recommended are 'Blue Ridge', which bears masses of lilac-blue flowers, 'Pink Ridge', a rose-pink, and 'Bruce's White', white with a yellow eye. For culture, see list 27, *Phlox.*

POLEMONIUM (pol-em-*moh*-ee-um)
Jacob's-ladder, Greek Valerian
A very hardy group that reaches to 36 inches in height. Leafy plants bear clusters of cup-shaped flowers in late spring or early summer. Usually a pretty lavender-blue, but there are clear pink, white, and yellow forms. Delightful in a wild or woodland garden, it is lasting as a cut flower. The leaves are organized rather like rungs on a ladder, which gives rise to the name given to some of the species—Jacob's-ladder. Flowers for many weeks in cooler climates.

Culture: Sow seeds in spring or set out root divisions in summer in partial shade, in very well drained soil. Intolerant of hot, humid climates.

P. caeruleum Jacob's-ladder, Greek Valerian, Charity   Zones 2-7
The foliage forms large, upright mounds, and in May showy clusters of yellow-anthered blue florets are borne in drooping terminal clusters on stems to 18 to 24 inches high. 'Album' is a white cultivar.

P. reptans   Zones 2-8
A sprawling, tufted form that makes a pretty green mat in the garden all season long. In late April and May, loose clusters of light blue flowers appear on stems 5 to 8 inches tall. Beautiful in a rock garden, by stone steps, and as a cover for tulips and daffodils. Self-sows. 'Blue Pearl', an excellent choice, which is 8 to 10 inches tall and has bright blue flowers.

POLYGONATUM, Solomon's-seal, King-Solomon's-seal. These large, graceful, spring-blooming wildflowers thrive in damp, light woodlands and are reliable plants for light shade to deep shade. The usually white, bell-like flowers scalloped in green appear in spring, pretty if not spectacular, followed in some species by blue-black berries in late summer. They form good sturdy clumps.

Recommended are *P. commutatum,* Great Solomon's-seal (often offered as *P. canauculatum*), a bold, big plant, 3 to 6 feet tall, with arching stems and 7-inch-long leaves with showy veins. In late May to mid-June come the slightly scented clusters of 2 to 10 pale yellow flowers tinged with green, followed by blue-black berries. Zones 4 to 9. Succeeds in light and deep shade and requires sustained moisture. *P. odoratum* 'Variegatum', 18 to 24 inches, has soft green leaves trimmed with an edge of cream white. The white-green flowers appear in mid-April for 2 or 3 weeks. Recommended for the South. *P. odoratum* var. *thunbergii,* Japanese Variegated Solomon's-seal, Zones 3 to 9, is a striking plant 24 to 36 inches tall with pink-tinted stems. Fragrant in the evening. *P. multiflorum,* known as Eurasian Solomon's-seal, is 24 to 36 inches tall with arching leaves and flowers in late May to mid-June. Prefers neutral to slightly acid, moist soil. For other species and culture see list 65, The Woodland Garden.

PRIMULA, Primrose. Charming little plants 3 or 4 to 10 inches tall that bear cup-shaped or flat-faced flowers above or nestled in a basal clump of crinkled leaves in moist, cool seasons, mostly spring. They bloom in jewel-bright colors including yellow, pink, crimson, blue, and purple. The following are recommended for spring, in the order of preference. *P. vulgaris,* English Primrose, is handsome massed in a woodland situation. An early plant, it bears masses of lightly fragrant, pale yellow flowers on single stems up to 6 inches tall. Modern cultivars come in every color and many forms. The Barnhaven strains are superior. *P. veris,* Cowslip. has strongly fragrant flowers clustered at the top of 6- to 8-inch stems; there are many colors available. *P. japonica* gives a remarkable display in late spring and early summer, but must have moisture. It's a tall "candelabra" type whose flowers mass elegantly around the top quarter of sturdy 10- to 15-inch stems. Large leaves form handsome basal mounds that will go dormant if allowed to dry out in summer. Two of the loveliest are 'Postford White' (late spring), which has large white flowers, and 'Miller's Crimson'. This is one of the hardiest and easiest to grow; it often self-sows. *P. sieboldii* blooms in late spring and is perhaps the prettiest primrose with the most intricate and delicate flowers. Some look like snowflakes. Typically, the flowers are pink with a light cast of lavender. There's also a white form. Usually the plants go dormant in early summer and survive heat this way. See list 29, Primrose.

PULMONARIA saccharata, 'Mrs. Moon', Bethlehem Sage. A very popular ground cover for semishade. The large, silver-spotted leaves are covered with soft bristly hairs that often blend into large patches. In early to mid-spring, tubular flowers bloom, pink at first then turning toward blue. About 12 inches high, it is attractive as a single specimen or massed for ground cover. For culture see list 44, Flowering Ground Covers.

THALICTRUM aquilegifolium. A charming meadow-rue 2 to 4 feet tall with tufts of dainty scalloped blue-green leaves topped for a few weeks in spring by airy sprays of plumy lilac florets. The foliage makes it a valuable filler for the back of the border and in wild gardens, whether in or out of bloom. This species succeeds in the warmer regions, Zones 5 to 8. 'Album' has white flowers. For culture, see list 67, Rare and Choice.

TIARELLA cordifolia, Foamflower. A charming wildflower whose underground stems form small clumps of crinkled leaves that are evergreen in milder areas. They are topped in spring by fluffy little white flowers on tall stems. An excellent woodland ground cover 10 inches high. *T. wherrryi,* 6 to 12 inches high, forms mounds of bronze-green, heart-shaped leaves that turn reddish in fall. In early May and June it bears creamy pink flowers that are larger than the species above. For culture, see list 48, Wildflowers to Naturalize.

SOURCE: ROBERT HEBB, A HORTICULTURIST, IS DIRECTOR OF THE LEWIS GINTER BOTANIC GARDEN IN RICHMOND, VIRGINIA, AND WAS FORMERLY WITH THE ARNOLD ARBORETUM, LONGWOOD GARDENS, THE NEW YORK BOTANICAL GARDEN, AND OTHER DISTINGUISHED ARBORETA.

Handsome silvery spring foliage of *Lychnis coronaria* is followed by brilliant rose-red flowers in early summer. This ideal low-care self-sower is suited to casual borders and cottage gardens. (Woodham)

15. SUMMER PERENNIALS FOR SUN

. . . .

■ Here are the best flowers to plant for lasting color through a most difficult time—the hot, dry months when the spring show is over. Achillea, the daisies, coreopsis, rudbeckia, and sedum are the indestructibles. Plant ceratostigma for its glossy low foliage and the eye-catching scraps of blue blossoms that appear over many weeks in late summer and in fall. Daylilies make statements in shades of yellow, orange, and rusty red. Phlox is essential for lasting midsummer pastels.

The border will also need tall, bold plants for the background and colorful foliage plants to anchor the design—see lists 50 and 51. Plant ornamental grasses for their lasting linear forms.

Some summer perennials purchased in containers and planted in early spring bloom that year, but most that come into full bloom will have been planted the year before. Their foliage rises as the spring bulbs and spring perennials fade. Experiment with exotic summer-flowering bulbs for real excitement!

Follow-on Plants: Asters, mums, fall-flowering crocus, and *Colchicum* are good successors. Or consider attractive cool weather crops—carrots, Swiss chard, ornamental kale, and cabbage. Other possibilities include *Onopordum acanthium*, Scotch Thistle; *Rodgersia*; *Ruta graveolens*, Rue, Herb-of-grace; *Salvia argentea*, Silver Sage; blue salvias; and lavender.

. . . .

ACHILLEA (ak-il-*lee*-uh)
Yarrow

Excellent. Highly valued for drought and heat resistance, and long-lasting flowerheads in bright yellows, golds, strong pinks, and occasionally white. It grows exuberantly in heights from 8 inches to 3 feet, and is especially useful for early and midsummer color. The showy flowers are borne in branching flat-topped heads (corymbs) several inches across that last well when cut. The yellows are among the best of all flowers to dry for winter arrangements and wreaths. The excellent ferny foliage adds texture to the garden before and after flowering.

Culture: Takes full sun even in hot climates and requires occasional watering only in the worst drought. Set container plants 10 to 12 inches apart in very well-drained; ordinary soil in spring or late summer. Excellent for sandy and poor soils as either very rich or moist soil encourages lax growth and causes some specimens, such as *A. millefolium*, to spread excessively. Divide every 4 or 5 years. Remove spent blossoms promptly to encourage an intermittent succession of bloom.

A. 'Coronation Gold'   Zones 3-8
Bright yellow flowers 5 inches across for 2 to 3 months starting in late spring, combined with deeply divided silvery foliage. Taller—to 3 feet—than the popular 'Moonshine', it belongs in the middle of the border and may be slightly less desirable since it usually requires staking.

A. filipendulina Fern-leaved Yarrow
Zones 3-8
Silvery green, deeply cut foliage and great, flat, mustard yellow flowerheads to 5 inches across. Good cutting flowers. Recommended for sandy places and by the sea.

A. millefolium Yarrow, Millfoil   Zones 3-8
A durable species with white, pink or red flowers, it is more likely to spread than the golden achilleas, especially in light and fertile soil—sandy places and by the sea—but it succeeds in heavy clay as long as it is well drained. Never needing coddling, it is happy with poor soil, drought, and neglect. At its height in July, it forms large clumps up to 18 inches tall. 'Cerise Queen' bears excellent cerise-red flowers. 'Paprika', a relatively new and superb cultivar from Germany, is a spicy rose-red. Also recommended are 'Fire King', deep rose-red, and the Galaxy hybrids, which flower in shades of peach and salmon. Others of note appear on list 75, Herbs with Showy Flowers. Space plants 2 feet apart.

A. 'Moonshine'   Zones 3-8
Similar to 'Coronation Gold', this superb plant is 12 to 24 inches high with large, lemon yellow flowers from late spring through summer above deeply divided silvery foliage. Doesn't perennialize well where summers are hot and humid and is best treated as an annual in the warm South. Succeeds by the seashore.

Two of the most resistant and long-flowering of all summer perennials:
TOP *Coreopsis verticillata* is mat-forming and literally smothers itself with tiny starry daisies. This is 'Zagreb', a dainty cultivar that does well in the South. (Viette)
RIGHT *Achillea*'s showy blooms persist in heat and drought. It performs exceptionally well in low-maintenance situations, and stands out in wild and meadow gardens. (Viette)

A. taygetea   Zones 3-7

Cool, sulphur yellow flowers and beautiful, finely divided, woolly, silvery leaves make this one of the best plants for the front of the border in early summer. About 18 to 24 inches tall. The foliage is gray-green. Succeeds by the seashore.

ASCLEPIAS (ass-*kleep*-ee-ass) **tuberosa**
Butterfly Weed, Pleurisy Root, Tuberroot, Indian Paintbrush, Chigger Flower   Zones 3/4-9

A fresh orange accent for the meadow that keeps butterflies coming. This is a 24- to 36-inch perennial look-alike for milkweed with long-lasting fragrant, showy flowerheads in summer. Interesting seed pods follow. There are yellow hybrids and bicolors. Good cut flower, especially if the stem is seared immediately after cutting, then put into water. *Asclepias incarnata*, Swamp Milkweed, is recommended for damp meadows.

Culture: Transplanting is difficult but asclepias grows fairly easily from seed and is charming when naturalized. Mark the plants, for they are slow to break dormancy and, once disturbed, may disappear. Set out container plants or root divisions in full or partial sun in spring, or sow seed for next year's bloom in late summer or spring in well-drained, light, ordinary, rather acid soil. Be patient—the plants are slow to start but will bloom in 3 to 4 months. Drought resistant.

CAMPANULA **carpatica**, Tussock Bellflower. This is the Carpathian bellflower, a species that blooms in summer. It is 9 to 12 inches tall and short-lived, but it bears masses of blue flowers and is quickly and easily grown from seed. Best in rock gardens and raised beds and intolerant of extremes—too dry, too wet, or too hot. Not a good choice where slugs are a problem. See list 22, Campanula.

CHRYSANTHEMUM. The main show for the big mums is in the fall, but the species mums are our beautiful summer daisies and belong in every flowering border. *C. coccineum*, Pyrethrum, Painted Daisy, bears showy 3-inch red, pink, or white single or double, daisylike flowers with yellow centers on plants 12 to 24 inches tall in early summer. *C. leucanthemum*, Oxeye Daisy, White Daisy, Marguerite, the common field daisy, blooms in early summer and is ideal for meadow gardens and wild plantings. *C. parthenium*, Feverfew, is a lovely old-fashioned mum 12 to 36 inches tall that in late summer bears masses of little 1-inch, daisylike white or yellow button-type flowers with yellow centers. *C. × superbum*, Shasta Daisy, is the beautiful, big, shaggy daisy that flowers in early summer on plants 2 to 4 feet tall. There are singles and doubles. See list 23, Mum—Daisy.

CERATOSTIGMA **plumbaginoides**, Blue Ceratostigma, Plumbago. Pretty foliage plant that spreads vigorously under good conditions, forming 6- or 8- to 12-inch high mats of almost evergreen, glossy, dark green leaves. From midsummer to frosts electric blue flowers appear, then with the cold, the foliage turns bronzy red. Excellent as a ground cover, edger, or in rock and wall gardens. Good in sun or bright shade. Listed in some catalogs as *Plumbago larpentae*. See list 51, Foliage for Color.

TOP Spike gayfeather, *Liatris spicata*, easily wild. (Viette)
RIGHT Coneflower *Rudbeckia fulgida* variety *sullivanti* 'Goldsturm' withstands heat and drought. (Viette)
BELOW Exotic *Stokesia*, a late summer drought resistant beauty. (Viette)

COREOPSIS (ko-ree-**op**-sis) Tickseed. Excellent. This is one of the easiest and most rewarding garden flowers. In late spring and throughout the summer, masses of sunny, starry flowers bloom above the narrow, dark green foliage. There are many species but the *C. verticillata* cutlivars described here are recommended as among the very best garden perennials.

Culture: Full sun, but half a day of semishade or bright shade are acceptable, especially in hot regions. In spring, sow seeds indoors or outdoors. Set out root divisions in spring or late summer 15 to 18 inches apart in light, loamy, or sandy soil that is slightly acid, pH 6.0 to 7.0. Resists drought, but appreciates water during dry spells. When, or if, flowering slackens in midsummer cut back to within a few inches of the ground and plants sprout back and bloom for the rest of the season.

C. auriculata 'Nana'   Zones 3-9
Small and long-lived with attractive green foliage over which, in late spring and early summer, sparkling orange-gold flowers are borne on 6- to 8-inch stems. Cut back, it repeats sporadically through summer.

C. grandiflora   Zones 5-9
Large-flowered species. 'Badengold', 24 inches high, is a beautiful gold and flowers all summer. 'Schnittgold' is a large-flowered, long-blooming cultivar. 'Goldfink', under 9 inches, is a lovely dwarf for the front of the border. 'Sun Ray' and 'Early Sunrise' have double flowers.

C. lanceolata Tickseed   Zones 3-8
Sunny, long-lasting, and covers itself with fluffy, pretty 2½-inch yellow flowers that appear in late spring or summer, according to region, on plants 1 to 2 feet tall. The deeply cut foliage, light or somewhat coarse, is attractive. 'Sterntaler' is 24 inches tall, and has fully double blooms. 'Goldteppich', 14 inches high, is a golden yellow.

C. rosea   Zones 3-9
To 2 feet tall and similar to *C. verticillata* 'Moonbeam', but with rosy or purple petals surrounding the yellow center. The species is very tolerant of wet situations and hot summers.

C. verticillata 'Moonbeam', Dwarf Threadleaf Tickseed   Zones 3-9
Excellent for the front of the border, it flowers from June to fall frosts if cut back in midsummer. The plants are 15 or 18 to 24 inches tall, covered with pale butter yellow blossoms on slender stems with threadlike leaves. Combines beautifully with anything that grows behind it. Light soil is essential—the plants may be lost in heavy soil after a wet season. Set plants 1½ feet apart. For the South, choose the mat-forming 'Zagreb', which literally smothers itself with tiny starry daisies of the brightest yellow, and 'Golden Showers', which is larger. Cut back, it has the same long period of bloom as 'Moonbeam'.

ECHINACEA purpurea, Purple Coneflower. The coarse dark green foliage sets off and balances large daisylike flowers in rich, dusky rose-purple with an orange-bronze cast. Characteristically, the petals droop a little backwards. Extremely long-flowering, it comes into bloom in the South in May or June and continues intermittently into November if faded flowers are removed. Usually 24 to 36 inches tall, but it rarely needs staking. Makes a good cut flower, blends well in mixed borders and perennializes readily in a meadow garden; bees and butterflies love it. For culture, see list 64, The Meadow Garden.

ECHINOPS ritro 'Taplow Blue', Small Globe Thistle. This big-leaved plant grows from 2 to 4 feet tall. Its interesting gray-green, hairy undersides have very handsome, dryish, thistlelike heads of steely blue flowers in summer and early autumn. Use it in groups in the wild garden or in front of tall shrubs. It is attractive to bees and nocturnal moths. 'Blue Globe' is a dark blue cultivar 36 inches tall and 'Veitch's Blue' is even taller, up to 40 inches. For culture, see list 58, Urban Conditions.

GAURA lindheimeri. A graceful bushy perennial that blooms from May to October. The plant is 4 feet tall, with hairy, gray-green, willowlike leaves. Long-blooming, loose panicles of pink buds open to 1-inch, tubular, pink-tinted white flowers. It is a good perennializer and withstands drought. For culture, see list 57, Seashore and Sandy Soils.

GYPSOPHILA paniculata, Baby's-breath. Excellent. This species is the traditional Baby's-breath for bouquets; it is 24 to 36 inches tall and blooms all summer. Airy and many-branched, spangled with tiny, dainty, roselike flowers in summer. In the garden it spreads like a cloud, filling spaces left empty by, for instance, the big Oriental poppies, and ties everything together. In the warm south it is grown as an annual or biennial planted in fall. 'Bristol Fairy' is the favorite double-flowered white. 'Pink Fairy' is similar, about 18 inches tall, an almost-white pink. 'Red Sea', 3 to 4 feet high, bears double rose-pink flowers. For culture see list 71, The Cutting Garden.

HELIOPSIS (hee-lee-*opp*-sis) **helianthoides**
Zones 3-9
The species is a sturdy, hardy native that resembles a small sunflower. Recommended is the smaller subspecies, *H. scabra*, which grows to about 3 feet tall and bears showy bright yellow flowers about 2 inches across all summer long. It is easily grown—nice with white annuals and blues in an informal mixed bed or a sunny wild garden. The cultivars have more and better flowers in colors from citron to true yellow. Choose semi-double or doubles for a better show. 'Gold Greenheart' is fully double chrome yellow with a greenish center. 'Summer Sun' is a 2 to 3 foot plant with 4-inch sunny yellow flowers and it tolerates Southern heat.

Culture: In early spring sow seed or set out root divisions in full sun in well-drained soil. Drought tolerant. This is an easy but short-lived plant that requires divisions every two to three years.

HEMEROCALLIS, Daylily. Modern daylilies anchor the sunny perennial garden through midsummer with lovely lilylike flowers in intense colors. They're easy to grow and long lasting; whether you plant 4- to 5-foot giants with huge 8-inch flowers at the back of the border, or 8- to 12-inch dwarfs with 1-inch blooms near the front, each plant offers a brilliant, nonstop show for 3 to 4 weeks. Some rebloom in late fall. The strap-shaped leaves fountain up, screening the yellowing remains of spring bulbs. An established 3-year-old clump of daylilies produces many blooms on stalks (scapes) averaging 2 to 3 feet tall. There are many different solid colors and patterned types and colors, including some that qualify as whites; forms include round or triangular, recurved, flat, trumpet, ruffled, or double. Some daylilies are fragrant. See list 24, Daylily.

HIBISCUS (hye-*bisk*-us) Excellent. The genus includes tall, woody shrubs like the glamorous tropical hibiscus grown as a container plant in the North, and a few shrublike herbaceous perennials 3 to 6 feet tall with huge flowers. These big plants are wonderful at the back of the border or cornering a property.

Culture: Succeeds in full sun in well-drained, humusy, sandy loam, pH 5.5 to 7.0. It also survives in clayey situations, and withstands wet soils. Early spring is the best time for planting and transplanting. Set dormant roots (bare root) with the crown a few inches below the soil surface. Mulch with decayed leaves. Established plantings resent disturbance. Tolerates some drought.

H. coccineus Zones 7-9
The flowers are scarlet red, 5 to 6 inches across, with long stamens. The plant is slender, 6 to 8 feet tall, with an open growth habit and deeply divided, narrow blue-green leaves. Rather tender but wonderful when it can be grown. The species is native to swampy areas in Florida and Georgia.

H. moscheutos Rose Mallow Zones 5-9
Shrubby perennial that in midsummer bears flowers 7 to 10 inches across. Very useful in warm regions. In late spring new growth shoots up 3 to 6 feet and never needs staking. Striking cultivars include 'Appleblossom', featuring light pink flowers that have deeper rose margins; and 'Cotton Candy', an exceptional bicolor with soft pink on white flowers. The Dixie Belle strain is a seed-raised group of compacts a few feet high with flowers varying from red-eyed to red, rose, and pink. The Lord Baltimore strain has masses of bright red flowers and beautifully lobed leaves. 'Satan' bears large fire-engine red flowers on 5-foot plants.

LIATRIS (lye-*ay*-triss) **spicata**
Spike Gay-feather Zones 3-9
Excellent in a wild garden and quick to perenialize near water. In mid- to late summer the dense tufts of grasslike foliage are topped by 24- to 36-inch-tall, narrow, decorative spikes of ragged-edged, pink-purple florets. The florets open from the top and the flowers last well when cut. 'Kobold', lilac-mauve and 18 inches high, is a good cultivar that blooms earlier. 'Floristan White' is 36 inches tall and perennializes well. *L. pycnostachya* is a very large plant for the wild garden; see list 48.

Culture: Catalogs offer both seeds and the cormlike rootstocks of various types, but liatris is most easily set out as a container plant. It tolerates heat and drought but thrives in light, well-drained, fairly moist soil. Plant the rootstocks in spring in sun or semi-sun 4 to 6 inches deep and 18 to 24 inches apart. Maintain moisture, although the plant can tolerate some dryness.

LIGULARIA. These are majestic plants grown for their bold foliage and soaring spikes of ragged yellow or orange-yellow flowers in midsummer. Choice for back of the border and to naturalize at the edge of a woodland. It is also a good container plant and can be grown indoors. Accepts some direct sun or semishade. See list 16, Summer Perennials for Shade.

LYCHNIS (*lik*-niss)
Campion, Catchfly
Fine, upright summer bloomers 12 to 24 or 36 inches tall that generally reseed themselves and perennialize. The species recommended here bear brilliant, beautiful flowers excellent for cutting and have handsome foliage.

Culture: Sow seed indoors in March or outdoors in April. Or set out root divisions. All species prefer full sun—light shade in the South—and somewhat rich, well-drained soil.

L. × arkwrightii Zones 6-8
Brilliant orange-red flowers on bushy plants 18 to 24 inches high. The foliage is a dark bronze. Pinch back early to encourage branching and more flowers. Seedpods add interest.

L. coronaria Mullein Pink, Rose Campion, Dusty-miller Zones 4-8
Showy species with a spreading rosette of woolly silver-gray leaves and silvery wide-branched stems topped in spring by brilliant rose-red flowers beginning in early summer. 'Abbotswood Rose' bears intense pink flowers beginning in late spring.

L. flos-jovis Flower-of-Jove Zones 4-8
Woolly gray-white basal rosettes all season and, in early to late summer, densely clustered, long-lasting, small, cerise to purple flowers on branching stems that rise 18 to 30 inches above the foliage.

L. viscaria German Catchfly Zones 4-8
Handsome compact foliage in grasslike clump, evergreen in mild regions, 6 to 18 inches tall, for the front of the border. In early summer loose clusters of small, purplish pink flowers appear. The common name refers to the stems and leaves, which are sticky.

LYTHRUM (*lith*-rum) cultivars
Purple Loosestrife, Spiked Loosestrife Zones 3-9
Long-lived, water-loving species whose many cultivated varieties thrive in rich, moist soils, even with their feet in water, North or South. All summer, rigid flower stalks stand tall above interesting, slightly hairy, heart-shaped leaves and cover themselves with small, fluffy, purple-pink blooms. 'Robert', deep pink, and 'The Beacon', rose-red, are 3½ feet tall. These are environmentally sound cultivated varieties, not to be confused with *Lythrum salicaria*, which has become a weed along roadsides and in wet meadows.

Culture: In early spring sow seeds or plant root divisions in full or semi-sun, in well-worked soil. Provide plenty of water.

MONARDA didyma, Bee Balm, Oswego Tea. Attractive whorls of shaggy scarlet petals surrounded by red-tinted bracts bloom through summer on this plant's stiff stems. The plants are 24 to 36 inches tall and attract butterflies, hummingbirds, and bees. Deadheading lengthens bloom time. Among monardas ranging through shades of cerise to red, white, and violet, 'Croftway Pink' is notable. 'Sunset' is a mildew-resistant purple-red. For culture, see list 75, Herbs with Showy Flowers.

PEROVSKIA atriplicifolia, Russian Sage. Excellent. A good plant to bring that coveted blue color to the border for the longest period—summer through late summer. Tall and beautiful, with silvery stems and foliage grayish down below, it is topped by airy spikes of tiny florets that are a subtle powder blue. It is also one of the most heat- and drought-resistant perennials. To 36 inches tall. There is a delightful scent of sage when the foliage is crushed. For culture, see list 57, Seashore and Sandy Soils.

PHLOX. The most luscious pastels of summer belong to the upright phloxes, American natives that thrive almost everywhere. The big silky-soft flowerheads of the upright types bloom for a long time and are preferred fillers for the middle or back of sunny summer borders. The cut flowers are lovely in bouquets. Recommended are: *P. maculata*, Wild Sweet William, which is a very fragrant, upright phlox 24 to 36 inches tall, quite mildew-resistant; and *P. paniculata*, Summer Perennial Phlox, Fall Phlox, the most important upright phlox for the middle of the border. For the home garden there are durable, sparkling plants from 6 to 36 inches tall with big, lush panicles of flowers in a range of colors—white, pink, salmon, scarlet, and purple, many with a contrasting eye. See list 27, *Phlox*.

PLATYCODON grandiflorus var. **mariesii**, Dwarf Balloon Flower. This 12- to 24- and 28-inch variety is outstanding, reliable, durable. Easily one of the best summer flowers. The distinctive balloon-shaped buds studded along graceful wandlike stems open to starry, blue, white, or lilac-pink flowers up to 2 inches across. Very free-flowering, from early summer to early fall, with glossy foliage. As cut flowers, they are long-lasting if the stems are seared before they are put in water. *P. grandiflorus* 'Apoyama' has violet flowers on plants 15 to 18 inches tall and is recommended for planting with herbs. For culture, see list 57, Seashore and Sandy Soils.

RUDBECKIA (rud-*bek*-ee-uh) Coneflower. Excellent. There are many very good rudbeckias and the two perennial species here are among the finest summer-flowering herbaceous plants for moderate climates. The blossoms are typical daisies, having outer, often drooping, ray florets around a central elevated cone of disk florets. They flower for 2 to 3 months and grow to be 1½ to 4 or 5 feet tall. Leave the flowerheads to ripen for the birds, for winter interest, and to reseed. In difficult southern climates, *R. hirta*, Black-eyed Susan, a biennial or perennial grown as an annual, may be the best choice. It blooms from August to October the second year after sowing.

Culture: Self-sows aggressively, a good naturalizer for wild places. The rudbeckias withstand high heat and thrive in full sun in moderately fertile soil that is humusy, evenly moist, and has a pH in the range of 5.0 to 6.5. In the early spring, plant root divisions 15 to 18 inches apart. Some irrigation during droughts assures the best flowering.

R. fulgida var. **sullivanti 'Goldsturm'** Coneflower
Zones 3-9
Finest of the Black-eyed Susan type, this cultivar blooms freely through midsummer into fall on compact, bushy plants that are 18 to 30 inches high. The ray florets are deep yellow and the cone-shaped centers are bronze-black. Tolerates light shade and is nice in a large grouping in the middle of the border.

R. nitida 'Herbstonne' ('Autumn Sun') Zones 4-11
Very dense, 4- to 5-foot clump with many upright, branching stalks, imposing as a backdrop for the border. The rather coarse leaves are leathery and divided and there's a nonstop, abundant flower display throughout July and August no matter how hot the weather. The flowers are big,

showy heads of drooping, clear yellow ray florets surrounding a greenish central disk. Support early with sturdy stakes or summer storms may knock the plants over, especially in the South. Set plants 2½ feet apart.

SEDUM, Stonecrop. This group of indestructible and sometimes invasive herbaceous perennials 2 to 15 inches tall is valued for its pretty evergreen, succulent-like light green foliage and, in some important larger hybrids, its beautiful autumn color (see list 17.) The flowers are tiny and star-shaped, yellow or pink-red, quite modest in ground-hugging species but showy flowerheads in taller forms. The importance of these plants can be judged by their appearance on lists 45, 46, 49, 56, 57, and elsewhere in this book.

Where a low-grower is wanted, one of the easiest is often the invasive *S. acre*, Golden-carpet or Golden Moss. In late spring or early summer it bears clusters of yellow flowers on slim, trailing stems 2 to 3 inches high with tiny, pointed, upright leaves. Not showy, but thrives in dry places where nothing else grows. Invasive in moist fertile soil. The tips and new shoots of 'Aureum' are edged with gold. For culture see the full discussion on list 56, Dry, Hot Conditions.

STOKESIA (stoh-*keez*-ee-uh) **laevis**
Zones 4/5-9
Durable, drought-resistant, very beautiful flower presented in late summer by a clump 12 to 24 inches high of sprawling but upright stems. Evergreen in mild regions. The flower somehow combines the precision of a thistle with the softness of an aster. The common name for the genus is Stoke's Aster. The color is a delicate lavender-blue, and there are also pinks and whites. Good for cutting. It is a hardy perennial native to the southeastern U. S. 'Blue Star' is a 12-inch, blue cultivar. 'Blue Danube' bears 5-inch lavender flowers.

Culture: In spring, set out root divisions in full sun or light shade, in moist, well-drained, sandy soil. Provide a winter mulch in Zone 4.

VERONICA, Speedwell, Brooklime. First-rate fillers, these invulnerable plants with attractive semi-evergreen or evergreen foliage have abundant flowers in densely packed spikes. Cultivars recommended for summer flowers include 'Icicle', a 20-inch white, and 'Blue Charm', a 24-inch lavender-blue. Low-growers and culture are given on list 66, The Rock Garden. Spring bloomers are described on list 13, Spring Perennials for Sun.

SOURCE: ROBERT HEBB, A HORTICULTURIST, IS DIRECTOR OF THE LEWIS GINTER BOTANIC GARDEN IN RICHMOND, VIRGINIA, AND WAS FORMERLY WITH THE ARNOLD ARBORETUM, LONGWOOD GARDENS, THE NEW YORK BOTANICAL GARDEN, AND OTHER DISTINGUISHED ARBORETA.

16. SUMMER PERENNIALS FOR SHADE

■ Once you get beyond spring, showy flowers that bloom in shade are more scarce, but there are real beauties from which to choose. Heuchera is a favorite, a nice plant for the front of the border. It has a long season of bloom and the foliage is low and attractive. Ceratostigma's glossy leaves reach high in bright shade, and the scraps of brilliant blue flowers bloom for many weeks in late summer and fall.

Don't overlook the woodland and colorful foliage plants for shady places on lists 50 and 51. Caladium leaves are as showy as flowers and last all summer. Coleus and some very good flowering annuals do well in semishade—impatiens, nicotiana, and ageratum, as well as wax, angel-wing, and tuberous begonias. Many vines can have their feet in sun and expand into semishade without losing their ability to bloom. And astilbes flower on into summer—see list 21.

As summer heads into cooler weather and tree leaves thin out a bit, bringing more light to the garden, replant annuals that have died in heat and drought. Geraniums come back to life with cool nights, and herbs enjoy a renewal, too.

Follow-on Plants: *Hosta plantaginea*, the best and most indispensable companion plant for semi-shade; also ferns, *Digitalis* (Foxglove), and *Epimedium × rubrum*.

ACONITUM (ak-oh-*nye*-tum) Aconite, Monkshood
This is one of the great tall perennials for the back of the garden, an upright leafy plant with strong stalks 3 to 4 feet high. The deeply divided, dark green leaves are topped in summer and late summer and, in one popular species, in fall by spires of blue flowers. The plants increase slowly and go on for years. All parts of the plant, including the roots, are poisonous if ingested.

Culture: Started from seed, it takes three years to come into flower. Set out container plants in early spring in sun (North) or semishade (South) in rich, humusy, moist soil. They thrive at the edge of a bog garden. Don't disturb or divide unless you must.

A. × bicolor (syn. *cammarum* but usually listed as **A. napellus 'Bicolor'**) Zones 3-7
This 40-inch hybrid bears spires of blue and white flowers June through August. 'Bressingham Spire' has violet-blue blossoms and flowers July through August.

A. napellus Zones 3-8
Handsome strong stalks 3 to 4 feet high are topped in July and August by showy dark blue flowers.

ASTILBE, Spiraea, Perennial Spiraea. The plants may be 6 inches to 6 feet tall and have feathery flowerheads in late spring or summer that stand above deeply cut green or bronzed foliage. The colors are shades from palest pink through coral to bright red and cream white. Cultivars of *A. × arendsii* offer a range of colors and bloom periods. The one that appears on most every list is

Tall summer flowers for the back of the border:

ABOVE Riotous yellows of 'The Rocket', *Ligularia*, brighten a border of daylilies. (Viette)

FAR LEFT Tall, strong 3- to 4-foot stalks of *Aconitum napellus* are topped in July and August by showy dark blue flowers. (Viette)

LEFT Improved *Cimicifuga racemosa*, one of the finest of all hardy perennials, raises tall spires and in mid- to late summer covers them with small fluffy white flowers. This is 'Atropurpurea' from Germany, which has reddish foliage. (Viette)

Lobelia cardinalis is called the cardinal flower for its color. It thrives in moist, lightly shaded soil and near water. (American Horticultural Society)

'Fanal', 24 inches high, early, blood red. Also recommended are 'Koblenz', 'Vesuvius', 'White Gloria', 'Erica', 'Fanal', 'Red Sentinel', 'Ostrich Plume', and 'Cattleya', in that order. The vigorous 'Superba', 24 to 48 inches, a lilac cultivar of *A. taquettii*, blooms in late summer and fall and is considered best for its exceptional heat resistance. For culture see list 21, *Astilbe*.

BEGONIA grandis, Hardy Begonia. Hardy in Zones 6 to 11, this modest flower is not easy to find, but its flowers and foliage are very attractive in light shade all summer and well into cold weather. It grows from a small bulblike tuber and with some protection survives winters in the ground as far north as New York. There are white- and pink-flowering types to 24 inches tall, with a rounded leaf that is bronzy flushed maroon-crimson underneath. Also known as Evans Begonia (formerly *B. evansiana*).

CERATOSTIGMA plumbaginoides, Blue Ceratostigma, Plumbago. Pretty foliage plant that spreads vigorously under good conditions, forming 6- or 8- to 12-inch-high mats of almost evergreen, glossy, dark green leaves. From midsummer to frost electric blue flowers appear, then with the cold, the foliage turns bronzy red—in California almost red. Excellent as a ground cover, an edger, or in rock and wall gardens. Good in sun or bright shade. Listed in some catalogs as *Plumbago larpentae*. See list 51, Foliage for Color.

CHELONE glabra
Turtlehead, Snakehead, Balmony   Zones 3-8
The turtleheads are tall plants especially useful in moist shady areas with somewhat acid soil. For several weeks in late summer the leafy upright stems are topped by spikes of hooded white flowers tinged with pink or rosy red. Tolerates full sun in cool regions, but must have constant moisture. For culture see list 48, Wildflowers to Naturalize.

CIMICIFUGA (sim-iss-*siff*-yew-guh)
Bugbane, Rattletop
Excellent. Tall, handsome spires of small fluffy white flowers comprised mostly of stamens open from rounded pearl-like buds in mid- to late summer. These are arranged densely on spiky stems rising from generous clumps of shiny, compound leaves. Excellent for the back of the border, in wild gardens, and for cutting. Given two or three growing seasons to become established, these plants are among the very best and most permanent maintenance-free perennials—almost completely pest and disease free. The display can dominate a garden and there are choices for early summer, midsummer, and autumn.

Culture: Bright shade is ideal for all species, or morning sun and some shade in the afternoon. In cool northern summers, full sun is suitable with sustained moisture. They may be increased in early spring, which is the best time for planting, but they hardly ever need division. Set the plants 24 to 30 inches apart, according to height, in deep, humus-rich, moisture-retentive soil with average fertility and a pH range of 5.0 to 6.0. The soil must not be allowed to dry out, and irrigation during droughts is essential. A mulch of decomposed leaves helps in hot summers.

C. americana American Bugbane, Mountain Bugbane, Summer Cohosh   Zones 4-8
Slender, arching spires of white flowers to 3 or 3½ feet. Not quite as showy as the next species, but it blooms in mid-August when virtually nothing else is in flower in a semishaded garden.

C. racemosa Black Cohosh, Black Snakeroot
                                        Zones 3-8
The best. One of the fullest and most imposing summer perennials and one of the finest of all perennials. The stiff, slender, towering, branching spires of white flowers will dominate any planting for a month or more beginning in early or midsummer. Height is 6 to 8 feet.

C. simplex   Zones 4/5-8
Fluffy bottlebrush-like spikes of flowers on gracefully arching stalks, 3½ to 4 feet tall and nicely fragrant. Known as Kamchatka Bugbane, it blooms in early fall—October in the East. The last of the perennials, it stays in flower about 3 weeks or until frost. This species loses its leaves if it goes dry, and in Zones 4 to 5 frost takes the flowers 2 seasons out of 4, but in Zone 6 and south it is very reliable. The variety *ramosa* is a magnificent plant with upright spikes 6 to 7 feet tall. 'White Pearl' is the best cultivar, a free-flowering plant with thick, feathery wands of blossoms.

FILIPENDULA rubra 'Venusta', Queen-of-the-prairie. Often sold as false spirea, these are big, architectural plants 6 to 8 feet tall with bold foliage and, in summer, towering spires of deep pink to carmine flowers that toss in the wind. See list 75, Herbs with Showy Flowers.

HEMEROCALLIS, Daylily. This is a big, almost indispensable lilylike flower for sun that also tolerates light shade, especially in the South. Each plant offers a brilliant, nonstop show for 3 to 4 weeks—in late May in Florida, June 5 in South Carolina, July 10 in Virginia. Depending on type, some rebloom in fall. Flowers can be 8 inches across, plants 4 to 5 feet tall, but dwarfs have 1-inch flowers and are 8 to 12 inches tall. The color range is vast and some flowers are fragrant. Long-lived, easy to grow, durable. Choose a miniature such as 'Stella De Oro' that has a high bud count; it often reblooms and its foliage withstands summer heat. They are splendid as specimen plants, or in a group, ideal companions in a mixed border, good ground cover for big spaces, and excellent edging plants. See list 24, Daylily.

HEUCHERA (*hew*-ker-uh) sanguinea
Coralbells   Zones 3-8

In late spring and early summer this plant's tiny but eye-catching bell-shaped flowers sway on 12- to 24-inch wiry stalks that are held high above its semievergreen cluster of scalloped, dark green leaves. The foliage contrasts well with late bloomers such as *Echinops ritro*, Small Globe Thistle. Suited to containers and a delightful cut flower. Bressingham hybrids, such as 'Bressingham Blaze', bloom in shades of coral to deep red, pink, and white. Deadheading encourages blooms.

Recommended for lasting summer bloom and ability to withstand direct sun are: 'Firebird', deep scarlet; 'Fire Sprite', smaller; 'Mount St. Helen's', fiery red flowers, blooms all summer; 'Pluie de Feu', cherry red; 'June Bride', superb white that flowers May through midsummer; 'Red Spangles', red; 'Scarlet Sentinel', scarlet; 'Scintillation', bright pink tipped with red; and 'Snowflake', white.

For foliage primarily, 'Palace Purple' (which is actually a cultivar of *H. micrantha*) is recommended. It has 12-inch-high, rich burgundy red, ivy-shaped foliage that takes on a bronze cast in hot summers. The 18-inch-high flowers are off-white. It thrives in cool climates, is cold hardy in Zones 5 and even 4, and prefers slightly acid soil.

Culture: Set out container plants or root divisions in spring in semi-sun in the North, partial shade in the South. Coralbells requires well-drained, humusy soil and sustained moisture. Divide every 4 or 5 years. In cold climates mulch for winter after a solid frost.

LIGULARIA (lig-yew-*lay*-ree-uh)
These are majestic plants grown for their bold foliage and soaring spikes of ragged yellow or orange-yellow flowers in midsummer. Choice for back of the border and to naturalize at the edge of a woodland. It also is a good container plant and can be grown indoors. A species used in Japanese garden design is *L. tussilaginea* (see list 61, The Japanese Garden).

Culture: Easy to grow. In early spring, set out root divisions in semi-sun in well-drained soil and keep them very well watered.

L. dentata 'Desdemona'   Zones 4-8
Excellent, compact (to 4 feet) plant that forms clumps of 12-inch-long, heart-shaped, leathery, brownish green leaves that are mahogany underneath. The long, flowering stems branch and bear large orange flowers from mid- to late summer.

L. × hessei (syn. Senecio × hessei)
'Gregynog Gold'   Zones 4-8
The best. The plant is 5 to 6 feet tall, with large, heart-shaped, leathery leaves that have small teeth. The daisylike flowers are large and orangish yellow. Also described as a hybrid of *L. dentata* and *L. veitchiana*.

L. przewalskii 'The Rocket'   Zones 5-8
Next best. Suited to watery sites and moist borders, a large, tall plant that develops generous mounds of handsome, dark-stemmed, slightly rounded leathery leaves and, in summer, long spikes of ragged lemon yellow flowers. 'The Rocket' grows to 6 feet when in bloom. Good companion to Japanese Iris and large-leaved hostas. Also is given as a cultivar of *L. stenocephala*.

LOBELIA (loh-*beel*-ee-uh)
A diverse group of brilliant flowers on elegant plants. They are often short-lived and must have sustained moisture, but they are too exquisite to do without.

Culture: Self-sows in good conditions. In spring in the North, spring or fall in the South, sow seeds or set out container-grown plants in shade or semishade in moist, humusy soil enriched with compost. Maintain moisture. Adapts to some direct sun in the North and elsewhere if moisture is maintained evenly.

L. cardinalis Cardinal Flower   Zones 2-8
A tall, upright, romantic wildflower 24 to 30 or 36 inches high topped by up to 50 loosely spaced, bright red blossoms. It thrives by woodland streams and flowers in late summer and fall. With its feet in water, it can stand some sun but prefers semishade. The flower spikes are long and slender and the foliage dark green. Lovely with ferns.

L. erinus Edging Lobelia
This may be an annual or a short-lived perennial. Delicate plants 6 to 8 inches high produce a cloud of thin, fragile stems spangled from late spring to mid-fall (in the right conditions) with tiny florets in luminous intense blues and purples, often with a white eye. There are whites and wine reds as well. The upright types are vibrant edgers, and the compacts and dwarfs belong in every small container. The blue cascades make unforgettable basket plants. Cut back after every flush of blooming to encourage continued flowering. See also list 32, Annuals for Shade.

L. siphilitica Great Lobelia, Blue Cardinal Flower
Zones 4-8
A stately, rather stiff plant 24 to 36 inches tall that bears slender, leafy racemes with blue flowers larger than those of the Cardinal Flower. Needs to be divided and moved every few years. 'Blue Peter' is expected to last longer than the species.

TROLLIUS chinensis Globeflower. Often offered as *T. ledebourii*. Wonderful gold or golden orange, buttercup-like flowers that bloom in late spring and early summer in damp, shady places. About 24 inches high, it is charming massed on moist banks in light woodlands. For culture, see list 59, Wet, Boggy Soils.

SOURCE: ROBERT HEBB, A HORTICULTURIST, IS DIRECTOR OF THE LEWIS GINTER BOTANIC GARDEN IN RICHMOND, VIRGINIA, AND WAS FORMERLY WITH THE ARNOLD ARBORETUM, LONGWOOD GARDENS, THE NEW YORK BOTANICAL GARDEN, AND OTHER DISTINGUISHED ARBORETA.

17. SUMMER-INTO-FALL PERENNIALS

■ **Fall does a lot for the garden all by itself. As daylight decreases and cool, moist weather settles in, the early evening sky burns that almost incandescent blue and many summer perennials that shriveled in August come back to life. With the slow onset of cold, the annuals such as ageratum, nicotiana, and begonias color up. Impatiens matures and alyssum sweetens the air noon and night. The feathery heads of ornamental grasses catch the light and dance in the wind.**

A handful of perennials and an annual or two planted just for fall color can pull the autumn scene together and keep the garden bright until winter shuts it down. The most interesting fall bloomers look deceptively fragile—the roselike blossoms of the tall Japanese Anemone, for instance. Perennial Ageratum is a tender blue and the asters have turned into bushes now covered with powder puff florets. They stand out in contrast to the gold and burgundy red foliage and the strong earth tones of *Sedum* 'Autumn Joy', Goldenrod, sunflowers and mums. They do take over, the mums—cushion mums you planted (or divided) last spring and drop-in instant mums sold everywhere—along with pumpkins and bright squashes and gourds.

It's when the mums start to go that you know it's time to plant the bulbs for next year—to make perfect everything that didn't quite live up to last year's dreams.

Follow-on Plants: Ornamental grasses, annual asters, fall crocus and colchicum, very early daffodils, and late winter bloomers such as *Galanthus nivalis* (Snowdrop), ornamental cabbages and kales, and colorful hot peppers.

For semishade, in mild climates, set out V. × wittrockiana (Pansy) and primroses in mid-fall to flower on into winter and spring. Ferns, hostas, pumpkins, and gourds are also good follow-on plants.

FOR SUN

ASTER. A very important perennial for late summer and fall color, bushy plants that literally cover themselves with small, fluffy, daisylike flowers in wonderful shades of blue, lavender, dark purple, pink, rose, rosy red, and white. *A. × frikartii* 'Wonder of Staffa' is the earliest and has large flowers in shades of blue on plants 1½ to 2 feet tall. Easy to grow and good for cutting. *A. novae-angliae*, New England Aster, is a shrubby plant 4 to 6 feet tall covered in late summer and early fall with pink and purple-pink blooms. Survives early frosts. Colorful cultivars have been developed. 'Harrington's Pink' flowers in September, and is one of the best. 'Hella Lacy' is frost hardy, 40 inches high, purple, and lasts into October. *A. nova-belgii*, often called New York Aster, is 1 foot to 6 feet tall and flowers in early fall—September in the Northeast. 'Blue Lake', to 36 inches tall, is a spectacular medium blue with a yellow eye on sturdy stems, good for cutting, to 36 inches high. The 15-inch 'Red Star' is red-purple and blooms from August to October. See list 20, Aster.

BOLTONIA (bolt-*toh*-nee-uh) **asteroides**
Zones 3-8

This is an airy American native that bears masses of little 1- to 1½-inch flowers with raised, rounded yellow centers surrounded by ray petals that may be white, violet, pink, or purple. It resembles an aster and like asters provides masses of color in late summer and early fall. The strong branches grow from 3 to 5 feet or more in the wild and often need staking in gardens. The stalks and leaves are a rich brown in winter. Nice massed, and especially attractive behind *Physostegia virginiana*—there's a pale pink cultivar. The species is weedy, but the 4-foot-tall 'Snowbank', a pure white that flowers from early August into September, is trim.

Culture: In spring sow seeds or set out root divisions in well-drained, humusy soil in some sun or light shade. Maintain moisture. Provide winter mulch where there is some frost. Divide every two or three years. An excellent plant for naturalizing.

CHRYSANTHEMUM. Fall is mum time. For instant fall color, plant disposable cushion mums offered already in flower from September until frosts. Or, in spring, plant your own cushion mums and pinch and nurture them until fall blooming, then divide them next year and start over again. The great football and florist's mums are for collectors and connoisseurs. Some of the species chrysanthemum daisies flower in fall, too. Fresh as mint are cultivars of *C. nipponicum*, the Nippon Daisy, a hardy perennial from 3 to 5 feet tall that bears loads of white daisylike flowers with greenish centers, from early fall to the first frosts. *C. pacificum*, 12 inches tall, is grown as much for its year-round foliage, which is backed and edged thinly with silver, as for the very small tansy-like flowers it produces in October. See list 23, Mum—Daisy.

HELENIUM (hel-*leen*-ee-um) **autumnale**
Zones 3-8

A big, hardy native 4 to 5 feet tall that flowers freely for months, bearing masses of yellow daisies in late summer and fall on well-branched plants. Excellent in groups at the back of the garden, in islands, and for naturalizing. Cultivated varieties display a broad range of gold, orange, red, brown, and bronze shades. 'The Bishop', 24 to 30 inches high with clear yellow flowers, is choice for smaller borders. Typical of some striking new cultivars is one from Germany, 'Moerheim Beauty'—the flowers have brownish red petals and a black central disk.

Culture: Grows easily from seed, but root divisions usually are planted in spring. Full sun and well-drained, humusy soil with sustained moisture. May require staking.

HELIANTHUS (hee-lee-*anth*-us)
Sunflower

Excellent. Beginning in the late summer, these very tall, coarse plants with bold yellow flowers lift huge heads to the sun and follow its course. Perfect for the vegetable and wild garden. The annual sunflower, *H. annuus,* is described with the flowers for cutting on list 71.

Culture: Thrives in poor soil, and tolerates drought. Sow seeds where the plants are to grow in full sun—they grow very rapidly there. Or, set out tubers or root divisions in early spring.

H. angustifolius Swamp Sunflower Zones 6-9
Superb October and November flower in warmer regions, 5 to 7 feet tall, and covered with brown-centered yellow daisies 2 to 3 inches across. Requires frequent fertilizing.

H. multiflorus 'Flore-plena' Zones 4-8
Very hardy cultivar 3 to 5 feet tall with showy, double, 4-inch flowers with darker yellow centers. It flowers all summer and prefers slightly alkaline soil.

H. salicifolius Willow-leafed Sunflower
Zones 3-8

Native to the Western Plains, about 4 feet tall in the garden, with daisylike yellow flowers in September and October. Attractive in big borders, or naturalized with ornamental grasses.

H. tuberosus Jerusalem Artichoke Zones 3-8
For the food garden—small, fluffy flowerheads on plants to 12 feet. The edible root was a food for native Americans. Invasive unless the tubers are dug and reduced every fall.

SALVIA Sage, Ramona. An important and diverse group for summer and fall color. It includes the red, blue, and culinary sages. Most of the ornamentals—leafy stems topped by colorful florets or bracts—are late to bloom and go on into late fall. Recommended for late color are the various blue sages—by September they can be counted on to overflow borders with a show of dainty green leaves topped by slim, soaring spires of lavender-blue and purple- or violet-blue. There are also whites. Lovely with pink dahlias and roses, in the garden or in arrangements. Recommended for fall are *S. azurea* var. *grandiflora*, Blue Sage, which has striking deep blue flowers and narrow leaves prominently veined with lighter green on plants 3 to 4 feet high. And *S.* × *superba* cultivars are among the best late blues. See list 41, *Salvia*.

SEDUM *sieboldii*, October Daphne, October. Plant. Indestructible plant up to 15 inches tall; very highly valued for its evergreen, succulent-like, light green foliage and unusual autumn color. The species is a trailer 6 to 9 inches long that has bluish green leaves with faint reddish margins and is excellent for filling corners and for autumn color. It bears flat flowerheads in late summer that in fall turn bright pink. Tolerates light shade. The flowers are tiny and star-shaped, but remarkable in the tall hybrids as they change color with the cold. Several cultivars are recommended: *S.* 'Autumn Joy', 18 to 24 inches tall, often naturalized with ornamental grasses and bulbs. Its lovely spring and summer show of gray-green foliage is followed by fresh apple green flowerheads in early summer, slowly changing to rich pink, through rose to salmon-bronze, and finally with cold to rosy russet. *S.* 'Ruby Glow', to 12 inches, bears iridescent ruby red flowers in autumn. *S.* 'Vera Jameson', 9 to 12 inches tall, with darkish leaves and 2- to 4-inch-wide flowerheads, colors a pleasant rose pink in fall. One of the best for hot sun. See list 56, Dry, Hot Conditions.

SOLIDAGO *odora*, Sweet Goldenrod. Sweetly scented species of the lovely field goldenrod, a wonderful filler for the late summer and fall garden. The golden yellow plumes top plants 24 or 36 inches high for 3 or 4 weeks. A fast-spreading perennial, it may be hard to find but seeds are offered for other goldenrods such as the showier but less fragrant *S. canadensis* and *S. virgaurea*. Goldenrods do not cause hay fever. See list 64, The Meadow Garden.

FOR SHADE

ACONITUM, Aconite, Monkshood. This is one of the great tall perennials for the back of the flowering border, an upright leafy plant with strong stalks 3 to 4 feet high. The deeply divided, dark green leaves are topped in summer and fall by spires of dark blue flowers. For culture and summer bloomers, see list 16. For fall, plant *A. fisheri* (*A. carmichaelii*), 24 to 36 inches tall, the last of the monkshoods to bloom. Especially beautiful as a background plant for pastel mums. Sun is suitable in the North. For culture, see list 16.

ANEMONE (an-*nem*-on-ee)
Excellent. The fall flowering anemones are perhaps the most beautiful late summer and fall flowers. Two to 3 feet tall with ferny foliage, these are superb low-maintenance perennials for gardens with semishade. For several weeks they bear deep rose, pink, white, or purple flowers 2 to 3 inches in diameter on multibranched stems. The dried winter form is also interesting. And throughout the growing season, dense clumps of attractive, rather coarse compound leaves are formed. Nice contrast with ferns, epimediums, and hostas. The little, very early spring anemone, *A. blanda*, and the beautiful summer poppy anemone, *A. coronaria*, are described on lists 1 and 4, respectively.

Culture: The Japanese anemones need 2 or 3 seasons to become established, and they resent disturbance. Divide every 10 years. Good winter drainage is essential. Where summers are hot, summer mulch is helpful. Plant in spring only 24 inches apart in a rich, neutral-range soil to which lots of compost has been added; mulch over winter. Maintain moisture. In cool regions they tolerate sun most of the day, or bright shade. South of Zone 6 they need consistent bright shade. Established older clumps are fairly drought-resistant, but the best results are obtained when plants are well watered during dry periods.

A. hupehensis var. **japonica**, Japanese Anemone
Zones 5-8

This is similar to the beautiful hybrid below but has 5 to 7 petals and is hardy in Zone 5. It blooms earlier, midsummer to fall, bearing single pink flowers copiously on plants 2 to 2½ feet high. Tolerates sun better than the other species.

A. × **hybrida** Japanese Anemone Zones 5/6-8
The single-flowered forms have 5 rounded petals around a central heart of bright yellow stamens. Winter hardiness will be lessened if the drainage is not good. Winter mulch for Zone 5 is advisable. There are semidouble and double forms.

Long-blooming fall flowers:
ABOVE *Boltonia* 'Snowbank'.
(Viette)

RIGHT German cultivar of
Helenium autumnale,
'Feuersiegel'. (Viette)

BELOW *Sedum* 'Autumn Joy' in
its late fall color. (Viette)

KIRENGESHOMA palmata. The large maple-like leaves are carried on purplish stems that arch at the tips. In early autumn, nodding bell-shaped yellow flowers appear in the leaf axils. The mature height is 36 inches. This slow-growing plant is one of the few late-flowering perennials for the semishaded garden and does best in cool regions. For culture, see list 67, Rare and Choice.

LIRIOPE platyphylla (formerly *muscari*), Big Blue Lilyturf. Standard landscape plants and one of the best ground covers for Zones 6 to 10. The graceful, tough, and resistant semievergreen or evergreen grasslike foliage is ¼ to ¾ inch wide and 8 to 12 or 18 inches high. In summer or early fall, thin spikes covered with grainlike lavender or white flowers rise well above the grassy tufts. Shiny black fruits develop in late fall and persist into winter. Hybrids may bear green, bluish, blue, red, lavender, white, or purple flowers. Recommended for the fall border are: 'Christmas Tree', to 8 inches tall, with the largest lavender flower spikes; 'Lilac Beauty', to 12 inches tall, an excellent bloomer with dark lilac flowers; 'Gold Banded', to 12 inches tall, with variegated foliage and lilac flowers; and 'John Burch', to 12 inches tall, with variegated foliage and crested lavender flowers. For culture, see list 44, Flowering Ground Covers.

PHYSOSTEGIA (fye-sos-*teej*-ee-uh) **virginiana**
Obedience   Zones 3-9
An outstanding native that produces flower spikes 12 to 18 inches tall on straight, squarish stems; ideal for cutting and very handsome in the late summer border. The plant forms a large clump to 4 feet high that spreads in good conditions. 'Summer Snow', a clean white to 24 inches tall, is less invasive than the species. 'Vivid' is 24 to 36 inches tall, a brilliant late-blooming pink that lasts well when cut and is a good companion to *Boltonia* 'Snowbank'. The common name refers to the curious way in which individual florets hold whatever position they are turned to.

Culture: Set out root divisions in spring in semi- or light shade in rich, moist, well-drained soil. May need staking.

TRICYRTIS, Toad Lily. Unusual and exotic close up, these semishade plants are valued for their bloom from mid-September to frost in the South. Graceful, from 12 to 18 inches tall, its flowers are heavily spotted and rather showy, and often borne in the leaf axils. Some self-sow and spread by underground stolons, in time forming imposing colonies. *T. formosana* var. *amethystina* flowers in the South from late July until frost, displaying small, red-spotted, whitish flowers. Elsewhere, they are fall blooming. See list 18, Perennials for the South.

SOURCE: ROBERT HEBB, A HORTICULTURIST, IS DIRECTOR OF THE LEWIS GINTER BOTANIC GARDEN IN RICHMOND, VIRGINIA, AND WAS FORMERLY WITH THE ARNOLD ARBORETUM, LONGWOOD GARDENS, THE NEW YORK BOTANICAL GARDEN, AND OTHER DISTINGUISHED ARBORETA.

Recommended are:
'Honorine Jobert', a superb, glistening white single, is perhaps the all-time best. A historic anemone 3 to 4 feet tall.
'Margarete' is a double or semidouble bright rose pink, with abundant blooms on stems 2 to 3 feet tall.
'Konigin Charlotte' ('Queen Charlotte') is a lovely semidouble, 3 feet tall, with 3-inch deep pink flowers.
'Whirlwind' is a semidouble pure white, 4 to 5 feet tall with 4-inch flowers.

EUPATORIUM coelestinum, Mist Flower, Hardy Ageratum, Blue Boneset. A wonderful perennial 24 to 36 inches high, with dense heads of tiny, fluffy flowers resembling blue ageratum. It blooms from late summer into early fall and is especially pretty with asters, white mums, and *Sedum* 'Autumn Joy'. The cut flowers last. Recommended are 'Alba', a white, and 'Cori', a blue, 24 inches tall. Very different is the 4- to 7-foot-tall native *E. purpureum*, Joe-Pye Weed, Zones 4 to 7, a wild plant for moist, shady places. It bears attractive purple flowerheads in fall. *E. rugosum*, Zones 3 to 7, is a hardy but not easily found white whose flowers last well into fall. For culture, see list 63, The Container Garden.

18. PERENNIALS FOR THE SOUTH

■ The plants recommended here present an overview of the perennials that are the most successful in Zones 8 and 9. But other flowers recommended in the book succeed all the way south to Zone 11.

In Zones 8 and 9 perennials bloom earlier than predicted for northern gardens because heat comes sooner than in the North and often everything colors up at the same time. Flowers don't necessarily last longer or even as long as in the North. Heat shuts down plant productivity just as cold does. Excessive watering during dormancy can rot the plants. But with the coming of cool, moist weather in fall, some flowers color up again and there are many weeks of quiet beauty ahead.

Be aware that a Zone 8 garden on a breezy headland near water will be five to ten degrees cooler than its counterpart surrounded by asphalt and skyscrapers. Crape myrtles don't do well in British Columbia's Zone 8 because, though the temperature is right, the light requirements aren't met. There's more twilight in the North, and light has everything to do with flowering.

See the related list 6, Best Bulbs for the South, which recommends bulbs for as far south as Zone 11.

Culture: Late summer and early fall are the best planting times for many flower seeds and young perennials in the South. After the last frost in very early spring is good, too. Early fall is the best time to divide established perennials for this region, but those that transplant badly may start more easily in spring.

The mild winters of the South can play havoc with perennials. Often the cold isn't enough to throw plants into dormancy, and when they do go dormant there's no cozy snow cover to keep them asleep. They respond to winter hot spells by growing and then freeze back. When that happens, cut plants back to the ground and let them start over again. A winter mulch (see Growing Flowers) affords some protection and is advised for the northern edges of a plant's hardiness zone. Zone 8 winters can be especially variable.

Remember that in hot regions, plants can't stand as much direct sun as in cool regions. Plants growing in improved (see Growing Flowers), moist but well-drained, humusy soil can stand more direct sun than those growing in hot, dry, sandy soil. Noon sun in the South is too hot.

Watering at ground level rather than from overhead is recommended in areas where mildew is prevalent. Avoid watering at night.

. . . .

ASTER × **frikartii.** The blooms are long-flowering, minute powder puffs in shades of blue during July and August in the North, and September in the South. This hybrid is the earliest, a compact 18- to 24-inches tall. Easy to grow and good for cutting. 'Wonder of Staffa' is a handsome cultivar with big lavender-blue flowers; 'Monch' is similar, though a darker blue—it flowers later and is considered the best. See list 20, Aster.

Red Valerian, *Centranthus ruber*, a good background and cutting flower, benefits from shade in warm climates, as do many other flowers. (Viette)

CENTRANTHUS (sen-*tranth*-us) **ruber**
Red Valerian, Jupiter's-beard, Fox's-brush

Zones 4-9

An easy, sun-loving plant from 18 to 36 inches high, with attractive gray-green foliage setting off globes of fragrant, airy, pink-red flowers. There is also a good white form. It blooms for a long time beginning in early summer and, if cut back, may rebloom until frosts. It is a good backdrop for a mixed border. Excellent cut flower.

Culture: Sow seed in spring or set out root divisions—sun in the North, semi-sun in the South. Best in well-drained, not too rich, alkaline soil. Space the plants 10 to 12 inches apart. It tolerates moistness. Divide every year in spring or fall to maintain good color. Nice companion for campanula and crocosmia.

CHRYSOGONUM (kriss-*og*-on-num) **virginianum**

Zones 5-9

Called golden star. Easy, low, fast-spreading, trouble-free native about 8 inches high that covers itself with masses of small, bright yellow star-shaped flowers in spring and then sporadically through late summer and fall. The foliage is neat, compact, attractive. There are several selections from a totally prostrate form to one with flower stems 4 inches tall.

Culture: In late spring sow seeds or plant root divisions—sun in the North, light shade where summers are long and hot. Best in humusy, moisture-retentive soil that is somewhat acid. Maintain moisture. Mulch for winter in Zone 5.

COREOPSIS, Tickseed. Excellent. This is one of the easiest and most long-lasting garden flowers. In late spring and throughout summer masses of sunny, starry flowers bloom above the narrow, dark green foliage. Recommended for the South: *C. auriculata* 'Nana', small and delightful with attractive green foliage covered in late spring and summer by sparkling orange-gold flowers on 6- to 8-inch stems; *C. rosea*, a rosy species extremely tolerant of wet situations; *C. verticillata* 'Zagreb', Dwarf Threadleaf Tickseed, which bears masses of lemon yellow flowers on compact plants 12 to 15 inches tall and is very tolerant of heat; and 'Golden Showers' ('Grandiflora') which is largest and the best bloomer. Coreopsis are discussed on list 15, Summer Perennials for Sun.

TOP Fast-spreading, trouble-free native *Chrysogonum virginianum*, Golden Star. (Harper)
ABOVE *Bibalsamita major*, Costmary or Bible Leaf, a charming herb, spreads readily in the South. See list 76, Fragrant Herbs for Drying and Potpourris. (Harper)
ABOVE, RIGHT Exotic *Tricyrtis formosana* variety *amethystina*, blooms in shade mid-September to frosts. (Viette)

DIANTHUS gratianopolitanus, Cheddar Pink. Pretty, spicily scented, 1- to 1½-inch miniature pink or rose carnations 2 or 3 to a stem flower all summer in mounds of grassy gray-green foliage 6 to 9 or 12 inches high. A charming plant for rock gardens and edging walks, it is almost indestructible. 'Petite', a dwarf only 3 inches high, and 'Peppermint Polly' succeed even in dry seasons. See list 70, The Fragrance Garden.

DICENTRA 'Luxuriant', Turkey Corn, Staggerweed, Wild Bleeding-heart. The flowers are pendulous cherry red, heart-shaped blossoms set off by ferny foliage. A dainty long-lived semi shade plant 12 to 18 inches tall, it blooms freely all spring and sporadically through summer if moisture is maintained. Choice for mixed borders and wildflower and rock gardens. Very hardy. See list 14, Spring Perennials for Shade.

ECHINACEA purpurea, Purple Coneflower. The coarse, dark green foliage sets off and balances large daisy flowers in rich, dusky rose-purple with an orange-bronze central disk. Characteristically, the petals slant backwards a bit. In the South it comes into bloom in May or June and continues intermittently into November if faded flowers are removed. The height is 24 to 36 inches tall, but staking is rarely necessary. This is a very useful flower—good when cut, handsome in mixed borders, and easily perennialized in a meadow garden—and bees and butterflies love it. For culture, see list 64, The Meadow Garden.

GERANIUM. Cranesbill. Don't confuse it with *Pelargonium*, the flower whose common name is geranium. In spring and early summer this "true geranium" bears pretty 5-petaled pastel pink, mauve, purplish, magenta, violet, cerise, red, blue, or white flowers on wandlike stems above deeply divided foliage. In the South, the best performance is given by plants shielded from afternoon sun and growing in humusy, evenly moist, enriched soil. Recommended: *G.* 'Claridge Druce', to 18 inches with handsome gray-green foliage, bearing masses of 2-inch lilac-pink flowers all summer; *G.* 'Johnson's Blue', Zones 3 to 8, 15 to 18 inches high, with long-lasting, 2-inch lilac-blue flowers and handsome gray-green foliage—undemanding and vigorous; *G. psilostemon*, Zones 3 to 8, forming mounds to 4 feet tall and covering itself with black-eyed, purple-magenta blooms in spring—the leaves are red in fall; and *G. sanguineum* var. *prostratum*, Zones 3 to 8, 6 to 12 inches high, coming into flower early in the South and bearing small magenta-pink flowers with darker veins through summer. See also list 13.

GERBERA (*jerb*-er-uh) **jamesonii**
Transvaal Daisy, Baberton Daisy, African Daisy, Veldt Daisy   Zones 8-11
In warm regions this is an evergreen perennial 12 to 18 inches tall with bold, broad, dark green leaves; it blooms midsummer to winter depending on growing conditions. In the North it is grown as a container plant. The flowers are striking daisies 3 to 4 inches across on round stems. Brilliant colors are characteristic—reds and oranges to

clear or salmon pinks, white, and yellow. It is a superb cut flower and thrives in containers on a porch or patio.

Culture: Zone 8 and southward, handle it as a bedding perennial to produce flowers in late winter. Plant seeds in late fall or early spring in well-drained, slightly acid, humusy soil and move outdoors when frost is over. Or set out container plants in early fall. Fertilize regularly. Even moisture is absolutely essential, especially in pot culture.

HELLEBORUS, Hellebore. Evergreen plants 12 to 18 inches high with distinctive, shiny, leathery, deeply divided foliage that remains interesting in winter. The flowers they produce in December, January, or early spring—according to the climate—are the finest of any winter and late winter herbaceous perennial. The rounded, nodding, roselike white-green and pink flowers—actually 5 petal-like sepals—are also rather leathery for added resistance to bad weather and persist for 2 to 3 months. The two most famous hellebores are: *H. niger,* Christmas Rose, 12 to 18 inches tall, which in December through February bears large white flowers with yellow stamens from December through January; and *H. orientalis,* Lenten Rose, the best of the hellebores, which thrives in gardens from Maine to Georgia, producing loads of 2- to 4-inch, saucer-shaped flowers that range in color from white through pink to maroon, and are speckled, mottled, or streaked with various color configurations. See list 14, Spring Perennials for Shade.

HEMEROCALLIS, Daylily. This big, almost indispensable, lilylike flower enjoys the sun but tolerates light shade in the South. Each plant offers a brilliant, nonstop show for 3 to 4 weeks—in late May in Florida, June 5 in South Carolina, July 10 in Virginia. Depending on type, some rebloom in fall. Its flowers can be 8 inches across, the plants 4 to 5 feet tall; dwarfs have 1-inch flowers and are 8 to 12 inches tall. Colors are in the yellow-orange-maroon range and some are fragrant. Miniatures such as 'Stella De Oro' have high bud counts, often rebloom, and their foliage withstands summer heat. Splendid as specimen plants, or in a group, in a mixed border, as ground cover for big spaces, and as tall edgers. Long-lived, easy to grow, durable. See list 24 for information on daylilies for southern gardens (Zones 8 and below).

HOSTA, Plantain Lily, Daylily. Superb group of bold-leaved foliage plants that thrive in shade and bear spires of often fragrant lavender to white bells from summer through fall. The clumps are 18 to 30 inches tall with considerable spread—they are magnificent edgers and ground covers. Many cultivars merit planting as specimen plants or background in flower borders. Hosta leaves begin to unfurl just as fading bulb foliage needs screening, and the long-lasting flowers arrive when others are fading. *H. tardiflora* is one of the last perennials to bloom in autumn. In areas with hot summers hostas succeed if grown in well-prepared, humusy, damp soil. See list 54, *Hosta.*

IRIS. Many of the irises will do well in the South, including hybrids and species. The Dutch cultivars succeed for one flowering season. Recommended are hybrids or cultivars of the following: *I. × germanica,* Sweet Flag, Fleur-de-lys, which bears several blue-purple flowers on each stem in late spring and early summer; *I. ensata* (syn. *kaempferei*), Japanese Iris, which grow up to 3 feet tall in boggy places (shorter in garden soil), has orchidlike flowers 8 inches across, flat and ruffled, marbled and mottled in exotic combinations of blue, pink, reddish purple, mauve, and white—it flowers in early summer; and *I. sibirica,* Siberian Iris, which produces clusters of 2 or 3 flowers on stalks 24 to 40 inches tall backed by slender, grasslike, waving leaves in late spring and early summer. See list 25, Iris.

LIRIOPE, Lilyturf. Graceful and tough semievergreen or evergreen tufts with grassy leaves ¼ to ¾ inch wide and 8 to 12 or 18 inches high. In summer or early fall, thin spikes covered with grainlike lavender, blue, or white flowers stand above the grassy tufts. Shiny black fruits develop in late fall and persist into winter. It is an impenetrable ground cover and a good edging plant. There are variegated cultivars. See list 44, Flowering Ground Covers.

ORNAMENTAL GRASSES. Small mounds to giant clumps, these are used as linear accents and send graceful flowerheads soaring to catch the wind. Movement and sound and winter interest are among the grasses' many gifts to the garden. The colors are subtle but distinct—buff, tan, sea green, green, gold, pale gold—and the forms—straight-up or fountaining—are excellent foils for garden flowers. Many grasses, including *Carex* (a sedge usually included with grasses), thrive in Zones 8 to 9, and several striking specimens exist in frost-free Zones 10 to 11. Some grasses prefer sun and some shade. All are easy to grow and tolerant of poor soil. See list 53, Ornamental Grasses.

PHLOX. A major perennial on many lists. The creeping phloxes are important sources of spring color in the shade. The tall, upright perennials and annuals are prized for midsummer flowerheads in pastels or fluorescent blue, pink, crimson, purple, and white, often with a contrasting eye. The more you cut, the more the flowers come. The annual *P. drummondii,* Annual Phlox, Drummond Phlox, 18 inches tall, does well in the South. Even in hot, sandy soil it withstands considerable drought and goes on blooming. The fragrant *P. maculata,* Wild Sweet William, 24 to 36 inches tall, flowers in early summer. 'Miss Lingard' is an excellent pure white. *P. glaberrima* 'Triflora', Smooth Phlox, is a shorter, superior dwarf form 15 to 18 inches high with strong stems that easily support its big heads of lavender-pink flowers with a distinctive white eye. See list 27, Phlox.

POLYGONATUM. Solomon's-seal, King-Solomon's-seal. These graceful, spring-blooming wildflowers are reliable plants for a shade garden. The white bell-like flowers scalloped in green appear in spring, pretty if not spectacular, followed in some species by blue-black berries in late summer. Recommended is *P. odoratum* var. *thunbergii,* Zones 3 to 9, a handsome plant 24 to 36 inches tall with white flowers in spring and rich green leaves brushed with cream along the edges. Pink tinted stems add drama. Fragrant in the evening. For culture see list 65, The Woodland Garden.

SALVIA, Sage, Ramona. An important and diverse group for summer and fall color, it includes the red, blue, and culinary sages. The ornamentals flower in August and September in sunny gardens in the South. Blue Sage, *S. azurea* var. *grandiflora,* 3 to 4 feet high, is a striking specimen for mixed borders with its important midsummer-to-fall show of sky blue flowers. Mexican Bush Sage, *S. leucantha,* a 3- to 4-foot clump with exotic flowers, is a beautiful, regal plant for Zone 8. *S. officinalis,* the culinary sage, should not be banished to the herb harden for it is handsome in the perennial garden and a good edger and ground cover, particularly the little multicolored *S. o.* 'Tricolor'. The gray-green leaves of 'Icterina' are variegated with gold. See list 41, *Salvia.*

TRICYRTIS (trye-*surt*-iss)
Toad Lily
Unusual and exotic close up, these shade plants are valued for their bloom from mid-September to frosts in the South. Graceful and arching, from 12 to 18 inches tall, its flowers are orchidlike, heavily spotted with red and rather showy, and often borne in the leaf axils. Some self-sow and spread by underground stolons, in time forming imposing colonies. Nice by the edge of the woods near a path.

Culture: In early spring set out root divisions or divide and replant. Set in light shade in well-drained, humusy, somewhat acid soil and maintain moisture during droughts.

T. formosana var. **amethystina**   Zones 4-9
Early, July until frost, with heavily spotted red on white-pink flowers. Self-sows and also spreads by underground stolons.

T. hirta   Zones 4-8
Displays arching stems with close-set leaves, with flowers that appear in mid-September in the South, a little later farther north. The blossoms are whitish or light purple splotched and spotted with deeper purple.

SOURCE: VIKI FERRENIEA, ASSISTANT HORTICULTURAL DIRECTOR FOR WAYSIDE GARDENS IN SOUTH CAROLINA. A HORTICULTURIST AND LECTURER, VIKI WAS FORMERLY THE ROCK GARDEN CURATOR AT THE NEW YORK BOTANICAL GARDEN.

19. WINTERING PERENNIALS INDOORS

■ As the earth cools and we move into the warmth and light of our homes, it's tempting to bring still healthy plants indoors to make a winter garden. A few will flourish inside, but only if a cool, sunny place is available. Airing and frequent misting help. Thriving container plants can be trimmed down and brought in to cool, sunny windows. First, hose them clean and spray twice for insects two days apart.

Here are a few hardy perennials, several tender perennials, and some annual species of plants we think of as perennial that will live and bloom for some time indoors. Most can be started from seed or grown from cuttings.

In mid- or late spring the indoor perennials should go out to the garden after a hardening-off period of a week or so away from direct sun.

Companion Plants: Other garden plants that bring freshness into the home are discussed on lists 7, Exotic Bulbs, 8, Bulbs for Containers, and 35, Annuals to Start Indoors.

ABUTILON (ab-yew-til-on)
Flowering Maple

The abutilons recommended are leafy plants 24 to 36 inches high with foliage like maple leaves and, in spring and summer, bell-like flowers. They thrive as pot plants indoors and accept the move outdoors readily in late spring. Mature plants become shrubs or small trees.

Culture: Abutilon blooms from seed in about a month. Tip cuttings taken from bedding plants in late summer will root indoors. Indoors, abutilon prefers sun, rich soil, and monthly fertilization. Maintain even moisture and mist often. Outdoors, particularly in the South, provide protection from hot afternoon sun.

A. hybridum Chinese-lantern   Zones 9-11
A group that bears showy red, pink, purple, white, or yellow flowers. The leaves are sometimes speckled.

A. megapotamicum Trailing Abutilon   Zones 8-11
A delightful drooping plant with yellow flowers, handsome on a pedestal or in a hanging basket. The leaves of 'Variegata' are mottled with gold.

ANTHEMIS (anth-em-iss) tinctoria var. kelwayi
Hardy Marguerite   Zones 3-7
Aromatic, finely cut dark green foliage 12 to 24 inches high is topped by showy 2-inch, daisy-faced yellow flowers. Interesting and unusual indoors but it may need staking. Outdoors it blooms reliably from May to frost and is often used as a ground cover for slopes and in wild gardens in Canada and the northern U. S.

Culture: In spring, sow seeds or plant root divisions in full sun in a deep container in well-drained, rather gritty soil. Maintain on the dry side and don't fertilize.

AQUILEGIA, Columbine. A hardy perennial that in spring bears exquisite spurred, bicolored flowers that may be nodding or upright. In late winter sow seeds indoors in a large container in full sun in rich well-drained soil, and grow the plants in a cool, airy location. Fresh green scalloped foliage will develop and eventually reach 12 to 36 inches. Moved to the garden in spring, aquilegia will bloom either the first or following year. Species recommended for starting indoors include: *A. caerulea*, Zones 3 to 8, which is blue and white, long lasting, and long spurred; *A. canadensis*, Zones 3 to 8, with pink and yellow or orange-red flowers, an elegant native of the Northeast that blooms early in moist, semishaded places; *A. chrysantha*, Zones 3 to 9, with big yellow flowers; and *A. flabellata* 'Nana Alba', Zones 3 to 9, with small, exquisite white flowers. See list 13, Spring Perennials for Sun, for culture.

ASTILBE × arendsii. A hardy perennial 18 to 48 inches high with handsome foliage in either green or bronze, which is topped in late spring and early summer by tall, feathery flower spikes. The colors are white, pink, red, or purple. Root divisions taken in early fall thrive indoors in humusy moist soil in either sun or semishade and usually bloom. 'Deutschland', white, to 24 inches, and the early, pale pink 'Europa', over 24 inches tall, are recommended as a good indoor pair. For culture see list 21, *Astilbe*.

BEGONIA *Semperflorens-Cultorum Hybrids*, Bedding Begonia, Wax Begonia. This charming little tender perennial flowers nonstop from spring until frost in hues of pink, salmon, red, or white. The crisp, shiny brownish or bright green (or both) leaves are attractive. Potted up in fall and moved indoors to a sunny windowsill it blooms all winter. In early spring, root 6-inch cuttings and plant them outdoors when the weather warms. Replant the parent, too. Provide rich, moist, well-drained humusy soil in the acid range, and fertilize often. Among recommended plants are 'Pygmy White' and the sun-resistant, bronze-foliage Cocktail compacts. See also list 36, Begonia.

BROWALLIA speciosa 'Major', Sapphire Flower. This is a tender perennial with upright-then-cascading branches about 12 inches long, dainty leaves, and lavender-blue starfaced flowers. It blooms indoors or out in filtered sun. Container plants may be brought indoors in fall. Seeds started indoors in late winter flower in summer. Fertilize with 5-10-5 to keep blooms coming. See 63. The Container Garden.

CALCEOLARIA (kal-see-oh-lay-ree-uh)
Slipperwort, Slipper Flower, Pocketbook Flower, Pouch Flower   Zones 9-11
A familiar little tender perennial we know as a florist's plant that grows 6 to 12 inches high. In spring it covers itself with flowers like miniscule purses in dazzlingly bright, often spotted colors—yellow, orange, red, brown, and purple.

Culture: Sow seeds from August to October. Blooms in fine-milled sphagnum moss; maintain even moisture and fertilize monthly. Set in a cool, sunny window it will bloom in spring. Complements primroses.

C. integrifolia
A woody plant to 12 inches tall, particularly popular for spring bloom in California flower beds. The flowers are yellowish to red. Grows from cuttings or seed.

A. mexicana
This is an annual species that bears ½-inch yellow flowers in summer on a plant 12 inches tall. Usually grown from seed.

CHAMAEMELUM (kam-muh-mee-lum) nobile
Chamomile, Russian Chamomile, Roman Chamomile   Zones 4-9
A rather invasive perennial outdoors. In late spring small yellow flowers stand above lacy, semievergreen foliage that smells slightly of apples when crushed. Reaches 12 inches in height. In mild areas it is a lawn substitute. Formerly known as *Anthemis nobilis*.

Culture: In early spring sow seeds or plant root divisions in full sun in sandy or gritty soil and keep on the dry side.

COLEUS, Flame Nettle, Painted Leaves. The many brilliant cultivars of *C. × hybridus*, a tender perennial, displays almost infinite variegations of red-mahogany, green, yellow, white, blue, and rose on plants 6 to 24 inches tall. Grows easily from seed in sun or semi-sun, and cuttings root and flourish indefinitely in water or in rich, moist, well-drained loam. Keep the flowers and foliage pinched back for best results. An excellent basket, pot, or border plant that may be brought indoors for winter. See list 51, Foliage for Color.

CUPHEA (kew-fee-uh) ignea
Cigar Flower, Firecracker Plant, Red-white-and-blue Flower   Zones 10-11
This is an attractive tender perennial with trailing branches up to 36 inches in length. Grown as a basket plant and, sometimes, in a planter or a flower bed. It covers itself with small, bright green leaves and from spring to autumn bears orange-red flowers shaped like minute cigars. After the weather warms the plant may be moved outdoors to semi-sun in the North, semishade in the South.

Culture: In early spring, start the seeds indoors in rich, well-drained, humusy soil and good light. Maintain even moisture as it grows, reducing water as growth slows. Maintain evenly moist soil.

FUCHSIA × hybrida, Lady's-eardrops. Unforgettable pendulous flowers not unlike long earrings in fanciful color combinations of creamy white and cerise-red, purple, or pink on cascading branches. A challenging but very beautiful basket plant. It can be maintained indoors for winter in a cool, semishaded space if even moisture is maintained. Pinch back during growth to encourage compact growth, and fertilize lightly once a week. Cuttings taken in spring will root. See list 63. The Container Garden.

ABOVE Flowering ground cover, the hardy marguerite, *Anthemis tinctoria* variety *kelwayi*, can bloom indoors. (Harper)

ABOVE, RIGHT Pocketbook plant, *Calceolaria*, one of many greenhouse flowers grown in the home. (Longwood Gardens)

RIGHT 'Lava', a new tropical hibiscus, blooms on a windowsill if it has summered outdoors. (Yoder Brothers, Inc.)

GERBERA **jamesonii**, Transvaal Daisy, Baberton Daisy, African Daisy, Veldt Daisy. In warm regions this is an evergreen perennial 12 to 18 inches tall with bold, broad, dark green leaves and striking daisylike flowers 3 to 4 inches across on round stems. The colors are brilliant—clear reds and oranges, salmon pinks, white, and yellow. Blooms midsummer to winter, depending on growing conditions. Challenging to grow indoors, but the potted houseplants sold in early fall do relatively well if they have full sun and the soil is evenly moist. This is a striking cut flower. The plant thrives in containers on a porch or patio in summer. See list 18, Perennials for the South.

HIBISCUS (hye-**bisk**-us) **rosa-sinensis**
Chinese Hibiscus   Zones 9-11
This long-lived tropical hibiscus is sold during the fall and spring as a 24- to 30-inch houseplant and in tree form. The exotic blooms last a day and are borne in profusion outdoors during the summer and more sparsely indoors in winter. Colors may be white, pink, rose, lavender, or red and there are bicolors. 'Lava', a fiery orange, and 'Vista', a rosy red, have been bred for windowsill gardens. Ultimate height in a container is 6 to 8 feet. This is actually a shrub grown as a herbaceous garden plant and is related to the shrubby hibiscus with large blossoms recommended on list 15, Summer Perennials for Sun.

   Culture: In late summer prune branch tips back 4 inches to encourage branching and maintain size. Repot in spring and summer the plant outdoors in full sun, then bring it indoors in fall. It needs well-drained sandy loam, pH 5.5 to 7.0, with a high organic content, sustained moisture, and warmth. Fertilize monthly March through November and a few times in between. White and black flies may be troublesome indoors—mist often.

NIEREMBERGIA (nee-rem-*ber*-gee-uh)

strumosa var. **violacea**

Cupflower   Zones 9-11

Mat-forming, 12-inch-high tender perennial that in summer and fall covers itself with 1- to 2-inch-wide blue, violet, or purple flowers shaped like cups. A perennial bedding plant in warm climates, in the North it is grown indoors as a winter pot plant and moved outdoors to window boxes in warm weather.

Culture: Sow seeds in February in full sun in fertile, sandy, humusy soil; maintain moisture.

PELARGONIUM, Geranium. Ivy geraniums,

scented-leaved geraniums, and most other geraniums are tender perennials that produce showy blooms all summer in shades of pink, red, fuchsia, and white, as well as bicolors. Some varieties have beautiful variegated foliage. A superb container plant indoors, on a cool sunny windowsill it will produce a few blooms in winter. Cuttings taken from January on root quickly. New plants may be started from seed indoors in late winter. Most successful in rather poor, dryish, well-drained soil. See list 37, Geranium—Ivy Geranium—especially *P.* × *domesticum*, Fancy Geranium, Lady Washington, or Martha Washington Geranium, and *P.* × *hortorum*, Fish Geranium, Zonal Geranium, House Geranium, Horseshoe Geranium, Bedding Geranium.

PORTULACA grandiflora, Rose Moss, Sun

Plant, Eleven-o'clock. A low-growing annual with short, trailing branches and fat needlelike leaves, it bears pretty, bright, single or double roselike blooms all summer. It is a good basket plant and suited to any hot, dry, sunny situation. Sow seeds indoors in mid-spring in well-drained soil and move outdoors when the weather warms. For culture see list 63, The Container Garden.

PRIMULA, Primrose. A charming little perennial 3

or 4 to 10 inches tall that bears cup-shaped or flat-faced flowers above or nestled in a basal clump of crinkled leaves in moist cool seasons, mostly spring. It blooms in jewel-bright colors including yellow, pink, crimson, blue, and purple. The recommended species thrive in a cool greenhouse and bloom from seeds sown indoors. *P. malacoides*, Fairy Primrose, Zones 10 to 11, is an attractive 8- to 12-inch primrose that has rounded leaves and dainty pink, lavender-blue, or white flowers in late winter or early spring. *P. sinensis*, Chinese Primrose, a 6- to 12-inch primrose, blooms in late winter or early spring. See also list 29, Primrose.

SOURCE: EVERETT L. MILLER, LANDSCAPE DESIGNER, SOURCE DIRECTOR TO LIVE OAK GARDENS, LOUISIANA, FORMER DIRECTOR OF LONGWOOD GARDENS, IS THE COAUTHOR OF VOLUMES 1 AND 2 OF *THE AMERICAN GARDEN GUIDEBOOK*.

20. ASTER

■ **Asters are best known as fall flowers, but there are attractive spring-blooming asters, too. The blossoms are small and daisylike, usually with bright yellow or purple centers, and are borne singly or in sprays. In bloom, the plants are covered with blue, dark purple, lavender, pink, rosy red, or white flowers. Asters are good companion plants with autumn's earthy browns, russets, golds, oranges, and crimsons. The light blue 'Professor Kippenburg', which is only 15 to 18 inches tall, can have 300 to 400 of the tiny flowers on one plant.**

The plant itself is a leafy bush and, depending on height, is handsome at the back or front of a small border and a good green filler during the months before it comes into bloom. Nice used as a lone specimen plant, or in massed plantings. Set shorter types at the front of the border and the taller sorts at the back. The height of tall fall asters can be reduced a little by pinching or shearing in the spring when they are 6 to 8 inches high.

Spring-flowering asters such as *A. alpinus* are well suited to the rock garden and the front of a perennial border, though they are less vigorous than the fall bloomers. This type sets bud the previous season, which accounts for the early bloom. In contrast, the two best summer-fall asters, the quite similar *A. novi-belgii* and *A. novae-angliae*, set buds on the current season's growth and bloom in late summer and autumn.

Sprays of asters—wild as well as the domesticated types—are superb in fresh arrangements; they're nice when dried, too. Pale pink asters are especially lovely with the big pale and deep pink dahlias that bloom in late summer and fall.

Follow-on Plants: Follow spring-blooming asters with annual edgers like Sweet Alyssum, Ageratum, *Catharanthus roseus* (Rose Periwinkle, Madagascar Periwinkle), and *Sanvitalia procumbens* (Creeping Zinnia, Trailing Zinnia).

ASTER (ass-ter)

Michaelmas Daisy, Starwort, Frost Flower

Asters grow almost everywhere on this continent. They flourish wild along the roadside and in open meadow gardens where they spread and form big thickets. One of the most popular white asters in Europe is *A. ericoides*, a wildflower that grows luxuriantly in open fields and along roadsides from Maine to Florida.

The much larger, mumlike flower sold as an annual aster is *Callistephus chinensis*, China Aster. It is a member of the Aster Family and a great late summer to fall flower in the aster color range—lavender-blues, pinks, rosy reds, and white. For information, see list 33, Annuals for Fall.

Culture: Perennial asters grow so vigorously they are considered weeds in some areas. Sow seed in spring for bloom the following year. For bloom this year set out divisions spaced 12 inches apart.

Site them in full sun in well-drained, somewhat acidic soil—moderate fertility is best for most types. Plants growing in very fertile soil may need staking. Asters require good drainage—wet winter soils will rot most of them. Although soils wet in winter may shorten the life of many, some asters can live in slightly damp meadows; they can withstand some drought and flower in bright shade.

Pinch the short tips back 2 to 3 inches once in spring and again a month later to keep the plants stocky and avoid the need to stake. Some asters that flower in summer may rebloom if deadheaded. Taller types may need staking to stand upright.

Divide aster plantings every 2 or 3 years. Discard the main section and replant the outer portions. In areas where powdery mildew is a problem, choose resistant cultivars.

A. alpinus   Zones 4-7

A late spring or early summer bloomer according to region, it is 6 to 8 inches high and bears solitary purple blossoms with yellow centers. Near-neutral, well-drained soil is best, and it prefers a cool climate. 'Goliath' is 15 inches high and bears 2½- to 3-inch flowers.

A. amellus Italian Aster   Zones 5-8

The flowers are purple with orange-yellow centers and bloom in late spring and early summer. 'Framfieldii', 24 to 30 inches tall, has lilac-blue flowers. Better in cooler climates and nice in the rock garden.

A. × frikartii   Zones 5-8

Excellent. The lasting, scented, powder puff flowers are 2 to 3 inches across, mostly blue or lilac-blue with bright yellow centers. In cool regions they bloom during summer and fall on loose, bushy mounds with lots of branches; in the South they last even longer. The cultivars are upright, 18 to 24 or 30 inches tall. Provide a winter mulch of evergreen boughs beginning around Christmas. Divide every 3 to 4 years in spring. Somewhat mildew-resistant.

The following cultivars are recommended:
'Wonder of Staffa', to 36 inches, a handsome plant with big, clear lavender-blue flowers.
'Mönch', 24 to 36 inches, is similar but darker blue with stronger stems and later flowers. It is considered the finest.

A. novae-angliae New England Aster

Zones 3-8

In a meadow, these hardy plants develop into thickets 4 to 6 feet tall, covered in late summer and early fall with lasting, daisylike, fluffy little violet-purple blooms. The leaves may be rough or hairy. Survives early frosts. New cultivars may be white, rose, or ruby red.

The following are recommended:
'Harrington's Pink', an unusual salmon-pink, late-blooming.
'Alma Potschke' has rose pink flowers on stiff stems that are 3 feet tall. This is one of the showiest, most striking asters and well worth planting.
'Purple Dome' is 18 inches high with a spread of 36 inches. The flowers are semidouble with deep violet ray florets surrounding a bright yellow central disk. Blooms from August to the first frosts.

TOP Double 'Marie Ballard' aster, an old favorite, is a cultivar of *Aster novi-belgii*, New York aster, a valuable fall flower. (Viette)

ABOVE New England aster, 'Alma Potschke', is recommended as one of the showiest asters. Similar to the New York aster, but somewhat taller. Outstanding in a meadow. (Beattie)

RIGHT *Aster* × *frikartii*, an excellent scented blue hybrid, flowers all summer in cool regions, and is an excellent choice for the South. (Viette)

A. novi-belgii   Zones 4-8

Known as the New York Aster, it is violet, blooms in early fall, and is similar to the New England Aster above. The species may be 1 foot to 6 feet tall, according to variety and location. The cultivars are generally shorter than *A. novae-angliae* and the leaves are nearly smooth; provide these with fertile soil. Pinch out the tips early in the season to encourage bushier plants.

The following are highly recommended:

'Alert', 12 to 15 inches tall, with masses of ruby red flowers; one of the best dwarf reds.

'Blue Lake', 36 inches tall, a spectacular medium blue with a yellow disk and sturdy stems, choice for cutting.

'Fellowship', 24 to 30 inches tall, with double light pink flowers.

'Marie Ballard', 36 inches tall, an old favorite with large, fluffy, double powder blue flowers.

'Patricia Ballard', 30 inches tall, a double rose-pink.

'Professor Kippenburg', 15 to 18 inches tall, light blue, sometimes semi double. There can be 300 to 400 flowers on one plant.

'Rose Serenade', 15 to 18 inches tall, a dwarf rose pink.

'Snow Cushion', 12 inches tall, a clear white.

'Snowsprite', 12 to 15 inches tall, with white semidouble ray flowers around a yellow disk.

A. tartaricus Tartarian Aster   Zones 4-8

This is a very late aster, 3 to 6 feet tall. During fall it bears many blue to purple flowers with yellow centers that last until frost.

A. thomsonii 'Nanus'   Zones 4-9

A neat, bushy late-summer aster that bears very pretty 1- to 2-inch, daisylike lilac flowers on plants 12 to 18 inches high. It blooms from late summer until frost. Lovely at the front of the garden.

A. tongolensis 'Wartburg Star'   Zones 5-8

One of the early asters, it is 12 or 15 to 24 inches tall, and forms mats of hairy deep green leaves 3 to 5 inches long. Solitary 2-inch blue or violet flowers with orange or yellow disks are borne in summer. Divide after flowering. Short-lived in the South.

SOURCE: DR. DAVID J. BEATTIE, DEPARTMENT OF HORTICULTURE, PENNSYLVANIA STATE UNIVERSITY, MAINTAINS TEST GARDENS AND HAS PUBLISHED MORE THAN 100 SCIENTIFIC AND POPULAR ARTICLES AND TEXTBOOK CHAPTERS ON HORTICULTURE.

21. ASTILBE

■ **Astilbes are open, airy plants of great beauty whose spike-like flower plumes brighten semishaded areas for four to six weeks in late spring and summer. The flowerheads are composed of masses of small florets ranging from palest pink and coral to bright red and creamy white. There are dwarfs suited to the rock garden, but most cultivars are 18 to 36 inches, occasionally to 4 feet tall. The deeply cut foliage may be green or bronze, is attractive both before and after flowering, and makes a good filler for the middle or back of the border. Standing alone, a mature astilbe in full bloom is a stunning accent plant. A mass of astilbes in bloom is a glorious tapestry of color, and the cut flowers are lasting and good for drying.**

Although most astilbe cultivars flower from June through the middle of July, season-long color can be achieved by planting both early and late bloomers. For instance, use the early white 'Washington' and pink 'Europa' with the later light pink 'Sprite', and late bloomers such as the lilac-flowered 'Superba' and 'Pumila'.

Companion Plants: Astilbes are nice in a bold texture of bergenia and hosta; they are also complemented by fine ferns and bleeding hearts.

ASTILBE (ass-*till*-bee) Spiraea, Perennial Spiraea

With their triangular, upright, sometimes nodding, plumes, the astilbes resemble some *Spiraea* shrubs. Botanically, astilbe is closest to *Aruncus*, Goatsbeard, and *Filipendula*, Meadowsweet. There is an American native, *A. biternata*, a gangly 6-footer, but most of the cultivars in our gardens are descendants of Asian species. The largest group of cultivars were developed by George Arends of Rondsdorf, Germany, and named for him—*Astilbe × arendsii*.

The name astilbe means "without color" and refers to the leaves. A few cultivars have simple leaves, but most have compound, three-part leaves. Those that are shiny likely to belong to the species *A. simplicifolia*.

Culture: Crown divisions may be set out in spring or late summer. Grows best in light shade in rich, moist, well-drained, humusy soil, but it also succeeds in moderate climates in full sun, so long as they are kept moist. Astilbes tolerate a wide range of soil types, but they seem to prefer a slightly acid pH. They are heavy feeders. Fertilize before growth starts and again lightly after the first real frost. Apply a complete fertilizer at the rate of 30 to 40 pounds for each 1000 square feet, or scratch a small handful of

Astilbe trials show the color range and beauty of these airy plants that bloom in semi-shade in late spring and summer. The deeply-cut leaves make it a good filler for the middle or back of the border. Dried plumes and handsome foliage last all summer. (Beattie)

TOP 'Fanal', the first cultivar with bronze leaves and red flowers, is the most popular. (Beattie)

TOP, LEFT A spreading astilbe, little 'Pumila', which is very drought-resistant, makes a good ground cover. (Beattie)

BOTTOM, LEFT Vigorous 'Veronica Klose' is recommended for edging. (Beattie)

ABOVE Big *A. taquetii* 'Superba' can grow to 4 feet high. It is one of the last astilbes to flower and is more tolerant of heat than most. (Beattie)

fertilizer into the soil around each plant. Some suppliers ship crowns bare root in early spring; follow their instructions for planting. The keys to success, particularly in summer gardens, are sustained moisture and summer mulches.

Early bloomers may get frostbitten at the northern edge of their hardiness zones; in areas where late spring frosts are prevalent provide a winter mulch of pine boughs.

Astilbes are not long-lived—they must be renewed by division every 3 or 4 years. Division is successful almost any time from early spring to August. Crown divisions potted up in early fall and moved indoors in late fall to either sunny or semishaded areas will usually bloom.

A. × arendsii cultivars — Zones 4-8

This is a big, beautiful plant for the middle and back of the border. Its many graceful cultivars flower from late spring through midsummer. The height is 18 to 24 inches or 4 feet. The foliage of many cultivars is red in spring and some remains distinctly reddish through summer.

The following cultivars are recommended:

WHITES

'Deutschland', to 24 inches, creamy white. It is one of the earliest, an old favorite and a good indoor astilbe.
'Snowdrift', to 24 inches, whiter, very floriferous. Midseason.
'Professor van der Wielen', to 36 inches, a beautiful white with open, graceful flower spikes. Midseason.
'Bridal Veil', about 30 inches, off-white. Also recommended for containers. Midseason.
'Europa', over 24 inches, pale pink. Also recommended for containers. Provide a winter mulch in Zone 4. Early.
'White Gloria', 24 inches tall, white with tight, blocky flowerheads. Early.

PINKS

'Europa', 15 to 24 inches tall, a soft pink that usually begins the flowering season. Good indoors, too.
'Cattleya', 36 inches tall, orchid pink. One of the best, it combines vigorous growth with graceful bloom in slightly nodding plumes. Blooms with 'Peach Blossom'. Early.
'Erica', 30 to 36 inches tall, vigorous bloomer with very long plumes. The young leaves are displayed at an upward angle and the foliage is distinctly reddish. Midseason.
'Ostrich Plume', over 36 inches, with arching, bright pink blooms. Midseason.

ROSE TO RED

'Fanal', 24 inches, one of the earliest, best, and most popular astilbes. This was the first cultivar developed with bronze leaves and red flowers. Also recommended for containers .
'Montgomery', to 23 and 30 inches, red, with full, wide plumes. Early to midseason.
'Red Sentinel', 30 to 36 inches, carmine red, narrow, and erect. Midseason.

A. chinensis — Zones 3-8

A small, dense, late-blooming plant 8 or 12 to 16 inches high that spreads by creeping stolons. Suitable for ground cover and for edging the front of a tall border. After the popular A. × arendsii cultivars have gone by, these plants raise tall mauve-pink flowerheads on stiffly narrow panicles high above the foliage clump. Easily divided and moved in spring or fall.

The following cultivar is recommended for ground cover.
'Pumila', to 12 inches, lilac; begins to bloom in late summer and continues until fall. It is the only one that spreads. Probably the most drought-tolerant astilbe and a good ground cover substitute for the overused juniper "rugs." The only astilbe that spreads.

For edging, plant the following cultivars.
'Finale', 14 to 18 inches, pale mauve-rose. Late.
'Serenade', 14 inches tall, rose red. Late.
'Veronica Klose', to 20 inches, purple-rose with purple-tinged stems. Outstanding; this is among the newest and best cultivars, very vigorous and floriferous. Late.

A. × rosea 'Peach Blossom' — Zones 4-8

Choice for damp places. One of the early bloomers, it is 36 to 48 inches tall with elongated salmon-pink plumes.

A. simplicifolia 'Sprite' — Zones 4-8

If you had to choose a single astilbe, this would be the one. It has much-divided, bright green foliage, masses of light-pink florets borne on slightly pendulous panicles, followed by attractive rust-colored seedheads. The total height of the plant is 12 inches. It begins blooming in midsummer and continues for several weeks. Another attractive cultivar of the species is the bright rose-red 'Afrodite', 18 to 20 inches tall.

A. taquetii (syn. A. chinensis var. taquetii) 'Purpurkerze' (Purple Crown) — Zones 4-8

A big late bloomer nearly 4 feet tall; vigorous and floriferous. The florets are deep pink, and the stems are tinged purple. It is an outstanding improved selection of the popular 'Superba'. 'Superba', 24 to 48 inches, produces lilac blooms in late summer and fall. More tolerant of heat and drought than most astilbes, but avoid them where Japanese beetles are a problem.

SOURCE: DR. DAVID J. BEATTIE, DEPARTMENT OF HORTICULTURE, PENNSYLVANIA STATE UNIVERSITY, MAINTAINS EXTENSIVE TEST GARDENS, AND HAS PUBLISHED MORE THAN 100 SCIENTIFIC AND POPULAR ARTICLES AND TEXTBOOK CHAPTERS ON HORTICULTURE.

22. CAMPANULA

■ These gossamer cups—most often blue but also lavender, white, and sometimes pink—are called bell-flowers, but in some of the small forms the flowers are more like stars spangled on a canopy of green. From a few inches to a few feet tall, they have an airy dancing grace. There are some 250 species and the group has great appeal for collectors. Erect types are often showy enough for use in mixed flower borders but collectors, seekers of charm rather than glamor, delight in more subtle species. Many are good cutting flowers.

Generally, small species withstand warm southern nights best, although *C. persicifolia* is a tall campanula that performs well in the South, best for beginners. Where heat precludes campanulas, try look-alikes *Platycodon* or *Adenophora confusa*, which is called Ladybells.

The species here are presented in the order of preference of our Source, Pamela Harper.

Companion Plants: Hostas are good companions in warm regions where campanulas need protection from hot sun; try blue Siberian irises where they flower together; combine campanulas with gray artemisias, white flowers, and either yellow or pink flowers, but not both. Campanulas can be preceded by crocus.

CAMPANULA (kam-*pan*-yew-luh)
Bellflower
The flowering period can be 2 or even 3 months in late spring or early summer and into fall, according to species and region. Where winters are mild some are evergreen and form mats or mounds of foliage that brighten the dull months. Taller types with graceful, trailing flower stems develop in the romantic disarray suited to cottage gardens. There are low, mounded forms for rock gardens and creepers that flourish in, around, and through dry stone walls. A few are hardy in alpine gardens. On the whole, they're long lasting and many species multiply and naturalize quite rapidly.

Culture: Well-prepared, neutral-range garden soil and full sun are all most campanulas require to thrive where summers are cool. In warm climates they need rich, moist, well-drained soil with lots of humus and shade in the afternoon. Six hours of afternoon sun kills most campanulas in Zone 7 and southward. Single-flowered campanulas grow readily from seed and most multiply from root cuttings and divisions planted in early spring. Provide a permanent mulch as protection against summer heat and deadhead to prolong the flowering period.

CHOICE CAMPANULAS

C. persicifolia Willow Bellflower, Peach Bells — Zones 3-8

Flowers in summer, 24 to 36 inches tall. Pretty, with upright stems excellent for cutting, it lacks only a long bloom season to be a perfect plant. The flowers are single or double, blue or white, and 'Telham Beauty' is a large-flowered pale lavender (frequently is not true to the name as supplied by American nurseries). Where winters are mild, the good basal foliage is evergreen, forming neat mats that spread steadily out around the edges without being invasive. The white form is beautiful with blue Siberian irises where they come into flower together. Moving and dividing are easy but unnecessary, unless performance drops off. Needs no fertilizing or other regular attention. Tolerant of most sites and any reasonable fertile soil. *C. grandis* (syn. *latiloba*), sometimes included under this species, is a good plant that spreads more rapidly, sending up new shoots that need corralling 6 inches or more from the parent.

C. portenschlagiana   Zones 4-8
Upward-facing lavender flowers in spring on clumps 4 to 6 inches tall. Nice in dry walls, where it weaves its way along the cracks. If the cold isn't excessive, it maintains a green mist of little leaves over the earth in winter. Excellent ground cover at the front of the border over early *Crocus chrysanthus* hybrids. Very adaptable to cool summers. Spreads fast but is not invasive. In the South, where it needs shade, it is especially attractive growing with yellow-leaved hostas. Nice with snowdrops and coming up through crocuses.

C. carpatica Tussock Bellflower   Zones 3-8
Flowers in summer, 9 to 12 inches tall. Short-lived but bears masses of blue flowers and is quickly and easily grown from seed. Best in rock gardens and raised beds. In cool regions the flowering season is lasting but the plant is intolerant of extremes—too dry, too wet, or too hot. Not a good choice where slugs are a problem. Also called Carpathian harebell.

C. lactiflora   Zones 5-7
Milky blue or white flowers are borne in summer on plants 3 to 5 feet tall. Very variable in color—the flowers also may be deep blue. Where the spring is long and cool, this is one of the best perennials, an easy, long-lived plant that self-sows and tolerates even poor, dry soil. It has a cloud-soft look and usually needs staking. There's a delightful pale pink form, 'Loddon Anna'. Perfect for a mixed border.

C. poscharskyana   Zones 3-7
Flowers in spring, 8 to 12 inches high. Evergreen in mild regions. Long stems of starry blue-lilac flowers radiate out from the clump. Blooms into fall, especially if sheared at midsummer. Tolerant of poor soil and drought where summers are cool. Spreads rapidly enough for ground cover but too quickly for rock gardens or borders. The milky white 'Elizabeth Frost' is less rampant.

C. garganica   Zones 6-8
Flowers in spring, 5 to 6 inches tall. Features masses of tiny, starry blue flowers and clumps of gray-green foliage that increase fairly slowly. Good in rock gardens and walls, and excellent at the front of raised beds. It flattens tiny ivy-shaped leaves against earth or wall and sends out trailing stems. *Hortus Third* classes this as a variety of *C. elatines*, Adriatic Bellflower.

C. glomerata Clustered Bellflower Zones 3-8
Deep, rich purple or white flowers in early summer, 12 to 18 inches tall. A robust plant north of Philadelphia, it is tolerant of wet soil and showy enough to be a strong accent in the flower border. Nice with ferns and with orangish apricot tones as in some hybrids of *Lychnis,* for instance. The cut flowers are lasting. Somewhat coarse and overabundant foliage in proportion to the flowers. Spreads quite rapidly in good soil and likes moisture. 'Superba' is a strong violet-blue; 'Joan Elliot' is paler. There's a white and

FACING PAGE Tall willow bellflower, *Campanula persicifolia*, for beginners, with poppies and lupines. (Harper)

TOP, LEFT *C. poscharskyana* with *Chrysogonum virginianum*, lasts spring to fall, if sheared at midsummer. (Harper)

TOP, RIGHT The Italian bellflower, *C. isophylla*, trailing evergreen species, choice for collectors. (Harper)

ABOVE *C. portenschlagiana*, an excellent bellflower for rock walls and as ground cover. (Harper)

LEFT Canterbury bells, cottage garden favorites that flower in spring. (Harper)

a dwarf form, variety *acaulis,* 3 to 6 inches high. Both seeds and plants are available.

C. latifolia   Zones 3-7

Flowers in early summer on spiky stems 4 to 5 feet tall, a welcome vertical for mixed borders and mounded forms. First-rate in the Pacific Northwest, but not where summers are hot. The white 'Alba' is particularly attractive. Most of the foliage is in short basal clumps and the running rootstock spreads rapidly.

OTHER BELLFLOWERS OF NOTE

C. rapunculoides Rampion   Zones 3-11

Summer-flowering, 2 to 4 feet tall. Multiplies too rapidly for gardens, but is ideal for naturalizing.

C. trachelium Nettleleaved Bellflower, Throatwort   Zones 5-8

Summer-flowering on erect stems 24 to 36 inches tall. Similar to rampion but not invasive. A nice single- or double-flowered plant, white or lilac. Hard to find but can be grown from seed.

C. pyramidalis Chimney Bellflower Zones 8-11

Summer-flowering, 5-foot tall variety that usually requires staking. Quite beautiful, an erect, branching perennial best considered as an annual or biennial and used as a short-term container plant.

C. rotundifolia Bluebell, Harebell   Zones 2-7

Gracefully nodding blue flowers in late spring and summer, 6 to 18 inches tall. Dainty but too insubstantial for the border. Thrives in moist soil, pH 5.5 to 6.5. In the Pacific Northwest it self-sows generously and is ideal for naturalizing in the casual garden or rock garden.

C. cochleariifolia   Zones 6-7

Summer-flowering, 4 to 6 inches tall. A mat-forming, dainty but sturdy little charmer for the rock garden, where it quickly weaves its way among rocks and other plants.

C. isophylla Italian Bellflower, Star-of-Bethlehem, Falling-stars   Zone 8

Summer-flowering, a trailing evergreen species about 4 inches tall. Choice for ardent collectors. This is the loveliest campanula of all, but it is not hardy where temperatures fall below freezing for long, and it doesn't thrive in extreme heat. Pretty for hanging baskets and greenhouses. Looks like a refined *C. poscharskyana.*

C. medium Canterbury-bells   Biennial

Flowers in spring, 2 to 4 feet tall. Best in cool regions and glorious when massed, a cottage garden favorite. Where summer nights are warm, performs well only if started very early and set out in the garden before the heat arrives. Sow seeds every spring for bloom the following year.

SOURCE: PAMELA HARPER, A HORTICULTURAL AUTHOR, PHOTOGRAPHER, AND LECTURER, HAS GARDENED IN ENGLAND, CONNECTICUT, MARYLAND, AND VIRGINIA. SHE IS THE AUTHOR OF *PERENNIALS: HOW TO SELECT, GROW AND ENJOY,* WITH FREDERICK MCGOURTY, AND OF *DESIGNING WITH PERENNIALS.*

23. MUM—DAISY (CHRYSANTHEMUM)

■ **When the leaves begin to fall and earth tones take over the garden, it's chrysanthemum time. Little bright yellow button mums, great fancy spider mums, fat round football mums, cushion mums in lavender, pink, white, and even real red (which is surprisingly good with the others), all the glowing earth tones to deep maroon—these and their daisy relatives have been celebrities since they first were taken up in China 500 years before the birth of Christ.**

All the mums are rather easy to grow and all can be moved to where color is wanted in almost any season without much harm to the plants.

Companion Plants and Follow-on Plants: Dusty-miller, 'Silver Mound' artemisia, miniature zinnias, and French marigolds are all good companions. Sweet Alyssum makes a cool living mulch. To follow-on, try ornamental grasses, list 53. They're beautiful as the mums come into flower and remain attractive into winter before being cut down in January.

CHRYSANTHEMUM (kriss-*anth*-em-um)

For the home gardener, mums divide into four groups: disposable cushion mums to pop into the garden for instant fall color; the very similar hardy garden mums for those who grow their own fall color and retain the plants; florists' mums for collectors and connoisseurs; and summer-flowering species mums with daisy flowers such as the Shasta Daisy, Pyrethrum, and Feverfew. An unusual little creeping mum, *C. weyrichii* 'White Bomb', flowers late and is recommended for rock gardens (see list 66).

Culture: Chrysanthemums will live for at least 3 years if the weather is reasonable and the garden soil well prepared. However, for the best plants and flowers, renew your mums every year or at least every 2 years, as described below. Move mums to another area of the garden every 3 years. Plant the big hedge or climax marigolds in their place for a year or 2 to give the soil organisms a change of diet, then replant the mums. They require full sun. Winter dormancy is vital; a winter mulch applied after the ground has frozen guarantees it.

Well-drained soil is essential to mums. If drainage is a problem, create a raised bed. Chrysanthemums prefer loamy soil but tolerate any reasonably good, deeply dug garden soil that is slightly acid, in the area of pH 6.5. Digging in rotted manure, compost, peat moss or leaf mold enhances plant performance. In early spring, work super-phosphate into the soil; broadcast at the rate of 3 pounds per 100 square feet. Every few years scratch some dolomitic agricultural limestone into the soil around the roots of established plantings. It is rich in calcium and magnesium, which are very beneficial to mums.

Plant mums in spring—March to June, according to region. Soak the plants first if they appear wilted. Dig holes twice as big as the plants. Set the root balls at the level at which they were growing, 12 to 18 inches apart according to the size of the plant. Firm the soil around each plant and water thoroughly.

An inch of rain or hose water each week is enough for mums. They enjoy a regular monthly feeding of liquid 20-20-20 until August. A timed release fertilizer can be applied early in the growing season,. There are formulations of organic fertilizers timed for release in 3, 4, 8 and 12 months. Stop fertilizing when the buds begin to show color.

Winter care is simple: when flowering stops, or after a frost, cut the plants back to between 3 and 6 inches above the ground. After the ground has frozen, water the plants thoroughly and mulch to 3 inches deep with salt hay, pine boughs, bark, or cut-back mum branches if they are thick. Remove this temporary mulch when new growth comes shooting up through it in spring.

In the North plant early and midseason mums. The catalogs give bloom dates. Plants that winter over in the South will bloom in spring or early summer unless trained back by pinching, as described below. Pinching stops about July 1 in the North; in the South, July 15.

QUICK FALL COLOR— CUSHION MUMS

These potted mums are sold already flowering in early fall and are used to fill holes left by the passing of summer flowers. Tightly budded, usually smallish plants to 16 inches, though sometimes much bigger, they cover themselves with flowers 2½ to 3 and 4 inches across. The blossoms may be formed like asters, or have a raised (cushion) center, and there are also perky, bright button mums. Cushion mums bloom into early frosts with watering and minimal care. They'll drape themselves over a wall or, planted closely, the dense foliage and stiff stems support each other. Staking and pinching aren't necessary.

This type of mum is set out without much preparation. Generally they are treated as annuals and discarded after flowering. In most regions the cushions don't have time to develop good root systems before winter. But if left in the garden, some will come back, especially if winters are mild and the autumn was warm and long. They tend to sprawl and grow wild the second year, and will bloom in spring and early summer if not severely pinched back. There are innumerable cultivars. Look for plants loaded with buds and healthy green leaves right to the soil line, and buy by color. If they come back and you like them, handle them as hardy mums (see below).

LASTING PLANTS— HARDY GARDEN MUMS

This is the important group for gardeners interested in growing rather than buying a fall display. The plants are similar to cushion mums, but with larger flowers. In this group the buttons become pom pons. In early spring, root cuttings are set out in the flowering border, containers, or anywhere fall color or cutting flowers are needed in the landscape. The flowers are 2½ to 3 or 4 inches across and the mature height about 36 inches unless another description is given. Some hardy garden mums are offered in fall with flowers already opening. These big sizes are a lot more expensive than the spring plantlets. They need to be set out in early fall to survive winter in good condition.

TOP, LEFT Painted daisy, or pyrethrum, 'Scarlet Glow', *Chrysan-themum coccineum*. (Viette)

TOP, RIGHT Marguerite, *C. leucanthemum*, the field daisy, a great naturalizer. (American Horticultural Society)

BOTTOM, LEFT Dainty, daisyflowered feverfew is *C. parthenium*. (Viette)

BOTTOM, RIGHT Nippon daisy is *C. nipponicum*, a popular autumn mum. (Viette)

All hardy mums that winter over and grow at will are woody as well as leggy, and flower long before the desired time in fall. To get a worthwhile display from last year's mums, follow a procedure called "scotch cutting"—dig up the plants in spring, pull off and replant strong new side shoots, and discard the old central crown.

To make the plants produce more flowers, encourage branching by pinching back the branch tips beginning about 2 weeks after they have been planted in spring. This is called "stopping" and will cause 3 new shoots to form on each branch tip. Stopping can be continued until the new growth slows about midsummer—July 1 in cold areas, July 15 in warm areas.

The plants recommended here are heat tolerant. With watering and care they will grow all over the U.S. They are recommended for performance and durable beauty, ease of care, and resistance to pest and diseases.

The form called Decorative is a larger cushion mum.

RED

'Antoinette Ladygo', velvety red.
'Mischief', red semidouble.
'Remember Me', red spoon.

PINK

'Carrousel', 3- to 4-inch aster-purple quill petals, 24 inches tall.
'Small Wonder', dwarf pink pom pon.
'Stardom', very hardy pink daisy.

YELLOW

'Charles Nye', yellow pom pon.
'Ginger', yellow-bronze decorative.
'Ruby Breithaupt', yellow decorative.
'Sea Urchin', greenish yellow.
'Sombrero', 3- to 5-inch flowers, bright lemon yellow with good sprays.
'Sunburst', golden yellow spider.
'Yellow Starlet', very hardy.

WHITE

'Ballerina', 2½ inch, pure white, quill form flowers. Prolific bloomer.
'French Vanilla', strong , 24 inches tall.
'Frolic', 2½-inch flowers, strong spreading plant.
'Pearls,' frost-tolerant white pom pon.
'Raggedy Ann', snow white.
'Starfire', pure white, strong stems.

FOR COLLECTORS— FLORISTS' MUMS

C. × morifolium (syn. *Dendranthema grandiflora*) Florist's Chrysanthemum, Mum Zones 5-8
This species is considered a parent of the fall mums—the cushions, the hardy garden mums, and the florist's mums. Florist's mums are plants for collectors and experienced gardeners with time to spend training them. They are classed in 13 groups according to flower form; several of them are big, extravagant flowers.

But for ordinary flower borders there are many interesting mum forms—mums with petals that are incurved (football mums), reflexed, quilled, spoon-shaped, or spidery. There are singles and semidoubles and anemone-flowered blooms as well. Any of these may be trained for bonsai or to a cascade form. They are set out as small plants in spring and grow so fast almost daily training is required to turn them into the show plants they are meant to be.

Disbudding is the key to the size of mums. For the largest blooms, a plant is kept to 3 main stems, each of which will have just one huge flower. All lateral branches appearing at the leaf axils are removed at regular intervals of about 10 days. Every branch removed eliminates a flower. Untrained, the florist's mums will have many more, but smaller, flowers.

HARVEST GIANT FOOTBALL MUMS

Recommended here are tall chrysanthemums with large football blooms from mid-September to killing frosts. For mum suppliers, see the Appendix.
'Golden Arrow', large incurved bright gold-yellow.
'Golden Promise', large incurved, warm gold.
'Indian Summer', 4- to 5-inch scarlet flower with a bronze reverse.
'September Song', 6 inches across, incurved, medium-deep rose pink.
'Silver Song', huge, stunning ivory white.
'Touchdown', huge rose pink flower.

SPECIES MUMS

The main show for the big mums is in the fall, but the species mums are our beautiful summer daisies and belong in every flowering border. They are delightful cut flowers. No special training is needed for these plants and most will repeat for 3 years. Plants from seed usually come into bloom the second year. Easier is to set out root divisions in early spring.

C. coccineum Pyrethrum, Painted Daisy Zones 3-7
Showy 3-inch red, pink, or white single or double daisylike flowers with yellow centers on plants 12 to 24 inches tall. They bloom in early summer and thrive in sandy loam in cool regions, but may need winter mulch. The foliage is rich green. Choose dwarf cultivars which need no support.

C. leucanthemum Oxeye Daisy, White Daisy, Marguerite Zones 3-9
This is the common field daisy that blooms in sunny places in early summer all over the U.S. and Canada. The plants spread by rootstock and seeds. Recommended for meadow gardens and wild plantings.

C. nipponicum Nippon Chrysanthemum, Nippon Daisy Zones 5-9
A good border flower and hardy perennial that reaches 3 to 5 feet in height. It bears white, daisylike flowers with greenish centers from September or October, according to region, until killing frost.

Earth-toned cushion mums are planted already blooming for instant fall color. (Frease)

C. pacificum Zones 5-9
Ground cover mum with nice little green leaves edged thinly with silver on a 12-inch-high plant. It spreads rapidly to make a 3½-foot mat, and bears very small tansy-like flowers in October. Introduced recently by the National Arboretum from Japan.

C. parthenium Feverfew Zones 4-9
Lovely old-fashioned mum 12 to 36 inches tall that bears masses of little 1-inch, daisylike white or yellow button-type flowers with yellow centers in late summer. Self-sows generously. Dwarf forms are used for edging but not in the warm South. 'Aureum', Golden-feather, 8 to 12 inches tall, has yellow foliage that turns green when the plant blooms.

C. × superbum Shasta Daisy Zones 5-9
Big, beautiful, shaggy daisies that flower in early summer on plants 2 to 4 feet tall. There are singles and doubles. Plant shastas 12 inches apart in deep, rich soil. Remove spent blooms. Keep soil evenly moist. Single types need full sun; doubles do better in light shade. 'Aglaya', the Lace Daisy, 24 inches tall, has long-lasting, fully double flowers. 'Alaska', 24 to 36 inches tall, the best-known older shasta, has pure white flowers 3 inches across on yellow centers; very hardy, even in Zone 3. 'Cobham Gold' is almost yellow, 15 to 18 inches tall. 'Little Miss Moffat', 14-inch semidouble, flowers July and August. 'Marconi', 24 inches with double-frilled, 6-inch blossoms, blooms in June and is a superb cut flower. 'Polaris', 28 inches, flowers in June and July, and later if cut back; the large, single flowers are up to 7 inches across.

SOURCE: BARBARA C. VAUGHAN AND THE OLD DOMINION CHRYSANTHEMUM SOCIETY, INC. OF FALLS CHURCH, VIRGINIA, A CHAPTER OF THE NATIONAL CHRYSANTHEMUM SOCIETY.

24. DAYLILY (HEMEROCALLIS)

■ Modern daylilies anchor the perennial garden through late spring, summer, and into fall with lilylike flowers in many warm shades, and the plants are easy to grow and long-lived. Whether you plant 4- to 5-foot giants with huge 8-inch flowers at the back of the border, or 8- to 12-inch dwarfs with 1-inch blooms near the front, each plant offers a brilliant, nonstop show for 3 to 4 weeks. Some rebloom immediately, extending their flowering period to six weeks, while others rebloom in the fall. A bonus is daylily foliage—as the plants develop, strap-shaped leaves fountain up, screening the yellowing remains of spring bulbs.

An established three-year-old clump of daylilies produces many blooms on stalks (scapes) averaging 24 to 36 inches tall. There are solid colors and patterned types. Patterns include a contrasting eyezone, a lighter watermark near the center, a deeper color edge on segments. Daylilies come in all colors except blue—yellow, gold, orange, lavender, purple, pink, peach, coral, salmon, persimmon, melon, red, almost-black, and white. The flowers may be round or triangular, recurved, flat, trumpet-shaped, single, or double. Some are fragrant, for instance 'Fragrant Light', 'Hyperion', 'Ida Jane', and 'Citrina'.

In the text that follows, the asterisk * indicates cultivars that perform well in both the North and the South.

Follow-on Plants: Japanese anemones, asters, chrysanthemums, boltonia, and liatris are some tall late-bloomers that flower into autumn after the major daylily show goes by.

HEMEROCALLIS (hem-er-oh-*kal*-iss)
Daylily

A few old-fashioned species are of interest to collectors and for planting with herbs: *H. fulva,* the Tawny or Orange Daylily that blooms wild in moderate and cool regions; *H. lilioasphodelus* (syn. *H. flava*), a fragrant yellow recommended on list 62, The Historic Garden; and *H. minor,* a little 18-inch-high daylily that has fragrant lemon yellow flowers. You will probably have to go to specialists to find them.

The popular daylilies are the big modern cultivars. The average daylily blooms over a period of three to four weeks with new flowers every day, or every other day, 1 to 3 per stem, each lasting a day. Every year new plants are introduced that have enhanced blooming habits and fascinating flower variations. All these improvements have given rise to a daylily vocabulary that needs to be understood to make the best plant choices.

"Multiflora" types and some others cover the daylily clump with 3 to 5 blooms per stem every day rather than just one flower every other day. "Extended" bloomers flower in the morning and remain open until 11 P.M. or 1 A.M., a total of 18 to 24 hours. "Nocturnals" open at some point between late afternoon and dawn, and are a good choice in climates with cold summer nights. They stay open throughout the next day.

Another type of daylily is called "reblooming"; these are plants that produce more than one round of flowers per clump. Rebloomers usually flower a second time in late summer or fall, but some rebloom immediately after the initial flowering period, prolonging the display.

Daylilies bloom in the Viettes' front garden in late spring, summer, and into fall in near-whites and shades of melon, pink, orange, yellow. (Viette)

LEFT 'Red Spinel', very showy, opens in the evening. (Viette)
BELOW 'Joyful Occasion', a green-throated, ruffled daylily. (Viette)
BOTTOM, LEFT 'Pandora's Box', one of the daylilies "evergreen" in frost-free climates. (Viette)
BOTTOM, RIGHT 'Prester John', hose-in-hose-double. (Viette)

Other special words used in identifying daylily performance are diploid and tetraploid. A tetraploid has twice as many chromosomes as a diploid, and often shows intense colors, petals with heavier texture, and stronger stems. Some of the more exotic color patterns are emerging from the tetraploids.

The plants below are divided into daylilies recommended for the cool North, and those that do best in the warm South. "Dormants" give the best performance for the North. They lose their foliage in winter, as do other perennials. Daylilies identified as "evergreen" maintain attractive green foliage only in frost-free climates. Semievergreen plants are hardy in the North. A few evergreen daylilies also are hardy in cold climates and should be mulched for winter. Evergreens in mid-regions may start to grow in an early spring warm spell and be damaged by late frost. Cut the damaged foliage back to below the frosted area—to the ground in extreme cases. They regrow unharmed.

Small-flowered and miniature daylilies are lovely as the sole plant in a small bed or in large containers. The larger tall daylilies are handsome at the back of mixed perennial borders. To make a good show, group 3 to 6 of the same kind, 18 to 24 inches apart. In a mixed border, allow 3 to 6 feet between groups of daylilies and other plants.

Culture: Plant, and when necessary divide, the tuberous roots in mid-spring or early autumn. They flourish in bright sun or under tall trees such as pines, but never succeed near maples or willows that provide only filtered light. Clumps need dividing when bloom production decreases, usually after five years.

Set the crowns of the plants ½ to 1 inch below soil level on a mound of soil, and spread the roots out and down. They tolerate a wide range of soils—poor, rich, sandy, clayey—and moisture can range from wet to moderately dry. Ideally, they should get an inch of water every week or two during the growing season. A year-round light mulch is beneficial.

The seasons of bloom indicated below vary somewhat with climate. Mulch for winter where hardy in Zones 3 through 6.

DAYLILIES FOR NORTHERN (ZONES 7 AND ABOVE) GARDENS

EARLY

'Dancing Shiva', to 22 inches, 5-inch flowers, medium pink with green-yellow throat. Tetraploid; rebloomer; open evenings; dormant.
'Little Cherub', to 22 inches, 3½-inch flowers, light yellow. Evergreen.
'Stella De Oro', 10 to 20 inches, 2¾-inch flowers, gold with a green throat. Hundreds of blooms in a mature (3-year) clump with a height of 20 inches. Rapid increase; rebloomer; open evenings; fragrant; dormant.

EARLY MIDSEASON

'Condilla', 20 inches, 4½-inch flowers, deep gold, hose-in-hose double, serrated segment edges. Excellent bloomer; dormant.

'Jakarta', 32 inches, 5-inch flowers, light yellow with green throat. Round, flat, ruffled shape, very heavy substance. Good bloomer; rebloomer; open evenings; dormant.
'Mary Todd', 26 inches, 6-inch flowers, buff yellow. Good bloomer; tetraploid; semievergreen.
'Ruffled Apricot', 30 inches, 7-inch flowers, apricot, lavender-pink ribs, gold throat. Tetraploid; open evenings; fragrant; dormant.
*'Siloam June Bug', 23 inches, 2¾-inch flowers of deep yellow-gold, dark maroon eyezone, green throat. Rapid increase; dormant.
'Virachoca', 28 inches, 7-inch flowers, bright tangerine, deeper throat. Tetraploid; fragrant; dormant in the North.

MIDSEASON

'Anzac', 28 inches, 6-inch flowers, true brilliant red, yellow-green throat. Rebloomer; open evenings; dormant.
*'Baltimore Oriole', 28 inches, deep velvety red, green throat. Tetraploid; dormant.
'Country Club', to 18 inches, 6-inch flowers, ribbon pink, lavender shading, green throat. Excellent form; dormant.
'Ed Murray', 35 inches, 5-inch flowers, black-red, green throat. Open evenings; dormant.
'Joyful Occasion', 20 inches, 6-inch flowers, medium pink, green throat. Ruffled. Open evenings; evergreen but hardy in the North.
*'Puddin', 24 inches, 2½-inch flowers, lemon yellow, green throat. Rapid increase; nocturnal; dormant.
'Quinn Buck', 26 inches, 7-inch flowers, medium lavender, green throat. Tetraploid; dormant.

LATE MIDSEASON

'Catherine Woodbery', 30 inches, 6-inch flowers, palest orchid-pink, green throat. Very fragrant; open evenings; dormant.
'Cherry Cheeks', 28 inches, 6-inch flowers, deep rose pink, yellow-green throat. Tetraploid; dormant.
'Golden Prize', 26 inches, 7-inch flowers, deep gold. Flat, rounded. Tetraploid; dormant.
'Pardon Me', 18 inches, 2¾-inch flowers, bright cerise-red, green throat. Heavy bloomer; rapid increase; immediate rebloomer; nocturnal; fragrant; dormant.
'Rahotep', 28 inches, 5-inch flowers, rose red with yellow throat; round, ruffled shape. Tetraploid; rebloomer; open evenings; fragrant; dormant.
'Red Spinel', 36 inches, 5½-inch flowers, bright deep red. Very showy. Open evenings; dormant.
'Real Wind', 30 inches, 6½-inch flowers, light orange, rose halo, gold throat. Tetraploid; dormant.
'White Temptation', 24 inches, 6-inch flowers, near-white, light green throat. Ruffled. Nocturnal; semievergreen.

LATE

'Bountiful Valley', 28 inches, 6-inch flowers, lemon yellow, lime throat. Many blooms. Excellent landscaping variety; vigorous; dormant.
'Lady Recurve', 32 inches, 6-inch flowers, light creamy yellow, light green throat. Recurved; open evenings; nocturnal; dormant.
'Fall Farewell', 28 inches, 7-inch flowers, lavender-pink, yellow-green throat. Open evenings; tetraploid; dormant.
'Fall Glow', 28 inches, 6-inch flowers, golden orange, corduroy ribbing. Open evenings; nocturnal; dormant.
'Court of Honor', 25 inches, 5-inch flowers, hot tangerine-pink. Rebloomer.

DAYLILIES FOR SOUTHERN (ZONES 8 AND BELOW) GARDENS

Many of the cultivars listed for northern gardens will also do well in Zones 8 and 9.

EARLY

'Green Glitter', 34 inches, 7-inch flowers, pale yellow, chartreuse throat. Good bloomer; rebloomer; evergreen in the South.

EARLY MIDSEASON

'Baja', 28 inches, 6-inch flowers, deep red, green throat. Tetraploid; rebloomer; evergreen in the South.
'Double Cutie', 18 inches, 4-inch flowers, chartreuse-yellow, hose-in-hose double. Rebloomer; open evenings; evergreen in cooler regions as well as the South.
'Joan Senior', 24 inches, 6-inch flowers, near-white, lime green throat, round, ruffled form. Rebloomer; open evenings; evergreen in cooler regions as well as the South.
'Little Fantastic', 22 inches, 3-inch flowers, rose pink, green throat. Multiflora bloomer with many blooms open at once. Looks like a cushion mum. Evergreen in the South.
*'Lullaby Baby', 25 inches, 3½-inch flowers, lightest pink to white, green throat, rounded form. Good bloomer; open evenings; fragrant; evergreen in the South.
'Pandora's Box', 22 inches, 4-inch flowers, showy cream with a purple eyezone. Evergreen.
*'Prester John', 26 inches, 5-inch blooms of bright gold-orange, green throat, hose-in-hose double. Long blooming season; rebloomer; fragrant; dormant. good in Zones 3 to 9.
'Sebastian', 22 inches, 5½-inch flowers, deep purple, lime green throat. Rebloomer; evergreen even in cooler regions.
*'Siloam Bo Peep', 18 inches, 4½-inch flowers, orchid-pink with a plum eye.
'Sun's Eye', 32 inches, 5-inch flowers, bright yellow, green throat. Round form. Tetraploid; rebloomer; fragrant; evergreen in the South.

MIDSEASON

'Elizabeth Yancey', 30 inches, 5½-inch flowers, light pink with a green throat. Rebloomer; open evenings; evergreen in the South.
'Lavender Dew', 26 inches, 5½-inch flowers, light blue-lavender, chartreuse throat. Fragrant; evergreen in the South.

LATE

'Green Flutter', 22 inches, 3-inch flowers, canary yellow, green throat. Heavy bloomer; rebloomer; open evenings; evergreen in the South.
*'Tender Love', 24 inches, 6½-inch flowers, flesh pink, green throat. Open evenings; dormant.

SOURCE: JOHN MASON ALLGOOD, A HORTICULTURIST, GROWS OVER 3,500 CULTIVARS IN HIS DAYLILY GARDEN IN WALTERBORO, SOUTH CAROLINA, AND SOME OF HIS DAYLILY INTRODUCTIONS HOLD INTERNATIONAL AWARDS. HE HAS BEEN THE EDITOR OF SEVERAL DAYLILY PUBLICATIONS, INCLUDING THE NATIONAL *DAYLILY JOURNAL*.

25. IRIS

■ The stars of late spring and early summer are the spectacular bearded, Siberian, and Japanese irises. With blossoms as big as 8 and 10 inches across, they play variations on the classical iris form—three uprising "standards" and three horizontal or downward-turning "falls"—a form whose elegance made it the emblem of kings. The French fleur-de-lys is an iris. Iris colors cover the rainbow except for true red, and new color combinations are introduced every season.

But there are other wonderful irises. The magnificent 5-foot *Iris pseudacorus* and its relatives lend springtime beauty to damp or watery places. For rock gardens and naturalizing, there are lovely little species and miniatures with foliage like grass and flowers only an inch across. A whole other group of small irises that grow on bulbous roots and bloom very early are described with the other spring bulbs on lists 1 and 2.

The plants recommended below grow from rhizomes or fibrous roots and are classed with perennials rather than bulbs. The plants are arranged within each group according to bloom sequence. With careful selection, you can have irises in bloom for two-thirds of the year.

The American Iris Society has divisions devoted to each of the major types of iris and can be reached through the American Horticultural Society. The best-performing modern irises are available primarily from specialists. The names of distributors appear in the quarterly *Bulletin* of the American Iris Society, and in other nationally distributed garden publications such as *Flower and Garden*, *Horticulture*, and *Fine Gardening*.

Companion Plants: hardy ferns, peonies, *Heuchera*, columbines, lilies, and daylilies make good companions, as does *Stachys byzantina*, Woolly Betony, Lamb's-ears, and, in sunny locations, herbs—both annual and perennial. Hostas are often used in shady areas associated with iris beds.

IRIS (eye-riss)

The peak flowering period is 3 to 5 weeks; by careful selection an iris collection can be in flower from spring to fall. The irises that fit best into a mixed perennial border are the Siberians, whose foliage is attractive all season. The Japanese irises have all the advantages of Siberians except that they require more specific growing conditions; they will not tolerate alkaline soil and need more water than other irises.

Culture: Irises grow from thick, fleshy, elongated roots called rhizomes that have something of the texture of a potato. The rhizome can remain out of the ground for one to several weeks, but should be planted as soon as possible. The best period for planting and transplanting most irises (see beardless below) is midsummer to early fall. Midsummer—July or August—also is the time to divide irises.

Most irises prefer full sun and light, well-drained soil that has been worked to a depth of at least 10 inches. Two to 3 weeks before planting, work bonemeal and a low-nitrogen fertilizer into the top layer of soil. Bury the rhizome with the top just barely beneath the surface of the soil, but with the roots anchored deeply enough to be held firmly in place. Space the plants 8 to 18 inches apart, depending on the type, Dwarf to Tall Bearded. All irises are heavy feeders and need regular fertilization.

FACING PAGE Bearded iris trials at the Viette nursery in Virginia. (Viette)
TOP Fluted Japanese iris, 'Wine Ruffles'. (Lowe)
ABOVE Crested iris, 'Summer Storm'. (Viette)

All the beardless irises, except the Louisianas, require a permanent site as they resent being disturbed. The beardless irises are best planted or transplanted in fall. Never allow the roots to dry out, and water them heavily after transplanting. Set these slightly deeper in the soil than the tall bearded. Beardless irises are happy when mulched, making for reduced garden maintenance.

Bearded irises need to be divided when the rhizomes begin to crowd each other, usually in 2 to 3 years.

FAVORITE BEARDED HYBRID IRISES   Zones 3-8

Successful most anywhere, these colorful spring to early summer flowers display the classical iris form—three upright standards that meet, and three colorful bearded falls. The "beard" is a fuzz of filaments. Straight, strong stems fork to show several buds. Suitable as cut flowers and beautiful naturalized in groups of 3 to 5 in a small garden or 10 or 12 in a large garden. The sword-shaped leaves remain crisp through summer, a fine asset at the middle or back of the border.

Culture: Beardeds do not tolerate "wet feet"—don't place them in borders that require constant moisture. In the North, protect them with winter mulch.

In Southern states the beardeds bloom from mid-March to mid-May; in the North, late April to late May. Some are "rebloomers" and bloom again in summer, fall, or winter in milder regions. Additional water and fertilizer applied to rebloomers in summer encourages repeat flowering. Keep weeds away.

Following are some recommended cultivars.

DWARF BEARDED IRISES

The dwarf bearded, to 15 inches high, are the earliest and usually have a single, unbranched stem and 2 or 3 buds. They are good specimens for the rock garden and naturalize and multiply well.

'Baby Blessed', to 12 inches, yellow with a white spot; rebloomer; early.

'Sapphire Gem', to 14 inches, smooth, medium blue; early.

'Chubby Cheeks', to 12 inches, white stitched with violet; early.

'Michael Paul', to 10 inches, very ruffled, very dark purple; early.

'Hush Puppy', to 15 inches, medium yellow with blue beard; early midseason.

'Plum Wine', to 11 inches, dark violet-red; rebloomer; early to late.

'Cotton Blossom', to 12 inches, superb ruffled warm white with a white beard; midseason.

'Cherry Pop', to 12 inches, crimson-red bitone; midseason.

'On Fire', to 12 inches, orange-red with white beard; midseason.

'Little Episode', to 12 inches, dark violet, light violet rim; midseason.

'Brown Wave', to 12 inches, two-toned brown with violet beard; midseason.

'Bright Vision', to 12 inches, peach with darker peach spot; late.

TALL BEARDED IRISES

Tall stalks 28 to 40 inches high whose candelabra-branched stems bear numerous buds. Suited to the middle or back border. Many are ruffled or veined with other colors. The period of flowering spans the entire iris season, mid- to late spring.

'Lady Friend', to 38 inches, garnet-red; very early.

'Holy Night', to 35 inches, deep violet-purple; early and reblooms in late fall.

'Corn Harvest', to 30 inches, yellow; early-midseason. Top favorite rebloomer that flowers midseason to fall.

'Generosity', to 36 inches, cream, falls washed with lemon; early midseason.

'Titan's Glory', to 37 inches, huge, ruffled, silky purple flowers; early midseason. One of the best.

'Vanity', to 35 inches, creamy pink; early late-season bloomer.

'Anna Belle Babson', to 36 inches, intense deep pink; midseason.

'Hindenburg', to 35 inches, orange; midseason.

'Sapphire Hills', to 36 inches, the bluest medium blue; midseason.

'Sultan's Palace', to 34 inches, rich maroon-red; midseason.

'Superstition', to 36 inches, black with red undertones; midseason.

TOP, LEFT Louisiana iris, 'Acadian Miss', for moist wild places in warm regions. (Lowe)

TOP, RIGHT Water iris *I. pseudacorus*, flourishes on riverbanks. (Viette)

BOTTOM Roof iris, *Iris tectorum* 'Album', grows on sod roofs in Japan. (Viette)

'Lorilee', to 37 inches, rose-orchid with a white patch; midseason late.

'Song of Norway', to 38 inches, powder blue with a blue beard; midseason-late.

'Stepping Out', to 38 inches, white stippled and rimmed with dark blue-violet; midseason-late. Long-time established favorite and excellent performer.

'Immortality', to 30 inches, pure white, ruffled; midseason. Rebloomer that can bloom from spring until frost.

SIBERIAN IRISES

I. sibirica Siberian Iris   Zones 3-8

Successful in cold, wet climates, these bloom in late spring and early summer, clustering two or three flowers on stalks 24 to 40 inches tall backed by slender, grasslike, waving leaves. The standards are small and don't quite meet, the large falls are exquisite. Excellent cutting flowers. Colors are blue-purple, lavender, maroon, white, pinkish, and yellowish tones. Mass for best effect.

Culture: They bloom best in rich, evenly moist garden soil with good drainage and nearly full sun. In the South, they tolerate light shade or late afternoon shade. They succeed in soil with a pH range of 5.0 to 8.0, but prefer moderately acid soils. Once established, they can stand some drought.

'Soft Blue', to 30 inches; repeat bloomer; one of the earliest.

'Rejoice Always', to 35 inches, light lavender and lilac; very early midseason.

'Reddy Maid', to 30 inches, dark wine red; early midseason to midseason.

'Silver Edge', to 28 inches, medium blue with silver edge; early midseason.

'Early Bluebird', to 32 inches, blue with yellow and white blaze; early late-season.

'Butter & Sugar', to 27 inches, yellow and white; midseason.

'Cambridge', to 36 inches, turquoise blue; midseason.

'Pink Haze', to 38 inches, pink; midseason; a top Siberian.

'Earthshine', to 38 inches, creamy white, flaring form; midseason to late.

'Dewful', to 40 inches, blue; midseason to late.

'Shirley Pope', to 28 inches, red-purple and white; midseason to late.

'VI Luihn', to 40 inches, deep violet; late.

JAPANESE IRISES

I. kaempferi, Japanese Iris   Zones 4-8

The flowers are like spectacular orchids, often measuring 8 inches across, and are flat and ruffled, marbled and mottled in exotic combinations of blue, pink, reddish purple, mauve, and white. They have slender stems and grasslike leaves. Valuable cut flowers, border specimens, and container plants, they sulk if the soil dries out. The bloom period is early summer, about a month after the tall beardeds.

Culture: Japanese irises are best planted in a distinct depression in heavy soil, and require full sun and moisture during the summer months. They thrive in moist soil at streamside, or under as much as 4 inches of water, or in a border if the roots are kept evenly moist. Ideal pH is between 5.5 and 6.5. Divide in late summer. Never, ever use lime!

The following cultivars are recommended.

'Geisha Gown', to 36 inches, white veined with deep rose-purple; early midseason.

'Freckled Geisha', to 36 inches, ruffled white with wine freckles; early midseason.

'Wine Ruffles', to 37 inches, fluted royal purple; midseason.

'Ipsus', to 36 inches, ruffled navy blue; midseason.

'Hegira', to 36 inches, white striped with deep blue; midseason.

'Anytus', to 38 inches, ruffled lavender-blue; midseason.

'Agrippinella', to 38 inches, deep rose pink on white; midseason.

'Snowy Hills', to 48 inches, white; midseason to late.

'The Great Mogul', to 46 inches, huge, blackish purple; early midseason.

'Dancing Waves', to 42 inches, dark violet or mulberry purple with white edging; midseason to late.

'Ocean Mist', to 36 inches, light and medium blue with a white center; midseason.

'Prairie Velvet', to 42 inches, ruffled dark violet-red; early midseason.

LOUISIANA IRISES

I. hexagona Louisiana Iris   Zones 6-9

Cultivars and hybrids of *I. fulva, I. foliosa, I. giganticaerulea,* or *I. nelsonii,* they flower in every shade of blue, red, yellow, cream, and white. The foliage is sword-shaped. In the South, the bloom period is early May through June, farther north, from mid-May to late June. From 18 inches to 5 feet tall.

Culture: Place in full sun and provide moisture during summer. Recommended for moist, wild places in warm regions where bearded irises don't do well. Best in moderately acid soil. Louisianas creep and need dividing every few years.

EASY SPECIES IRISES

I. cristata Crested Iris   Zones 3-8

Best in partial shade, this is a creeping native dwarf 3 to 4 inches high. It is very appealing naturalized on rocky wooded slopes and in rock gardens and light woodlands, especially in the South, where it blooms late April to late May. In the North, it blooms early May to early June in light shade. The lavender-blue, 4-inch-wide flowers have narrow falls with a central white or yellow ridge (also available in white and dark blue). The shiny, arching foliage may die back in summer. The plants grow vigorously soon after flowering, spreading in all directions. Divide every 4 years, just before growth begins. Deteriorates when crowded. Prefers somewhat acid soil, pH 4.5 to 5.5.

I. sibirica var. **alba 'Nana'**   Zones 3-8

Midseason to late-flowering white dwarf Siberian iris.

I. tectorum Roof Iris   Zones 4-8

To 10 inches tall, crested and and easy to grow, the Roof Iris has arching, evergreen, grassy foliage; it naturalizes readily. The falls have a central ridge and the standards are level with the falls, which gives the blossoms a wide, open look. The frilled 3- to 6-inch flowers appear in late spring to midsummer on stems almost as tall as the foliage and forked to carry 2 or more blooms. Colors are elegant lavender-blues speckled with dark blue to black blotches. In Japan, they grow on the edges of sod roofs. A white form, *I. tectorum* 'Alba', is lovely but hard to grow.

Culture: Plant in spring just before growth begins in moist, well-drained, humusy, moderately acid soil. Prefers full sun, but tolerates partial shade. These are heavy feeders—fertilize each spring.

I. versicolor Wild Iris, Blue Flag   Zones 3-8

The beautiful 2- to 3-foot-tall wild iris found in wetlands in Canada and the eastern U.S. is rather like the Yellow Iris, *I. pseudacorus.* In late spring and early summer, it bears purplish blue flowers, and the falls are often veined and blotched. It is a good cutting flower, with 3 to 5 blooms on branched stems up to 3 feet tall. Ideal for naturalizing on stream banks and in wet places, but it also succeeds in humusy, evenly moist soil. Full sun to partial shade.

I. pseudacorus Yellow Iris   Zones 5-8

This is the tallest of the water irises and it is magnificent in pools and ponds and in a humusy, evenly-moist flowering border. In late spring or early summer, it bears bright yellow canna-like flowers that may be blotched or veined with violet or brown. There is a handsome variegated form.

Culture: Grows from a fleshy root. Produces dense clumps of stately, 1-inch-wide leaves on plants up to 5 feet tall, in full sun and up to 6 feet of water. Also succeeds, but is smaller, in consistently moist garden soil. Plant rooted divisions in early spring or fall in full or half sun. The soil should be heavy, humusy, and moderately acid, but this species does tolerate some lime. Naturalized in the northeastern U.S. and easy to grow.

SOURCES: ANNE S. LOWE, PRESIDENT OF THE HISTORIC IRIS PRESERVATION SOCIETY AND EDITOR OF *ROOTS: JOURNAL OF THE HISTORIC IRIS PRESERVATION SOCIETY;* MICHAEL B. LOWE, EDITOR OF THE *REBLOOMING IRIS RECORDER;* AND CLARENCE E. MAHAN, AN IRIS HYBRIDIZER, THE OWNER OF THE IRIS POND NURSERY, AND PRESIDENT OF THE SOCIETY FOR JAPANESE IRISES.

26. PEONY (PAEONIA)

■ Few spring flowers can match the big, satiny peonies for showy beauty and ease of culture, particularly in cooler regions. Revered in the Orient for 2,500 years, thousands of elegant modern peonies attract collectors, botanists, taxonomists, horticulturists, and beginning gardeners. Peonies are among the most bountiful of the important perennials, and they make superb cut flowers.

There are two major types, shrub-size herbaceous peonies, and woody tree forms. The herbaceous types are the first big blossoms to flower. In New England and Canada, when the soil has warmed enough so the smell of the earth begins to rise, they rush into bloom. One day a hardy bud tip glistens at the surface of the soil. With just a little warmth, the stem stretches up—overnight it seems—to 4 inches, and then there are lots of stems 6 to 8 inches tall unfurling their first leaves. In April and May—depending on the region, plant, and weather—they bloom for four to six weeks, producing great globes of crinkled silk with an unmistakable fragrance in creamy whites, pinks, blush pinks, brilliant yellows, corals, and crimsons. Some reds are so rich they're nearly purple. All are remarkably beautiful.

The American Peony Society publishes a bulletin and may be contacted through the American Horticultural Society.

Companion and Follow-on Plants: *Geranium himalayense* 'Johnson's Blue' sets off peonies very well. Peony foliage usually looks good all summer and does not need screening, however, *Hemerocallis*, 'Autumn Joy' sedum, annual asters, and achillea can be planted for later color, (but don't plant so close that they rob the peonies of nutrients or moisture).

PAEONIA (pay-*oh*-nee-ah)

Peony   Zones 3-8

Both types of peony bear masses of huge, many-petaled flowers. The herbaceous peony dies back to the ground in fall. The woody stems of the tree peony (more shrub than tree) reach about 4 feet and remain after the leaves fall.

Culture: To bloom well, all peonies require 6 hours of sun, generous planting holes, rich, humusy, well-drained soil, and sustained moisture. They are more successful in neutral or slightly alkaline soils, but tolerate an acid range. Add a handful of dolomitic limestone to each planting hole and a pound of bonemeal. Manure is not used with peonies. A dressing of fertilizer in late fall raked in during the early spring is beneficial and so are fall and early spring applications of ash from wood fires. Keep invasive ground covers and weeds away from peonies—they need all the fertilizer and water available. Remove seedheads until the plants are well established. When taking peonies for bouquets, cut only a few from each plant.

Peonies prefer cold winters and indeed must have a chilling period at below 40° F to flower. Best choices for Zone 8 and warm regions are peonies that flower early and midseason. The Japanese and Single herbaceous peonies will open more successfully in warm regions than the late, large semidoubles or doubles.

FACING PAGE Large-flowered single Japanese peony 'Krinkled White'. (Klehm)
TOP Small double fern-leaf peony *Paeonia tenuifolia* 'Plena', often used as edger. (Klehm)
ABOVE 'Tria', the earliest Daphnis tree peony. (Klehm)
RIGHT 'Age of Gold', fragrant Saunders tree peony. (Klehm)

HERBACEOUS PEONIES

The herbaceous peonies are used in clumps of 4 to 8 in low-maintenance lawns and landcapes and in groups of 2 or 3 to anchor paths and flowering borders. In snow country they are planted in rows to hedge walks and even driveways because the foliage dies away in fall, leaving space for snow removal. The flowers are produced on stems 24 to 36 inches tall. The foliage is a strong green and stays fresh through summer in the Northeast and much of the Mid-Atlantic area. In warm regions, it remains attractive if given some shade by tall trees.

Culture: It's a healthy practice to cut the foliage of herbaceous peonies to the ground in fall and burn it. If desired, divide peonies in the fall after the foliage has turned from green to brown. Cut the stems to the ground, then insert a spading fork as deeply as possible under the root ball and lift it our. Wash the dirt away with a hose to expose the root crown and eyes. Divide the crown so that each section has 3 to 5 eyes, along with a balanced root system and crown tissue. Use a good sharp butcher knife to cut the crown apart. Trim the roots back to about 8 inches. Cut out any rotted, diseased, or dead tissue. In regions with a moderate to cold climate, plant the divisions with the eyes 2 inches below the soil surface. In southern areas, plant with the eyes right at the soil surface. Failure to bloom is one effect of planting too deeply. Peonies a century and older are not uncommon, but after transplanting, they need a year or two to reestablish themselves for good bloom. So don't divide them needlessly.

The most popular herbaceous peonies are the many-petaled Doubles, but interest is growing in the exotic Single and Japanese peonies.

DOUBLE AND SEMIDOUBLE PEONIES

The doubles are huge puffs of countless petals that just keep unfolding. A big fluff of narrow petals fills the center. Among the most durable and elegant are:
'Miss America', semidouble, white with a mound of golden stamens. Early.
'Coral Charm', semidouble, intense true coral. Early. This one is a modern breakthrough in peony hybrids and an American Peony Society Gold Medal Winner.
'Raspberry Ice', double, raspberry with silver highlights. Early.
'Red Grace', very double, dark red, fragrant. Early.
'Bowl O' Cream', double; huge bowl-shaped, creamy white blossoms. Midseason.
'Honey Gold', double, white and gold with a slight fragrance. Good cutting flower. Midseason.
'Pillow Talk', double, pink with a hint of rose at the base. Midseason.
'Moonstone', classical blush double, fragrant. Midseason.
'Felix Supreme', double, light red with frothy petals. Superb cut flower. Midseason.

TOP Japanese Moutans tree peony 'Hinode-sekai', semi-double with crinkled petals, is an early-blooming natural dwarf. (Klehm)

TOP, LEFT Gorgeous, fragrant 'Moonstone', a classical blush double peony. It is shown in a bouquet on page 254. (Klehm)

BOTTOM, LEFT Fragrant peony 'Red Grace', has very double petals. (Klehm)

JAPANESE AND SINGLE-FLOWERED PEONIES

These are big flowers, with mounds of silky anthers in their centers surrounded by satiny petals.

'Dawn Pink', raspberry pink with gold fringed center. Lush foliage and a slight fragrance. Early.

'Flame', single, brilliant rose-peach. Excellent cut flower. Early.

'Krinkled White', typical of the large-flowered single peonies, has broad, pure white petals like crinkled paper, and a golden central mound. Early.

'Barrington Belle', Japanese, very dark red, anemone-form flowers with ruffled, bright gold margins. An attention-getter. Midseason.

'Cora Stubbs', raspberry pink with a vanilla center. Lush foliage. Midseason.

'White Cap', raspberry with an ivory and pale pink center. Midseason.

P. tenuifolia 'Plena' Double Fern-leaved Peony
Zones 3-8

This species peony is 12 to 15 inches high, perfect for the front of the border, and has brilliant, double, dark red flowers and dense ferny foliage that remains decorative all season. Very early blooming. Mark its place in fall to avoid disturbing the plant in spring.

TREE PEONIES

The shrubby tree peonies were derived from the Chinese Moutan Peony, *P. suffruticosa*, over 1,400 years ago and bloomed in Japanese gardens in the seventh century A.D. The big flowers, 6 to 10 inches across, have satiny, crinkled petals. As many as 75 flowers can bloom on one plant through mid- and late spring. The flowers may be single or double. A single tree peony is a lovely specimen for an estate or park, and elegant as the centerpiece of a formal flower bed.

Culture: The tree peonies require cold winters and hot summers. In the Northeast protect them against winter by covering the plants or wrapping them in straw. The Northwest may have neither enough chilling time nor enough warm weather for tree peonies to bloom fully. Zone 7 is as far south as most horticulturists feel full blooming can be assured.

The tree peonies are slow-growing and slow to reestablish after transplanting, but they are rewarding to grow. If possible, order plants that are 3 years old. Allow a tree peony to have only 4 or 5 main stems and only 3 to 4 shoots at the tip of each main stem. Remove suckers that rise from the rootstock.

After the leaves fall in autumn, plant in a big, generous hole in rich, well-dug, well-drained soil, but don't add fertilizer except bonemeal—2 pounds per planting hole. Provide at least 6 hours of direct sun daily in the North. In the South, give shelter from the noon sun. Plant grafted peonies 6 to 12 inches below the graft union. After the first frost remove all leaves on the tree peony.

DAPHNIS HYBRIDS

These tree peonies have large single, semidouble, or double blooms, like those of the herbaceous peonies.

'Tria', single, a soft, clear, silky yellow, often has three blossoms to each stem. The earliest Daphnis.

'Iphigenia', semi-double, deep red with dark maroon flares. Delicate olive foliage. Midseason.

'Leda', large semi-double blossoms in striking mauve-lavender with deeper flares. Midseason.

JAPANESE MOUTANS

The Japanese Moutans have satiny, crinkled petals and narrow foliage.

'Hinode-sekai', semidouble, rosy carmine blooms with crinkled petals. Early-blooming natural dwarf.

'Kamada Nishiki', semidouble, rich, dark purple in a vigorous, free-blooming plant. The buds are shaped like tea roses. Early.

'Shintenchi', semidouble, large cameo pink blossoms, ruffled and airy. Early.

SAUNDERS HYBRIDS

These are the first American hybrids achieved by the late Professor A. P. Saunders at Hamilton College in New York. He combined the yellow of the *P. lutea* species with the very floriferous Japanese Mountans. These bloom about the time the Japanese tree peonies are fading

'Age of Gold', spectacular semidouble with a central rosette of creamy gold anthers. Fragrant; blooms at an early age; late spring.

'Banquet', semidouble, brilliant strawberry red with the undersides blushed gold. Attractive cut-leaf foliage. Midseason.

'Black Pirate', single, dark crimson with dark inner flares. Late spring.

'Savage Splendor', single, large ivory flower flushed and edged with deep rose and lavender. Each petal is twisted and turned and accented with deep flares. Midseason.

SOURCE: ROY G. KLEHM, A FOURTH-GENERATION HORTICULTURIST, PEONY BREEDER, AND NURSERYMAN, IS PAST PRESIDENT AND DIRECTOR EMERITUS OF THE AMERICAN PEONY SOCIETY.

Upright phlox, the perennial most trusted to produce lasting color in the hot months of midsummer, in field trials at the Viette farm in Fishersville, VA. (Viette)

27. PHLOX

■ **The most luscious pastels of spring and summer belong to the phloxes. American natives that thrive almost everywhere, the big silky-soft flowerheads of upright types fill the middle ground of sunny borders with color all through mid- and late summer. For me no perennial garden is complete without them. The cut flowers are lovely and have a special fragrance all their own.**

Just as important for spring are the little creeping phloxes—mats of lavender-blue, purple, pink, or white that spill down slopes and over rock gardens and masonry walls. When the flowers have gone by the foliage of the better types remains as ground cover.

Follow-on plants: Set asters near the upright phloxes to take over in late summer and fall; backdrop them with fall-flowering *Anemone bupehensis* var. *japonica*, Japanese Anemone, and its hybrids; in mid-fall, heel in potted cushion mums in white and lavender. The creeping phloxes become too dense to be interplanted, but an impatiens or two can be tucked in among them for summer color.

PHLOX (flocks)

The greatest display of summer color comes from the big upright perennial phloxes, but the annual type offers quick summer color for the middle of the border. Recommended on list 18, Perennials for the South, is *P. glaberrima* 'Triflora', Smooth Phlox, a shorter, superior dwarf form 15 to 18 inches high with strong stems.

The little creeping phloxes bloom in early to mid-spring and are valuable for ground cover, rock gardens, tumbling over ledges, or edging.

Culture: For the perennials, set out root divisions in early spring. Most of the upright phloxes thrive in open, sunny spaces. The low-growers grow in sun or shade, according to species. All phloxes are easy to grow as long as the soil is very well-drained and rich in leaf mold, peat moss, or other humus. Most phloxes require a slightly acid, moist soil.

Don't plant the creeping phloxes as ground cover for bulbs—their dense growth will choke out the bulbs.

The upright phloxes are susceptible to mildew in warm, wet August weather. The low phloxes, *P. stolonifera* and *P. subulata*, are less susceptible. To avoid mildew space plants 18 to 24 inches apart and after flowering cut them back to the ground. Avoid stress by keeping the ground damp enough (but don't overwater) so the plants never wilt; water the soil, not the plants. Where mildew is a threat

choose resistant varieties, and when the plants have been in the ground 2 or 3 weeks spray with the fungicide Benomyl (it has EPA approval). Repeat every 10 days and after rain.

Many upright phloxes self-sow and the volunteers usually revert to magenta. This is generally seen as an asset only for cottage gardens. To avoid the magenta invasion, prevent the seeds from setting by deadheading consistently; that also encourages branching and gives another flush of flowers, smaller than those that went before. To prolong the phlox display, pinch back one or two weaker stems in each clump early on, so secondary flowers will be growing as the main stems fade. Stake tall phloxes before wind and weather-flatten them.

Maintain even moisture during droughts. In hot climates, mulch phlox before the heat of summer. Divide the clumps every 3 to 5 years, preferably in mid-fall or in very early spring.

Other miniature phloxes are recommended on list 66, The Rock Garden.

P. carolina (syn. *suffruticosa*) Thick-leaf Phlox
· Zones 4-8
Upright early blooming perennial 12 to 36 inches tall with long-lasting, luscious cream-white to rose-pink flowers. The species thrives in its native South and Southwest and is not too susceptible to mildew. The white 'Miss Lingard' (also attributed to *P. maculata*), a highly regarded, long-established, mildew-resistant plant, does not set seed and so avoids the magenta seedlings self-sowers produce.

ABOVE Mat-forming mountain phlox, *Phlox subulata*, blooms in spring. (Viette)
RIGHT 'Miss Lingard', famous disease-resistant phlox, doesn't revert to magenta. (Viette)
FAR RIGHT Fragrant 'Alpha' *P. maculata*, Wild Sweet William, blooms wild in early summer. (Viette)

BELOW Close-up of the rare white miniature, 'Bruce's White', a creeping phlox. *P. stolonifera.* (Viette)

RIGHT Close-up of 'Graf Zeplin', upright summer phlox *P. paniculata.* (Viette)

P. divaricata 'Fuller's White' Wild Sweet William, Blue Phlox Zones 4-9

Low-growing, leafy mats that produce iris-scented, upright, lavender-blue flowers 9 to 15 inches tall in April to June. A hardy perennial that spreads by creeping rootstock, it is native to the moist woodlands of the Northeast (often listed as *P. canadensis*). 'Fuller's White' is 14 inches tall and covers itself with sparkling white flowers. The subspecies *Laphamii,* has large, rich blue-violet flowers. 'Dirgo Ice', 8-12 inches tall, is a fragrant pale blue. *P. × chattahoochee,* a 12- by 18-inch cross between the species and subspecies, is lavender-blue with a striking purple-red eye. Hardy from Zones 5 to 9; when flowering ends, cut it back to encourage growth.

P. drummondii Annual Phlox, Drummond Phlox Annual

Upright and popular annual 18 to 20 inches tall with a meadowy scent. From summer to fall the flowers appear in shades of red, pink, blue, soft yellow, violet, and white, some with a contrasting eye. It is a native Texan that grows easily from fresh seed sown in spring. Even in hot, sandy soil, it withstands considerable drought and goes on blooming, especially if given a permanent mulch. It self-sows and has naturalized in the sand of the Outer Banks of North Carolina, Zones 8 to 9. The more you cut, the more the flowers come. Star Phlox is the common name given to a strain with fringed petals.

P. maculata Wild Sweet William Zones 3-9

Upright phlox that blooms wild in early summer in fields and sunny woodlands of the Northeast, and west to Minnesota and Arkansas. It is very fragrant, 24 to 36 inches tall, and quite mildew-resistant. Recommended are 'Alpha', a deep rose pink with a slightly darker eye, and 'Rosalinde', a dark pink. 'Omega' is white tinged with violet and has a lilac eye. Tends to rebloom.

P. paniculata Summer Perennial Phlox, Fall Phlox Zones 3-8

Upright phlox, and probably the most popular. In July and August sweetly fragrant purplish pink flowerheads 2 to 4 feet tall bloom in sunny meadows from New York to Georgia, and westward into Illinois and Arkansas. There are beautiful durable cultivars 6 to 36 inches tall with big, lush panicles of flowers in white, pink, salmon, scarlet, and purple, many with a contrasting eye. Deadhead the cultivars or the garden will fill up with magenta seedlings. Withstands drought and urban environments within its hardiness zones. In hot, humid climates, choose mildew-resistant cultivated varieties. Set plants 24 inches apart.

Among the excellent performers are:

'Brigadier', to 32 inches, salmon- or orange-red.
'Bright Eyes', 24 inches, pale pink with a crimson eye. Noted for intense color. Mildew-resistant.
'Dodo Hanbury Forbes', 36 inches, huge heads of clear pink flowers with a red eye.
'Fairest One', 20 inches, shell pink with a dark red eye.
'Katherine', to 28 inches, light blue with a white eye. This is the best blue phlox, and moderately mildew-resistant.
'Leo Schlageter', to 28 inches, red.
'Mia Ruys', 20 inches, a beautiful rare white.
'Mount Fujiyama' ('Mount Fuji'), 26 inches, sparkling white with a soft golden eye that shines at a distance. Moderately mildew-resistant.

'Orange Perfection' ('Orange'), 24 inches, large, luminous orange flowers. Mildew resistant.
'Progress', 30 inches, soft lavender-blue with a blue-purple eye.
'Pinafore Pink', 12 to 16 inches, pink blossoms with a crimson eye.
'Prime Minister', to 28 inches, icy white with a sparkling red eye. Vigorous grower.
'Sandra', 20 inches, sparkling scarlet. Mildew-resistant.
'Sir John Falstaff', 30 inches, huge salmon-pink flowers with enormous florets.
'Starfire', 30 inches, striking cherry red that comes into flower early.
'Sternhimmel', to 30 inches, light blue with a lavender eye, good grower. Mildew-resistant.
'The King', 30 inches, good purple.
'White Admiral', 36 inches, giant white flowers.

P. stolonifera Creeping Phlox Zones 3-8

A superb mat-forming ground cover for semishade or shade, 5 to 12 inches tall. Some varieties are evergreen in warm winters. The flowers are purple or violet with a lilylike scent, borne in dense clusters in mid- to late spring. May bloom again intermittently. The species grows wild from Pennsylvania to Georgia and westward to Kentucky. In rich, acid (pH 5.0 to 6.0), peaty soil the creeping stems spread rapidly. Handsome 12-inch-tall late-bloomers are 'Blue Ridge', with large, light blue flowers, and 'Irridescens', lavender. 'Bruce's White', a rare white miniature only 4 to 6 inches tall, has a yellow eye and blooms in early mid-spring. 'Home Fires' is a clean, clear pink, 5 to 12 inches tall.

P. subulata, Moss Pink, Moss Phlox, Mountain Phlox Zones 2-9

Charming, mat-forming, needle-leaved creeper 6 inches tall that has a mossy look and is semievergreen in warm regions. In early to mid-spring it covers itself with clusters of tiny, starry, honey-scented flowers in pink, bright pink with a darker eye, light or dark blue, or white. Planted in well-drained soil and full sun, it quickly carpets banks and slopes and cascades down rock walls. After flowering, shear halfway back and top-dress with compost. Space plants 12 inches apart. Thrives in pH of 5.0 to 6.0.

Recommended cultivars include:

'Apple Blossom', 6 inches, pale pink with a dark pink eye.
'Coral Eye', 6 inches, blush pink with a coral-red central ring, hardy to Zone 3.
'Crimson Beauty', 8 inches, wonderful rosy red.
'Emerald Cushion Blue', 8 inches, lavender-blue.
'Millstream Jupiter', 6 inches, intense blue flowers.
'Millstream Daphne', 6 inches, bright pink.
'Red Wings', 6 inches, light red.
'Scarlet Flame', 8 inches, bright red.
'White Delight', 6 inches, sparkling white.

SOURCE: MARK VIETTE, A THIRD-GENERATION HORTICULTURIST, IS GENERAL MANAGER OF THE ANDRE VIETTE FARM AND NURSERY, FISHERSVILLE, VIRGINIA, SPECIALISTS IN HERBACEOUS PERENNIALS. HE ALSO LECTURES AND WRITES ON HORTICULTURAL SUBJECTS.

28. POPPY (PAPAVER)

■ The members of the poppy family are sun-loving, often finicky plants, but they have petals of shimmering silk in luminous, changeable, sometimes iridescent colors, and an ephemeral beauty that is breathtaking. Grouped 6 to 10 in the border they develop rich tangles of low-lying, deeply cut foliage, wandlike stems, and glorious flowers in displays that are among the most exciting of spring and early summer. Every garden needs poppies, both little annuals and big perennials.

One of the most exotic flowers in the world is the huge Oriental Poppy, *Papaver orientale*, a perennial 2 to 4 feet tall with big flowers like silky crepe paper that can be 10 inches across—but it is challenging to grow. Easier are the sunny Iceland Poppy, *Papaver nudicaule*, and the little California poppy, *Eschscholzia californica* (see list 34, Annuals That Self-sow). Another member of the poppy family commonly grown in rock gardens and as an edger is *Platystemon californicus*, Creamcups, but it is not particularly showy and seed is hard to find, so it is not featured in this work.

Poppy stems exude a milky or colored juice. The cut flowers last well if 6 inches of the cut end is immediately seared and charred black with a hot gas (not candle) flame before it is placed in warm water.

Preceding and Follow-on Plants: Precede poppies with medium-tall, spring-flowering bulbs and low-growers such as *Aurinia saxatilis*, polyantha primroses, *Phlox divaricata*, and pansies. Follow the big Oriental poppies with *Boltonia*, *Gypsophila*, or *Perovskia*, but don't plant any of them close enough to shade the poppy growth that begins with cooler weather. See notes on the summer dormancy period, below.

PAPAVER (pap-*pay*-ver)

Poppy

This genus includes poppies as small as those that grow wild in Flanders' fields as well as the extraordinary, dramatic Oriental poppies. Colors may be red, scarlet, pink, melon, coral, orange, gold, or white, often with dark blotches at the base of the petals. Heights range from 8 inches to 3 feet. The hairy leaves die down soon after the spring or early summer flowering period and the plant goes dormant.

Culture: Plant in full sun and soil that is deeply dug, very well-drained, light, somewhat sandy, and humusy enough to hold moisture. Poppies grown from seed are planted where they will bloom—in cool regions they are planted in early spring for midsummer flowering; in warm regions they are planted in late summer or early fall for spring flowering.

Maintain moisture during the growing period but allow poppies to run dry during dormancy and until new growth begins. Don't plant them close to flowers that will require constant moisture during dormancy. Poppies transplant with difficulty; do not divide or transplant until late summer after the foliage has died down completely.

In the garden, disbud after blooming; in a meadow, allow the seedheads to remain for reseeding.

A field of Oriental poppies shows the sooty black splotches characteristic of the type—pink 'Cedar Hill' and red 'Bonfire' and 'Glowing Embers'. (Viette)

P. alpinum Alpine Poppy   Zones 2-7

This is a low-growing poppy—to 10 inches or so—for alpine and rock gardens, the front of the border, and moist, gravelly, well-drained soils in cool regions of Zone 7 and north. The delicately textured white, pink, or yellow flowers are an inch or two across and very silky. Short-lived plant but it self-sows.

P. commutatum   Annual

The flowers are brilliant crimson with a dark blotch at the base of each petal, and plants grow 18 to 20 inches high. Seed for this may be easier to find than for the similar and popular *P. rhoeas* described below.

P. nudicaule Iceland Poppy, Arctic Poppy
          Zones 2/3-8

Small, sunny species 12 to 24 inches tall with some fragrance and wonderful colors—white-green, yellow, coral, pink, and red. There are double-flowered types. Among the long-established plants are 'Champagne Bubbles', with 3-inch flowers in mixed colors, and 'Coonara Pink', with 2-inch flowers in luscious shades of pink. Generally grown from seed.

P. orientale Oriental Poppy   Zones 2/3-6/7

These are the stars—big crinkled-silk blossoms 5 to 8 and 10 inches across that unfold in spring and early summer in vibrant reds, exquisite pinks, oranges, whites, and combinations, usually with a dark or sooty center. The petals of some are splotched at the base in a contrasting color, usually black, and others have contrasting edges. The deeply cut foliage dies in late summer but reappears in fall and is evergreen or semievergreen in winter according to climate.

Culture: Set out container plants in mid-fall in the South, early spring in the North. Set the plants 24 to 36 inches apart with the top of the crown 1 to 1½ inches below the soil surface. Fertilize in early spring if the soil is poor and water in persistent spring droughts. Orientals are long-lived but hate to be disturbed and die if transplanted while flowering. Old foliage and stems must be allowed to ripen on the plant, then removed to make way for the growth of new foliage in fall. In cool climates, mulch the plants for winter with evergreen boughs or salt hay.

Oriental poppies are cold-hardy but not very successful south of Zone 7. In the cooler regions of Zone 7 and northward, the late spring/early summer display is dramatic, and they succeed in Zone 8 in the bright shade of tall trees.

For warmer regions, the strain known as Mohn hybrids and the 'Minicap' series are recommended. They are known by their small seed capsules and bloom over a 2- to 4-month period bearing as many as 50 and more flowers per plant. 'Allegro' is a dwarf with black-blotched scarlet flowers on plants 16 inches high. 'Tara', pink, and 'Maya', salmon, may reach 6 feet.

Among recommended plants 3 to 3½ feet tall are: 'Big Jim', crinkly petals in deep carmine-red with black splotches.

Oriental poppies:
TOP, LEFT 'Doubloon'. (Viette)
TOP, RIGHT 'Carousel'. (Viette)
ABOVE 'Pinnacle'. (Viette)
BOTTOM, LEFT 'Helen
Elizabeth'. (Viette)
BOTTOM, RIGHT Shirley Poppy.
(McDonald)

'Bonfire', huge, brilliant orange-red flowers with small black splotches at the base.

'Carmen', sparkling deep red with black splotches.

'Carousel', 9-inch blooms, ruffled, white with a vivid red border.

'Cedar Hill', early blooming with crimped and ruffled petals in silky shell pink with black splotches.

'China Boy', 8- to 10-inch, ruffled orange flowers with creamy white centers.

'Doubloon', one of the first to bloom, 6-inch, fully double, clear orange flowers.

'Glowing Embers', vigorous, crinkly orange-red flowers with black splotches.

'Joyce', deep rose pink double.

'Harvest Moon', 8- to 10-inch blooms, orange-yellow. Midseason.

'Helen Elizabeth', 30 inches, ruffled and crimped clear, light, salmon-pink.

'Maiden's Blush', 6-inch, very ruffled white flowers with 1-inch blush pink edge. Midseason to late.

'Mrs. Perry', compact salmon-pink.

'Perry's White', silky white.

'Pinnacle', large, ruffled, white flowers with an orange edge.

'Raspberry Queen', brilliant raspberry pink with black splotches. Midseason to late.

'Springtime', large pure white flowers trimmed with a ½-inch border of true pink. Outstanding.

'Snow Queen', pure white with a black eye.

'Turkenlouis', 2 to 3 feet, bright Chinese red with serrated, pointed edges.

'Warlord', vibrant red.

P. rhoeas. Corn Poppy, Field Poppy   Annual

This is the little red poppy that grows wild in the fields of France and is celebrated by the World War I poem "In Flanders Field." The 24-inch-high Shirley Poppy is the most popular modern strain and includes full begonia- and ranunculus-flowered forms in melting shades of pink, coral-pink, and rose. Needs full sun and light, sandy, well-drained soil to flower well. Sow the very fine seeds sparsely in little drifts where the plants are to flower. Deadhead to keep the flowers producing. Self-sows under good conditions.

SOURCE: MARK VIETTE, A THIRD-GENERATION HORTICULTURIST, IS GEN-ERAL MANAGER OF THE ANDRE VIETTE FARM AND NURSERY, FISHERSVILLE, VIRGINIA, SPECIALISTS IN HERBACEOUS PERENNIALS. HE ALSO LECTURES AND WRITES ON HORTICULTURAL SUBJECTS.

29. PRIMROSE (PRIMULA)

■ Once the crocuses have gone, spring's prettiest colors belong to the primroses—strong, fresh yellows, pinks, crimsons, blues, purples, and whites, some with contrasting eyes. The julianas, English primroses, and a little Russian variety bloom in the moist, chilly weather of very early spring, appearing seemingly from nowhere—bright little clusters of cup-shaped or flat-faced flowers in nests of crinkled, sometimes hairy, blue-gray-green leaves 3 or 4 to 10 inches high. They evoke the damp meadows, light woodlands, and stream banks of their origins and need similar conditions to be as beautiful as they can be. The plants are exquisite nestled in groups of 3 to 5 among gnarly old tree roots, by rock outcroppings and near ferns, and in rock gardens and wild gardens. The damp cool of the West Coast is ideal, but even in the Southeast where many die out or go dormant in high summer heat, their early beauty makes replanting worth the effort.

Companion and Follow-on Plants: Pastel and white tulips and miniature daffodils are good companion plants. Annuals and tender perennials that replace primroses just as the heat begins to fade them include Edging Lobelia *(Lobelia erinus)*, Forget-me-not *(Myosotis sylvatica* 'Victoria Blue'), and impatiens. See also list 32, Annuals for Shade.

PRIMULA *(prim-yew-luh)*
Primrose

Some primrose species and cultivars bloom in fall, others in early and mid-spring, and still others in late spring and summer. A few are suited to greenhouses and indoor gardens, for instance, *P. malacoides*, Fairy Primrose, Baby Primrose, which has rounded leaves and dainty pink or lavender-blue flowers. The dwarf known as *P.* × *hybrida* is also sold as a houseplant, and seeds for the 6- to 12-inch *P. sinensis*, Chinese Primrose, are sown in pots for growth on a cool, semi-sunny sill.

The primroses that follow are easy to grow and suited to the gardens of many regions in North America. Most often seen are the types called candelabra (flat-faced flowers borne in tiered whorls up tall stems), and Polyantha (large blooms clustered around the top of stout stems). A third group, the alpine Auriculas, are cold-hardy in Zone 3 and challenging to grow; collectors can find them with the help of the American Primrose Society.

Culture: Primroses grow easily from seed. Seed can be harvested from the garden primrose as soon as it is ripe and should be sown at once. It germinates in 10 to 15 days in moist, peaty soil and temperatures of 60° to 65° F. To start primroses from purchased seeds, sow the seeds in spring 2 weeks after the last frost date, or in late summer or fall up to 2 months before the first frost is expected. Container-grown primroses are sold for fall planting in mild regions, and in early spring in cooler areas.

Primroses thrive in England on full sun (on those occasions when it shines) beside water. Here they tolerate direct sun only in the North, New England, and the Pacific Northwest, but except for *P. japonica* they do not require waterside sites. They do thrive near running water, but most fail in stagnant, boggy soils. In warm regions filtered light is essential—heat is the enemy—and primroses always require constant, ample moisture and rich, well-drained, humusy soil. In droughts deep watering is essential.

Established clumps of primroses benefit from division every 3 or 4 years. Divide after flowering and before dormancy. Use a sharp trowel and very carefully separate offsets from the main clump and replant.

Some primroses naturally go dormant in any sort of summer weather, and many self-sow or come back in the cool season as long as the roots haven't dried out.

P. acaulis 'Mark Viette'   Zones 5-8
This 6-inch primrose developed by the Viettes is a full carnation-like double in deep rose. It flowers in May and is very showy. Hardy, and a wonderful addition to the shade garden.

P. denticulata   Zones 5-8
One of the very earliest primroses to bloom, a true harbinger of spring and generally easy to grow. The round terminal clusters of flowers are lavender-pink or pure white. Selections with more intense colors have been developed. Blooming starts almost at ground level and continues as the stems extend to 8 to 10 inches during flowering. All parts of the plant are covered with a silvery gray meal that adds to its beauty. It is recommended for moist spots. A winter mulch is advantageous where there is not much snow cover.

P. elatior Oxlip   Zones 6-8
A pretty English species 6 to 10 inches tall that blooms in late spring with flattish, sulphur yellow florets in graceful clusters on 8- to 12-inch stems. There are also whites and purples. Recommended for mass planting in woodlands—the flowers are modest and flow well together.

P. japonica   Zones 6-7
This species gives an incredible display in late spring and early summer, but it must have moist soil. It's a tall candelabra type whose flowers mass elegantly around the top quarter of sturdy 10- to 15-inch stems. The colors range from pure white to pink, wine red, and lavender to white with colored eyes. Large leaves form handsome basal mounds that will go dormant if allowed to dry out in summer. Two of the loveliest are the late spring, large-flowered 'Postford White' and 'Miller's Crimson'. Most candelabra primroses can be raised from seed. This is one of the hardiest and easiest to grow. Often self-sows.

P. juliae   Zones 6-8
This hardy species leads off the primrose season. It is a low, mound-forming, compact plant particularly good for small spaces and rock gardens. Hardy, to 6 inches tall, it requires shade and rich, well-drained soil. The flowers are lovely and there are lots of them, usually rose or bright wine red. It grows from a creeping rootstock near the soil surface and benefits from a permanent mulch. The oldest and most widely distributed juliana is 'Wanda', 3 to 5 or 6 inches tall, a small-leaved plant with bronzy foliage that produces blankets of purplish red flowers all spring. Look for other cultivars in shades of carmine, red, maroon, pink, salmon, lavender, and lilac-mauve. There are also miniatures in a gorgeous array of colors.

LEFT Carnationlike double primrose, *Primula acaulis* 'Mark Viette', blooms April or May and is just 6 inches high. (Viette)
BELOW *P. juliae* 'Wanda', widely-distributed cultivar of a very early primrose. Suited to small spaces and rock gardens. (Ferreniea)
BOTTOM Distinctive candelabras of Japanese primroses flourish in moist woodlands. (Ferreniea)

TOP Pacific Giant strain of the easy, popular polyanthus prim-rose, *P. × polyantha*, has very large flowers. (Ferreniea)
ABOVE *P. kisoana* has exceptionally pretty flowers and downy gray-green scalloped foliage. Recommended as one of the very best. (Ferreniea)

P. kisoana   Zones 4-7

The foliage is very distinctive and the flower incredibly pretty. One of the very best, it is sturdy yet ornamental, with an attractive gray-green scalloped foliage heavily coated with hairs and prominent veins. The large flowers are a good pink with a touch of lavender. Stoloniferous, it forms a clump more quickly than most primroses and spreads rapidly. Somewhat less affected by heat than the others.

P. × polyantha Polyanthus, Polyantha Primrose
Zones 4-8

As the flowers of *P. vulgaris* reach their peak, the popular, easy-to-grow polyanthus primroses begin their long season of bloom. They offer an extraordinary diversity of forms and colors. The flowers are bunched on 10- to 12-inch stems and range from pastels to vibrant shades of gold, red and blue. Some notables are laced with gold or silver, with a colored ruff edging the petals that contrasts with the main flower color. There are doubles and some with intense golden eyes. The Pacific Giants strain, somewhat less cold-hardy than the species, has mixed colors and very large flowers. In the South they bloom in mid-winter. Barhaven hybrids have large flowers and diminutive foliage that puts them among the finest primroses.

P. sieboldii   Zones 5-8

It blooms in late spring and is perhaps the prettiest primrose, with the most intricate and delicate flowers. Some look like snowflakes. The downy, scalloped foliage forms a nice clump, each delicate 3- to 4- inch stem carrying a terminal flower ¾ to 1 inch across. Typically, the flowers are pink with a light lavender cast. There's an exquisite pure white, too. The plants usually survive summer heat by going dormant.

P. veris Cowslip   Zones 6-7

A spring-flowering species native to England's open glades and wet meadows, this primrose is one of the parents of the popular Polyantha Primrose. The strongly fragrant flowers cluster at the top of 6- to 8-inch stems and come in many colors.

P. vulgaris English Primrose   Zones 3-8

This true primrose of English woods and gardens follows the early julianas into bloom. Lovely massed in woodlands. It bears many lightly fragrant, pale-yellow flowers on single stems up to 6 inches tall. Modern cultivars come in every color imaginable, including blues and purples. There are doubles, hose-in-hose (cup and saucer), and other charming forms. Provide light mulch for winter. Easily divided. The Barnhaven strains are recommended.

P. v. var. abschasica   Zones 4-7

Very strong early color for the woodland garden. This is an enduring, compact little plant from Russia, one of the earliest to bloom. It bears many fragrant flowers on 3- to 4-inch stems above mounded foliage over a long season. The blossoms are rosy purple but become a rich, deep purple when touched by frost. It often blooms again in fall and is budded and ready to go again when the snow melts.

SOURCE: VIKI FERRENIEA, ASSISTANT HORTICULTURAL DIRECTOR FOR WAYSIDE GARDENS IN SOUTH CAROLINA. A HORTICULTURIST AND LEC-TURER, VIKI WAS FORMERLY THE ROCK GARDEN CURATOR AT THE NEW YORK BOTANICAL GARDEN.

30. VIOLET— PANSY (VIOLA)

■ The perky woodland violets that flash purple-blue in spring from 8- to 12-inch clumps of dark green leaves are kissing cousins to the big, beautiful, charismatic pansies whose faces are velvety works of art. The little tricolor violets we call Johnny-jump-ups also are related. All flourished in English herb gardens before America was discovered and belong to the genus *Viola.*

Many of the violets love shade and are delightful as accent plants and edgers for moist places in rock gardens, wild gardens, and other woodsy places. Though violets flower for only a few weeks where summers are not too hot—Connecticut, for instance, and the West Coast—the foliage clumps remain fresh throughout summer. So don't crowd them with follow-on annuals.

Pansies are the dramatic beauties of this group, the "heartsease" beloved of Elizabethans. Most prefer some shade but accept some sun, and their flowers are showy enough for patio containers, flower borders, and sunny rock gardens. They bloom in cool spring weather, or mild fall weather, or both, and some are hardy in moderate winters (not more than five days of frost) and summers.

Follow-on Plants: Shade-loving followers include Edging Lobelia, *Lobelia erinus;* Forget-me-not, *Myosotis sylvatica* 'Victoria Blue'; wax begonias; and impatiens. See also list 32, Annuals for Shade.

VIOLA (vye-oh-luh)
Violet

The "real" violets generally are grown as perennials—these are the small, nodding, violet-colored (there are also pinks and whites) flowers on stems that barely top neat mounds of usually heart-shaped leaves.

Culture: Violets start easily from seed or divisions planted outdoors in mid-fall in the South, early fall or spring in the North. Packed clumps of violets benefit from division every 3 or 4 years. Or, start seeds indoors about 14 weeks before warm weather; they germinate and transplant without difficulty. Violets, except *V. pedata,* prefer semishade and rich, well-drained soil that contains enough humus to retain moisture.

Violets often self-sow. They produce two kinds of flowers—the showy but infertile spring flowers we know and love, and rudimentary summer flowers hidden by the leaves. These develop capsules that shoot the tiny seeds a great distance from the parent plant; violets can be a pest.

V. cornuta Horned Violet, Viola   Zones 5-8
This is a woodland violet that blooms in spring and even into fall, bearing small, pansy-like flowers, star-shaped or spurred, some with outstanding beauty and fragrance. In the South and Pacific Northwest it is planted for winter bloom. Be sure to cut back this plant after the first round of flowering to encourage more bloom. Provide a permanent mulch in summer. The species blooms the first year from seed sown in early spring and is so vigorous it is used as low ground cover along walls and fences. Recommended are:

Spectacular spring blooms of pansies, *Viola × wittrockiana*, and lily-flowered tulips with forget-me-nots. (Viette)

RIGHT Tiny Johnny-jump-ups, *Viola tricolor*. (Viette)
BELOW Lovely new pink Imperial pansies. (McDonald)
BOTTOM Blue pansy, Universal series. (McDonald)

Common violets thrive in containers if soil moisture is maintained. (McDonald)

'Arkwright Ruby', spring through summer, a crimson flower with a black blotch in the center; 'Nellie Britain', which blooms from spring through summer with masses of rich lavender-pink flowers; 'Eatin', which flowers generously in summer, displaying large, lemon-colored blossoms with contrasting lavender margins.

V. cucullata Marsh Blue Violet   Zones 5-8
This strong, easy-to-grow native woodland violet spreads by means of scaly branching rhizomes that slowly form large colonies. It blooms from early spring until hot weather; its small flowers are dark lavender-blue to pale violet. Damp, humusy soil and light shade are important. Recommended is the unusual 'Freckles', with pale blue flowers flecked with tiny purple marks.

V. labradorica Labrador Violet   Zones 3-8
Small, native to woodlands in the northern U.S. and Greenland, this low-grower bears mauve flowers suffused with dark purple. Its culture is easy; it blooms in early spring, and occasionally in summer, and spreads rapidly on creeping rhizomes. Does well in southern states given shade, moisture, and a pH between 5.0 and 6.5. Charming with ferns, yellow grasses, and white snowdrops. Purple leaves add a nice splash of color, especially in summer when shade gardens have a lot of green.

V. odorata Sweet Violet, Florist's Violet, English Violet   Zones 6-9
A sweetly fragrant woodland violet that comes to us all the way from ancient Greece and Rome, it is still candied for bonbons and pastry garnishes, and is raised to make perfume. Heart-shaped, dark green leaves half hide flowers that may be white or blue-purple, sometimes pink. The spring blooming is heavy and often repeats in fall. It grows in partial sun but flowers well only in full sun, and it prefers sweet soil. Easily perennialized. Recommended are 'White Czar' and 'Royal Robe', which has pansy-like, deep violet-blue or purple flowers. The large-flowered, lavender-

violet double Parma violet is exquisitely perfumed and found in cultivars such as 'Duchesse de Parme' and 'Lady Hume Campbell'. If possible, buy from a nursery specializing in fragrant plants.

V. pedata Bird-foot Violet, Pansy Violet
Zones 3-8
A durable native species that blooms in spring and again through summer into fall. The foliage is dark green and heavily divided (like a bird's foot), and the flowers are exquisite. There are also bicolors and a rare white. It requires well-drained, slightly acid soil less fertile than for most violets and thrives in sun if heat spells are not prolonged. In the South, partial shade is recommended. 'Eco-Artist Palette' has lavender flowers with a deep purple central flare.

V. tricolor Johnny-Jump-up
An easy-to-grow viola that in spring bears masses of tiny multicolored blooms with whiskered pansy faces in yellow, white, and blue. Height is 6 to 12 inches. It is a short-lived perennial usually treated as an annual. Self-sows and perennializes profusely in moist, humusy soil where summers aren't too hot.

THE PANSIES
. . . .

V. × wittrockiana Pansy, Ladies'-delight, Heartsease, Stepmother's Flower
Annual/Tender Perennial
Usually just 6 to 9 inches tall, but those with painted faces in combinations of white, yellow, pink, blue, purple, black, and mahogany-red—attract every eye. Among modern strains there are smaller-flowered tall pansies in melting solid colors—coral, peach, lavender, yellow, blue, and many more. Just-planted pansies bloom continuously in spring and early fall if they are deadheaded. Some continue to flower in warm summers and bloom through mild winters.

Culture: In most regions the pansies are treated as annuals and some act as biennials. They grow readily enough from seed, as violets, above. A yellow biennial I knew in Manhattan reseeded itself for years. In moderate regions of the Northeast seed is sown in late summer and they survive temperatures to 5° F, especially if covered with salt hay (marsh grass).

In cooler regions pansies are sold in flats or pots in early spring for spring and summer bloom. Where winters are mild and summer heat intense, they are set out in mid-fall for late fall, winter, and spring bloom.

As spring advances, pansies become leggy. With shearing and constant deadheading—and in moist, mild climates—some pansies bloom all summer. Here in Washington, D. C., about half are gone by August.

Recommended cultivars include:
'Crystal Bowl', clear colors for massed plantings.
'Delft', white and porcelain blue blooms marked with "whiskers" and bright yellow eyes. Compact habit.
'Joker', early to bloom and very heat tolerant. 'Jolly Joker' is a striking 3-inch, orange and purple color with whiskers, excellent for containers or bedding. 'Joker Light Blue', a delight for anyone who loves blue flowers.
'Majestic Giant', summer-blooming 4-inch flowers that have charming "faces" and are offered in many colors. These flower profusely on vigorous plants that often last through summer.
'Maxim Marina', an All-America Selection award winner, has 2-inch, pansy-faced, lavender-blue blossoms; flowers when 4 inches tall and tends to bloom freely in full sun in hot summers.
'Universal', early-blooming fall to spring flowers in a range of bright, clear colors, some with "faces."
'Black Devil', an unusual pansy for collectors, with 2-inch flowers in purple-black on mounded, free-flowering plants.
'Baby Lucia', miniature pansies for pots, containers, and rock gardens. The blooms are 1½ inches, warm lavender, and are produced generously on mounded 4- to 5-inch plants, rather like very flowery violets.

SOURCE: VIKI FERRENIEA, ASSISTANT HORTICULTURAL DIRECTOR FOR WAYSIDE GARDENS IN SOUTH CAROLINA. A HORTICULTURIST AND LECTURER, VIKI WAS FORMERLY THE ROCK GARDEN CURATOR AT THE NEW YORK BOTANICAL GARDEN.

CHAPTER THREE:
Annuals—The Once-Only Flowers

Summer is show time for annuals. True annuals are pop-up, once-only flowers that germinate rather quickly from seed, come into bloom six to eight weeks later, and complete their life cycle in one season. There are a few excellent foliage plants in this group, notably the silvery Dusty-miller, *Senecio cineraria*. Tender perennials, which freeze in winter and are grown as one-season plants, are included here along with true annuals. The colors of annuals are vivid, and the summer-to-fall performance is unbeatable. Flowering begins just when yellowing spring bulb foliage needs screening and the garden is running out of color. Most annuals bloom for a month or two and even longer if deadheaded regularly. The few that have brief flowering periods, *Nigella*, for instance, are handled by making several successive sowings in early and mid-spring.

In a border combining perennials, bulbs and annuals, the annuals go into the ground in late spring, summer, and early fall as needed to screen or fill empty spaces. Stocky seedlings offered already in flower at garden centers in late spring, summer, and fall hardly ever fail if given reasonably good soil and moisture. Annuals also are easy to start outdoors or indoors from seed. Because annuals are readily hybridized, new colors and color combinations of the seven major genera are introduced each year. The following annuals are considered the most important, and each is given its own list: list 36, *Begonia*, list 37, Geranium and Ivy Geranium *(Pelargonium)*; list 38, *Impatiens*, list 39, Marigold *(Tagetes)*; list 40, *Petunia*; list 41, *Salvia*; and list 42, *Zinnia*.

Choose from lists 31 through 42 when your garden needs quick, new, late spring, summer, or fall color—you won't be disappointed.

Helping Self-sowers

Though annuals live for only a year, some come back like perennials because they self-sow. List 34 describes some very good self-sowers. The plants will naturalize if conditions are good, but everything has to come together in just the right way.

A seed is the ripened ovule of a flower. It has a hard outer shell to protect the embryo. Cold and moisture are required in many cases to break down the seed shell and expose the embryo to oxygen, water, and the sequence of temperatures that encourages growth. But each flower has its own sequence. Some seeds germinate in days; others take months. A few seeds sprout as soon as they ripen and others need a rest or a chilling time between ripening and planting. Follow the recommendation for planting seasons given with each flower.

You can give self-sowers an assist. Spread a 1- or 2-inch layer of well-prepared soil around the feet of the parent plants, dampen the soil, gather the seeds as they ripen, and scatter them over the fresh dirt. Or, monitor the seeds as they ripen and when they are dry and loose in their casings, shake the flowerheads vigorously over the soil to spread the seeds where you want them to grow.

Harvesting Seeds

Harvesting seeds combines the joy of picking flowers with the satisfaction of winning a small lottery. And it's a way of touching the past—our great grandparents and their neighbors relied upon their gardens as the source for seeds. Seeds of species plants produce new plants like the parents in type and color. The seeds of hybridized plants are likely to revert poor forms, and produce plants unlike the previous generation. Such plants are said not to come true from seed.

Harvesting flower seed is simple, but timing is important. Each plant has its own type of seed and ripens it at its own pace. Petunia seeds are tiny and black, and packed into a pointed green envelope that swells where the flower once met the "receptacle" or stem tip. The envelope dries and splits, and the seeds explode outward. Marigold seeds are different—tiny, feathered darts whose pointed tips are buried in the drying tops of the flower stems. Eventually, they'll fall to the ground.

The famous Butchard Gardens, in Victoria, BC, Canada, use the familiar annuals—begonias, salvia, dusty-miller, marigolds and many more—to keep glowing color in a formal garden from late spring until frost. (Viette)

Early in the flowering season, allow one blossom to ripen on each plant you hope to harvest. Study its seed development—then you'll know when and what to harvest at the end of the flowering season. Tag plants you plan to harvest. Keep an eye on those that explode and gather the seedheads into a large brown paper bag when they look as though they're read to let go.

Dry the seeds on newspaper in a room at 45° or 50° F for up to six weeks. Place them in a dry, clean jar with a small cheesecloth bag filled with flour to absorb any moisture. Poke two or three holes in the lid. Store the jar in the refrigerator at about 40° F (the vegetable crisper is a good place). After a year of storage the seeds will have reduced vigor and germination rates—10 or 15 percent instead of 90 percent. Try to plant the seeds the season after you collect them.

Starting Seeds Indoors

In cold regions with a short growing season, start annuals indoors to get earlier flowers, and choose types billed as early; they need less time to come into flower. Some of the easiest annuals with which to experiment are given on list 35.

Start fast-growers six to eight weeks before the plants are to be set outdoors. Seed packets give the number of days to maturity, which indicates which plants are fast and which slow to bloom.

Transplanting time generally is two weeks after the date of the last annual frost in the area. Many annuals won't start growing until temperatures are around 55° F. Don't set them out in the cold—they will sulk for weeks and may rot.

Most seeds germinate well at indoor temperatures around 65° to 70° F—if they aren't up in 20 days, start over again with a fresh batch of seed.

For containers, choose shallow peat or plastic flats that have drainage holes. Sow the seeds of flowers that transplant with difficulty in individual peat pots; before transplanting, soak and then break the bottoms of the pots so you can transplant without disturbing the roots.

Fill the containers to within ¼ inch of the top with moistened, sterilized, commercial potting mix. Press the seeds into the medium to a depth equal to their diameter. Very fine seeds can be sprinkled over the soil surface and covered with a thin sifting of the growing medium. Mist the surface and tent the flats with pliofilm (a dry

Color on color, in a small city garden: blue *Lobelia erinus* and tall blue salvia; low-growing white alyssum and silvery dusty-miller; dwarf red snapdragons and red geraniums. A scattering of marigolds holds the composition together. (Viette)

cleaner's bag). Label all the flats—it's easy to confuse seedlings. Keep the containers in strong, indirect light. Maintain even moisture, watering from the bottom.

When the seeds germinate, poke small holes in the tent for ventilation and to prevent overheating. When they get their second set of leaves, remove the tenting, reduce humidity, and expose the seedlings to full sun. Turn the containers often to keep the stems growing straight.

Thin seedlings as they become crowded; the leaves of adjoining plants should not touch. Seeds unfold a rudimentary root as they open their first primitive leaves. That root—called a radicle—is their fail-safe system and it mustn't be disturbed. When the second pair of leaves develop, the roots are growing. Then you can transplant.

After transplanting, watch for the first perky movement toward growth. That indicates the root system is growing again and it's time to fertilize. At this stage, make sure the seedlings get plenty of bright light. Before transplanting occurs, harden off seedlings—that is, allow them a week in a sheltered position in bright shade to adjust to the harsher outdoor environment.

Planting Outdoors

Outdoors, after all danger of frost is past, sow seeds directly where they are to bloom. Most plants will come into flower soonest if planted where they are to bloom. Transplanting tends to check growth, though not for very long if the weather is mild and the soil moist. For transplanting of container plants and seedlings, see Growing Flowers.

To Encourage Flowering:

The secret of greatly increased flowering in most branching annuals and some perennials that put up a strong central stem or leader, such as snapdragons, is to pinch out the first 3 or 4 inches of the lead stem early in the growing season and, after blooming begins, deadhead relentlessly.

But don't use this technique on all your flowers. The key words here are *branching* and *leader*. This practice does not benefit flowers rising from bulbs, corms, or rhizomes, or any of the major perennials except asters.

31. ANNUALS FOR SUN

■ When the night air loses its cold edge late spring has arrived—time to set out the annuals. Their mission is to screen the final ripening of bulb foliage and to bring instant color to spaces where the spring flowers once bloomed. They will bloom brightly through summer until mid-autumn or the first frost, then it will be their turn to go, making way for next spring's display.

Summer annuals become available at garden centers in spring and late spring, already blooming in flats and individual containers. Many start easily from seed sown indoors 6 to 10 weeks before outdoor planting time. Some flower so quickly from seed they may as well be sown directly in the garden. The annuals lists in this book include true annuals and tender perennials grown as annuals.

The plants recommended here are arranged in order of bloom strength. The plants that bear the most flowers for the longest time are at the top. But even *Cleome*, the tall, elegant Spider Flower—last on the list—blooms all summer until frost and is a lovely and undemanding filler for the back of the border.

A reminder about sunlight: plants that flourish in full sun in Zone 7 and north need protection from hot afternoon sun in Zones 9 through 11; the closer your garden is to these warm zones, the more important is the neeed for protection.

Follow-on Plants: Fall-flowering bulbs, potted mums, and the plants on list 33, Annuals for Fall, are good successors to summer annuals.

Annuals carpet a hot, sunny slope with color—red zinnias, bicolor purple petunias, yellow marigolds, and pink wax begonias. Most will bloom through August heat and drought and on into the cool autumn months. (Viette)

BEGONIA Semperflorens-Cultorum Hybrids, Bedding Begonia, Wax Begonia. Excellent. A crisp and colorful low edger that succeeds in sun if temperatures stay under 90° F but thrives in filtered light. It flowers from spring until frost—growing bigger and brighter with the return of cool weather—in hues of pink, salmon, red, or white. The crisp, shiny leaves are attractive all season. There are also variegated-leaved strains. Among superior cultivars are the sun-resistant, compact Cocktail series, with their deep bronze foliage. Seedlings are readily available in late spring. See also list 36, Begonia.

TAGETES, Marigold. Excellent. These fluffy globes of gold, mahogany, orange, or pumpkin orange grow quickly, bloom summer to frost in hot sun, never look wilted, and withstand the worst summer storms. The foliage is lacy and pungent-smelling. One of few annuals that bloom through southern Florida summers, their tolerance of drought and heat are exceptional. The small French marigolds often self-sow. As cut flowers they last well. Blooms quickly from seed sown indoors 4 to 6 weeks before the weather warms. *T. erecta* × *T. patula*, Triploid (Mule) Marigold, is a 12- to 15- inch cross between French and African marigolds; its big yellow or orange flowers seem indestructible. 'Red Seven Star F₁' and 'Yellow Mighty Marietta' are especially good. *T. patula*, French Marigold, bears single or double flowers wonderfully enduring as edgers and in containers. Height is 8 to 12 inches. There are many forms, including strains with mahogany markings. This species is rated below *Salvia splendens* for bloom strength, but bears lots of flowers summer to frost and may self-sow. Especially good are the super-petite, reddish 'Harmony Boy' and the early, compact 'Aurora Gold', a rich yellow. For culture, see list 39, Marigold.

PETUNIA × hybrida F₁ Single Multiflora Class Excellent. The trumpet-shaped flowers on droopy stems boldly bloom all summer in dozens of colors and combinations. For lavish all-summer bloom, few petunias equal these hybrids and they stand up to summer storms better than most. There are cascading and supercascading types for baskets and window boxes and uprights for bedding. The colors range through pink, red, white, lavender and bicolors. Keep dead blooms picked if you can, and be sure to trim the plants back a third after the first great rush of flowers to encourage continuing bloom. One of the best is the Pearls series of single-flowered dwarfs, 'Azure Pearl', 'Pink Pearl', and others. Flowering stems last rather well when cut. For culture, see list 40, *Petunia*.

IMPATIENS wallerana, Zanzibar Balsam, Busy Lizzy. Excellent. Masses of sparkling little flowers from summer to frost and delicate, pointed leaves make this the most popular low-growing annual (actually a tender perennial) for shaded places—and more are being bred to withstand sun. By autumn they are tall, and the show grows brighter until frost. 'Tempo Blush', 'Accent Pink', and 'Super Elfin Blue Pearl' are excellent for semi-sunny situations and can withstand sun if moisture is constant. New Guinea Impatiens withstands more sun, but must have humusy soil and water. For culture, see list 38, *Impatiens*.

NICOTIANA (nik-oh-shee-**ay**-nuh) alata Jasmine Tobacco, Flowering Tobacco

Tender Perennial

Lush, semirecumbent, 15 to 24 inches tall, with big leaves. An excellent filler. Blooms lavishly in July or August and into early frosts, sending up clusters of tubular white flowers that open and release a faint lilylike scent late in the day. There are some colorful hybrids: 'Lime Green' is a fresh greeny white; 'Nicki White', 'Nicki Rose', the earlier 'Domino Crimson', and 'Domino White' bloom earlier and branch more fully than the species, but are scentless.

Culture: Plants start easily from seed and transplant well but the seedlings must be hardened off gradually. Heavy rains will damage young foliage. Flowers well in full or partial sun and almost any soil. Prefers roots evenly moist but tolerates dryness. Species and hybrids will self-sow, sometimes in their original colors, occasionally producing several colors on one plant.

SALVIA splendens, Scarlet Sage. The reddest summer red there is. A perennial subshrub known here as an annual 8 or 12 to 24 inches high with glossy green foliage and small tubular red flowers clustered at the top of leafy stems in thick, showy spikes from early summer until frost. Modern colors include white, pink, salmon, purple, and bicolors, as well as bright red. It is most effective in

ABOVE 'Yellow Mighty Marietta', persistent French marigold. (Goodwin)

LEFT 'Nicki Red', shade-loving, long-blooming *Nicotiana alata*. (Goodwin)

BELOW Tall *Cleome*, a romantic filler. (Goodwin)

small groups and easily grown from seed. 'Tally-Ho', 15 to 18 inches tall, flowers from July, as do the early 19-inch, bright red 'St. John's Fire' and the scarlet dwarf 'Primco'. See list 41, *Salvia*.

IBERIS (eye-*beer*-iss) **amara, Rocket Candytuft.** Also called Hyacinth-flowered Candytuft, this is a good edger, fast-growing and bushy. It has attractive foliage and from summer to mid-fall bears showy, rounded, elongated racemes of scented, 4-petaled, pure white flowers about 12 inches tall. May be started from seed indoors or outside. Adaptable to any soil, it withstands some drought and will self-sow. *I. umbellata,* **Globe Candytuft,** the other popular annual, comes into bloom within 6 weeks of sowing, producing tightly clustered lavendar, violet, pink, or red flowers. Perennial species and culture are discussed on list 43, Flowers for Edging.

CELOSIA (sel-*loh*-shee-uh) **cristata**
Cockscomb   Tender Perennial
Colorful, durable, in varieties 4 to 24 inches tall with striking, velvety, crested blooms (Cockscomb) or feathery plumes (Plumosa Group, Feathered Amaranth). The colors are vibrant shades of red, rose, pink, yellow, apricot, burgundy red, gold, or cream. Blooms all summer to frost. The foliage is green or bronze. There are dwarfs and also taller types that may need staking, for the plumes are huge. Celosia dries with little loss of color. The dwarf Fairy Fountains has 4- to 6-inch plumes on 12-inch plants that make charming edgers. The larger Century celosias are for massed beds or cut flowers. The scarlet-plumed 'New Look' endures hot climates.

Culture: Sow seeds thinly indoors in late winter, or as soon as the soil has warmed; sow directly in full sun in fertile, well-drained soil. Transplant closely in groups 12 inches apart. The plants start well but sulk if the roots are disturbed. Don't let the seedlings dry out, but don't overwater indoors, either, or a fungicide to prevent damping-off may be necessary. Established plants withstand some drought.

LOBELIA erinus, Edging Lobelia. Very delicate plants 6 to 8 inches high with a cloud of thin, fragile stems spangled with tiny florets from late spring to mid-fall in luminous intense blues and purples, often with a white eye. There are whites and wine reds as well. 'Crystal Palace', 'Blue Moon', 'Cambridge Blue', and 'White Lady' bloom all summer to mid-fall. The trailing types, such as 'Blue Cascade', make exquisite hanging baskets. The upright types are vibrant as edgers, and the compacts and dwarfs belong in every small container. Prefers semi-sun but in cooler climates tolerates full sun. See list 32, Annuals for Shade.

VIOLA × wittrockiana, Pansy, Ladies'-delight, Heartsease, Stepmother's Flower. Just 6 to 9 inches tall, but so charismatic are the velvety painted faces in their fine, strong colors, that each seems a work of art. Among modern strains there also are tallish pansies with small flowers in melting solid colors, coral, peach, lavender, yellow, and blue. Blooms in fall and winter in mild regions and in spring in the North. Some heat-hardy strains continue through mild summers and into fall. Perennial in some areas but usually grown as an annual or biennial for fall or early spring color. Removing spent flowers and cutting back leggy plants encourages contin-

ABOVE *Phlox drummondii* 'Cecily Mix', an annual phlox as pretty as the popular perennial. (Goodwin)

RIGHT Bright reds of feathered amaranth—*Celosia cristata* Plumosa Group—combine well with other colors. (McDonald)

ued blooming. The F$_1$ hybrids tolerate summer heat better than many. The patented Universal series—'Blue Blotch', 'Yellow Blotch', and others—are among the winter-to-spring bloomers that can also tolerate summer heat. Among the many beautiful hybrids the exquisitely marked, spring-to-frost-flowering 'Joker Light Blue' is a star. For culture, see list 30, Violet—Pansy.

AGERATUM (aj-er-**ray**-tum) **houstonianum**
Flossflower   Annual
A low-growing, mounded plant 6 to 12 inches high that provides an indispensable puff of soft blue in the garden summer through fall and is available in shades of pink and in white. The dainty arrangement of the bright green pointed leaves suggests a nosegay. This indispensable blue is becoming available in sizes at least 18 inches tall—great with pink snapdragons and Dusty-miller *(Senecio cineraria,* 'Silver Dust'). Recommended are the compact, lavishly blooming, lavender-blue 'Blue Danube' (Blue Puff), the extra-early, bright blue 'Adriatic', and 'Blue Surf', which grows to 9 inches tall and blooms from June to frost. (The flower called Hardy Ageratum is *Eupatorium coelestinum.)*

Culture: After the last spring frost, sow seed indoors or outdoors. In cool regions plant in full sun in well-drained, humusy soil, and sustain moisture. In hot climates, plant in partial shade. Pinch out the tops of the first shoots to encourage branching. Deadhead to promote flowering. Ageratum browns in extreme heat, but if the dead material is removed and fertilizer and a little extra care are given, it blooms again with cooler weather and lasts until a hard frost. Usually self-sows.

PELARGONIUM × **hortorum**, Fish Geranium, Zonal Geranium, House Geranium, Horseshoe Geranium, Bedding Geranium. Beloved old-fashioned tender perennial grown as an annual and started from seed quite successfully now. The big, round flowerheads come in shades of red, salmon, pink, shocking pink, white, and more. With sunny days and cool nights it flowers all summer long and into fall. Zonal markings can be prominent and there are white-variegated cultivars. Recommended are 'Sprinter', a scarlet, and the early-blooming All-America Selections winner 'Rose Diamond'. Geraniums are among the most successful container, window box, and basket plants, and excellent in well-drained flower beds. See list 37, Geraniums—Ivy Geraniums.

PHLOX **drummondii**, Annual Phlox, Drummond Phlox. The straight leafy stems up to 18 inches tall bear loose panicles of silky pastel flowers as pretty as the Perennial Phlox. Blooms midsummer to fall—white, pink, rose, red, lavender, magenta, cerise, and fuchsia, some with a contrasting eye. It grows easily from fresh seed and often self-sows. Deadheading encourages blooming. Recommended are the 10-inch 'Dwarf Beauty' in white, pink, or blue and the 16-inch 'Cecily Mix'. For culture, see list 27, *Phlox.*

ZINNIA **elegans**. Loved for the brilliance of its daisylike flowers and free-blooming habit, the zinnia has been bred to many vibrant colors, shapes, heights, and forms. There's a beauty for every garden use and they're unbeatable as cut flowers. Where mildew is a problem, however, they are not recommended. See list 42, *Zinnia.*

CLEOME (klee-*oh*-mee) **hasslerana,** Spider Flower. This is a wonderfully airy, back-of-the-border filler 3 to 5 feet tall that bears big, open white, pink, or lavender-pink flowers. It peaks in late summer and early fall. Perfect background for a mixed flowering border. Absolutely trouble-free but may need staking.

Culture: Cleome flowers readily from seed sown in midspring in full sun in light, slightly sandy soil. Maintain moisture—but the plant is adaptable. Self-sows freely. 'Rose Queen', 'Purple Queen', and 'Helen Campbell', a white, are recommended (often attributed to *C. spinosa,* a similar species). Self-sows generously.

MORE ANNUALS FOR SUN

The following annuals are also good for sunny gardens:

ANTIRRHINUM majus, Snapdragon, see list 71, The Cutting Garden.

COSMOS bipinnatus, see list 33, Annuals for Fall.

COSMOS sulphureus, Yellow Cosmos, Orange Cosmos, see list 69, To Attract Butterflies and Hummingbirds.

CUPHEA ignea, Cigar Flower, Firecracker Plant, see list 19, Perennials Wintering Indoors.

DIANTHUS chinensis, Princess Mix, Rainbow Pink, see list 70, The Fragrance Garden

DYSSODIA tenuiloba, Dahlberg Daisy, Golden-fleece, see list 34, Annuals That Self-sow.

HELIOTROPUM arborescens, Heliotrope, see list 70, The Fragrance Garden.

PENSTEMON hartwegii hybrids (gloxiniodes), Beard-tongue, see list 69, To Attract Butterflies and Hummingbirds.

PORTULACA grandiflora, Rose Moss, see list 63, The Container Garden.

RUDBECKIA hirta, Black-eyed Susan, see list 15, Summer Perennials for Sun.

SALPIGLOSSIS sinuata, Painted-tongue, see list 35, Annuals to Start Indoors.

SALVIA farinacea 'Victoria', Mealycup Sage, see list 41, Salvia.

SANVITALIA procumbens 'Mandarin Orange', Creeping Zinnia, Trailing Santivitalia, see list 43, Flowers for Edging.

SOURCE: TALENTED AMATEUR GARDENER CHARLES H. GOODWIN, SHERRILL, NEW YORK, HAS SINCE 1974 DEVOTED HIS TIME TO LOOKING FOR THE PERFECT ANNUAL. THE CHOICES HERE ARE FROM TRIALS HE HAS MADE OF APPROXIMATELY 900 TYPES OF ANNUALS IN SOME 2,500 SEPARATE PLANTINGS.

Bright shade-lovers—hot pink impatiens, orange and red tuberous begonias in baskets, pink wax begonias alternating with clumps of blue lobelia. (Viette)

32. ANNUALS FOR SHADE

■ **These are the seedlings offered by garden centers in late spring already flowering and ready to provide instant color for shady places left empty by fading spring flowers. They bloom all summer to fall and some last through the first light frosts.**

All are most successful in semi-sun or filtered light; 4 to 6 hours of sun a day is ideal. A place in the bright or filtered light under the tall trees or shrubs is fine. So are spots shaded from the hottest hours of noon to 4 o'clock sun—which is hotter than morning sun. Most may be grown in sun in northern areas as long as the soil maintains a constant supply of moisture. The closer these shade-loving plants get to Zones 9 through 11, the more they need protection from hot afternoon sun.

Companion and Follow-on Plants: The annuals are nice with shade-loving foliage plants such as ferns, hostas, galax, *Salvia argentea,* or Dusty-miller; in the background use polygonatums, *Cornus canadensis,* shade-loving ornamental grasses, or *Rodgersia.* Nice for later on are fall-flowering bulbs, potted mums, and the plants on list 33, Annuals for Fall.

BEGONIA **Semperflorens-Cultorum Hybrids,** Bedding Begonia, Wax Begonia. A crisp and colorful low edger that succeeds in sun if temperatures stay under 90° F, but thrives in filtered light. It flowers from spring until frost in hues of salmon, pink, red, or white, and the crisp, shiny brownish green or bright green leaves are attractive. There are also variegated strains. Among the recommendations for some shade are the Prima Donna hybrids, including 'Pizzazz', a green-leaved 10-inch mound that bears masses of 1½-inch blooms in vibrant shades, and 'Party Fun', 12 to 15 inches high, which bears 2-inch flowers from the last frost in spring to the first in fall. See list 36, *Begonia.*

BROWALLIA speciosa 'Major', Sapphire Flower. A lovely little plant with cascading branches about 12 inches long, dainty leaves, and lavender-blue (most often) or white star-faced flowers. A good basket or box plant that blooms indoors or out in filtered sun. See list 63, The Container Garden.

CATHARANTHUS roseus, Rose Periwinkle, Madagascar Periwinkle. Also called *"Vinca rosea"*— it does resemble a pink vinca—this is a 12-inch-high, bushy mound that spreads to 18 and 24 inches in a season. The shiny leaves are dark green and evergreen in warm climates, but farther north the plant is handled as an annual. All summer it displays upright flowers like small

TOP Heat-resistant *Catharanthus roseus* 'Pretty in Pink', a popular sunplant that will flower in shade and has extraordinary stress resistance. (All American Selections)

LEFT Lovely, bright impatiens, the most-planted shade flower, peaks late summer and early fall. (Viette)

BELOW *Lobela erinus*, exquisite edger, has many colors but dark blue is best. (Goodwin)

phlox in mauve-pink or white, usually with a darker rose or red eye. Excellent for baskets, borders and as ground cover. Recommended is 'Pink Panther', which is under 12 inches tall and has clear rose-red flowers with a darker eye; and the Little Series, 23 inches tall with a spread of up to 24 inches. 'Pretty in Pink', 'Pretty in Rose', and 'Parasol'—white with a rose-red eye—are exceptionally heat- and drought-tolerant All-America Selections and continue to flower even in full sun. For culture, see list 58, Urban Conditions.

DIGITALIS purpurea 'Foxy', Foxglove. The foxgloves are strikingly tall, very narrow spikes of pendulous thimble- or finger-shaped white, cream, yellow, or rosy red flowers, usually with dark spots. They bloom spring and early summer according to region and species and are outstanding in clumps or singly. 'Foxy' is a biennial dwarf 30 to 36 inches tall that flowers in early summer from seed sown 5 months before. Perennials and culture are described on list 60, The Cottage Garden.

EXACUM (ex-ak-um) affine
German Violet, Persian Violet.
A bushy, free-flowering biennial 12 to 24 inches high with tiny, fragrant, long-lasting, saucer-shaped flowers in summer, usually light violet-blue with yellow or white eyes. The foliage is waxy. Excellent as a pot plant.
   Culture: In late winter, sow seed in semi-sun in humusy soil, and maintain moisture. Transplant after the air warms. Flowers bloom in about 6 months.

IMPATIENS. Summer-long bloom in filtered light and semishade is the exceptional gift of these low-growing tender perennials and annuals that cover themselves with glowing flowers backed by delicate, pointed leaves. By autumn they are tall, and the show grows brighter until frost.
   The familiar impatiens is *I. wallerana*, Zanzibar Balsam, Busy Lizzy, the most popular low-growing flower for shaded gardens and containers. A sprawling habit makes it a good basket plant, too, especially cascading types such as 'Blitz' and 'Showstopper' and the low-growing, big-flowered Super Elfins. The array of colors increases yearly—dark red, hot pink, intense coral, orchid, white, pale lavender—and there are bicolors and strains with variegated leaves. The height of standard size plants by fall is to 36 inches; compacts stay at 6 to 8 inches. Recommended are: 'Shady Lady' pastels, which often have a darker center in 2-inch flowers on 12- to 15-inch plants; the very early 'Tempo Blush'; the 10-inch, early 'Accent Pink', which thrives in real shade; the compact Super Elfin group, including 'Blue Pearl', a rather sprawling, delicate lilac-blue. More upright and more adaptable to sun if their roots are kept moist are the upright New Guinea Spectra hybrids; the flowers are to 4 inches across and much of the lush foliage is variegated.
   I. balsamina, **Garden Balsam**, is a leafy, upright plant 30 inches high with bright little flowers that sparkle through dense foliage from midsummer through frost. Recommended are dwarf types with double blooms. Sow seeds indoors and set the plants out when the weather warms. See list 38, *Impatiens*.

LOBELIA erinus, Edging Lobelia. Very delicate plants 6 to 8 inches high with a cloud of thin, fragile stems spangled with tiny florets from late spring to mid-fall in beautiful, luminous, intense blues and purples, often with a white eye. There are whites and wine reds as well. The upright types are vibrant edgers, and the compacts and dwarfs belong in every small container. The blue cascade types such as 'Blue Cascade' make exquisite basket plants. Recommended compacts include 'Crystal Palace', dark blue with bronzed foliage; 'Blue Moon'; 'Cambridge Blue', a lighter blue; and 'White Lady'. Sow seeds in sandy soil indoors, 10 weeks before the weather warms. Transplant— or set out container plants—with roots intact into light, humusy soil and maintain moisture. Thrives in light shade but survives partial sun. See also list 16, Summer Perennials for Shade.

MIMULUS (*mim*-yew-lus) **luteus**
Monkey Flower   Zones 4-9
This is a delightful and tough little native found from Canada to Mexico. About 12 inches high, in summer it bears long-blooming snapdragon-like yellow flowers splotched with red. It flourishes in baskets, borders, and damp pockets in woodlands and rock gardens. Pretty multicolored hybrids are grown as annuals because they are not winter hardy. They are early blooming with 2-inch flowers in red, orange, pink, or yellow, and some are splotched.

   Culture: Seeds sown indoors germinate fairly easily. May also be sown outdoors in fall or early spring in semi-sun or shade in well-drained moist soil amply supplied with peat moss or leaf mold. Maintain moisture.

MYOSOTIS (mye-oh-*soh*-tiss) **sylvatica** 'Victoria Blue'
Forget-me-not   Zones 3-8
An endearing, shade-loving flower 6 to 8 inches high that is grown as an annual or biennial and blooms from seed in 6 weeks—late spring and early summer. The dainty little blossoms are an unforgettable gentian-blue, very effective in drifts around late-flowering bulbs. There are pinks and whites, but the blue is the favorite. The very similar species *M. alpestris* is perennial.

   Culture: In early spring sow seeds or set out seedlings in light shade in moist, somewhat acid soil. Maintain even moisture. Fertilize every other month during the growing season. Self-sows generously once established. In the North, full sun is acceptable.

NICOTIANA alata, Jasmine Tobacco, Flowering Tobacco. Tender perennial, lush, semirecumbent, 15 to 24 inches tall, with big leaves. An excellent filler. The species blooms lavishly from July and August to early frosts, sending up clusters of tubular white flowers that open and release a lilylike scent late in the day. 'Lime Green' is a fresh greeny white. Modern hybrids such as 'Nicki White', 'Nicki Rose', and the earlier 'Domino Crimson' and 'Domino White' bloom sooner and have better branching than the species. Nicotiana flowers well in sun or partial sun, almost any soil and tolerates damp situations. See also list 31, Annuals for Sun.

Source: Viki Ferreniea, Assistant Horticultural Director for Wayside Gardens in South Carolina. A horticulturist and lecturer, Viki was formerly the Rock Garden Curator at the New York Botanical Garden.

Big, bold ornamental cabbages are planted in early and mid-fall, instant color replacement for fading garden flowers. (Frease)

33. ANNUALS FOR FALL

■ **These are the ultimate follow-on plants—cold-weather flowers, great colorful cabbages and kales, and an annual "bush"—that brighten the garden from late summer until killing frosts. Some of the best fall displays come from flowers that bloom first in summer and then color up again in the cooling temperatures and additional moisture of autumn. Don't pull up anything that isn't dead—wait and see what nature is going to do next. In October, flowers that burn out in the hot summers of the Southeast are still flourishing on the West Coast and along the Gulf, and may bloom into winter.**

   Companion Plants: The greatest fall color comes from the already-blooming potted cushion mums sold in late summer and early fall. They're perennials usually discarded in spring—see list 23, Mum-Daisy. Some bulbs, perennials, ornamental grasses, and foliage plants put on a great show when cold weather comes—look for them on lists 4, 17, 49, 51, 53, and 54. In the Northwest and Southeast, where winters are mild, set out pansies and primroses in fall.

BRASSICA (*brass*-ik-uh) **oleracea Acephala Group, Ornamentals**
Flowering Cabbage, Flowering Kale
Showstoppers to start from seed, or pop into the garden or containers as potted plants in early fall. The jade green leaves of these fabulous cabbages and kales are streaked, splotched, and edged with deep red, purple, and cream. The colors become more vibrant as temperatures cool. Real vegetables bred for exquisite, subtle, and fanciful effects, they're between 12 and 24 inches high.

   Culture: Like kitchen cabbages, these need cool air and flourish through mild winters, often all the way to spring. Keep the flowerheads pinched out. Brassicas thrive in deeply dug, well-drained, fertile soil that holds moisture. Sow seed outdoors in late spring or early summer in full sun, or purchase potted plants in early fall. Maintain moisture.

Ornamental Cabbage
It's a cabbage but it looks more like a huge rose edged with red, pink, or cream. Recommended is 'Color Up Hybrid', 12 inches across, whose brilliant splotching and streaking occupies a full 80 percent of the head.

Flowering Kale 'Peacock Hybrid'
This cultivator has feathery leaves and is extra compact—about 12 inches tall. The leaves are extravagantly serrated or notched and make a remarkable display in red or white.

CALENDULA (kal-*lend*-yew-luh) **officinalis,** Pot Marigold
An old favorite about 24 inches tall grown for the brilliant gold and orange flower petals that once colored and flavored desserts—and for the fresh green of its foliage. (This is the "marigold" of Shakespeare and ancient herbals. One tablespoon of minced petals transforms cream-cheese dips and desserts.) Does best in cool weather and even withstands light frosts—in the East it blooms in summer and fall and on the West Coast and along the Gulf, February through late spring. In the garden, group the plants in minimums of 6. Handsome in big tubs. Recommended for the front of the border is 'Bon Bon', a compact 12-inch plant with 2½- to 3-inch blooms in clear, bright colors. 'Kablouna', 12 to 24 inches tall, has elegant crested flowers.

rather alkaline soil well supplied with humus. Don't plant in the same place on successive years. Where mildew is prevalent, choose improved, mildew-resistant cultivars. Pinch out the leader to encourage branching, and deadhead consistently.

CAPSICUM (*kap*-sik-um) **annuum** var. **annuum**
Ornamental Pepper
The ornamental peppers belong to the variety *annuum* and add touches of sparkling red and yellow to the fall scene. The very good Fasciculatum Group includes the Cluster Pepper hybrid, 'Treasure Red', 8 inches tall with conical fruit clusters that stand well above the deep green foliage. The little peppers change from white to bright red as they mature. Nice with herbs.

Culture: Seeds germinate in about 2 weeks after the weather has warmed (70° to 80° F) and thrive in fertile, well-drained soil in full sun. Fertilize regularly with 5-10-5 and maintain soil moisture in droughts. Good container plants, indoors or outdoors.

CLEOME **hasslerana**, Spider Flower. A tall, airy,
back-of-the-border filler with white, pink, or lavender-pink flowers that peak in late summer and early fall. 'Rose Queen', 'Purple Queen', and 'Helen Campbell', a white, are recommended. Perfect background for a mixed flowering border. Absolutely trouble-free and usually volunteers the next season. See list 31, Annuals for Sun.

COSMOS (*kos*-moss) **bipinnatus**. A tall, willowy
plant with many dispersed but showy 2- to 4-inch-wide, open-faced flowers in clear colors—crimson, rose, yellow, and white—with crested or tufted centers held above delicate ferny foliage. The plants are 3 to 4 feet high. They flower in summer and continue in vigorous bloom until killed by frost. Very decorative grouped at the back of a mixed border with asters and Japanese anemones. Lasting and lovely as cut flowers—cutting encourages growth. Recommended for its fall display is the Early Wonder series, a mix of big-flowered cosmos in vibrant rose, pink, crimson, and white. For smaller gardens, try the Sunny series (*C. sulphureus*), 16 to 18 inches tall, with bright scarlet flowers.

Culture: In the North, sow seeds indoors and transplant to full sun and well-drained, humusy soil after the ground has warmed in early spring. Early-flowering strains bloom from seed in 8 to 10 weeks. Cosmos withstands drying winds, but it flops without sufficient sun and may need staking. Self-sows in good conditions.

DAHLIA × **hybrida** Unwin Hybrids. These are
bushy, pretty little plants that in late summer and fall bear small many-petaled blossoms in strong, usually showy colors. Tender perennials, they are usually planted in late spring and discarded at the end of the season. Garden centers offer flats of seedlings and container plants, but they are easily raised from seed sown indoors 6 to 8 weeks before the weather warms. Recommended is the Rigoletto Mix that produces 12-inch plants with double and semidouble flowers 2½ inches across in yellow, red, orange, pink, and white. For a discussion of these and the big show dahlias, see list 10, *Dahlia*.

FACING PAGE Bright orange *Cosmos sulphureus* shows its late summer–fall color in a bed interplanted with lavender-blue *Salvia farinacea*. (Frease)
ABOVE *Cosmos bipinnatus* cultivars, 'Seashells'. A handsome cutting flower, cosmos usually is started from seed sown indoors in spring. It self-sows regularly. (Stokes Seed Co.)

Culture: Sow seeds in the garden in June and July for fall color in the East. For spring bloom, sow seeds indoors in January. On the West Coast and along the Gulf, plant seeds in October for bloom from February through late spring. Plant in full sun or very bright shade in well-drained soil that sustains moisture. Deadhead to prolong flowering.

CALLISTEPHUS (kal-*liss*-tef-us) **chinensis**
China Aster, Annual Aster
This looks like a big aster or a small cushion mum and provides showy late summer and fall color in the aster spectrum—lavender-blue, purple, pink, rosy red, and white. The plants are well-branched and bushy, 12 to 30 inches high. The more flowers you cut (on short stems) the more blooms you get. Dwarfs are especially charming when half-blanketed by the last fall leaves.

Culture: For late summer blooming, start the seeds indoors in early spring. For fall flowers, sow seeds outdoors after danger of frost. Best in full sun in well-drained,

IMPATIENS balsamina, Garden Balsam. From midsummer until frost, colorful little flowers, single or double, white, red, yellow, or bicolor, sparkle from lush foliage on upright stalks to 30 inches high. This cousin of the sprawling impatiens, *I. wallerana*, thrives in a lightly shaded garden, but in cooler regions it tolerates the sun if the soil is rich, humusy, and evenly moist. Sow seeds indoors and set the plants out when the weather warms. Recommended are the bush-flowered dwarf types with double blooms. For culture see list 38, *Impatiens*.

KOCHIA scoparia forma trichophylla 'Childsii', Burning Bush, Fire Bush, Red Summer Cypress. A tough annual which even in hot, polluted areas develops in a single season from seed into what seems to be a full-grown dwarf evergreen, columnar, pyramidal, or round, 24 to 36 inches high. With cold weather, the 2-inch leaves burn purplish to bright red. Valuable for fall color, for quick, temporary hedges, and in groups as a filler for the back of the border. 'Childsii', an improved plant, is recommended. For culture see list 51, Foliage for Color.

LOBULARIA maritima, Sweet Alyssum. This is a very sweetly scented and dainty flowering edger 4 to 8 inches high that grows into a low mound 12 to 18 inches across and covers itself with tiny, sparkling white, rosy violet, or purple florets in summer and fall. A midsummer slump in flowering can occur in extreme heat, but flowering resumes when cooler weather returns. Self-sows. For culture see list 43, Flowers for Edging.

LYSIMACHIA (lye-sim-*may*-kee-uh) congestiflora 'Eco Dark Stain'
Tender Perennial/Zones 4/5-7/8
A wonderful flowering ground cover 6 to 12 inches high that blooms in summer but comes into its own in the cooling temperatures of fall and lasts until November. It covers itself with clusters of cup-shaped, rich golden flowers with red throats. The foliage forms dense mats of apple green leaves edged in dark red. It is becoming generally available.

Culture: Sow seeds in spring in semi-sun in good neutral-range garden soil well supplied with organic matter to retain moisture. Needs lots of space, and may become a nuisance. Mulched for winter, it goes on.

NICOTIANA alata, Jasmine Tobacco, Flowering Tobacco. Tender perennial, lush, semirecumbent, 15 to 24 inches tall, with big leaves. An excellent filler. Blooms lavishly from July into August to early frosts, sending up clusters of tubular white flowers that open and release a lilylike scent late in the day. 'Lime Green' is a fresh greeny white. Modern hybrids such as 'Nicki White', 'Nicki Rose', and the earlier 'Domino Crimson' and 'Domino White' bloom sooner and have better branching than the species. For culture see list 31, Annuals for Sun.

Source: Viki Ferreniea, Assistant Horticultural Director for Wayside Gardens in South Carolina. A horticulturist and lecturer, Viki was formerly the Rock Garden Curator at the New York Botanical Garden.

34. ANNUALS THAT SELF-SOW

■ Annuals and biennials that reseed themselves will naturalize—or at least repeat well for a few years—if conditions are right.

The seedlings of self-sowers are called "volunteers." Petunia, snapdragon, and some zinnia volunteers turn up in my Washington, D.C., garden every year. In northern gardens the growing season usually is too brief to make nurturing them worthwhile. But farther south snapdragons, four o'clocks, and even petunia volunteers can make a nice show toward the end of summer when fresh color is so welcome.

The volunteers of the self-sowers that follow do everything right. They bloom about as they would if you had sown the seeds yourself. But be aware: in some situations self-sowers are so productive they become weeds—Morning-glory comes to mind.

Culture: For plants to self-sow successfully, everything has to come together in just the right way. Some seeds germinate as soon as they ripen. Others need a rest or cold and moisture to break down the shell that protects the embryo and expose it to oxygen, water, and the sequence of temperatures that encourages growth.

To encourage volunteers, spread a 1- or 2-inch layer of well-prepared soil around the feet of the parent plants, dampen the soil, gather the seeds as they ripen, and scatter them over the prepared soil. Or, monitor the seeds as they ripen and when they are dry and loose in their casings, shake the flowerheads vigorously over prepared soil.

AGERATUM houstonianum, Flossflower. A low-growing, mounded plant 6 to 12 inches high that provides an indispensable puff of soft blue in the garden summer through fall and is also available in shades of pink and in white. The dainty arrangement of the bright green pointed leaves suggests a nosegay. Volunteer in modest numbers when moisture is consistent. See list 31, Annuals for Sun.

CENTAUREA (sen-taw-*ree*-uh) cyanus Cornflower, Bachelor's-button, Bluebottle. The shaggy or fluffy little flowerheads (1½ inches across) are a characteristic bright, deep blue (though there are also purples, pinks, and whites), intensified by a dark-brown eye. This is a fast-growing annual excellent for cutting. Improved plants have larger double flowers, for instance 'Blue Diadem', 2½ inches across on stems to 24 inches tall. See also list 60, The Cottage Garden.

Culture: Easily grown from seed sown in the garden in early fall or spring where the plants are to grow. Or in early spring start seeds indoors. Blooms all summer and in early fall if successive sowings are made. Successful in full sun, in any well-drained, even poor, soil. In warm regions often self-sows.

CLEOME hasslerana, Spider Flower. A tall, airy, back-of-the-border filler with white, pink, or lavender-pink flowers that peak in late summer and early fall. 'Rose Queen', 'Purple Queen', and 'Helen Campbell', a white, are recommended. Perfect background for a mixed flowering border. Absolutely trouble-free and usually volunteers the next season. See list 31, Annuals for Sun.

COSMOS bipinnatus. These are tall, delicate but tough flowers with 2- to 4-inch, wide-petaled daisy faces in clear colors blooming on willowy stems 3 to 4 feet tall—nice in large pots or boxes. The centers may be crested or tufted. Long lasting in arrangements—bloom is from summer until frost, and cutting encourages new growth. Self-sows. For culture see list 33, Annuals for Fall.

DYSSODIA (diss-**oh**-dee-uh) tenuiloba Dahlberg Daisy, Golden-fleece. This daisy grows from seed into a bushy plant 9 to 12 inches tall in just 4 months, and blooms through summer in shades of red, orange, yellow, and sometimes white. A good soil binder but can be temperamental.

Culture: Best in cool climates and self-sows easily in well-drained, sandy soil. A good bedding plant for full sun. Tolerant of drought.

ESCHSCHOLZIA (esh-**sholt**-see-uh) californica
California Poppy   Tender Perennial
These lovely, silky poppies 3 to 4 inches across bloom all summer in luminous colors ranging from deep orange, coral, pink, and scarlet to golden yellow and white. There are bicolors, double, semidouble, and frilled forms. The plants are 12 to 18 inches tall and the flowers are borne on sinuous, wandlike stems above low-lying, blue-green, deeply cut foliage. Tender perennials grown as annuals. See also list 28, Poppy.

Culture: For flowers in the North in June and July, sow seeds outdoors in early spring where the plants are to bloom. In warmer areas, sow seeds in fall for spring flowering. Plant in full sun in light, sandy, somewhat dry soil. Self-sows generously and naturalizes in regions such as its native southern California.

LAVATERA (lav-at-*teer*-uh) trimestris
Tree Mallow
A bold, branching, very bushy annual up to 5 feet tall with big leaves and showy, trumpet-shaped pink or red flowers, to 4 inches wide, that bloom all summer until killed by frost. Modern mallows include dwarfs and some handsome whites. Need lots of space—a good corner anchor in the garden.

Culture: A sunny spot protected from wind is ideal. Sow seeds in late April or early May where plants are to grow; use ordinary, well-drained garden soil enriched with humus.

LINARIA (lye-*nay*-ree-uh) maroccana 'Fairy Bouquet'
Toadflax, Spurred Snapdragon
A fast-growing hybrid 8 to 10 inches tall that produces masses of snapdragon-like flowers on short spikes in carmine, primrose, white, purple, or pink with white throats. Flowering is lush in early summer and it sometimes repeats in fall. An excellent small plant for the front of the border and the cutting garden.

Culture: Sow seeds outdoors in April and keep faded flowers picked. It grows easily in full sun and ordinary, well-drained garden soil. Often self-sows.

Some of the prettiest annuals self-sow:
BELOW *Linum perenne*, Perennial Flax. (Goodwin)
TOP, RIGHT *Lavatera trimestris*, Tree Mallow. (Goodwin)
BOTTOM, LEFT *Linaria maroccana* 'Fairy Bouquet'. (Goodwin)
BOTTOM, RIGHT *Nigella damascena*, Love-in-a-mist,
'Persian Jewels Mix'. (Goodwin)

LINUM (*lye*-num) **perenne**

Perennial Flax   Zones 5-9

This willowy perennial 12 to 18 inches tall is included here because it will bloom the first year from seed. The flowers are an arresting shade of sky blue and borne from early to midsummer. There's also a white variety. Though the blooms are short-lived, masses of them are constantly appearing.

Culture: Sow seeds in April in light, well-drained, well-prepared soil in full sun where plants are to bloom. Often self-sows. Nice in rock gardens and perennializes well. Tolerates drought.

MYOSOTIS **sylvatica**, Forget-me-not. A shade-loving little flower 6 to 8 inches high that blooms from seed in 6 weeks, in late spring and early summer. The dainty little blossoms are an unforgettable gentian-blue, charming in drifts around late-flowering bulbs. There are pinks and whites, but blue is the favorite. In a slightly shaded, moist situation in well-worked, acid soil it self-sows and naturalizes. See list 32, Annuals for Shade

NEMOPHILA (nee-*moff*-ill-uh) **maculata**

Five-spot

Fast-growing, charming, and showy small plant that in summer covers itself with white petunia-like flowers, each petal spotted purple at the outer edge. About 4 to 8 inches tall, excellent for lightly shaded rock gardens.

Culture: Sow seeds where plants are to bloom in sun or semi-sun—in autumn in warm regions and in early spring in the cool North. Light, loamy soil with added humus is best, and protection from strong winds helps maintain it. Self-sows and spreads easily but doesn't last well in very hot weather. Tolerates some drought.

NICOTIANA **alata**, Jasmine Tobacco, Flowering Tobacco. Tender perennial, lush, semirecumbent, 15 to 24 inches tall, with big leaves. An excellent filler. Blooms lavishly from July or August to early frosts, sending up clusters of tubular white flowers that open and release a lilylike scent late in the day. The species, particularly the whites, are fragrant; hybrids, less so. It flowers well in sun or partial sun, almost any soil, and tolerates damp situations. Often self-sows and grows readily from seed. The hybrids also self-sow, sometimes in their original colors, occasionally producing several colors on one plant. For culture see list 31, Annuals for Sun.

NIGELLA **damascena**, Love-in-a-mist, Wild Fennel. The flowers of this very pretty, fast-growing annual 18 to 24 inches tall are spidery, 1 to 2 inches across, and bloom all summer in blue, pink, or white if successive plantings are made. The finely divided bright green foliage is a good filler for hanging baskets and boxes of mixed flowers. Excellent cut flower, and the dried seedpods are attractive in winter arrangements. Dwarfs such as 'Blue Midget' are 8 to 10 inches tall. The standard 12- to 18-inch 'Persian Jewels' has white, pink, red, and purple flowers. 'Miss Jekyll' is blue. For culture, see list 72, To Dry for Winter Bouquets.

PAPAVER **rhoeas**, Corn Poppy, Field Poppy. The Shirley Poppy, a strain of this small, pastel flower, has been hybridized to produce begonia- and ranunculus-flowered plants in wonderful shades of pink, rose, and coral-pink. It is a hardy annual grown from seed sown outdoors—late summer or early fall in warmer regions where it blooms in spring, early spring in cooler regions where it blooms in midsummer. It needs full sun and light, sandy, well-drained soil to flower well. Sow the very fine seeds sparsely in little drifts where the plants are to flower. Deadhead to keep the flowers producing. Self-sows under good conditions. See also list 28, Poppy.

PHLOX· **drummondii**, Annual Phlox. The straight, leafy stems reach up to 18 inches high and bear loose panicles of silky, pastel flowers as pretty as the perennial phlox; the colors may be white, pink, rose, red, lavender, magenta, cerise, or fuchsia, some with a contrasting eye. It blooms from midsummer to late fall and grows easily from seed as long as the seed is fresh. Deadheading encourages continued blooming. It self-sows and has naturalized in sand in the Outer Banks of North Carolina, Zones 8 to 9. Recommended are the 10-inch 'Dwarf Beauty' in white, pink, or blue, and the 16-inch 'Cecily Mix'. See list 27, Phlox, and list 31, Annuals for Sun.

PORTULACA **grandiflora**, Rose Moss, Sun Plant, Eleven-o'clock, is a pretty little trailing plant with fat needle leaves. It blooms generously all summer; the flowers are single or double, in red, pink, yellow, coral, or white. It thrives on hot, dry slopes and in baskets. Modern portulacas stay open through the day; the old-fashioned species plants tend to close their blooms after bees have visited. The plant is a hardy annual grown from seed sown outdoors—late summer or early fall in warmer regions where it blooms in spring, early spring in cooler regions where it blooms in midsummer. Types like 'Cloud-beater' and 'All-Day Mix' seldom live up to their names in dull weather. See list 63, The Container Garden.

TALINUM **paniculatum**, Jewels-of-opar, Fame-flower. A prolific self-sower up to 24 inches high with waxy, succulent, bright green leaves. Sends up airy panicles of pink flowers followed by burgundy-colored seedpods. It blooms profusely in June and is popular in rock gardens. See list 55, Easy Alpine Plants.

SOURCE: TALENTED AMATEUR GARDENER CHARLES H. GOODWIN, SHERRILL, NEW YORK, HAS SINCE 1974 DEVOTED HIS TIME TO LOOKING FOR THE PERFECT ANNUAL. THE CHOICES HERE ARE FROM TRIALS HE HAS MADE OF APPROXIMATELY 900 TYPES OF ANNUALS IN SOME 2,500 SEPARATE PLANTINGS.

35. ANNUALS TO START INDOORS

■ **Where the growing season is short, seeds started early indoors can provide seedlings that will have time to mature in the garden before summer shuts down. Where weather isn't a factor, economy can be a motive for starting your own annuals. Seeds cost less than seedlings and nothing at all if you harvest your own. Seeds of petunias, marigolds, and zinnias are very easy to collect. And starting seeds indoors is a way to be in the garden before the weather invites you outdoors.**

The annuals recommended here are especially easy to start from seed and provide an assortment of follow-on flowers for the summer border. Avoid leaning on wax begonias and lantana, which need more care than other annuals, and gomphrena, which can be difficult.

BEGONIA **Semperflorens-Cultorum Hybrids**, Bedding Begonia, Wax Begonia. A crisp and colorful low edger that succeeds in sun but thrives in filtered light. It flowers from spring until frost in hues of salmon, pink, red, or white, and the crisp, shiny leaves are attractive. It is more difficult than many to start from seed, but when potted up in fall and brought indoors to a sunny windowsill, it continues to bloom. In late winter root 6-inch cuttings in water; when the weather warms set out the rooted cuttings and the cut-back parent, too. New seedlings will be required annually. See list 36, *Begonia*, for information about the rhizomatous begonias that start well indoors.

CELOSIA **cristata, Plumosa Group**, Feathered Amaranth, is a colorful, durable plant with beautiful feathery plumes in bright shades of red, pink, yellow, apricot, burgundy red, gold, or cream. Sow these seeds thinly indoors in late winter. The plants start well but sulk if the roots are disturbed. Don't let the seedlings dry out but don't overwater, either, or a fungicide to prevent damping-off may be necessary. See list 31, Annuals for Sun.

CLARKIA (*klark*-ee-uh)

Farewell-to-spring, Godetia

Showy, hardy annual that prefers cool nights and bears spikes of charming, delicately frilled, upward-facing single or double flowers in 3 months from seed. The long-lasting summer to fall blooms are good for cutting.

Culture: The plant blooms from seed in 3 months but must be sown where it is to grow as it doesn't stand transplanting. Sow seeds thickly in fall in warm regions, early spring in cooler areas, in well-drained, gritty soil that is not rich; allow to dry between waterings. Not good in high heat, but thrives in full sun or semi-sun in cool regions such as the Pacific Northwest. Keep fading flowers cut to encourage a long season of bloom and allow the plants to set seed for next year's display.

C. amoena Satin Flower

Small, fast-growing, 9 to 12 inches tall, with masses of satiny single flowers with wavy petals.

Try these annuals as pot plants indoors:
TOP Showy *Salpiglossis* blooms indoors in a cool room.
(Longwood Gardens)
BOTTOM, LEFT *Nemesia strumosa* covers itself with
trumpet-shaped blooms from June to September.
(Longwood Gardens)
BOTTOM, RIGHT *Felicia dubia*, a fall bloomer indoors,
grows wild along the cool New England coast. (McDonald)

'Daddy Mix' *Petunia*, an annual of many uses, is easy to start indoors. (Ball Seed Co.)

C. concinna Red-Ribbons
A California native that flowers all summer in pink and purple on stems to 24 inches tall.

C. pulchella
Semidouble and double flowers in white, lavender, and carmine on stems 12 to 15 inches tall.

FELICIA (fel-*lish*-ee-uh) dubia
Pretty little blue daisy 12 inches high. Seeds sown indoors in pots in early spring form low mounds of foliage that may be moved outdoors after frost danger is past, and will bear sky blue daisylike flowers in summer to early fall. It may be brought back indoors for winter flowering.

Culture: Grows best in well-drained, evenly moist soil in full sun. Remove spent flowers to extend the bloom season.

IMPATIENS wallerana, Zanzibar Balsam, Busy Lizzy.
Masses of sparkling little flowers from summer to frost and delicate, pointed leaves make this the most popular low-growing annual (actually a tender perennial) for shaded places—porch gardens, under the canopy of trees and tall shrubs, in the shadows of city buildings. By autumn the plants are tall, and the show grows brighter until frost. Excellent for baskets and boxes. The array of colors grows every year—dark red, hot pink, intense coral, orchid, and white are now included, and there are bicolors and strains with variegated leaves. The bigger New Guinea Impatiens has more substantial foliage and withstands more sun if it is grown in humusy soil with sustained moisture. New Guinea Spectra hybrids bloom from seed, producing 2- to 3-inch flowers with much of the foliage variegated. Impatiens seed is not difficult to start, but the seedlings are very sensitive to cold and hot sun so carefully and gradually harden them off before planting them outside. See list 38, *Impatiens*.

LOBELIA erinus, Edging Lobelia,
blooms late spring to mid-fall in beautiful rich blues, some with a white eye, and is an exquisite edger for filtered sun. There are also white forms, wine reds, compacts, and dwarfs. Blue cascade types make superb basket plants. Sow these very fine seeds thinly indoors 10 weeks before the weather warms. Generally, lobelia is a strong sprouter. Allow the seedlings to get large enough to handle easily before transplanting. Transplant with care to light, humusy soil in semishade. Set the crown a fraction above the soil line and maintain even moisture. See also list 32, Annuals for Shade.

MYOSOTIS sylvatica, Forget-me-not,
is a small, shade-loving plant 6 to 8 inches high, considered annual or biennial, that blooms from seed in 6 weeks—in late spring and early summer. The dainty little blossoms are an unforgettable gentian blue, delightful in drifts around late-flowering bulbs. There are pinks and whites, but the blue is the favorite. The very similar species *M. alpestris* is perennial. See also list 32, Annuals for Shade.

NEMESIA (nem-*meesh*-ee-uh) strumosa
A fast-growing, bushy annual 12 to 24 inches high, sometimes called "large-flowered primrose." It covers itself with trumpet-shaped blooms from June to September. The foliage is finely toothed and attractive. Colors are white, yellow, orange, pink, red, and purple, and there are bicolors.

Culture: In early spring, sow seeds indoors in rich, moist, well-drained soil. When plants reach 4 inches, pinch tips back to encourage bushiness. Feed plants every 2 weeks. 'Grandiflora' is a large-flowered form and there are dwarfs. Plant closely in full sun for a showy display and maintain moisture.

NICOTIANA alata, Jasmine Tobacco, Flowering Tobacco.
Tender perennial, lush, semirecumbent, 15 to 24 inches tall, with big leaves. An excellent filler. The species blooms lavishly from July or August to early frosts, sending up clusters of tubular white flowers that open and release a lilylike scent late in the day. The species, particularly the whites, are fragrant, hybrids less so. Plants start easily from seed and transplant well, but the seedlings must be hardened off very gradually and carefully. Heavy rains will damage young foliage. For culture, see list 31, Annuals for Sun.

PETUNIA × hybrida
is the indispensable all-summer bloomer whose colors range through pink, red, white, blue, and lavender, and there are bicolors, cascading and supercascading types for baskets and window boxes, and uprights for bedding. Thinly sow the very fine seeds indoors 10 weeks before the last frost. At 6 inches, pinch out the central stem tip, and repeat at every 4 inches until the plant is many-branched. See list 40, *Petunia*.

SALVIA splendens, Scarlet Sage.
The reddest summer red there is. A perennial subshrub known here as an annual 8 or 12 to 24 inches high with glossy green foliage and small, tubular, red flowers clustered at the top of leafy stems in thick, showy spikes from early summer until frost. Hummingbirds sip nectar from the deep-throated blossoms. Modern colors include white, pink, salmon, purple, and bicolors, as well as bright red. This is not difficult to start from seed, though the germination of the seeds is only fair. Good light helps. Start seeds approximately 8 weeks before frost-free weather. See also list 41, Salvia.

SALPIGLOSSIS (sal-pee-*gloss*-iss) sinuata
Painted-tongue
A showy, colorful, rather fast-growing branching annual that bears 2- to 3-inch outward-facing, trumpet-shaped blooms in yellow, bronze, blue, pink, or purple, with prominent veins. The plants are 12 to 36 inches tall with pale green leaves and often need staking.

Culture: Blooms in winter from seeds sown indoors in September; blooms in June and July from seed sown indoors in March; blooms in late summer from seed sown outdoors after all danger of frost is past. Provide cool conditions and rich, sandy loam that has lots of humus and is slightly alkaline. Plant in full sun and keep the soil damp. Deadheading helps flowers continue.

TAGETES, Marigold,
blooms vigorously all summer until frost in sizes tall or small, even in hot sunny places. The full ruffled flowerheads are yellow, gold, pumpkin, or reddish orange, and there are bicolors marked with mahogany. One of few annuals that blooms through southern Florida summers. Seedlings transplant strongly and are quick to come into bloom from seeds started indoors 4 to 6 weeks before the weather warms. See list 39, Marigold.

VIOLA × wittrockiana, Pansy, Ladies'-delight, Heartsease, Stepmother's Flower.
Loved for strains whose velvety faces are painted in fine, strong colors, but the solid shades are charming, too. All bloom generously in spring and fall, and some strains continue in mild summers and winters. Perennial in much of the country, pansies usually are grown as annuals or biennials for fall or early spring color. Some self-sow. Where winters are mild and summer heat intense, they are set out in mid-fall or late fall for early spring bloom. They germinate easily and transplant without difficulty. Or, start seeds indoors about 14 weeks ahead of warm weather. See list 30, Violet—Pansy, for planting and bloom times.

ZINNIA elegans.
Loved for the brilliance of its daisylike flowers and free-blooming habit, the zinnia has been bred to many vibrant colors, shapes, and heights. There's a beauty for every garden use and they're unbeatable flowers for cutting. The seeds germinate quickly and grow into strong plants. Start them indoors 3 weeks before the weather warms. Harden off with care and when transplanting, disturbing the roots as little as possible. See also list 42, *Zinnia*.

SOURCE: TALENTED AMATEUR GARDENER CHARLES H. GOODWIN, SHERRILL, NEW YORK, HAS SINCE 1974 DEVOTED HIS TIME TO LOOKING FOR THE PERFECT ANNUAL. THE REPORTS HERE ARE FROM TRIALS HE HAS MADE OF APPROXIMATELY 900 TYPES OF ANNUALS IN SOME 2,500 SEPARATE PLANTINGS.

36. BEGONIA

■ **Begonias are nonstop summer flowers superb in window boxes, baskets, beds, or edging—some are for sun, some for semi-sun. The leaves are fresh green or rosy bronze or both, and the blossoms just keep coming from mid-spring to early frost. The wax begonias and the big tuberous hybrids once were the only begonias for outdoor gardens, but new crosses are encouraging new uses of those that we traditionally knew as greenhouse plants and houseplants. Even the Rex Begonia turns up now and then in outdoor window boxes.**

Companion Plants: Backdrop wax begonias with spires or spikes—for instance, small rosy astilbes. In partial shade, begonias combine well with impatiens, coleus, and salvia. Combine tuberous bedding begonias with caladiums in complementary colors.

BEGONIA (beg-*oh*-nee-uh)

Begonias are a diverse group from 6 inches to 4 feet tall, mostly perennials grown as annuals and grouped here by type and use. They have in common multibranched, succulent stems and handsome foliage.

Culture: A few things are true of most of the popular begonias. The ideal climate is cool and moist with even temperatures, and grown as annuals the plants succeed almost everywhere and tolerate some drought. Plant in the cool of early mid-spring for better root development, in very well-drained, rich, humusy soil. Fertilize often.

FIBROUS-ROOTED BEGONIAS

B. Semperflorens-Cultorum Hybrids Bedding Begonia, Wax Begonia   Tender Perennial

These are wonderfully carefree small plants with fibrous roots and crisp, waxy, rounded leaves that stay handsome all season. The flowers are in shades of cool white to pink, coral, bright red, and there are bicolors. Some strains have maroon-bronze leaves, others are bright green, and plants turn up now and then with green and white foliage.

Culture: Semperflorens begonias are plants for partial shade or full sun in moist soil, but in hot climates they definitely do better with some shade. The leaves darken in full sun. Bronze-leaved begonias withstand the hot, humid South better than green-leaved types. With the cool, moist weather of early fall, wax begonias brighten and grow bigger. Often they withstand early frosts. Now and then, buried under fall leaves, they live through milder winters in my Washington, D.C., garden, Zone 7. In hot regions, space seedlings closer together.

Seeds are available, and in late spring seedlings already in flower are offered. Starting wax begonias from seed is challenging, but possible. Mix a teaspoon of sugar or sand into the packet of dustlike seeds to make them easier to sow, and broadcast over a damp, well-drained, soilless planting mix. Do not cover the seeds, but press them gently into the medium; keep the surface uniformly moist with warm water. When the second pair of leaves appears, apply a light solution of houseplant fertilizer. Six weeks after sowing, transplant the seedlings to a flat filled with well-drained, humusy soil. Transplant to the garden after danger of frost is gone.

To keep a wax begonia over winter, before frost cut it back by one-third, pot it, and move it to a sunny indoor windowsill. In late winter root 6-inch cuttings in water. Rooted cuttings and the cut-back parent can be set out when the weather warms.

The Semperflorens types most useful for the home garden are described below. In addition to the tall and dwarf varieties, there are some hybrids with somewhat cascading branches 12 to 18 inches long, that are pretty in hanging baskets.

TALL SEMPERFLORENS

Big-flowered Semperflorens types 10 to 12 inches high are outstanding in beds in groups of 5 to 7. In a small border, plant sets of 3. For edging, set seedlings out singly, 6 inches apart.

Party series, 12 to 15 inches tall, 2-inch flowers, bronze or green leaves, outstanding among large-flowered garden begonias.

Wing series, 10 to 12 inches, 3-inch flowers, green leaves. These are F$_1$ hybrids. 'Picotee Wings' is white edged in rose.

DWARF SEMPERFLORENS

Similar to the tall Semperflorens but smaller in every way. Ideal for window boxes, pots, small borders, and edging.

Cocktail series, 6 to 8 inches, bronze-maroon leaves that withstand sun and hot southern summers. 'Rum' has white flowers edged in red.

Olympia series, 6 to 8 inches, green leaves. Early blooming, ball-shaped, compact plants with flowers in vivid colors.

Prelude series, 5 to 6 inches, green leaves. Early, excellent flower color and foliage. There's a very handsome bicolor, white blooms with delicate coral-pink edges.

Pizzazz series, to 10 inches, 1½-inch flowers, green leaves. Tidy mounds with masses of vibrant flowers that withstand full sun. 'PizzazzWhite' is fresh and lively.

ANGEL-WING BEGONIAS

Angel-wing begonias have canelike, branching stems, pendulous clusters of large flowers in the coral and pink and white begonia range. The leaves are wide at the top and pointed at the tip, like a wing. Usually seen as greenhouse or indoor plants, but a few woody evergreen types that thrive in warm California gardens are planted as annuals in the East. Some are 4 feet tall and useful at the back of the border. Smaller hybrids are sometimes used as ground cover around the base of large potted plants.

Culture: Same as for the Semperflorens begonias, but these plants do not tolerate frost. The following cultivars are recommended.

'Irene Nuss', to 4 feet, medium pink flowers.

'Sophie Cecile', to 12 inches, a spreading hybrid for baskets.

'West Newton', to 12 inches, a spreading plant with salmon-orange flowers suited to basket culture.

SHRUBLIKE BEGONIAS

B. 'Richmondenses': The name represents a group of spreading, showy shrublike hybrid begonias to 24 inches tall of unknown parentage that have small, pointed, angel-wing leaves and are good bedding plants. Best known on the West Coast, but they thrive in eastern gardens when conditions are right. They bloom in white and rosy colors that deepen according to the intensity of the sun. Excellent container and basket plants with tolerance for drought. Grow in sun or shade.

Shrublike Semperflorens Begonia, to 12 inches, is a very showy plant with rounded green Semperflorens leaves and big flowers in hanging clusters. Use it as a specimen in containers, beds, greenhouses, and indoors. Some exceptional cultivars cascade or spread and have brilliant colors. The following 2 are recommended.

'Christmas Candy', to 12 inches, has striking, orangy red blossoms. It is sold only as a rooted cutting.

'Pink Avalanche', to 12 inches, is available in seed form.

TUBEROUS BEGONIAS

B. × tuberhybrida Hybrid Tuberous Begonia
Tender Perennial

The stars of the begonia world, these are challenging bedding or basket plants with large, often pedulous flowers 2 to 6 or 7 inches across on plants 12 to 20 or even 30 inches tall, with big, silky leaves. The upright forms are absolutely gorgeous in flower beds and boxes. The cascading forms make extraordinary hanging baskets. The large, sensuous, double-petaled flowers may be crested, frilled, or daffodil-flowered. There are some with blossoms like ranunculus, camellias or ruffled camellias, roses or double roses, or carnations. There are singles, doubles, reds, yellows, oranges, pinks, whites, picotees, and color-blotched forms. Each season the mail-order catalogs present classics and the newest plants, and nurseries devoted to begonias offer them all.

Culture: The plants develop from roundish tubers started indoors in spring and dried down for indoor storage in fall. They thrive in cool, moist places but don't do well in cities that hold heat after sundown, or in southern gardens. Direct sun in the morning and very late afternoon is not a problem, but noon and midafternoon sun scorches the leaves. They need protection from sweeps of wind.

Tuberous begonias started from seed in winter will produce 1 or 2 blooms late the first season. However, it is more usual to plant tubers, or plants already in bloom. Suppliers (see Sources, in the Appendix), generally don't ship begonia tubers after April 15.

Look for thick tubers 1½ to 2 inches across. A single tuber will fill a 10-inch container. Press tubers 1 to 2 inches deep into the top layer of a damp soilless mix, or a mix of 2 parts leaf mold, forest humus, or sphagnum peat moss, and 1 part sand or sandy loam. When they start growing, move them to bright light, but not direct sun, at temperatures between 60° to 75° F. Maintain even moisture but don't fertilize until they have been potted, then fertilize every 3 weeks with a light application of Osmocote slow-release fertilizer or a similar product. When growth begins, move the containers to cooler temperatures, about 55° to

FACING PAGE Tuberous begonias thrive in cool shade.
(Viette)

ABOVE Non-stop orange tuberous begonia.
(Ball Seed Co.)

LEFT Prelude bicolor wax begonia. (Ball Seed Co.)

BELOW *Begonia grandis* at River Farm.
(American Horticultural Society)

65° F; when they are 4 inches tall, transplant to 8- to 10-inch baskets or azalea pans.

If mildew is a problem in your area, choose only mildew-resistant plants.

To plant upright tuberous begonias in a bed, replace the top 10 inches of soil with one of the mixes described above. To guarantee good drainage make the finished bed 3 or 4 inches higher than surrounding soil surface. Water thoroughly several days before planting and set the begonias 18 inches apart. When planting in boxes, space the tubers 15 inches apart.

With tuberous begonias, it is essential to maintain the soil evenly moist but not soaking and to clear away dying foliage. Deadhead consistently. The showy blooms are male, and most are backed by a single female flower; it isn't necessary to remove the latter. Stake stems more than 5 or 6 inches tall, tying them with old rags rather than string or anything that can cut into the soft stems. Do not cultivate around tuberous begonias.

In fall when potted plants begin to yellow, bring them indoors, let the soil dry to barely damp over 5 or 6 weeks, then remove dead foliage and wipe and store the tubers in a cool, dry place. They must never freeze. In February, move the tubers that don't show a pink bud to a warm, dark place. When sprouts appear, but no later than March, set them in a soilless mix 4 inches apart. Sprinkle enough sphagnum over the tubers to cover them, and keep the mix moist by sprinkling the surface.

Lift bedding begonias before the first frost. Store the whole dirt ball in a dry place until the foliage has dried, then clean and store the tubers indoors.

UPRIGHT TUBEROUS BEGONIAS

These are spectacular in planters and beds. Grow them in partial shade; in full shade, they get leggy and need staking.

Pacific or California strains, 12 to 14 inches, 6-inch fluffed and fully double flowers. One of the finest big-flowered, tuberous-rooted types. These are raised by nurseries from seed and are less expensive than the following group.

Blackmore and Langdon strains, 12 to 14 inches, with the largest flowers of all. The British nursery that created them raises them from cuttings, so they are more costly. 'Allan Langdon', one of many remarkable plants, covers itself with dark red flowers.

Nonstop Hybrids, 8 to 10 inches tall, 2- to 3-inch medium and semidouble flowers on multibranched plants in intense shades of scarlet to apricot, orange, yellow, rose, pink, and white. These very popular, free-flowering plants require no staking. Recommended for bedding, window boxes, and baskets. They bloom earlier, but do not reliably set tubers to dig and save in the fall. Plan to buy these new each year.

Clips series, 7- to 9-inches, masses of 2½-inch flowers begin early—scarlet, orange, yellow, and white. Similar to Nonstops but more compact, and they do not reliably set tubers to dig and save in the fall. Plan to buy these new each year.

Midnight Beauty series, 8 to 10 inches, lots of many 2½-inch double flowers and similar to Nonstops but the leaves are very dark bronze. Plan to buy these new each year.

CASCADE OR HANGING BASKET TUBEROUS BEGONIAS

The Pendula Group tuberous begonias (often listed as *B. × lloydii pendula*) are bushy, trailing plants with flowers 2 to 4 inches across. Many, but not all, of the exotic flower forms found in the upright tuberous begonias appear in this group. Hang baskets in shady spots on the north side of the house. Classed under *B. × tuberhybrida*, these need good overhead light but not direct hot sun.

Blackmore and Langdon strains, the trailing forms of this famous strain, have double flowers. 'Gold Cascade' has brilliant chrome-yellow flowers. There's also an 'Orange Cascade'. 'Lou Anne' has big, pale pink flowers.

REIGER BEGONIAS

The Reiger begonias sold by florists are hybrid, semituberous, tender plants that bloom indoors for several months in winter. The flowers are somewhere between Semperflorens and tuberous begonias in size and type. These are not recommended for bedding and usually are discarded when they lose their appeal.

SPECIES BEGONIAS OF NOTE

The flowers are as small as 1½ inches, but have extraordinary blooming vigor. Of interest primarily to collectors.

B. grandis Hardy Begonia   Zones 6-11
A modest flower and not easy to find, but its flowers and foliage are attractive for lightly shaded gardens in regions where it is hardy. It grows from a small bulblike tuber and with some protection survives winters in the ground as far north as New York. There are white- and pink-flowering types to 24 inches tall, with a rounded leaf that is bronzy flushed with maroon-crimson underneath. Also known as 'Evans begonia' (formerly *B. Evansiana*).

B. sutherlandii   Zones 9-11
Basket begonia with small, single, 1-inch, bright orange flowers in summer. The vivid green foliage sprawls to 24 inches and often is scarlet-veined. Beautiful when grown well, but susceptible to mildew.

SOURCES: GEORGE C. BALL, JR., PRESIDENT OF THE FLOWERSEED GROUP, GEORGE J. BALL, INC., WHO PRESENTLY SERVES AS PRESIDENT OF THE AMERICAN HORTICULTURAL SOCIETY; MICHAEL DODGE, HORTICULTURIST, WHITE FLOWER FARM, LITCHFIELD, CONNECTICUT; BYRON MARTIN, LOGEE GREENHOUSES, DANIELSON, CONNECTICUT; MICHAEL KARTUZ, KARTUZ GREENHOUSES, VISTA, CALIFORNIA; AND ELVIN MCDONALD, BROOKLYN BOTANIC GARDENS, BROOKLYN, NEW YORK.

37. GERANIUM— IVY GERANIUM (PELARGONIUM)

■ **Geranium is a common name for species of *Pelargonium*—the familiar window box and trailing pot plant whose vibrant reds, pinks, and sparkling whites bloom from spring through fall. The name causes confusion—*Geranium* also is the botanical name of the very different cranesbills, or hardy geraniums, spring bloomers that balance delicate cup-shaped flowers on extended wandlike stems. Geraniums bloom almost continuously from spring through summer—though real heat can slow them up a little—and into fall, when their colors brighten again. They'll flower in winter if brought indoors to a sunny window in a cool room. The leaves are attractive—bright green and shaped like a horseshoe or a crinkled palm or an ivy leaf, according to species. There are hundreds and perhaps thousands of eye-catching forms—some variegated, many with zoned leaves, dwarfs, miniatures, cascades, and scented-leaved types. Some are rosebud-, tulip-, cactus-, or carnation-flowered, and there are elegant bicolors. The more exotic are sought after by collectors.**

Specialists in unusual geraniums may be located through the American Horticultural Society. Those recommended here are familiar garden forms.

Companion Plants: In window boxes grow geraniums with trailing vinca, petunias, verbena, and indoor foliage plants; for bedding, include Dusty-miller and carpet with white Sweet Alyssum.

PELARGONIUM (pel-ahr-*goh*-nee-um)
Geranium
The popular geraniums divide into three major groups, all grown as annuals in cool regions: geraniums for containers and bedding, trailing geraniums for baskets, and scented-leaved species for herbal use. Many of the big-flowered semidouble and double zonal geraniums are propagated from softwood (new growth) cuttings and come into full bloom 6 to 8 weeks later, depending on species. They are noticeably larger than the geraniums grown from seed.

Culture: All geraniums prefer western exposure in summer with some protection from the heat of afternoon and in winter, indoors, full southern sun. They tolerate hot, dry windy exposures in containers, but flourish with as little as 3 hours of summer sun if facing south. They need lots of air, benefit from cool nights, and are most successful in soil that is sandy or at least well-drained, rather poor, and neutral to slightly acid. Allow the soil surface to dry between deep waterings. Deadhead to encourage flowering.

CONTAINER GERANIUMS

For potted plants (florist's plants) and indoor gardens in winter, 2 species are popular—the familiar zonal or house geranium, and the exotic, longer-lasting Martha Washington or Regal Geranium, identified by its attractively splotched blossoms.

P. × hortorum Zonal Geranium, House Geranium, Horseshoe Geranium, Bedding Geranium, Fish Geranium   Zones 10-11
Popular window box plant 12 to 24 inches tall, with large, slightly fuzzy leaves shaped like a horseshoe and usually banded with a dark red-purple or bronze zones. The flowerheads (or flowering umbels) are globe-shaped and appear from spring through summer in brilliant shades of pink, salmon, red, fuchsia, and white, as well as bicolors. Seed-grown plants of this group are also used as bedding plants. These are tender evergreen perennials grown in southern California—and in hot, dry lands such as Corsica—as flowering evergreen ground cover. In cool regions they are planted as annuals for quick summer color in boxes, pots, and hanging baskets and wintered indoors as flowering houseplants.

Rooted cuttings or seedlings are planted out in window boxes and beds as soon as danger of frost is past, and are usually discarded at the end of the season. Wintered indoors in their container, the plants can be trained to espalier or tree form and also may be used to provide softwood cuttings for next year's planting. Tip cuttings root easily in late winter, spring, and summer. Smaller geraniums also are wintered bare-root, hanging upside down in a cool room. For winter bloom indoors, start cuttings in summer.

Culture: Set out rooted cuttings or seedlings after the air has warmed. Or sow seeds indoors 10 to 12 weeks before planting time and keep at temperatures under 80° F during germination. Maintain uniform moisture during germination, which occurs within 7 to 10 days. After germination the best results are obtained from seedlings set in bright sunlight or under fluorescent lights that are 12 to 18 inches above the trays. Temperatures should drop to about 62° F at night.

FROM CUTTINGS

Some excellent plants sold as rooted cuttings are:
'Blues', a large, semidouble, rose pink flower with a white eye; compact and vigorous; a Fischer cultivar.
'Schone Helena' bears masses of large, semidouble salmon pink blooms; a Fischer cultivar.
'Tango', is a fiery scarlet; a Fischer cultivar.
'Irene', an old favorite that is strong, well-branched, and bears big, semidouble cherry red flowers; a Fischer cultivar.
Satisfaction series, top-quality, floriferous plants for tubs, pots, patios, and planters in the usual geranium colors. 'Sincerity' blooms profusely, with semidouble flowers that are an intense, brilliant red.
Sunbelt series, standard favorites; large semidouble flowers held well above the foliag of large plants developed to withstand the hot nights and humidity of midwestern summers. 'Sunbelt Coral' is a deep coral-orange double. 'Yours Truly', semidouble flowers that are scarlet-red.

Martha Washington geraniums, *Pelargonium × domesticum*, flower most heavily around Easter. Like the beautiful fuchsias, they need cool weather. (Viette)

VARIEGATED LEAVES

Also propagated from cuttings are several geraniums whose leaves are unusual.
Recommended are:
'Ben Franklin', which has leaves edged with crisp white markings. The flowers are semi-double, rosy pink.
'Mrs. Quiller', rare coloring in yellow leaf zones coupled with reddish brown and pink flowers.

BEDDING PLANTS FROM SEEDS

Seed is offered for the plants that follow. Plants grown from seed tend to branch more freely, thus providing more flowering tips, but they start the season as smaller plants, 6 to 10 inches, with strong zonal markings. The florets are single, sometimes with a white eye, and stand higher than the leaves. They are offered in many colors. Any of the following thrive in sunny garden beds as well as containers.

Bandit series, early, tops for flower beds, with big globe-shaped flowerheads in red, salmon, pink or white.
'Freckles', All-America Selections winner, warm rose pink, each floret splotched or freckled with bright red.
'Hollywood Star', early, compact to 12 inches, free-flowering, beautiful bicolor, white banded with rose-red.
'Lone Ranger' is a superb bedding and container plant that blooms in cardinal-red, an unusual shade.
Orbit series, compact, strongly zoned with red or bronze, large well-branched, flowerheads in a range of colors, soft white through apple blossom, pinks to salmon, red and cherry red.

P. × domesticum, Regal Geranium, Show Geranium, Fancy Geranium, Lady Washington or Martha Washington Geranium, Pansy-flowered Geranium, Summer Azalea

Except in southern California, these are sold as potted florist's plants that bloom for 3 weeks or so. The leaves are 2 to 4 inches wide, not very clearly divided and without zonal markings. The flowers are large and conspicuous, white, pink, or red; the upper 2 petals have characteristically dark blotches. The period of heaviest flowering is at Easter. Those with somewhat ruffled petals are known as summer azalea, and the flat-faced, smaller-flowered type are called pansy geraniums. An exceptionally attractive plant with much potential.

Culture: In the past, Regals only set buds at night temperatures below 60° F, which limited their value as patio plants in much of the U. S., though they are excellent flowering plants for indoors. Softwood cuttings taken in late fall or winter produce flowers for next spring. Breeders are currently working on new Regals that will flower in any season, continue to bloom at warmer night temperatures, and last up to a month indoors.

The following cultivars are recommended.
'Majestic', compact, early-blooming; melon with a garnet red blotch on the upper petals.
'Crystal', early-blooming compact single; crisp, lovely white flowers with a dash of red; lots of blooms.
'Brendon', exotic, a marvelous deep red.
'Leslie Judd', exotic, with coral-orange splotches; the trumpet-shaped flower is much like an azalea.
'Purple Emperor', exotic, intense purple-pink.
'Tip-top Duet', ray-lined white eye.

VAVRA REGALS

The new Vavra Regals are expected to become increasingly popular. They are well-branched, compact plants that flower very heavily. Three examples are:
'Dolly', an early coral-red with a white eye.
'Josey', a rose pink single with red blotches on the upper petals; compact.
'Mary', white with pink feathering on the upper petals and a more vigorous growth habit.

HANGING BASKET GERANIUMS

P. peltatum Ivy Geranium, Hanging Geranium
Zone 10

A shape like ivy identifies the leaves of this first-rate basket and window box plant with handsome evergreen, stiff, waxy, shiny leaves and a naturally trailing habit. Stems 3 to 4 feet long cascade from the window boxes of Europe, where they are most popular. The blossoms are white to deep rose with darker markings in single and semidouble forms. They bloom from late winter to early fall and are especially floriferous.

Culture: Best in partly sunny exposures and cooler temperatures—about 80° F—and somewhat dry, well-drained soil. They winter indoors rather well, though without much flowering. Water only moderately, but don't allow to dry out in either summer or winter. Softwood cuttings root readily in early spring.

The following cultivars are recommended.
'Amethyst', double flowers in a light mauve-purple.
'Admiral Bouvet', an exceptional, imported semidouble; compact, light red, with zoned ivy foliage.
Balcon series, These European imports originally were introduced as Alpine Ivy geraniums. There are many colors and sizes. All bear many masses of dainty single flowers that stand high on slender stems above trailing,

TOP, LEFT Silver Medal winner 'Summer Showers', ivy geranium. (Ball Seed Co.)

TOP, RIGHT All American Selections winner, 'Freckles'. (All American Selections)

ABOVE Variegated semi-double zonal geranium, 'Ben Franklin'. (Ball Seed Co.)

RIGHT Bedding and window-box geranium, 'New Dawn' *P. × hortorum*. (Ball Seed Co.)

dense, deeply cut foliage. 'Princess Balcon', to 60 inches, is lilac; 'King Balcon', to 60 inches, is salmon pink; 'Mini Rose' is light pink, to 24 inches. Striking container plants. 'Solidor', spectacular in spring baskets, is a pink semidouble.

'Sybil Holmes', bright pink, roselike, tightly curled double flowers borne profusely on compact plants.

FROM SEED

Seeds for the superb ivy geranium described below are available—it is the only ivy geranium so far for which seed is offered:

'Summer Showers', a mix of many bright colors—reds, pink, lavenders, magenta, burgundy, and near white—that blooms in 3½ to 4 months from sowing. Winner of the Fleuroselect Silver Medal (the European equivalent of the All-America Selections). The flowers are single, bigger than most single zonal flowers, dainty, and held high above ivy-like leaves. The mixed colors make a riot of lasting color in a basket or window box. Like other seed-grown plants, these branch immediately and often, producing bushier plants and many more flowering stems. Excellent choice for along retaining walls, rocky slopes, as annual ground cover, and in pots, window boxes, and baskets.

SCENTED HERBAL GERANIUMS

Several species geraniums have crinkly, sweet- or spicy-scented leaves. Tender perennials, they flower sparsely compared to the big zonal geraniums, but are treasured for foliage that is scented like, among other things, nutmeg, mint, rose, and lemon. Their long-lasting fragrant oils give them a place in potpourris and, in the past, in jams, jellies, and sweets.

P. crispum Lemon Geranium, Finger Bowl
Pelargonium   Zone 10
A wonderful lemony scent comes from the small, crinkly leaves when pressed or brushed; two-toned pink flowers. 'French Lace' has variegated leaves.

P. graveolens Rose Geranium   Zones 9-10
The best-known rose geranium, sweetly scented, with rose-colored flowers having a dark purple spot in the middle of the upper petal; gray-green leaves.

P. odoratissimum Apple Geranium, Nutmeg
Pelargonium   Zones 10-11
Sweetly scented, with small, velvety, ruffled leaves and white flowers. 'Gray Lady Plymouth' is variegated.

P. tomentosum Peppermint Geranium,
Woolly Pelargonium   Zones 10-11
Peppermint-scented, with large, fuzzy, grapelike leaves and tiny, purple-veined white flowers. Interesting texture.

SOURCE: GEORGE C. BALL, JR. IS PRESIDENT OF THE FLOWERSEED GROUP, GEORGE J. BALL, INC., HE PRESENTLY SERVES AS PRESIDENT OF THE AMERICAN HORTICULTURAL SOCIETY.

38. IMPATIENS

■ **The ability to flower generously in shade, rare among flowers, has made *Impatiens* a star annual from coast to coast. These carefree plants also bloom early and sustain lavish displays until frost with practically no effort on the gardener's part. With autumn's cool, moist weather, impatiens' colors intensify and the plants attain their mature height, an impressive display. A broad range of vibrant colors has been developed in recent years—solid pastels, pinks, reds, whites, orange, salmon, melon, color-spotted forms, and bicolors. Double-flowered types are becoming more available, some as pretty as miniature roses. The stems are succulent and somewhat brittle, the leaves glossy, dark green, bronze, or variegated—delicate, pointed, and pretty. If flower production slows in high heat, the leaves sustain the garden tapestry until the flowers come again. In fact, these shade-lovers are so desirable that breeders are moving them out into the sun with new cultivars.**

Impatiens are great follow-on plants for corners vacated by bulbs and which become shady as branches leaf out.

Companion Plants: Gray-white *Senecio cineraria* (Dusty-miller) or *Artemisia* is a good companion for light and dark, pink and white impatiens; white impatiens can be a carpet for miniature white cushion mums; interplant impatiens with blue ageratum; plant mixed pastel shades with maroon and green coleus; team white and green caladiums with white and coral impatiens. Ferns are also good companions for impatiens. Or combine *Hosta sieboldii* 'Kabitan', or *H. fortunei* 'Piedmont Gold', or *H. undulata* 'Univittata' ('Medio-variegata') with white impatiens.

IMPATIENS (im-**pay**-shee-enz)
The genus is widely distributed in the tropics and sub-tropics although some species are native North American wildflowers, for instance the orange-spotted, yellow Touch-me-not, *I. noli-tangere*, and Jewelweed, *I. pallida*.

The best-known impatiens is the low-growing, wide-branching *I. wallerana*, a pretty plant that flowers under trees, low shrubs, big perennials, at the edge of leafy flowering borders, in hanging baskets, and window boxes. But two taller upright impatiens are gaining attention. One is the leafy Garden Balsam, a Victorian favorite with flowers that are half-hidden in pretty foliage. The other is the bushy New Guinea Impatiens which withstands direct sun reasonably well in moist, humusy soil, and is chosen for its rather showy variegated leaves as well as for its larger flowers.

Impatiens is a very "plastic" flower. It reaches varying heights in the garden depending on temperature, length of growing season, and water.

Culture: Seed for good impatiens are becoming more available. In frost-free regions sow the seeds outdoors in fall or very early spring. In cool regions, plant them indoors in late winter. Sow the seeds thinly over a sterile, soilless growing mix and set the flats 12 inches under cool white fluorescent lamps. Burn the lights 16 hours a day in temperatures between 70 and 75° F. After germination, the seedlings do best in nighttime temperatures of 68° F. They generally start to flower 9 to 12 weeks after sowing.

After the air has warmed, plant seedlings in light, well-drained, very humusy, rich soil. Pinch young plants to promote dense growth.

Tall and filtered shade are best for impatiens, but modern cultivars tolerate some direct sun if they are set out as young seedlings, mulched thinly, and watered often with a dilute liquid-soluble fertilizer. In sandy, hot regions, grow impatiens in containers in shady corners.

Water impatiens early in the day and avoid wetting the foliage. The succulent stems wilt quickly if deprived of water, but soon regain their form after watering.

I. balsamina Garden Balsam   Annual
This rather straight-up favorite of the Victorians is less well-known than the popular species below, but it is an excellent foliage and flowering plant up to 30 inches high, lovely in clumps of 4 or 5 in a lightly shaded border of mixed flowers. The colorful little blossoms, single or double, white, red, yellow, or bicolored, sparkle from dense foliage from midsummer through frost.

Culture: Sow seeds indoors and transplant after the danger of frost has passed. Remove the first flowers and early side shoots.

Recommended are:

Extra Dwarf Tom Thumb Mixed, 8 to 12 inches high, with 3-inch camellia-flowered blossoms in purple-rose, salmon, shell pink, and white. Good container plants, very tolerant of drought.

Camellia-flowered Mixed: 16 to 28 inches high, camellia-flowered plants in a mix of rose and bicolors.

New Guinea Impatiens   Tender Perennial
These are tall, upright plants, hybrids of a sort of "species complex" including *I. platypetala*, *I. hawkerii*, and *I. herzogii* native to New Guinea, Java and the Celebes Islands. They are known for very large flowers in white through pastel shades of pink, lavender, orange to magenta, scarlet, and vermilion. The whites are excellent in a mixed border. The large, pointed leaves range from dull to bright green above and from pale to dark red below. Some are bronzed or variegated with shades of green, yellow, pink and red. They make attractive fillers.

Culture: Modern cultivars are tolerant of direct sun—a half day of full sun is ideal, but not noonday sun. They must have moisture-retentive, humusy soil and extra watering in high heat. In frost-free areas, they may grow year-round.

Seed-grown plants are new and have many more branches and flowers, and have less tendency to hide flowers beneath the foliage. The first seed-grown selection was the 1989 All-America Selections winner, 'Tango'.
Spectra Mixture: the first New Guinea color mixture from seed, with flowers 2 to 3 inches across in shades from violet and deep red to rose, salmon, pink, and white. The plants are 10 to 14 inches tall and have the basal branching of seed-grown impatiens. The leaves may be green, bronzed, or variegated.
'Tango', vigorous, 18 to 24 inches high, with attractive, dark bronze leaves and bright orange flowers 2½ inches across. A very showy garden ornament when massed.
Sunshine series, grown from cuttings and sold as seedlings. There are over 30 choices of flower and foliage combinations with names such as 'Quasar', orange; 'Comet', hot pink; and 'Sunburst', a red and white bicolor. Lasting Impressions series, larger flowers and better branching, grown from cuttings.

TOP Impatiens, companioned by shade-loving ferns and hostas, blooms in dappled light all summer and into late fall. Impatiens withstands some direct, hot, sun as long as it is growing in damp, humusy soil. (American Horticultural Society)

ABOVE Super Elfin 'Red Velvet', a well-branched type handsome as a basket plant. (Ball Seed Co.)

RIGHT AAS winner, 'Tango', bronze-leaved New Guinea impatiens. (All American Selections)

I. wallerana Zanzibar Balsam, Busy Lizzy
Annual

This is the impatiens covered with big, flat blooms that is planted everywhere in shaded spots—porch gardens, under the high shade of trees and tall shrubs, in the shadows of city buildings, and in container gardens. Plants grow 12 to 24 inches tall with a wide spread; dwarfs are between 6 and 8 inches tall. A vigorous breeding program started in 1974 has introduced hundreds of new hybrids that can stand some direct sun. The flower is shaped rather like a phlox floret with a soft, suede finish, and the colors are pale or intense pastels—dark red, hot pink, intense coral, orchid, and white. There are bicolors and striped types, and strains with variegated leaves.

Culture: The seeds are expensive but not difficult to start. The seedlings are very sensitive to cold and hot sun, so carefully and gradually harden them off before planting them outside.

All perform well in shade to part sun. There is no *I. wallerana* hybrid able to take full sun and heat across North America, although Super Elfins and Dazzlers will handle a wide range of conditions. Water sparingly to keep the plants compact and fertilize rarely, if at all, and very lightly.

Recommended are:

Accent series, 6 to 8 inches high, early, thrives in shade and has a very large color range, including bicolors and blossoms with contrasting eyes 2 inches across.

Dazzler series, 8 to 10 inches high, shade lovers that share the wide branching characteristics of the Super Elfins, are uniform in height, and come in very intense shades including cranberry, orange, and the brilliant 'Scarlet Plush.'

Super Elfin series, under 10 inches, is the best low-bedding type, a new hybrid descended from the original bedding work done by Claude Hope of Linda Vista, Costa Rica. Covered with big flowers in melting shades all season long, the plants branch freely at the base, allowing for many more flowers per plant than other types, and stay close to the ground with a spread of 12 inches or more. Among designer shades are 'Velvet', a bronze-leaved red; 'Lipstick', bright red; 'Blush', a very tender pink with a darker eye; and 'Blue Pearl', lavender-pink, pale blue (best alone or in a color mix).

Showstopper, 10 to 12 inches high, very vigorous growers, especially recommended for hanging baskets and tubs. A favorite is 'Flair', pale pink with a hot pink eye.

Shady Lady strain, pastels, often with a darker center, in 2-inch flowers on 12- to 15-inch plants.

Blitz series, 14 to 16 inches high, good for bedding. The orange is an All-America Selection.

Double Impatiens, very beautiful little flowers on plants 12 to 14 inches high, choice for viewing close up in big pots or baskets. The blooms are a mixture of fully double, single, and semidouble.

Rosette Hybrid Mixed, 12 to 14 inches high, a mix of double, single, and semidoubles in red, scarlet, rose, pink, orange, salmon, blush white, and bicolors.

'Tempo Blush', very early.

SOURCE: GEORGE C. BALL, JR. IS PRESIDENT OF THE FLOWERSEED GROUP, GEORGE J. BALL, INC. HE PRESENTLY SERVES AS PRESIDENT OF THE AMERICAN HORTICULTURAL SOCIETY.

39. MARIGOLD (TAGETES)

■ **Marigolds are those early-flowering fluffy globes of gold, orange, or pumpkin orange that keep blooming throughout the summer and well into autumn in hot sun, never look wilted, and withstand the worst storms. The foliage is lacy and the fragrance distinctive, clean, and pungent. One of few annuals that flowers through southern Florida summers, their tolerance of drought and heat is natural—they're natives of the hot, dry regions of America and were first brought to Europe from Mexico by the Spanish explorer Cortez. In Spain, the devout placed the gold blooms on altars to the Virgin Mary and in time "Mary's gold" became Marigolds.**

Along with zinnias, marigolds are probably the best annuals for low-maintenance gardens, from small window boxes to huge municipal plantings. There are two main types—the big, fluffy, round, African or Aztec marigolds that come in several heights, and the small French marigolds that are often blotched with mahogany red.

Marigolds are great follow-on flowers for spaces left empty by spring bulbs. They make good cut flowers, too, if you strip leaves from the part of the stem that will be immersed.

Follow-on Plants: Plant the big marigolds where they will be followed by *Japanese anemone*, the Cosmos Early Wonder series, or the hardy *Amaryllis belladona*, Belladonna Lily. When the small marigolds are touched by frost, replace them with ornamental cabbages, kales, and peppers, or with small mums potted and already coloring up.

TAGETES (taj-*jeet*-eez) Marigold

Hundreds of modern hybrids have been developed from the species described below, the African (or Aztec) marigolds and the French marigolds—all American natives. The flowers may be single or double and there there are bicolors, and even a few almost-whites. For nonfans of the pungent marigold scent, odorless hybrids are available.

Marigolds resist almost every pest and disease, and themselves are natural enemies of root-knot nematodes, which cause a disease that attacks bulbs and many other plants.

Culture: Sow marigold seeds indoors 4 to 6 weeks before outdoor planting time. Seeds germinate quickly indoors (3 to 4 days) at 65° F in full sun in any moist, light-growing medium, and they transplant well. Small, early marigolds bloom in as little as 6 to 7 weeks from seed sown directly where they are to grow after the air has warmed. The larger types need 12 or 13 weeks to bloom, and these are started indoors or purchased as mature seedlings in cool regions.

Deadhead to keep blooms coming, and drench with liquid fertilizer in August.

The little French marigolds often self-sow, even in window boxes, and may perennialize. One volunteered and bloomed year after year in a roof garden at the author's Manhattan penthouse terrace, subsisting on trickles from the watering of the roof garden.

AFRICAN MARIGOLDS

T. erecta African Marigold   Annual

The big marigolds evolved from this species. The hybrids bear double, fluffy, ruffled blooms 2 to 4 inches across on plants in sizes from 10 to 36 inches tall. Some typical series are described below. The "Odorless" and the white marigolds were developed from this group, whose color range is yellow to gold, orange, and pumpkin-orange. The whites are the only marigolds that prefer shade. Among them is 'Snowdrift', with flowers 3½ inches across on wide-spreading plants 22 inches high. It blooms early to late summer. 'Snowbird' is a more compact white, to 18 inches tall. Plant seedlings of the large marigolds 12 inches apart.

SEMIDWARF

These are small, compact plants 10 to 12 inches tall that carry big, long-lasting flowers well above the dense, ferny foliage. Just right for pots, window boxes and low, wide edgings. Among several types are:

Crush series, 10 to 12 inches, double 3½- to 4-inch flowers. 'Discovery Yellow', slightly taller free-flowering F_1 hybrid with big blooms. Good ground cover around newly planted trees and for large boxes.

MEDIUM TALL

Compact, weather-resistant plants 14 to 16 or 18 inches tall, with long-lasting, double blooms to 4 inches across. Good in big pots and the front middle border. The following are among the best.

Inca series, lots of flowers and strong colors. Withstands rain exceptionally well and are the best marigolds for southern summers.

Space Age series, big 3-inch blooms and lots of flowers. The gold 'Sunshot' blooms earlier and is recommended as a companion to the golden orange 'Apollo.'

TALL

Big flowers on plants 16 to 20 inches high. Good for the middle or back of the border and for big planters, municipal flower beds, and low hedges.

Galore series, 16 to 18 inches, big fully double blooms. Lady series, to 20 inches, early-blooming double flowers 3½ inches across on strong plants. Great for pots and borders.

HEDGE TYPES

These are the biggest marigolds, strong, shrubby plants 30 to 36 inches tall and more, with thick branches that hold masses of huge, fluffy blooms in the yellow-to-deep-orange range. They make splendid, fast-growing backdrops for flowering borders, and handsome low hedges. Especially useful in snow country.

Climax series, big, strong plants with dramatic flowers 4½ inches across and exceptionally suitable for cutting.

Crackerjack, to 24 inches spreading 12 to 18 inches, with extra-large flowers.

FACING PAGE A border of the big Climax marigolds. (Ball Seed Co.)
TOP, LEFT 'Red Marietta', French marigold. (Ball Seed Co.)
TOP, RIGHT 'Inca Gold', medium African marigold. (Ball Seed Co.)
ABOVE 'Yellow Boy', French marigold. (Ball Seed Co.)
RIGHT, CENTER Climax marigolds. (Ball Seed Co.)
RIGHT, BOTTOM 'Snowdrift', man-made white marigold, prefers shade.
(W. Atlee Burpee Co.)

TRIPLOIDS

These are early-blooming crosses between the species above and below, durable as the French marigolds and full as the Africans. They're called "mule" marigolds because they don't set seed. One effect is flowers that are almost indestructible and keep blooming on in high heat. Another effect is that fewer seeds germinate and fewer flowers are produced. They're a good choice for municipal beds.

Nugget series, 10 to 12 inches, showy 2-inch, very full, fluffy flowers, good germinators for the type; they can be counted on to perform well in high heat. These often bloom from seed in 6 weeks.

Fireworks series, 12 to 14 inches, bushy, covered with spectacular 2¾-inch double flowers. Showy when massed in borders and containers.

FRENCH MARIGOLDS

T. patula French Marigold   Annual
These are the durable, compact little plants 12 inches tall or less that bear lots of small orange, gold, or mahogany red marigolds 1½ to 2 inches across. They're great for low edgings, the front of the border, and small window boxes. Beautiful when massed for ground cover. Often self-sows. The single-flowered forms make a very attractive display, covering themselves with flowers. For showier displays there are double-flowered types as many-petaled as a rose, and ruffled fluffies like the big African marigolds. When transplanting, space the seedlings 9 inches apart. 'Golden Gate' is a very early French marigold to 2½ inches across with a gold-edged mahogany center, the largest blooms in this group to date.

Boy series, 8 to 10 inches, long established solid and bicolor dwarfs, amazingly self-sufficient massed in large plantings. Early bloomer with full, fluffy flowers.

Disco series, large, dainty single flowers up to 2 inches across in an array of gold and mahogany combinations.

Fiesta series, showy bicolored single flowers on dainty little plants. 'Red Marietta', mahogany red edged with gold, and 'Granada', gold with a mahogany red blotch, make an interesting pair.

Hero series, 10 to 12 inches, early, with fluffy 2-inch crested flowers in deep, vibrant shades, or bicolor combinations. Withstand the hottest weather.

SIGNET MARIGOLD

T. tenuifolia (syn. *signata*) Signet Marigold
                                                  Annual
Stocky, bushy plants to 24 inches tall almost covered with dainty little single flowers. The fine, lacy foliage has a lemon scent. The plant is spreading and erect, perfect for edgings and rocks gardens. Self-sows. 'Pumila' is a group name covering various plants of dwarf habit.

Gem series, some 'Pumila' dwarfs grow 8 to 10 inches tall with a 12-inch spread and bear sweet, single flowers in shades of gold and orange. Perfect for small window boxes, pots, and gardens of miniatures.

SOURCE: SUZANNE FRÜTIG BALES IS A DIRECTOR OF W. ATLEE BURPEE & CO., AND A GARDEN DESIGNER NOTED FOR HER INTEREST IN LONG-SEASON BEAUTY.

Petunias bring brilliant color to a window box. The most important box and basket annual, it comes in both upright and cascade forms. (Yang)

40. PETUNIA

■ The lovely old-fashioned, trumpet-shaped petunia is a sprawling—and sometimes upright—perennial grown as an annual. You see its fabulous hybrids and cultivars everywhere—cascade types in baskets and window boxes, upright types as edging and in flower beds. This is an easy plant, just blooms and blooms in every shade needed to make other flower colors work. The sparkling whites are especially useful in groups of mixed colors, and a window box of the small, single multifloras in mixed bright colors is one of summer's prettiest displays. Some of the color combinations are amazing. The scarlets are breathtaking. Petunias are fairly long lasting as cut flowers, too; individual blossoms fade but others on the branch open indoors.

There are fragrant petunias, including Double Grandifloras and singles, but you must read the fine print in the catalogs to locate them. Generally in their background is the night-scented *Petunia axillaris*, Large White Petunia.

Follow-on Plants: Petunias are follow-on plants for spring flowers and begin to phase out in early fall. Discard and replace them with potted mums and later with winter pansies. *Sedum* 'Autumn Joy' is a good companion plant that comes into color as the petunias fade. See list 5, Fall and Winter Bulbs.

PETUNIA (pet-*tew*-nee-uh) **x hybrida**
                                    Tender Perennial
An array of new petunias has been introduced through hybridizing. Modern flowers are between 2 and 5 inches across. There are large and small singles, and some doubles are as full as a turkey-feather muff. There are fringed, ruffled, picoteed, veined, starred, striped, and streaked petunias. The multifloras and floribundas bear masses of smaller flowers. Grandifloras produce fewer but very large flowers.

For flower beds and edging choose the upright petunias and plant them in groups of 3 to 5 in one color. For hanging baskets, containers, massing on ledges and along edges, and window boxes, choose cascading types with long, drooping, blossom-studded stems.

The one place petunias don't belong is where heavy falls of water will hit during a rainstorm. The branches are as tender as poppy stems and need protection from heavy winds and showers.

By mid-spring garden centers are offering a representative selection of budded petunia seedlings 4 to 6 inches tall, just right for spaces left empty by the passing of spring flowers. Many gardeners start their own seeds to take advantage of a wider choice of petunia colors and forms. The seeds are tiny, slow to germinate—start early—and require warmth.

TOP Jewel-bright single floribunda petunias, 'Total Madness', bloom "like mad." (Ball Seed Co.)

LEFT 'Purple Pirouette', giant Double Grandiflora petunia. (Ball Seed Co.)

ABOVE 'Hullahoop Red', Single Grandiflora bicolor. (Ball Seed Co.)

'Summer Sun', new man-made yellow petunia in the Single Multiflora class. (Ball Seed Co.)

Culture: Ten weeks before the last frost, sprinkle the seeds over dampened soilless potting mixture. Tamp them into place—don't bury them. To retain moisture, cover the flats with clear pliofilm (as in a dry cleaner's bag) or glass. Water from the bottom and don't let the seedlings dry out. Keep the flats in full sun at 65° to 75° F until the seeds sprout, then move them to a situation 10 degrees cooler. At 2½ inches, transplant seedlings to individual peat pots, disturbing the roots as little as possible. When the stems are 6 inches long, pinch out the tip of the central stem. Repeat with every 4 inches of growth until the plant has many branches. Transplant seedlings to the garden as soon as the weather warms to 60° to 65° F, in well-drained, humusy soil in the pH range of 6.0 to 7.0. Petunias will tolerate cold dips as low as 50° F. A light summer mulch in borders saves blooms from soil spatters and helps maintain even moisture.

Remove faded petunias as quickly as you can—they form seeds and stop flowering. Trim plants back by a third at midseason to encourage late blooming, and again later if blooms become sparse.

Petunias, especially those in containers, dry out quickly and need ample water during hot weather to bloom well. Where summers are very hot, choose strains that bloom in spite of the heat—F₁ Hybrid Single Multifloras are recommended. In very hot areas, cuttings may be rooted in water in late summer to start pot plants for winter bloom.

Petunias self-sow and in warmer regions may produce flowering volunteers by summer's end—just when other petunias may be fading. It takes 10 weeks for a petunia to come into bloom from seed.

SINGLE GRANDIFLORA

These are early-blooming, vigorous plants to 12 inches tall that bear flowers with big trumpets 3 to 4 inches across. They need good drainage, cool temperatures, and lots of sun. Among recommended types are the following.

Supercascade series, 14 to 15 inches; this strain is the one most grown, ideal for edging containers, baskets and rocky ledges. There are many showy colors. 'Supercascade Lilac' is an exquisite lilac-pink shaded to white in the eye.

Daddy series, 12 to 14 inches, early, recommended for mass plantings and for the beauty of the flowers. Blooms profusely in many distinctive colors veined in intense colors. 'Sugar Daddy' has been a best-seller for years—bright orchid background color with wine-red veins. 'Orchid Daddy' is a light orchid with darker veins. 'Strawberry Daddy', an All-America Selection, has deep red veins contrasting with a rosy salmon background color.

Magic and Supermagic series, to 12 inches; early, compact, and well-branched with slightly ruffled, medium-size blooms. Choice for mass planting in flower beds and borders. There's a 'Yellow Magic', a color rare in petunias, and a fresh white tinged with green in the center, as well as blues, coral, pink, and many other colors.

Flair series, 10 to 14 inches spreading to 24 inches, with a profusion of 3½- to 4-inch flowers from early summer to frost. Good for baskets and edging. The colors are bright and clear.

Americana series, 12 inches; bushy plants that bloom all summer without deadheading and show remarkable tolerance for rainstorms. The colors are bright and clear. Recommended for carefree mass plantings, edging, and the front of the border.

SINGLE FLORIBUNDA

These bear as many flowers as the Multifloras, but the flowers are larger, 2½ to 3 inches across. The plants are to 12 inches tall, spreading to 16 to 20 inches, and bounce back after heavy rains. Recommended for mass plantings and for hanging baskets and containers.

Madness series, so named because the plants bloom "like mad" all summer. The colors are either clear or veined. 'Summer Madness' is coral with rose veins. 'Sugar Madness' is orchid with darker veins. A good choice when lots of color is the goal.

Picotee series, big, single blue, red, or rose flowers with frilled edges, each exquisitely marked with a pure white border.

SINGLE MULTIFLORA

These are compact plants to 12 inches high that bear a profusion of 2½-inch, rounded blooms that are showy in flower beds and open borders. These are long-lasting in mass plantings, and are recommended for their ability to bloom through hot spells.

Joy series, very early and compact with masses of flowers. They come in all colors, from pure white to intense red, hot pink, and striking bicolors.

Plum series, similar to the Joy series, but the distinguishing characteristic is the deep veining of the blooms. Very resistant to heat and diseases. 'Plum Pudding' is a mix of these veined beauties.

DOUBLE GRANDIFLORA

Twelve-inch plants with the giant blooms of the Single Grandifloras, but these are riveting—all are fully double, some are bicolored, and many are fringed and very fragrant. Recommended for show-stopping displays in containers and beds. They need good drainage, prefer cool temperatures, and lots of sun. All doubles require more fertilizing than singles. Double F₁ Hybrids are dwarf doubles as frilled as a big carnation, and they come in a brilliant array of color variations and many forms, some upright.

'Circus' is a warm salmon-red with variable white picotee. 'Blue Danube' has lavender-blue flowers with dark violet veining, an outstanding performer.

'Purple Pirouette' is a velvety violet-purple with a bright white edge.

DOUBLE MULTIFLORA

These are fragrant hybrids with flowers to 2½ inches across, smaller than the big doubles above, but handsome, and noted for more flowers and more resistance to weather. Height is 12 to 13 inches. Showy in window boxes and pots.

Tart series, a colorful array of 2- to 2½-inch flowers covers the plants all season.

Delight series display softly ruffled 2- to 2½-inch blooms in bright clear colors and showy bicolors.

SOURCE: SUZANNE FRUTIG BALES, A DIRECTOR OF W. ATLEE BURPEE & CO., IS A GARDEN DESIGNER NOTED FOR HER INTEREST IN LONG-SEASON BEAUTY.

Empire series *Salvia splendens*, Scarlet Sage, have an exceptional color range. The showy spikes bloom from midsummer until frost and are favorites of hummingbirds. (Pan American Seed Co.)

41. SALVIA

■ The red salvias are stocky spikes covered with flamboyant red flowers—scarlet sages, summer's hottest reds. The blues are tall, slim wands covered with lavender-blue florets, usually in late summer and fall, beautiful with anything pink and great with roses. (There's one blue sage hybrid that appears in late spring and goes on all summer.) Species of these flower and foliage plants are so different from each other they often seem unrelated, but they are so useful that they are recommended on more than a dozen lists in this book.

In addition to the reds and blues, a third group is known for its aromatic and very interesting foliage; it includes the popular culinary herb, sage, and the woolly, silvery white foliage plant called Silver Sage.

Salvias are leafy and square-stemmed as are other members of the mint family; they are outstanding fillers for the front or middle of the border, especially valuable towards the end of the season. They go on until the autumn frosts arrive and are wonderful in fresh flower arrangements; many are excellent dried.

Companion Plants: With red sages, plant oregano or summer savory, and green and silver variegated thyme. Precede blue salvias with campanula, and join them with roses and dwarf white and pink snapdragons. Try French marigolds, calendula, Dustymiller, artemisia, and lavender with the silvery sages.

SALVIA (*sal*-vee-uh)
Sage, Ramona

The salvias bring essential color to the garden from midsummer to—and often through—the first frosts. They are grouped here according to category—Red Sages, Blue Sages, Herbal Sages—rather than alphabetically by species, as in other lists.

Culture: The flowering annuals and tender perennials grown as annuals may be purchased as seedlings in spring. Though germination is only fair, they're easy enough to grow once started. Sow seeds approximately 8 weeks before frost-free weather. For germination, good light and temperatures of 70° F are essential. Set the seeds, uncovered, on top of a well-soaked, sterile, soilless mix, and cover the trays with glass or plastic to maintain moisture. Don't water unless the surface dries. After germination, move the trays to a cooler place, about 55° F if possible.

The hardy perennial salvias are usually set out as root divisions in early mid-spring.

For most salvias to thrive, the soil has to be fairly fertile and very well-drained or they rot, especially *S. officinalis* types, the foliage sages. Plants set in full sun give the best performance, though some blue sages flower moderately well with only morning sun, particularly in the warm South. The sages are drought-resistant, but flourish best when watered during prolonged dry spells.

RED SAGES

S. splendens Scarlet Sage   Zones 9-10

The red sages derive from this species. In its native, frost-free Brazil it is an attractive flowering perennial subshrub 6 to 8 feet high. Here, it is known as an annual 8 or 12 to 24 inches tall, with glossy green foliage and small, tubular red flowers clustered at the top of leafy stems in thick, showy spikes from early summer until frost. Hummingbirds sip nectar from the deep-throated blossoms. This species provides the red in many public plantings and in red, white, and blue designs. But recently breeders have devoted time and attention to this seed-propagated class and its colors now include white, pink, salmon, purple, and various bicolors, as well as the traditional bright red.

Another scarlet salvia of somewhat narrow interest is *S. rutilans*, Pineapple Sage, which has a fruity fragrance attractive to certain species of butterfly. See list 69, To Attract Butterflies and Hummingbirds.

The plants recommended for this group are organized according to mature height. Dwarfs flower in early summer. Midsize plants bloom a few weeks later and hold up better than most dwarfs through summer heat and into fall. The big salvias bloom in late summer and last until autumn's frosts.

'Red Hot Sally', 8 to 12 inches, is a very popular early bloomer with deep red flowers that stand well above its compact, lush foliage; excellent for landscaping and garden borders.

Carabiniere series, to 12 inches, a very popular red now cultivated in other colors. An excellent performer.

Empire series, 10 to 12 inches, has an exceptional color range, including unique shades of white, light and dark salmon, lilac and purple, and red.

'St. John's Fire', to 12 inches; popular early, fire-engine red with deep green leaves. It is an older plant used for landscaping and borders.

'Flare', to 18 inches; midseason, good foliage color, uniform plant height, and many big, bright-red flower spikes. Good as a specimen or as a background for white begonias and blue petunias. It is new, bred for landscape and garden performance.

'America' ('Globe of Fire'), 18 to 20 inches, midseason, with bright red flower spikes. Popular landscaping plant.

'Bonfire' ('Clara Bedman'), to 26 inches, late, a traditional favorite with bright-red flower spikes, used for landscaping and massing.

BLUE SAGES

S. azurea var. grandiflora Blue Sage Zones 5-9
Perennial with striking deep blue flowers and narrow leaves prominently veined with lighter green on plants 3 to 4 feet high. Blooms in midsummer to mid-fall, providing a lasting late show of blue, especially in the South.

S. farinacea Mealy-cup Sage Zones 8-9
This is the most popular blue sage. It's a bushy plant that bears slim wands clustered with blue flowers in whorled spikes from midsummer to autumn frosts. A heat- and drought-tolerant perennial in its native Texas and the southern U.S., it is grown as an annual in the North. 'Victoria', 18 to 20 inches tall, lavender-blue, is the best landscaping and garden plant. It dries a lovely Wedgwood blue and is also available in a silvery white. A similar dwarf is 'Rhea', 14 inches tall, a free-flowering specimen for smaller spaces. 'Blue Bedder', 24 inches tall, is a superior plant in bright Wedgwood blue. It may need staking or shearing.

S. leucantha Mexican Bush Sage Zones 8-11
A robust, tender perennial 3 to 4 feet tall with fragrant velvety leaves, it is grown as an annual in the North for its sheer beauty and regal stature. From late summer through autumn frosts it covers itself with lavender flowers that have white corollas.

S. × superba cvs. Zones 5-8
A blue for spring, 18 to 24 inches tall. This is a somewhat hardy perennial also known as *S. nemerosa*. In the cool nights and moist weather of late spring and early summer it stages a brilliant show of deep violet-blue flower spikes. The leaves are pungent, crenulate, and leathery. A staple for durable blue color until early fall. Deadhead to keep the

TOP Mealy-cup sages, *Salvia farinacea*, beautiful blue lasts all season. This is the dwarf 'Rhea'.
(All American Selections)

ABOVE, LEFT *S. argentea*, Silver Sage, planted for its foliage. (Viette)

ABOVE, RIGHT 'May Night', very drought resistant cultivar of *S. × superba*. (Viette)

flowers coming. Two very drought-resistant plants are 'May Night' ('Mainacht'), which has deep indigo flowers on plants about 12 or 14 to 18 inches high, and 'Blue Queen', which has intense violet flowers on stems 18 to 24 inches high. 'East Friesland' ('Ostfriesland') has deep purple flowers. The species and 'Blue Queen' may easily be raised from seed, but plant root divisions of the others.

S. viridis (syn. *S. horminum*) — Annual

An 18-inch annual species topped by compact spires of substantial bracts. There are shades of rich violet-blue, brilliant pink, purple, or white. Dries well.

FOLIAGE SAGES
. . . .

S. argentea Silver Sage — Zones 5-11

To 24 inches tall. The basal rosette of its low-growing, 6-inch-long, hairy, silvery gray-white leaves glows in the midst of the garden's usual greens. The flowers, which are white with a pink or yellow tint, bloom on tall, strong stems in summer. They usually are removed to enhance leaf production. This is a perennial grown as a biennial and started from seed.

S. elegans Pineapple-scented Sage Zones 9-11

Shrubby, branching plant 3 to 4 feet tall with light green leaves deliciously scented of pineapple. Slender, velvety red flowers about an inch long emerge just before frost. Cuttings root easily in spring and summer. Tender perennial grown as an annual. Also fragrant but scarce is the species *S. dorisiana*, which bears attractive spikes of pink flowers and has thick, fuzzy, heart-shaped leaves with a peach scent.

S. officinalis Sage — Zones 4-9

This is the best-known culinary sage, an erect subshrub to 24 inches tall with violet, blue, or white flower spikes in summer and downy, sharply aromatic gray-green foliage. It should not be banished to the herb garden for it is handsome in the perennial garden, and a good edger and ground cover. Pinch back taller sorts to keep them trim— some need staking. Plant rooted cuttings in spring in very well-drained, neutral-range soil. There are new sages with brightly variegated leaves. Particularly pretty is the little *S. o.* 'Tricolor', 6 to 10 inches high, with leaves that are red, pink, gray, cream, and purple. The gray-green leaves of the often-seen 'Icterina' are variegated with gold. These are less hardy than the species. In California, a handsome gray plant, *S. clevelandii*, is often used as a substitute for *S. officinalis* in cooking.

SOURCE: GEORGE C. BALL, JR. IS PRESIDENT OF THE FLOWERSEED GROUP, GEORGE J. BALL, INC. HE PRESENTLY SERVES AS PRESIDENT OF THE AMERICAN HORTICULTURAL SOCIETY.

The hot zinnia colors—scarlet, cherry, yellow, pink with white—in the medium tall Ruffles series that blooms until early frosts. (Ball Seed Co.)

42. ZINNIA
. . . .

■ The zinnia captures the essence of summer in its hot, radiant colors—reds, pinks, oranges, magentas, yellows, white, and bicolors. Like that other great summer annual, the marigold, it's a native of the warm southwestern U.S., Central and South America. It blooms from early summer to fall, is carefree except for areas in which mildew is a problem—and with care, that can be avoided—needs heat, likes being rather dry, and holds its color in blazing sun. It's adaptable to conditions that are less than ideal, an easy-going, easy-to-care-for plant.

Its many forms make zinnia the ideal follow-on flower for quick summer color. It blooms in as little as four to five weeks from seed sown outdoors. Seedlings popped into holes left by the passing of spring flowers go right on blooming.

Even a few plants in a mixed border provide flowers for cutting. The more blooms you cut, the more the flowers will come, rising between each pair of leaves and the main stem. Some zinnias are called "cut and come again." Cut zinnias last well if they are in a roomy vase with lots of water. They last even longer if the stem ends are stripped of leaves, plunged in boiling water for 30 seconds, then soaked in warm water several hours before being placed in an arrangement.

Companion and Follow-on Plants: Replace finished medium and tall zinnias with ornamental cabbages, kales, peppers, and potted white mums. Grow medium zinnias with yellow *Helianthus*, the tall sunflowers, and *Sedum spectabile* 'Autumn Joy' that colors up as the zinnias come to an end. Plant *Callistephus* in mixed colors and sizes matched to the zinnias.
. . . .

ABOVE Medium tall Splendor series for cutting.
(W. Atlee Burpee Seed Co.)

TOP, RIGHT Tiny 'Peter Pan' for edging.
(W. Atlee Burpee Seed Co.)

BOTTOM, RIGHT 'Rose Pinwheel', mildew-resistant singles.
(W. Atlee Burpee Seed Co.)

FACING PAGE Cut-and-come-again zinnia 'Candy Cane'.
(W. Atlee Burpee Seed Co.)

ZINNIA (zinn-ee-uh)

Most modern zinnias have *Z. elegans* in their background, a rather stiff annual with hairy leaves and flowerheads to 4½ inches across.

There's a size of zinnia for every purpose—from tiny 6-inch plants with 2-inch flowers to 30-inch plants with 6-inch flowers. Some have petals quilled like a cactus, some curled as dahlias, some both; and there are ruffled and flat-petaled forms, and doubles and singles. Generally speaking, the large-flowered zinnias, flower less freely than the small-flowered zinnias and the large plants require a few more weeks to come into bloom.

Culture: All garden zinnias may be started indoors 3 to 4 weeks before planting time—they germinate in 4 to 5 days—and the fast-growing seedlings will be ready to set out when temperatures warm. But they flower almost as quickly from seed sown where they are to grow after the weather has warmed. Outdoors sow pairs of seeds ½ to ¾ inch below well-prepared, well-drained soil. Keep the soil moist until the seedlings are thriving.

Zinnias growing 12 inches apart in full sun in an airy site generally avoid mildew. Other ways to keep zinnias healthy: plant resistant types; avoid stress by keeping the ground damp enough (but don't overwater) so the plants never wilt; always water the soil, not the plants; water only on sunny days; water only in the morning. Where mildew is a threat choose mildew-resistant zinnias.

Early in the season pinch out the lead tip on each zinnia to force branching.

DWARF

Small mound-shaped plants 6 to 10 or 12 inches tall, ideal for edging and for fronting mixed borders and small window boxes. Set them out in groups of 3 to 7.

Thumbelina Mixture, a 6-inch plant in muted zinnia colors that starts to bloom when only 3 inches tall. The single flowers are about 1¼ inches across. Makes a charming, very low mound for narrow edgings.

Dasher series, 10-12 inches, an early, compact, rounded plant with blooms to 3 inches across in bright colors. Great edger.

Dreamland series, to 12 inches, a compact dahlia-flowered zinnia with fully double 3½-inch flowers borne freely. Blooms starting 6 weeks from sowing and is a good choice for color-patterned beds.

Mexican Zinnias, *Zinnia angustifolia* (syn. *linearis*) is offered in catalogs with a few other small species described as "old-fashioned" or "Mexican" zinnias. This one bears masses of single, golden orange, daisy-shaped flowers on compact 8-inch plants that are great for edging or use as a ground cover. Very durable little plant.

Peter Pan series, 10-12 inches, the best large-flowered dwarf, a free-flowering bushy plant with big double and semidouble flowers up to 3 inches across. Starts to flower at 7 inches.

'Rose Pinwheel', to 12 inches, with single daisylike flowers 2½ to 3 inches across with raised yellow centers. The blooms open pink and deepen to rose. Pretty in beds and good for cutting. Mildew-resistant even where summers are humid.

SEMIDWARF

Slightly taller mounded plants, 13 to 14 inches, for the front of the border. They produce a profusion of flowers 3½ inches across on stems long enough for cutting.

Pulchino series, 12 to 14 inches, an early, disease- and mildew-resistant plant with semidouble and double flowerheads in clear colors. Good for cutting.

MEDIUM TALL

The striking, large-flowered, 3½- to 5-inch zinnias recommended here are borne on upright plants to 20 inches tall. Mass in beds of mixed colors or plant in groups of 4 to 6 in mixed borders.

Cut-and-come-again series, 17 to 18 inches, double flowers, 2½ inches across borne on long stems. 'Candy Cane' has striped or flecked bicolor blooms. The more these are cut, the more they bloom—exceptionally floriferous.

'Candy Cane Mixed', to 17 inches, a seed mixture offering several 3¾-inch bicolors, including bright pink, rose, and cerise stripes on white zinnias, and gold blooms striped or flecked with orange-scarlet.

Marvel series, to 18 inches, sturdy plants with rather formal, dahlia-flowered blooms in clear, bright colors.

Splendor series, 20 to 22 inches, produces semi-ruffled, very full double 5-inch flowers that are superb for cutting. Blooms more freely than most other large zinnias.

Border series, 20 to 22 inches, dahlia-type, semidouble and double flowers 3½ inches across on bushy plants. Choice for cutting. 'Border Beauty Rose' is an All-America Selections winner, a lovely rose-pink-salmon.

TALL

These upright plants grow to 24 to 36 inches tall and bear magnificent big blooms that are excellent for cutting. Group them 12 to 20 in the back of the border, or mass in big beds.

Giant-flowered Double series, 24 to 36 inches; striking dahlia or cactus forms, fully double blooms to 5 inches across. 'Envy Double' is a chartreuse zinnia suited to semishaded, sheltered sites.

Ruffled series, to 27 inches, gorgeous, ruffled cactus-flowered giant with blooms 6 to 7 inches across. Flowering begins at 18 inches and continues until early frosts. 'Big Tetra' bears dahlia-flowered blooms 5 to 6 inches across.

Scabious-flowered series, 24 to 30 inches, these have a crested center surrounded by a row of true zinnia petals. Decorative in the border and superb for bouquets.

State Fair mixture, 30 to 36 inches, with broad-petaled, single blooms 5 to 6 inches across. Highly resistant to mildew.

SOURCE: SUZANNE FRUTIG BALES IS A DIRECTOR OF W. ATLEE BURPEE & CO., AND A GARDEN DESIGNER NOTED FOR HER INTEREST IN LONG-SEASON BEAUTY.

CHAPTER FOUR:
Workhorses Of The Garden

Special Performance Flowers

This chapter contains three groups of lists. Lists 43 through 49 cover Special Performance Flowers. Lists 50 through 54 are devoted to Foliage Plants for Contrast. Lists 55 through 59 recommend Flowers for Challenging Sites.

Flower gardens often have a vegetable plot in their background. One year some sweet peas and mums crept in beside the lettuce and pumpkins the way they used to on the farm—and the following year there were more. Then Aunt Jessie divided her prize irises and shared them. Another way to become a flower gardener is to move into a new home that has a nice flower garden that will die if you don't take care of it, or a garden that has been badly neglected. In the beginning, you're grateful when things bloom. But after you live with a landscape for a few years, it begins to talk back. This set of lists and the next describe flowers and foliage plants traditionally used to complete and focus garden designs without necessarily making them formal.

For instance, the edging flowers bring a crisp finish to sprawling beds. The edging satisfies the eye and says "Stop!" to the lawn. Most flowering edgers—begonias and ageratum, for instance—bloom the entire season. The most popular edging plant, Sweet Alyssum, makes a white ribbon that perfumes the late afternoon until the first frost.

The flowering ground covers have several important functions, some of which call for low plants, some for tall. They crowd out weeds invading empty spaces, and ajuga adds to its carpet an amazing show of spring blue. Liriope looks like grass, but in late summer and fall puts up flowers like little sticks of lavender. Lily-of-the-valley flourishes in light shade and in spring exhales a perfume that is legendary. *Lamium maculatum,* the silvery spotted dead nettle, trails silver leaves up hill and down dale under shrubs and low flowering trees. Some wonderful ground covers color up in autumn.

The native flowers that naturalize and grow wild—monarda, for instance—will bind steep slopes and sandy wastelands, and maintain nesting places for birds. Asclepias thrives in damp meadows and attracts butterflies as bright as its blossoms.

Queen-Anne's-lace, daisies, and fall-blooming asters can be gathered by the armful and will come back next year with more.

The creepers on the lists for rocky plants tie walls and naked stepping-stones into the landscape with mounds that nestle, climb up, tumble down, carpet, and make everything look as though it had always been there—a comforting lived-in look.

High-flying climbers have the same knack—they are especially worthwhile in urban gardens and not used as much as they should be. They do a lot that a tree does in less space, and are perfect screening for balcony and roof gardens. At ground level, vines can be directed to swallow up that which should be hidden—like a discontinued gate post—and they are lovely in their own right. One beautiful day and night combination is lavender-blue morning-glories intertwined with fragrant, pure-white moonflowers.

And, when everything else is growing in harmony, consider the winter garden. Warmth is not solely the province of the fireplace. Windows should look out on

FACING PAGE Ornamental grass, *Miscanthus gracillimus*, brings important foliage contrast to a flowering border of easy-care daylilies and lythrum. (Viette)
ABOVE Patterned leaves of 'White Nancy' *Lamium maculatum*, one of the prettiest ground covers. (Still)

Planted with flowers that grow in crevices, a wall becomes a garden for all seasons. In the background, flowering quince and viburnum; growing in the wall, *Aurinia saxatile*, basket-of-gold, aubrieta, and candytuft, *Iberis*, Alexander's 'White' and 'Snowflake'. (Viette)

changing, growing things that lift the heart in winter as well as summer. Golden grasses moving with the wind, binding snow at their feet; semievergreen and evergreen edgers and ground covers spiked with leaves; boltonia's little browned asters; liriope's grassy greens; seedpods of baptisia in gunmetal gray—all bring interest to the winter landscape.

Foliage Plants for Contrast

The importance of foliage to the beauty of a garden can't be overestimated. Plants chosen for their leaves are included in all good garden designs. Some foliage plants are chosen for their color (see list 51), while others are valuable sources of contrast in form and texture (see list 50).

The big advantage of colorful foliage is that it is in perpetual "bloom." The silvery Dusty-millers and artemisias have the presence of white flowers from the moment they come into the garden in spring. Coleus and caladiums are splashed all season long with crimson, orange, and coral. The dazzling purple-cream-rose ornamental kales and cabbages can be propped into the bed in autumn and remain bright through the first frosts.

The foliage plants on list 50 add the essential elements of texture and form. A bed whose every leaf is small and oval—many flowering plants have such leaves—is boring. The garden picture gains much more interest when it includes big, bold leaves, such as those displayed by *Angelica archangelica* and *Cimicifuga*. Joseph's-coat, an annual, brings color as well as form and texture. And find a place for a few ferns and hostas—these very beautiful foliage plants thrive in spots that don't have enough light for many of the flowers, in the shade cast by taller flowers, shrubs, trees, or buildings.

Hostas will spread and cover blank spaces under trees and in other shady places. Their mounds of bold leaves come in a dizzying array of textures; they can be puckered, smooth, quilted, or slightly twisted. The colors are many; leaves can be bluish, pale green, deep green, or variegated with blue or green or yellow or white. There are hostas in a range of sizes: small, medium, and large. And the hosta flowers rise up in late summer and fall and can be both fragrant and beautiful.

Many modern garden designs include at least a few ornamental grasses. They introduce long verticals, the element of gold in autumn, and sound and movement. The foliage can be counted on to whisper and flow, and the dance of the feathered plumes magnifies the autumn breeze. In the landscape design style we are calling the "New American Garden," grasses are massed with bulbs and perennials. Even a small city plot can benefit from a few tufts that bend in the wind. The tallest grasses are very effective against a blank masonry wall in place of labor-intensive espaliers.

Flowers for Challenging Sites

The lists at the end of this chapter describe flowers that flourish in especially challenging places: in heat and drought, sand, the seashore, cities, or wet and boggy places. These aren't the only flowers in the book that will succeed in such sites, but when others that should succeed are failing, these workhorses will prevail.

43. FLOWERS FOR EDGING

■ **Finish your border with flowering edgers.** The most colorful approach is to use repeating modules of several flowers. But that can be too much, and sometimes a more effective edging combines flowers and green plants—trailing *Vinca minor,* oregano, or green or variegated thyme. Or alternate one flowering edger with half a dozen herbs and repeat the pattern.

A finish that displays just one plant and color—white alyssum, for instance—appears more formal than combinations—for instance, white alyssum and blue ageratum, or those two plus pink wax begonias. An edger that flowers only in spring and may lose its foliage early, *Bellis perennis,* for example, must be combined with a second or follow-on edger that will bloom throughout the summer—for instance, the charming, rustic little creeping zinnia.

Almost any low-growing flower that blooms all season gives a pretty finish to a flower garden or path. Many annuals are popular edgers—for instance, the little French marigolds (sun), tuberous begonias (semi-sun), and low growing impatiens (shade.) But the edging plants recommended here are those with pretty foliage that remains crisp and colorful even when flowering hesitates or stops. Quiet color has more lasting appeal than a riot of bold hues.

Culture: Space edging plants a little closer together than bedding plants for a continuous ribbon of color. Edgers set in perfect alignment are boring. Rather, set the plants in a zigzag pattern within the line or the curve. That gives the plants space to spread, and the final effect is far more satisfying to the eye.

AGERATUM houstonianum, Flossflower. A low-growing mounded plant 6 to 12 inches high that provides an indispensable puff of soft blue, or pink or white, in the garden from late spring through fall. The dainty arrangement of the good green, pointed leaves is reminiscent of a nosegay. Recommended for edging are the compact, lavishly blooming, lavender-blue 'Blue Danube' ('Blue Puff'), the extra-early bright blue 'Adriatic' and 'Blue Surf', which grows to 9 inches tall and blooms from June to the first frost. See list 31, Annuals for Sun.

ALCHEMILLA mollis, Lady's-mantle. A 12-inch-high, clump-forming ground cover with crinkle-edged leaves—round as nasturtium foliage and covered with silky hairs—that sparkle when drops of rain or dew collect on them. Sprays of tiny chartreuse or yellowish green flowers stand above the leaves in late spring or early summer. Attractive as an edger or massed as ground cover. For culture see list 75, Herbs with Showy Flowers.

ASTILBE chinensis. A small, dense plant 8 or 12 to 16 inches high that spreads by creeping stolons and has low, compact foliage suitable for ground cover or for edging the front of a tall border. From summer to fall, after the flowers of the popular *A.* × *arendsii* have gone by, this plant raises spiky mauve-pink flowerheads on stiffly narrow panicles high above the foliage clump. Recommended for edging are 'Pumila', 12 inches tall, lilac-rose; 'Finale', 14 inches tall, rose; 'Serenade', 14 inches tall, rose-red; and 'Veronica Klose', to 20 inches, purple-rose. See also list 21, *Astilbe.*

FACING PAGE Marigolds edged with blue ageratum. (McDonald)
BELOW Silvery-white dusty-miller, *Senecio cineraria*. (Still)
RIGHT *Bellis perennis* with lily-flowered tulips. (McDonald)
BOTTOM, LEFT Creeping zinnia, *Sanvitalia procumbens*. (Woodham)
BOTTOM, RIGHT *Alchemilla*, Lady's-mantle. (Viette)

BEGONIA Semperflorens-Cultorum Hybrids, Bedding Begonia, Wax Begonia, is a pretty little tender perennial planted as an annual filler or edger for walks and small window boxes. It flowers from spring until frost in hues of salmon, pink, red, or white, and the crisp, shiny leaves are attractive. Best grown in filtered light where summers are hot, but withstands full sun if temperatures stay under 90° F and adequate moisture is assured. Among superior plants are the sun-resistant, compact, deep bronze foliaged Cocktail hybrids. See also list 36, Begonias.

BELLIS (*bell*-iss) **perennis**
English Daisy   Zones 3-11
A dainty, perky little mound that bears masses of 4- to 5-inch-tall, completely charming, tiny single or double pink, white, or red-, white- or pink-edged daisy-like flowers in early spring. The foliage is decorative, sometimes hairy. It is choice as a low edger, a rock garden specimen, an underplanting for daffodils and tulips, or a pot plant for late winter bloom indoors. Where summers are cool and moist it will likely flower again in autumn. 'Pomponette' is a pretty semidouble with quilled rays to 6 inches high.

Culture: In hot climates this is best replanted every spring from seed for the species. Or set out spring or early fall root divisions. Plant in full sun, in moist, rich, well-drained soil with lots of humus added. Maintain even moisture.

CATHARANTHUS roseus, Rose Periwinkle, Madagascar Periwinkle. Also called 'Vinca rosea'—it does resemble a pink vinca—this is a 12-inch-high bushy mound that spreads to 18 and 24 inches in a season. The shiny leaves are dark green. Evergreen in warm climates, but farther north the plant is handled as an annual. All summer it blooms on upright stems, producing small phlox-like flowers in mauvy pink or white, usually with a darker eye, either in rose or red. This is the bedding plant that best tolerates heat, drought, and pollution—it truly thrives in grim city conditions, including neglected tree boxes. 'Pretty in Pink', 'Pretty in Rose', and 'Parasol' (white with a rose-red eye) are exceptionally heat- and drought-tolerant All-America Selections, and flower in full sun. For culture, see list 58, Urban Conditions.

IBERIS (eye-*beer*-iss)
Candytuft
Low-growing, spreading, clump-forming, narrow-leaved plants with attractive foliage on semiwoody stems, 6 to 12 inches high with a 24-inch spread. They blanket themselves with short spikes of upright florets over a long period, usually in spring. There are evergreen perennials and annuals. Valuable as ground cover in rock and wall gardens and as edging for spring borders.

Culture: Set out container plants in early spring. Full sun and well-drained soil are essential to good growth. In cold climates with little snow cover the evergreens benefit from a light winter covering of evergreen branches to reduce sunscald and keep the plants from drying out. After flowering, cut back the stems of perennial types to promote vigorous growth and density.

I. amara Rocket Candytuft   Annual
Also called hyacinth-flowered candytuft, this is a good annual edger, about 12 inches high, fast-growing, and bushy. It has attractive foliage and in summer to mid-fall bears showy, rounded, elongated spikes of scented 4-petaled, pure white flowers. May be started from seed indoors or outside. Adaptable as to soil, it withstands some drought and will self-sow.

I. saxatilis   Zones 2-7
A small evergreen form just 3 to 6 inches tall, ideal for growing on rocks and exceptionally hardy. Prefers alkaline soils.

I. sempervirens Edging Candytuft   Zones 4-8
Early to mid-spring it is blanketed with dense heads of white flowers. Thrives without care in full or semi-sun and somewhat acid soil. Recommended are 'Autumn Beauty', 8 inches tall, which flowers in spring and reblooms in fall; 'Alexander's White', 8 to 10 inches tall, a very dense, floriferous plant; 'Little Gem', 5 to 8 inches tall, a delightful rare plant; and 'Snowflake', 8 to 10 inches tall, late-blooming with large leaves and flowers.

I. umbellata Globe Candytuft   Annual
This is the other popular annual candytuft. Within 6 weeks of sowing the tightly clustered flowerheads come into bloom. There are various shades of lilac, violet, red, and pink. Good until frost.

LOBULARIA (lob-yew-*lay*-ree-uh) maritima
Sweet Alyssum   Annual
This is a very sweetly scented and dainty flowering edger, 4 to 8 inches high, that grows into a low mound 12 to 18 inches across and covers itself with tiny, sparkling white, rosy violet, or purple florets in summer and fall. Often used as a continuous low border. A midsummer slump in flowering can occur in extreme heat, but when cool weather returns, the flowers glow with new color and perfume the whole garden. 'Carpet of Snow' is just 4 inches tall.

Culture: Set out container plants in spring, or sow seeds indoors early or outdoors as soon as the soil has warmed—and be patient. Thrives in full sun or partial shade, in well-drained soil in the neutral range. Versatile as to moisture and withstands heat. Self-sows. Excellent near the sea. Shear spent blooms to encourage continued flowering.

SANTOLINA chamaecyparissus, Lavender Cotton. A highly valued, dense, pine-scented evergreen 18 to 30 inches high as multibranched as coral with needlelike foliage—white-woolly underneath, silvery in moonlight, and whiter when growing in dry conditions, sandy soil, and full sun. In late spring and summer small, bright yellow flowers stand well above the foliage, but they aren't often seen as the plant usually is tightly sheared. Useful in gravelly dry places, as a low hedge, in the rock garden, or to carpet flowering beds. 'Nana' is a dwarf to 14 inches high. The related *S. virens* is a handsome green. For culture, see list 73, Herbs with Colorful Foliage.

SANVITALIA (san-vi-*tay*-lee-uh) **procumbens**
Creeping Zinnia, Trailing Zinnia   Annual
A bushy mound 6 inches high with an 18-inch spread, covered with nonstop, purple-brown centered, golden yellow flowers similar to small zinnias from early summer to frost. Used to edge borders, along paths, in rock gardens, and hanging baskets and as a summer ground cover. 'Gold Braid' is a double golden yellow with purplish centers; 'Mandarin Orange' has large, semidouble flowers.

Culture: Sow seeds in early spring in full sun where the plants are to bloom. In the warm South, seeds may be planted in early fall. Thrives in loose, well-drained soil. Tolerates drought, heat, and humidity.

SENECIO cineraria, Dusty-miller. The stiff, white-woolly leaves are divided into blunt segments, especially in 'Silver Lace'. The species is 8 to 12 inches tall and the ornamental foliage is most conspicuous when dry—and lovely dried in winter arrangements. In summer there are daisylike yellow flowers in groups of 10 or 12 unless the plants are sheared. Serves well as an edging, in containers, or as a specimen for color contrast in a mixed border. It winters over in frost-free climates and grows into a sizable, shrublike plant. Recommended are the compact 'Silver Lace', 6 to 8 inches tall, and 'Silver Dust', 8 inches tall, which has very finely cut foliage. This also is sold as *Cineraria maritima*, and is not to be confused with 2 other silvery plants that share its common name—*Artemisia* and *Centaurea cineraria*, Dusty-miller. For culture, see list 50, Foliage for Form and Texture.

TEUCRIUM (*tewk*-ree-um) **chamaedrys**
Germander   Zones 5-8
A semiwoody herbal subshrub, evergreen to semievergreen in mild climates, that forms clumps 12 inches tall and 24 inches wide. It branches very densely and is used primarily as a foliage plant for edging or low hedges, sometimes clipped like boxwood. The 2-lipped, pale to deep purple flowers bloom in early to midsummer in loose spikes. See also list 73, Herbs with Colorful Foliage.

MORE EDGING PLANTS
....
The following plants can also be used as edgers.

AJUGA genevensis, A. pyramidalis, list 44, Flowering Ground Covers.

ALCHIMELLA mollis, list 75, Herbs with Showy Flowers.

ALTERNANTHERA ficoidea.

ASTILBE chinensis 'Pumila', list 21, *Astilbe*.

CHRYSOGONUM virginianum, list 18, Perennials for the South.

COLEUS × hybridus, list 51, Foliage for Color.

DIANTHUS gratianapolitanus 'Tiny Rubies', list 70, The Fragrance Garden.

DYSSODIA tenuiloba, Dahlberg Daisy, Golden-Fleece, list 34, Annuals That Self-sow.

SOURCE: DR. STEVEN STILL IS A PROFESSOR OF HORTICULTURE AT OHIO STATE UNIVERSITY AND THE AUTHOR OF THE *MANUAL OF HERBACEOUS ORNAMENTAL PLANTS*.

Little French marigolds cover a meadow with sheets of gold—'Boy O Boy Mixed'. The French marigolds often self-sow and repeat the following year. (Denham Seed Co.)

44. FLOWERING GROUND COVERS

■ **The best ground covers are low-growing plants that clothe the earth with beauty, perennialize rapidly, and are dense enough to crowd out weeds. Combine flowering types with foliage plants for a rich, tapestried effect that brings an excitement to the changing seasons never achieved by plain green ground covers alone. Be cautious with ground covers that spread rapidly—plant them in confined spaces, away from the lawn.**

Culture: Choose plants matched to their soil and site so they'll thrive with little help. Good drainage is the single most important factor in the success of all but the boggy plants. Prepare the soil carefully as described in Growing Flowers and provide sustained moisture the first season. Be patient! It can be two summers before the plants grow together enough for good coverage.

AJUGA (aj-**yew**-guh) **reptans**
Carpet Bugle   Zones 3-8/9
Effective, fast-growing, semievergreen cover with low, upright, leafy stems 4 to 8 inches high that may be green, green-purple, bronze, or multicolor according to species and variety. In spring it covers itself with little stubs of blue, pink, white, or purple flowers. 'Burgundy Glow' has variegated foliage—white, pink, rose, and green—and blue flowers. 'Pink Spire' has green foliage and pink flowers 7 inches high. 'Gaiety' has bronze-purple leaves and lilac flowers. The species is prostrate, spreads very quickly by underground runners, and should be confined to its own territory. Keep it away from the lawn. *A. genevensis*, Geneva Bugle, is more upright, less invasive, hardy to Zone 4, and a healthier plant for the South.

Culture: Sow seed or set out root divisions in late summer, fall, or very early spring. In the North, plant in full sun; partial shade is recommended in the South. Prefers evenly moist, well-drained, humusy soil.

BRUNNERA (**brunn**-er-uh) **macrophylla** (syn. *Anchusa myosotidiflora*)
Siberian Bugloss   Zones 4-7
A deciduous ground cover that includes a long-lasting—up to 6 weeks—spring display of true blue flowers. The 12-inch-high foliage remains fresh all season. Easily perennialized, adaptable in most of the country, and a good choice for large spaces. 'Variegata' is boldly variegated with creamy white. It grows slowly, scorches in dry areas, and often reverses to the green of the species, but it is very beautiful when it's successful.

Culture: Sow seeds in early fall, or in early spring set out root divisions in partial shade in moist, well-drained soil. Often self-sows.

CONVALLARIA **majalis,** Lily-of-the-valley. Creamy little white bells with haunting perfume bloom on 4- to 8-inch stems rising from furled green leaves. It is loved for its fragrance and is among the plants forced into early bloom indoors. Exquisite in bouquets. The rhizomatous roots set out in early spring or fall densely carpet the ground if planted in humusy, somewhat acid soil and in the light shade of trees or tall shrubs. Spreading ground cover for shady corners, woodlands, and wild gardens. 'Fortin's Giant', 10 to 12 inches tall, is a favorite full-flowered white. In catalogs, it may be grouped with bulbs for forcing and/or with perennials. For culture see list 70, The Fragrance Garden.

GERANIUM **macrorrhizum.** Not to be confused with *Pelargonium,* whose common name is geranium, this fast-growing, clump-forming herbaceous perennial 12 inches or taller is called bigroot geranium. The attractive, dense foliage is deeply lobed, has a slightly medicinal odor when crushed, and remains as an excellent ground cover after a spring show of pretty magenta flowers. Weed-smothering, noninvasive, and quite drought-resistant even in warm climates. In the hot summers of Zone 8 it grows best in partial shade, but elsewhere it thrives in the sun. Recommended are 'Album', 15 to 18 inches high, white, an excellent garden plant; 'Beven's Variety', to 12 inches high, with deep magenta flowers; and 'Ingwersen's Variety', 12 inches high, with excellent soft rose pink flowers. See list 13, Spring Perennials for Sun.

Outstanding flowering ground covers:
ABOVE *Brunnera macrophylla* 'Cheguers'. (Viette)
RIGHT *Liriope platyphylla* 'Christmas Tree'. (Viette)
BELOW, LEFT 'Shell Pink' *Lamium maculatum*. '(Viette)
BELOW, RIGHT *Pulmonaria saccharata* 'Mrs. Moon'. (Still)

GYPSOPHILA repens. Airy, many-branched, spangled with tiny roselike flowers in summer, this is a creeping form of baby's-breath, the florist's favorite filler for arrangements. It forms mats 8 to 12 inches high that are delightful in rock gardens and as ground cover. Gray-leaved, white-flowered, it blooms all summer into early fall. For culture, see list 71, The Cutting Garden.

LAMIUM (*lay*-mee-um) **maculatum**
Spotted Dead Nettle   Zones 4-8
This fast-growing member of the mint family has small, hooded, pink flowers in late spring to midsummer, trailing stems 6 to 8 inches long, and dark green oval leaves blotched with white along the midrib. The cultivars are superior. Recommended are the attractively variegated 'Beacon Silver', 8 to 12 inches high, whose silver leaves are edged with a narrow band of green, and the similar 'White Nancy', 6 to 8 inches high, which has white flowers.

Culture: Plant seeds or root divisions in spring in partial to full shade in almost any site, but preferably in moist, well-drained soil. Tolerates drought and succeeds in light, calcareous soils even in rigorous climates.

LAMIASTRUM (lay-mee-*as*-strum)
galeobdolan
Yellow Archangel   Zones 4-9
The perfect answer to what will grow in the heavy shade of trees such as Norway Maple. A member of the mint family with trailing stems 6 to 8 inches long, this resembles *Lamium* but the late-spring to early-summer flowers are hooded and yellow. It has attractive, hairy leaves and is a very fast-spreading ground cover that roots at the nodes. To promote a compact habit, cut back after flowering. Recommended are 'Variegatum', 12 to 15 inches tall, which has silver leaves marked with green on the margins and midribs; and the slower-growing, compact 'Herman's Pride', 8 inches tall, which has smaller flowers and foliage and more distinct silver markings.

Culture: Plant seeds or root divisions in spring in partial to full shade in almost any soil. Best in moist, well-drained soil. Tolerates drought and succeeds in light, calcareous soils, even in rigorous climates.

LIRIOPE (lihr-*rye*-oh-pee) Lilyturf
Graceful, remarkably tough, and resistant semievergreen or evergreen plants grown primarily for the grasslike foliage which is ¼ to ¾ inch wide and 8 to 12 or 18 inches high. In summer or early fall, thin spikes covered with grainlike lavender or white flowers rise well above the grassy tufts. Shiny black fruits develop in late fall and persist into winter. It is an impenetrable ground cover and good edging plant, nice with daffodils and fall-blooming crocus coming up through it. Some have handsome variegated foliage. The other plant called Lilyturf, *Ophiogon*, is not as hardy, and its flowers are less visible.

Culture: In early spring, set out container plants or root divisions 6 to 8 inches apart in sun or shade in any but very wet locations. In late winter, mow the foliage to the ground to allow for fresh growth. Liriope spreads rapidly and tolerates heat, humidity, drought, and even dense shade.

L. platyphylla (formerly muscari)
Big Blue Lilyturf   Zones 6-9/10
A standard landscape plant in southern regions and one of the best ground covers—the flowers of the hybrids may be green, bluish, blue, red, lavender, white, or purple. The leaves are ½ to ¾ inch wide. Recommended are: 'Christmas Tree', to 8 inches tall, with large, lavender flower spikes narrow at the top and widening toward the bottom, like a Christmas tree; 'Lilac Beauty', to 12 inches tall, an excellent bloomer with dark lilac flowers; 'Monroe's White', to 12 inches tall, slower growing, with white flowers; 'Gold Banded', to 12 inches tall, variegated, with lilac flowers; 'John Burch', 12 inches tall, variegated, crested lavender flowers; and 'Silvery Midget', to 6 inches tall, variegated, with violet flowers.

L. spicata Creeping Liriope   Zones 4-9
For northern gardens, shorter, 8 to 12 inches tall, with ¼-inch leaves and rather sparse pale violet or white flowers. It spreads rapidly, requires evenly moist soil, and prefers semishade.

PHLOX. The little creeping phloxes described here are good ground covers. Low-growing, mat-forming perennials, one for sun, one for shade, they are very effective cascading over banks and slopes and down rock walls. Usually 5 to 12 inches tall, in spring they cover themselves with small blooms in rosy reds, pinks, shades of blue or purple-blue, and white. Shearing the plants back halfway after flowering promotes denser foliage. The creeping stolons of *P. stolonifera*, Creeping Phlox, which is evergreen in some varieties in mild winters and blooms in spring, spread moderately fast in partial or full shade. Recommended are 'Blue Ridge', 12 inches tall, 'Bruce's White', 6 inches tall, and 'Home Fires', a 6-inch-tall pink. *P. subulata*, Moss Pink, Moss Phlox, Mountain Phlox, is a moderate- to fast-spreading species that prefers full sun and is semievergreen in warm regions. In early to mid-spring it covers itself with small clusters of starry flowers. Recommended are: 'Crimson Beauty', a red: 'Millstream Jupiter', blue; 'Red Wings', light red, and 'White Delight'. See also list 27, *Phlox*.

PULMONARIA (pull-mon-*nay*-ree-uh)
saccharata
Bethlehem Sage   Zones 4-8
A lovely foliage plant recommended on several of the lists in this book. The dark green leaves are covered with soft, bristly hairs and conspicuously marked with white splotches that often blend into large patches. In early to mid-spring, tubular flowers bloom, pink at first then turning toward blue. About 12 inches high, it is attractive as a single specimen or massed for ground cover. The popular 'Mrs. Moon' has large, silver-spotted leaves. 'Margery Fish' has larger and more uniform spots. 'Sissinghurst White' has white flowers. *P. angustifolia* has intense blue flowers.

Culture: Set out root divisions in early spring or very early fall, in partial to full shade, in a soil that is cool and moist, and to which a lot of organic material has been added. Water during summer droughts.

SYMPHYTUM grandiflorum. This very good plant is called ground-cover comfrey and may be offered in catalogs as *Pulmonaria lutea*. The leaves are dark green, crinkled, and have a rough, bristly texture. The cream and white flowers in late spring are a bonus. Few weeds find their way through massed plantings. An excellent cover for dry sites, but it spreads faster in moist soils. For culture, see list 73, Herbs with Colorful Foliage.

MORE GROUND COVERS

The following plants can also be grown for ground cover:

CHRYSOGONUM virginianum, list 18, Perennials for the South.

EPIMEDIUM spp., list 51, Foliage for Color.

GALIUM odoratum, Woodroof, Sweet Woodruff, list 76, Fragrant Herbs for Drying and Potpourri.

HYPERICUM calycinum, Rose-of-Sharon, Aaron's Beard, Creeping St-John's-wort, Goldflower.

SEDUM 'Vera Jameson', list 15, Summer Perennials for Sun.

STACHYS byzantina 'Silver Carpet', Woolly Betony, Lamb's-ears, list 50, Foliage for Form and Texture.

TIARELLA cordifolia, list 48, Wildflowers to Naturalize.

VERONICA incana, list 66, The Rock Garden.

VERONICA repens, list 66, The Rock Garden.

WALDSTEINIA fragarioides, Barren Strawberry.

SOURCE: DR. STEVEN STILL IS A PROFESSOR OF HORTICULTURE AT OHIO STATE UNIVERSITY AND THE AUTHOR OF THE *MANUAL OF HERBACEOUS ORNAMENTAL PLANTS*.

45. ROCK WALLS AND CREVICES

■ A spill of green leaves spangled with little flowers can transform even a grim masonry wall into a garden whose seasons rival the flower borders. There's something so appealing about the contrast between the strength of masonry and the delicacy of plants.

A double dry stone wall—two parallel tiers of stones separated by a core of soil and humus—offers unlimited opportunities for the plants here. The entire top and all the crevices and pockets are plantable. Trailing plants go into the pockets, and low growers, or a whole collection of rock garden plants, fit in the soil between the double stone walls. A retaining wall can be just as striking. The wall is best built with a backward slant of about 1 inch per foot of height to allow the face to collect falling rain.

These are two major opportunities for the plants here. But almost any crevice open to rain that can give roots access to an inner core of cool, damp earth can be successfully planted—brick or cement block walls can be designed to hold planting pockets; stone steps invite fuzzy things to bloom in earthy angles. Or try planting in strawberry jars!

Culture: Wait until the wall is finished to plant, even though it means digging out and replacing some of the soil. A gritty loam composed of equal parts of sharp sand, humus, and good garden soil is used for planting pockets—and, when possible, as mortar. To plant, use a small, flat stick to dig out the dirt, then push the roots into the emptied space, pack it about half full with soil, then wet the soil and add more soil, wetting it in until the surface is level with the crown. The crown of the plant must not project beyond the face of the wall, and is better set a little below it.

In early spring and once during the summer, check the planting pockets and, if necessary, refill them with humus and gravel, and reset crowns or roots loosened by rain and wind.

Feed heavy bloomers several times in the growing season with a liquid houseplant fertilizer.

For sources of hard-to-find plants, see the Appendix.

AUBRIETA (au-*bree*-tuh) deltoidea
                                     Zones 4-8
An ideal wall plant rather like the one called Rock Cress, *Arabis*. It forms low, leafy mats of grayish foliage that in mid-spring bear masses of 6- to 8-inch stems topped by 4-petaled flowers in shades of pale pink to dark purple. There are many beautiful single and double forms. When the plants become leggy in summer, cut them back to 6 to 8 inches, particularly in the warm South, to keep the foliage full.

Culture: In early spring, sow seed or set out container plants in semi-sun in nearly neutral garden soil with lots of sand, grit, and humus—enough to sustain moisture. Succumbs to excessive heat and drying out. Most successful in cool, moist climates.

RIGHT *Aubrieta* bears masses of flowers in mid-spring. (Viette)

BOTTOM Exotic *Corydalis lutea*, excellent for wall crevices and walkways, blooms in mid-spring. (McDonald)

BOTTOM, RIGHT *Sempervivum*, live-forever, a workhorse of the rock garden, spreads into the least inviting cracks and crannies. (Viette)

CAMPANULA, Bellflower. The small forms of these delicate cups in blue, lavender, white, and sometimes pink are like stars spangled on a canopy of green. Long lasting, and many species multiply and perennialize very well. Chose species that make low mounds and creepers that flourish in, around, and through dry stone walls and rock gardens. The flowering period can be 2 even 3 months in late spring or early summer and into fall, according to species and region. Where winters are mild, some are evergreen. Recommended for the walls and crevices are: *C. dasyantha*, a very hardy (to Zone 2) mat-forming plant composed of rosettes of small leaves and, in early summer, violet flowers on 6-inch stems; *C. rotundifolia*, Bluebell, Harebell, 6 to 18 inches tall, with graceful, nodding blue flowers in late spring and summer. A dainty plant for moist soil, pH 5.5 to 6.5. It self-sows generously in the Pacific Northwest. Long-lasting bloomer. For culture, see list 22, *Campanula*.

CORYDALIS (kor-*rid*-al-iss) **lutea**
Zones 5-7
Excellent exotic plant for wall crevices and cracks in walkways. Wiry stems bearing 6- to 8-inch spikes of spurred, soft yellow flowers about 12 inches tall are held above light blue-green, ferny foliage for weeks in mid-spring.
  Culture: Sow fresh (only) seeds or plant root divisions in early spring or fall, in moist, very well-drained soil with a pH of 5.5 to 6.5. Self-sows. Best in the shade of taller deciduous plants, it flourishes when given spring sun and summer shade.

GENTIANA (jen-shee-*ay*-nuh) **scabra**
Zones 5-9
The gentians are beautiful but sometimes difficult little plants that cover themselves with remarkably blue flowers (in most species) in late summer and/or early fall. This is an easy gentian from Japan that blooms October to November at heights from 6 to 12 inches. Thrives in rock gardens, rock walls, and stony crevices. The form *saxatilis* is particularly desirable.
  Culture: Set out root divisions in early fall or early spring in sun or semishade in scree—gravel rich in leaf mold, with a pH of 6.0 to 7.0—and maintain constant moisture. Best in cool places; not so good in hot, dry situations. Self-sows.

PETRORHAGIA (pet-roar-hay-*gee*-uh)
saxifraga (syn. *Tunica saxifraga*)
Coat Flower, Tunic Flower   Zones 5-7
For most of the summer, pretty, tiny pale pink flowers sometimes veined with deeper pink float on 8-inch stems above creeping mats of tufted, grassy leaves. Excellent in the rock garden or wall and as an edging plant.
  Culture: Plant seeds or root divisions in autumn in full sun, in near-neutral, fertile, well-drained humusy soil. Self-sows.

SEDUM, Stonecrop. These species are indestructible, succulent-like, and evergreen. The flowers are tiny and star-shaped, modest but charming in the ground-hugging species recommended here. *S. kamtschaticum* subsp. *middendorfianum*, hardy in Zones 3 to 8, 4 to 9 inches tall, has grooved leaves and unbranched, pale green stems topped in summer by flat little yellow florets; *S. sieboldii*, October Daphne, October Plant, hardy to Zones 4 and 5, has a trailer 6 to 9 inches long with bluish green leaves that have faint reddish margins. Tolerates light shade and bears large, flat flowerheads that in late summer and fall turn bright pink; similar is 'Vera Jameson', 9 to 12 inches tall, with darkish leaves, 2- to 4-inch-wide rose pink flowerheads. For culture and a full discussion of this valuable genus, see list 56, Dry, Hot Conditions.

SEMPERVIVUM (sem-per-*vye*-vum)
Houseleek, Live-forever
A staple for rock gardens, but the plant is chosen more for the evergreen, succulent, tightly-clustered, bright green rosettes. Performs very well in dry, poor soils, rocky pockets, between stepping-stones and in cracks and crevices.
  Culture: In spring, plant rooted offsets in full sun or light shade, in neutral-range soil and any well-drained situation. Withstands high heat and multiplies steadily, but require a fairly constant supply of moisture.

S. arachnoideum Cobweb Houseleek
Zones 5-10
Small, the leaf tips of its rosettes are connected by a dense webbing of cobwebby hairs and it bears rose-red flowers. Otherwise it resembles *S. tectorum*. These are the 2 most-grown species.

S. soboliferum Hens-and-chickens Zones 6-9
Develops into a sheet of densely packed, small green rosettes with yellow flowers.

S. tectorum Common Houseleek, Roof Houseleek, Hens-and-chickens, Old-man-and-old-woman   Zone 4-8
These thick rosettes 1½ to 3 inches high and 4 inches wide have red-purple pointed tips. In summer, clusters of soft purple-red flowers grow from the centers.

SOURCE: DR. NICKOLAS NICKOU, M.D., IS A TALENTED GARDENER WHOSE TWO THIRTY-YEAR-OLD ROCK GARDENS HAVE BENEFITED FROM COLLECTING TRIPS TO ICELAND, GREENLAND, THE HIMALAYAS, CHINA, NEW ZEALAND, AUSTRALIA, TURKEY, THE ALPS, THE CANADIAN AND U.S. ROCKIES, SOUTH AFRICA, AND OTHER PLACES.

46. STEPPING-STONES AND WALKS

■ Flagstone paths and stepping-stones are beautifully softened by the small-leaved creeping plants recommended here—there's an instant "belonging" effect. To do their best, these plants require suitable soils and an early start. They are not sold in every garden center but can be found through mail-order nurseries and by persistent search—the effect is worth the effort. The American Horticultural Society can be helpful.
  Culture: Since they will be in place for many years, go to whatever lengths are necessary to set these plants in generous, well-worked planting holes filled with soil that has been improved as described under Culture for each plant. If sowing seeds, plant them in flats and transplant only when the seedlings are growing vigorously. Plants set between stones should not be walked on until they are showing signs of strong new growth.

HERNIARIA (her-knee-*air*-ee-uh) **glabra**
Rupturewort   Zones 4-9
Minute, mossy, evergreen ground cover under 1 inch high, slow but effective filler for between flagstones. Easy to grow and a nice carpet for perennialized small bulbs.
  Culture: Set out closely spaced root divisions in early spring in full sun, in ordinary, well-drained, humusy soil and maintain moisture until the plants are well started.

HYDYOTIS (hi-dee-*oh*-tis) **michauxii**
(syn. *Houstonia serpyllifolia*)
Creeping Bluets   Zones 3-8
Forms a creeping deep-pile carpet with, in spring or early summer, masses of tiny, sweetly scented, single dark blue or violet flowers on slender 2- to 3-inch stems. Can handle only light traffic, but spreads and needs little care. Nice for edging walks and stepping-stones.
  Culture: Plant root divisions in early spring in a shaded, moist area in well-drained, peaty soil.

MAZUS (*may*-zus) **reptans**   Zones 4-8
Delightful long-lasting, mat-forming, creeping ground cover with tiny leaves, ideal for rock gardens, steps, and between stones. In spring, 2- to 4-inch stems bear clusters of blue-purplish flowers with yellow, white, or purple spots on the lower lip. Evergreen in warm regions.
  Culture: Plant seeds in early spring or root divisions in fall, in a sheltered, lightly shaded moist spot in ordinary, well-drained soil. Does not withstand drought.

SAGINA (saj-*jye*-nuh) **subulata**   Zones 5-8
One of the most successful ground covers between stepping-stones. It is low, mossy, well branched, with many creeping stems that form a dense evergreen mat 2 inches high. In summer, minute white flowers appear on hairlike stems to 4 inches high. There is a yellow variety.
  Culture: Sow seeds or plant root divisions in early spring in sun or shade, in well-drained, humusy soil; provide sustained moisture.

TOP, LEFT The tangy scent of durable creeping thyme fills the air when walked on. In late spring, minute flowers appear. (Viette)

TOP, RIGHT Less than an inch high, *Hernaria glabra* is a mossy evergreen filler for flagstones. (Harper)

ABOVE Spring flowers of *Mazus reptans,* a delightful creeper. (Viette)

BOTTOM Mossy *Sagina subulata* 'Aurea', in summer bears tiny white flowers on hairlike stems. (Viette)

SEDUM acre var. **minus**, Golden-carpet, Gold Moss. In late spring or early summer, clusters of tiny yellow flowers appear on slim, trailing stems rarely more than 1 inch high with minute, pointed, upright succulent-like leaves. Not showy, but thrives—and can be invasive—on rock walls and in pockets where nothing else grows. Two years are required to reach flowering size. The variety *minus* is less invasive than the species, even in moist, fertile soil. See also list 56, Dry, Hot Conditions.

SEMPERVIVUM tectorum, Common House-leek, Roof Houseleek, Hens-and-chickens, Old-man-and-old-woman. A workhorse made for rock gardens and wonderful in cracks and crevices. Clusters of soft purple-red flowers grow from the center in summer, but the plant is valued most for the evergreen, succulent, tightly clustered rosettes with red-purple pointed tips, 1½ to 3 inches tall and 4 inches wide. The tiny *S. arachnoideum*, Cobweb Houseleek, is suited to growing between high stepping-stones and flagstones and can handle limited foot traffic. For culture, see list 45, Rock Walls and Crevices.

THYMUS, Thyme. The thymes are low, attractive, evergreen herbs with trailing branches and tiny leaves that release a "clean" aromatic scent when crushed. The species recommended are heat- and drought-resistant, and tough enough to thrive in crevices in stone walks and walls and carpet rocky slopes. *T.* × *citriodorus* is about 8 inches high and has lemon thyme-scented leaves; 'Aureus' is gold-variegated. The silver-variegated 'Argenteus' is pretty between big dark stones. For flagstones, use the very small thymes. *T. praecox* subsp. *arcticus*, Mother-of-thyme, to 4 inches high, which stands a lot of abuse, is choice for walkways. 'Albus' is white-flowered, 'Coccineus' is a lovely crimson, and 'Splendens' is red. 'Lanuginosus' is a mat-forming creeper barely ½ inch high that bears a few pale pink flowers in the leaf axils and is perfect between low flagstones. *T. serpyllum* forms an excellent ground-hugging carpet about 2 inches high, and from spring to fall bears small flowerheads in white or pink or dark red, but is hard to find in the U.S. Most plants offered under this name in the U.S. are incorrectly named. 'Minus' is 1 inch high; there are also variegated forms. See also list 74, Herbs with Fragrant Foliage.

VIOLA aetolica. This is a clump-forming, tiny, bright yellow violet that loves a gravel path or terrace. It starts blooming in early May, continues into summer, and self-sows freely. The flowers face south so place plants with this in mind—they are barely visible when seen from the north. A truly first-rate acquisition; plant in groups between stepping-stones. For culture, see list 30, Violet—Pansy.

SOURCE: NICKOLAS NICKOU, M.D., IS A TALENTED GARDENER WHOSE TWO 30-YEAR-OLD ROCK GARDENS HAVE BENEFITED FROM COLLECTING TRIPS TO ICELAND, GREENLAND, THE HIMALAYAS, CHINA, NEW ZEALAND, AUSTRALIA, TURKEY, THE ALPS, THE CANADIAN AND U.S. ROCKIES, SOUTH AFRICA, AND SO ON.

Morning glory, *Ipomoea purpurea*, a hardy annual, reaches 8 to 10 feet in just two months. This is the cultivar 'Heavenly Blue.' (Viette)

47. CLIMBERS

■ **Flowering vines bring to the small garden the elegance, lift, and screening of a tree, and do it in less time and space. Climbing a trellis or guide wires, a vine brings interest to a bare masonry wall and will cover with foliage anything from an architect's mistake to the neighbor's ugly woodpile. Just as willingly, a vine will clamber down to soften a lower-story drywall, for instance, or to disguise leftover tree stumps and foundations. A few, like the Moonflower, are to be planted just for their night beauty and fragrance.**

The vines recommended climb either by means of vining stems that wind around sturdy supports, or tendrils that twine around strings or wires. Those with vining stems need a wooden post, a pipe, or sturdy string or wire. A wire or mesh string is sufficient support for a vine with twining tendrils.

Culture: Provide deeply dug, generous planting holes and well-drained soil rich in humusy materials. Set the plant 6 inches from its support so there will be air space for maturing foliage.

In winter, prune flowering vines that bloom on this year's growth. Prune those that bloom on year-old wood after the flowers fade. Annual vines are cut to the ground, dug, and discarded after the foliage fades in fall.

CLEMATIS (*klem*-at-iss) × **jackmanii**
Jackman Clematis   Zones 4-8
The twining tendrils of this lovely vine cover walls, trellises, posts, fences, and arbors with slender stems, dainty leaves, and large, velvety flowers 4 to 6 inches across in a range of purples, pinks, and whites. The largest are borne singly; smaller-flowered types bloom in panicles of 3. The height of the vines varies from 8 to 20 feet. Recommendations include: 'Alba', about 10 feet tall, white with a blue tinge around each sepal on flowers 4 to 5 inches across; 'Comtesse de Bouchaud', 8 to 12 feet tall, rosy lilac, summer-flowering; 'Ernest Markham', 12 to 16 feet tall, red, flowers in summer and fall; 'Elsa Spath', 8 to 12 feet tall, lavender-blue, flowers in late spring and summer; 'Lady Betty Balfour', 12 to 20 feet tall, purple, flowers in summer and fall; 'Lord Neville', 8 to 12 feet tall, purple, summer-flowering. The Sweet Clematis, *C. maximowicziana* syn. *paniculata*, a rapid-screening, dainty-leaved vine that covers itself with a fuzz of little whitish flowers, is planted for its fall fragrance.

Culture: Set out container-grown plants in early spring. Clematis thrives in fertile, well-drained alkaline soil and

TOP, LEFT Quick-growing *Nasturtium majus*, a climbing or trailing annual species, blooms all summer. (Still)

LEFT The flowers of *Ipomoea alba*, the fragrant, lovely moonflower, are open evening till noon—nice with morning glories. (Harper)

ABOVE Dainty Sweet Clematis, *Clematis maximowicziana*, is planted for its fall fragrance. (Still)

full sun or partial shade. The roots must be kept cool and moist with cover plants or mulch if grown in full sun. Adding humus to the soil before planting and an organic mulch after planting provides a cool root zone. The hybrids recommended above flower on the current season's wood, so in early spring cut last year's woody shoots back to 2 to 4 feet.

IPOMOEA (eye-poh-*mee*-uh)
Morning-glory

The species recommended below are fast-growing vines that climb by means of twining stems, providing quick cover for screens, trellises, or the urban chain-link fence. The flowers are trumpet-shaped and bloom all summer, opening in the morning and closing in the afternoon, except for the beautiful night-blooming Moonflower. Cloudy days promote extended bloom during the afternoon.

Culture: Soak seeds overnight in warm water before planting for best germination. Sow the seeds where the plants are to bloom, or start them indoors 4 to 6 weeks before the weather warms. Plant out in full sun in well-drained, rather dry soil.

I. alba Moonflower   Zones 9-11

Formerly classified as *Calonyction aculeatum,* this robust, tender perennial with 8-inch leaves is cultivated for its large, beautiful, very fragrant white flowers, which grow up to 6 inches across on longish robust stems. They open toward evening and remain open until about noon the following day. In most of the country it is grown as an annual and can reach 10 to 20 feet in a single season. Prefers moderately fertile soil. Very beautiful and the foliage is handsome.

I. purpurea Morning-glory   Annual

Fast-growing, hardy annual that reaches 8 to 10 feet in just two months after sowing. The color range includes blue, pink, rose, carmine, or white, often with white markings. Many improved morning-glories are available. Morning-glory grows wild in many areas and should not be planted where it is known to be invasive. 'Heavenly Blue' has sky blue flowers 4 to 5 inches across, with a white throat. 'Scarlet Star', a 36-inch climber, has 3½-inch flowers of scarlet-red marked with a central white star and white edging. High fertility and moist soil will produce abundant foliage but few flowers.

LATHYRUS (*lath*-ihr-us)
Vetchling, Wild Pea

The old-fashioned Sweet Pea, *L. odoratus,* a fresh, delicately scented little flower, blooms on a long, slender stem borne on a leafy vine that grows 4 to 6 feet in a season, like its cousin the edible pea. It can bloom all summer if given shade for the hottest part of the day. In the South, look for heat-resistant sweet peas. May self-sow. Mixed colors make delightful bouquets. The flowers appear in early to mid-spring, masses of blooms from purple to pale lavender, ruby red, pale pink, and white, and there are bicolors.

The 2 species recommended below are fast-growing vines that bear big flowers resembling those of peas, but in bright colors and pastels. They are most effective planted in mixed colors including pink, red, purple, white, and blue. Long, slender stems make the flowers good for cutting.

Culture: They climb by tendrils and need to be supported, either with a set of training strings or wires, or planted to clamber at will over rocks and walls. They do best during cool weather, and in hot climates afternoon shade extends the flowering period. Start seeds indoors in late winter and transplant outdoors as soon as the ground can be worked. Or, as soon as the ground can be worked, sow seeds where the flowers are to bloom in full sun in well-drained, fertile soil. Before sowing the seeds, soak them in warm water overnight or lightly file the seed coats to facilitate germination.

L. latifolius Perennial Pea, Everlasting Pea
Zones 4-8

A vigorous perennial that flowers mid- to late summer and easily grows 10 feet a year. Garden centers sell these as container plants.

L. odoratus Sweet Pea   Annual

This is the fragrant or "sweet" pea, an annual that grows 4 to 6 feet in a season and can bloom all summer if given shade for the hottest part of the day. It requires consistently moist soil. Cultivars include nonclimbing dwarfs suitable for small gardens and containers. In the South, look for heat-resistant sweet peas. May self-sow.

THUNBERGIA (thun-*berj*-ee-uh) alata
Black-eyed Susan Vine, Clock Vine   Annual

This flowering vine serves well as a screen when encouraged to climb on a trellis or fence. It also is useful as a trailing plant for window boxes, urns, and hanging baskets. A dense grower, it literally covers its supports with foliage and flowers to a height of about 5 feet. In southern regions, it may be perennial but it does not perform particularly well in excessive heat. The best flower displays are usually in late summer or early fall, when the weather cools.

Culture: Sow seeds in partial shade in a moist, well-drained, fertile soil, or start them indoors 6 to 8 weeks before the weather warms enough for transplanting. Climbs by means of vining stems.

TROPAEOLUM (trop-*pee*-ol-um) majus
Garden Nasturtium, Tall Nasturtium,
Indian Cress   Annual

This is a fast-climbing or trailing vine with stems 6 to 8 feet long. Like the common bush nasturtium, it blooms all summer in a range of orangy reds and yellows. Both flowers and foliage are edible—pretty, peppery garnishes for salads and sandwiches. 'Fordhook' is recommended, a vigorous plant with single flowers that mix yellow and orange.

Culture: As soon as the weather warms, sow seeds in full sun where the plants are to bloom. In well-drained, inhospitable soils, including gravelly banks, the plants flower lavishly. High fertility produces abundant foliage and few flowers. Attaches itself by twisting leaf stems around slender supports such as string or mesh.

SOURCE: DR. STEVEN STILL IS A PROFESSOR OF HORTICULTURE AT OHIO STATE UNIVERSITY AND THE AUTHOR OF THE *MANUAL OF HERBACEOUS ORNAMENTAL PLANTS.*

48. WILDFLOWERS TO NATURALIZE

■ A wildflower garden can be sited almost anywhere. Evocative plants—not site, not size—express the theme. A fringe tree with bleeding-hearts and a clump of ferns at its feet fits easily into a pocket of Manhattan or San Francisco, and a small suburban hillside lot can accommodate all the flowers recommended here, from Prairie Gay-feather to Butterfly Weed and the butterflies that flit around them.

Fresh beauty is the great gift of a wildflower garden—a landscape unexpectedly rural, where the unusual blooms. And there are dividends, too. Low maintenance is one. Wildflower gardens make even the weeds look good. Once established in conditions similar to those of their native habitats, wildflowers resist adversity and bring a measure of healthy variety to the environment. They have deep roots and thrive without a lot of watering. Most are willing to spread.

The plants recommended here—some for sun, some for shade—are interesting as well as easy to grow, closely associated with wild gardens but nonetheless tamed. Most are available from regular nurseries, but make sure your source offers propagated plants, not plants collected in the wild. And don't take your own plants from the wild—many are protected by conservation laws.

Culture: If the conditions are less than ideal for the plants you choose, modify the soil as described in Culture for each plant. Add leaf mold or peat moss to improve its capacity to hold moisture and lower the pH—most of the flowers here flourish in somewhat acid conditions. As soon as the soil is workable, set out container plants. Generally, April and early May are best for transplanting wild plants; in cool regions, wait until after May 24. Set the crown a bit above soil level, firm the plant, and water liberally.

Some wildflowers grow easily from seed, usually fresh seed sown as soon as it has ripened on the plants in late summer or early fall. Wildflowers benefit from a sprinkling of fertilizer during the growing season; for most, an acid fertilizer is best.

Companion Plants: A lot of these wildflowers bloom early and leave good foliage to green the spaces they occupy, so follow-on plants are not needed. Ferns are essential to wild gardens. Other candidates are described on lists 33, Annuals That Self-sow; 64, The Meadow Garden; and 65, The Woodland Garden.

SUN OR PART SUN

These natives thrive in a sunny area if they are given sufficient moisture, and will naturalize. Most will also do well in very light shade, such as found under tall trees.

ASCLEPIAS tuberosa, Butterfly Weed, Pleurisy Root, Tuberroot, Indian Paintbrush, Chigger Flower. Sunny orange flowerheads that attract butterflies. This is a 24- to 36-inch perennial look-alike for milkweed with long-lasting, fragrant, showy flowers in summer. Interesting seedpods follow. There are yellow hybrids and bicolors. Good for bouquets, especially if the stem is seared immediately after cutting and then put into water. For culture, see list 15, Summer Perennials for Sun.

Tamed Queen-Anne's-lace, *Daucus carota*, bee balm, *Monarda*, and black-eyed Susans, *Rudbeckia*, flourish with little care in Ryan Gainey's Atlanta cottage garden. (Woodham)

ASTER **novae-angliae,** New England Aster. In a meadow, these shrubby plants grow into great patches 4 to 6 feet tall. Covered in late summer and early fall with long-lasting pink and purple-pink daisies. Sprays of the flowers are excellent fillers for flower arrangements, especially with pink dahlias. Survives early frosts. Colorful asters have been developed—white, rose, ruby red, and salmon. 'Harrington's Pink' is one of the best. For culture, see list 20, *Aster.*

BAPTISIA **australis,** Blue False Indigo, Plains False Indigo, Wild Blue Indigo. Bears lovely spikes of indigo-blue flowers in early summer, followed by prominent dark seedpods that remain for winter. The plants are vigorous, 3 to 4 feet tall and have attractive gray-green leaves. A good cut flower. See list 13, Spring Perennials for Sun.

CAMPANULA **rotundifolia,** Bluebell, Harebell. Graceful, nodding blue flowers in late spring and summer, 6 to 18 inches tall. Dainty and lovely in a woodland setting. Thrives in well-drained moist soil with a pH between 5.5 and 6.5. It self-sows generously in the Pacific Northwest. Ideal for perennializing in sun or light shade. See list 22, *Campanula.*

CHELONE (kee-*loh*-nee) **lyonii**
Pink Turtlehead   Zones 4-9
In September and October, rigid spikes to 24 inches tall bear lilac-pink flowers shaped like a turtle's head, or a snapdragon. The dark green, basal foliage extends up the stems, setting off the flowers very well. Good for cutting. A popular garden species, *C. glabra,* is discussed on list 16, Summer Perennials for Shade.

Culture: This hardy perennial grows wild in moist southern woodlands and marshes where there is dappled sun, and it tolerates some direct sun in cooler regions. Plant root divisions in spring in moist, humusy soil with a pH between 4.0 and 6.0.

DODECATHEON (doh-dek-*kayth*-ee-on) **meadia**
Shooting-star   Zones 5-9
A showy wildflower whose sinuous stems are topped by a half dozen or so 1-inch white, lavender, or dark rose pink flowers like miniature cyclamens with tightly folded petals. Flowers appear in late spring above 6- to 12- or 18-inch plants with basal tufts of long green leaves that disappear in summer. Nice in a rock garden.

Culture: Finicky, but successful when planted in well-drained, humusy soil, pH 5.0 to 7.0, in full sun or partial shade. Set out root divisions in spring, or sow seed where the plants are to grow in fall—they'll germinate in spring. Takes 3 years to bloom.

GILLENIA (gil-*leen*-ee-uh) **trifoliata**
Indian-physic, Bowman's-root   Zones 4-8
In late spring or early summer, loose panicles of delicate starry 1- to 1½-inch pinkish or white flowers cover branching plants to 36 inches tall with wiry, reddish stems and sharply serrated leaves. Charming massed in a woodland garden.

Culture: Set out root divisions or in fall sow seeds in the wild garden to germinate in spring—requires partial sun or light shade and well-drained, humusy, moist soil with pH 5.0 to 6.0.

LIATRIS (lye-ay- triss) **pycnostachya**
Prairie Gay-feather   Zones 3-10
Showy and useful violet-lavender spikes that open from the top down in late summer and early fall, on plants 3 to 6 feet tall with dense grassy basal foliage. Valuable at the back of the border and very hardy. Good cut flower and dries well. *L. spicata,* the more familiar Spike Gay-feather, is discussed on list 15, Summer Perennials for Sun.

Culture: Tolerates heat and drought, but thrives in full sun in well-drained, fairly moist soil with a pH of 6.0 to 7.0. Plant root divisions in early spring.

LEFT Starry panicles of *Gillenia trifoliata*, Indian-physic, Bowman's-root. (Viette)
BOTTOM, LEFT One of the most beautiful wildflowers, *Sanguinaria canadensis*, Bloodroot, Red Puccoon. (New England Wild Flower Society–Long)
BOTTOM, RIGHT *Dodecatheon meadia*, Shooting-star, bears showy cyclamenlike flowers—nice in a rock garden. (Viette)

LOBELIA (loh-*beel*-ee-uh) **cardinalis**
Cardinal Flower, Indian Pink　　　　Zones 2-8
Lovely slender wildflower named for spikes of blossoms red as a cardinal's feathers. Blooms on stems 24 to 30 inches tall in late summer and early fall. The plant thrives when perennialized by a small rocky stream, but is also successful in a wildflower border. The genus is discussed on list 16, Summer Perennials for Shade.

Culture: Sow seeds outdoors in fall. Or put cleaned seeds into a sealed jar and chill in the refrigerator for 2 months and sow outdoors any time. Or, in early spring set out root divisions. With its feet in moist, humusy soil, pH 4.0 to 6.0, it withstands direct sun, but thrives in light shade.

MONARDA **didyma**, Bee Balm, Oswego Tea. Whorls of shaggy scarlet petals surrounded by red-tinted bracts bloom through summer on stiff stems above neat plants 3 to 4 feet tall with pointed, bright green leaves. Attractive to hummingbirds, butterflies, and bees. Among plants ranging through shades of cerise to red, white, and violet, 'Croftway Pink' is notable. For culture see list 75, Herbs with Showy Flowers.

OENOTHERA (ee-noh-*theer*-uh) **fruticosa**
Sundrops　　　　　　　　　　　Zones 3-9
Delightful yellow flowers like delicate little cups with a silky sheen open during the day at the top of very slender, slightly drooping stems 12 to 24 inches high. The foliage is refined—pointed and often flecked or tinged with bright red. The plant makes a charming tangle sprinkled over with blossoms for many weeks in summer.

Culture: Plant root divisions in spring in full sun in sandy or very well-drained soil pH 5.0 to 6.0. Very drought-resistant, it spreads and perennializes rapidly.

PENSTEMON (pen-*steem*-on) **digitalis**
Smooth White Beard-tongue　　　　Zones 3-9
Also called white penstemon, this is a stately, durable wildflower with 36-inch stems bearing panicles of open bells, white with a touch of purple at the throat, late spring to midsummer. With its lush basal foliage and purple flower stems, it's an attractive addition all season long.

Culture: Sow seed in fall or early spring, or plant root divisions in spring. Set in sun or light shade, in moist, humusy soil with a pH range of 5.5 to 6.5.

RUDBECKIA **fulgida** var. **sullivantii** 'Goldsturm', Coneflower. Finest of the golden yellow black-eyed Susan flowers, this rudbeckia blooms freely through midsummer into fall on compact, bushy plants 18 to 30 inches high. The ray florets are deep yellow and the cone-shaped centers are bronze-black. Self-sows aggressively and is a good perennializer in wild sites. Leave the flowerheads to ripen for the birds, for winter interest, and to reseed. Tolerates light shade. See also list 15, Summer Perennials for Sun.

SHADE AND WOODLANDS
....
These are plants for naturalizing in a woodland where little or no maintenance will need to be given. Many perform well as ground covers and will seed themselves.

ANEMONELLA (an-em-on-*nell*-uh)
thalictroides
Rue Anemone　　　　　　　　　Zones 4-8
In early to late spring, this delicate little perennial about 6 inches tall bears white blossoms 1 inch across in a loose terminal cluster above low-growing, ferny leaves. There are pinks and some double-flowered forms. Excellent in shady corners of a rock garden.

Culture: Plant root divisions in spring, or sow fresh seed in summer, in well-drained, moist, humusy soil with a pH between 6.0 and 7.0.

ASARUM (*ass*-uh-rum) **canadense**
Wild Ginger　　　　　　　　　Zones 2-9
Handsome heart-shaped leaves about 5 inches across make this a delightful deciduous foliage plant and ground cover for a wild garden in shade. The 1-inch, purplish brown flowers appear in spring close to the ground. The aromatic rhizomatous root is used as a substitute for ginger. This species is easy to grow and very hardy. Several other species are evergreen in mild winters in Zones 4 to 7, including *A. europaeum*, *A. shuttleworthii*, which is wonderfully mottled, and, in the West, *A. caudatum* and the silver-veined *A. hartwegii*.

Culture: Plant root divisions in early spring in shade in moist, rich, humusy soil with a pH of 5.0 to 6.5. Self-sows.

DICENTRA. The bleeding-hearts are named for the shape of the pink blossoms, hardy old-fashioned favorites for spring and early summer that bloom in shade. The foliage is deeply cut and lacy, and the pretty pink, white, or red heart-shaped flowers dangle from gracefully arching stems. Height is 9 to 24 inches. Mass planting among ferns, hostas, and Solomon's-seal is very effective, especially for those whose foliage dies to the ground in summer. Delightful with wildflowers and in rock gardens. Two species are recommended for naturalizing in shade: *D. cucullaria*, Dutchman's-breeches, Zones 3 to 9, which bears racemes of small, white, nodding hearts tipped with yellow on 6- to 8- or 10-inch plants whose foliage dies down in summer; and *D. eximia*, Turkey Corn, Staggerweed, Wild Bleeding-heart, Zones 2/3 to 9, a plumed, or fringed, bleeding-heart, with rosy pink flowers on stems 12 to 18 inches long and ferny blue-green foliage. It blooms heavily in mid-spring to early summer and tends to retain its foliage. With extra moisture, it may continue to flower intermittently until midsummer. For culture, see list 14, Spring Perennials for Shade.

GERANIUM **maculatum**, Wild Geranium, Wild Cranesbill, Spotted Cranesbill, Alumroot. In spring and early summer in Zones 5 to 8 this native "true" geranium 18 to 24 inches tall produces an abundance of clusters of showy, saucerlike, pale to deep rosy purple flowers on wandlike stems above loose mounds of deeply divided foliage. The common name of cranesbill refers to the beaklike fruit which follows. The plant is mat- or clump-forming, about 12 inches tall, and is excellent in groups. Dormant in summer. Thrives in evenly moist, well-drained, humusy soil with pH 4.0 to 5.0. Don't confuse this with *Pelargonium*, whose common name is geranium. For culture see list 13, Spring Perennials for Sun.

Double pink Rue Anemone, *Anemonella thalictroides* variety *rosea*. (New England Wild Flower Society)

IRIS **cristata**, Crested Iris. Very showy creeping dwarf that is most appealing naturalized on rocky wooded slopes, in rock gardens and light woodlands. Only 3 to 4 inches high, the lavender-blue, 4-inch wide-spreading flowers have narrow falls with a central white or yellow ridge. The foliage is shiny and arching. In the South it blooms in late April to late May; in the North, early May to early June in light shade. Plants may die back in summer. Excellent for edgings, and good ground cover for partial shade. See list 25, *Iris*.

MERTENSIA (mer-*ten*-see-uh) **virginica**
Virginia Bluebells, Virginia Cowslip, Roanoke-bluebells　　　　　　　　　　Zones 3-9
Early spring flower to 24 inches tall with nodding sprays of pink buds that open to bell-shaped violet-blue blossoms. Fresh, pale green foliage disappears during summer. Nice with *Aquilegia* and *Dicentra*.

Culture: Plant root divisions in early spring or fresh seeds in summer, in light shade in moist, well-drained soil with a pH of 5.0 to 6.0.

PHLOX. In spring, the little creeping phloxes spill mats of lavender-blue, purple, pink, or white florets over sunny or shady slopes, rock gardens, or masonry walls. Several thrive in wild gardens and woodlands in Zones 3 to 8/9. *P. divaricata*, Wild Sweet William, Blue Phlox, is one of the best. It forms leafy mats that bear fragrant, soft lavender-blue flowers 9 to 15 inches tall, April to June. This is a hardy perennial that spreads by creeping rootstock but must have an open, airy site as it is subject to mildew. *P. ovata*, Mountain Phlox, can stand more direct sun and flowers later. It bears lavender flowers 12 inches tall. *P. stolonifera*, Creeping Phlox, a mat-forming ground cover 5 to 12 inches tall, is very hardy in semishade or shade. Some varieties are evergreen in mild winters. The flowers are purple or violet, borne in dense clusters in mid- to late spring. May bloom again intermittently. See list 27, *Phlox*.

SANGUINARIA (san-gwi-*nay*-ree-uh)
canadensis
Bloodroot, Red Puccoon   Zones 5-8
A very early spring favorite with flowering stems 8 inches tall that cover themselves with a fluff of white, starry flowers. The foliage is rich, dark green. Double forms are available.

   Culture: Plant root divisions in early spring in bright shade or shade in light, well-drained, humusy soil in the pH range between pH 5.0 and 6.0. Needs sustained moisture.

SMILACINA (smye-las-*sye*-uh) **racemosa**
False Spikenard, Solomon's-zigzag, Treacleberry
                                Zones 3-9
The feathery, fragrant flower plumes 3 to 5 inches long bloom in spring on clumps of arching, leafy stems. They are followed in summer by showy clusters of pink-red berries. Lovely in mass plantings.

   Culture: Plant root divisions in early spring in shade in moist, humusy soil with a pH between 4.0 and 6.0.

STYLOPHORUM (stye-*loff*-or-um)
diphyllum
Celandine Poppy   Zones 6-8
This charming 12- to 19-inch spring wildflower has graceful clusters of poppy-like, showy yellow flowers 2 inches across that develop into loosely hanging seedpods. The light green leaves are deeply lobed and remain well into fall if grown in evenly moist conditions. The yellow sap that comes from the stems and leaves was used as dye by North American Indians. Good ground cover.

   Culture: Set out container plants or root divisions in early spring or sow fresh seed in summer in partial sun or shade in rich, moist, well-drained soil with a pH between 5.0 and 6.0. It spreads steadily and also self-sows.

TIARELLA (tye-uh-*rell*- uh) **cordifolia**
Foamflower   Zones 3-9
Small mounds of crinkled leaves, evergreen in milder areas, are topped in spring by flowering stems that cover themselves with fluffy little white flowers. An excellent woodland ground cover 10 inches high.

   Culture: Plant root divisions in early spring in shade in moist, humusy soil with a pH between 5.0 and 6.0.

VIOLA   **labradorica**, Labrador Violet. Low-growing violet with dark purple leaves and mauve flowers suffused with dark purple. Blooms in early spring and occasionally in summer, and spreads rapidly on creeping rhizomes. Does well even in southern states when given shade, moisture, and soil with a pH between 5.0 and 6.5. Charming with ferns, yellow grasses, and white snowdrops. See list 29, Violet—Pansy.

SOURCE: WILLIAM BRUMBACK, OF THE GARDEN IN THE WOODS, FRA-
MINGHAM, MASSACHUSETTS, A BOTANICAL GARDEN OWNED BY THE NEW
ENGLAND WILD FLOWER SOCIETY.

Ornamental cabbages and grasses in their fall gold brighten garden designer Lynden Miller's New England yard. (Miller)

49. *INTERESTING IN WINTER*

■ **A garden that looks nice in May is easy to achieve—but will it still be appealing when the leaves fall?**

   Even in the gray seasons, the view from the window should draw the eye and lift the spirit. Choose plants that are transformed by the elements of winter into something wonderful—plumy ornamental grasses that dance with the cold wind, or woolly betonies that cover their beds with fallen leaves. Semievergreen and evergreen edgers and ground covers rimmed with ice will catch the sun and sparkle. Hummocks of *Ajuga* 'Burgundy Glow', dark-needled candytuft, grassy liriope, and the daring Christmas and Lenten roses shake off snow flurries to send out color signals.

   Even old flower stalks denuded by autumn have gifts to give. Seed-bearers feed the birds, sow next year's flowers, and color their architectural branches rust, or rich brown, or—in the rain—sooty black. *Sedum* 'Autumn Joy', Siberian iris in its rusty winter brown, the coreopsis bramble, the dry, whispering leaves of *Allium tuberosum*, all give the garden form and quiet beauty while the earth rests.

   Then, if you have planned well, in late winter the first little bulbs come up, all white, blue, purple, and yellow, to tell us spring is coming!

   Here are a few of many interesting forms that emerge as the storm of falling leaves gives way to wintry blue skies and creaking cold.

   Companion Plants: Ornamental grasses, colorful shrubs such as weeping hemlock and other evergreens, the red-stemmed *Cornus alba*, brown oak-leaved *Hydrangea quercifolia*, junipers, bright-berried cotoneasters, and the barberries 'Rosy Glo' and 'Crimson Pygmy'; native briar roses, and wild honeysuckle. The small, early-flowering bulbs are ideal follow-on plants; see list 1, Early Spring, Specialty Bulbs.

TOP, LEFT Silvery Russian Sage, *Perovskia atriplicifolia*, with Siberian iris foliage, catmint, *Nepeta*, and maroon barberry. (Miller)

TOP, RIGHT *Miscanthus*, a superb ornamental grass, transformed by snow and ice. (Viette)

BOTTOM *Helictotrichon*, with 'Crimson Pygmy' barberry, russet *Sedum* 'Autumn Joy' and white *Helchryssum*. (Miller)

AJUGA reptans 'Burgundy Glow', Carpet Bugle. A fast-growing, prostrate semievergreen ground cover that has low, upright leafy stems to 8 inches high with variegated foliage—white, pink, rose, and green. In spring, stubby blue flowerheads top the foliage. Spreads very quickly by underground runners and should be confined to its own territory. Keep it away from the lawn. See list 44, Flowering Ground Covers.

ALLIUM tuberosum, Chinese Chives, Garlic Chives, Oriental Garlic. Handsome white seedheads in winter. This is an ornamental onion with grassy leaves. In late summer, it bears spreading clusters of fragrant white flowers with a green midriff on 18-inch stems. Excellent in dried arrangements. See list 72, To Dry for Winter Bouquets. Ornamental onions are described on List 3, Spring, Large-flowered Bulbs.

ANEMONE × hybrida or A. hupehensis var. japonica. The lean, branching stems are covered in winter with seedheads similar to cotton balls. The tall fall anemones have ferny foliage, and bloom in summer and autumn for several weeks, seemingly impervious even to whipping winds, bearing deep rose, pink, white, or purple flowers 2 to 3 inches in diameter. The plants form dense clumps of attractive leaves that are effective throughout the growing season. See list 17, Summer-into-fall Perennials.

ASTILBE, Spiraea, Perennial Spiraea. The flower stalks remain a rich brown in winter, handsome in the snow. The plants are 6 inches to 6 feet tall and produce flowerheads in late spring or summer that stand well above deeply cut green or bronzed foliage. The colors are shades from palest pink and coral, to bright red and cream white. Many lovely cultivated varieties are described on list 21, *Astilbe*.

BAPTISIA australis, Blue False Indigo, Plains False Indigo, Wild Blue Indigo. In winter, the plant has gunmetal gray or black seedpods and leaves. This is a tall, vigorous plant that produces masses of pretty gray-green foliage in spring. In early summer there are spikes of pea-like, indigo-blue flowers used in arrangements. Mature height is 3 to 4 feet. See list 13, Spring Perennials for Sun.

BOLTONIA asteroides. In winter, the stalks and leaves are a rich brown. This is a sturdy, easy-to-grow daisylike Midwest native with strong upright stems, small gray-green leaves and in summer masses of small 1- to 1½-inch asterlike flowers that are white, violet, pink, or purple. It reaches 3 to 5 feet and is airy and colorful at the back of the border. A good cutting flower. 'Snowbank' is a pretty, full white that reaches 4 feet high. For culture, see list 17, Summer-into-fall Perennials.

COREOPSIS verticillata. 'Moonbeam' retains its stems in winter, providing an interesting, dark, feathery texture in the garden. One of the most popular perennials and one of the very best for the front of the border. Its period of flowering is longer than most—June to frost if cut back in midsummer. The plants are about 18 inches tall and cover themselves with pale yellow blossoms on many slender stems clothed with delicate threadlike leaves. The subtle color combines perfectly with anything that grows behind it. See list 15, Summer Perennials for Sun.

HELLEBORUS, Hellebore. Evergreen plants with distinctive, deeply divided foliage that remains interesting in winter. In the warm South, the nodding flowers bloom in late winter in light shade and damp, humusy woodland soil. Undisturbed, handsome colonies form and self-sow. *H. foetidus*, 18 to 24 inches, bears panicles of drooping, bell-like pale green flowers edged with red. *H. lividus* subsp. *corsicus* is another hellebore grown in the South, a shrubby plant with gray-green, holly-like foliage and clusters of pale, lichen green flowers suffused beneath with purple. From December through February, *H. niger*, Christmas Rose, 12 to 18 inches tall, bears beautiful, large white flowers that have yellow stamens. It will bloom in the snow during the lengthening days of early spring. *H. orientalis*, Lenten Rose, 15 to 18 inches tall, is one of the finest low-growing, very early flowers. Its long-lasting, nodding blooms are 3 to 4 inches wide, in green, creamy white, pink, or purple. The leathery, nearly evergreen foliage is especially valuable in winter. See list 14, Spring Perennials for Shade.

HELICTOTRICHON sempervirens, Blue Oat Grass, a pretty little plant that, unlike other grasses, should never be cut down. It has gray-blue, semievergreen leaves that grow in 24-inch puffs. In early summer, delicate, golden, oatlike flowers sway high above the foliage and remain through winter. Many other ornamental grasses are cold weather assets and should be cut only in late winter or early spring. See list 53, Ornamental Grasses.

HOSTA, Plantain Lily, Daylily. The seedheads remain on the flowering stems, an interesting sight in winter. These are superb foliage plants for shade that bear spires of often fragrant lavender to white bells in summer and fall. The clumps of bold, handsome leaves are 12 to 30 inches tall with considerable spread—they're magnificent edgers and ground covers. Hosta leaves begin to unfurl just as fading bulb foliage needs screening, and the long-lasting flowers arrive when other summer flowers are going. *H. tardiflora* is the last perennial to bloom in autumn. See list 54, *Hosta*.

IBERIS sempervirens, Edging Candytuft. Remains dark green most winters. This is a low-growing, spreading, clump-forming, narrow-leaved plant with attractive foliage on semiwoody stems, 6 to 12 inches high with a 24-inch spread. In early to mid-spring it is blanketed with dense heads of white flowers. See list 43, Flowers for Edging.

IRIS siberica, Siberian Iris. In winter, the tall, flowering stems have attractive seedpods and the foliage turns rusty brown. In late spring and early summer, magnificent blossoms cluster in 2's and 3's on stalks 24 to 40 inches tall backed by the slender, waving leaves. The standards are small and don't quite meet, but the large falls are exquisite. Excellent cutting flowers. Colors are blue-purple, lavender, maroon, and white, along with pinkish and yellowish tones. See list 25, Iris.

LIRIOPE, Lilyturf, is evergreen until late winter, when it should be cut back right to the ground. Graceful and remarkably tough and resistant plants grown primarily for the grasslike foliage which is ¼ to ¾ inch wide and 8 to 12 or 18 inches high. In summer or early fall, thin spikes covered with grainlike lavender, blue, or white flowers rise well above the grassy tufts. Shiny black fruits develop in late fall and persist into winter. Some have handsomely variegated foliage. See list 44, Flowering Ground Covers.

MISCANTHUS sinensis can soar to 8 feet and in winter is all fine foliage and flowery tassels, lovely with snow at its feet. It has broad, grassy, gracefully arching leaves and in midsummer sends flower plumes high above the foliage. For flowering borders choose smaller plants such as 'Yaku Jima', 24 to 30 inches in height. See list 53, Ornamental Grasses.

PEROVSKIA atriplicifolia, Russian Sage. It is like a huge white bird's nest all winter. A good plant to bring that coveted color, blue, to the border for the longest period—July, August, and most of September. Tall, beautiful, with silvery stems and grayish foliage down below, it is topped by airy spikes of tiny florets that are a subtle powder blue. Foliage releases a lovely scent of sage when crushed. See list 57, Seashore and Sandy Soils.

SALVIA officinalis retains its purple-gray foliage all winter. This is the best-known culinary sage, an erect subshrub up to 24 inches tall with violet, blue, or white flower spikes in summer, and downy, sharply aromatic foliage. It should not be banished to the herb garden, for it is handsome in the perennial garden and a good edger and ground cover. Particularly pretty is the little *S. o.* 'Tricolor', 6 to 10 inches high, which features leaves that are variegated red, pink, gray, cream, and purple. The gray-green leaves of the often-seen 'Icterina' are variegated with gold. These are less hardy than the species. In California a handsome gray plant, *S. clevelandii*, is often used as a substitute for *S. officinalis* in cooking. See list 41, Salvia.

SEDUM, especially 'Autumn Joy', seedheads are good all winter. One of the most valuable flowers for fall. The lovely spring show of gray-green foliage up to 18 to 24 inches tall is followed by fresh apple green flowerheads in early summer, slowly changes to rich pink on through rose to salmon-bronze, and finally, with the cold, to rosy russet. See list 56, Dry, Hot Conditions.

STACHYS byzantina (syn. *lanata*), Woolly Betony, Lamb's-ears. The big, gray, semievergreen leaves from 12 to 15 inches long, are almost luminous in moonlight, and so woolly they invite stroking; a wonderful contrast in color, an outstanding texture, and lovely in tussie-mussies and wreaths. From midsummer until frost they are topped by small, usually violet or white flowers, which some gardeners prefer to remove to keep the focus on the leaves. The nonflowering 8-inch-high 'Silver Carpet' spreads rapidly and is choice. See list 50. Foliage for Form and Texture.

Source: A distinguished artist and garden designer, Lynden B. Miller holds the National Landscape Design Award and is widely recognized for the design and installation of Manhattan's Central Park Zoo. She serves as the director of the Central Park Conservatory Garden and is garden designer for the New York Botanical Garden. Mrs. Miller is also a popular writer and lecturer on garden design.

50. FOLIAGE FOR FORM AND TEXTURE

■ Flowers paint the colors in a garden composition, but leaves and stalks provide the texture and structure that hold the picture together. Flower colors rise and fall, but the plant's leafy texture and branches remain constant, an architecture that comforts the eye in all seasons. This is especially true in warm regions where deep snow cannot be counted on for winter cover-up.

When choosing flowers, try to visualize their foliage in spring, summer, fall, and winter. Imagine leaf buds unfurling, clothing the stems, stems branching and rebranching, shooting out flower buds. Will the leaves attract your curiosity in all seasons, draw your eye with ever-changing patterns? Will the mature architecture of the plants add character and grace to the fall and winter garden? Will there be seedheads?

Using the same leaf and plant shapes again and again—even if their blossoms are different—makes a boring garden. Ten or fifteen plants all with the same one-half inch, somewhat oval leaf, sets you to wondering why the garden has no impact. A flowering border needs big, bold leaves on structurally strong plants to contrast with the small ones. Combine leaves of various textures: very rough, very smooth, some shiny, some spiky. Put together forms that are round, skinny, airy, sturdy, assymetrical, and symmetrical; constrast sword-shaped leaves with the dancing lines and wonderful fountain effects of ornamental grasses.

With the right combination of foliage keeping the garden interesting in every season, the flowers will be a bonus.

On this list with the classical foliage plants are some challenging strangers, marvels of architecture that bring excitement especially to late summer and fall, such as the Scotch Thistle, *Onopordum acanthium*, verbascum, angelica, and macleaya.

Many more small plants useful for foliage effects appear on list 44, Flowering Ground Covers. See also list 51, Foliage for Color.

Companion Plants: Good companions include Foxgloves, Hollyhocks, *Alcea rosea; Rheum palmatum*, a rhubarb purely for ornament, or the edible one, *R. rhabarbarum*; and little bright red peppers, vining tomatoes, asparagus gone to fern, and ferns.

AMARANTHUS (am-ar-*ranth*-us) Amaranth
Two annual species are used in large, dramatic compositions for their amazing texture and colors. They are coarse, weedy annuals, big and fast-growing, suited to the border or a big container.

Culture: Sow seeds outdoors in late spring where they are to grow, in full sun and well-drained, fertile soil with plenty of humus. Fertilize often and maintain moisture.

A. caudatus Love-lies-bleeding, Tassel Flower
Unique texture and form. A dense, bushy annual 3 to 5 feet tall that cascades clusters of slim, tassel-like, crimson or green flower tails, 18 inches long or more, toward the ground against a backdrop of big, oval, pale green leaves. The flower tails are excellent for drying. In 'Green Thumb', the spikes are green and upright. 'Viridis' is the form with long, drooping, green spikes.

A. tricolor Joseph's-coat
This is probably the most dramatic foliage plant for texture and color. Growing to 4 feet tall, the big, pointed green leaves are wildly splashed with yellow and scarlet patches. 'Molten Fire' is deep crimson splashed bright red and bronze—amazing by summer's end.

ANGELICA   archangelica. A stout architectural herb 4 to 6 feet tall with dense, fist-sized, green-white flowers. The large green leaves are coarse and thin and have cut-edged leaflets. All parts of the plant are aromatic—the flavor is like anise. Nice backdrop for lavender, bee balm, or iris. See list 75, Herbs with Showy Flowers.

ARTEMISIA, Sagebrush, Wormwood. Important perennials for foliage color and texture that appear on several lists in this book. Some species are good ground covers, some are strongly scented herbs, some are tall plants good for the back of the border. *A. lactiflora*, White Mugwort, is a tall, textural plant 4 to 5 feet high that bears magnificent, creamy white, plumy flowers from summer into fall. The dark green leaves are paler underneath. Evergreen in milder regions. *A. ludoviciana*, Western Mugwort, Cudwort, White Sage, is 24 to 36 inches tall, airy, with delicately divided gray leaves that are woolly white underneath on white, branching stems. In late summer there are panicles of gray florets. A beautiful plant of the variety *albula* is 'Silver King', a fragrant, frosty compact that has a hint of red in autumn. See list 73, Herbs with Colorful Foliage.

ARUNCUS   dioicus, Goatsbeard. Zones 3 to 6. Outstanding, big, clump-forming perennial 4 to 6 feet tall and almost as wide with handsome light green leaves 4 to 16 inches long. In early summer, it bears tall, feathery, light-catching, off-white panicles of florets. The male plumes are more upright and showier than female plumes. They occur on different plants, so to choose correctly buy container-grown plants already blooming. Used as a background plant and for foliage accents in big flowering borders. For smaller gardens, 'Keniffi' is less showy but a better choice; it grows to 36 inches tall. A smaller form and culture are discussed on list 67, Rare and Choice.

BRASSICA   oleracea Acephala Group of Ornamentals, Flowering Cabbage, Flowering Kale. Amazing texture and color in fall comes from these cabbages and kales whose jade green leaves are streaked, splotched and edged red, purple and cream. The sea kale, 'Crambe Maritima', is blue-gray and sculptural. See list 33, Annuals for Fall.

CALADIUM, Elephant's-ear. They are called "dancing ladies." In a breeze these large, shield-shaped leaves colorful as flowers dance on slender stems—all movement and form through the long, hot days of summer. Superb bedding and pot plants, the fanciful leaf patterns are variations on combinations of pink, red, and/or white on green, almost see-through. Lasting in flower arrangements. See list 51, Foliage for Color.

CIMICIFUGA   racemosa, Black Cohosh, Black Snakeroot. Great clumps of divided green leaves are formed and from them ascend like tall white candles, sometimes to 8 feet high, spires of tiny airy white florets that dominate any planting for a month or more beginning in early or midsummer. Good cutting flowers, though the scent is not liked by all. For culture see list 16, Summer Perennials for Sun.

FILIPENDULA,   Meadowsweet. Often sold as false spirea—these are big architectural plants with bold foliage and in summer soaring sprays of showy sweetly scented small flowers that toss in the wind. *F. palmata*, a small species, to 36 inches, with pink flowers. *F. rubra* 'Venusta', Queen-of-the-prairie, is similar but much bigger, 6 to 8 feet high, with towering spires of deep pink to carmine flowers. *F. ulmaria*, Queen-of-the-meadow. The foliage is bold and textural and lasts all season if moisture is maintained. Height is 2 to 4 feet. 'Aurea' has golden yellow foliage. For culture see list 75, Herbs with Showy Flowers.

GALAX   urceolata, Galax. The plants are slow-growing, wonderful tufts of thick, evergreen, heart-shaped basal leaves 12 inches high valued by florists and for their year-round textural interest in the garden. The leaves turn bronze in autumn. In late spring and early summer, small white flowers rise on slender stems. Excellent ground cover. See list 65, The Woodland Garden.

HOSTA, Plantain Lily, Daylily. Outstanding foliage plants for shade. Recommended especially for form and texture are: *H. sieboldiana* 'Frances Williams' ('Aureo-marginata'), also known as 'Gold Edge' or 'Golden Circle'; its leaves are puckered, very large, rounded, heavy-textured, blue-green with a gold border that deepens with the season; 'August Moon' has large, rounded, crinkled yellow leaves that are prominently veined. *H. tokudama* is a pretty, diminutive species that forms a low, wide clump 18 inches high. The leaves are rounded, crinkled, and cup-shaped, and their deep blue-green sets the standard for blue hostas. 'Krossa Regal', a popular silvery gray-green type, has big, crinkly, pointed, upright leaves that expose the blue undersides and stems. See list 54, *Hosta*.

IRIS,   Flag, Fleur-de-lys. Irises are the stars of late spring and early summer—blossoms of tuberous rhizomes that produce the spectacular bearded, Siberian, and Japanese irises. The swordlike leaves of most remain all summer long, welcome linear shapes for the middle or back of the border. In warmer regions the tops often need a summer trim. See list 25, *Iris*.

MACLEAYA (mak-*lay*-uh) **cordata**
(syn. *Bocconia cordata*)
Plume Poppy, Tree Celandine   Zones 3-8
Handsome, impressive, shrubby perennial 5 to 8 feet tall with large heart-shaped leaves 6 to 8 inches across, deeply cut, gray-green, whitish underneath. The flowers appear in early summer, graceful 12- to 20-inch plumes of buff-cream-pink florets with colorful stamens. Airy, bold texture

The several forms and textures of *Caladium*, ferns and green and variegated hostas—some in flower—carpet a shaded green garden. (Viette)

TOP, LEFT Felted basal foliage of gray-green *Verbascum hybridum* 'Silver Candelabra'. (Harper)

TOP, RIGHT Big, feathery goatsbeard, *Aruncus dioicus*, background plant. The male flower has the showiest plumes. (McDonald)

LEFT Foliage and flowers of plume poppy, *Macleaya cordata*—airy, bold texture for large borders. It needs room to spread. (Harper)

The common names Lamb's-ears and Woolly Betony describe the texture of *Stachys bizantina*, an ancient herb. It invites stroking. This is the rapid spreader 'Silver Carpet', best for foliage. (Viette)

for the back of the border, a center island, or other big spaces.

Culture: Sow seeds or set out root divisions in spring in full sun and rich, well-drained, humusy soil. Tends to outgrow its space, so it must be kept in bounds early.

ONOPORDUM (on-oh-*pord*-um) acanthium

Cotton Thistle, Scotch Thistle, Silver Thistle, Oat Thistle, Argentine Thistle   Biennial

Very ornamental, asymetrically branched thistle up to 9 feet tall with a bright silver-blue look and sharply toothed, hairy leaves 12 inches long or more. The fuzzy, typically thistlelike flowers are white or purple, and disk-shaped. A choice piece of gray architecture.

Culture: Sow seeds in early fall or spring in full sun or semishade in rich, well-drained soil. Deadhead to prevent self-sowing.

ORNAMENTAL GRASSES are extremely

useful—they stand upright, catch the light, throw up great feathery heads that dance in the wind, and bend to the snow. See list 53, Ornamental Grasses.

RODGERSIA (rod-*jerz*-ee-uh)

Magnificent ornamentals to 5 feet wide grown for the big, bold leaves. Pale, feathery flower panicles 12 inches long in shades of yellow, white, or red are held above the foliage in summer. Choice for adding texture to a wild garden in a moist woodlands or by a stream. Nice with the tall yellow flowerheads of *Ligularia stenocephala* 'The Rocket'.

Culture: In early spring before growth starts, plant pairs of root divisions in light shade along moist banks or in well-worked, rich, very humusy soil. Soil must remain very moist.

R. aesculifolia   Zones 5-6

Big shrubby plant 3 to 6 feet tall with coarse, showy, toothed leaves. The flower panicles are 18 to 24 inches long, composed of flat clusters of off-white florets; shaggy brown hairs cover the flower stalks and major veins.

R. pinnata   Zones 5-7

Very similar, but in cool spring or fall the leaves turn bronze. The flowers are dense, branched panicles of rose-red florets.

R. podophylla   Zones 5-6/7

Resembles *R. aesculifolia*. Can be 36 inches tall and spread to 5 feet wide. It is grown for the bold leaves that start out bright green and turn to bronze in autumn. In summer, feathery white flower panicles rise 12 inches above the foliage.

RUTA graveolens, Rue, Herb-of-grace. Dense,

nearly evergreen subshrub, 12 to 24 inches or taller with flattish, delicately cut, blue-green leaves. 'Variegata' is edged with white. In summer, modest blooms make a haze of yellow-green—pleasantly impressive and an excellent foil for gray in the garden. Attractive seedpods enhance textural value when the flowers have gone by. 'Jackman's Blue', 18 to 24 inches tall, is a more intense blue; lovely in fall. *R. chalapensis*, Fringed Rue, is scarce and slightly less hardy. See list 73, Herbs with Colorful Foliage.

SALVIA argentea, Silver Sage. To 24 inches tall,

the basal rosette of low-growing, hairy-textured, 12-inch-long, silvery gray-white leaves glows in the midst of the garden's usual greens. In summer, the flowers—cream, pink, or purple—bloom on tall, upright stems. They are usually removed to encourage lavish leaf production. See also list 41, *Salvia*.

SENECIO (sen-*nee*-shee-oh) cineraria

Dusty-miller   Tender Perennial

Author's favorite for instant silver-white foliage contrast. The stiff, woolly white leaves are divided into blunt segments, especially in 'Silver Lace'. The species is 8 to 12 inches tall and the ornamental foliage most conspicuous when dry; perfect dried in winter arrangements. Daisylike yellow flowers, in groups of 10 or 12, appear in summer but these are usually removed. Suitable as edging, container plant, and specimen in a mixed border. Recommended in addition to the 6- to 8-inch 'Silver Lace', is 'Silver Dust', 8 inches tall, for its finely cut foliage. Also offered as *Cineraria maritima*; do not confuse this with 2 other silvery plants that share its common name—*Artemisia* and *Centaurea cineraria*. 'Silver Dust' is like a finer-textured *Chrysanthemum ptarmiciflorum*. 'Cirrus' has a rounded, scalloped leaf.

Culture: In early spring, sow seeds or set out rooted cuttings or divisions in full sun in well-drained soil. Tolerates drought. It winters over in frost-free climates and grows into a sizable shrublike plant.

STACHYS (*stay*-kiss) byzantina (syn. *lanata*)

Woolly Betony, Lamb's-ears   Zones 4-8

The big, semievergreen, gray leaves 12 to 15 inches high are almost luminous in moonlight and so woolly they invite stroking—a wonderful contrast in color, and a unique, outstanding texture in the garden. Violet flower racemes bloom from summer to frost—they are usually removed to keep the focus on the leaves. This is a favorite for edging and leafy accents. The nonflowering, 8-inch-high 'Silver Carpet' spreads rapidly and is the best for foliage. Nice with *Sedum* 'Ruby Glow' or 'Vera Jameson'.

S. macrantha and *S. officinalis*, Betony, mat-forming species 12 to 24 inches tall, are grown for their showy purple or pink flowers; the foliage is dark green.

Culture: Sow seeds in spring, or set out container plants or root divisions in early fall or spring in full or partial sun in moist, well drained soil. In hot humid climates, avoid overhead watering.

VERBASCUM (ver-*bask*-um) Mullein

Group of biennials with bold basal rosettes of imposing feltlike, gray-green leaves. In late spring and early summer of the second year, its soaring, rigid spikes of white, yellow, orange, red, or purple florets are followed by interesting seedpods. Handsome in a center island or in the wild garden. Stems and pods dry well and are arresting in arrangements.

Culture: Sow seeds in spring or fall, or in spring set out root divisions in full sun in very well-drained, somewhat dry soil. Often self-sows.

V. bombyciferum 'Polar Summer'
                  Biennial, Zones 5-9

Spectacular; 5 feet tall with rosettes of 12- to 18-inch-long, white-silver, felted leaves. The small yellow flowers bloom on soaring candelabras.

V. hybridum 'Silver Candelabra'
                  Biennial, Zones 5-9

Rosettes of 18-inch-high, gray-green leaves and flowering candelabras of rose or yellow flowers.

VERONICASTRUM (ver-on- ik-*kast*-rum) virginicum

Culver's-root, Bowman's-root, Blackroot
                  Zones 3-8

Another big, bold plant, 4 to 7 feet tall, with an architectural structure, interesting foliage, and a generous late-summer display of soaring flower spikes. The florets are tiny and white or pale blue. Spectacular at the back of a border and in the wild garden. 'Album' has very white flowers and dark foliage.

Culture: Set out root divisions in early spring in full sun and moist, well-drained, fertile soil. Maintain moisture and fertilize regularly.

YUCCA. Very contemporary and exotic with huge

evergreen rosettes of silvery sword-shaped leaves and astonishing flower spikes. In early summer, these long-lasting, 4- to 6-foot woody stems rise up and unfold big bell-shaped flowers, white or flushed violet or purple on the outside. *Y. filamentosa* 'Bright Edge', Adam's-needle, is a magnificent stylized plant to feature in contemporary settings with 1- by 15-inch gold-rimmed leaves edged with shaggy threads. The flower stem reaches 5 feet and bears creamy white blooms. *Y. glauca*, Soapweed, has narrow, white-edged, gray-green leaves 36 inches long and ½ inch wide. The flowers are greenish white on a 36-inch spike. See list 57, Seashore and Sandy Soils.

SOURCE: J. BARRY FERGUSON, A BOTANIST, FLORAL DESIGNER, LECTURER, AND HORTICULTURIST, DESIGNS FLORAL ARRANGEMENTS FOR MAJOR SOCIAL EVENTS IN MANHATTAN AND HOLDS THE AMERICAN HORTICULTURAL SOCIETY FRANCES JONES POETKER AWARD FOR CREATIVE FLORAL DESIGNS. HE IS ALSO THE AUTHOR OF *LIVING WITH FLOWERS*.

51. FOLIAGE FOR COLOR

■ Flowering plants whose leaves color with the cold bring new vitality to the fading fall display. No garden is complete without a few of these plants. Even more valuable are the foliage plants whose showy, season-long color stabilizes the spring-to-autumn tapestry. Silver-leaved plants and the wildly variegated coleus and caladiums are among the best.

But choose the all-season foliage plants with caution. The colors can clash with flowers, and if there are too many colors, the garden focus is lost. The silver foliage plants, particularly *Artemisia*, which is recommended on many of our lists, do wonderful things. From spring to late fall they stand like cool splashes of white on a colorful canvas—beautiful with low, pale pink and tall, true pink impatiens and blue-purple ageratum, for instance. By moonlight, combined with white petunias, they're magical. But even silver can be overdone. Unless a whole bed is to be white, or white and yellow, or white and one other color, one silver accent or two is probably all it will take.

In a mixed garden, set the smaller foliage plants in groups of 3 or 4 together to make an splash of color, but repeat the group with caution. One or 2 of the larger plants growing at the back of the border will make a unit of color.

AMARANTHUS tricolor, Joseph's-coat. A big, coarse, dramatic foliage plant 1 foot to 4 feet tall with green leaves wildly splashed by yellow and scarlet patches. 'Molten Fire' is deep crimson splashed bright red and bronze. See list 50, Foliage for Form and Texture.

AMSONIA tabernaemontana, Bluestar. Slow growing, easy-care native perennial that forms clumps 12 to 36 inches tall and for several weeks in late spring bears drooping or upright clusters of small, persistent, truly blue flowers. Pods follow the flowers and are attractive in flower arrangements. The willowlike foliage sways with every breeze, remains green and lush all season, and turns a striking yellow-gold in fall. Pruning after flowers fade helps maintain the foliage. For culture, see list 13, Spring Perennials for Sun.

ARTEMISIA (art-em-*miz*-ee-uh)
Sagebrush, Mugwort
The best group of perennials for season-long silver or gray foliage in a mixed border. The effect is that of a mass of cool white flowers—exquisite next to shades of pink, purple, and light blue. The silver unifies discordant color combinations, lightens the border when nothing else is in bloom, and provides months of stable color. The small yellow or white flowers are sweet but not a factor. Some species are good ground covers, others are strongly scented herbs. There's an annual, *A. annua,* but the perennials are preferable and easy to grow. See also list 73, Herbs with Colorful Foliage.

Culture: Transplant root divisions or divide established artemisias in early spring or late summer (except for the woody 'Lambrook Silver' and 'Powis Castle', which are propagated by cuttings). Plant in moderately fertile, very well-drained soil in full sun or, in the South, bright shade.

Coleus hybrids in combinations of crimson, maroon, yellow, green, and white bring extravagant color to partial shade—here with impatiens. (Still)

Heat- and drought-resistant. Water sparingly. Invasive species are restrained by planting in heavier clay soils or in 3- to 5-gallon containers buried in soil up to the rim. In hot, humid areas foliage may die back in midsummer; prune to promote new growth.

A. absinthium 'Lambrook Silver' Absinthe, Wormwood   Zones 3-8
This is a subshrub with divided, very silvery leaves on a bushy plant 24 inches tall. It lives for years but is prettiest if you cut the woody stems back to a few inches from ground level in early spring. This severe pruning also keeps the plant vigorous and long-lived. 'Lambrook Silver' is the best artemisia for the North.

A. ludoviciana var. **albula** Silver-king Artemisia
                                  Zones 4-9
This is the best of the invasive artemisias, an upright, bushy plant 36 inches tall, airy, with frosty foliage on silvery stems, a lacy effect best used with restraint. There are tiny grayish white florets. It is somewhat fragrant,

valuable for edging, borders, as ground cover in larger landscapes; choice for sandy, dry places. Space 24 inches apart.

A. 'Powis Castle'   Zones 5-8
Silky soft and feathery, it makes a rounded clump 18 to 24 inches high.

A. schmidtiana 'Silver Mound'   Zones 3-7
For the front of the border and edging paths. It makes a mound 12 inches tall and 18 to 20 inches wide and has lacy, silvery green leaves with a bluish green undertone. Don't encourage with overly rich soil. If the clump opens at the center and flops by midsummer, cut the stems to the ground—recovery is quick and the foliage will remain in good condition till frost. Choice for dry, sandy places.

TOP, LEFT 'Silver Mound' *Artemesia schmidtiana*. (Viette)
TOP, RIGHT Plumbago, *Ceratostigma plumbaginoides*, bears blazing blue flowers. (Viette)
ABOVE Fast-growing annual Burning bush, *Kochi scoparia* forma *trichophylla*, turns red in fall. (Still)
RIGHT *Heuchera* 'Palace Purple' is burgundy in cool weather, bronze in heat, especially in the South. (Viette)

A. splendens   Zones 4-8

This is the best artemisia for the intermediate mixed border, a mounded filigree of curly, silvery leaves 12 inches tall. Superb delicate foliage contrasts with other plants or as bands of edging. Best divided every 4 years to maintain vigor. (Similar in appearance and use is *A. canescens*, syn. *A. versicolor*.)

A. stellerana Beach Wormwood, Old-woman, Dusty-miller   Zones 3/4-9

A perennial 24 to 36 inches tall with thick, wolly-white, finely divided leaves. Handsome as an edger or grouped in fours in a flowering border, and as a ground cover by the shore. It flourishes on sandy beaches in the Northeast. Tiny yellow flowers in summer.

BERGENIA cordifolia.

This vigorous plant 12 to 16 or 18 inches high bears graceful spires of dark pink flowers in mid-spring. It is prized in particular for its clumps of glossy, leathery, evergreen leaves, which turn bronze in winter sun. There's a white-flowered variety and a tall, purple-toned 'Purpurea' with dark pink blossoms whose leaves color burgundy in cold. Bergenia makes a bold backdrop for ferns and other delicate-looking woodsy plants. It is not invasive and is most effective in groups. Recommended for foliage are: 'Abendglut' ('Evening Glow'), 9 inches tall, with crimson-purple flowers; 'Bressingham White', to 14 inches, pinkish flowers that later turn white; and 'Evening Bells', to 14 inches, pink flowers with hardy red winter foliage. For culture, see list 13, Spring Perennials for Sun.

CALADIUM (kal-*lay*-dee-um)

Elephant's-ear   Zones 9/10-11

Excellent for semishade. Grown for the large, shield-shaped leaves as colorful as flowers on slender stems 12 to 24 inches tall. They're called "dancing ladies" because they flutter in the wind. Superb bedding and pot plants, the fanciful leaf patterns are pink, red, and/or white on green, translucent leaves. Caladiums brighten late spring/summer/early fall borders with color that is often more reliable than flowers. The leaves are used in flower arrangements. Remove the flowers. May be grown indoors at high temperatures in a humid atmosphere with good light. Great in planters, as a ribbon of color edging a mixed flower border, and in groups with impatiens and coleus.

Culture: Start the tubers in a warm room indoors in mid-spring in 2 to 3 inches of moistened peat moss or sterile soilless mix. Once rooted, transplant to soil-filled pots and set outdoors when nights are above 60° F and days at 70° F. Or, when temperatures are right outdoors, plant the tuber knobbled side up in groups of 4 to 6 about 2 inches deep in rich, well-drained, humusy soil in a semi-sunny location. Maintain root moisture. Above Zone 9, as the temperature drops in fall, gradually dry out the tubers and store them in dry peat moss, vermiculite, or perlite at 70° to 75° F .

C. × hortulanum Fancy-leaved Caladium
Zones 9/10-11

The most available caladiums are these colorful hybrids of *C. bicolor* and *C. picturatum*—dense, compact plants patterned with red, rose, salmon, white, or green.

C. humboldtii

Oblongish, heart-shaped, bright green leaves splotched and spotted with white.

CERATOSTIGMA (ser-at-oh-*stig*-muh) plumbaginoides

Blue Ceratostigma, Plumbago   Zones 5-9

One of the bluest blue flowers in the world is borne by this pretty foliage plant. It spreads vigorously under good conditions, forming 6- to 8- or 12-inch-high mats of almost evergreen, glossy, dark green leaves. From midsummer to frost scraps of electric blue flowers appear, then with the cold the foliage turns bronzy red—in California, almost red. Excellent as ground cover, edger, and in rock and wall gardens. Listed in some catalogs as *Plumbago larpentae*.

Culture: Set out root divisions in spring in sun or bright shade in ordinary but very well-drained soil. Soggy conditions are fatal, but it multiplies rapidly in humusy, moist soil and tolerates drought. Stays in top form when sheared annually in spring with the mower set high.

COLEUS (koh-*lee*-) × hybridus
Tender perennial

A leafy, upright plant 6 to 24 inches tall grown for foliage that all year long displays combinations and variegations of brilliant red-mahogany, green, yellow, white, blue, and rose. The panicles of insignificant pale blue or lavender flowers usually are removed to keep the plants bushy. The perennial 'Concord' has velvety purple leaves on 24-inch stems; 'Highland Fling' is yellow splashed with light green; 'Molten Lava' is red with a red margin; and 'Salmon Lace' is salmon with lacy edgings of green and cream-white. For baskets, use the red and gold 'Scarlet Poncho', which has trailing stems. Also recommended for baskets are *C. blumei*, Painted Nettle, whose leaves include dashes of white, red, purple, yellow, and green, and *C. pumilus*, a well-branched, green-edged dark purple creeping or trailing species whose cultivars are choice basket plants.

Culture: Grows easily from seed at any season—indoors in sun or outdoors in semi-sun, and cuttings 8 inches long or more flourish indefinitely in water. Without enough sun the color fades. Plant outdoors after the weather warms in rich, well-drained loam and maintain even moisture.

EPIMEDIUM × rubrum.

Dainty, durable, 6- to 12-inch-high, clump-forming evergreen plant for shade, which in late spring bears graceful sprays of charming, irregular, bicolored flowers, red with yellow. It is grown primarily for its foliage—the leaves turn bronzy red in cold weather. Excellent for rock gardens and in the heavy shade of trees. Rather similar are *E. grandiflorum* 'Rose Queen', 10 inches tall; *E.* × *versicolor* 'Sulphureum', 12-inch yellow, evergreen in the South; 6-inch-tall *E.* × *youngianum* 'Roseum', lilac; and 'Niveum', a late-blooming white. See also list 14, Spring Perennials for Shade.

GERANIUM, Cranesbill.

In spring and early summer this "true" geranium produces an abundance of small, cup-shaped flowers on wandlike stems above deeply divided foliage. Noted for fall foliage color are: *G.* × *magnificum*, a sterile hybrid 24 inches tall, cultivated for more than a century, that has dark-veined, violet-blue flowers and very ornamental, rather hairy leaves richly tinted orange-scarlet in fall; and *G. sanguineum*, Blood-red Cranesbill, nearly indestructible, exceptionally tough plant 9 to 12 inches tall, easy to grow and long-blooming, with red-purple to bright magenta flowers and attractive spreading foliage that forms a mound and in fall turns crimson-red or maroon. 'Album', a pure white, is recommended. For culture, see list 13, Spring Perennials for Sun.

HEUCHERA 'Palace Purple'.

Low-growing plant for shade recommended for its striking, 12-inch-high, ivy-shaped burgundy foliage. During the hot months it has a bronze cast, especially in the South. In late spring and early summer tiny bell-shaped, off-white flowers bloom on wiry stalks about 18 inches tall. Some beautiful combinations include 'Palace Purple' with *Artemisia.* 'Powis Castle, or *Oenothera missouriensis* 'Green Court', or *Liatris spicata*, or *Geranium* 'Johnson's Blue', or *Sedum* 'Vera Jameson'. For culture, see list 16, Summer Perennials for Shade.

KOCHIA (koh-kee-uh) scoparia forma trichophylla

Burning Bush, Fire Bush, Red Summer Cypress
Annual

A tough annual which even in hot, polluted areas develops from seed in a single season into what seems to be a full-grown columnar, pyramidal, or round dwarf evergreen 24 to 36 inches high. With cold weather the 2-inch leaves burn purplish to bright red. Valuable for fall color, for quick, temporary hedges, and in groups as a filler for the back of the border.

Culture: In the North, sow seeds indoors in March; in the South, sow seeds outdoors in April where the plants are to mature. Develops best in well-dug, light soil and full sun. Also performs well in moist, well-drained soil. Self-sows in warm climates and can be a nuisance. To prevent spreading, cut back before the seed matures in fall. Naturalized in the dry Western states.

SENECIO cineraria, Dusty-miller.

The stiff, white-woolly leaves are divided into blunt segments, especially in 'Silver Lace'. The species is 8 to 12 inches tall and the ornamental foliage most conspicuous when dry. Serves well as an edging, or as a specimen for color contrast in a mixed border and containers. Recommended are the compact 'Silver Lace', 6 to 8 inches tall and 'Silver Dust', 8 inches tall, which has very finely cut foliage. Also sold as *Cineraria maritima*, and not to be confused with 2 other silvery plants that share its common name—*Artemisia* and *Centaurea cineraria*. See list 43, Flowers for Edging.

SOURCE: DR. STEVEN STILL IS A PROFESSOR OF HORTICULTURE AT OHIO STATE UNIVERSITY AND THE AUTHOR OF THE *MANUAL OF HERBACEOUS ORNAMENTAL PLANTS*.

52. FERNS FOR THE GARDEN

■ Ferns have a cool, graceful presence that no other type of plant quite duplicates. Their lush greens evoke woodlands and romantic glades, and no cottage garden is complete without them. They also offer practical solutions to a number of landscaping challenges. Ferns flourish in cool, moist places—the north side of a house, the north slope of a wooded stretch, a sun-dappled stream edge with poor drainage.

Because most ferns are native to shaded places, they are perfect backdrops to a flower bed that backs into the shadow of the building behind. And, because they're generally shallow-rooted, they compete successfully with tree roots for moisture and space where other plants fail.

Many are evergreen or semievergreen, particularly in warmer regions. But even in the North ferns linger into early winter, greening wooded lots long after the leaves have fallen. Most are acid-loving and can be established where otherwise only mosses will grow.

Not all ferns require moisture and shade—a few flourish by the roadside in sandy, dry, sunny places.

The American Fern Society was founded in 1893 and the *American Fern Journal* is published quarterly, as is its newsletter. You can reach them through the American Horticultural Society.

Companion Plants: Ferns fill their spaces throughout the year and make charming backgrounds for garden plants as well as wildflowers: begonias, columbines, the very fragrant Lily-of-the-valley, primroses, Solomon's-seals, trilliums, and lady's-slippers are all lovely companions. See lists 14, Spring Perennials for Shade; 32, Annuals for Shade; 29, Primrose; 30, Violet—Pansy; 38, *Impatiens;* 64, The Meadow Garden; 65, The Woodland Garden; and 54, Hosta.

Culture: Generally, ferns are easy to grow and adaptable to new situations. Container-grown ferns adapt more quickly to garden life than those taken from the wild. They're sold by nurseries, garden catalogs, and wildflower specialists. Please insist on purchasing only plants propagated by nurseries, not gathered from the wild. Local species and varieties of the ferns recommended here are usually the better choice. Some ferns thrive in sunny meadows, but most prefer partial or complete shade.

Ferns may be planted in a flower border with special preparation. They live long and multiply all around, so dig a wide planting hole. Most require somewhat acid, moist soil consisting of 50 to 75 percent humusy forest soil or decayed, shredded leaves fertilized with composted cow manure. In following years, in late winter scatter a light application of acid fertilizer under the foliage. Allow the duff (the layer of decaying vegetation that covers the soil) to remain undisturbed.

Plant a fern just a little higher than the level at which it was growing before, and just a little below the soil surface. Mulch all around with shredded leaves, leaf compost, or peat moss. Avoid deep cultivating—pull weeds by hand, gently. Fern rhizomes must be free to creep over or just under the surface soil and colonize their territory. A little overhead watering in high heat is helpful.

Some species are evergreen and others will tolerate sun and some drought, especially if growing in moist, humusy soil.

Divide in early spring or fall in the South, by digging and separating the rhizomes, each with a good root system, or cutting them apart, and replanting.

ADIANTUM (ad-ee-*an*-tum) **pedatum**
Maidenhair Fern   Zones 3-8
One of our prettiest ferns, about 24 inches tall. Delicate fronds 12 inches across with bright green leaves are borne at the forked ends of wiry, strong, black-purple stems. Airy enough to dance in every breeze and hardy enough for the rocky north woods. Good ground cover if thickly planted.

Culture: In early spring, plant crown divisions in shade under tall trees in rich, humusy, well-drained soil with a pH of 6.0 to 7.0. Must be kept moist.

ATHYRIUM (ath-*theer*-ee-um)
Tall, graceful ferns with light green, lance-shaped fronds that have many leaflets. They form good clumps and are among the easiest ferns to grow.

Culture: Successful in partial shade almost anywhere. Set out root divisions in early spring in moist, humusy soil in the pH range of 5.0 to 6.0.

A. filix-femina Lady Fern   Zones 3-8
Forms thick clumps of graceful, finely divided fronds 12 to 20 inches long that appear throughout the growing season. Spreads at a moderate rate in moist conditions, but is tolerant of fairly dry soils.

A. goeringianum 'Pictum'
Japanese Silver Painted Fern   Zones 3-8
Beautiful, exotic variegated fern with a gray-silver central stripe on green fronds, wine red stems, and a weeping habit. It fairly shines in dark corners of the wild garden. Grows vigorously to at least 18 inches, and competes well with other roots.

CYRTOMIUM (ser-*toh*-mee-um) **falcatum**
Holly Fern, Japanese Holly Fern   Zones 9-10
Durable, upright, spreading fern 12 to 24 inches high with glossy, holly-like leaves on dark green fronds 8 inches wide and to 30 inches long. Long-lasting, easy to grow, slow spreading; in Florida it is used as a ground cover under trees and on partially shaded banks and slopes.

Culture: Set out root divisions in late fall or early spring in light shade in well-drained, humusy, moist, somewhat acid soil. Tolerates some salt and drought.

DENNSTAEDTIA (den-*stet*-ee-uh)
punctilobula
Hay-scented Fern, Boulder Fern   Zones 2-8
The delicate, arching, finely cut, leathery 20- to 32-inch fronds of this hardy fern form solid masses and are fragrant when crushed. Spreads vigorously even in rocky places, and is choice for naturalizing, but not good for small gardens.

Culture: Set out divisions of the creeping rootstock in sun or shade, in moist, humusy soil that is somewhat acid.

DRYOPTERIS (drye-*opp*-ter-iss)
Wood Fern, Shield Fern
Big deciduous and evergreen species with delicate, much-divided fronds rising gracefully to form symmetrical groups or nice clumps.

Culture: Many species grow wild in American woodlands and are among the easiest ferns to grow. Plant crown divisions in early spring in light shade in moist, humusy soil that is somewhat acid.

D. erythrospora Japanese Shield Fern
                                                   Zones 5-9
Outstanding and colorful species from Japan that has fronds 24 to 36 inches tall and with rounded red spores.

D. filix-mas Male Fern   Zones 3/4-9
A favorite for fern gardens, the deeply cut, nearly evergreen fronds form dense crowns 24 to 36 inches high. There are varieties with crested, forking, or curled fronds, and also dwarf varieties.

D. goldiana Goldie's Fern   Zones 3-9
Most striking of the group, stately, to 4 feet tall, with blue-green fronds in graceful clumps of 6 or more.

D. marginalis Marginal Shield Fern,
Leather Wood Fern   Zones 3-9
Handsome plants formed by a dozen or so usually evergreen, feathery, dark green 15- to 20-inch fronds that are upright in the growing season but may lay flat during winter. Not a rapid spreader.

NEPHROLEPIS (nef-*frol*-ep-iss)
Sword Fern
Species of evergreen tropical ferns that form dense crowns of delicate, narrow, arching, drooping fronds 12 to 36 inches long. Indoor or greenhouse ferns except in tropical climates such as Florida, where they are used as ground cover under trees, and on shady banks and slopes.

Culture: Plant crown divisions in summer or early fall in light shade. Prefers moist, humusy soil that is somewhat acid. Tolerates drought, waterlogging, and poor soil.

N. cordifolia Erect Sword Fern,
Ladder Sword Fern   Zones 10-11
Semievergreen with arching dark green fronds to 18 inches high. Nice border plant in its hardiness zones.

N. exaltata 'Bostoniensis' Boston Fern
                                                   Zones 10-11
The most popular and successful house fern, a fluffy, full plant that is long-lasting if divided every year. Give it a little water often and never let it dry out. There are variations, some with extremely fine leaves. Superb container plant for the shaded porch or patio and charming in borders.

OSMUNDA (os-*mund*-uh) **cinnamomea**
Cinnamon Fern   Zones 3-8
Striking, big fern with fountainlike, sterile, green outer fronds and stiff, thick-stemmed, upright, fertile inner fronds. These inner fronds have a green felt covering of spores that turns to cinnamon-brown, then darkens and withers. To 5 feet tall, an excellent choice to backdrop wild and woodland gardens. Magnificent massed.

Culture: Plant crown divisions in early spring in light shade in moist, humusy soil in the pH range of 4.0 to 5.0. Transplants easily and spreads slowly. The Royal Fern, *O. regalis,* can stand some sun if growing in a wet place, Zones 3 to 9.

POLYPODIUM (pol-ip-*poh*-dee-um)
virginianum
Rock Polypody, American Wall Fern   Zones 7-9
Semievergreen fern with vertical or horizontal frond stalks to 12 inches tall rising from creeping rhizomes; in time, it forms a dense ground cover.

LEFT Evergreen Christmas fern, *Polystichum acrostichoides*, choice textural plant.

BELOW Beautiful weeping Japanese painted fern, *Athyrium goeringianum* 'Pictum', has a gray-silver central stripe, wine red stems. (Viette)

BOTTOM, LEFT The big cinnamon fern, *Osmunda cinnamomea*, has upright inner fronds whose felt green covering of spores turns to cinnamon. (McDonald)

BOTTOM, RIGHT Dainty fronds of maidenhair fern, *Adiantum*, dance in every breeze but are surprisingly durable. (McDonald)

Culture: Plant root divisions in early spring in partial shade in moist, well-drained, humusy, somewhat acid soil.

POLYSTICHUM (pol-*list*-ik-um) Shield Fern
Narrow ferns with lustrous green leaves growing in arching, circular clusters from the crown. Most are evergreen.

Culture: Excellent for damp, shady places where soil is rich in humus.

P. acrostichoides Christmas Fern, Dagger Fern, Canker Brake Zones 3-8
Often seen in rock gardens, a wonderful evergreen fern with deep green, lance-shaped, leathery fronds to 24 inches long. Tolerates some sun if given adequate moisture.

P. braunii Shield Fern, Braun's Holly Fern Zones 3-8
Semievergreen ferns with graceful, arching fronds 2 to 36 inches tall, and with twice-divided leaves covered with hairlike scales at the edges. Needs cool, deep shade and tolerates somewhat alkaline soil.

THELYPTERIS (thel-*lip*-ter-iss)
Hardy, bold ferns with good color, often narrower at the base. The species here spread rapidly in fair conditions and make a bright green ground cover.

Culture: Plant root divisions in early spring in shade and moist, humusy soil in the acid range.

T. hexagonoptera Beech Fern, Broad Beech Fern Zones 3-9
Triangular fronds tapered at the base, 10 to 24 inches long.

T. noveboracensis New York Fern Zones 2-8
Finely divided fronds tapering toward the base, 12 to 24 inches tall.

T. palustris forma pufferae Marsh Fern Zones 3-8
A slow-spreading form 18 inches tall. Prefers sun and wet soil in the pH range of 4.0 to 5.0.

T. simulata Massachusetts Fern Zones 3-7
A native species 18 inches tall, recommended for moist-to-wet marshy areas, in either sun or light shade, and soil with a pH of 5.0 to 6.0.

SOURCE: WILLIAM BRUMBACK, OF THE GARDEN IN THE WOODS, FRAMINGHAM, MASSACHUSETTS, A BOTANICAL GARDEN OWNED BY THE NEW ENGLAND WILD FLOWER SOCIETY.

53. ORNAMENTAL GRASSES

■ In a flower garden, the willowy ornamental grasses create linear accents that whisper and toss with the wind. Interesting at every season, dynamic in their changes and caprices—dried, they can bend or flatten or break like the straw man in *The Wizard of Oz*—they play with their spaces, a quality of nature. Buff, tan, sea green, green, gold, or pale gold in color, straight up or fountaining, grasses are perfect foils for the busy foliage and bright spires, the rounds and clumps of flowers. Together, they make a four-season show planned by nature when the world was young.

Grasses are the mainstay of the meadowlike garden design that has become widely known as the New American Garden—the new "natural" garden. The accepted ratio is ⅓ flowers to ⅔ grasses for sunny places; ⅓ grasses and ⅔ flowers for shade. The seedheads—inflorescences—make striking displays in the garden in late summer and winter, as well as in dried arrangements. Combine both fine and coarse-textured grasses for contrast. Use fewer varieties and more of each rather than lots of varieties and few of each. They really are very different from one another in color as well as form and texture.

In season one, spring, the first green grass spears thrust up through just-cut clumps to green the earth around flowering bulbs and shrubs. In summer, the grasses, tall now, are topped by delicate flowerheads dancing on slender stems. In autumn, summer greens fade and the grasses blaze gold against the cold blue sky. Finally, in the fourth season, winter, the golden stalks bind snow at their feet, whistle and rustle in the wind. Then it's January, time for most grasses to be cut back to the ground—but not *Helictotrichon*.

The recommendations that follow group grasses for sun into small, medium-tall, and tall sizes. Grasses for the home garden can grow up to 20 feet tall. Most grasses succeed in full sun or some shade; a few thrive in real shade, and are covered—both large and small—at the end of this list. The genera, species, and cultivars are presented in the order of preference of plant finder Kurt Bluemel, not alphabetically.

Companion Plantings: With grasses, plant flowers that naturalize readily and stand some neglect. Include spring-flowering bulbs such as: daffodils; *Allium giganteum*, Giant Onion; *Camassia quamash*, Quamash, or Camosh, also known as Foxtail Lily; species tulips and Water-lily, Lily-flowered, Fringed, red Parrot, Greigii, and Bunch-flowering tulips. Plant tall, fragrant herbs or ground covers.

Other good companions are sturdy perennials such as: *Achillea* 'Coronation Gold'; *Astilbe × arendsii* 'Fanal'; *Hemerocallis* species and hybrids, daylilies; *Rudbeckia fulgida* var. *sullivanti* 'Goldsturm'; *Sedum spectabile* 'Autumn Joy'; *Lysimachia punctata*, Yellow Loosestrife; *Macleaya cordata*, Plume Poppy; *Perovskia atriplicifolia*, Russian Sage; peonies; Siberian, Japanese, and bearded irises. For comprehensive lists of flowers that combine well with grasses in naturalized plantings, see lists 64, The Meadow Garden, and 48, Wildflowers to Naturalize.

Culture: Grasses are shipped bare-root or in containers. Soak bare-root plants thoroughly before setting them out. Plant in early spring or early fall in well-drained soil that is one-quarter to one-half humus. Set the crowns ½ to 1 inch higher than the soil surface. Don't "drown" the grasses in mulch—1 to 2 inches is enough.

Allow the seedheads to ripen and remain through fall and winter to encourage birds. A garden that includes grasses can resemble a naturally evolved ecosystem that welcomes insects, the majority of which—in a healthy garden—are beneficial.

In late winter or early spring, most of the grasses should be cut to the ground and a light mulch applied. As new foliage emerges, fertilize with partially organic 10-6-4 at the rate of 5 pounds per 100 square feet. Or, better yet, apply organic compost instead of fertilizer. Water deeply during summer's worst droughts.

BEST LOW-GROWING GRASSES

Use small grasses in a collage of flowering and foliage plants on the low plane—a few inches to 8 or 10 inches in height. Combine small grasses whose textures contrast as ground cover, a step beyond pachysandra and vinca.

BRIZA (*brye*-tza) media
Quaking Grass Zones 5-9
For the front or middle of the border, a tufted meadow grass that in spring bears short, oatlike panicles of flowers that rustle with every slight breeze. The mature height is 24 to 36 inches. Other species of interest are *B. maxima*, to 30 inches tall, an annual that is good for cutting; and *B. subaristata*, a tender perennial 12 inches high, hardy only to Zone 8.

Culture: In spring or fall, set out in mass plantings in full sun, in ordinary, well-drained soil. Tolerates droughts. This perennial usually self-sows.

FESTUCA (fes-*tew*-kuh)
Fescue
Festucas are true clump-forming grasses planted for their fine textured foliage. They vary in color from bright green to silver-blue. The upright flowers dry to a tawny brown, but can be removed to promote the foliage.

Culture: Well-drained soil is essential. Plant spring or fall in full sun and maintain moderate moisture.

F. amethystina var. superba Blue Sheep's Fescue Zones 4-8
The flower stalks are the color of amethyst and the 24-inch flowers are pendulous. The foliage is 8 to 12 inches tall. Some excellent cultivars are 'Elijah Blue', a rich olive green bloomer; 'Bronzeglanz', which is silvery green; and 'Aprilgrun', a fresh green.

F. cinerea Blue Fescue Zones 6-9
Foliage height is 8 inches, the flower stalk 14 inches. Outstanding cultivars include 'Azurit', a true blue; 'Meerblau', sea blue; and 'Palatinat', silver-blue.

F. mairei Maire's Fescue Zones 7-9
Native to North Africa, the fresh green leaves have silvery undersides and stiffly arching inflorescences up to 30 inches long. The plant spread is from 24 to 30 inches, and the height is about 18 inches. Attractive as a featured specimen or in mass plantings.

Among the most colorful ornamental grasses:
RIGHT Evergreen silver variegated Japanese sedge, *Carex morrowii* 'Variegata'. (Viette)
BOTTOM, LEFT Intensely blue wild rye grass, *Elymus racemosus* 'Glaucus', stabilizes dunes and dry, sandy land. (Viette)
BOTTOM, RIGHT Brilliant red when the sun shines through it, Japanese blood grass, *Imperata cylindrica* 'Red Baron', is a good edger. (Viette)

F. tenuifolia Zones 5-9

An excellent clump-forming ground cover with velvety, fresh green foliage. It contrasts well with other silver-blue fescues. The hummocks are 8 inches tall and the flower stalks reach to 14 inches.

OTHER CHOICE LOW-GROWING GRASSES

DESCHAMPSIA (des-*shamp*-see-uh)
caespitosa
Tufted Hair Grass Zones 4-9

A vigorous, versatile grass that naturalizes readily in dry or moist areas. Semievergreen in warm regions, though the tips still brown out. It grows from to 24 to 36 inches. The foliage is fresh green and the golden inflorescences reach high above the tufted mound. Recommended are: 48-inch-high 'Schottland', which is dark green; 'Goldschleier', ('Golden Veil'), a light green whose flower stalk rises to 30 inches; and 'Tautrager' ('Dew Carrier'), dark green, a rich bloomer whose flowers may be up to 36 inches tall.

Culture: Plant in spring or fall in full sun or partial shade, in ordinary, well-drained soil.

PHALARIS (fuh-*lar*-iss) **arundinacea var. 'Picta'**
Gardener's Garters, Ribbon Grass Zones 4-9

Variegated green and white, this is a rapid-spreading ground cover in use since early times and very tolerant of moisture. The height is about 24 inches. A superior cultivar is 'Feecey', which has almost white foliage—new growth is pink.

Culture: Spreads rapidly by underground rhizomes. Plant in spring or fall in full sun. It also tolerates partial shade. The foliage tends to brown out in dry summer heat.

ELYMUS (*ell*-lim-us) **racemosus**
(syn. *giganteus*) **'Glaucus'**
Blue Wild Rye Grass Zones 4-9

This is the best grass for stabilizing dunes and sandy dry lands. An intense blue, the height is 30 inches. Flowers appear in July and August, up to 48 inches tall.

Culture: Spreads rapidly by underground rhizomes. Plant in spring or fall in full sun, in average to dry soil.

MOLINIA (moh-*lye*-nee-uh) **caerulea**
Purple Moor Grass Zones 4-7

This is a clump-forming grass for cool climates, and it performs well in boggy situations. Excellent for the wild meadow and to create natural effects. Green flowers appear in May and June, turning to golden brown as the season progresses. Mature height is 8 inches for the foliage, 24 to 36 inches for the flowers. The variegated subspecies *caerulea* 'Variegata' is a beautiful specimen for the small garden or as an edger. Recommended are cultivars 'Heidebraut', ('Heather Bride'), 24 to 36 inches tall, and 'Moorhexe', ('Bog Witch'), 18 to 24 inches tall.

Culture: Plant in spring in full sun in average to boggy soil.

GLYCERIA (glye-*ser*-ee-uh) **maxima**
'Variegata'
Manna Grass Zones 4-9

A mounded, slow-spreading, golden variegated grass valued for its colorful foliage. Mature height is 18 to 24 inches. In moist areas, it grows more rapidly and is ideal for stabilizing soil at the water's edge. The new spring growth emerges pink and purple, bleaching out in midseason.

Culture: Set out spring or fall in full sun, in average soil. Tolerates a wide range of moisture conditions.

HELICTOTRICHON (hel-lik-toe-*try*-kon)
sempervirens
Blue Oat Grass Zones 4-8

Colorful. The wiry, shining, semievergreen, gray-blue leaves grow in 24-inch puffs. In spring, delicate, oatlike golden flowers sway high above the foliage and remain through winter. Very nice next to Russian Sage, *Perovskia atriplicifolia*, and *Sedum* 'Ruby Glow'. Foliage reaches 18 inches, the flowers 3 to 4 feet. A hardy plant that is best massed or planted in large groups. The cultivar 'Saphiresprudel' is an excellent blue.

Culture: Set out in early spring or fall in full sun or very light shade, in well-drained, ordinary soil. Tolerates drought. Don't cut this one in spring—let it be.

IMPERATA (im-*per*-rah-tuh) **cylindrica**
Japanese Blood Grass Zones 6-9

Striking color. A low-growing, slow-spreading spiky grass that turns bloodred with summer temperatures and stays red until winter. Must be grouped or massed to be effective. A good edger that is brightest when backlit with evening sun. Mature height is 12 to 24 inches. Plant only the cultivar—the USDA bans interstate shipment of the species, which is very invasive..

Culture: Hardy, it succeeds in any good garden soil. Plant in spring in semi-sun in hot regions, or full sun farther north. Provide good drainage and maintain moisture around the roots.

SESLERIA (sess-*lair*-ee-uh)
Ornamental, drought-tolerant grasses that thrive in small city gardens. Growth rate is medium to fast.

Culture: Plant spring or fall in sun or semi-sun according to species, in ordinary, well-drained soil.

S. autumnalis Autumn Moor Grass Zones 5-8
Attractive, chartreuse-green tufts that in fall bear airy, pale panicles that lighten the whole plant. Good rock garden specimen and edger for shrubs. Mature height is 12 to 18 inches. Prefers semi-sun.

S. heuffleriana Zones 5-8
The bluish green foliage appears in March. topped by striking black buds that develop into white puffs as the weather warms. Prefers full sun.

BEST MEDIUM-TALL GRASSES

A medium-tall grass clump has the effect of a shrub—a kinetic, four-dimensional structure. It is big enough to attract attention in the middle of the border and looks good in an island bed. Moving in the wind in a small city garden backlit by street lights or the sun, these grasses have marvelous texture and luminosity.

CALAMAGROSTIS (kal-a-muh-*gros*-tis) × **acutiflora**
Feather Reed Grass Zones 5-9

An upright, early-blooming grass with long-lasting, feathery panicles that are exceptionally decorative. It makes an easy-care substitute for an espalier on a blank wall, and is excellent for screening. 'Stricta', from 5 to 7 feet tall, bears fluffy bluish panicles in early summer that develop into light-catching, golden-tan reeds. They remain until the following spring. The seeds are sterile, so the grass never is invasive. The cultivar 'Karl Foerster', from 5 to 6 feet tall, is a little smaller and blooms earlier.

Culture: Plant in groups in spring or fall, in full sun and ordinary soil. Succeeds in a wide range of soils, but requires moisture around the roots.

MISCANTHUS (mis-*kanth*-us)
Bold plants with broad, grassy, gracefully arching leaves. In late summer or fall they send up silky, silvery plumes that stand high above the foliage and make good cut flowers. The species and cultivars recommended here are moderate in size and look best in groups or when massed. Maintenance is minimal. Taller miscanthus are described in the section on tall grasses, below.

Culture: All miscanthus develop rapidly in full sun and any good garden soil. Plant in spring or fall.

M. sinensis cultivars Zones 5-9
Many cultivars are now offered in medium height, 3 to 5 feet or so, including the flowers. Textures range from fine to coarse. Taller types are described among tall grasses.

Recommended cultivars are:

'Yaku Jima', Zones 7 to 9, 24 to 30 inches tall, with flowers to 48 inches. Blooms early, in August.

'Adagio', Zones 7 to 9, is similar to the above, with soft-looking, pendulous silvery foliage. A rich blooming habit. Flowers in August.

'Nippon', Zones 5 to 9, one of the earliest, blooms in early August. The foliage reaches 24 inches and the flowers, to 4 feet tall, are narrow, upright, and wispy.

'Purpurascens', Red Silver Grass, Zones 5 to 9, is 36 inches tall with, in August, flowers to 5½ feet tall. The dark green leaves turn, after the first frost, to maroon-orange.

M. transmorrisonensis Zones 7-10
Smaller, with fine, almost evergreen foliage to 24 inches high. The long-lasting flowers appear in late July, carried high above the leaves.

PANICUM (*pan*-ik-um) **virgatum**

Switch Grass   Zones 4-9

Upright, narrow, clump-forming plants 3 to 6 feet tall. In midsummer, they lift clouds of dark red to purple spikelets on long, open panicles high above the foliage. The leaves turn bright yellow in autumn and last through winter. 'Haense Herms', Red Switch Grass, Zones 5 to 9, 3 to 4 feet tall, turns red in fall and remains all winter; attractive perennialized with purple asters. 'Heavy Metal', Zones 4 to 9, is an erect, stiff plant 4 to 5 feet tall, with blue-gray foliage and pink flowers.

Culture: Thrives in a moist or wet site in full sun, but is tolerant of sandy soils. Plant in spring or fall, in groups.

PENNISETUM (pen-nis-*seet*-um)

Slender grasses that come in various greens; there are also a few burgundy cultivars. Rounded mounds of graceful, arching foliage with flower spikelets that have conspicuous bottlebrush bristles. Mature height is 3 to 4 feet. Best used in large drifts.

Culture: Easy to grow. Plant in spring in full sun, in any soil. Keep the soil surface damp. Multiply by spring division.

P. alopecuroides Chinese Pennisetum

Zones 6-9

This is the most popular species. The foliage is 24 to 30 inches long, and the flowers reach up to 4 feet. It bears quantities of golden maroon brushes from early August to late fall, dispersing in winter. 'Hameln' is a compact form choice for smaller gardens. It blooms three weeks earlier than the species and is about 18 inches tall.

P. incomptum Fountain Grass   Zones 6-9

An arching grass 3 to 4 feet tall whose very fine leaves fountain upward. Starting in July, tannish flower spikelets with conspicuous bristles rise above the leaves and bloom continuously to frost. In spring, mass plants in full sun; it also tolerates less light. Fountain grass spreads at a run, and needs lots of space—it is very invasive.

P. orientale Oriental Fountain Grass Zones 7-9

The light gray-green foliage has the finest texture of all the pennisetums and nearly pink, delicate, fluffy flowerheads from May until frost. Height is 16 inches for the leaves, 24 inches for the flowers. Tolerant of drought.

OTHER CHOICE MEDIUM-TALL GRASSES

SORGHASTRUM (sore-*gas*-strum)

avenaceum (syn. *nutans*)

Wood Grass, Indian Grass   Zones 4-8

A clump-forming grass whose foliage is often blue. The 6-foot flower stalks carry beautiful inflorescences accented with distinctive golden anthers. Shines in the sun. The foliage is 24 inches high. Native to moist ditches in the prairies.

Culture: Plant in spring in full sun and ordinary soil. Maintain moisture.

SPOROBOLUS (spore-ub-*boh*-lus)

heterolepis

Prairie Drop Seed   Zones 4-8

A prairie plant that grows slowly and forms a fresh, green mound of fine, arching foliage topped by slender flower stalks. From July on, the stalks are accented by tiny rounded beads. Colors nicely in fall. The foliage at maturity is 18 to 24 inches high; the flowers reach up to 4 feet.

Culture: Plant in spring or fall in full sun in ordinary, well-drained soil. Drought tolerant.

SPARTINA (spar-*ti*-nuh) **pectinata**

Prairie Cord Grass   Zones 5-9

This plant's gracious, drooping habit shows off best when it is massed on a slight incline or at the water's edge. The leaves are wide and so tough they can almost function as cord. Grows rapidly to a height of 4 to 6 feet and is chosen for its graceful leaves—it rarely flowers. The foliage of the popular 'Aureo-marginata' is edged with yellow.

Culture: It spreads rapidly in moist soil. Plant in spring or fall, in masses or groups, in full sun at water's edge. Maintain moisture around the roots.

SPODIOPOGON (spoh-dee-oh-*poe*-gon)

sibiricus

Graybeard Grass, Frost Grass   Zones 5-9

This is a clump-forming, architectural grass with reedlike green foliage that turns reddish then golden as autumn approaches. Stately, upright, purple-tinged spikelets appear in July and August and remain through fall. Mature height is 3 to 4 feet. Good naturalizer for slopes.

Culture: Plant in spring or fall in ordinary, well-drained soil. It thrives in full sun, but handles light shade—prefers moisture but tolerates drought.

STIPA (*stye*-puh) **gigantea**

Giant Feather Grass   Zones 7-9

Graceful and impressive, this is very successful on the West Coast, but more difficult in the East. The foliage clumps reach 24 inches and produce light, feathery panicles that are greenish, then gold, and can reach 7 feet tall. Combines beautifully with *Allium giganteum*.

Culture: Plant in spring in full sun. It is sensitive to excess moisture and must have well-drained soil.

BEST TALL GRASSES

Tall grasses explode upward as the growing season advances. They become positively tropical-looking in summer when their inflorescences catch the light. In fall, they become dried bouquets of gold. They are easy-care substitutes for espaliers on barren walls, and are great for screening. Those recommended here are durable and able to withstand storms. Plant in pairs or groups of 3 where space permits.

ARUNDO (ar-*run*-do) **donax**

Giant Reed   Zones 7-11

Giant Reed has woody stems that develop large leaves like those of corn in a bold, upright clump 7 to 18 feet high. Spreads slowly but steadily to become a massive, long-lived clump. It makes a dependable screen. In warm climates, the stalks are evergreen and last for years, and in late summer big tassels of 12- to 24-inch flowers and seeds rise.

The 5- to 7-foot variegated 'Versicolor', Giant Stripe, or Striped Giant Reed, is hardy only in Zones 7 to 11.

Culture: Cut to the ground annually in cold climates. Plant in spring in rich, moist soil and full sun. Good drainage is essential. Keep the soil surface damp.

CORTADERIA (kor-ta-*deer*-ee-uh) **selloana**

Pampas Grass   Zones 8-11

This is true pampas grass, but the common name often is applied incorrectly to cultivars of miscanthus. The plants show great variations in height—from 5 to 15 feet—and the plumes may be pink or white or gray. Beautiful flowers harvested for dried arrangements.

Recommended cultivars are:

'Pumila', the most desirable, has olive green foliage that forms 4-foot clumps and many dense 6-foot plumes. Hardier than most, it survives normal Zone 7 winters.

'Sunningdale Silver' is the best pure white cultivar. It has large, open plumes from 10 to 12 feet tall above foliage 4 to 5 feet tall.

'Rendatleri' is the best pink cultivar. The foliage height is 6 feet, the inflorescence 8 feet.

'Goldband' is grown for its golden-variegated foliage; about 36 inches tall.

'Silver Comet' has beautiful white-variegated foliage and open, pure white plumes. Very attractive.

Culture: Plant in spring or fall in full sun in ordinary, well-drained soil. Tolerant of soil and moisture.

ERIANTHUS (air-ee-*anth*-us) **ravennae**

Ravenna Grass   Zones 5-9

Imposing. A magnificent plant with arching, silvery leaves from 9 to 12 feet tall and, in late summer, 24-inch silvery purple flowerheads. The forms is an elegant vase shape, best displayed as a specimen. Good substitute for cortaderia in cold climates.

Culture: Plant in spring in full sun. Provide rich soil for optimum growth. Maintain moisture at the roots during growing.

MISCANTHUS (mis-*kanth*-us)

Big, bold plants with broad, grassy, gracefully arching leaves. In late summer or fall, they send silky, silvery plumes soaring above the foliage. Use boldly in big spaces, either in groups or massed.

Culture: Plant spring or fall in full sun in ordinary soil. Prefers moisture at the roots.

M. 'Giganteus' Giant Silver Grass   Zones 5-9

Often sold as *M. floridulus*. This is a tall, arching, wide-leaved, rather coarse species 8 to 12 feet high that fills with silvery light when the wind catches it. It changes form with the seasons—winter blows the leaves away, but the canes remain. In a sunny spot in moist soil, or at the water's edge, it becomes a dense screen. Use as a specimen or plant closely for screening. Blooms in late September in southern regions, infrequently in the North.

M. sacchariflorus   Zones 5-9

Use this spreading, 4- to 6-foot species boldly in big spaces. The tall, silky, silvery tan plumes sway above the foliage in late summer and fall. Plant in groups, or mass in sun or semi-sun by the water's edge.

TOP, LEFT Lovely, cascading *Hakonechloa macra* 'Albo-aurea', handsome with Japanese blood grass. (Viette)

ABOVE Japanese eulia grass, *Miscanthus sinensis*, a very beautiful grass. (Viette)

LEFT Fine, gray-green Oriental fountain grass, *Pennisetum orientale*, bears light-catching flowerheads from May until frost. Drought-tolerant. (Viette)

M. sinensis Eulalia   Zones 5-9

Desirable, versatile, and robust, this species forms a dense, open-upright clump to 8 feet tall and develops slowly into effective screening. The drooping, pale pink to red flower clusters open on panicles up to 12 inches long. Plant in spring in groups, or mass in sun or partial shade.

Recommended cultivars are:

'Variegatus', 4- to 5-foot foliage with white longitudinal stripes. Blooms September to October.

'Cabaret', 5-foot foliage which is a bolder silver than that of the species, and 7-foot flowers. Very choice.

'Cosmopolitan', 5-foot foliage with a new look in wide leaves that have white margins. The flowers reach up to 7 feet. Strong growth habit and a good bloomer.

'Zebrinus' was popular in the Victorian era. It has unusual banding.

'Strictus' is called Porcupine Grass and grows from 6 to 7 feet tall. It has strong banding, narrow leaves and, when young, a more upright growth habit than the species.

'Gracillimus' is the miscanthus most often planted because of its fine foliage and vase shape. The leaves are 5 to 6 feet long, its flowers from 7 to 8 feet tall. Blooms occasionally, and late in the season.

'Morning Light', a variegated form of 'Gracillimus', reaches from 5 to 6 feet tall. The bright silvery midrib and margins create a misty, gray effect.

'Graziella' is upright with a graceful, arching form and, in August, snow white flowers. The height is 5 to 6 feet.

'Malepartus' has horizontally branching leaves. The pink-purplish flowers soar to 7 feet above 5-foot foliage. This is one of the best cultivars.

MOLINIA (moh-*lye*-nee-uh)   **caerulea** subsp. **arundinacea**,

Tall Purple Moor Grass   Zones 5-8

The inflorescence of this subspecies (see species above) soars from 5 to 9 feet above 24- to 36-inch foliage. It is used as a specimen grass with *Aster dumosus, Calluna vulgaris,* and low-growing sedums. 'Skyracer' is one of the tallest cultivars—the flowers reach up to 9 feet. 'Transparent' gets its name from long, airy panicles; the height is 7 feet. 'Windspiel' is 6 to 7 feet tall with narrow, upright, slightly arching stalks.

Best Grasses For Shade

Big and small, these grasses flourish in semishade—some in full shade.

CAREX (kah-*rex*) Sedge

The genus has gracefully arched leaves and usually forms well-defined, neat, rounded clumps. Good for naturalizing under trees.

Culture: Plant in spring. The species here succeed in light shade in ordinary well-drained soil, spread rapidly, and require little attention. Maintain moisture at the roots.

C. buchananii Fox Red Curley Sedge

                                                 Zones 6-10

An upright, wiry sedge, architectural in structure and well-defined—24 to 36 inches high. The foliage is reddish bronze and the blade ends curl at the tips. Beautiful with black Mexican smooth rock. Plant as a specimen or in groups.

C. nigra   Zones 5-9

This lovely, gray-blue sedge raises black inforescences. It is small, to 6 inches high, and neat; a good choice for modular gardens and flower borders. Plant in sun or light shade, wet soil or dry. Like a reed, it spreads rapidly; massed in big spaces, it can take over. Succeeds in wet or dry soil, sun or light shade.

C. hachijoensis (syn. *oshimensis*) **'Evergold'**

                                                 Zones 5-9

Colorful, soft foliage striped with gold. Often seen as edging in California. Height is 12 inches.

C. humilis   Zones 5-9

A grassy clump 6 to 8 inches tall. Well suited for use as a ground cover in naturalized areas of a rock garden. It hugs the ground, holds the soil, and has great charm. Set out in spring or fall, in sun or shade.

C. morrowii 'Variegata' Silver Variegated

Japanese Sedge   Zones 5-9

Forms a pretty, evergreen clump of foliage that is stiff, broad, and leathery; 12 to 24 inches tall. The color is fresh green marked by bright silver stripes down the center and along the margins. Plant in spring or fall in partial to deep shade.

C. muskingumensis Palm Sedge   Zones 4-9

Interesting low-clumping grass from 24 to 36 inches high, upright but arching in a manner reminiscent of the individual leaves of a palm frond. Nicely textured and a good, bright green. The pretty brown seedheads are just a little taller than the leaves. Mass in spring or fall in partial shade. Needs sustained moisture.

C. pendula Drooping Sedge   Zones 5-9

A 36-inch or taller arching, drooping sedge to mass for ground cover where it has lots of space. Very handsome year-round and almost evergreen until late winter, when it browns off. Great quantities of flowers are produced in spring and remain throughout the season. Plant in spring in shade where moisture is assured. Prefers somewhat acid soil, but is versatile.

C. grayi Morning Star Sedge   Zones 4-9

Large, vigorous, clump-forming, "spiked club" fruiting sedge to plant by the edge of the water. The height is 12 to 36 inches.

C. elata 'Bowles Golden'   Zones 5-9

Grown for the luminous effect created by the chartreuse-green margins of the leaves; 24 to 36 inches tall. Thrives in moist soils and even in shallow water.

C. phyllocephala 'Sparkler'   Zones 7-10

A white, variegated sedge from 24 to 36 inches high; reminiscent of *Cyperus papyrus.* A vigorous specimen plant for moist, shaded locations. Nice indoors.

CHASMANTHIUM (chas-*manth*-ee-um)

latifolium (syn. *Uniola latifolia*)

Northern Oats, Wild Oats   Zones 5-9

The fresh green leaves turn bronze in fall; height is 3 to 5 feet. Flat fruits with oatlike heads an inch wide and an inch long are spangled on slender, drooping stems that stand above the foliage and rustle in the breeze. Delightful at the edge of woods. Plant in groups, or mass.

Culture: Set out in spring, in semi-sun, in ordinary soil. Maintain moisture around the roots.

FARGESIA (far-ges-*see*-uh)   **nitida**

(syn. *Sinarundinaria nitida*)

Blue Clump Bamboo   Zones 5-8

Graceful, evergreen bamboo with elegant, arching, purple canes up to ¾ inch thick from which spring small, pointed leaves that are green on one side, bluish on the other. It never needs cutting back and isn't invasive. Mature height is 12 feet. A green-stemmed, clumping species, *F. murielea,* is suited to shade as well as semishade.

Culture: Plant in spring in semishade. Maintain moisture around the roots.

HAKONECHLOA (ha-kun-eh-*clo*-uh)   **macra**

                                                 Zones 4-9

A lovely, cascading, light green grass great for massing in woodlands; 24 inches high. One of the most desirable of all available ornamental grasses is the variegated 'Aureola', a yellow-gold striped with green; 12 to 24 inches tall, this form is hardy only in Zones 5 to 7. The species and cultivar are attractive planted together and with *Imperata cylindrica,* Japanese Blood Grass.

Culture: Plant in spring in semishade in ordinary soil. Maintain moisture around the roots. Difficult in warm climates.

LUZULA (*loo*-zul-ah)   **nivea**

Snowy Wood Rush   Zones 4-9

A delicate grass 24 inches high that grows in low tufts that are topped in spring and early summer by nodding clusters of dainty, white-green flowers on arching stems. It spreads rapidly.

Culture: In spring, plant in groups or mass in ordinary, well-drained soil in semi-sun. Prefers dryish situations and is very tolerant of drought.

Sources: Kurt Bluemel, the founder and president of Kurt Bluemel, Inc., Landscape Design-Construction and Nurseries, in Baldwin, Maryland, helped to introduce the use of ornamental grasses to this country in the 1960s. He is sought after as consultant to the trade and a frequent speaker at colleges, universities, garden clubs, and seminars. Other contributors were Wolfgang Oehme and James van Sweden, of Oehme, van Sweden, Washington, D.C., landscape architects whose names are closely associated with grass gardens.

54. HOSTA

■ Hostas are the outstanding foliage plants for shade. Low, leafy clumps with bold foliage, usually 12 to 30 inches tall, they succeed even in the dim stretches under trees, and are magnificent as edgings and ground covers. Flower stalks appear late in summer covered with sometimes very fragrant bell-like blossoms; in new forms, such as the pure white 'Aphrodite', the flowers can be remarkably beautiful.

For variety of foliage form, hostas are almost unbeatable. Leaves may be broad or tall, narrow or small, smooth-textured, quilted, puckered, or somewhat twisted, and their colors range from rich or muted shades of blue-green to yellow-white. Countless variegations have been developed. There are green leaves with narrow or broad white or gold edges or splotches, and yellow-green leaves with dark green splotchings and edgings.

A massed planting of a single hosta cultivar has sweep and harmony; combinations of contrasting colors and forms create exciting textures. The smaller hostas grow well in large tubs and planters and some are recommended for window boxes.

The American Hosta Society, which publishes a bulletin and newsletter, may be reached through the American Horticultural Society.

Follow-on and Companion Plants: Hostas thrive under crab apples, cherries, and other ornamental fruits; their early flowers protect the hostas from late chills, while the mature summer foliage filters the sun during the hottest season. Lovely also with dogwoods, which bloom as the last of the hostas appear above ground. For follow-on plants, interplant hosta tubers with early bulbs or winter-blooming cyclamen where it is hardy.

HOSTA (hoss-tuh)

Plantain Lily, Daylily

Many of the new hostas, such as 'Aphrodite', merit planting as specimens or backgrounds in flower borders. All have good timing. They unfurl their leaves just as fading bulb foliage needs screening, and they send up 6 inch- to 6-foot-tall, long-lasting lavender, purple, or white flowers in summer and fall when other flowers are finishing. *H. tardiflora* is the last perennial to bloom in autumn.

It takes a hosta plant 3 years to achieve maturity. The older it gets, the more impressive and pleasing it will be. Clumps have been recorded that are 8 feet across but, depending on type, hostas generally range from clumps 30 inches tall by 60 inches wide to little fountains of green 3 by 6 inches wide.

Culture: Hostas do not succeed south of Zone 9, and the larger hostas do not like Zone 8. No hosta is recommended for full sun, but good light improves flowering and some tolerate more sun than others, especially in cooler regions. Ideal light is filtered. The tips of early-flowering hostas push up early; where there are late frosts, these are safer planted under the canopy of trees.

Set out container plants, and divide established clumps, in early spring or early fall. If you are planting rhizomes, do that in early to mid-spring. Set the rhizomes with their tops an inch below the soil surface, in a large hole in rich,

Small hostas in full bloom edge a shaded bed where big hostas and hanging baskets thrive. The miniatures are tidy plants with great charm. (Viette)

well-drained, humusy soil. Even moisture is important, especially in the beginning, but established plants will tolerate drought, wet feet, and neglect.

FOR FRAGRANCE

These are vigorous plants attractive enough to be featured as specimens. The leaves have excellent color and the flowers are larger and more fragrant than those of other hostas. Place near paths or entrances.

H. plantaginea Fragrant Plantain Lily Zones 4-8
The beautiful "August lily" bears strongly fragrant white flowers in late summer. The leaves are heart-shaped, light green, to 10 inches long by 6 inches wide, and form big clumps about 18 inches tall by 30 inches wide. The following varieties are recommended.

TOP, LEFT *Hosta ventricosa* 'Aureo-marginata', hardy blue plantain lily, an eye-catcher. (Klehm)

ABOVE 'Aphrodite', *H. plantaginea*, grown for its beautiful fragrance, flowers mid-August through September. The leaves look like smaller 'Sum and Sub-stance', a spectacular large-leaf hosta. (Viette)

TOP, RIGHT Miniature *H. sieboldii* 'Kabitan' is choice for window boxes and rock gardens. (Viette)

RIGHT *H. undulata* 'Gene's Joy', a new, small-leaf hosta for edging. (Klehm)

'Honeybells' has wavy grass green leaves and, in July and August, fragrant 36-inch lavender-lilac flower spikes.

'Aphrodite' is a new hosta from China with racemes of breathtakingly beautiful, very fragrant, pure white flowers—something like a cross between a lily and a double gardenia. The leaves are large and a glossy green. It flowers in mid-August through September and is about 24 inches high. Zones 5 to 8.

'Summer Fragrance' is a handsome, all-purpose hosta with large, lavender-blue flowers in midsummer. The base is light green to yellow and the leaves are edged with creamy white. Grows rapidly and is pest-resistant. Tolerates half a day in sun.

FOR LARGE LEAVES

Large- and small-leaved hostas are included in this group; all make good ground covers. For commanding attention at a distance, the large hostas are recommended.

H. sieboldiana 'Frances Williams'
('Aureo-marginata') Seersucker Plantain Lily
Zones 3-8

Known also as 'Gold Edge' or 'Golden Circle', the clumps are 24 inches tall by 30 inches wide and the leaves are puckered, very large, rounded, heavy-textured, and blue-green with a gold border that deepens with the season. Very showy next to white flowers. In early summer it bears foliage-height soft lilac flowers. 'Northern Halo' is similar but the edging starts creamy yellow and changes to cream-white.

Other recommended ground covers are:

H. tokudama, closely related to *H. sieboldiana* and perhaps a variety of it, this pretty, diminutive species forms a low, wide clump 18 inches high. Rather slow growing, the leaves are rounded, crinkled, and cup-shaped, and their deep blue-green sets the standard for blue hostas. In early summer it bears lots of white flowers on stems that stand above the leaves. Zones 4 to 8.

'Flavo-circinalis' has heavily puckered leaves and wide, irregular, cream-yellow margins. Zones 4 to 8.

'Great Expectations' and 'Paul's Glory' reverse the variations above; their leaves are gold-centered with irregular blue-green edges. Good background plants.

'Great Expectations', a sport of *H. sieboldiana*, forms a clump 22 inches high by 30 inches wide. The flowers are a mass of white just taller than the foliage.

'August Moon' forms a 24-inch-high clump of large, rounded, crinkled yellow leaves that are prominently veined. The flowers are off-white, to 20 inches tall. Nice planted as contrast with blue hostas.

TALL, LARGE-LEAVED

Very imposing plant used as background in the flower border and to screen the base of tall spring flowers that are fading. Large hostas are better in Zone 7 than 8. The best one is 'Krossa Regal', a popular silvery gray-green type, with crinkly, big, pointed, and upright leaves that expose the blue undersides and stems. The leaves form a vase-shaped clump 30 inches tall by 24 inches wide. In late summer, 4- to 5-foot lilac-blue spires stand 24 inches above the foliage.

MEDIUM-LEAVED

These hostas are suited to the middle border, ideal for edging lawns and as ground cover for small spaces.

H. fortunei 'Aureo-marginata'
Zones 3-8

The heart-shaped green to gray-green leaves have irregular yellow margins and form a clump 18 to 24 inches wide. In summer mauve blossoms stand well above the foliage.

Other recommended medium-leaved hostas are described below.

'Blue Wedgewood' is the fastest-growing of the best blues, a good edger, ground cover, and container plant that forms a clump 18 inches tall by 24 inches wide. The leaves are heavily textured and the pale lavender flowers appear in early summer.

'Francee' is a fast-growing but tidy *fortunei* type 18 inches high by 30 inches wide. It forms a mound of dark green, heart-shaped puckered leaves with narrow, irregular, clear white edges of varying width. The lavender flowers open in mid- to late summer.

'Gold Standard', which may be a cultivar of *H. fortunei*, is another rapid grower. It forms an extensive clump 18 inches high by 30 wide with heart-shaped green leaves edged yellow. Spectacular when mature. Pale lavender flowers in midseason. Tolerates more sun than most hostas.

'Piedmont Gold', one of the best golden hostas, is a rapid grower that forms clumps 18 inches tall by 30 inches wide. White blooms appear in midsummer, and the large golden leaves with no green in them have an attractive twist. Tolerates more sun than most hostas. The gold dulls in deep shade.

H. ventricosa 'Aureo-marginata'
Blue Plantain Lily
Zones 3-8

A magnificent hosta for specimen planting with large, glossy, very dark green, heart-shaped leaves with chartreuse centers and yellow to white broad, irregular margins. It bears dark blue-violet blooms in midseason. To 20 inches tall by 30 inches across.

SMALL-LEAVED

For planting close to the house, the small-leaved types are very appealing; good edgers and specimens for small spaces. Most succeed in Zones 3 to 8.

H. undulata 'Univittata' ('Medio-variegata'), very common and eye-catching with a creamy white center with irregular edges like a candle flame rising, and a demi-twist to the leaves, which form a small mound 10 to 14 inches high. Pretty as flowers.

'Allen P. McConnell', a neat, compact edger, has small, medium-green, ovalish leaves with fine white margins. Grows vigorously.

'Gene's Joy', very new; white-centered leaves with slashing green margins form dense mounds 8 to 12 inches tall by 10 to 14 inches wide. Flowers are blue and come in midsummer.

'Ginko Craig', a dwarf introduction from Japan, is less than 12 inches tall and has light green, lance-shaped leaves edged with a thin band of bright white. The plants flower freely and in summer produce blue-lilac flowers that stand well above the flattened clump of leaves. Rapid grower.

LATE-FLOWERING

Many new introductions in late-flowering types are now appearing. The species described here is a classic form that can be counted on.

H. tardiflora
Zones 4-8

The original October bloomer and often the last perennial to bloom. It is a small plant with lustrous, narrow, lance-shaped leaves in dense clumps 12 inches tall by 12 inches wide. Attractive lavender flowers face in all directions at about foliage height and hold well into fall. Nice in a large container garden.

FOR QUICK COVER

This is a stoloniferous hosta that spreads rapidly and quickly covers the ground; it requires isolation or will become invasive.

H. clausa
Zones 4-8

The plant is 10 inches high with narrow green leaves. It develops from underground shoots 12 inches long or more that quickly spread to make a thick ground cover. Attractive snapdragon-like flowers in midsummer have a reddish purple cast.

FOR WINDOW BOXES

These 2 species are recommended for window box planting. They can stand considerable neglect.

H. nakaiana
Zones 3-8

Fine, durable, textured clump of deep green foliage 6 inches tall by 9 inches wide. The leaves are small and heart-shaped, choice for window boxes. In midsummer plant bears lavender blooms 24 inches tall.

H. sieboldii 'Kabitan'
Zones 3-8

A delightful miniature just 8 inches tall, suited to rock gardens and window boxes. The narrow, lance-shaped, ruffled yellow leaves have a thin dark green edge. In late summer there are 12-inch spikes with soft lavender-purple flowers. Vigorous.

BETWEEN TREE ROOTS

Hostas generally are successful in shaded spaces under trees. This durable species may even be planted between the aggressive roots of a maple tree.

H. lancifolia Narrow-leaved Plantain Lily
Zones 3-8

The shiny, narrow, lance-shaped green leaves form low, dense clumps 12 inches high by 12 to 24 inches wide. The flowers are blue-lavender on stems 24 inches tall, and appear in late August and September. Better soil will give quicker growth.

SOURCE: ALEX SUMMERS, A RETIRED PROFESSIONAL GARDENER, FOUNDED THE AMERICAN HOSTA SOCIETY AND WAS ITS PRESIDENT FOR 10 YEARS. MORE THAN 1,000 HOSTA SPECIES AND CULTIVARS THRIVE IN HIS 4-ACRE GARDEN.

55. EASY ALPINE PLANTS

■ Alpine plants are collectors' items, low-growing, rock-hugging natives of high mountains where big winds blow and the streams run cold and clear. Collectors grow them in rock gardens that evoke their natural habitats. Granite, sandstone, and limestone or dolomite stones are used to provide varying degrees of acidity and density. Blends of chips from these stones combined with peat, soil, and a little fertilizer fill the planting pockets.

Culture: The soil mixture and moisture are vital to the success of these plants, which tend to be finicky outside their native environment. Advanced growers create a scree or moraine to meet the needs of their chosen plants. Scree is the loose, deep layer of rock chips and humusy rubble that collects below the face of a mountain cliff, and plants growing there depend on surface water. The accumulation of small stones and grit pushed up by a glacier is moraine. In the garden a moraine is constructed so it can be watered from below to simulate a melting glacier.

Alpine plants also are grown in clay pots set in gravel or coarse sand in troughs sheltered inside an "alpine house," a low-roofed, cool greenhouse.

The mountain plants recommended in this list are among the easiest to grow—good "beginner" plants for an alpine collection. All will do fairly well in ordinary rock gardens providing soil and moisture are right.

ALCHEMILLA alpina, Alpine Lady's-mantle. Low, neat plant grown in borders and rock gardens for the handsome, deeply divided, silver-edged leaves. In spring there are sprays of small yellow-green flowers. For culture, see list 75, Herbs with Showy Flowers.

ANACYCLUS (ann-ass-*sye*-klus) **depressus**
Zones 6-7
Low, mat-forming, trailing plant 1 to 2 inches high with flat rosettes of gray-green leaves. In summer it bears sparkling, yellow-centered, daisylike flowers with a crimson reverse. The flowers tend to close under gray skies.

Culture: Sow seed in fall or plant root divisions in early spring in full sun in very well-drained, deep, gravelly alkaline soil. A covering of loose evergreen boughs helps the plants through freezing winters.

ANDROSACE (an-*dross*-a-see)
Rock Jasmine
Tufted, cushion-forming little plants with small rosettes of pointed leaves that have hairy margins. A pretty, challenging genus; the species recommended below are the easiest.

Culture: Sow fresh seed in fall or set out container plants in early spring; plants require full sun in the North, afternoon shade in warmer regions. Difficult where summer temperatures go over 90° F. Provide very well-drained, sandy or gritty soil that includes stone chips but is humusy enough to hold sustained moisture during warm weather. Must not get too wet in winter.

Inula ensifolia covers itself with blooms in late summer. In a perennial border, it will be taller than its normal 12 inches. The low alpine plants come from rocky soil and high, windy places above the timberline. (Harper)

A. carnea   Zones 4-7
About 1 to 2 inches high, in spring it lifts 2 or more loose umbels of pink or white flowers another inch or two above each leafy rosette. Pretty, self-sows, and spreads if growing in a very well-drained, gritty, moist scree soil with neutral to slightly acid pH. Suitable for a trough in an alpine house or a rock garden.

A. sarmentosa   Zones 4-7
Evergreen, very attractive, 1½ to 4 inches high with small, hairy rosettes of leaves; in spring, showy, flat, bright pink flowers with yellow eyes appear on stems 6 to 8 inches tall. Good rock garden plant, but must not dry out in summer or face soggy, wet soil.

ANEMONE pulsatilla (syn. *Pulsatilla vulgaris*)
Pasque-flower   Zones 5-7
First class. A very early anemone about 12 inches high with nodding blue, purple, or reddish flowers with bright yellow centers, followed by feathery seeds. The plants are tufted, with delicate light green leaves. Easy to grow and attractive in rock gardens. The early *A. blanda* is a another anemone for the rock garden, see list 1, Early Spring, Specialty Bulbs.

Culture: Sow fresh seeds as soon as they ripen in full sun and well-drained but rich, humusy soil. Self-sows.

ARABIS (*ar*-ab-iss)
Rock Cress
Wonderful evergreen, gray-green tufted mats ideal for spilling over the top of a rock wall, in crevices, in rock gardens, or naturalized on rocky slopes. Covered in spring with masses of small, sweet-scented white flowers. There are also rose pink cultivars.

Culture: Sow fresh seed or plant root divisions in early autumn. Gritty, well-drained soil and full sun are essential.

A. caucasica (syn. *A. albida*) Wall Rock Cress
Zones 4-8
Loose, hairy mat with succulent leaves 8 to 12 inches high and in early spring masses of little spires of bright white flowers. Cut back heavily after blooming to maintain full foliage. Plan to divide every 2 to 3 years.

A. blepharophylla   Zones 6-9
The purplish pink flowers appear in spring on stems 6 to 12 inches tall above flat rosettes of dark green leaves. Rather susceptible to frost and best mulched over winter. Popular in California.

A. sturii   Zones 4/5-9
A fine ground cover 2 to 4 inches high with glossy foliage, it spreads on creeping stolons. The white flowers are large in proportion to the plant. Showy in small spaces.

ARENARIA (ar-ren-*nay*-ree-uh) **tetraquetra**
Zones 3-5
Cushion-forming, tufted creeper tiny enough to pass for moss except in late spring when it is covered with white flowers on 2-inch stems. Good for the narrowest crevices, between stepping-stones, and for a trough in an alpine house.

Culture: Sow seed in fall or spring, or set out root divisions in summer in full sun and well-drained, deep, loose, gritty soil with lots of rock chips and enough humus to hold moisture consistently. Not successful where summers are hot and humid.

RIGHT Trailing alpine, *Anacyclus depressus*, only an inch or two high. (Harper)

BELOW *Arabis* species thrive in rocky, difficult situations and in spring are covered with sweet-scented white or rose-pink flowers. (McDonald)

BOTTOM Edelweiss, whose enduring presence in harsh circumstances inspired a song, is *Leontopodium alpinum*, from the high Swiss Alps. (Harper)

ERYSIMUM (ee-*riss*-im-um) **kotschyanum**
Zones 6-9

Evergreen, 3 to 4 inches high, with rather grassy leaves and, in spring, clusters of fragrant, bright yellow flowers, similar to wallflowers, *Cheiranthus.*

Culture: Sow the fast-sprouting seeds in early spring or set out root divisions in full sun or partial shade in well-drained, gritty limestone soil or rocky crevices. Tolerates some drought.

FESTUCA, Fescue. Tufts of these colorful ornamental grasses embellish alpine gardens as well as rock gardens with fine, wiry leaves that sometimes are rolled. The flowers are green-white or purplish—like a lawn gone to seed. *F. glaciales,* hardy to Zone 5, is 2 inches high by 10 inches wide, with icy, blue-green foliage. *F. ovina* var. *glauca,* Blue Fescue, is a very pretty tufted grass about 10 inches tall, with bright silvery blue leaves, hardy to Zone 4 or 5. For culture, see list 53, Ornamental Grasses.

GENTIANA **scabra.** Charming little plant that covers itself with remarkably blue flowers in October and November. An easy gentian from Japan, it comes in several sizes up to 12 inches tall. Thrives in rock gardens, rock walls and stony crevices, and scree beds. For rock gardens the form *saxatilis* is particularly desirable. For culture, see list 45, Rock Walls and Crevices.

GLOBULARIA (glob-yew-*lay*-ree-uh)
cordifolia   Zones 8-9

One of the easiest of the genus, a cushion-forming, evergreen subshrub about 4 inches high, with heart-shaped leaves and, in spring, flowers like little lavender-blue buttons. Delightful in alpine collections and rock gardens, and sometimes used as a ground cover in warm regions.

Culture: In midsummer to autumn sow fresh seed or set out root divisions in full sun in well-drained, humusy soil. Many other species are scalded in winter sun but this one withstands it.

HYPERICUM (hye-*pehr*-ik-um) olympium
                                               Zones 6-8

A thick subshrub just 6 to 12 inches high. All summer it bears masses of big silky, buttercup yellow flowers like single roses with long stamens. Excellent for rocky slopes since it grows and blooms all season in poor soil and most dry, sun-baked locations.

Culture: In early fall, sow fresh seeds or set out container plants in full or semi-sun, in very well-drained soil that is gravelly. Early spring mowing or shearing encourages masses of blooms. It self-sows sparingly, so there are always some plants around.

IBERIS   saxatilis. Low-growing, spreading, narrow-leaved evergreen plant that for most of the spring covers itself with upright, bright white flowers. Valuable ground cover in rock and wall gardens and as edging for spring borders. This species is just 3 to 6 inches tall and exceptionally hardy. For culture, see list 43, Flowers for Edging.

INULA (*in*-yew-luh)   ensifolia
                                               Zones 4-9

A clump-forming, full-flowered plant about 12 inches tall (taller in a perennial bed) that in late summer bears daisylike, bright yellow flowers 1 to 2 inches across. Nice background plant for a low border.

Culture: Sow seeds or plant root divisions spring or fall in full sun, in well-drained soil. This perennial blooms the first season from an early spring sowing.

LEONTOPODIUM (lee-on-toh-*poh*-dee-um)
alpinum Edelweiss   Zones 4-9

Easy to grow conversation piece, this is the small wildflower found in the Swiss Alps and celebrated by the song named for it. The plant is a low rosette of off-white, 6-inch-long leaves topped in early summer by 8-inch flowering stems with petal-like bracts—all covered with fine woolly hair, like flannel. Keeps well when dried.

Culture: In the average lowland garden it will require replanting every year. Sow seeds in late summer or set out root divisions in early spring, in full sun, in well-drained, deep, gritty, dry soil with space for long roots.

LEWISIA (lew-*iss*-ee-uh)   cotyledon
                                               Zones 6-8

Low rosettes of thick evergreen leaves that in early summer send up 6-inch-high stems bearing pink flowers with red stripes—like small water lilies. Fussy outside its native Northwest, but a true beauty.

Culture: Sow seeds in fall or plant root divisions in early spring. Easily grown in a north-facing crevice or wall in full sun and soil that is perfectly drained, coarse, and gritty but contains generous amounts of humus. Prefers to be moist in spring and dry in summer.

SAPONARIA   ocymoides. This spreading mat of delicate stems and small leaves sends up 3- to 6-inch sprays of pink to purple flowers from mid-spring to late summer. There are several forms, including white, all easy to grow and long-lived. An excellent plant. For culture, see list 66, The Rock Garden.

SOLIDAGO   spathulata var. nana, is a 6-inch-high goldenrod, found in the western mountains, that blooms for a long period beginning in midsummer. It is easy to grow, self-sows, and is somewhat weedy but controllable. For culture, see list 64, The Meadow Garden.

TALINUM (tal-*lye*-num)
Fameflower

Small, fleshy plants often seen in rock gardens, with waxy bright green leaves covered for a long period in summer with soft panicles of short-lived pink flowers.

Culture: Starts easily from seed sown indoors or outdoors in full sun after the ground has warmed, in well-drained, gritty soil where it is to grow. Add enough humus to sustain moisture. Or, sow seed outdoors in fall. Talinum grows wild in this country, self-sowing freely in good soil even after 4 or 5 years in the ground.

T. calycinum   Zones 6-8

A fleshy little plant 8 inches high with pink flowers in season; used in alpine houses and rock gardens.

T. paniculatum Jewels-of-Opar, Fameflower
                                            Tender Perennial

A prolific self-sower to 24 inches high with waxy, succulent, bright green leaves that sends up airy panicles of pink flowers in summer, followed by burgundy-colored seedpods. It blooms profusely in June and is popular for the rock garden.

SOURCE: NOCKOLAS NICKOU, M.D., IS A TALENTED GARDENER WHOSE TWO THIRTY-YEAR-OLD ROCK GARDENS HAVE BENEFITED FROM COLLECTING TRIPS TO ICELAND, GREENLAND, THE HIMALAYAS, CHINA, NEW ZEALAND, AUSTRALIA, TURKEY, THE ALPS, THE CANADIAN AND U.S. ROCKIES, SOUTH AFRICA, AND OTHER PLACES.

56. DRY, HOT CONDITIONS

■ These are some of the best plants for gardens in situations that bake and dry out and probably will be neglected in summer—urban gardens and hot downtown locations. There are large and small flowers, some for fragrance and cutting, low-growers to carpet bare corners, and spectacular plants to use as specimens.

Other drought-tolerant perennials to seek out are plants with fleshy stems and leaves, those with gray or silvery leaves, ornamental grasses, and members of the pea family.

A number of cultural practices are especially helpful in hot, dry sites. Arrange soil levels to retain as much rainwater as possible and prevent runoff; for instance, terrace sloping areas and create saucers in the earth or mulch around the base of plants to keep moisture in the area of the roots. Improve soil as described in Growing Flowers. Provide permanent mulches in summer. Water deeply but infrequently, as suggested in Growing Flowers, to encourage plant roots to go deeper into the soil. Use fertilizers very sparingly.

Companion Plants: Many herbs come from the dry, hot regions of the Mediterranean and make good companions—see lists 73 through 77.

Related lists are 57, Seashore and Sandy Soils, and 58, Urban Conditions.

ACHILLEA 'Moonshine'. Drought-resistant plant 12 to 24 inches tall whose handsome, flat, lemon yellow flowers stand well above the ferny, silvery green foliage in spring and summer. Succeeds by the seashore. Similar to the popular 'Coronation Gold', but shorter and lighter in color. Both flourish in dry, hot situations and have the same cultural requirements. See list 15, Summer Perennials for Sun.

ALLIUM   senescens 'Glaucum'. Also called curly chives. This is one of the ornamental onions that flower in spring and summer bearing attractive round flowerheads above grassy leaves. Durable if well fertilized and moisture is maintained in early spring. 'Glaucum' (or variety *glaucum*) bears a showy little lavender-pink flower ideal for the rock garden in late summer. Mature height is 8 inches. The species itself is attractive and, though hard to find, worth the effort. Plant in fall or spring in large groups with the bulbs set 6 inches apart. For culture and other recommended ornamental onions, see list 3, Spring, Large-flowered Bulbs.

ARTEMISIA   schmidtiana 'Silver Mound'. The sagebrushes (mugworts) are very useful, mostly drought-resistant herbs with small flowers. The very fine foliage makes a silky, silvery mound 12 by 18 inches wide. In summer, inconspicuous, drooping, yellow flowers appear. See list 51, Foliage for Color, and 73, Herbs with Colorful Foliage.

Thoughtful plantings of heat- and drought-resistant sedums, cacti, and marigolds make a dramatic statement about beauty in an arid place—and where neglect is likely. (American Horticultural Society)

BAPTISIA australis, Blue False Indigo, Plains False Indigo, Wild Blue Indigo. A tall, vigorous plant that produces masses of pretty gray-green foliage in spring, followed in early summer by spikes of pea-like, indigo blue flowers. They are used in arrangements, as are the attractive black seedpods that develop later. Interesting in winter. Mature height, 3 to 4 feet. See list 13, Spring Perennials for Sun.

COREOPSIS verticillata. 'Moonbeam' is one of the most popular perennials and one of the very best for the front of the border. It has eye-catching pale yellow flowers and lovely threadleaf foliage, and is long-lived and long-flowering. It is about 18 inches tall and excellent for dry, hot situations. See list 15, Summer Perennials for Sun.

DIANTHUS gratianopolitanus, Cheddar Pink. Pretty, fragrant little 1- or 1½-inch miniature pink or rose carnations, 2 or 3 to a stem, flower in summer in mounds of grassy gray-green foliage 6 to 9 or 12 inches high. Charming in rock gardens and for edging walks, and almost indestructible even in the hot South. 'Tiny Rubies' is a superior, rich pink, double-flowered form about 4 inches high. For culture, see list 70, The Fragrance Garden.

ERYNGIUM (ee-*rinj*-ee-um) amethystinum Amethyst Sea-holly   Zones 2-8
In summer this very cold-hardy, sea green, thistlelike plant with colorful stems produces heads of small blue flowers surrounded by long, spiky, darker blue bracts. About 18 to 24 inches tall and handsome in groups of 3 to 5 in a big border. Exceptional with soft pink or yellow flowers, and excellent for drying.

Culture: In early spring, separate and set out the plantlets that develop at the base. Or, plant root divisions in full sun, in dry, sandy soil.

HELICTOTRICHON sempervirens, Blue Oat Grass. An excellent little ornamental grass that, unlike others, should never be cut down. It has semievergreen, gray-blue leaves that grow in 24-inch puffs. In early summer, delicate, oatlike flowers sway high above the foliage; they remain through winter. For this and other drought-tolerant ornamental grasses, see list 53, Ornamental Grasses.

RUDBECKIA fulgida var. sullivantii 'Goldsturm', Coneflower. Finest of the yellow black-eyed Susans, this one blooms freely through midsummer into fall on compact, bushy plants 18 to 30 inches high. The ray florets are deep yellow and the cone-shaped centers are bronze-black. Blooms for 2 to 3 months, self-sows aggressively, and is a good perennializer for wild places. Tolerates light shade and is nice in a large grouping in the middle of the border. For culture, see list 15, Summer Perennials for Sun.

SALVIA × superba cultivars. A blue sage that comes into flower early and goes on into fall bearing showy, violet-blue flower spikes on plants 18 to 24 inches tall. Notably drought-resistant are 'Blue Queen', an intense violet; 'East Friesland' ('Ostfriesland'), deep purple; and 'May Night' ('Mainacht'), deep indigo. A staple for durable blue color, indispensable with roses. Lasts well as a cut flower. See list 41, *Salvia*.

SEDUM (*seed*-um)
Stonecrop
Indestructible, heat- and drought-resistant, and sometimes invasive (*S. acre* in particular) herbaceous perennials 2 to 15 inches tall. The many forms are valued for their pretty, evergreen, succulent-like, light green foliage and, in some important hybrids, beautiful autumn color. The flowers are tiny and star-shaped, yellow or pink-red, quite modest in ground-hugging species, but become showy flowerheads in taller forms. The ground huggers are used in rock gardens, for filling nooks, crannies, and pockets in rocks and walls, and by steps. The taller types are indispensable in perennialized plantings and a treasured addition to gardens of ornamental grasses. Sedums are recommended on many lists including 15, 45, 46, 57, 67, 72, and as companion or follow-on plants.

Culture: Withstands heat and drought, even in sand and by the sea. Some self-sow, some volunteer, some perennialize easily. Sedums flourish in full sun north of Zone 6, but prefer afternoon shade in the warm South, where they are at their best during cool weather. They grow readily from root divisions set out in early spring or late summer, in well-drained soil. Prefer average moisture during growth period, somewhat dry soil later. Divide clumps every 3 or 4 years.

S. acre 'Aureum' Golden-carpet, Gold Moss
Zones 4-9

A somewhat weedy but useful little mat 1 to 2 inches high, with tiny, fleshy light green leaves edged with gold in spring. Clusters of tiny yellow flowers appear in late spring or early summer. Less invasive than the species, 'Aureum' spreads rapidly and, in late spring and early summer, covers itself with yellow florets. Plant it between stones, to spill over the edge of a wall, and in places where little else grows.

S. 'Autumn Joy' Zones 3-10

One of the most valuable flowers for fall—the fresh spring show of gray-green foliage 18 to 24 inches high is followed by fresh apple green flowerheads in early summer, slowly changing to rich pink, then rose to salmon-bronze and, finally, with the cold, to rosy russet. Indispensable with ornamental grasses and in perennialized plantings. Prefers dry soil but tolerates moisture.

S. kamtschaticum subsp. middendorfianum
Zones 3-8

Recommended for rock gardens and filling pockets in walls, for steps, and for autumn color. The plants are 4 to 9 inches tall with grooved leaves and unbranched, pale green stems topped in summer by flat little yellow florets.

S. 'Ruby Glow' Zones 3-8

A beautiful autumn flower almost as popular as 'Autumn Joy', but slightly smaller—12 inches tall—that bears iridescent ruby red flowers.

Outstanding performers in dry sites: TOP, LEFT *Eryngium yuccifolia*, colorful sea holly. (Viette) ABOVE *Sedum* 'Autumn Joy', fall, at River Farm. (McDonald) RIGHT Large, ornate flowers of *Eryngium giganteum*. (Viette) BOTTOM Trailing *Sedum sieboldii*, October Plant, whose blooms turn bright pink in fall. (Viette)

S. sediforme (syn. *nicaeense*)   Zones 9-11
A small succulent, 6 inches high, with attractive foliage; often used as ground cover in sandy places. Bears cream-colored flowers in August and is very tolerant of heat and drought.

S. sieboldii October Daphne, October Plant
                                              Zones 5/6-9
A trailer 6 to 9 inches long that has bluish green leaves with faint reddish margins, excellent for filling corners and for autumn color. It bears flat flowerheads in late summer that turn bright pink in fall. Tolerates light shade.

S. spectabile   Zones 3-11
Trouble-free, 18 to 24 inches tall, with large fleshy leaves. Tiny heart-shaped flowers form a dense, flat-topped flowerhead in late summer and fall. Easy to grow in containers and thrives in sun or shade.

S. spurium   Zones 3-8
A rapidly spreading ground cover and rock garden creeper 2 to 6 inches tall. In summer it bears showy white to rose flowers on stems 4 inches high. Good cover for stony or unsightly patches of packed, sandy dirt. The popular 'Dragon's Blood' ('Splendens') bears dark red, starry flowers in spring and summer, and the foliage turns wine-red-bronze by summer's end. Not successful in the South. The flowers of the similar 'Bronze Carpet' are pink, and the foliage turns bronze in late summer to early autumn.

S. 'Vera Jameson'   Zones 3-10
Small, 9 to 12 inches tall, with darkish leaves and 2- to 4-inch-wide flowerheads, it colors a pleasant rose pink in fall. One of the best for hot sun.

STACHYS byzantina, Woolly Betony, Lamb's-ears. The big, semievergreen gray leaves, 12 to 15 inches long, are almost luminous in moonlight and so woolly they invite stroking—a wonderful contrast in color, outstanding texture, perfect in tussie-mussies and wreaths. From midsummer until frost, they are topped by small, usually violet or white, flowers. Prettiest foliage is found on the nonflowering, 8-inch-high 'Silver Carpet'. See list 50, Foliage for Form and Texture.

YUCCA. Very drought resistant and exotic. Grown for its huge evergreen rosettes of silvery sword-shaped leaves and secondarily for its astonishing flower spikes. In early summer, these long-lasting, 4- to 6-foot woody stems rise up and unfold big bell-shaped flowers, white or flushed with purple or violet on the outside. *Y. filamentosa* 'Bright Edge', Adam's-needle, is a magnificent, stylized plant to feature in contemporary settings; 1- by 15-inch gold-edged leaves edged with shaggy threads. The flower stem reaches 5 feet and bears creamy white blooms. *Y. glauca*, Soapweed, has narrow, white-edged, gray-green leaves 36 inches long and ½ inch wide. The flowers are greenish white on a 36-inch spike. See list 57, Seashore and Sandy Soils.

SOURCES: MARY ANN AND FRED MCGOURTY, OWNERS OF HILLSIDE GARDENS, NORFOLK, CONNECTICUT, SPECIALIZE IN UNCOMMON PERENNIALS AND GARDEN DESIGN.

57. *SEASHORE AND SANDY SOILS*

■ **Of the 459 plants tested by Andre Viette Farm and Nursery in Zones 7 to 8 over a five-year period both at the shore and 600 feet from the ocean, those recommended here gave the best performance. They were grown in pure sand with Osmocote and fertilized once yearly. The plantings were deeply watered three times each month from June through October, but not at all from November through May. Among them are plants for every purpose—ground covers, edgers, herbs, showy flowers, and many that last well when cut.**

The seashore is not a standard environment. There are varying intensities of saltiness, light, sand in the soil, and wind. It is the wind that carries the salt spray, dries the soil, and shifts the sand around. A new garden at the seashore begins with the establishment of durable plants that will survive the wind and perennialize. The best way to reclaim the land is to multiply what already is thriving.

Companion Plants: Herbs, and many plants on list 53, Ornamental Grasses, are excellent in sandy soils; among them are *Elymus glaucus* (Blue Wild Rye), *Phragmites australis* (Reed), *Uniola paniculata* (Sea Oats), and *Ammophila* (Beach Grass). Behind this barrier, dig humus into the soil to improve its moisture retention and set out the garden's foundation plants—American holly, amelanchier, sourgum, Eastern cedar, *Viburnum dentatum*, and the perennials described below are recommended.

Add annuals for quick color. Tolerant of sandy soils and salt spray are calendula, coreopsis, cornflower, cosmos, cottage pinks, globe amaranth, marigolds, annual phlox, and verbena. Many popular herbs such as thyme and oregano, which are native to the Mediterranean, thrive in somewhat dry soils and high heat.

ACHILLEA, Yarrow. This marvellously durable plant is resistant to sun, drought, and heat, grows exuberantly to heights from 8 to 36 inches, and is especially useful for early and midsummer color. It develops excellent, ferny foliage before flowering and retains it afterward. The showy yellow, gold, pink, or white flowers are borne in branching, flat-topped heads (corymbs) several inches across, and they last well as cut flowers. The yellows are among the best of all flowers for dried arrangements and wreaths. Recommended for sandy places and by the sea are *A. filipendulina*, Fern-leaved Yarrow, which has deeply divided silvery foliage and beautiful mustard-yellow flowers; the big-flowered, deep gold 'Coronation Gold', 36 inches tall, and 'Moonshine', 12 to 24 inches tall; *A. millefolium*, Yarrow, Millfoil, and 'Cerise Queen', 'Paprika', spicy rose-red, 'Fire King', deep rose-red, and 'Hoffnuny', pale yellow flowers with peach overtones. See list 15, Summer Perennials for sun.

AMSONIA tabernaemontana, Bluestar. This is a slow-growing, easy-care native perennial that forms clumps 12 to 36 inches tall. It bears drooping or upright clusters of persistent small truly blue flowers for several weeks in late spring. Pods follow the flowers and are attractive in arrangements. The willowlike foliage sways with every breeze, remains green and lush all season, and turns a striking yellow-gold in fall. Pruning after the flowers fade helps maintain the foliage. For culture, see list 13, Spring Perennials for Sun.

ANEMONE hupehensis, Japanese Anemone, is a wonderful tall species, 12 to 36 inches high, that blooms for several weeks in July and early August, earlier than most fall-flowering anemones, bearing quantities of single, pink, 2- to 3-inch flowers. The plant forms dense clumps of attractive, rather coarse compound leaves that are effective throughout the growing season. An excellent low-maintenance perennial for sandy gardens with shade, and it tolerates more sun than most autumn anemones. See list 17, Summer-into-fall Perennials.

ARTEMISIA, Artemisia. This is the best group of perennials to bring season-long silver or gray foliage to a mixed border. The effect almost equals that of a mass of white flowers—exquisite next to shades of pink, purple, and light blue. The silver unifies discordant color combinations and lightens the border when nothing else is in bloom. The small flowers are sweet, but not a factor. Recommended for sandy places are *A. ludoviciana* var. *albula*, Silver-king Artemisia, 'Silver King', 36 inches tall, and 'Silver Queen', 24 inches tall; and *A. schmidtiana*, 'Silver Mound', a dwarf 12 inches high. See list 51, Foliage for Color.

CERASTIUM (ser-*rass*-tee-um) **tomentosum**
Snow-in-summer   Zones 2/3-7
A mat of low-growing, silvery gray leaves 6 to 8 inches tall that, in late spring and early summer, is covered with dainty white flowers. Charming in a rock garden and a pretty ground cover for small spaces.

Culture: It is an aggressive spreader in well-drained, rich soil, but it fails in hot, humid climates. Set out divisions in early spring, in full sun in cool regions, partial shade in warmer areas. Grows well in pure sand.

CERATOSTIGMA plumbaginoides, Blue Ceratostigma, Plumbago. A pretty foliage plant that spreads vigorously under good conditions, forming 6- to 8- or 12-inch-high mats of almost evergreen, glossy, dark green leaves. From midsummer to frost, electric purple-blue flowers appear, then, with the cold, the foliage turns bronzy red—in California, almost red. Excellent as a ground cover, an edger, or in rock and wall gardens. Listed in some catalogs as *Plumbago larpentae*. See list 51, Foliage for Color.

CHRYSOPSIS (kriss-**op**-siss) **'Golden Sunshine'**
Golden Aster   Zones 5-9
A handsome cultivar 3 to 4 feet tall of a big, broad, native species that from summer to frost bears masses of 2-inch-wide, sunny yellow, daisy-faced flowers. Good choice for the wild garden.

Culture: Plant seeds or root divisions in spring or fall, in full sun, in ordinary soil. Thrives in dry, sandy soils and tolerates drought. Cut back to the ground after frost. May be divided after 2 or 3 years.

Drought-tolerant *Achillea* in pinks combined with the foliage of silvery Scotch thistle make a garden even in sand. (Viette)

CHRYSANTHEMUM (kriss-*anth*-em-um)
The fall-blooming species mums recommended here have daisy flowers and perennialize for at least 3 years, even in sandy soils. The potted cushion mums sold by the thousands for fall color will do well in sandy locations and are usually grown as annuals. For recommendations, see list 23, Mum—Daisy.

Culture: Plant root divisions in early spring in full sun, in well-drained soil or raised beds. Chrysanthemums tolerate sandy situations with annual additions of humus as long as the soil is slightly acid, about pH 6.5. Some sustained moisture is necessary. An inch of rain or hose water each week should be enough.

C. pacificum   Zones 5-9
Ground cover with nice little green leaves edged thinly with silver on 12-inch plants. It spreads rapidly to make a 3½-foot mat and bears very small, tansy-like flowers in October. Introduced recently from Japan by the National Arboretum.

C. weyrichii   Zones 4-9
Small, blooms in late fall, and spreads by underground stolons. 'White Bomb' and 'Pink Bomb' bear 1- to 2-inch single flowers above shiny green leaves on plants 14 or 16 to 18 inches tall.

COREOPSIS   lanceolata, Tickseed. Excellent. Sunny, long-lasting, and trouble-free; covers itself with fluffy, pretty 2½-inch yellow flowers in late spring or summer, according to region, on plants 12 to 24 inches tall. The deeply cut foliage, light or somewhat coarse, is attractive. See list 15, Summer Perennials for Sun.

EUPHORBIA (yew-*forb*-ee-uh)
Spurge
The genus includes widely differing plants—for instance, poinsettias *(Euphorbia pulcherrima)* and the cactuslike Crown-of-thorns. All contain a milky juice that can cause allergies, but generally have different cultural needs. The look-alike species here are useful ground covers and rock garden plants that have colorful, flowerlike bracts in spring. See also list 71, The Cutting Garden.

Culture: Plant divisions in spring, in well-drained soil, in full sun. Tolerates drought and some shade in the warm South. Self-sows.

E. epithymoides (syn. *polychroma*) Zones 5-9
Bushy clumps of stems about 15 to 18 inches high, packed with narrow leaves and topped all spring with long-lasting, bright yellow bracts. The leaves turn reddish in fall. Best with afternoon shade in the warm South.

E. myrsinites   Zones 5-9
Prostrate evergreen plant with fleshy, blue-gray-green leaves that grow in attractive spirals up the woody 8- to 10-inch stems. Displays colorful 2- to 4-inch yellow bracts over a long period in spring. Good cutting flower. Tolerates heat.

GAURA (gow-ruh) **lindheimeri**   Zones 5-9
A graceful, bushy perennial that blooms from May to October. The plant is 4 feet tall, with hairy, gray-green, willowlike leaves. Long-blooming, loose panicles of pink buds open to 1-inch tubular, pink-tinted white flowers. Good perennializer.

Enduring color for sandy sites:
TOP, LEFT Russian sage, *Perovskia atriplicifolia*. (Viette)
TOP, RIGHT Dwarf balloon flower, *Platycodon grandiflorus*. (Harper)
LEFT *Chrysopsis* 'Golden Sunshine'. (Viette)
ABOVE Sea lavender, *Limonium latifolium*. (Viette)

Flower spikes of red-hot-poker, *Knifovia uvaria*, are yellow where early-blooming florets are aging; red where new florets are just opening. The sword-shaped gray-green, semi- or evergreen foliage is attractive when new. Lasts well when cut. (McDonald)

Culture: Sow seeds or plant divisions in early spring, either in full sun or partial sun, in rich, light, very well-drained, even sandy soil. Tolerates a great deal of drought, heat, and humidity. Deadhead to keep flowers coming, and in midsummer the second year, cut back to 8 to 10 inches to improve growth.

HEMEROCALLIS, Daylilies. Modern daylilies anchor the perennial garden through midsummer with handsome lilylike flowers in intense colors; they're easy to grow and long lasting. Whether 4- to 5-foot giants with huge 8-inch flowers or 8- to 12-inch dwarfs with 1-inch blooms, all offer a brilliant, nonstop show for 3 to 4 weeks, and some rebloom in late fall. Some daylilies are fragrant. A bonus is daylily foliage—as the plants grow the strap-shaped leaves fountain up, screening the yellowing remains of spring bulbs. See list 24, Daylily.

IRIS, Tall Bearded. These magnificent flowers are among the most important of spring bloomers, huge blossoms that often are ruffled or veined or laced with other colors. The "beard" is a fuzz of filaments. Straight strong stems from 28 to 40 inches tall fork to show several buds. They last well as cut flowers, and are wonderful perennialized in groups of 3 to 5 in a small garden or 10 or 12 in a large garden. The sword-shaped leaves remain crisp through summer, a fine asset at the middle or back of the border. In southern states, the beardeds bloom in mid-March to mid-May; In the North, late April to late May.

Some are "rebloomers" and bloom again in summer, fall, or winter in milder regions. See the discussion on list 25, *Iris*.

KNIPHOFIA (nip-*hoh*-fee-uh) **uvaria** (syn. *Tritoma uvaria*)
Poker Plant, Torch Flower, Red-hot-poker
Zones 6-9

In late spring and summer these bold flower spikes, several per plant, stand straight as a poker on plants from 18 to 36 inches tall. The "pokers" are yellow at the bottom, where early-blooming florets are aging, and red at the top, where new florets are just opening. The sword-shaped, gray-green, semievergreen or evergreen foliage is attractive when new. Lasts well when cut. There are several good poker plants, including 'Springtime', coral with muted yellow.

Culture: In cooler regions set it out in early spring in very well-drained or sandy soil and full sun. In warm regions, plant in fall, in semi-sun. Deadhead consistently and, when the blooms fade, trim the plants back by half to get rid of some of the unsightly foliage.

LIMONIUM (lim-*moh*-nee-um) **latifolium**
Sea Lavender
Zones 3-9

A cloud of tiny lavender flowers blooms on up to a dozen delicately branched stems—if baby's-breath were lavender it would look like this. The foliage is wide and low-lying on

plants from 24 to 30 inches tall. Superb cut flower in fresh or dried arrangements, 'Violetta' is an outstanding 18-inch violet-blue that flowers in July and August.

Culture: An easy plant. Sow seeds indoors in March and transplant in May, or sow seeds outdoors in April or when the ground has dried, and thin seedlings to stand 18 inches apart. Prefers full sun and ordinary, well-drained, somewhat acid soil. Tolerates drought and, in the South, semi-sun.

LINUM **perenne**, Perennial Flax. Attactive perennial 12 to 18 inches tall that blooms the first year from seed. The blossoms are an arresting shade of sky blue, and flower from early to midsummer on tall, slim, willowy stems. Though the blooms are short-lived, masses of them are constantly appearing. Especially useful for rock gardens and perennializing. There's also a white form. Tolerates considerable drought. For culture, see list 34, Annuals That Self-sow.

LYTHRUM **cultivars**, Purple Loosestrife, Spiked Loosestrife. Long-lived, water-loving species whose many cultivated varieties thrive in rich, moist soils, even with their feet in water, in the North or South. All summer, rigid flower stalks stand tall above interesting, slightly hairy, heart-shaped leaves and cover themselves with small, fluffy, purple-pink blooms. 'Robert', deep pink, and 'The Beacon', rose-red, are 3½ feet tall. 'Morden's Pink' is a 36-inch lavender. These are environmentally sound cultivated varieties, not to be confused with *Lythrum salicaria*, which has become a weed along roadsides and in wet meadows. See list 59, Wet, Boggy Soils.

NEPETA × **faassenii**, Persian Ground Ivy. Lovely upright, gray-green herb from 12 to 15 inches tall with strongly aromatic foliage and fuzzy spikes of deep or pale lavender-blue flowers all summer. Used for edging, as a filler, and in the wild garden. This is a relative of Catnip, *N. cataria*. See list 74, Herbs with Fragrant Foliage.

PEROVSKIA (pehr-*roff*-skee-uh)
atriplicifolia
Russian Sage   Zones 5-9
A good plant to bring that coveted color, blue, to the border for the longest period—July, August, and most of September. Tall, beautiful, with silvery stems and grayish foliage down below, it is topped by airy spikes of tiny florets that are a subtle powder blue. It is also one of the most heat- and drought-resistant perennials. To 36 inches tall. Foliage releases a delightful sage scent when crushed.

Culture: In early spring or fall, plant rooted softwood cuttings 24 inches apart in full sun, in well-drained, moderately fertile soil in the neutral range. Heavy clay soils are inappropriate. This is a subshrub with a woody base; cut back to 6 inches above ground in early spring just before new growth commences to renew vigor and improve growth habit. Defies heat and drought, and even does well when summers are humid.

PHLOX **drummondii**, Annual Phlox, Drummond Phlox. The straight, leafy stems—usually 12 to 14 or 18 inches tall—are topped by loose clusters of silky, star-shaped flowers, some with a contrasting eye and a meadowy scent. The flowers appear in midsummer and may be white, pink, rose, red, lavender, magenta, cerise, or fuchsia. The more you cut it, the more it blooms. Even in hot, sandy soil this annual phlox withstands considerable drought and goes on blooming. It self-sows and often naturalizes. See list 27, *Phlox*.

PLATYCODON (plat-ik-*koh*-don)
grandiflorus var. **mariesii**
Dwarf Balloon Flower   Zones 3-8
An outstanding 12- to 24- and 28-inch variety—reliable, durable, and easy, one of the best summer flowers. The distinctive balloon-shaped buds studded along wandlike, graceful stems open to starry blue, white, or lilac-pink flowers up to 2 inches across. Very free-flowering, from early summer to early fall, with glossy foliage. As cut flowers, they are long lasting if the stems are seared before they are put in water. *P. grandiflorus* 'Apoyama' has violet flowers on plants 15 to 18 inches tall and is recommended for planting with herbs.

Culture: Sow seeds in spring in well-drained, sandy, or loamy soil in full sun in the North, semi-sun in the South, and be patient. Long-lived, but it does not always transplant well, and it's slow to grow in spring—mark the place.

ROSMARINUS **officinalis 'Arp'**, Rosemary. Hardy as far north as New Jersey, the familiar herb for scenting potpourris and flavoring lamb and pork. It has needlelike evergreen leaves with a lasting minty-piny scent and in early spring, clusters of pleasant, light blue edible flowers. Nice filler for bare spots in walls or the rock garden. May be pruned and is a good bonsai subject. Hardy spreading rosemaries are used as ground cover. The tender (Zone 8) *R. o.* 'Prostratus' is grown in southern California. For culture see list 77, Popular Culinary Herbs.

SANTOLINA
Low evergreen shrubs and subshrubs from 12 to 30 inches high whose cool, gray, pine-scented leaves edge with silvery softness rock gardens, formal plantings, knot gardens, mixed flower borders and roses. The flowers appear in late spring and summer and are buttonlike and inconspicuous. Good container plants. Recommended for sand and seashore are *S. chamaecyparissus* 'Nana', Lavender Cotton, a dwarf to 14 inches high with foliage that is white-woolly underneath, silvery in moonlight, and whiter when growing in dry conditions, sandy soil, and full sun. *S. virens*, Green Santolina, is a 15-inch species with yellowish white flowers and brilliant green foliage. Nice as a clipped hedge. For culture, see list 73, Herbs with Colorful Foliage.

SAPONARIA (sap-on-*nay*-ree-uh)
officinalis 'Rosea Plena' and **'Rubra Plena'**
Bouncing Bet   Zones 2-8
An old-fashioned and very pretty rhizomatous perennial that grows wild and spreads quickly. Throughout summer, these cultivars bear clusters of double flowers that look like shaggy pinks on plants 24 to 36 inches tall. 'Rosea Plena' is pink; 'Rubra Plena' is red. Both are very fragrant and last well when cut.

Culture: Plant rooted cuttings at any time in full sun, in well-drained, ordinary soil. Upright in poor, sandy soil, it sprawls in rich soils. When it gets leggy in late spring, pinch back to trim it up and increase flowering sprays. Divide established plants at will.

SEDUM, Stonecrop. This group of indestructible and sometimes invasive (*S. acre* in particular) herbaceous perennials from 2 to 15 inches tall is valued for its pretty, evergreen, succulent-like, light green foliage and, in some important larger hybrids, attractive autumn color. The flowers are tiny and star-shaped, yellow or pink-red, quite modest in ground-hugging species, but become showy flowerheads in taller forms. The ground-huggers are very useful in rock gardens, for filling nooks and crannies and pockets in rocks and walls, and by steps. The taller types are indispensable in naturalized plantings and a treasured addition to gardens of ornamental grasses. The following plants are recommended.

S. sediforme (syn. *nicaeense*), a small succulent with attractive foliage planted as ground cover in sandy places. Just 6 inches tall with cream-colored flowers in August, it is very tolerant of heat and drought. *S.* 'Autumn Joy', 12 to 24 inches tall, is excellent with ornamental grasses and when naturalized. The flowers start light pink in summer, turn to salmon, then change in fall to rosy russet. *S.* 'Ruby Glow' is a slightly smaller plant, about 12 inches tall, that bears ruby red flowers in autumn.

S. spurium is a rapidly spreading ground cover and rock garden creeper from 2 to 6 inches tall, with showy white to rose flowers in summer on stems 4 inches tall. Good cover for stony or unsightly patches of packed, sandy dirt. The popular 'Dragon's Blood' ('Splendens') bears dark red, starry flowers in spring and summer, and the foliage turns wine red-bronze by summer's end. Not successful in the South. The flowers of the similar 'Bronze Carpet' are pink, and the foliage turns bronze in late summer to early autumn. See also lists 45, 67, and for culture, 56, Dry, Hot Conditions.

TANACETUM **vulgare 'Crispum'** (syn. *Chrysanthemum vulgare* 'Crispum'), Fern-leaf Tansy. The colonists established the species by their front doors so the strong, sharp aroma could repel insects, and to serve medicinal purposes (the leaves and stems are actually toxic). It is used today to scent potpourris and winter arrangements. 'Crispum', which is 24- to 36-inches tall, has pretty, very lacy leaves and buttonlike, bright yellow flowers in flat-topped clusters in summer. It makes a handsome, aromatic filler. For culture, see list 74, Herbs with Fragrant Foliage.

YUCCA (*yukk*-uh)
Very contemporary and exotic, with huge evergreen rosettes of silvery sword-shaped leaves and astonishing flower spikes. In early summer, these long-lasting, 4- to 6-foot woody stems rise up and unfold big bell-shaped flowers, white or flushed with violet or purple on the outside.

Culture: In fall or spring, plant root divisions in full sun, rather poor, sandy, well-drained, preferably neutral-range soil. Maintain on the dry side.

Y. filamentosa 'Bright Edge' Adam's-needle
                                              Zones 5-11
Magnificent stylized plant to feature in contemporary settings and in hedges. The flower stem reaches 5 feet and bears creamy white blooms, but it is grown for the ornamental leaves, 15 inches long, 1 inch across, with a golden edge and shaggy threads along the edges.

Y. glauca Soapweed   Zones 4-11
One of the toughest, with narrow, white-edged, gray-green leaves that are 36 inches long and ½ inch wide. Suited to the Midwest and more tolerant of some shade. The flowers are greenish white on a 36-inch spike.

Y. recurvifolia   Zones 6-11
A native plant seen in the South, it reaches 6 feet tall and has 2-inch-wide recurving leaves. Flowers on branching stems. There's a remarkable variegated variety with a central yellow stripe.

SOURCE: ANDRE VIETTE IS SENIOR CONSULTANT FOR THIS BOOK. AN AUTHOR, LECTURER, AND SECOND-GENERATION HORTICULTURIST, HE OWNS THE NURSERY IN FISHERSVILLE, VIRGINIA, THAT BEARS HIS NAME. AT THIS WRITING, HE SERVES ON THE ADVISORY COUNCIL OF THE U.S. NATIONAL ARBORETUM, AND IS A DIRECTOR OF BOTH THE AMERICAN HORTICULTURAL SOCIETY AND THE LEWIS GINTER BOTANICAL GARDEN. HE IS ALSO PRESIDENT OF THE PERENNIAL PLANT ASSOCIATION. A LIFETIME DEVOTED TO THE STUDY AND DEVELOPMENT OF PERENNIALS HAS EARNED HIM NUMEROUS HORTICULTURAL AWARDS.

58. *URBAN CONDITIONS*

■ These are among the many beautiful but tough annuals and perennials that thrive in city conditions. Included here are long-blooming plants for every purpose—sun lovers that withstand drought and neglect, shade lovers for planting under shrubs and in the lee of light-blocking walls. There are wildflowers and bold-leaved herbs, grasslike ground covers, and little clumpy plants to edge walks and fill boxes.

Hose your plants with a fine spray in early morning to keep the leaves clean. Renew the flower beds annually with top dressings of fresh soil, and turn under composted leaves or dried cow manure purchased from garden centers. Mulch to keep the roots cool through summer heat. Cities may be 5° to 10° F warmer than the surrounding countryside, and exposed rooftops and balconies can be subject to severe drying winds.

Related lists are 63, The Container Garden, and 56, Dry, Hot Conditions.

Companion Plants: *Ligustrum*, *Kerria japonica*, *Pinus mugo* (Mugho Pine), *Potentilla fruticosa*, and *Skimmia* are some of the shrubs that do well in city conditions.

ACHILLEA, Yarrow. This pungent ancient herb from 8 to 36 inches tall bears great, flat flowerheads in yellow, gold, pink, or white that stand well above its woolly gray-green foliage in late spring and summer. The cut flowers are handsome in bouquets, fresh or dried. It succeeds in drought, sand and by the seashore. 'Coronation Gold' is a striking deep gold hybrid, 24 to 36 inches tall, that blooms for 2 to 3 months starting in late spring. *A. millefolium* 'Cerise Queen', (Yarrow, Milfoil), which never needs coddling, is happy with poor soil, drought, and neglect. It bears cerise-red flowers in summer on plants up to 18 inches tall. The Galaxy hybrids flower in shades of peach and salmon. For culture, see list 15, Summer Perennials for Sun.

ALCHEMILLA mollis, Lady's-mantle. Woodsy plant 12 inches high or taller for edging and massing in shaded gardens and under trees. This low-growing, wonderfully durable species has scalloped, silvery leaves that hold shimmering drops of rain after a shower. In spring, it bears sprays of tiny, star-shaped, chartreuse-yellow flowers. For culture, see list 75, Herbs with Showy Flowers.

BERGENIA cordifolia. Vigorous, 12 to 16 or 18 inches high, it bears graceful spires of dark pink flowers in mid-spring and is particularly prized for its clumps of glossy, leathery evergreen leaves, which turn bronze in winter sun. There's a white-flowered variety and a tall, purple-toned 'Purpurea' with dark pink blossoms whose leaves turn a burgundy color in cold weather. Bergenia makes a bold backdrop for ferns and other delicate-looking woodsy plants. It is not invasive and is most effective in groups. For culture, see list 13, Spring Perennials for Sun.

CATHARANTHUS (kat-ta-*ranth*-us) **roseus**
Rose Periwinkle, Madagascar Periwinkle
                                        Tender Perennial
A bedding plant that tolerates heat, drought, and pollution, it truly thrives in the city. Also called 'Vinca rosea'—it does resemble a tall pink vinca—it develops into a 12- to 18-inch-high bushy mound that spreads from 18 to 24 inches in a season. The shiny leaves are dark green and evergreen in warm climates, but northward the plant is handled as an annual. All summer it displays flowers like small, flat phlox in mauvy pink or white, usually with a darker, rose or red eye. Excellent for baskets, borders, edging, and as a summer ground cover. 'Bright Eye' is a dwarf, white with a carmine eye. 'Pink Panther' is under 12 inches and has clear rose-red flowers with a darker eye. The 'Magic Carpet' strain is small, 6 to 9 inches high, with flowers in white and shades of pink and rose—very heat tolerant.

Culture: Seeds started indoors bloom in summer and fall. Seed germination can be difficult as the plants are extremely sensitive to cold and overwatering; a surer method is to set out container-grown nursery plants. Prefers semi-sun, but modern cultivars tolerate full sun as long as the soil is well-drained and rich in humusy material that holds moisture.

CLEOME hasslerana, Spider Flower, is a wonderfully airy and decorative back-of-the-border filler 3 to 5 feet tall with white, pink, or lavender-pink flowers that peak in late summer and early fall. Self-sows. 'Rose Queen' and 'Helen Campbell', a white, are recommended (and often attributed to *C. spinosa*, which is very similar.) See list 31, Annuals for Sun.

COREOPSIS, Tickseed. Excellent. This is one of the easiest and most rewarding garden flowers. In late spring and throughout summer masses of sunny, starry flowers bloom above the narrow, dark green foliage. *C. grandiflora* is a large-flowered species. 'Goldfink', under 9 inches, is a delightful dwarf for the front of the border. 'Early Sunrise' is compact and has charming double flowers. Seed is available. *C. verticillata*, Threadleaf Tickseed, is one of the parents of several long-lived, long-flowering plants resistant to drought. Among the best is 'Moonbeam', 15 to 18 or 24 inches tall, which has eye-catching pale, butter yellow flowers. 'Golden Showers' is a bolder yellow. See list 15, Summer Perennials for Sun.

ECHINOPS (ek-in-ops) **ritro 'Taplow Blue'**
Small Globe Thistle   Zones 3-8
This big-leaved plant, 2 to 4 feet tall, has interesting foliage with gray-green hairy undersides and bears dry, somewhat very handsome, thistlelike heads of steely blue flowers in summer and early autumn. Use it in groups in the wild garden or in front of tall shrubs. Attractive to bees and nocturnal moths.

Culture: Set out container plants in spring, in well-drained soil, in full sun. Tolerant of drought. Don't divide plants until they are at least 3 years old.

GALIUM odoratum, Woodruff, Sweet Woodruff. Sometimes still listed as *Asperula odorata*, its old name. The shiny, star-shaped leaves are fragrant when dry, and in spring, dainty white flowers are arranged in layers along the stems. A neat plant from 6 to 12 inches high, it

makes a fine ground cover. Longtime favorite of herbalists for flavoring May wine and liqueurs, and for garnishing pastry and desserts. Dried, it acts as a fixative for dried perfumes and potpourris; the aroma invokes vanilla. For culture, see list 76, Fragrant Herbs for Drying and Potpourri.

GERANIUM sanguineum var. prostratum (syn. *lancastriense*). The "true" or "hardy" geraniums don't look at all like the *Pelargonium* we call geranium and grow in hanging baskets and window boxes. This common garden species is 6 to 12 inches high and has a long spring/summer sequence of airy, magenta-pink flowers with deeper veining held above a sprawl of delicate foliage. The pointed leaves are touched with bright red or maroon in cold weather, and the plant withstands heat and cold. Two others recommended for urban use are 'Ingwersen's Variety', which has pale pink flowers and glossier leaves, and 'Johnson's Blue', which has clear blue flowers. For culture, see list 13, Spring Perennials for Sun.

IMPATIENS. Summer-long bloom in filtered light and semishade is the exceptional gift of these tender perennials and annuals with sparkling little flowers and delicate, pointed leaves. The familiar impatiens is *I. wallerana*, Zanzibar Balsam, Busy Lizzy, a superb container and basket plant. The array of colors expands every year—now including dark red, hot pink, intense coral, orchid, white—and there are bicolors and strains with variegated leaves. By fall, standard sizes can attain a height of 36 inches; compacts stay at 6 to 8 inches. Recommended are: Shady Lady pastels, which bear 2-inch flowers, often with a darker center, on 12- to 15-inch plants; the very early 'Tempo Blush'; the 10-inch early 'Accent Pink', which thrives in real shade; compact 'Super Elfin Blue Pearl', a delicate lilac-blue. The sturdy New Guinea strain is more upright, has brightly variegated, more substantial foliage, larger blooms, and withstands more sun. New Guinea Spectra hybrids bloom from seed, with 2- to 3-inch flowers, and much of the foliage is variegated. For culture see list 38, *Impatiens*.

LIRIOPE, Lilyturf. This is a wonderful semi-evergreen or evergreen edger and ground cover that looks like tufts of grass ¼ to ¾ inch wide and 8 to 12 or 18 inches high. In late summer or early fall, lavender, blue, or white flower spikes rise above the leaves and are followed by shiny black berries. The other plant called Lilyturf, *Ophiogon* (see below), is not as hardy, and its flowers are less visible. Recommended for urban gardens are: *L. platyphylla* (formerly *muscari*), Big Blue Lilyturf, cultivars with green, bluish, blue, red, lavender, white, or purple flowers. 'Variegata', which has creamy margins and blue flowers, is one of many variegated cultivars—they are showiest in full sun. *L. spicata*, Creeping Lilyturf, is the choice for northern gardens—it is shorter, 8 to 12 inches tall, has ¼-inch leaves, and rather sparser pale violet or white flowers. It spreads rapidly. See list 44, Flowering Ground Covers.

Linda Yang's romantic backyard garden between high Manhattan walls includes flowers for sun and shade—among them, coreopsis, canna, herbs. Photo from Linda Yang's *The City Gardener's Handbook: From Balcony to Backyard*, Random House 1990. Reprinted with permission. (Yang)

Real city slickers:
TOP, LEFT 'Pretty in Rose',
Catharanthus roseus.
(All American Selections)
TOP, RIGHT Foliage tufts of Lily-
turf, *Ophiopogon japonicum*.
(Viette)
RIGHT Small globe thistle,
'Taplow Blue' *Echinops ritro*.
(Viette)

NICOTIANA alata, Jasmine Tobacco, Flowering Tobacco. Tender perennial; lush, semirecumbent, 15
to 24 inches tall, with big leaves; an excellent filler. From
midsummer to frost the plant produces a constant show of
fragrant, tubular white flowers that open after sundown
from a nest of luxuriantly large leaves. A large relative, *N.
sylvestris*, produces unusually long clusters of white
flowers. See also list 31, Annuals for Sun.

NIGELLA damascena, Love-in-a-mist, Wild
Fennel. The flowers of this fast-growing annual, 18 to 24
inches tall, are spidery, 1 to 2 inches across, and bloom all
summer in blue, pink, or white if successive plantings are
made. The finely divided bright green foliage is a good
filler for hanging baskets and boxes of mixed flowers.
Lovely as cut flowers and the dried seedpods are attractive
in winter arrangements. There are dwarfs, such as 'Blue
Midget', 8 to 10 inches tall. The standard 12- to 18-inch
'Persian Jewels' has white, pink, red, and purple flowers.
'Miss Jekyll' is blue. For culture, see list 72, To Dry for
Winter Bouquets

OPHIOPOGON (off-ee-oh-**poh**-gon)
japonicus
Lilyturf, Mondo Grass   Zones 7-10
A low-growing, clumping plant with semievergreen or
evergreen grassy leaves ¼ inch wide and 8 to 12 inches
high. It bears discreet spikes of light lilac flowers in late
summer and fall, followed by metallic blue berries. For
moist, shady areas, it is preferred to the similar but showier
Liriope platyphylla, Lilyturf, above, which has taller
flowers and shiny black berries. *O. planiscapus* 'Ebony

King' is a striking, 10-inch-high, purple-black plant whose flowers are flushed with pink. It is rated hardy in Zone 6.

Culture: In spring in cool areas, or fall in warm areas, set out container plants or root divisions in partial shade and moist soil. Tolerates sun in well-drained soil with sustained moisture. Resists salt spray and drought and flourishes in sandy, humusy soil.

PELARGONIUM, Geranium. Ivy geraniums, scented-leaved geraniums, and most other geraniums produce showy blooms all summer in shades of pink, red, fuchsia, white, and bicolors. These superb container plants may be brought indoors for the winter. Some types may be started from seed indoors in late winter. For sun or semi-sun. See list 37, Geranium—Ivy Geranium.

PHLOX. The most luscious pastels of spring and summer belong to the phloxes, American natives that thrive almost everywhere. The big, silky-soft flowerheads of the upright types bloom for a long time and are the preferred filler for the middle or back of sunny summer borders. Recommended is *P. paniculata*, Summer Perennial Phlox, Fall Phlox, an upright, durable, sparkling plant 6 to 36 inches tall with big panicles of flowers in a range of colors—white, pink, salmon, scarlet, and purple, many with a contrasting eye. The sweetly fragrant cut flowers are lovely in bouquets. In hot, humid climates, choose mildew-resistant cultivars.

Essential for spring color are the little creeping phloxes whose cascading branches bloom in lavender-blue, purple, pink, or white florets. Their foliage remains as a ground cover through summer. Recommended is *P. stolonifera*, Creeping Phlox, for semishade or shade, a superb, mat-forming ground cover 5 to 12 inches tall. Some varieties are evergreen in mild winters. The flowers are dense clusters of purple or violet that have a lilylike scent and may bloom again intermittently. See list 27, Phlox.

STACHYS byzantina (syn. *lanata*). Woolly Betony, Lamb's-ears. The gray, oval semievergreen leaves of Lamb's-ears are so furry-looking they invite stroking and are almost luminous in moonlight. Violet flower racemes bloom from summer to frost, although some gardeners prefer to remove them to keep the focus on the leaves. A favorite plant for edging and leafy accents, 12 to 15 inches high. The nonflowering, 8-inch-high 'Silver Carpet' spreads rapidly and is the best for foliage. Nice with *Sedum* 'Ruby Glow' or 'Vera Jameson'. For culture see list 50, Foliage for Form and Texture.

TORENIA (tor-**reen**-ee-uh) **fournieri**
Bluewings   Annual
The bushy little annual wishbone plant is 12 inches high and has light green leaves. From late spring to frost it bears masses of bicolored blooms like tiny blue snapdragons. In autumn, the foliage turns a warm reddish purple in sun. Excellent for baskets, window boxes, and rock gardens.

Culture: Start seeds early indoors and plant outside, in semi-sun after all danger of frost is past. In frost-free zones, plant any time of the year. Fertile, well-drained soil and abundant, sustained moisture are important.

Source: Linda Yang, a garden columnist for the Home Section of The New York Times, tills her own city plot in Manhattan. She is the author of The City Gardener's Handbook: From Balcony to Backyard.

Irises, blue hostas, ferns, and artemisia are among many beautiful garden plants that flourish in moist soil and shade. (Viette)

59. *Wet, Boggy Soils*

■ These plants thrive in very moist situations. They also grow well in humusy, evenly moist soil, but they will be smaller. Those that prefer shade—ferns for instance—generally succeed in sun, or some sun, as long as the soil is very moist. "Evenly moist" soil can be found next to a running stream, or it can simply be well-drained soil with enough spongy humus in it to be water-retentive. "Boggy" soil is consistently wet but not necessarily well-drained.

Most of the plants recommended in this section are summer bloomers whose foliage is a lingering asset—they don't need follow-on plants. One exception is the primrose, which usually fades in hot summers. To follow primroses, plant impatiens and deep blue edging lobelia, *Lobelia erinus*, an exquisite little annual that blooms in late spring and again later on if sheared.

Other lists in the book contain some perennial species that are more tolerant of moist soils than other members of their genus; for instance, *Coreopsis rosea*. But the plants recommended here tolerate situations close to boggy.

Companion Plants: Big, leafy companions for the web-footed flowers on this list are Royal Fern, Umbrella Plant, and Rodgersia.

ASTILBE, Spiraea, Perennial Spiraea. The flower stalks of astilbe remain a rich brown in winter, handsome in the snow. The plants may be 6 inches to 6 feet tall, and in late spring or summer produce feathery flowerheads that stand above deeply cut green or bronzed foliage. The colors range from palest pink, through coral, to bright red and creamy white. The flowers are good for cutting and smaller varieties grow well in containers. It flourishes in moist, shady conditions. See list 21, Astilbe.

CANNA × hybrida, Water Canna. Superb for damp places and water gardens, a big plant up to 4 feet tall with lush leaves and exotic orange or reddish or yellow flowers. Plant in early spring in containers up to 6 inches under water. In cold regions, store the containers indoors for winter. For more about other types of canna see list 4, Summer-into-fall Bulbs.

IRIS ensata (syn. *kaempferi*). Japanese Iris, and *I. pseudacorus*, Yellow Iris, Yellow Flag, Water Flag, are early summer-blooming species irises that grow to 3 feet tall in boggy places. In humusy garden soil they may be somewhat shorter. The Yellow Iris can thrive 6 feet under water. *I. versicolor*, Wild Iris or Blue Flag, and the iris class called Louisianas, crosses of *I. fulva*, Copper or Red Iris, must have wet feet and are smaller, though not less beautiful, than the more vigorous Yellow Iris hybrids. For culture, see list 25, Iris.

Water lovers:
LEFT Little marsh marigold, *Caltha palustris*, a hardy bog or streamside native. (Viette)
BOTTOM, LEFT The flower of the umbrella plant, *Peltiphyllum peltatum*, a big, bold foliage plant. (Viette)
BOTTOM, RIGHT *Lythrum virgatum* cultivars at River Farm. (Viette)

Globeflower, *Trollius chinensis* (Ledebourii) blooms in late spring and early summer. (Viette)

LIGULARIA stenocephala 'The Rocket'. This plant has bold, leathery leaves and, in summer, tall slender spikes of ragged lemon yellow flowers. Suited to watery sites and moist borders, 'The Rocket' grows to 6 feet tall when in bloom. Good companion to Japanese iris and large-leaved hostas. For culture, see list 16, Summer Perennials for Shade.

LOBELIA cardinalis, Cardinal Flower. A tall, upright, romantic wildflower from 24 to 30 and 36 inches high, topped by up to 50 loosely spaced, bright red blossoms. It thrives by woodland streams and flowers in late summer and fall. With its feet in water, it can stand some sun, but it prefers semishade. The flower spikes are long and slender, and the foliage is dark green, lovely with ferns. Culture (for this and the blue lobelias) is discussed on list 16, Summer Perennials for Shade.

LYTHRUM virgatum cultivars
Purple Loosestrife, Spiked Loosestrife   Zones 3-9
Long-lived, water-loving species, whose many cultivated varieties thrive in rich, moist soils, even with their feet in water, in both North and South. All summer, rigid flower stalks stand tall above interesting, slightly hairy, heart-shaped leaves and cover themselves with small, fluffy, purple-pink blooms. 'Robert', deep pink, and 'The Beacon', rose-red, are 3½ feet tall. These are native, environmentally sound cultivated varieties, not to be confused with *Lythrum salicaria,* the European species, which has become a weed along roadsides and in wet meadows.

Culture: In early spring, sow seeds or plant root divisions in full or semi-sun, in well-worked soil, and provide plenty of water.

OSMUNDA regalis, Royal Fern. Elegant, deep green fern 4 to 6 feet tall that spreads slowly and can reach 36 inches wide. In spring, the fronds are pinkish. Established plants produce brown flower stalks at the ends of the taller fronds. For culture, see list 52, Ferns for the Garden.

PELTIPHYLLUM (pel-tif-*fill*-um) peltatum
Umbrella Plant   Zones 5-9
Big, bold foliage plant for wet places and bog gardens, with huge, rounded leaves 24 by 36 inches long. In spring, it bears flat clusters of showy, pale pink or white flowers on stalks to 36 inches high.

Culture: Set out root divisions in early spring, or sow seeds in early fall, in full or semi-sun, in humusy moist soil.

PRIMULA japonica 'Postford White'. This late-spring-flowering primrose is a captivating little plant with candelabra-type clusters of flat-faced, yellow-eyed white flowers 10 to 15 inches high, held above mounds of crinkled green leaves. Arresting massed in moist, shaded, or woodland gardens. See list 29, Primrose.

RODGERSIA podophylla. Can be 36 inches tall and spread to 5 feet wide—it is grown for the bold leaves that start out bright green and turn to bronze in autumn. In summer feathery white flower panicles 12 inches high rise above the foliage. See also list 50, Foliage for Form and Texture.

TROLLIUS (*troh*-lee-us) chinensis
(Ledebourii)
Globeflower   Zones 3-8
Charming gold or golden orange, buttercup-like flowers that bloom in spring and summer in damp, shady places; plants grow about 24 inches high. Charming massed on moist banks in light woodlands.

Culture: Set out container-grown plants, in early spring or fall, in semi-sun or shade in fairly heavy garden soil. Maintain even moisture. Seeds are slow to germinate.

CONSULTANTS: MARY ANN AND FRED McGOURTY, OWNERS OF HILLSIDE GARDENS, NORFOLK, CONNECTICUT, SPECIALIZE IN UNCOMMON PERENNIALS AND GARDEN DESIGN.

CHAPTER FIVE:
Theme Gardens

Traditional Themes

A garden is never completed. No matter how perfect it is, every season you end up promising next time to change at least one or two plants. For one thing, the flowers perform differently every year. We say it's because the January thaw lasted long, or March was cold. I have found myself thinking that plants (like Manhattan elevators) have group consciousness and share epidemics. Actually, it's the garden's wonderful unpredictability that draws us outdoors before the morning coffee has finished brewing. Gardeners are more interested in new experiences than in reproducing perfection. That's why plant collections and theme gardens are popular.

In the first part of this chapter, I describe the three dominant garden themes—The Cottage Garden, The Japanese Garden, and The New American Garden. The Cottage Garden (and The Meadow Garden) are lavish, romantic celebrations of color and form. Tom Woodham's photos of designer Ryan Gainey's own very sensual cottage garden in Atlanta says it all. Osamo Shimizu's Japanese garden in Glen Echo, Maryland, is the opposite experience—a private green place whose mystical serenity invites contemplation. The sword-like foliage of a few irises evokes their moment of bloom and once the cherries, dogwoods, and azaleas have gone by nothing shouts—everything evokes. The New American Garden is a prairie garden combining bulbs, durable and long-blooming perennials, and grasses.

To my mind the cottage and Japanese gardens are the twin poles of landscape design. Design comes first, specific plants second. In the other theme gardens suggested, the plant collection is the first consideration, design second.

....
Intricately woven ribbons of herbs and barberry shape a knot garden, one of the classical horticultural themes. "Knott" was the term used for the small beds in a formal garden of many beds separated by walks or grass. (McDonald)

Sensual Gardens

The most seductive theme gardens are those that appeal strongly to the senses. The five herb lists will attract anyone who is intrigued by new taste combinations and aromas. And if you have a full-sun space for a food garden, Rosalind Creasy's photos of flower-and-vegetable combinations on list 78 are irresistible.

The most sensual garden of all is one whose flowers have been chosen to perfume noon and moonlight in every season—from the heady hyacinths in spring to sweet alyssum in the last drowsy days of Indian summer. A garden of flowers for cutting is a close second. Imagine holding a great armful of just-cut peonies; against your cheek, the petals are softer than silk. Even flowers without marked perfume have a scent-signature to which we respond. A garden of flowers to dry for winter has the same sensual appeal: think of sleeping in linens from a closet filled with lavender sachets. Huge dried arrangements of gold, buff, and blue flowers from the garden and the wild recall strewing herbs and the smell of new-mown hay.

The seductions of a woodland garden are less blatant but no less strong—you want to touch the ferns, get down and smell the humusy soil, set the blossoms of Solomon's-seal to nodding. I must have loved a woodland garden as a child for that is the one that moves me most deeply. (Though the best flowers to start a child with are others, suggested on list 68 by Dr. H. Marc Cathey, Director of the U.S. National Arboretum.) Collections of flowers that attract butterflies and hummingbirds appeal to the senses—and to the sense of self-preservation. We must sustain the ecosystems that sustain us.

If you have an appropriate site for either of these collections, chances are you already also have suitable native materials. Before moving natives, even in your own backyard, be sure they aren't protected by state law. If they are protected, learn to propagate and share the seedlings with local garden groups.

Gardens for Collectors

The other theme gardens appeal more to the mind. Collecting specific types of plants is like eating salted peanuts—the more you have, the more you want. A growing world of specialty catalogs feeds the collector's enthusiasm. Woodsy and wild plants can be found through horticultural and plant societies—for instance, the New England Wild Flower Society's Garden in the Woods. Rock garden plants and the rare and choice wildlings have their own distribution systems, too.

One of the most interesting is The Historic Garden. All gardening tunes you in to the earth and others who love plants. Working with historic species, you experience a closeness with gardeners who grew them long ago. These conversation pieces are becoming easier to find. Bulb specialist Brent Heath adds more historics to his catalogue every year and the Dutch growers are joining in.

The most challenging theme garden is one the real horticulturist is apt to

TOP Fenced door yard and combined vegetable and flower beds in a typical historic garden in Colonial Williamsburg, VA. This is the Prentice House.
(Colonial Williamsburg).

ABOVE Dahlias at River Farm invite the butterflies.
(American Horticultural Society)

choose—a one-flower collection. The few lovely campanulas Pamela Harper recommends on list 22 are only a beginning —there are about 250 known campanula species. Only the popular garden types are sold by the usual sources. A collector inevitably is going to want to grow rare species. The more you know about a group of flowers, the more fascinating it becomes, but the rewards of collecting go beyond that. Collectors travel to unusual places, create new friendships, and expand their horizons. And, while some garden space is sacrificed, the new plants needn't limit the design. Collectibles are prettiest when they are preceded, followed, and companioned by other plants. So you end up, as Pam Harper did, with a superb all-season garden surrounding the stars.

Irises, peonies, poppies—all the major perennials and bulbs are superb subjects for collections and there are plant societies for each to prove it. The American Horticultural Society headquarters in Alexandria, Virginia, publishes *North American Horticulture: A Reference Guide*, with lists of names and addresses of plant societies and horticultural organizations.

The Eclectics

Though theme gardens are the focus of the next part of this book, some lists in the preceding chapter (4, Workhorses of the Garden) also invite collectors. Study the photo of Linda Yang's own Manhattan garden, in list 58, Urban Conditions. Her plantings have created a sunny glade and a small woodland between high city walls. It's a mix of several themes, including Linda's Container Garden (list 63), The Woodland Garden, Rare and Choice, and others.

Most landscapes, large and small, are like Linda—eclectic. A variety of garden experiences is the goal. Our garden makes an L around a corner of Capitol Hill and includes high noon sun and varying degrees of shade. Under flowering plums and a young Chinese dogwood, the front garden is green and serene, woodsy, floored with pachysandra, hostas, and silvery ground covers. Clumps of daffodils add a brief touch of spring gold, and a sprinkling of low-growing impatiens bloom under the star magnolia in summer. Along the length of the redbrick living room wall, there's a narrow semi-sunny flower border with astilbes, ferns, and in spring, drifts of tulips set the fall before.

From the kitchen gate, a path of flagstones leads past a hot, gravelly slope where herbs grow—lavenders, mints for flavoring desserts, and scenting bouquets. I'm coaxing a tiny-leaved thyme to spread among stones; last year it gained about four square inches. The path leads through a tunnel created by the weeping cherry to the next patch of color—a little cottage garden opposite the steps to the kitchen door and the veranda. Everything that flowers goes into it, but it is all low in scale. There's not enough space between the street and the steps for Ryan Gainey's towering foxgloves and hollyhocks, darn it. A fringe tree and azaleas screen the veranda from the street, and in its light shade, low impatiens repeat the summer colors of the front yard, and in cool weather I set out pansies and primroses.

If there was a bog or water I'd have some of those plants. If I lived in high, cool country, I'd try alpine plants. If I lived near the shore, I'd plant a garden of bulbs, perennials, and ornamental grasses to whip in the wind and turn golden russet in winter.

If I owned the world, there probably wouldn't be much room for houses.

60. THE COTTAGE GARDEN

■ A major theme in landscape design is the cottage garden, an interpretation of the English country garden. Here columbines and poppies and zinnias lap at the feet of foxgloves and hollyhocks, while night-blooming moonflower vines compete with morning-glories for the woodpile and arbor. Fall anemones, cleome, and cosmos come on together, with wild magenta phlox filling the middle ground. Creeping in and out are low-to-the-ground forget-me-nots and Johnny-jump-ups. In the spring shadows, clumps of violets and primroses duskily shine. All are meant to look as though they had escaped from the woods and multiplied here—tulips with forget-me-nots with Wild Sweet William. A cottage garden is pretty and romantic; the look inspires lush, gentle watercolors.

Cottage garden flowers are spring, summer, and fall annuals that are bedded in as the spring flowers fade away, and biennials that self-sow and come back. There are a few old-fashioned perennials like peonies and irises, too. Simple, single-flowered species are preferred to elaborate double cultivars, except for peonies. In time, birds and the wind will sow butterfly weed, Queen-Anne's-lace, wild bluebells, and asters, and most of the plants will be allowed to remain.

Culture: Wanting things to self-sow means you must let the flowers ripen their seeds. The seedheads must dry and release the seed to the earth to be worked over by winter cold and wet until it germinates. Don't cultivate until the seedlings have popped up—then a little careful hand weeding is possible. When the poppies announce, you can pull out self-sown larkspur if it's too crowded—but not before.

When possible, plant in fall; the plants will be bigger and sturdier in spring.

Companion and Follow-on Plants: For nostalgia, plant antique roses such as the pest-and-disease-resistant China rose 'Old Blush' that flowers all summer, or fragrant cabbage roses like *R. centifolia* 'Gloire des Mousseuses'. Old-fashioned purple and lavender irises are useful for their lasting sword-shaped foliage. A few clumps of ornamental grass such as *Miscanthus sinensis* 'Gracillimus', look handsome in a cottage garden, as do ferns, in shaded places. Other good companions for the flowers on this list are lacecap hydrangeas and *Hydrangea arborescens*, Hills-of-snow; Hardy *hibiscus syriacus* 'Helene' and 'Minerva; figs; silvery dusty-miller (*Senecio cineraria*); fragrant herbs; daffodils and spring-flowering bulbs; and thistlelike plants such as *Stokesia*.

ALCEA (al-*see*-uh) rosea (syn. *Althea rosea*)
Hollyhock   Biennial
Soaring verticals 3 to 7 feet high studded all summer with large, pretty, open-faced flowers that have crinkly petals. The blossoms open from the bottom and may be single or double in shades of white, yellow, pink, red, and maroon. 'Powder Puffs' is a beautiful double strain in lovely pastel shades.

Culture: In fall, sow seeds in well-drained, rich, moist soil; or set out container plants in early spring. Self-sows and may become perennialized. Though it is a biennial, it often blooms from seed the first year.

ANEMONE hupehensis var. japonica, Japanese Anemone.
For several weeks in late summer and early fall this perennial, 24- to 30-inch anemone bears single pink flowers 2 to 3 inches across on multibranched stems. The foliage is attractive throughout the growing season and the dried winter form is interesting. Nice contrast with ferns, epimediums, and hostas. This is a plant for semishade but it tolerates direct sun, especially in cool climates. The very similar but slightly later *A.* × *hybrida* is offered in white and pink forms. For culture, see list 17, Summer-into-fall Perennials.

AQUILEGIA vulgaris, European Crowfoot.
No cottage garden is complete without perennial columbines. The pretty, lush, blue-green scalloped leaves are beautiful most of the year and in early summer the nodding blue flowers with short spurs are delightful. A good cutting flower. Self-sows lavishly. For culture, see list 13, Spring Perennials for Sun.

ASTER.
Very useful perennials with sprays of small flowers that fill the late summer and fall garden with violet, lavender, purple, pink, blue, and white. Superb in bouquets with pink dahlias. There are species that flower in late spring and early summer as well. Hybridizing has made cultivars available in sizes from 6 inches to 6 feet. Recommended for late flowers is *A. tartarica*, Tartarian Aster, 3 to 6 feet tall, a very pretty blue-purple. Tolerant of shade (if you can find it) is *A. divaricatus* (syn. *A. corymbosus*); the flowers are whitish with yellow centers. For additional recommendations and culture see list, *Aster*. The much larger, very full flower sold as an annual aster is *Callistephus chinensis*, China Aster. See list 33, Annuals for Fall.

BOLTONIA asteroides.
An asterlike, airy American native perennial that bears masses of little 1- to 1½-inch flowers with raised, rounded yellow centers surrounded by ray petals that may be white, violet, pink, or purple. It provides masses of color in late summer and early fall on strong plants 3 to 5 feet or more. In winter, the stalks and leaves are a rich brown. The species is weedy, but the 4-foot-tall 'Snowbank', a pure white that flowers from early August into September, is trim. For culture, see list 17, Summer-into-fall Perennials.

ADENOPHORA (ad-en-*off*-o-ruh) confusa
       Zones 3-8
A ladybell often taken for a bluebell, adenophora flowers for several weeks in places where heat destroys *Campanula*. It is a charming plant with bell-shaped, nodding, lavender-blue blossoms on upright stems 24 to 30 inches tall. Blooms in late spring and early summer, a real cottage garden plant found in old and abandoned gardens. It resembles that other sturdy campanula substitute, *Platycodon*. Most effective in closely spaced groups.

Culture: Dislikes transplanting but once established is tough and long-lived. After temperatures reach 70° to 75° F, sow the fine seeds where the plants are to flower. Maintain moisture for the 2 to 3 weeks required for germination. Or, set out root divisions in full sun or partial shade (especially in the South), in well-drained, humusy soil.

CENTAUREA (sen-taw-*ree*-uh)
Knapweed
The group includes useful, silvery leaved, thistlelike perennials in lavender, rose, pink, yellow, and violet, and some bright blue annuals like the Bachelor's-button, *C. cyanus*, discussed on list 34, Annuals That Self-Sow. Centaureas bloom in spring or summer and are valued as fillers and for cutting. Attractive with *Verbena bonariensis*.

Culture: In moderate climates, the plants are easily grown from seed sown in the garden, where the plants are to grow, in early fall or spring. Or, in early spring, start seeds indoors. Successful in full sun and any well-drained, even poor, soil.

C. dealbata   Zones 4-7
Called the Persian cornflower, this leafy, upright perennial 18 to 30 inches tall bears solitary 2- to 3-inch flowers that resemble the annual cornflower. The undersides of the leaves have long, whitish hairs.

C. macrocephala   Zones 3-7
Thistlelike yellow flowers 3 to 4 inches across on coarse plants 3 to 4 feet tall. Long-lasting cutting flower.

C. montana Mountain Bluet   Zones 3-8
Often called the perennial cornflower, this stoloniferous species can be invasive in good conditions. The little 2- to 2½-inch flowers are deep blue on plants 12 to 18 inches high, and the new foliage is silvery.

CHRYSANTHEMUM leucanthemum, Ox-eye Daisy, White Daisy, Marguerite.
All types of perennial mums fit a cottage garden, but this common field daisy is especially appropriate. It blooms in sunny places in early summer all over the U.S. and Canada. The plants spread by rootstock and seeds. Another cottage garden favorite is *C. coccineum*, Pyrethrum or Painted Daisy. Showy 3-inch red, pink, or white single or double flowers with yellow centers on plants 12 to 24 inches tall bloom in early summer. Thrives in sandy loam in cool regions, but may need winter mulch. The foliage is rich green. For fall color, plant cushion mums. For recommendations and culture, see list 23, Mum—Daisy.

CLEOME hasslerana, Spider Flower,
is a big, airy, back-of-the-border filler with white, pink, or lavender-pink flowers that peak in late summer and early fall. Perfect background for a mixed flowering border. Absolutely trouble-free and usually volunteers the next season. Recommended is 'Purple Queen'. For culture, see list 31, Annuals for Sun.

COREOPSIS, Tickseed.
Excellent. This is one of the easiest and most long-lasting garden perennials. In late spring and throughout summer masses of sunny, starry flowers bloom above the narrow dark green foliage. Recommended are: *C. verticillata* 'Zagreb', Dwarf Threadleaf Tickseed, which bears masses of yellow flowers on compact plants 12 to 15 inches tall and is very tolerant of heat; *C. grandiflora* 'Goldfink', under 9 inches, a lovely dwarf for the front of the border, 'Sun Ray' which

Looking as though they had escaped from the woods and multiplied here, foxglove, larkspur, lavender irises, and poppies bloom in the romantic tangle typical of one of the great themes, the cottage garden. (Woodham)

Old-fashioned flowers for a cottage garden:

TOP, LEFT Larkspur with lavender clematis billowing over the wall. (American Horticultural Society)

TOP, RIGHT *Centaurea dealbata*, the Persian cornflower. (Viette)

LEFT Musk mallow, *Malva moschata* 'Alba' looks like a daintier hollyhock. (Viette)

ABOVE Double-flowered hollyhock, *Alcea rosea*. (Viette)

Adenophora takes the place of bluebells where heat is a problem. It is most effective in closely spaced groups.
(Viette)

has double flowers; and *C. verticillata* 'Moonbeam', Dwarf Threadleaf Tickseed, 15 or 18 to 24 inches tall and covered with pale butter yellow blossoms on slender stems with threadlike leaves. Coreopsis are discussed on list 15, Summer Perennials for Sun.

COBAEA (koh-*bee*-uh) scandens
Mexican Ivy, Monastery-bells, Cup-and-saucer
Vine   Tender Perennial/Zone 9
This vine grows quickly to 25 feet, climbs by means of tendrils, and from late summer until frost bears showy, bell-shaped, usually purple-lavender flowers. There is a white cultivar.

Culture: A woody perennial in warm climates, it is grown as an annual in the North from seed started indoors in late winter. In warm regions, sow seeds outdoors in fall or late winter where plants are to flower, in full sun and moist, sandy soil.

COSMOS is a tall, willowy annual that flowers from late summer into fall, comes easily from seed, and reseeds freely; the more flowers you cut, the more come up. Lay the plants over on the ground and they send up lateral stems that bloom. *C. bipinnatus* has many dispersed but showy 2- to 4-inch-wide, open-faced flowers in clear colors—crimson, rose, yellow, and white—with crested or tufted centers held above delicate, ferny foliage. The height is 3 to 4 feet. Early Wonder, a mix, and 'Sunny Red', a dwarf about 24 inches tall that has single, bright scarlet flowers, are recommended. Another wonderful cosmos is *C. sulphureus* 'Bright Lights', which bears a great number of orange-red and bright yellow flowers on wiry stems. For culture, see list 33, Annuals for Fall.

DELPHINIUM (del-*fin*-ee-um)
Larkspur
Excellent in cool, moist climates, summer-blooming, stately, unforgettable; 4- to 6-foot-tall spikes densely covered with beautiful open-faced, spurred florets loosely arranged on slender stems. The colors are intense shades of blue and contrasting pale pinks, lavenders, and white. Some strains have a dramatic black "bee" at the center. A superb flower for arrangements, fresh or dried. Stake single specimens at the back of the border, or center groups in an island. Single forms hold up best against rain. Attractive to bees and butterflies.

In hot regions where the big perennials fail, the annual Rocket Larkspur, *Delphinium ajacis*, now renamed *Consolida ambigua*, is grown. See list 62, The Historic Garden.

Culture: In areas of moderate winters, sow seeds in the fall so they can freeze and sprout in spring. In the South, provide semishade. In cool regions, in early spring, plant root divisions in full sun, in rich, humusy, well-drained soil with a near-neutral pH. Remove spent flowers to encourage rebloom. Fertilizer is essential. When plants are 4 to 5 inches tall, pinch out the central bud to encourage branching—the flowers will be smaller but more prolific, and the plants stronger.

D. elatum   Zones 2-7
Called the candle larkspur, this memorable perennial is 4 to 8 feet tall. It forms clumps of several upright flowering stems that in summer are covered with large, flat flowers in strong purples, blues, and white, often with a dark contrasting "bee." It is grown as an annual or biennial in hot, humid areas. The Blackmore and Langdon strain is superior to early cultivars. The beautiful Pacific Hybrid Round Table series is successful in cooler climates, especially along the moist West Coast. Mid-century hybrids are recommended in areas where mildew is a nuisance. The Connecticut Yankee series are well-branched, sturdy plants successful in the Northeast.

D. grandiflorum (syn. *D. chinense*) Zones 2-7
Called Siberian larkspur, this old multistemmed sky blue (or white) delphinium succeeds in semishade in warm regions. In late June to August, it bears spurred florets 1 inch long, loosely arranged on slender stems 12 to 18 inches high. Although most plants are short-lived, they may flower the first year from seed. Deadhead to prolong flowering.

DIANTHUS barbatus, Sweet William, a short-lived, old-fashioned flower 18 inches high that for a brief time in spring bears flat-topped flowerheads of small toothed or fringed, carnation-type florets, often with a distinct crimson eye. There are reds, pinks, and bicolors with flashes of white. See list 71, The Cutting Garden.

DIGITALIS (dij-it-*tay*-liss)
Foxglove
In spring and early summer, the foxgloves dangle pendulous thimble- or finger-shaped flowers from tall, narrow spikes. The flower colors are white, cream, yellow, or rosy red, usually with dark spots. They are striking planted singly or in clumps. The leaves grow in rosettes. Though the biennial, *D. purpurea*, is remarkably big and handsome, the perennials are recommended for the cottage garden.

Culture: In early spring or fall, sow seeds or set out container plants in partial shade in rich, moist soil with lots of humus. Provide sustained moisture.

D. ferruginea Rusty Foxglove   Zones 4-7
Beautiful, lanky perennial to 6 feet tall that in spring or early summer bears spikes of coppery yellow flowers with a distinctly furry lower lip.

D. grandiflora (syn. *D. ambigua*)
Yellow Foxglove   Zones 3-8
A tidy clumping perennial to 2 feet tall with typical foxglove flowers in a pleasing creamy yellow; delicate and refined.

D. lutea   Zones 3-8
Perennial with slender spikes to 3 feet tall of small, greeny lemon flowers, excellent in a woodland garden, and especially charming in arrangements.

D. × mertonensis   Zones 3-8
Called strawberry foxglove in some regions. It is 3 to 4 feet tall, a biennial tetraploid of superior quality with big flowers in a lovely coppery rose. Attractive even when not in bloom. Self-sows freely.

D. purpurea Foxglove   Zones 4-9
A biennial 4 to 5 feet tall with 2- to 3-inch flowers in white, cream, yellow, or rosy red. It blooms the second season in spring or early summer, and even a single plant dominates the garden. 'Foxy', a dwarf 2½ to 3 feet tall, flowers in early summer from seed sown 5 months before. 'Alba', a beautiful white, is grown as an annual. See also list 71, The Cutting Garden.

ESCHSCHOLZIA californica, California
Poppy. Lovely silky poppies 3 to 4 inches across that bloom all summer in luminous colors ranging from deep orange, coral, pink, and scarlet to golden yellow and white. There are bicolors, double, semidouble, and frilled forms. The plants are 12 to 18 inches tall and the flowers are borne on sinuous, wandlike stems above low-lying, blue-green, deeply cut foliage. Tender perennials grown as annuals. See list 34, Annuals That Self-sow.

GAURA lindheimeri. A graceful, bushy perennial that flowers from May to October. The plant is 4 feet tall, with hairy, gray-green, willowlike leaves. Long-blooming loose panicles of pink buds open to 1-inch tubular, pink-tinted white flowers. A good perennializer that withstands drought. For culture see list 57, Seashore and Sandy Soils.

HELIANTHUS. Integrate the huge sunflowers, singly or in large groups, somewhere at the back of the garden. The giant daisy face with its dark central disk surrounded by yellow petals turns to follow the sun all day. There are crimson cultivars, but the old-fashioned yellow types are best for a cottage garden. When dried, the seedheads become bird supermarkets and have a nice homely look like shower heads talking to each other. Harvest the heads, give them handles of grapevine or twined grass, and hang them in trees as bird feeders. The annual, *H. annuus* (see list 71, The Cutting Garden), is 12 feet tall and its pale yellow flowerheads are 12 inches across. 'Teddy Bear' is a 2-foot dwarf with double golden flowers 6 inches across. Perennial forms, including a very hardy little sunflower whose roots are edible tubers, the Jerusalem Artichoke, *H. tuberosus*, are discussed on list 17, Summer-into-fall Perennials.

HOSTA *plantaginea*, Fragrant Plantain Lily. Once called funkia and August lily, this lush green perennial grown for its foliage still flourishes in shade gardens everywhere. In late summer, slender stems rise bearing strongly fragrant, white, bell-like flowers. The leaves are heart-shaped, light green, about 10 inches long by 6 inches wide, and grow in big clumps 18 inches tall by 30 inches wide. See also list 54, *Hosta*.

IPOMOEA, Morning-glory. These fast-growing annual vines climb by twining stems and provide quick cover to soften screens, trellises, or the chainlink fence. The flowers are trumpet-shaped and bloom all summer—opening in the morning and closing in the afternoon, except for the night-blooming Moonflower, *I. alba*. The familiar Morning-glory, *I. purpurea*, reaches 8 to 10 feet just 2 months after sowing; do not plant where it is known to be invasive. The color range includes blue, pink, rose, carmine, or white, often with white markings. A superb day-night flowering combination is 'Heavenly Blue' Morning-glory, which has 4- to 5-inch sky blue flowers with a white throat, and the creamy white Moonflower. High fertility and moist soil will produce abundant foliage but few flowers. For culture, see list 47, Climbers.

MALVA (*mal*-vuh) *moschata* 'Alba'
Musk Mallow   Zones 3-5
Bushy and branching like daintier hollyhocks 24 to 36 inches high, the clump produces many upright stems that bear a succession of pure white, satiny, 2-inch flowers. The species is rose pink and combines beautifully with wildflowers. The foliage is downy and deeply cut. This and other species have naturalized in the U. S. *M. sylvestris*, High Mallow or Cheeses, a favorite in European cottage gardens, is hardy in Zones 4 to 9 and has small rose-purple flowers.
   Culture: Plant root divisions or seed outdoors in early to midspring, and thin to stand 15 inches apart. Can be slow to germinate. Thrives in full sun or partial shade in well-worked soil. Self-sows generously.

MYOSOTIS *sylvatica*, Forget-me-not. An endearing, shade-loving flower 6 to 8 inches high that is grown as an annual or biennial and blooms from seed in 6 weeks during late spring and early summer. Dainty, an unforgettable blue, it is very effective in drifts around late-flowering bulbs. For wet, shaded places, plant *M. scorpioides*. For culture, see list 32, Annuals for Shade.

OENOTHERA *fruticosa*, Sundrops. Beautiful yellow flowers like delicate little cups with a silky sheen open during the day at the top of very slender, slightly drooping stems 1 to 2 feet high. The foliage is refined, pointed, and often flecked or tinged with bright red. The plant makes a charming tangle sprinkled over with blossoms for many weeks in summer. Night-flowering species of this American genus are commonly called evening primroses. Perennial. For culture, see list 48, Wildflowers to Naturalize.

PAEONIA, Peony. Few spring flowers can match these big, satiny blossoms for showy beauty and ease of culture, particularly in cooler regions. Peonies are among the most bountiful of the important perennials, and are superb cut flowers. For the cottage garden, choose double and semidouble herbaceous types, such as the magnificent midseason 'Felix Supreme', a light red with frothy petals. Culture and excellent cultivars are described on list 26, Peony.

PAPAVER, Poppy. Sun-loving, often finicky plants that have petals of shimmering silk in luminous, changeable, sometimes iridescent colors. Planted in groups of 6 to 10 they develop rich tangles of low-lying, deeply cut foliage, and wandlike stems, among the most exciting displays of spring and early summer. Every garden needs poppies, both the little annuals and the big perennials. The most exotic is the big *P. orientale*, a perennial 2 to 4 feet tall whose flowers can be 10 inches across; but it is challenging to grow. Small poppies are easier. Try the Iceland or Arctic Poppy, *P. nudicaule*, a small, sunny species 12 to 24 inches tall with some fragrance and wonderful colors—white-green, yellow, coral, pink, red; there are double-flowered types; generally grown from seed. The annual, *P. rhoeas*, Corn or Field Poppy, includes the 24-inch-high Shirley Poppy, a popular modern strain, and full begonia- and ranunculus-flowered forms in melting shades of pink, coral pink, and rose; doubles are delightful. See list 28, Poppy.

PHLOX. Recommended are both the perennial, starry-blossomed, spring-flowering creeping phloxes and the upright types that fill the middle of the best summer borders with long-lasting, rich pastels. But even phlox reverted to species shades of magenta are welcome in a cottage garden.
   The easiest upright phlox is *P. drummondii*, Annual Phlox, Drummond Phlox, 18 to 20 inches tall; in summer, it bears flowers in shades of red, pink, blue, soft yellow, violet, and white, some with a contrasting eye. The popular upright perennial is *P. paniculata*, Summer Perennial Phlox, Fall Phlox, which has given rise to many beautiful cultivars 6 to 36 inches tall in white, pink, salmon, scarlet, and purple, many with a contrasting eye. Deadhead the

cultivars or the garden will fill up with magenta seedlings. 'Miss Lingard', a long-established, mildew-resistant white cultivar, is recommended.
   The creeping phloxes make beautiful mats of color in spring and early summer. *P. divaricata*, Wild Sweet William, bears iris-scented, upright, lavender-blue flowers on stems 9 to 15 inches tall, from April to June. The subspecies *Laphamii* has large, rich, blue-violet flowers. *P. stolonifera*, Creeping Phlox, is a mat-forming ground cover for semishade or shade, 5 to 12 inches tall with purple or violet flowers in mid- to late spring. *P. subulata*, Moss Pink, Moss Phlox, Mountain Phlox, a mossy, needle-leaved creeper for sunny places, is 6 inches tall; it blooms in early to mid-spring in pink, bright pink with a darker eye, light or dark blue, or white. For cultivars and culture, see list 27, *Phlox*.

RUDBECKIA, Coneflower. In the worst conditions, rudbeckia comes through with yellow daisylike flowers on stems 1½ to 4 or 5 feet tall. They flower for 2 to 3 months in summer, and are among the finest and most durable herbaceous perennials. See list 15, Summer Perennials for Sun.

SANVITALIA *procumbens*, Creeping Zinnia, Trailing Zinnia. A bushy, mounding annual 6 inches high with an 18-inch spread that from early summer to frost is covered with nonstop, purple-brown-centered, golden yellow flowers similar to perky little zinnias. Used to edge borders, along paths, in rock gardens, in hanging baskets, and as a summer ground cover. 'Gold Braid' has double, golden yellow flowers with purplish centers; 'Mandarin Orange' has large semidouble flowers. For culture see list 43, Flowers for Edging.

SCILLA *siberica*, Siberian Squill. Excellent little bluebell 4 to 6 inches tall that in early and mid-spring raises slender stems covered in mid- to late spring with pendent, bell-like blossoms. The species is also known as blue squill, and the color is magnificent when plants are massed. 'Spring Beauty' is a superb blue with large blossoms. Perennialize in sheets while the pretty green grassy foliage will have time to ripen before mowing begins, and under shrubs or trees. See list 1, Early Spring, Specialty Bulbs.

SOLIDAGO *odora*, Sweet Goldenrod. Sweetly scented goldenrod, a wonderful filler 24 or 36 inches high for the late summer and fall garden. The golden yellow plumes bloom for 3 or 4 weeks. A fast-spreading perennial, it may be hard to find, but seed is offered for other types such as the showier but less fragrant *S. canadensis* and *S. virgaurea*. Goldenrods do not cause hay fever. See list 64, The Meadow Garden.

TULIPA Species or Botanical Tulips. The brilliant cup-shaped tulips on their round jade green stems are the garden's big showstoppers from late March through May. They have been bred for centuries by the Dutch to create an extraordinary range of colors and forms. Favorite groups for a cottage garden are the very early species tulips (called botanical tulips in the trade) described on list 1, Early Spring, Specialty Bulbs. They're interesting, bright, and informal. Particularly recommended are *T. clusiana,* a dainty, eye-catching flower 12 inches high called Lady tulip, pink and white with a deep purple base, that tends to perennialize on the dry West Coast; *T. marjolettii,* 20 inches tall, a slim-leafed, midseason tulip with ivory white petals brushed red on the edges; and *T. pulchella* 'Violacea', 3½ inches tall with pointed purple-red petals, the lower outer segment tinged green with a green-black basal blotch. See also list 12, Tulip.

VERBENA bonariensis. Deep purple flowers bloom from May to October on well-branched stems backed by rough, dark green leaves. The height is 4 to 5 feet. Especially attractive in mass plantings; almost as appealing to butterflies as *Buddleia.* A good cut flower, too—from South America, but naturalized here. For culture, see list 63, The Container Garden.

VIOLA. Pansies and Violets. The woodland violets that flash purple-blue in spring from 8- to 12-inch clumps of dark green leaves are kissing cousins to the big, beautiful, charismatic pansies whose faces are velvety works of art. The little tricolor violets we call Johnny-jump-ups are also related. All flourished in cottage gardens before America was discovered and belong to the genus *Viola.* Recommended for cottage gardens are white pansies, *V × wittrockiana,* backed by dwarf white irises. See list 30, Violet—Pansy.

ZINNIA. This daisylike annual comes in sizes from a few inches to several feet tall. Its form, hot colors, and drought-resistance are hard to beat. It blooms from early summer to fall, is carefree except where mildew is a problem—with care that can be avoided—and needs heat; likes being rather dry, and holds its color in blazing sun. It blooms in as little as 4 to 5 weeks from seed sown outdoors. Even a few plants in a mixed border provide flowers for cutting. The more you cut, the more the flowers come, rising between each pair of leaves and the main stem. For a cottage garden, try *Z. angustifolia* (syn. *linearis),* which is offered in catalogs with other small species described as "old-fashioned" or "Mexican" zinnias. It bears masses of single, golden orange daisy-shaped flowers on compact 8-inch plants, great for edging or as ground cover.

SOURCE: RYAN GAINEY, A HORTICULTURIST, DESIGNS CLASSIC GARDENS THAT EMBRACE THE CHARM OF COTTAGE GARDENS. WITH TOM WOODHAM, WHO TOOK THE PHOTOS HERE, HE IS CO-OWNER OF THE POTTED PLANT, THE COTTAGE GARDEN, AND THE CONNOISSEUR'S GARDEN, GARDEN AND PARTY DESIGN AND RETAIL CENTERS IN ATLANTA, GEORGIA.

Still black water in a small reflecting pond mirrors irises in this harmonious Japanese-American garden design by Osamu Shimizu. Japanese maples, ferns and other green plants with stones and trees are traditional. (Shimizu)

61. THE JAPANESE GARDEN

■ The concept of the Japanese garden is the perfect model for a garden in a very small space—and the opposite of the cottage garden. It is not intended to replicate nature but to express its moods. Where there's no room to re-create a chunk of forest or a patch of prairie, the whole effort is to give meaning to every inch of garden space. A clump of grass in sand patterned by the sea, a windswept tree with gravel raked by a waterfall, an azalea and its mountain, a fern and its valley—these are moods of nature that Japanese gardens seek to evoke in the viewer.

In this context, the Japanese garden expresses its purpose using only a few herbaceous—primarily green—plants. Several of the plants will be grasses and textured foliage plants. There are no bold, brash color statements. A water-loving iris is more important as a season-long linear accent for a pond than for its color in its season of bloom. Ferns between stones with a few—but not too many—forest flowers is a suitable expression of woodlands. Ornamental grasses with a flower or two near a sandy hummock evoke a pond.

Water is never far from the Japanese garden designer's mind, as you will realize from the plants recommended on this list.

Companion Plants: The camellia and some 25 to 35 shrubs are commonly used in Japanese gardens, among them: azaleas for texture; *Ilex crenata* (Japanese holly) and young evergreens (including *Chamaecyparis obtusa,* Hinoki Cypress, and *Cryptomeria japonica,* Japanese Cedar) for structure. *Acer palmatum,* Japanese Maple—especially weeping forms—adds texture and color. Other companions for the plants listed below are ferns, hostas, *Osmanthus,* bamboo, *Ardesia japonica,* and *A. crenata.*

The Japanese cherry tree is not recommended for residential gardens, but it is planted in Japan in parks surrounding temples and shrines. The ornamental cherry form suitable for a Japanese garden is the result of pruning. When pruned, the tree oozes, inviting disease, and for this reason it is not recommended for home gardens.

CAREX morrowii, Japanese Sedge. The plant thrives in boggy situations. Plant it between rocks, beside a stream or along a walk near a pond. It is a pretty, clumping, low-growing, evergreen ground cover 12 to 24 inches tall. The color is a fresh green marked by a bright silver central stripe. Hardy in Zones 5 to 9. For culture, see list 53, Ornamental Grasses.

EQUISETUM (ek-wih-**zee**-tum) **hyemale**

Scouring Rush, Horsetail   Zones 3-9

Equisetum forms an upright clump 3 to 4 feet tall of jointed, rushlike stalks without leaves or flowers. It is evergreen in warm climates and a good plant for contrast and for holding the soil on a bank. Plant this along a path by a pond, or between rocks. May be poisonous to livestock.

Culture: Prefers some shade, but tolerates full sun if growing in water and a cool climate. Plant divisions, in spring or fall, in wet soil up to 6 inches under water. Containerize the plant—it is invasive!

IRIS. Water is a vital element of a Japanese garden. When it isn't present as a physical property it is invoked by plants that flourish in it, for instance, the iris species *I. ensata* (syn. *kaempferi),* the Japanese Iris, thrives in damp woodlands in Zones 5 to 10, and blooms in early summer. The flowers resemble orchids up to 8 inches across and may be flat and ruffled, marbled and mottled in exotic combinations of blue, pink, reddish purple, mauve, and white. They are borne on slender stems and have grasslike leaves with a prominent midrib. In a boggy place the plant reaches 36 inches, but it will be shorter in the garden. It prefers rather acid soil, no lime, and full sun or partial shade. *I. laevigata* is a waterside iris, eloquent reflected in a quiet pond or at the edge of a stream or river. It is beardless, 24 to 36 inches tall, and in early to midsummer bears 2 to 4 blue, blue-purple, or white flowers that may be 2 to 5 inches across. It resembles the species above, but has smooth, unridged leaves. *I. sibirica* var. *orientalis* (syn. *sanguinea*), Zones 3 to 10, is 2 to 4 feet tall with dark blue to light purple flowers from 4 to 6 inches across. Prefers moist, moderately acid soil. For culture, see list 25, *Iris.*

LIGULARIA. In Japan, ligularia is used near a wash basin and lanterns, or with rock arrangements. It is a majestic plant with big, bold, basal leaves and soaring spikes of ragged yellow or orange-yellow flowers in mid-summer. Successful in containers. The species *L. tussilaginea,* hardy in Zones 6 to 8, forms loose, handsome clumps 24 inches high with large, rounded, toothed green leaves at the base. In late summer, woolly, branching, flowering stems soar above the leaves bearing clusters of daisylike pale yellow blossoms 2 inches wide. The leaves of 'Aureo-maculata', Leopard Plant, are variegated in gold and white. For culture, see list 16, Summer Perennials for Shade.

LYCORIS **radiata**, Spider Lily, Red Spider Lily, is a big, striking flower that grows from a bulb. It is used as an accent plant and with shrubs. Early in the season it produces handsome, strap-shaped leaves which die down, then in late summer or early fall a 15-inch flowering stem rises bearing exotic coral-red blossoms that have long, spidery, upcurved red stamens. For culture, see list 5, Fall and Winter Bulbs.

Traditional elements of a Japanese garden: TOP Sacred Lily-of-China, *Rohdea japonica,* foliage plant, a unifying agent among stones. (Harper)
LEFT For understated color, dwarf white Siberian iris. (Andre Viette)
ABOVE For contrast and as a bank holder, scouring brush, *Equisetum hyemale.* (Harper)

MISCANTHUS sinensis is one of the most beautiful grasses. A big plant, to 8 feet tall, it is open and upright with gracefully arching foliage. In midsummer, light-catching flower plumes rise high above the foliage. Attractive in winter. See list 53, Ornamental Grasses.

OPHIOPOGON japonicus, Lilyturf, Mondo Grass. Used as an expression of an island, as an accent plant, and as a contrast to stones. This is a low-growing, island-like mound with semievergreen or evergreen, arching, grassy leaves ¼ inch wide and 8 to 12 inches high. In late summer and fall it bears discreet spikes of light lilac flowers followed by metallic blue berries. For moist, shady areas, it is preferred to the similar but showier *Liriope platyphylla*, Lilyturf, which has taller flowers and shiny black berries. For culture, see list 58, Urban Conditions.

PLATYCODON grandiflorus, Balloon Flower. Hardy in Zones 3 to 8. The species is 24 to 36 inches tall, appears late in spring and produces graceful stems and gray-green foliage. From early summer to fall the stems are studded with distinctive balloon-shaped buds that open to blue, white, or lilac-pink starry flowers about 2 inches across. Balloon flower is used in the gardens and paths of a Japanese teahouse. For culture, see list 57, Seashore and Sandy Soils.

ROHDEA (**roh**-dee-uh) **japonica**
Lily-of-China, Sacred Lily-of-China   Zones 10-11
This is a most important foliage plant for the Japanese garden, especially appreciated when set among and between 2 or 3 stones as the unifying agent. It forms a basal rosette of arching, leathery leaves 12 to 24 inches long and 3 inches across. The flowers are pale yellow on short spikes, similar to Jack-in-the-pulpit, and partially concealed by foliage. Variegated forms are available.

Culture: In fall or spring, set out container plants in shade, in rich, well-drained, humusy soil. Maintain moisture.

TRICYRTIS hirta, Toad Lily. Used in a Japanese teahouse garden as an accent. It is unusual and exotic close up, a graceful shade plant with arching stems closely set with leaves. In mid-September in the South, and a little later in the North, flowers appear in the leaf axils; they are whitish or light purple blossoms splotched and spotted with deeper purple. For culture, see list 18, Perennials for the South.

SOURCE: OSAMO SHIMIZU, A BOTANIST, HORTICULTURIST, AND DESIGNER, WAS BORN AND TRAINED IN JAPAN. HE HAS WORKED FOR OUTSTANDING BOTANIC GARDENS ALL OVER BRITAIN AND EUROPE, AND PRESENTLY HEADS THE SHIMIZU LANDSCAPE CORPORATION, GLEN ECHO, MARYLAND.

62. THE HISTORIC GARDEN

■ Historic flowers have the lure of the restoration village. Working in a Colonial or Victorian garden you experience a feeling of an earlier time. Antique flowers generally are more modest than modern hybrids—like children who haven't been to finishing school—greener and more untidy, perhaps. The smaller, paler flowers have a way of claiming affection. The early species recommended here grow in restorations of Colonial and Victorian gardens, for instance at Colonial Williamsburg, in Virginia, and in collections of antique flowers. They and their modern counterparts are charming in herb gardens.

COLONIAL (BEFORE 1776)

Garden ideas for Colonial America came from England, Holland, and France. The prevailing tastes of the 17th century featured designs that were stylized, formal, and flat, denuded of timber, and open to the sun. After 1720, changing tastes gave rise to a more natural plant mixture that included more trees and fewer flowers.

But in America, where the land was wild and heavily forested, the bare, open formal design style took hold and held on well into the early 1800s. Ordered landscapes were a reassuring symbol of the settlers' ability to control and tame the wilderness.

In Colonial days, there was seldom a front yard, just a well-kept area of dirt, gravel, bricks, or stones. In back there was a dooryard, which was usually an enclosed work space. Beyond it was a functional kitchen garden. Boundaries were commonly fenced—also a practical measure to keep critters away—and the planting beds typically were laid out in rigid squares and rectangles. Occasionally, diagonal pathways appeared. Most plants were easily accessible from one side or another. There were food plants, berries, culinary herbs, and a few medicinal herbs. The beds around the perimeter of the gardens might be edged with tulips, daylilies, and other flowers. These were essentially kitchen gardens, so fruits were also common. Any turf areas were very small, coarse meadow grasses which had to be grazed by animals or hand-scythed.

The sources for plant materials were importation, propagation, and the wild. People dug wildflowers, harvested seeds, developed cuttings, and planted root divisions. Neighbors and families shared. Now and then seamen brought new plants from other lands, and these were very sought after.

Companion Plants: Roses make good companions for the plants on this list; consider simple species and wild roses, or climbers to grow over fences and woodpiles. For early bloom, plant *Crocus vernus*, with early, 3-inch flowers, pure white to deep purple, some striped or feathered (since 1765); white 'Joan of Arc' is one of the oldest. The following bulbs are also suitable companions: *Fritillaria imperialis* 'Rubra Maxima', a scarlet-red 2 feet tall (introduced in 1574); *Narcissus* 'Actaea,' (from the Middle Ages); *N. tazetta* 'Avalanche', one of the oldest; *N. poeticus* var. *recurvus*; and *N. obvallaris*. *N. jonquilla*, a deliciously fragrant daffodil, came with the early

colonists to America; 'Gracilis' is a fragrant, very late bloomer. Also consider *Tulipa* 'KeizersKroon', a single early tulip, bold orange-red edged in bright yellow (introduced 1750); *T. praestans* 'Fusilier,' which bears 4 red flowers to a stem (since 1600s); and *T. tarda*, yellow tipped with white, midseason, an old favorite to naturalize.

AQUILEGIA, Columbine. Exquisite foliage with flowers in purple, white and dark red, blue, or yellow. The delicate, intricate, nodding, or upright blossoms end in spurs usually in 2 shades, and are displayed against fresh, blue-green scalloped foliage on plants 12 to 36 inches tall. They are borne over many weeks in mid- to late spring. Usually self-sows. See list 13, Spring Perennials for Sun.

CONVALLARIA majalis, Lily-of-the-valley. Dainty, creamy white bells with a haunting, pervasive perfume are borne on slim 4- to 8-inch stems rising from furled green leaves. Exquisite in bouquets. It makes a cool, green ground cover for shady corners or in woodland and wild gardens. It is a perennial, but in catalogs may be grouped with bulbs for forcing and/or with perennials. For culture, see list 70, The Fragrance Garden.

DELPHINIUM ajacis, Lark's Heel, Larkspur. This is the beautiful annual delphinium, Rocket Larkspur, now renamed *Consolida ambigua*. The slender, upright 12- to 36-inch stems are densely covered with loosely arranged, beautiful, open-faced, spurred florets. The colors are intense shades of blue and contrasting pale pinks, lavenders, and white. For perennials and culture, see list 60, The Cottage Garden.

DIANTHUS, Pink, Gillyflower. The spicy clove scent of the genus is strong in both the large florists' carnations and the little grass or cottage pinks, and has been used since the Middle Ages as both flavoring and scent. Pink is just one of its several clear colors; others are red, salmon, white, yellow (*D. knappii*), and bicolors. Late spring or early summer is the usual flowering time, and some little pinks repeat sporadically if deadheaded or sheared. The slender, gray-green foliage tufts or mounds of the smaller types are usually evergreen, fine for edging and as ground cover. All the pinks are long lasting as cut flowers. See list 70, The Fragrance Garden.

INULA (**in**-yew-luh) **helenium**
Elecampane   Zones 3-8
This is a bold, stately perennial 4 to 6 feet tall with long, handsome, basal leaves; it is said to have been named for Helen of Troy. The roots were once used medicinally. Now naturalized in much of the U.S., in summer it bears bright yellow, daisylike flowers. Today it is used as a background plant for the herb or wild garden.

Culture: In early spring sow seeds or plant root divisions in sun in well-drained soil. Sustain even moisture.

GERANIUM, Cranesbill. Don't confuse it with the tender perennial whose common name is geranium, *Pelargonium*. In spring and early summer this "true geranium" bears pretty 5-petaled pastel pink, mauve, purplish, magenta, violet, cerise, red, blue, or white flowers on wandlike stems above deeply divided foliage. In colonial times the species grown were probably *maculatum,* the wild geranium, *robertianum,* which was called Herb Robert and Red Robin, and *G. lancastriense.* Today *lancastriense* is known as *G. sanguineum* var. *prostratum.* It is hardy in Zones 3 to 8, is 6 to 12 inches high, and bears small magenta-pink flowers with darker veins in summer. See also lists 13 and 14.

LYCHNIS chalcedonica, Maltese Cross, Red Campion. Upright summer perennial 12 to 24 or 36 inches tall that bears scarlet heads of closely packed florets resembling small crosses above dull green leaves. Deadheading prolongs bloom. For culture, see list 15, Summer Perennials for Sun.

NARCISSUS, Daffodil. Especially trumpets, poeticus, doubles, or multiplex. See list 9, Daffodil.

PAEONIA officinalis, Peony. These would have been the herbaceous perennial type, and double red and double purple forms are mentioned in the literature of the period. Few spring flowers can match the big, satiny flowers for showy beauty and ease of culture, particularly in cooler regions. The plants develop large clumps and produce their blossoms on upright, then branching, stems 24 to 36 inches tall. For cultivars and culture, see list 26, Peony.

VALERIANA officinalis, a perennial, is called Garden Heliotrope for its sweet perfume. This probably was the plant grown in colonial gardens, but it might also have been *V. polemonium* or *V. caeruleum,* Jacob's-ladder. Garden Heliotrope is a mounded, trailing plant that bears flat clusters of creamy white, pink, or lavender florets strongly scented of heliotrope. The branches are 2 to 4 feet long, and it blooms from late spring through summer until frost; lovely in baskets. For culture, see list 63, The Container Garden.

VIOLA odorata, Sweet Violet. This sweetly fragrant woodland perennial comes to us all the way from ancient Greece and Rome, and it still is candied for bonbons and pastry garnishes and raised to make perfume. Clumps of heart-shaped, dark green leaves half-hide flowers that may be white or blue-purple, sometimes pink. The spring blooming is heavy and often repeats in fall. A relative, *V. tricolor,* the little Johnny-jump-up, was also grown in Colonial gardens. For culture, see list 30, Violet—Pansy.

VICTORIAN (1850-1900)

Around the turn of this century, an era of opulent gardens was ushered in on big estates in England and America. Designs borrowed from Japan and Italy, France and England, were adapted or reproduced, and great sailing vessels brought plants from all over the world. At its height, the Sonnenberg estate employed 90 gardeners during the growing season.

New laborsaving technology and a growing middle class were behind many changes in the home garden. Urban homes were given porches and verandas—a step toward enjoying the now-tamed outdoors. Shrubs and ornamental trees crept back into the picture. With the invention of the lawn mower, manicured grass became a buffer between the street and the house. Shade trees were planted in the new lawns; in the North, the sugar maple was popular for its fall color. Greenhouse designs were refined and improved, and with them came the practice of removing fading spring flowers and "bedding in" annual seedlings already in bloom.

After about 1850, the keeping of the garden was increasingly seen as a pleasant family activity. The planting of flowers was accepted as a suitable pastime for the genteel. Seed catalogs elaborated on gardening as a healthy family pastime. The ladies quickly moved the flowers to the front lawn and created islands of peonies and beds of roses.

Hybridizing introduced new forms, and for the first time color became important. With the new emphasis on color, elaborate bedding schemes made an appearance.

A need for more efficient ways to nourish the earth drew attention to composting, and a few fertilizers and pesticides appeared. The modern era was launched. A century later, we're finding newness in old plants and styles, moving natives back into our gardens for health and variety, and deliberately re-creating the meadow in the New American Garden with its use of the tall, plumy, ornamental grasses.

Companion Plants: The following are recommended as companions for the plants on this list. Antique roses and bulbs such as *Crocus tomasinianus,* silvery gray lined with lavender, 6 inches tall, early, a great naturalizer (before 1850); *C. chrysanthus,* very early, low growing (before 1850); *Iris reticulata,* a dwarf from pale blue to rich violet-blue, early spring (since 1808); *Tulipa* 'Couleur Cardinal', single early, rich red with plum (since 1845); *T. kaufmanniana; T. greigii* 'Plaisir', red edged in creamy white; 'Red Riding Hood', fiery red petals and striped foliage; and *T. turkestanica,* creamy white star-shaped flowers touched with yellow-orange.

FACING PAGE Fences and gates enclose beds of mixed bulbs and perennials in a restoration garden typical of Colonial Williamsburg. (Viette)

TOP, LEFT *Delphinium ajacis*, Larks Heels, Larkspurs, the annual delphinium now known as Rocket Larkspur, *Consolida ambigua*. (American Horticultural Society)

ABOVE 'Rubra Maxima', *Fritallaria imperialis*, was introduced in 1574 from the Middle East.
(Netherlands Flowerbulb Information Center)

LEFT Historic *Tulipa tarda*.
(Netherlands Flowerbulb Information Center)

TOP The hardy lupines that flourished in Victorian gardens often escaped to the fields. These are modern Russell hybrids. (Viette) BELOW *Narcissus* 'Actaea', dates back to the Middle Ages. (Heath) BOTTOM, RIGHT *Tulipa* 'Keizerskroon', a Single Early tulip, was first introduced 1750. (Heath)

ACHILLEA ptarmica, Sneezewort. Wonderful ferny foliage and a summer-long supply of well-branched white flowerheads on plants about 24 inches tall. The dried roots were once ground for snuff—which accounts for the name. 'The Pearl' has been cultivated since the early 1900s. For culture, see list 15, Summer Perennials for Sun.

AURINIA saxatilis, Golden Tuft, Gold-dust, Basket-of-gold, Rock Madwort. Formerly known as *Alyssum saxatile*, this is a standard perennial for rock and wall gardens and ideal for carpeting steep slopes. It spreads rapidly on rambling, rubbery stems with silver leaves and in early spring covers itself with small, erect clusters of bright yellow florets. For culture, see list 66, The Rock Garden.

CHRYSANTHEMUM maximum, Daisy Chryanthemum, Max Chrysanthemum. This plant has been grown in many forms and under many names, including King Edward VII, Chrysanthemum Daisy, Shasta Daisy, Glory of the Wayside, and Parsons. The modern equivalent is probably *C.* × *superbum*, Shasta Daisy, beautiful, big, shaggy daisies that flower in early summer on plants 2 to 4 feet tall. There are singles and doubles. For cultivars and culture, see list 23, Mum—Daisy.

DELPHINIUM elatum, Tall Larkspur, Candle or Bee Larkspur. A memorable perennial that forms clumps of several upright stems which, in summer, are covered with large, flat blossoms in strong purples, blues, or white, often with a dark contrasting "bee." It is grown as an annual or biennial in hot, humid areas. See list 60, The Cottage Garden.

DICENTRA spectabilis, Bleeding-heart. A lovely shrublike, spring-flowering perennial that grows to 36 inches across and bears up to 20 or more arching racemes from which dangle perfect little pink hearts. Also known as live-forever, this old-fashioned perennial is beautiful and long-lived, a true aristocrat though the foliage tends to die out where summers are hot. See list 14, Spring Perennials for Shade.

DIGITALIS purpurea, Foxglove. In spring and early summer this biennial foxglove dangles pendulous thimble- or finger-shaped flowers 2 to 3 inches long from narrow spikes 4 to 5 feet high—in cream, white, yellow, or rosy red. It blooms the second season in spring or early summer, and even a single plant dominates the garden. For culture, see list 71, The Cutting Garden.

FILIPENDULA rubra var. venusta, Queen-of-the-prairie. Often sold as false spirea—this perennial is a big, architectural plant 6 to 8 feet tall with bold foliage. In summer it lifts towering spires of deep pink to carmine flowers that toss in the wind. See list 75, Herbs with Showy Flowers.

HELIANTHUS maximilianii, Maximilian Sunflower. The plants can reach 10 feet and the giant daisy face with its dark central disk surrounded by yellow petals follows the sun all day. Flowers in late summer; birds love the seeds. It is hardy in southern Canada. See lists 17, Summer-into-fall Perennials, and 60, The Cottage Garden.

HEMEROCALLIS lilioasphedelus, Yellow Daylily, Lemon Daylily, Lemon Lily. Formerly known as *H. flava*. Height is 30 to 36 inches, and in spring each stem bears 5 to 9 fragrant, 4-inch-long, lemon yellow flowers—a strong, sturdy daylily. Modern cultivars anchor the perennial garden through late spring, summer, and into fall in a whole new range of colors—melon, pink, orange, and white—but the old yellow daylilies have a special charm. For culture, see list 24, Daylily.

HIBISCUS moscheutos, Marsh Rose-mallow. A shrubby perennial that in midsummer bears extraordinary 7- to 10-inch flowers in white, pink, or rose. In late spring, new growth shoots up 3 to 6 feet and never needs staking. Big, sprawling, and very showy in bloom. For culture, see list 15, Summer Perennials for Sun.

HOSTA plantaginea, Fragrant Plantain Lily. Once called funkia and August lily, this lush green foliage plant still flourishes in shade gardens everywhere. In late summer, slender stems rise bearing strongly fragrant white bell-like flowers. The leaves are heart-shaped, light green, about 10 inches long by 6 inches wide and grow in big clumps 18 inches tall by 30 inches wide. Perennial. See also list 54, *Hosta*.

IRIS, probably × germanica types, Flower-de-luce, Sweet Flag, Fleur-de-lys. Sweet flags "blue and varied" were planted in Victorian gardens. The species flowers are blue-purple or violet, and there is a white form of the variety *florentina*, orris (the source of orris root, a fixative used in sachets and dried perfumes). Also recommended is *I. siberica*, which clusters 2 or 3 flowers on stalks 24 to 40 inches tall backed by slender, grasslike, waving leaves. The standards are small and don't quite meet; the large falls are exquisite. Excellent cutting flowers. Colors are blue-purple, lavender, maroon, white, and pinkish and yellowish tones. For modern cultivars, see list 25, *Iris*.

LIATRIS spicata, Burron Snakeroot, Blazing Star, Gay-feather. In mid- to late summer, the dense tufts of grasslike foliage are topped by 24- to 36-inch-tall, narrow, decorative spikes of ragged-edged, pink-purple florets. The florets open from the top and the flowers last well when cut. Nice grouped in a mixed border; good flower for cutting and for drying. For culture see list 15, Summer Perennials for Sun.

LUPINUS (lew-pye-nus) spp. Lupine
Hardy lupines flourished in Victorian gardens, and in early spring the erect 8-inch flowering spires of the old cream and purple lupines still bloom wild on plants 23 to 36 inches and taller in fields in cool, moist parts of New England and California. The florets are pea-like, thickly clustered at the tops of erect stems, and the deeply cut, palmate leaves are very attractive on their own. The genus includes shrubs and herbaceous annuals such as *L. annua*. Most often grown in modern gardens are the improved Russell hybrids, but the western native species, one of its parents, is more appropriate for a historic garden.

Culture: In early spring, sow seeds or set out container plants in full sun, or—in the South—part shade, in rich, well-drained, slightly acid soil. Mulch and sustain moisture.

Russell Hybrids   Zones 4-9
Clump forming hybrids 3 to 4 feet tall that have quite beautiful long-stemmed leaves and 18- to 24-inch flower spires in many glorious colors and bicolor combinations—purple, blues, reds and pinks, orange, cream, yellow, and white. 'Lulu' is a dwarf strain 24 inches tall. Flowers over a long period in spring to late summer, according to region. Avoid using lime in the planting area.

L. polyphyllus   Zones 4-9
Known as the Washington lupine, these hardy plants grow to 5 feet tall and bloom all summer in purple-blue combinations. The flower spires are 8 inches long and are followed by woolly seedpods.

MALVA moschata, Musk Mallow. The white cultivar 'Alba' is still grown today—a bushy, branching perennial 24 to 36 inches high. The many stems bear a succession of pure white, satiny, 2-inch flowers like daintier single hollyhocks. The foliage is downy and deeply cut. A hardy perennial. For culture, see list 60, The Cottage Garden.

MISCANTHUS sinensis 'Gracillimus'. Considered by some the most elegant of all the grasses, has fine texture and 5- to 6-foot-long, ¼-inch-wide, curly leaves with a prominent white midvein. The flowers are at first reddish pink to red then turn silvery white in autumn on curly branching panicles. Perennial. For culture, see list 74, Ornamental Grasses.

OENOTHERA. Evening Primrose. Judging from Allan M. Armitage in *Herbaceous Perennial Plants* (Athens, Ga.: Varsity Press, Inc., 1989), the species grown in Victorian gardens was probably the perennial *O. odorata*, which is open in the evening and hardy in Zones 4 to 8. Its delicate golden cups have a red tinge and are borne on slender stems 18 to 24 inches high. The foliage is refined, pointed, and often flecked or tinged with bright red. Modern gardens are more likely to display the showier day-blooming *O. fruticosa*, Sundrops. For culture, see list 48, Wildflowers To Naturalize.

PAEONIA spp. Peony. See above, under Colonial.

PHLOX paniculata, Summer Phlox. Upright perennial 2 to 4 feet tall, whose sweetly fragrant flowerheads have anchored the middle border through midsummer since Victorian times. Today the lush, pinkish purple flowers bloom wild in sunny meadows from New York to Georgia and westward into Illinois and Arkansas. There are many modern cultivars in wonderfully strong pastels. For culture, see list 27, *Phlox*.

PLATYCODON grandiflorus, Large Bell-flower, Balloon Flower. Reliable, durable, and easy, one of the best summer perennials and a good choice where campanula fails. The big, distinctive, balloon-shaped buds studded along graceful stems open to blue flowers veined with purple. The plant flowers freely from early summer to early fall and has glossy foliage. For culture, see list 57, Seashore and Sandy Soils.

SEDUM spectabile, Stonecrop. Trouble-free perennial 18 to 24 inches tall, valued for its pretty, evergreen, light green, fleshy foliage. Tiny heart-shaped flowers form a dense, flat-topped flowerhead in late summer and fall. Similar to, but not as showy as, the modern 'Autumn Joy', which burns rose and russett with the coming of cold. Easy to grow in containers and thrives in sun or shade. For culture, see list 56, Dry, Hot Conditions.

YUCCA filamentosa, Adam's-needle. A drought-resistant, huge, exotic clump 4 to 7 feet tall of evergreen, spine-tipped, silvery gray, sword-shaped leaves. In summer the soaring flower spikes bear big bell-shaped flowers that are white or cream flushed with violet or purple on the outside. It's surprisingly hardy; I first encountered it in northwestern Connecticut, where several very deep-rooted and ancient plants were anchoring the corners and entrances to a formal Victorian flower bed. For culture, see list 57, Seashore and Sandy Soils.

SOURCES: INTRODUCTORY NOTES FROM CONVERSATIONS WITH M. KENT BRINKLEY, ASLA, A LANDSCAPE ARCHITECT AND LECTURER, NOW GARDEN HISTORIAN FOR THE COLONIAL WILLIAMSBURG FOUNDATION, WILLIAMSBURG, VIRGINIA; PLANT NAMES PROVIDED BY RUDY FAVRETTI, ASLA, PROFESSOR EMERITUS, LANDSCAPE ARCHITECTURE, UNIVERSITY OF CONNECTICUT, STORRS, CONNECTICUT. AND PRACTICING LANDSCAPE ARCHITECT AND HISTORIAN.

63. THE CONTAINER GARDEN

■ Here's a movable feast of perennials and annuals for balconies, terraces, rooftops, doorsteps, under trees, and places where in-ground flowers don't succeed. The plants recommended are durable, long-flowering, and thrive in containers. Although more versatile than plants in the ground, container plants do require daily watering. This is true of small plants, plants in hanging baskets, and especially those located on balconies and terraces. Before planting a container-grown plant, loosen any roots binding the soil ball.

There are two major lists in this section; on the first list the most important annuals for small pots and baskets are discussed. With one or two exceptions these are discarded at the end of the season. Recommended on the second list are excellent perennials that usually survive winter if planted in large tubs or boxes. Between the two are listings of a few other plants that are very attractive in hanging baskets.

Follow-on and Companion Plants: Many of the bulbs on lists 1 through 12 succeed in containers, especially those on list 8, Bulbs for Containers. See also lists 56, Dry, Hot Conditions, and 58, Urban Conditions.

ANNUALS FOR BASKETS, WINDOW BOXES AND SMALL POTS

First are a number of colorful annuals and tender perennials that succeed in small containers. Those that cascade or droop are labeled as being well-suited to baskets, but they look good in pots or planters, too.

Flowers in small containers do best when given a dilute fertilizer solution with each watering. About midsummer, encourage them to rebloom by cutting back straggly branches by one-third or one-half. Perennials in small containers will not survive freezing winters, so discard them when they die back and plan to begin fresh next season.

Plants that are perennial in Zones 10 and 11 are grown as annuals in cooler regions and are replanted every year.

AGERATUM houstonianum, Flossflower. The fuzzy blue-purple flowerheads of ageratum rise above mounds of clear green foliage and bloom all summer and into late fall. The dainty arrangement of the pointed leaves is reminiscent of a nosegay. Blue ageratums are essential in the garden, but there are also pretty pink forms, as well as whites. A favorite at 6 to 12 inches tall for edging and containers of mixed flowers, ageratum now is also available in sizes at least to 18 inches. Deadhead to encourage more flowers. For culture, see list 31, Annuals for Sun.

BROWALLIA (broh-*wall*-lee-uh) **speciosa**
Tender Perennial/Zones 10-11
Good basket plant. It has slender upright-then-drooping stems about 12 inches long with dainty green leaves and summer-long, lavender-blue or white star-faced flowers with a white eye. Three or 4 plants fill a medium-size hanging basket. Bring indoors to a cool, semi-sunny window for winter. 'Major' is a large-flowered plant commonly called Sapphire Flower, that's especially colorful indoors in winter.

Culture: Seeds started indoors in late winter flower in summer. Set out seedlings after danger of frost. Keep the tips pinched out until the plants are well branched. Moist, well-drained, humusy soil and semi-sun are essential.

CELOSIA cristata Cockscomb hybrids. Eye-catching in window boxes. The velvety flowerheads of the showiest celosias resemble a rooster's crested comb. The colors are dazzling reds, yellows, salmon, oranges, apricots, and pinks. The Plumosa Group (Feathered Amaranth) are just as brilliant but have feathery flowerheads, something like goldenrod. The dwarf Fairy Fountains series bears 4- to 6-inch plumes on plants only 12 inches tall. Mass closely to hide the somewhat weedy leaves and hang upside down to dry for winter arrangements. See list 31, Annuals for Sun.

COSMOS bipinnatus. This tall, delicate-looking but tough flower has 2- to 4-inch, widepetaled, daisy-faced flowers that may be crested or tufted. It blooms from late summer into early fall in clear colors on willowy stems 3 to 4 feet tall; the plant is nice in large tubs or boxes. The cut flowers last well in arrangements and cutting encourages new growth. The Bright Lights series is yellow through gold and blooms early. 'Sunny Red', a dwarf about 24 inches tall, has single, bright scarlet flowers. For culture see list 33, Annuals for Fall.

GOMPHRENA globosa, Globe Amaranth. This is a colorful little annual whose long-lasting flowers look like fat clover heads in white, mauve, purple, pink, or orange. Use it to edge containers with long-lasting color. About 12 to 18 inches tall, it blooms in late summer and autumn and dries beautifully. Tolerates drought, wind, and searing sun. For culture, see list 72, To Dry for Winter Bouquets.

HEMEROCALLIS, Daylily. Modern daylilies anchor the garden through midsummer with magnificent lilylike flowers in many shades of melon, pink, orange, red, white, or yellow, and they're easy to grow and long lasting. Some rebloom in late fall. Medium and small daylilies are lovely featured as the sole plant in a big tub. The 8- to 12-inch dwarfs with 1-inch blooms set out in a large planter offer a brilliant, nonstop show for 3 to 4 weeks. A bonus is daylily foliage—as the plants grow the strap-shaped leaves fountain up, screening the yellowing remains of spring bulbs. They thrive in containers without any special care, except that they may need protection from the wind. Recommended for containers are 'Peach Fairy', 'Little Grapette', 'Pardon Me', 'Stella de Oro', 'American Revolution', 'Winning Ways', and 'American Belle'. Culture is described on list 24, Daylily.

FUCHSIA (*few*-shuh) × hybrida
Lady's-eardrops   Tender Perennial/Zone 9-11
Good basket plant. This woody shrub is included here because it has become almost synonymous with hanging baskets. The blossoms are like fanciful earrings dangling from slender branches 3 to 5 feet long with dainty, pointed leaves. The colors are seemingly endless combinations of creamy white and cerise-red, purple, or pink. Challenging to grow, but so beautiful they are worth trying if they can be given a cool, semishaded space. Lovely under small trees.

Culture: Buy mature basket plants in midspring, set in semishade and maintain moisture. Fuchsias flower on new wood, so to encourage blooming and maintain fullness pinch back the tips of the branches often. In fall, cut back the plants before moving them indoors to a cool place with just enough water to keep the wood from drying out. In spring, cut back again to maintain form and encourage branching; root the cuttings in water and repot the parent plant in fertile, well-drained, humusy loam in the mildly acid range, with a pH of 6.0 to 7.0.

IMPATIENS. Good basket plant. Summer-long bloom in filtered light and semishade is the exceptional gift of these tender perennials and annuals with sparkling little flowers and delicate, pointed leaves. The familiar impatiens is *I. wallerana*, Zanzibar Balsam, Busy Lizzy, which is wide-branched and superb in containers and baskets. The array of colors grows every year—dark red, hot pink, intense coral, orchid, and white—and there are bicolors and strains with variegated leaves. By fall standard sizes can attain a height of 36 inches; compacts stay at 6 to 8 inches. Recommended are: Shady Lady pastels, which bear 2-inch flowers, often with a darker center, on 12- to 15-inch plants; the very early 'Tempo Blush'; the 10-inch, early 'Accent Pink', which thrives in real shade; and the compact 'Super Elfin Blue Pearl', a delicate lilac-blue. The sturdy New Guinea strain of impatiens is branching but upright, has substantial, often brightly variegated foliage and larger blooms, and withstands more sun. New Guinea Spectra hybrids bloom from seed, bear 2- to 3-inch flowers, and much of the foliage is variegated. For culture see list 38, *Impatiens*.

LANTANA (lan-*tay*-nuh) camara
Yellow Sage   Tender Perennial/Zones 8-10
Good basket plant. This is a hairy shrub 2 to 6 feet tall that is grown as a tender perennial or annual. The cascading limbs are tipped by rounded or flat-topped flowerheads that start out yellow and turn to orange and rosy red. There are other colors as well. The nonstop, colorful blooms are attractive in hanging baskets and as edging in tubs and window boxes. Charming trained as a standard for the greenhouse or as a garden centerpiece. Lantana flowers until frost in the North, year-round in warm regions.

Culture: In early spring, set out container plants in full sun, in well-drained, rich soil. Pinch off branch tips of young plants to encourage bushy growth and maintain moisture in the early stages. Mature plants tolerate drought and thrive by the seashore.

Many of the most loved garden flowers flourish in pots, planters, and baskets—here, in a fountain full of containerized flowers, are tuberous begonias, impatiens, fuchsias and verbenas, petunias, pansies, ageratum, and *Lobelia erinus*. (Viette)

LOBELIA erinus, Edging Lobelia. Good basket plant. Succeeds in direct sun or some shade in cool, moist situations. These are delicate-looking plants 6 to 8 inches high whose thin, fragile stems are spangled from late spring to midfall with tiny florets in exquisite, luminous, intense blues and purples, often with a white eye. There are whites and wine reds as well. The upright types make vibrant edgers for planters and window boxes and the compacts and dwarfs belong in every small container. The blue cascades are unforgettable basket plants for semi-shade. See list 16, Summer Perennials for Shade.

MIRABILIS jalapa, Four-o'clock, Marvel-of-Peru, Beauty-of-the-night. An old-fashioned, leafy, bushy little plant 18 to 30 inches high that opens in the late afternoon with a burst of sweet, lemony scent that grows stronger in the cool of evening. The showy rose-red (most fragrant), bright yellow, white, or striped, veined, or spotted flowers resemble small petunias. The fresh green foliage is so full by summer's end that just 1 or 2 plants fill a corner of a big tub. Blooms in mid- to late summer and on until frost. For culture, see list 70, The Fragrance Garden.

NIGELLA damascena, Love-in-a-mist, Wild Fennel. The finely divided bright green foliage of this fast-growing, sturdy annual 18 to 24 inches tall is a good filler for hanging baskets and boxes of mixed flowers. Spidery 1- to 2-inch flowers in blue, pink, or white bloom all summer and provide charming cut flowers. Leaves with the dried seedpods are handsome in winter arrangements. There are dwarfs, such as 'Blue Midget', 8 to 10 inches tall. The standard 12- to 18-inch 'Persian Jewels' has white, pink, red, and purple flowers. 'Miss Jekyll' is beautiful blue. Successive sowings will give a longer season of bloom. For culture see list 72, To Dry for Winter Bouquets.

OCIMUM basilicum, Basil, Sweet Basil. Well branched, 12 to 24 inches tall, with somewhat puckered fresh green leaves whose fragrance and flavor combine anise and hot cloves. 'Crispum' and 'Minimum' are just 2 of the many flavorful, popular basils perfect for pots and baskets. Flowering branches of the big, dark 'Purple Ruffles' is a very aromatic and colorful addition to fresh flower arrangements. See list 77, Popular Culinary Herbs.

PELARGONIUM, Geranium. Good basket plant. Ivy geraniums, scented-leaved geraniums, and most other geraniums produce showy blooms all summer in shades of pink, red, fuchsia, white, and bicolors. They are superb container plants that may be brought indoors for the winter. Some types may be started indoors from seed in late winter. For sun or semi-sun. See list 37, Geranium—Ivy Geranium.

PETUNIA × hybrida. Good basket plant. This is the droopy-stemmed, trumpet-shaped annual flower that blooms boldly in just about every basket, tub, and window box—or so it seems. There's almost every color but true blue, and many, many combinations. Cascading types are exquisite edgers for containers. Flowering stems last rather well when cut. See list 40, *Petunia*.

PORTULACA (port-**yew**-lay-kuh) **grandiflora** Rose Moss, Sun Plant, Eleven-o'clock
Tender Perennial
Good basket plant. This is a trailing tender perennial about 8 inches high that is usually grown as an annual. The leaves are like fat needles and the flowers appear all summer, displaying bright single or double blossoms like small roses in red, pink, yellow, coral, or white. Modern portulacas stay open through the day; the old-fashioned species plants tend to close their blooms after bees have visited. Thrives in baskets and on hot, dry slopes.

Culture: Sow seeds indoors in mid-spring, in well-drained soil, and move outdoors when the weather warms. Or, in mid-spring sow seeds where they are to bloom, or set out container plants, in full sun and well-drained, humusy soil; thin so that the plants stand 6 inches apart. Tolerant of drought, but is at its best when moisture is maintained. Often self-sows.

TAGETES, Marigold. These fluffy globes of gold, orange, or pumpkin orange grow quickly, bloom from summer to autumn in hot sun, never look wilted, and withstand the worst summer storms. The foliage is lacy and pungent. One of few annuals that bloom through southern Florida summers, their tolerance of drought and heat are exceptional—and the small French marigolds often self-sow even in containers. See list 39, Marigold.

TROPAEOLUM (trop-**pee**-ol-um)
Nasturtium, Bitter Indian
Good basket plant. A fast-growing, old-fashioned plant whose spicy foliage and spurred flowers in sparkling yellow-orange-red combinations are edible. It blooms in summer until frost and comes in sizes from 8 inches high to climbers 3 to 4 feet high.

Culture: Plant both compact types and climbers in groups of 6 to 8 in full or partial sun. Sow seeds outdoors after the soil has warmed, where the plants are to bloom. If you buy nursery seedlings, choose those planted 1 to a pot and transplant without disturbing the soil. Poor, dry, soil usually produces the most flowers.

T. majus Tall Nasturtium, Indian Cress Annual
This is the common nasturtium, 1 foot to 4 feet high, whose flowers and peppery foliage garnish salads and sandwiches. The soft green seeds, when pickled, are a caper substitute. Seeds are offered for many low-growing types suited to pots and small window boxes, among them the red or yellow 'Alaska', which has pretty, variegated leaves. For bigger containers, try the rather fragrant Gleam series, whose branches trail to 36 inches.

T. peregrinum Canary-bird Flower, Canary-bird Vine, Canary Creeper
Tender Perennial/Zones 9-11
A good choice for rapid screening, this tender perennial grows to 8 to 10 feet from seed in a season. The flowers are small and light yellow with long green spurs.

VALERIANA (vall-eer-ee-**ay**-nuh) **officinalis** Valerian, Garden Heliotrope Zones 3/4-9
This mounded, trailing basket plant bears flat clusters of creamy white, pink, or lavender florets strongly scented of heliotrope. The branches are 2 to 4 feet long, and it blooms from late spring through summer until frost.

Culture: Sow seeds in early spring, or set out container plants or plant root divisions, in full sun, in well-drained soil after the soil has warmed. Self-sows and can be invasive.

VERBENA (ver-**bee**-nuh) **X hybrida** Verbena
Tender Perennial/Zone 11
Good basket plant. A fast-growing, vigorous, free-blooming creeper or trailer 8 to 18 inches long, verbena produces bright heads of small florets in white, red, pink, yellow, or purple through summer until frost. The leaves are oval or lance-shaped, serrated, and dark green. It is a superior basket plant, a great edger for boxes and tubs, and it thrives by the sea. The tall, spring-flowering V. *bonariensis* has deep purple flowers and attracts butterflies; see list 69, To Attract Butterflies and Hummingbirds.

Culture: In cooler regions it is grown as an annual from seed sown indoors in early spring. Prefers well-drained soil and tolerates drought, wind, and searing sun.

OTHER PLANTS FOR HANGING BASKETS AND WINDOW BOXES

The following plants are also suitable for hanging baskets and window boxes.

BEGONIA × **tuberhybrida Pendula Group**, see list 36, Begonia.

COLEUS blumei, Painted Nettle, and **C. pumilus**, see list 51, Foliage for Color.

CUPHEA ignea, Cigar Flower, Firecracker Plant, see list 19, Perennials Wintering Indoors.

OXALIS, Wood Sorrel, Lady's Sorrel, see list 2, Spring, Intermediate Bulbs.

THUNBERGIA alata, Black-eyed Susan Vine, Clock Vine, see list 47, Climbers.

PERENNIALS FOR PLANTERS AND TUBS

Here are some larger plants, beautiful, hardy perennials that can survive freezing winters where there is a generous buffer of soil to insulate them from frost. In Zones 6 and 7, a winter-safe, minimum container size is 14 to 16 inches (in all dimensions). In colder zones, this minimum should be increased. In warmer zones, it can be somewhat reduced. Large containers need water at least every second day in summer, and in full sun, maybe every day. Maintain some soil moisture in fall and winter. Fertilizing twice

For masses of flowers in containers:
LEFT *Portulaca* for hot places. (Yang)
BOTTOM, LEFT *Dianthus*, the scented pinks. (Yang)
BELOW Nasturtium, *Tropaeolum*, fast and spicy. (McDonald)

monthly during the growing season should be enough.

Included here are many lovely wildflowers as well as garden favorites in varied sizes suitable for the front, center, and back of a large container.

ASCLEPIAS tuberosa, Butterfly Weed, Pleurisy Root, Tuberroot, Indian Paintbrush, Chigger Flower. Butterflies and bees are drawn to the very fragrant reddish orange flowers on this stiff plant that resembles milkweed. After flowering, large, attractive seedpods develop. Height is 24 to 36 inches and it flowers in late summer. For culture, see list 15, Summer Perennials for Sun.

ASTILBE × arendsii, 18 to 48 inches high with good-looking foliage in either green or bronze, is topped in late spring and early summer by feathery flower spikes in soft shades of white, pink, red, or purple. The flowers are excellent for cutting and for growing in containers. Recommended cultivars for containers are 'Bridal Veil', about 30 inches, off-white; 'Europa', over 24 inches, early, pale pink; and 'Fanal', 24 inches, early, bloodred. These combine very well. For culture, see list 21, *Astilbe*.

CHRYSANTHEMUM nipponicum, Nippon Chrysanthemum, Nippon Daisy. This is known in the New York area as the Montauk daisy and is among the most desirable of the fall flowers. It bears fresh, white, daisylike flowers with greenish yellow centers in September or October, according to region, until frost. A good border flower and hardy perennial that reaches 3 to 5 feet in height. For culture, see list 23, Mum—Daisy.

DICENTRA eximia, Turkey Corn, Staggerweed, Wild Bleeding-heart. Heart-shaped blossoms on 12- to 18-inch plants bloom freely all summer—in shade, if moisture is sustained. The blue-gray foliage is fernlike and fine-textured. This fringed native is preferred especially in warm regions to the lovely old *D. spectabilis*, which goes dormant, leaving a foliage gap in midsummer. 'Alba' blooms are milky white, but sparser than 'Luxuriant', a pink-red hybrid. *D. formosa*, Western Bleedingheart, is very similar to *D. eximia*, and choice for dry regions. Its hybrids are more tolerant of drought but not suited to hot, wet summers. It is hardy in Zones 3 to 9, as are the other bleeding-hearts here. *Gypsophila paniculata*, Baby's-breath, is a good companion plant. See list 14, Spring Perennials for Shade.

ECHINACEA purpurea, Purple Coneflower. About 24 to 36 inches tall, the coarse, dark green foliage sets off and balances large daisylike, orange-bronze coned flowers with rich, dusky rose-purple petals. Extremely long-flowering, it comes into bloom in late spring (May or June in the South) and early summer and continues intermittently into fall if faded flowers are removed. This is one of the toughest, most durable, and longest-lived natives, showy in border or meadow and nice in fresh bouquets and dried arrangements. Recommended is 'Robert Bloom' which has very large purple-rose flowers with upright petals. 'Bright Star', a rosy-pink with maroon centers, is recommended for cutting. For culture, see list 64, The Meadow Garden.

EUPATORIUM (yew-pat-*toh*-ree-um) coelestinum
Mist Flower, Hardy Ageratum, Blue Boneset
Zones 6-10
A wonderful perennial 24 to 36 inches high with dense, fluffy flowerheads resembling blue ageratum. It flowers from late summer into early fall and is especially pretty with fall asters, white mums, and 'Autumn Joy' sedum. The cut flowers last.

Culture: Plant root divisions in early spring or fall, in full or partial sun, in well-drained, moist soil. Maintain moisture during growth. The plants tend to flop even with staking, so pinch back the tips once or twice during growth to encourage sturdy branching. Spreads easily and often self-sows.

GYPSOPHILA paniculata, Baby's-breath. This airy-looking plant bears its lilliputian white rosettes in early to midsummer. It is 24 to 36 inches high, a superior background filler for the border, and invaluable in most bouquets, fresh and dried. Cutting back after the first flowering encourages new blooms in fall. 'Bristol Fairy' is a double-flowered white, excellent for cutting. There's also a 'Pink Fairy'. The annual species is the smaller *G. elegans*. *G. repens*, a creeping form, is delightful in rock gardens and as a border ground cover. For culture, see list 71, The Cutting Garden.

HEUCHERA sanguinea, Coralbells. In late spring and early summer, this plant's tiny but eye-catching, bell-shaped flowers sway on 12- to 24-inch wiry stalks high above its semievergreen cluster of scalloped, dark green leaves. Bressingham hybrids, such as 'Bressingham Blaze', bloom in shades of coral to deep red, pink, and white. The plant makes a pretty and long-lasting edger for big containers in partial shade or sun. Deadheading encourages blooms. The foliage contrasts well with late bloomers such as *Echinops ritro*, Small Globe Thistle. For culture, see list 16, Summer Perennials for Shade.

HOSTA, Plantain Lily, Daylily. Superb group of foliage plants for shade that bear spires of often fragrant, lavender to white bells in summer and fall. The clumps of bold, handsome leaves are usually 12 to 24 inches tall with considerable spread—magnificent edgers and ground covers. *H. fortunei* 'Aureo-marginata', 'Blue Wedgewood', and *H. sieboldii* 'Kabitan' are first-rate shade-loving foliage plants recommended for large containers. *H. nakaiiana*, a textured green hosta 10 inches tall, is suggested for window boxes. *H. tardiflora* blooms in the fall. See list 54, *Hosta*.

LAVANDULA angustifolia 'Hidcote', 'Munstead', English Lavender. These hybrids are 18 inches tall with needlelike gray leaves, and all parts of the plants are sweetly fragrant. In late spring leafless shoots bear small, tightly packed, tubular flowers. According to species, these range from deep purple and blue to lavender, pink, white, and gray-blue. Pretty in containers—they'll need winter protection north of Zone 5—and delightful low foundation plant for flower borders and herb gardens in dry sunny places. See list 76, Fragrant Herbs for Drying and Potpourri.

MONARDA didyma, Bee Balm, Oswego Tea. Attractive whorls of shaggy scarlet petals surrounded by red-tinted bracts bloom through summer on stiff stems 24 to 36 inches tall. They attract butterflies, hummingbirds, and bees. Deadheading lengthens bloom time. Among monardas ranging through shades of cerise to red, white, and violet, 'Croftway Pink' is notable. For culture, see list 75, Herbs with Showy Flowers.

NEPETA, Catmint. The catmints are rather straggly herbs with slender flower spikes (usually blue) and aromatic silvery foliage. Good as edgers, fillers, and in the wild garden. *N. cataria*, Catnip, *N.* × *faassenii*, Persian Ground Ivy, and *N. mussinii* are all recommended for containers. Catnip is the one cats love best. See list 74, Herbs with Fragrant Foliage.

POLYGONATUM biflorum, Small Solomon's-seal. This is lovely and extremely easy to grow in Zones 3 to 9—a spring-blooming wildflower 12 to 36 inches tall for containers in deep shade. Rows of bell-shaped, yellow-white flowers, usually in pairs, line the arching stems through spring and are sometimes followed by blue-black berries. Attractive as a path edging, particularly opposite *P. odoratum* 'Variegatum', which is less vigorous but has cream-striped leaves. *P. multiflorum*, the European Solomon's-seal, is also quite beautiful—see list 14, Spring Perennials for Shade. For culture, see list 65, The Woodland Garden.

RUDBECKIA fulgida var. sullivantii 'Goldsturm', Coneflower. The finest of the yellow black-eyed Susans is 18 to 30 inches high, free-flowering through summer and, depending on season and place, into fall. Leave the sooty, cone-shaped flowerheads to ripen for the birds, for winter interest, and to reseed. For difficult warm climates *R. hirta*, Black-eyed Susan, which is grown as an annual, may be better. It flowers for 2 to 3 months, self-sows aggressively, and is a good perennializer for wild places. See list 64, The Meadow Garden. For culture, see list 15, Summer Perennials for Sun.

STYLOPHORUM diphyllum, Celandine Poppy, Wood Poppy. This charming 12- to 19-inch spring wildflower has graceful clusters of poppy-like, showy yellow flowers 2 inches across that develop into loose-hanging seedpods. The light green leaves are deeply lobed and remain well into fall if grown in evenly moist conditions. The yellow sap that comes from the stems and leaves was used as a dye by Native Americans. For culture, see list 48, Wildflowers to Naturalize.

SOURCE: LINDA YANG, A GARDEN COLUMNIST FOR THE HOME SECTION OF *THE NEW YORK TIMES*, TILLS HER OWN CITY PLOT IN MANHATTAN. SHE IS THE AUTHOR OF *THE CITY GARDENER'S HANDBOOK: FROM BALCONY TO BACKYARD* (RANDOM HOUSE).

64. THE MEADOW GARDEN

■ Do you have a field to spare, or a large lawn you are tired of mowing? There's room for a meadow garden in every gardener's dreams—a place, large or small, of tall grasses to come upon in sunshine, gilded by gold-enrod and spattered with poppies, where Queen-Anne's-lace gently nods. Here are some of the flowers that. make the show exciting, all recently tamed to garden life and ready to go wild without much food or water. All they need is about six hours a day of full sun and soaking rain two or three times a month.

The plants recommended here grow from seed, perennialize reliably, and can compete with wild grasses for a place in the sun. Once established, they withstand drought and are adapted to all regions of the country except the tropics. They guarantee the color a meadow garden must have year after year, and add a colorful splash to the wildflowers of your own region.

Wildflower seeds are sold by specialists, usually as mixes of the best regionals—from the tall, pink plumes of Wisconsin's Queen-of-the-prairie, *Filipendula rubra*, to California's evening primrose, *Geum triflorum*, and starry blue-eyed *Sisyrinchium bellum*.

The perennials and biennials, as well as the annuals listed here, self-sow. But keep your meadow garden exciting by giving it a yearly boost of new seed for the established plants, as well as seed for regional new-comers. Include lots of annuals, since many peren-nials require two seasons to come into full bloom.

Culture: To create a meadow garden, when the ground becomes workable in early spring till the sur-face, turning it over just an inch or so for good seed-to-soil contact. Rake the area smooth and discard weeds and roots. Till again every third year. Most experts recommend not fertilizing unless the soil is com-pletely sterile, because fertilizers encourage the grasses that crowd out wildflowers.

Mix the seeds and combine them with damp sand or sawdust, then broadcast them evenly over the site. Follow the seeding rates given on seed containers. Tamp down the seeds by walking lightly over the seeded area. Water with a fine spray. Maintain soil moisture until the seedlings are established. Even drought-resistant wildflowers need water to get started.

A little hand-weeding in the beginning and again early each spring will make a big difference as the years go by. Without some control, grasses and weeds tend to take over and obscure—and eventually engulf—the flowers.

Mow the meadow after the flowers have set seed, or in late winter. This opens up the area to more light and air and sets a healthy tone for another year of meadow gardening.

Related lists include 34, Annuals That Self-sow; 48, Wildflowers to Naturalize; and 53, Ornamental Grasses.

Companion Plantings: Look for sweetly scented regional wildlings to add, such as: *Asclepias incar-nata*, Swamp Milkweed; *Agastache foeniculum*, Giant Blue Hyssop; and *Sporobolus heterolepis*, Prairie Dropseed.

Purple coneflower, *Echinacea purpurea*, a tough, long-lived, native meadow flower, makes an outstanding, lasting, show in late spring and early summer. (Viette)

Showy and durable for meadow gardens:

TOP, RIGHT Purple coneflower, *Echinacea purpurea*, stands out even in a crowd. (Viette)

ABOVE Bright little 'Goblin', a dwarf *Gaillardia*. (Viette)

RIGHT Black-eyed Susans, *Rudbeckia*, with Queen-Anne's-lace and cornflowers. (American Horticultural Society–Martin)

FACING PAGE Long-lasting blooms of goldenrod, *Solidago*, with black-eyed Susans and grasses. Goldenrod's late summer bloom is increasingly appreciated now that it is known that it does not cause hayfever. (McDonald)

ASCLEPIAS tuberosa, Butterfly Weed, Pleurisy Root, Tuberroot, Indian Paintbrush, Chigger Flower. A fresh orange accent for the meadow, and it attracts butterflies. This is a 24- to 36-inch perennial look-alike for milkweed, with long-lasting fragrant, showy flowerheads in summer. Interesting seedpods follow. There are yellow hybrids and bicolors. Good cut flower, especially if the stem is seared immediately after cutting, then put into water. *Asclepias incarnata*, Swamp Milkweed, is recommended for damp meadows. For culture see list 15, Summer Perennials for Sun.

ASTER novae-angliae, New England Aster. In a meadow, these shrubby plants grow into great clumps 4 to 6 feet tall, covered in late summer and early fall with lasting daisylike, little fluffy pink and purple-pink blooms. Sprays of the flowers are excellent fillers for flower arrangements, especially with pink dahlias. They survive early frosts. Numerous colorful asters have been developed—white, rose, ruby red, and salmon. 'Harrington's Pink' is one of the best. For culture, see list 20, *Aster*.

CHRYSANTHEMUM leucanthemum, Ox-eye Daisy, White Daisy, Marguerite. The enduring, hardy perennial white-and-gold field daisy that blooms in early summer all over the U.S. and Canada—a meadow garden is hardly right without it. The plants are 12 to 24 inches tall and bear single flowers 2 inches across. Plant may flower from seed the first year and once established, spreads by rootstock. Cut flowers are delightful in bouquets. This is one of the most durable of the species chrysanthemums, but others on list 23, Mum—Daisy, also naturalize.

COREOPSIS lanceolata, Tickseed. Excellent. Sunny, long-lasting, and trouble-free, covers itself with fluffy, pretty 2½-inch yellow flowers in late spring or summer according to region, on plants 12 to 24 inches tall. The deeply cut foliage, light or somewhat coarse, is attractive. See list 15, Summer Perennials for Sun.

DAUCUS (daw-kus) carota
Queen-Anne's-lace   Zones 3-8
A much loved and widely spreading (sometimes invasive) wildflower that makes wonderful bouquets. The broad, flat, white-green flowerheads on 24- to 36-inch-tall, wandlike stems dance in every breeze above the pungent, ferny, carrotlike foliage. There's a tiny purple-red central floret.

Culture: Sow the seed of this biennial in well-drained soil, in early spring or fall; flowers the next year and self-sows generously. Where Queen-Anne's-lace is invasive, do not plant.

ECHINACEA (ek-in-nay-shee-uh) purpurea
Purple Coneflower   Zones 3-8
This is one of the showiest, toughest, and longest-lived native meadow flowers. About 24 to 36 inches tall, its coarse, dark green foliage sets off and balances large daisylike flowers in a rich, dusky rose-purple, with deep orange-bronze central cones. Characteristically, the petals droop a little backwards. Extremely long-flowering, it comes into bloom in late spring (May or June in the South) and early summer, and continues intermittently into fall if faded flowers are removed. Showy in borders and fresh bouquets and dry arrangements. Recommended for the cutting garden are 'Bright Star', rosy pink with maroon centers, and 'Magnus', whose petals are flatter than those of the species. 'White Lustre' is white-petaled with an orange center. Nice with *Rudbeckia*, which it resembles.

Culture: Sow seed or set out root divisions in early spring, in full sun, or dappled shade in the warm South. Prefers rich, moist, humusy, somewhat acid soil with a pH of 5.9 to 6.0. Do not fertilize when growing in semi-sun. Practically pest- and disease-free. Withstands dry conditions.

ESCHSCHOLZIA californica, California Poppy. This tender perennial 12 to 18 inches tall, usually grown as an annual, self-sows generously and naturalizes in regions like its native southern California. In colder areas it must be reseeded annually. The sunny, silky 2- to 4-inch flowers bloom all summer in luminous shades of pink, scarlet, orange, coral, red, white, and bicolors; single, double, or semidouble, some frilled. In the North, sow seeds in early spring; in warm areas, sow seeds in fall for spring flowering. For culture, see list 34, Annuals That Self-sow.

GAILLARDIA (gay-lard-ee-uh) pulchella
Blanket Flower   Annual
Bright, showy, yellow-tipped red, daisy-faced flowers also known as Indian Blanket. The 24-inch-tall species has the longest blooming period of any summer flower, especially if spent flowers are removed. Attractive to butterflies and has interesting seedheads. One of the best is the dwarf 'Goblin', 9 to 12 inches, which has 4-inch flowers with

yellow-edged red petals; grown from root divisions planted in spring. The species is recommended for meadow gardens, but for borders the preference is a large-flowered perennial hybrid, *G. × grandiflora*, and its variations.

Culture: Sow seeds of this annual in spring in full sun. Seeds of perennial species to be planted in a flower border are started indoors and set out after the weather warms. Prefers well-drained, ordinary soil but is versatile; impervious to heat and drought.

PHLOX drummondii, Annual Phlox, Drummond Phlox. The big, silky-soft flowerheads of this 18-inch annual appear in midsummer and may be white, pink, rose, red, lavender, magenta, cerise, or fuchsia; some have a contrasting eye and a meadowy scent. Deadheading prolongs bloom. Lovely in bouquets and the more you cut, the more the flowers come. Star Phlox is the common name given to a strain with fringed petals. Even in hot, sandy soil this phlox withstands considerable drought, and often self-sows and naturalizes. For culture, see list 27, *Phlox*.

RUDBECKIA hirta, Black-eyed Susan. The many rudbeckias are superb border flowers and naturalizers, but this is one of few that thrives even in the hot South. Biennial or perennial, it is grown as an annual and blooms the second year after seeding. It flowers from August to October, a typical yellow-gold daisy with outer ray florets around a central elevated cone of black disk florets on plants 18 to 36 inches tall. It self-sows aggressively and is choice for the meadow garden. *R. triloba* is recommended for damp meadows. Leave the flowerheads to ripen for the birds, for winter interest, and to reseed. For culture, see list 15, Summer Perennials for Sun.

SOLIDAGO (sol-id-day-goh) odora
Sweet Goldenrod   Zones 3-9
This species is recommended for its sweet scent. The golden-yellow plumes, on plants 24 or 36 inches high, flower for 3 or 4 weeks in late summer and early fall, a main event in the late wildflower displays of much of the continent. A fast-spreading perennial, it is valued as a filler in bouquets, fresh or dried. Seed for cultivated varieties and the showier but less fragrant *S. canadensis* and *S. virgaurea* may be easier to find and will serve the meadow garden as well as the flowering border. *S. nemoralis* is recommended for very dry meadows and *S. rugosa* for damp meadows. Goldenrods do not cause hay fever. Native Americans used it for medicinal teas and smoking materials.

Culture: Sow seeds in early spring, in full sun or part shade, in well-drained, ordinary soil. Blooms the first season and self-sows. Withstands drought and heat but prefers some moisture at the roots.

SOURCE: LAURA COOGLE MARTIN, A BIOLOGIST, NATURALIST, LECTURER, AND JOURNALIST, IS THE AUTHOR OF SEVERAL BOOKS ON WILDFLOWERS, INCLUDING *SOUTHERN WILDFLOWERS* AND *THE WILDFLOWER MEADOW BOOK*.

65. THE WOODLAND GARDEN

■ These superb flowers and foliage plants for woodland gardens and landscapes are all native aristocrats now propagated and sold by nurseries. Some grow a little slowly, but the plants described below are the best of the beautiful plants that grow in shade. Most are for dappled light found at the forest's rim; a few grow in the dim, secret reaches of the inner forest. They thrive in domesticity if they are provided with light and soil approximating that of their native haunts.

These plants are sold by nurseries that specialize in wildflowers. Do not dig them in the wild—many are protected by conservation laws. Make sure your source offers propagated plants, not those collected in the wild.

Companion Plants: When spent, most of these flowers leave behind attractive foliage to grace their places, so follow-on plants are not necessary. Other lists focused on flowers that thrive in shade include 14, Spring Perennials for Shade; 32, Annuals for Shade; 29, Primrose; 30, Violet—Pansy; 38, *Impatiens*; 64, The Meadow Garden; 52, Ferns for the Garden; and 54, *Hosta*.

Culture: Almost all of these plants require soil that is moist—as in woodlands—but well-drained. Forest soils are composed largely of humus from decomposed leaves. In the garden, compost made from shredded leaves is a better source of humus for these plants than purchased peat moss. Most but not all woodland plants prefer soils in the acid range, with a pH under 7.0. Adding humus increases soil acidity. If the soil is too acid for the plants chosen, add lime along with the humus.

If drainage needs improvement, see the section on improving the soil and building a raised bed in Growing Flowers.

Light shade, or semi-sun, is defined in this book as 2 to 6 hours of direct sun daily. Most of the wildflowers on this list thrive in semi-sun, preferably morning sun (afternoon sun is hotter). A few plants for deep shade are described below.

Set out container-grown wildflowers as soon as the soil is workable. Generally, April and early May are the best time for transplanting; in cool regions, wait until after May 24. Set the plant so the crown is a bit above soil level, firm the plant, and water liberally.

Some wildflowers are easily grown from seed, usually fresh seed sown as it ripens on the plants in late summer or early fall. Many wildflowers benefit from a sprinkling of fertilizer during the growing season. Use acid fertilizers for most of the plants listed here.

ACTAEA (ak-*tee*-uh)
Baneberry, Cohosh, Necklaceweed
Showy clusters of small, fluffy white flowers appear in spring on well-branched plants with handsome, deeply cut leaves; flowers are followed in late summer by striking glossy red or white berries. Long-lived, durable plants that perennialize well in woodlands and are good backdrops for low-growing rock garden plants.

Culture: Sow fresh seeds in fall, or in early spring set out root divisions, in light shade, in moist, humusy soil with a pH of 5.0 to 6.0.

A. pachypoda White Baneberry, White Cohosh, Doll's-eyes   Zones 3-9
Fluffy spring flowers on plants 36 inches tall are followed by white or pinkish berries, each with a dark eye.

A. rubra Red Baneberry, Snakeberry Zones 3-9
A little smaller, to 24 inches, with showy clusters of small white flowers in spring followed by red berries.

ANEMONELLA
thalictroides 'Schoaf's Double Pink', Double Rue Anemone. A superb pink double form of this delicate little perennial about 6 inches tall which, in early to late spring, bears blooms an inch across in a loose terminal cluster. A handsome plant with low-growing, ferny leaves. See list 48, Wildflowers to Naturalize.

CHRYSOGONUM
virginianum. It is called golden star. Easy, low, fast-spreading, trouble-free native about 8 inches high that covers itself with masses of small, bright yellow star-flowers in spring and sporadically through late summer and fall. Does especially well throughout summer in the North. Neat, compact, attractive foliage. There are several selections, from a totally prostrate form to one with flower stems 4 inches tall. For culture, see list 18, Perennials for the South.

CIMICIFUGA
racemosa, Black Cohosh, Black Snakeroot. One of the fullest, most imposing, and finest perennials. The stiff, slender, towering, branching spires 6 to 8 feet high with small, fluffy white flowers will dominate any planting for a month or more beginning in early or midsummer. The blooms are arranged densely on spiky stems rising from generous clumps of shiny, compound leaves. Excellent for the back of the border, in wild gardens, and for cutting. Given 2 or 3 growing seasons to become established, these plants are among the very best and most permanent maintenance-free perennials—almost completely pest- and disease-free. See list 16, Summer Perennials for Shade.

CLINTONIA (klin-*toh*-nee-uh) umbellutala
Speckled Wood Lily   Zones 4-8
Fleshy, broad-leaved perennial 12 inches high that bears graceful little clusters of nodding, jewel-like, white-spotted flowers in spring, followed by shiny ornamental blue berries. Handsome massed in woodlands or wild gardens.

Culture: Sow fresh seeds in early fall or set out root divisions in early spring, in shade, in moist soil with a pH in the range of 5.0 to 6.0. Slow to develop from seed.

CYPRIPEDIUM calceolus var. pubescens
Large Yellow Lady's-slipper, Large Yellow Moccasin Flower   Zones 3-8
Large, showy variety of the beautiful wild orchid of North American woods and bogs, and the most successful of this challenging genus in cultivation. The plants have strongly ribbed large leaves, and in spring the 12-inch stems are tipped with 1 or 2 very fragrant, pouchlike large yellow flowers streaked with brown. These are exotic, challenging specimen plants to be proudly featured in a wild or rock garden.

Culture: Can be transplanted successfully only if the brittle roots are handled with care and if the site duplicates the native habitat. Set out root divisions in early spring or fall in light shade, in moist, humusy soil with a pH in the range of 6.0 to 7.0.

DISPORUM (dis-*poh*-rum) maculatum
Nodding Mandarin   Zones 4-9
Elegant, showy, nodding greenish flowers speckled with white on plants 24 to 36 inches tall rise from forked stems that have narrow pointed leaves. Orange berries follow.

Culture: Sow seeds as soon as they are ripe, or in early spring set out root divisions, in shade in moist humusy soil with a pH in the range of 5.0 to 6.0.

EPIGAEA (ep-ij-ee-uh) repens
Trailing Arbutus, Mayflower   Zones 4-8
This is perhaps the most fragrant of all wildflowers, a slow-spreading 6-inch-high evergreen creeper with bright green leaves. In spring it bears clusters of pink-tinged flowers rather like tiny apple blossoms and almost hidden by the leaves. For the rock garden or woodland site.

Culture: Dislikes being disturbed, but can succeed with patient care in very well-drained soil, preferably sandy, with a pH of 4.0 to 5.0, and a light annual mulch of decayed leaves (oak is best). Plant container-grown, rooted divisions in partial to full shade, disturbing the root ball as little as possible.

GALAX (gay-lax) urceolata
Galax   Zones 3-8
The plants are slow-growing very attractive tufts of thick, evergreen, heart-shaped basal leaves 12 inches high; valued by florists, and for year-round textural interest. Bronze in autumn. Small white flowers rise on slender stems in late spring and early summer. Excellent ground cover.

Culture: Plant root divisions in early spring, in shade, in well-drained, moist, humusy soil in the acid range, with a pH of 4.0 to 5.0.

SANGUINARIA
canadensis 'Multiplex', Double Puccoon. Beautiful, showy, pure white double form of a very early spring favorite with flowering stems 8 inches tall. The foliage is rich, dark green. See list 48, Wildflowers to Naturalize.

POLYGONATUM (pol-ig-oh-*nay*-tum)
Solomon's-seal, King-Solomon's-seal. The species here are the smaller forms, graceful spring-blooming wildflowers found in damp, light woodlands and reliable for a shade garden. In spring, rows of white, pendulous, bell-shaped green- or yellow-white flowers, usually in pairs, line the arching stems and are followed by blue-black berries. Pretty if not spectacular, and some are fragrant. The foliage turns a fine yellow-brown in fall and persists. Good, sturdy clump. Other species are recommended in list 14, Spring Perennials for Shade, and list 67, Rare and Choice.

Culture: Set out root divisions in fall or spring in light to moderate shade in deeply dug, rich, well-drained, humusy, somewhat acid soil, about pH 5.0 to 6.0. Maintain even moisture.

P. biflorum Small Solomon's-seal   Zones 3-9
A lovely 12- to 36-inch-tall species attractive as a path edging, particularly opposite *P. odoratum* 'Variegatum', which is less vigorous but has cream-striped leaves.

P. humile Dwarf Solomon's-seal   Zones 4-7
A rare and choice spring-blooming perennial that is a pleasing companion for European Wild Ginger, *Asarum europaeum*. The plant is 8 inches high, stocky, vertical

Some of the superb woodland flowers now cultivated by nurseries:
TOP, LEFT *Trillium grandiflorum*.
TOP, RIGHT *Clintonia umbellulata*.
CENTER *Uvularia grandiflora*.
BOTTOM, LEFT *Galax urceolata*.
BOTTOM, RIGHT *Actaea rubra*.
(Photos by the New England Wild Flower Society)

TOP *Linnaea borealis.*
ABOVE *Cornus canadensis.*
RIGHT *Coptis groenlandica.*
(Photos by the New England Wild Flower Society)

with attractively grooved foliage. In mid-spring, it bears rather large, creamy, bell-shaped flowers. Clumps increase slowly and make a distinctive small-scale ground cover for the woodland or shaded rock garden. Available at this writing from sources 4, 5, 10, and 12 in the Appendix.

SHORTIA (*short*-ee-uh) galacifolia

Oconee-bells   Zones 4-8
Handsome, low-growing, stemless tufts of glossy green, rounded evergreen leaves that in very early spring send up stalks bearing nodding white bells with a cluster of white anthers in the center. The leaves redden as they mature, and in cold weather become dark red or purple. Excellent ground cover 4 to 8 inches high for deep shade.

Culture: Sow seeds as soon as they ripen and *do not cover them.* Or, set out root divisions of the creeping rootstock in early spring or after bloom, in shade in moist, peaty, well-drained, acid soil with a pH range of 4.0 to 5.0. Very slow from seed.

TRILLIUM (*trill*-ee-um)

Wake-robin, Birthroot
Beautiful orchidlike, early spring wildflower with large, showy flowers. Each rhizome sends up 1 stem with 3 leaves and a 3-leaved blossom which may be pure glowing white, deep maroon-red, or purple-brown. Spreads to form colonies in established woods; a good, tall ground cover for woods. The 3 species described here are only a few of the many that are much sought after for woodland and wild gardens in shade.

Culture: Set out container-rooted rhizomes, in early spring, in the light or dark shade of tall, deep-rooted trees in moist soil composed almost entirely of leaf mold or humus, with a pH of 6.0 to 7.0. Trilliums do not compete successfully with surface roots.

T. cunneatum Whippoorwill Flower Zones 7-9

To 10 inches tall, with deep maroon or brown flowers, this is suited to southern woodlands.

T. erectum Stinking Benjamin, Squawroot, Brown Beth   Zones 3-9

To 12 or 24 inches tall, the large flowers are 2 to 3 inches across, purple-brown or yellow and green, sometimes drooping, and have a rather unpleasant odor.

T. grandiflorum White Wake-robin Zones 3-8

Large, pure white flower that fades to pink as it matures. Do not cut. Mature height to 18 inches.

UVULARIA (yew-view-*lay*-ree-uh)

Merrybells, Bellwort, Haybells
Charming low-growing mats send up clusters of wiry, branching stems 18 inches tall, each tipped in spring with a single long, narrow, nodding, bell-shaped blossom. The plants attain their height after the blooms fade. Specimens to feature in rock or wild gardens.

Culture: In early spring or late fall set out root divisions in light shade in moist soil in the acid range.

U. grandiflora   Zones 3-9

Extremely showy yellow flowers on graceful stems. Prefers soil in the pH range of 6.0 to 7.0.

U. perfoliata Strawbell   Zones 3-9

Flowers are slightly paler and less showy than the species above. Prefers more acid soil, in the pH range of 5.0 to 6.0.

SPECIMENS FOR DEEP SHADE

Shade and deep shade are defined as only 2 hours of full sun a day, or dappled sun all day.

ARISAEMA (ar-riss-*seem*-uh) triphyllum

Jack-in-the-pulpit   Zones 4-9

One of the earliest wildflowers, sedate, to 24 inches tall, usually found in small colonies in shady woods. "Jack" stands in a "pulpit" like a small calla lily, purplish bronze inside and greenish outside. A small cluster of brilliant red berries follows. To put any part of the plant into one's mouth causes a long-lasting, painful pins-and-needles feeling.

Culture: Sow fresh seed or plant root divisions, in early spring, in light to moderate shade in moist, rich soil with a pH of 4.0 to 5.5. Perennializes. Maintain even moisture.

COPTIS (kop-tiss) groenlandica

Cankerroot   Zones 3-7

In late spring and early summer, slender stems bearing pretty, starry white flowers rise above a mound of low-growing, lustrous, evergreen basal leaves. The plant is about 5 inches high, an attractive ground cover for damp, shady woods.

Culture: Plant root divisions in early spring in shade, in cool, moist soil very well supplied with humus, and with a pH of 4.0 to 5.0.

CORNUS (korn-us) canadensis

Bunchberry, Dwarf Cornel, Crackerberry, Pudding-berry   Zones 2-8

Relative of the lovely spring-flowering dogwood tree, a neat and attractive herbaceous perennial that makes a good ground cover. In mid-spring, it carpets the ground with what look like 6-inch white dogwoods in bloom. In summer and fall, bunches of edible red berries appear, they were once used to make a pudding.

Culture: Plant container plants or divisions of the creeping rootstock in early spring, in shade, in cool, moist, well-drained, rich, soil with a pH of 4.0 to 5.0. Best in cool soil.

LINNAEA (lin-nee-uh) borealis

Twinflower   Zones 2-7

A small, dainty creeper just 4 inches high with rounded, 1-inch leaves that have a fine hairy fringe. In late spring and early summer, lovely little bell-shaped, fragrant pink flowers bloom in pairs, standing well above the leaves on slender stems.

Culture: Plant root divisions in early spring in shade, or part shade with morning sun only, in cool, moist, humusy soil with a pH of 4.0 to 5.0.

SOURCE: WILLIAM BRUMBACK, OF THE GARDEN IN THE WOODS, FRAMINGHAM, MASSACHUSETTS, A BOTANICAL GARDEN OWNED BY THE NEW ENGLAND WILD FLOWER SOCIETY.

66. THE ROCK GARDEN

■ **A good rock garden is a miniature mountain based on a core of rock and soil. It has pockets of loam for planting and areas of bare rock covered with gray-green lichen, pockets of loose-packed pebbles, and, at the bottom, if possible, a little pool where moisture-loving rock garden plants are at home.**

A rock garden is an ideal installation for a naturally existing stony terrain; a rocky slope falling away from a ridge, or ground sloping up from a valley or low point facing east, northeast, west, or northwest, with good light but not too much direct sun, is an ideal location. A rock garden can also be developed from a sheer drop gentled with a fill of rocks and soil.

Native rocks are the most effective and they must be placed to follow the stratification of rocks already there.

Culture: Before planting, be sure all the planting places and spaces behind are filled with soil; leave no hollows or caves that roots could creep into and die. Shallow pockets whose soil has no contact with the basic soil core are better left unplanted.

The texture of good rock garden soil is gritty. It includes lots of coarse sand composed of sharp-edged fragments of rock, along with liberal quantities of humus and loam. Plants requiring very good drainage belong in planting pockets angled to spill excess water. Most rock garden plants require slightly acid soil. In limestone areas, soil testing is necessary. Watering during droughts is indispensable.

Set out started seedlings or root divisions with 3 to 4 plants of each kind together in drifts or masses. When a pocket is so small it can hold only one plant, choose a showy one.

Companion Plants: Small shrubs and trees have a place in a rock garden, as do ornamental grasses such as *Festuca* (see list 55, Easy Alpine Plants). Low heaths and brooms, such as *Bruckenthalia spiculifolia* (Spike Heath), *Genista pilosa* 'Vancouver Gold', *G. dalmatica*, and *G. delphinensis* are also handsome in rock gardens. *Daphne cneorum* (Garland Flower), *Clematis integrifolia*, a nonvining clematis, and *Salix jesoalpina*, a prostrate willow 4 to 5 inches tall, all fit in well. Small bulbs, such as *Narcissus* 'Baby Moon', also work well.

ALLIUM thunbergii. This little ornamental onion 10 inches high for the fall border is one of the last to flower, beginning in late September and persisting beyond the first frosts. Hardy in Zones 4 to 9. Rounded heads of rose-violet blooms, urn-shaped like those of heaths, are held on slender stems above grassy foliage. Eye-catching in small groupings in the rock garden. For culture, see list 67, Rare and Choice.

AQUILEGIA, Columbine, is an exquisite spring-flowering plant 12 to 36 inches tall, with intricate nodding or upright flowers that have colorful spurs and fresh blue-green, scalloped foliage. If cut back when it begins to spoil, the foliage usually returns and becomes a low filler for the rest of the season. Some types flower in sun or shade. Species recommended for the partly shaded rock garden include: *A. bertolonii*, a fine, small plant, about 3 inches high with large, rich blue, upturned flowers; *A. canadensis*, Wild Columbine, Meeting-houses, Honeysuckle, delicate pink and yellow or orange-red flowers with long

spurs on plants about 12 inches high; *A. flabellata* 'Nana', white, 6 to 8 inches high, a handsome, easy-to-grow plant that self-sows. For culture, see list 13, Spring Perennials for Sun.

ARMERIA, Thrift, Sea Pink. Sturdy little evergreen plants that in spring form neat, dense mounds of grassy leaves and lift attractive globe-shaped flowers well above the foliage. Used especially for rock or wall gardens and edgings. The following are recommended. *A. juniperifolia*, Zones 4 to 8, 2 to 4 inches tall, is densely tufted and has interesting short leaves and lilac blooms. There's also a nice white-flowered form. *A. maritima* 'Dusseldorf Pride' is choice; its little pincushions of foliage produce tight heads of pink to carmine-red flowers on stems 6 to 12 inches high. Flowers in late spring in almost any soil or exposure. For culture, see list 13, Spring Perennials for Sun.

AURINIA (aw-*rin*-ee-uh) saxatilis (formerly *Alyssum saxatile*)

Basket-of-gold, Goldentuft, Madwort, Goldentuft Alyssum, Gold-dust, Rock Madwort   Zones 3-7

A standard rock garden and wall plant 6 to 12 inches high that shines hot yellow in early spring. The plant spreads rapidly on rambling, rubbery stems with silver leaves, and covers itself with small bright yellow flowerheads. Great carpet for steep slopes.

Culture: Sow seed in early spring or fall, in full sun, in well-drained, sandy or gravelly soil in the near neutral range. Trim back after flowering. Divide in the fall, or reseed. In the South, it is best in semishade, but tends to die out with high heat.

CAMPANULA, Bellflower. These small gossamer cups, usually in blue, but also seen in lavender, white, and sometimes pink, are like stars spangled on a canopy of green. There are low mounds for rock gardens and creepers that flourish in, around, and through dry stone walls. The flowering period can be 2 even 3 months in late spring or early summer and into fall. Some form evergreen mats. If any one genus can be said to provide the backbone plants for the rock garden, this would be it. Recommended are: *C.* 'Birch Hybrid', 6 inches tall, which covers itself with nodding, cup-shaped, purple-blue flowers, choice for walls and crevices; *C. carpatica*, Tussock Bellflower, a blue summer bloomer 9 to 12 inches tall, short-lived but fast-spreading, and quickly and easily grown from seed; and *C. glomerata* var. *acoulis*, a dwarf summer bloomer, violet-blue or white, 3 to 6 inches high. Also *C. rotundifolia*, Bluebell, Harebell, a graceful plant 6 to 18 inches tall with blue flowers in late spring and summer; a dainty plant for moist soil with a pH of 5.5 to 6.5, in the Pacific Northwest it self-sows generously. Longtime bloomer. For culture, see list 22, *Campanula*.

CHRYSANTHEMUM weyrichii 'White Bomb'. This is a small, creeping, clump-forming, 8- to 12-inch high stoloniferous species that bears 1- to 2-inch-wide white flowers above shiny green leaves. It flowers very late, is hardy in Zones 3 to 8, and ideal for the rock garden. There's also a pink form. Culture and the many other chrysanthemums are discussed on list 23, Mum—Daisy.

Among the best small flowers for rock gardens:
TOP, LEFT *Saponaria ocymoides*. (Harper)
BOTTOM, LEFT *Delosperma nubigenum*. (Harper)
TOP, RIGHT *Narcissus* 'Baby Moon'. (Heath)
CENTER, RIGHT *Veronica prostrata*. (Harper)
BOTTOM, RIGHT *Aurinia saxatilis*. (Viette)

DELOSPERMA (dee-loh-**sperm**-uh)
nubigenum   Zones 5-6
An easy, hardy, low-spreading succulent ice plant about 1 inch high with brilliant yellow flowers from spring to fall. The foliage is vivid green, turning red in winter.

Culture: Set out root divisions in early spring, in full sun, in very well-drained soil. Water well in summer, once established, watering requirements are minimal. Hardy to 25° F with snow cover or mulch.

DIANTHUS, Pink. This very fragrant, clove-scented genus includes florist's carnations and miniatures called grass or cottage pinks. For spring and intermittent summer bloom in rock gardens and wall plantings, the following are recommended: *D.* × *allwoodii* cultivars, 3 to 6 inches tall, including 'Mars', which has double, rounded, deep pink flowers, and 'Essex Witch' (also listed as a cv. of *D. plumarius*), in a range of pinks, whites, and salmons; 'Doris', a small semidouble, fragrant pink with red splotches at the base of the slightly fringed petals, compact, excellent for cutting, and widely grown; and 'Goblin', whose slender gray leaves form a 10-inch-high hummock, single pink flowers with a maroon-centered eye, Zones 3 to 9. *D. gratianopolitanus*, Cheddar Pink, has 2 or 3 tiny carnations on 6- to 9- or 12-inch stems, and 2 cultivars are especially recommended; 'Tiny Rubies', 4 inches high, a double-flowered deep pink, and 'La Bourbille', 3 inches high, with single clear pink flowers on compact, evergreen, silver-green grassy tufts, perfect for nooks and crannies and rock gardens, hardy to Zone 4. 'Warbonnet', also 10 inches high, has double deep red flowers. For culture, see list 70, The Fragrance Garden.

EUPHORBIA myrsinites. Unique, striking, prostrate evergreen plant with fleshy gray-green leaves that grow in attractive spirals up the woody 8- to 10-inch stems. It bears a bright 2- to 4-inch yellow inflorescence over a long period in spring. Should be used more in rock gardens. See list 57, Seashore and Sandy Soils.

GENTIANA scabra var. saxatilis. Beautiful little thing that covers itself with remarkably blue flowers in October and November. An easy gentian from Japan, it comes in several sizes up to 12 inches tall. Thrives in rock gardens, rock walls, and stony crevices. For culture see list 45, Rock Walls and Crevices.

GERANIUM, Cranesbill. Don't confuse this with *Pelargonium*, whose common name is geranium. These plants are mat or clump-forming herbaceous perennials, suitable for sunny rock gardens. In spring and early summer, this "true" geranium produces small, saucer-like, 5-petaled pastel flowers abundantly on wandlike stems above deeply divided foliage. Recommended for rock gardens are: spring-flowering *G. cinereum* var. *cinereum* 'Ballerina', a choice, long-blooming, award-winning plant 4 to 6 inches tall with 2-inch purple-veined, lilac-pink flowers, Zones 5 to 8; *G. cinereum* var. *subcaulescens* 'Splendens', 5 to 6 inches tall, a profuse bloomer with dark-centered, brilliant red flowers, Zones 5 to 8; and *G. sanguineum* var. *striatum* (usually sold as 'Lancastriense' or 'Prostratum'), 6 to 12 inches tall, with magenta-pink flowers that have darker pink veins and red or maroon foliage in fall, Zones 3 to 8. For late spring flowering, plant low-growing *G. dalmaticum*, 4 to 6

inches tall with mauve flowers and foliage that colors red to orange in fall and persists into winter, Zones 4 to 8; there is also an excellent white form. For culture, list 13, Spring Perennials for Sun.

HELIANTHEMUM (hee-lee-**anth**-em-um)
oelandicum subsp. **alpestre**
Sun Rose, Rock Rose   Zones 4/5-7
Dense mat 2 inches high by 10 inches wide, perfect for very small gardens or containers. It has tiny dark green leaves and bright yellow flowers on low stems from May to July. Most of the larger helianthemums do better if sheared back, and they live longer.

Culture: Sow seeds outdoors in early spring or root cuttings and grow them in a cold frame then put them out. Plant in full sun and deep, very well-drained soil that is somewhat alkaline, rather dry at the surface but moist at the root level. The plants resent being moved or divided. Hardy in Zone 4 if mulched.

IBERIS, Candytuft. Low-growing, spreading, narrow-leaved evergreen plants that in spring cover themselves with lasting, upright white flowerheads. It makes a sparkling ground cover for rock and wall gardens. Two perennials are recommended. *I. saxatilis*, 3 to 6 inches tall, blooms in spring and is exceptionally hardy. *I. sempervirens*, Edging Candytuft, about 10 inches high, covers itself in mid-spring with dense heads of white flowers; best cultivars are 'Little Gem', 5 to 8 inches tall; 'Purity', which is a little taller and bears a profusion of flowers; and 'Snowflake', 8 to 10 inches tall, with larger flowers. For culture, see list 43, Flowers for Edging.

IMPERATA cylindrica 'Rubra', Japanese Blood Grass, is a colorful, low-growing, spiky ornamental grass tipped with bloodred, most effective grouped or massed so the sun can shine through it. Mature height is 12 to 24 inches. For culture, see List 53, Ornamental Grasses.

IRIS, Flag, Fleur-de-lys. The 2 small, very showy irises described here flower in spring or early summer and are suited to rock gardens and moist woodlands. The foliage may die back in summer but often will remain as a ground cover in cool, light shade. *I. cristata*, Crested Iris, a creeping native dwarf, 3 to 4 inches high, is very appealing when naturalized. The lavender-blue, 4-inch-wide flowers have narrow falls with a central white or yellow ridge. Prefers acid soil with a pH of 4.5 to 5.5. *I. verna*, Dwarf Iris, Violet Iris, is a showy 6- to 8-inch-high violet-blue iris for light shade and moist, rather acid soil, pH 5.0 to 6.0. Culture is discussed on list 25, *Iris*.

PHLOX, Phlox. The most luscious pastels of spring and summer belong to the phloxes, American natives that thrive almost everywhere. Essential for rock gardens and walls are the little creeping phloxes that form mats and bloom in lavender-blue, purple, pink, or white. Several species are recommended. *P. bifida*, Sand Phlox, is a honey-scented, classic, 6-inch-high rock garden plant with deeply cleft, pale lavender-to-white petals. Best in sunny, well-drained acid soil, pH 5.0 to 6.0, blooms in April and May, hardy in Zones 4 to 8. 'Starbrite', 4 inches high, has flowers like blue and violet stars; 'Betty Blake' is

an 8- to 10-inch mound of spiny, reddish green leaves covered with deeply cut lavender-blue flowers; 'Coral Eye', 6 inches high, is blush pink with a coral-red central ring, hardy to Zone 3. *P.* 'Ellie B', a new, choice, compact spring-blooming selection, is white-flowered with cleft petals. *P. nivalis* 'Camla', Trailing Phlox, about 5 inches high, has dark green leaves, creeping stems, and rich pink flowers in late spring or early summer; hardy in Zones 6 to 9. *P. subulata*, Moss Pink, Moss Phlox, Mountain Phlox, semi-evergreen in warm regions, is a charming, needle-leaved, mat-forming creeper with a mossy look. In early to mid-spring it covers itself with small clusters of starry flowers that range in color from bright pink with a darker eye to blue, purple, or white. Planted in well-drained soil and full sun, it quickly carpets banks and slopes and cascades down rock walls. Excellent forms for the rock garden are 'Sneewichen', a miniature 3 inches high with compact mounds of tight foliage and small, pure, white, star-shaped flowers, hardy to Zone 3; and the very choice 'Whiteout', 6 inches high by 24 inches wide, that bears masses of extra-large snowflake-shaped white flowers. *P. s. sub. brittonii* forms a very tight mat of tiny leaves and bears small, bright pink flowers. Culture is discussed on list 27, *Phlox*.

PLATYCODON grandiflorus 'Apoyama', Balloon Flower. Balloon-shaped buds open to starry violet flowers 2 inches across on plants 15 to 18 inches high. Very free-flowering from early summer to early fall. Long-lasting as cut flowers if the stems are seared before they are put in water. See also list 57, Seashore and Sandy Soils.

RANUNCULUS gramineus. A cultivated buttercup that stands straight up and is a most attractive plant with long-lasting, blue-green, grassy leaves and cup-shaped brilliant yellow flowers in late spring and early summer. Height is 15 to 20 inches. Long-lived and different. The magnificent big Persian buttercup, *R. asiaticus*, for flowering borders in warm regions, is discussed on list 6, Best Bulbs for the South.

SAPONARIA (sap-on-**nay**-ree-uh)
ocymoides   Zones 4-7
This spreading mat with delicate stems and small leaves sends up 3- to 6-inch sprays of pink to purple flowers from mid-spring to late summer. There are several forms, including a white one, all easy to grow and long-lived. Recommended for seashore and sandy gardens are taller cultivars of the species, *S. officinalis* (see list 57).

Culture: Sow seed or set out root divisions in early spring, in sun or a little shade, in very well-drained, deep, rich soil humusy enough to sustain moisture.

SEDUM, Stonecrop. Some, but not all, of the sedums are quite invasive, *S. acre* in particular. This group is valued for its pretty, evergreen, light green, succulent-like foliage and, in some important larger hybrids, arresting autumn color. The flowers are tiny and star-shaped, yellow or pink-red, quite modest in ground-hugging species, but these become showy flowerheads in taller forms. Recommended for rock gardens and filling nooks, crannies, pockets in rocks and walls, by steps, and for autumn color are: *S. kamtschaticum* subsp. *middendorfianum*, hardy in Zones 3 to 8, 4 to 9 inches tall, with grooved leaves and unbranched pale green stems topped in summer by flat little yellow florets; *S. sieboldii*, October

Daphne, October Plant, hardy to Zone 4 or 5, with trailing stems 6 to 9 inches long and bluish green leaves that have faint reddish margins. It tolerates light shade and bears large, flat flowerheads that, in late summer and fall, turn bright pink; similar is 'Vera Jameson', 9 to 12 inches tall, with darkish leaves and 2- to 4-inch-wide rose pink flowerheads. Highly recommended. For culture, see list 56, Dry, Hot Conditions.

SEMPERVIVUM tectorum, Houseleek, Roof Houseleek, Hens-and-chickens, Old-man-and-old-woman. A workhorse made for rock gardens and wonderful in cracks and crevices. Clusters of soft purple-red flowers grow from the center in summer, but the plant is planted for the evergreen, succulent, tightly clustered fleshy rosettes with red-purple pointed tips, 1½ to 3 inches tall and 4 inches wide. For culture, see list 45, Rock Walls and Crevices.

VERONICA (ver-*ron*-ik-uh) Speedwell, Brooklime. First-rate fillers and invulnerable, these thrive in the rock garden. The foliage is attractive semi-evergreen or evergreen, and in mid-spring the plant bears an abundance of blue flowers in densely packed spikes. Recommended for flowers are *V. incana* and *V. repens*, which is called creeping speedwell and thrives on rocks and walls in full sun—the flowers are white-blue. See also taller veronicas on list 13, Spring Perennials for Sun, and 15, Summer Perennials for Sun.

Culture: Set out root divisions in early spring in very well-drained soil. Best in full sun but stands some shade and tolerates drought. Deadhead to keep flowers coming.

V. armena   Zones 4-8
Mat-forming, tufted evergreen to 4 inches high with pale green leaves and in early summer loose terminal spikes of deep blue to violet-blue flowers.

V. gentianoides   Zones 4-8
Mat-forming species approximately 6 inches or taller that in spring bears loose racemes of flowers that are pale blue, almost white, with darker veins.

V. prostrata (syn. rupestris)   Zones 5-8
Prostrate plant that forms mats of grayish green foliage with upright pale to dark blue flowers 3 to 8 inches tall in summer.

SOURCE: NICKOLAS NICKOU, M.D., IS A TALENTED GARDENER WHOSE TWO THIRTY-YEAR-OLD ROCK GARDENS HAVE BENEFITED FROM PLANT COLLECTING TRIPS TO ICELAND, GREENLAND, THE HIMALAYAS, CHINA, NEW ZEALAND, AUSTRALIA, TURKEY, THE ALPS, THE CANADIAN AND U.S. ROCKIES, SOUTH AFRICA, AND OTHER PLACES.

67. *RARE AND CHOICE*

■ **What makes a flower "rare and choice?" Our favorite flowers have been developed from the most noticeable wild flowers, the showy ones easily moved into the home garden and bred to the forms we know today. Those designated as rare and choice are more subtle; they come from hidden corners of the forest and failed to attract the plant hunter. Joy in them depends upon the mind, what the gardener brings to his or her contemplation. These are flowers for collectors, but rather easy to grow.**

Groups interested in rare and choice plants are found in every plant society. Among the very knowledgeable are members of the Rare Plant Group, a subgroup of The Garden Club of America. The American Rock Garden Society also has a dedicated interest in unusual plants and underwrites research trips to collect them.

Follow-on and Companion Plants: Low-growing bulbs on list 1, Early Spring, Specialty Bulbs, and small ferns are good companions.

ALCHEMILLA erythropoda, Dwarf Lady's-mantle. A choice, low-growing, shade-tolerant plant ideal for edging small borders or to tuck at the base of steps. Like the better-known *A. mollis*, it forms mounds of scalloped gray-green leaves, but in miniature—6 inches high. Especially attractive with drops of water held on the edges of the leaf pleats. In early summer it produces airy sprays of chartreuse flowers. Available at this writing from sources 3, 4, 4a, and 5 in the Appendix. For culture, see list 75, Herbs with Showy Flowers.

ALLIUM thunbergii. This ornamental onion, 10 inches high, is valuable for the fall border—one of the last to flower, beginning in late September, it persists beyond the first frosts. Hardy in Zones 4 to 9. Rounded heads of rose-violet blooms, urn-shaped like those of heaths, are held on slender stems above pretty, grassy foliage. Most effective in small groupings or grown as a container plant. 'Ozawa's Variety' produces more flowers than the species. Available at this writing from sources 2, 4, and 12 in the Appendix. For culture, see list 3, Spring, Large-flowered Bulbs.

ARISAEMA (ar-riss-*seem*-uh) sikokianum
Japanese Jack-in-the-pulpit   Zones 4-9
The flowers are like those of the beloved woodland plant, Jack-in-the-pulpit, *A. triphyllum*, but the large compound leaves are frequently marked with silver. In spring, the spathe, chocolate-maroon outside and white inside, surrounds a prominent white spadix that resembles ivory. Spikes of scarlet fruits follow in autumn. Mature height is 24 inches. Nicest in groups of 2 or 3. Available at this writing from sources 6 and 8 in the Appendix.

Culture: Sow fresh seed or plant root divisions in early spring, in light to moderate shade, in fertile, loose, well-drained, humusy soil. May be challenging to grow. Maintain even moisture.

ARUNCUS (ar-*runk*-us) aethusifolius
Korean Goatsbeard   Zones 4-7
At home in the shady rock garden or edging a shaded border, Korean Goatsbeard forms a tidy mound of bright green, finely cut leaves topped in early summer by feathery panicles of creamy white flowers. Mature height is 12

Massed *Allium thunbergii*, a small ornamental onion, makes a great show beginning in late September and persisting beyond the first frost. (Viette)

Flowers for collectors of the rare and choice:

TOP, LEFT *Phlomis russeliana* has heart-shaped sea-green leaves attractive throughout the season. (Harper)

TOP, RIGHT Masterwort, *Astrantia major*, is a good cutting flower. (Harper)

LEFT Lavender mist, *Thalictrum rochebrunianum*, is most effective planted in groups. (Harper)

ABOVE *Kirengeshoma palmata*, a slow-growing plant that is one of the few late-flowering perennials for a shaded garden. (Viette)

inches. When grown in a partly sunny or a lightly shaded location, a brilliant gold or reddish autumn foliage is a bonus. A fine companion for European Wild Ginger, *Asarum europaeum*. Available at this writing from sources 3, 4, and 5 in the Appendix. A larger form is discussed on list 50, Foliage for Form and Texture.

Culture: Sow fresh seeds in late summer or plant root divisions in early spring, in light shade and rich, humusy soil. May self-sow when established. Maintain even moisture.

ASTILBE (ass-*till*-bee) 'William Buchanan'
Zones 4-7

A refined plant for the shade garden, this dainty dwarf astilbe is thought to be a hybrid between *A. simplicifolia* and *A. glaberrima* var. *saxosa*. It forms low mounds about 8 inches high of glossy red-tinted, finely cut leaves that are topped in late summer by airy spikes of pale pink flowers which mature to a creamy white. Available at this writing from sources 2 and 7 in the Appendix. Other astilbes are discussed on list 21.

Culture: Plant in light shade in groups of no less than 3 to 5 in mid-spring, in rich, well-drained but moist soil. Divide every 3 or 4 years.

ASTRANTIA (ass-*trant*-tee-uh) major
Masterwort   Zones 4-7

A long-flowering perennial, to 24 inches tall. In midsummer, the slender branching stems bear several domed heads of tiny flowers surrounded by petal-like bracts in colors from greenish-white to pink. 'Rosensinfonie' ('Rose Symphony') is an attractive pink. A good cutting flower. Available at this writing from sources 1, 3, and 5 in the Appendix.

Culture: Sow fresh seed as soon as it's available, or plant crown divisions in spring in deep, woodsy soil. Thrives near a stream but does not require such a site. It is quite adaptable as long as it doesn't get hot, searing sun or deep shade all day. Maintain even moisture.

HAKONECHLOA macra 'Aureola', Hakonechloa, Japanese Forest Grass.
A slowly spreading, cascading, lovely light green grass with yellow-striped leaves to 12 inches high. Its graceful, arching habit is shown to best advantage in a raised planting area. The striking coloration makes it a distinctive specimen plant or ground cover. In autumn and winter, the foliage turns from pinkish to buff, a bonus. Available at this writing from sources 3, 7, 9, and 10 in the Appendix. For culture, see list 53, Ornamental Grasses.

KIRENGESHOMA (kye-reng-esh-*oh*-muh) palmata
Zones 4-7

The large maplelike leaves are carried on purplish stems that arch at the tips. In early autumn, nodding, bell-shaped yellow flowers appear in the leaf axils. The mature height is 36 inches. This slow-growing plant is one of the few late-flowering perennials for the shaded garden, and does best in cool regions. Available at this writing from sources 2, 5, and 9 in the Appendix.

Culture: Plant divisions in early spring, in light to moderate shade, in slightly acid, well-drained, humusy soil. Choose a site sheltered from strong winds and allow the plants to remain undisturbed. Maintain even moisture.

PHLOMIS (*floh*-miss) russeliana   Zones 5-8
Whorls of clear yellow hooded flowers appear along the stems in early summer, but the heart-shaped, sage green leaves are attractive throughout the growing season. Mature height is 36 inches. The plant's hefty appearance makes it a suitable shrub substitute for the wild garden. Seeds are available at this writing from The American Rock Garden Society.

Culture: Tolerates drought and poor soil. Set out root divisions in fall or spring, or sow fresh seed in late summer. Plant in full sun in the North, in light shade in the South. Needs average moisture to dry soil.

POLYGONATUM (pol-ig-oh-*nay*-tum) humile
Dwarf Solomon's-seal   Zones 4-7

A fascinating spring-blooming perennial that is a pleasing companion to European Wild Ginger, *Asarum europaeum*. The plant is 8 inches high, stocky and vertical, with attractively grooved foliage. In mid-spring, it bears rather large, creamy, bell-shaped flowers. Clumps increase slowly and make a distinctive, small-scale ground cover for the woodland or shaded rock garden. Available at this writing from sources 4, 5, 10, and 12 in the Appendix.

Culture: Set out root divisions in fall or spring, in light to moderate shade, in deeply dug, rich, well-drained, humusy soil. Maintain even moisture.

SANGUISORBA (san-gwis-*sorb*-uh) canadensis
Canadian Burnet   Zones 3-8

Nice with *Sedum* 'Autumn Joy' and late monkshood, *Aconitum carmichaelii*, the foliage is especially attractive when water drops catch on the toothed edges. In late summer and autumn, masses of creamy white bottlebrush flowers rise above the foliage mound and persist past early frosts. Mature height is 4 feet. Good for the wild garden or a border that does not dry out thoroughly. Available at this writing from source 2 in the Appendix.

Culture: Plant seeds in fall or root divisions in early spring in full sun in the North, but provide a cooling mulch; in the South, give it some protection from afternoon sun. Prefers humusy soils and requires even moisture. Deadhead to prolong flowering.

THALICTRUM (thal-*lik*-trum) rochebrunianum
Lavender Mist   Zones 4-7

Most effective planted in groups, this is an airy, graceful meadow rue from 5 to 6 feet high for the shaded garden. The finely cut leaves provide an interesting contrast to blockier foliage plants, such as hosta. In mid- to late summer, slender purple stems support soaring, airy sprays of light purple, long-lasting flowers. Available at this writing from sources 3, 4, 6, and 12 in the Appendix. A smaller meadow rue, *T. aquilegifolium*, is recommended on list 14, Spring Perennials for Shade.

Culture: May need staking but it is worth the effort. Plant fresh seeds in fall or root divisions in spring, in light shade, in well-drained garden soil. Maintain even moisture.

SOURCES: MARY ANN AND FRED MCGOURTY, OWNERS OF HILLSIDE GARDENS, NORFOLK, CONNECTICUT, SPECIALIZE IN UNCOMMON PERENNIALS AND GARDEN DESIGN.

68. THE CHILD'S GARDEN

■ **Early fun with flowers can lead to a rewarding lifetime interest in them. At the very least, it makes us aware of nature's fascinating cycles. Seeing what happens to a buried seed, nurturing the soil, watching butterflies, birds, and bees gather nectar, and harvesting and sharing flowers and seeds can all awaken a child's interest in gardening. Anticipation and the endless surprises of growing plants ease the process of learning the flowers' names (even the special Latin names). Gardening gives children stories to tell that make them proud.**

The steps for planting, growing, harvesting, and drying seeds are described under *Zinnia* and are the same for all the flowers suggested.

Consider the following flowers as the best candidates to give or make available to children. If your children are old enough, have them read the growing instructions under *Zinnia* and the other flowers for themselves.

ZINNIA

The colorful, easy-to-grow Zinnias are ideal flowers for children to grow.

Culture: Here's how to grow them.

1. Find a sunny spot in the garden and take away all the weeds.

2. Dig up the soil and make it crumbly.

3. Spread 3 inches of rotting leaves or peat moss on the earth and mix it into the soil.

4. Make the earth as level and smooth as you can.

5. Plant the seeds just under the top of the soil in groups 12 inches apart. Put 3 seeds in each group. Pat the soil down firmly over the seeds with your hands. Water the soil very gently with a sprinkler so it doesn't make puddles.

6. Check each day to see if the seedlings (baby plants) have come up. When the seedlings have put out their second set of leaves, gently pull up all but one seedling in each group.

7. Every month add a teaspoon of 5-10-10 organic or half-organic liquid fertilizer to a gallon of water and water the seedlings.

8. After the first flower on each plant blooms, cut it just above where the second pair of leaves is growing. Cut every flower as it begins to fade, always just down to the second set of leaves. Soon the plant will have many branches and flowers, and you can cut bouquets to give your family and friends.

9. When the cold weather comes and blooming slows, let the last few flowers stay on the plant and dry. The flower will become a head full of seeds. Gather the dried flowers and remove the seeds. Dry the seeds on newspaper in a room at 45° or 55° F for at least 6 weeks. Store in the refrigerator in a dry, clean jar. Put a mesh bag of flour inside to absorb any moisture. Poke 2 or 3 holes in the lid of the jar.

10. Wrap some seeds in small envelopes to give away, and keep some to plant next year.

Easy for beginners, the zinnia's bright colors attract children and provide lots of bouquets for gifts. This brilliant cultivar is 'Scarlet Splendor'.
(W. Atlee Burpee & Co.)

SNAPDRAGONS (ANTIRRHINUM majus)

Part of the fun of snapdragons is that you can snap (pinch) the flowers just about in the middle and the "dragon's" mouth will open and shut. And snapdragons have a nice smell. They are very pretty in bouquets.

Culture: Sow the seeds and when the young stems come up, pinch out the top 3 inches of each main stem (called a leader). Then the plants will branch out below and bear flowers on each branch. Harvest the flowers on short stems all summer long to keep the plants branching and flowering. Snapdragons may grow up again and flower the next year if your winters are mild.

SPIDER FLOWER (CLEOME hasslerana)

Measure this plant against your own height as it grows—by late summer it will be taller than you. The flowers are quite round. Watch the flowers on hot, sunny days in late summer—you'll see butterflies and moths dip into them to take nectar to make honey. The flowers coat the insects with pollen dust. When they go to the next flower, they drop the dust inside and that lets the flowers produce fertile seeds. Spider flowers produce lots of seeds. Even if you don't gather them, they will sow themselves and make more cleome plants next year.

ABOVE Part of the fun of growing snapdragons is that by pinching—snapping—a blossom just about in the middle you can make the "dragon's" mouth open and shut. (Frease) RIGHT The giant sunflowers, *Helianthus*, grow into living bird feeders and are fascinating to watch as the heads turn to follow the sun. (Viette)

PANSIES—JOHNNY-JUMP-UPS (VIOLA)

The big flowers that seem to have painted faces are the pansies. They are beautiful when dried. The little ones with painted faces are called Johnny-jump-ups and they do jump up everywhere once they start growing. These usually grow back again the next year.

Culture: In spring (and fall in warm regions) the seedlings (young plants) are sold already blooming in containers.

1. Choose a place that is a little shaded or has sun for only half the day. Follow steps 2, 3, and 4 under Zinnia.

5. Dig a hole just big enough for each plant. Space them a hand's-breadth apart.

6. Gently pull a plant out of its container. Set it in the hole so the top is just a little above the surface of the soil. Push the soil gently in around the plant and pat it down around the plant with your hands.

7. When the plants are blooming, pinch out faded flowers every day; that helps the plants to go on blooming.

SUNFLOWER (HELIANTHUS)

This grows into a living bird feeder taller than anyone you know. The flowers have really big round faces and face in the direction of the sun all day. After the plants bloom, let the big flowerheads dry. You can gather the seeds from some to feed birds in winter and to plant next year. Let others stay right there in the garden for the birds to eat. A single head can mature 1,000 seeds!

Culture: Plant these big seeds 36 inches apart in soil that is deeply dug. The roots need plenty of space.

NASTURTIUM (TROPAEOLUM majus)

These bright red and orange and yellow flowers are wonderful because they will grow where the soil is sandy and nothing much grows. In 50 or 60 days after you plant seeds, the plants will be covered with bright yellow and orange flowers with a nice sharp smell. The flowers keep blooming all summer. Pick as many as you want to make bouquets. Put them in sandwiches and salads—they are good to eat, and so are the leaves! Or, very carefully string the flowers on a shoe lace to make a necklace or a crown.

Culture: Soak the big seeds in water all night before you plant them. Nasturtium is a plant that likes poor soil so don't fertilize it (skip step 7 in the growing instructions).

SOURCE: DR. H. MARC CATHEY IS THE DIRECTOR OF THE U.S. NATIONAL ARBORETUM. AN EMINENT PLANT SCIENTIST, HE HAS BEEN THE RECIPIENT OF VIRTUALLY EVERY AWARD IN HIS FIELD.

69. TO ATTRACT BUTTERFLIES AND HUMMINGBIRDS

■ Butterflies and hummingbirds tend gardens of their own in the midst of ours, bringing beauty, color, and entertaining antics to lazy summer days. They also bring more tangible help—they pollinate flowers and fill an intricate but essential niche in the intricate food chains of our gardens, fields, and forests.

The flowers recommended here are among the most successful in the famous butterfly gardens of Callaway Gardens, Pine Mountain, Georgia.

BUTTERFLIES

As butterflies develop through their four stages—egg, caterpillar, chrysalis, and adult—they rely on plants in many ways. After mating, female butterflies look for "host plants" on which to lay eggs. Each species of butterfly searches for a specific kind of host plant. Monarchs lay eggs on milkweed; black swallowtails on parsley; tiger swallowtails on tulip and wild cherry trees. When the butterfly caterpillars emerge from their eggs and begin to feed they will starve if the desired host plant isn't available, rather than eat another kind of vegetation. Most feed on plants we classify as weeds (native plants).

Culture: To develop a butterfly garden, use large splashes of color in your design; butterflies are first attracted by color. Groups of flowers are easier to locate than isolated plants. Plant for continuous bloom; butterflies are active from early spring until late fall. Plant nectar-producing flowers that bear short, tubular blossoms and are flat-topped to provide "landing platforms." Many butterflies seem to prefer purple, yellow, orange, and red blossoms. Plant single- rather than double-flowered types; their nectar is more accessible.

Choose a sunny area. Butterflies and most plants that attract them need full sun.

Use biological controls and insecticidal soaps rather than garden pesticides which are toxic to butterflies.

Companion Plants: First choice is the shrub, *Buddleia davidii*, Butterfly Bush, a nectar-bearing magnet for butterflies. It has gorgeous, fragrant lavender flowers in summer and fall and performs best if deadheaded. The flowers are borne on new wood, so where it doesn't die to the ground, cut it back in late winter before growth begins. If you have only one plant for butterflies, this is it. Add lantana and you will have loads of them. *Passiflora* (Passionflower), a vigorous, exotic vine that bears fragrant flowers through fall, is the host plant for gulf fritillary, zebra, and Julia butterflies. Tropical passifloras such as *P. × alatocaerula* and *P. caerula* are grown as annuals.

ASCLEPIAS tuberosa, Butterfly Weed, Pleurisy Root, Tuberroot, Indian Paintbrush, Chigger Flower. Slow to start from seed and slow to emerge in spring, but worth the wait. The stiff stems, 24 to 36 inches tall, bear bright orange flowers in spring and summer. This is a host plant for the monarch butterfly and it

A compact garden planted to attract butterflies includes: *Buddleia davidii, Lantana davidii, Echinacea purpurea, Verbena tenuisecta, Lantana montevidensis, Zinnia elegans,* and marigolds, *Tagetes patula.*
(Calloway Gardens–Craighton)

provides nectar for many other butterfly species as well. *A. curassavica,* Bloodflower, a tropical milkweed grown as an annual, is also a host plant for monarch butterflies; it grows to 30 inches and bears striking orange-red, nectar-producing flowers; a good container plant. For notes on culture, see list 15, Summer Perennials for Sun.

COSMOS sulphureus 'Bright Lights'. In summer and fall it bears a great number of orange-red and bright yellow flowers on wiry stems to 4 feet tall. An annual that comes easily from seed and reseeds freely. Attractive in a mixed border or massed. For culture, see list 33, Annuals for Fall.

ECHINACEA purpurea, Purple Coneflower. Blooms from summer to fall and the spiny disk flowers provide ample opportunity for nectaring insects. The coarse, dark green foliage sets off and balances large daisylike flowers with rich, dusky rose-purple petals and an orange-bronze central disk. Characteristically, the petals slant backwards. In the South it blooms from May or June to November if faded flowers are removed. The height is 24 to 36 inches tall, but staking is rarely necessary. A very useful flower—good for cutting, handsome in mixed borders, easily perennialized in a meadow—and bees and butterflies love it. For culture, see list 64, The Meadow Garden.

FOENICULUM vulgare, Fennel. This host for the black swallowtail is anise-scented, 4 to 6 feet tall, a perennial grown as an annual. The foliage is a cloud of fine leaves softer even than dill. The stem develops a bluish cast in rich soil and the yellow flowers resemble Queen-Anne's-lace. A decorative form, 'Bronze Fennel', has a copper hue. For culture, see list 77, Popular Culinary Herbs.

LANTANA. Lantana is second only to *Buddleia* as a magnet for butterflies. Grown as an annual in most regions, it develops quickly and blossoms from summer through frost. It's a perfect butterfly flower in terms of color, shape, and nectar production. It also thrives as a container plant. Recommended are: *L. camara,* which bears tiny tubular florets in dense flowerheads that are cream-yellow, and in some plants change to orange, lavender, and red; *L. montevidensis* (syn. *L. delicatissima*), Weeping Lantana, Trailing Lantana, Pole-cat Geranium, whose drooping stems can reach 36 inches. For culture, see list 63, The Container Garden.

PENTAS (pen-tas) lanceolata
Star-cluster, Egyptian Star-cluster   Zone 10
A leafy, mounding plant which in summer and fall is covered with dense terminal clusters of starry flowers in vibrant red, pink, or white. Height is to 36 inches. It is familiar to south Floridians, but elsewhere it is grown as an annual. Especially attractive to swallowtail butterflies.

Culture: When nights remain above 55° F, set out container plants in full sun in well-drained, humusy soil. Maintain constant moisture.

Butterflies and some of their favorite flowers:

TOP, LEFT Gulf fritillary *Dione vanillae* on Butterfly Bush *Buddleia davidii*.
(Calloway Gardens–Craighton)

TOP, RIGHT Black Swallowtail *Papilio polyxenes* on *Lantana camara* 'Miss Huff's Hardy'.
(Calloway Gardens–Craighton)

RIGHT Buckeye *Precis coenia* on *Cosmos sulphureus* 'Bright Lights'.
(Calloway Gardens–Craighton)

PETROSELINUM crispum var. **crispum**, Parsley. A biennial which serves as a host plant for the black swallowtail. As a culinary herb it is grown as an annual, for it goes to seed quickly the second year. But butterflies use it in its first and second year. Fine in containers. For culture, see list 77, Popular Culinary Herbs.

PHLOX subulata, Moss Pink, Moss Phlox, Mountain Phlox. A low-growing pink species of creeping phlox that attracts the first butterflies of the growing season. In early spring, it carpets banks and ditches and is covered with clusters of tiny starry flowers in pink, bright pink with a darker eye, light or dark blue, or white. Honey-scented. Andre Viette reports that the sweetly scented upright perennial phlox that blooms in summer, *P. paniculata*, also attracts butterflies. For culture, see list 27, *Phlox*.

SALVIA rutilans, Pineapple Sage. Dark green leaves with a fruity fragrance on plants 24 to 36 inches tall. Bright scarlet blooms appear in autumn. It is not a typical butterfly flower in form, but its fruity fragrance attracts cloudless sulfur butterflies throughout the fall. For culture, see list 41, *Salvia*.

TAGETES patula, French Marigold. Durable, compact little plants about 12 inches tall that bear lots of small orange or gold flowers 1½ to 2 inches across. Many are mahogany red. Single varieties are much preferred to doubles by the skipper, buckeye, and painted lady butterflies that visit them. Deadheading is required. See list 39, Marigold.

TITHONIA (tith-*oh*-nee-uh) **rotundifolia**
Tender Perennial
A showy species of Mexican sunflower, this big, coarse plant gets to be 4 to 6 feet tall in a single season. In most regions it is grown as an annual. The bright orange or yellow flat-topped flowers bloom all summer long and appeal to many butterflies.
Culture: Start seeds indoors in small pots in late winter and set out after the air warms without disturbing the roots. Plant 1½ to 2 feet apart at the back of the border, in full sun and well-drained soil.

VERBENA bonariensis. Deep purple flowers bloom from May to October on well-branched stems backed by rough, dark green leaves. The height is 4 to 5 feet; especially attractive in mass plantings. It is almost as appealing to butterflies as *Buddleia*. A good cut flower, too; from South America, but naturalized here. For culture, see list 63, The Container Garden.

ZINNIA elegans. Loved for the brilliance of its daisylike flowers and free-blooming habit, the zinnia has been bred to a mind-staggering number of vibrant colors, shapes, heights, and forms. Single varieties are favorites of silver-spotted skippers and buckeyes. For culture, see list 42, *Zinnia*.

HUMMINGBIRDS

Hummingbirds are winged acrobats, masters of fast flight and surprising capers. Their days are spent looking for the food necessary to fuel their amazing energy output. They round out a diet primarily of nectar with tiny insects. In their travels between blossoms they serve as pollinators. Watch for hummingbirds whose foreheads are dusted with yellow pollen.

Culture: Hummingbirds are enticed by tubular, brightly colored flowers. Fragrances are not important because they rely on sight, not scent, to locate their food.

Hummingbirds prefer single flowers to doubles. Like butterflies, hummingbirds require a continuous supply of nectar, so plant flowers that bloom over a long season.

Companion Plants: Good companions for the plants on this list are flowering shrubs and vines, including *Buddleia davidii*, (Butterfly Bush); *Campsis radicans* (Trumpet Creeper, Trumpet Vine, Cow-itch, Trumpet Honeysuckle); *Fuchsia* spp.; *Hamelia patens* (Scarlet Bush, Firebush); *Hibiscus* spp.; and *Lonicera sempervirens* (Trumpet Honeysuckle, Coral Honeysuckle).

ALTHAEA (al-*thee*-uh) **officinalis**
Marsh Mallow, White Mallow   Zones 5-9
Various althaeas are loved by hummingbirds. This tall, narrow, upright species from 4 to 6 feet high has velvety leaves and in midsummer to mid-autumn bears rose or pale mauve flowers. It is best at the back of a large border and especially suited to wild and cottage gardens. See also *Alcea rosea* (syn. *Althea rosea*), Hollyhock, on list 60, The Cottage Garden.
Culture: Usually grown as an annual. In early spring sow seeds or set out root divisions in full sun in well-drained, moist soil.

AQUILEGIA spp., Columbine. The delicate, intricate nodding or upright blossoms end in spurs, usually in 2 shades, and are displayed against fresh blue-green, scalloped foliage on plants from 12 to 36 inches tall. Blooms over many weeks in mid- to late spring. Modern hybrids offer a wide range of heights, colors, and bicolors—white, yellow, blue, rusty pink, lavender, purple, and reddish orange. The wild-garden elegance of the old-fashioned A. *vulgaris*, European Crowfoot, Garden Columbine, is preferred for cutting and cottage gardens. See list 13, Spring Perennials for Sun.

IMPATIENS spp. The number one flowering plant for shady locations, it blooms from late spring until frost; usually 12 to 24 inches tall. A broad range of vibrant colors has been developed in recent years—solid pastels, pinks, reds, whites, orange, salmon, melon, color-spotted forms, and bicolors. Wonderful in containers and baskets and as bedding plants. The popular garden impatiens are discussed on list 38, *Impatiens*.

LOBELIA cardinalis, Cardinal Flower. A tall, upright wildflower from 24 to 30 or 36 inches high, topped by up to 50 loosely spaced, bright red blossoms. It thrives by woodland streams and blooms in late summer and fall. The flower spikes are slender and the dark green foliage is lovely with ferns. For culture, see list 16, Summer Perennials for Shade.

MONARDA spp. M. didyma, Bee Balm, Oswego Tea, is discussed on list 75, Herbs with Showy Flowers. Attractive whorls of shaggy scarlet petals surrounded by red-tinted bracts bloom through summer on this plant's stiff stems. There are also pinks and whites. The plants are 24 to 36 inches tall and attract butterflies, hummingbirds, and bees. Deadheading lengthens bloom time.

PENSTEMON spp. are attractive to hummingbirds. *P. digitalis*, Smooth White Beard-tongue, is discussed on list 48, Wildflowers to Naturalize. Called white penstemon, it is stately and durable, with 36-inch stems that in late spring to midsummer bear panicles of open bells, white with a touch of purple at the throat. Lush basal foliage and purple flower stems are attractive all season long. *P. hartwegii* hybrids (gloxinioides), Beard-tongue, bloom in summer, and those with bloodred flowers attract hummingbirds. For culture, see list 48.

PETUNIA spp. These trumpet-shaped flowers on droopy stems bloom boldly all summer in dozens of colors and combinations. There are cascading and supercascading types for baskets and window boxes, and uprights for bedding. The colors range through pink, red, white, lavender and bicolors. Keep dead blooms picked if you can and be sure to trim the plants back by ⅓ after the first great rush of flowers to encourage continuing bloom. For culture, see list 40, *Petunia*.

PHASEOLUS (fas-*see*-ol-us) **coccineus**
Scarlet Runner Bean, Dutch Case-knife Bean
Tender Perennial
This is a fast-growing twining vine that reaches 15 feet in a single season and bears brilliant red flowers followed by large edible beans. It is treated as an annual and often planted in containers as screening for porches and patios. There are also white varieties.
Culture: In early spring, sow seeds in full sun in rich, well-drained soil with a somewhat acid pH. Provide training wires or strings. Sustain moisture.

SALVIA. The reds are stocky spikes covered with flamboyant red flowers; blue salvias are tall, slim wands covered with lavender-blue florets usually in late summer and fall. Especially appealing to hummingbirds are the following: *S. leucantha*, Mexican Bush Sage, is a robust tender perennial 3 to 4 feet tall with fragrant velvety leaves and lavender flowers that have white corollas; *S. rutilans*, Pineapple Sage, has scarlet flowers and a fruity fragrance attractive to certain species of butterfly (see list 41, *Salvia*). Also recommended are 2 tender perennials, *S. coccinea*, Texas Sage, Scarlet Sage, 12 to 24 inches, a red sage that thrives in the Southwest; and *S. guaranitica*, a subshrub 3 to 5 feet tall which bears long, slender racemes of indigo blue flowers.

SOURCE: LUANN K. CRAIGTON IS AN INTERPRETIVE NATURALIST WITH THE EDUCATION DEPARTMENT OF CALLAWAY GARDENS, PINE MOUNTAIN, GEORGIA. SHE MANAGES THE CALLAWAY ORNITHOLOGY PROGRAM AND WORKS CLOSELY WITH ONGOING BUTTERFLY PROJECTS.

This garden includes some of the sweetest scented flowers: *Nicotiana*; stock, *Mathiola*; purple heliotrope, *Heliotropium arborescens*; sweet alyssum, *Lobularia maritima*. (Viette)

70. THE FRAGRANCE GARDEN

■ There are scented species and varieties of many flowers not usually associated with fragrance. Peonies have a pleasant aroma particular to them, especially 'Myrtle Gentry'. Many tall bearded irises are fragrant. Daylilies 'Fragrant Light', 'Hyperion', 'Ida Jane', 'Citrina', and several others are fragrant. *Saponaria officinalis* 'Rosea Plena' and 'Rubra Plena' are scented. *Phlox divaricata* has fragrance, especially 'Dirgo Ice'. But the 20 or so perfumed perennials and annuals described here are more than just scented—they are able to cast a fragrant spell over the whole garden.

Some forms—often white and purple flowers—are more intensely fragrant than others. The scents of many of the best fragrance plants become strongly intensified in the evening. For maximum enjoyment, plant those fragrant during the day close to doors and entrance paths. Plant those that wait for moonlight close to porches, patios, and bedroom windows.

Pick fragrant flowers in the early morning, or late afternoon. The volatile oils that carry the scent are evaporated by sun.

For the most intense experience of a flower's fragrance, lean close to it and breathe lightly into it before inhaling. The heat and rush of air releases the volatile oils. Fragrances you are inhaling seem to lose their scent after a few moments, but the flower hasn't run out of perfume. Rather, your olfactory system is saturated and you are numbed to the smell; the fragrance is still there in the flower for the next person.

The intensity of floral fragrances varies according to soil, climate, and season. If a plant appears not to have the fragrance promised, ask the nursery that sold it how to improve its performance.

Don't use chemical sprays on fragrant flowers in bloom. Chemicals affect the volatile oils. If possible, buy your fragrant flowers from nurseries that specialize in perfumed flowers.

Related lists are 74, Herbs with Fragrant Foliage, and 76, Fragrant Herbs for Drying and Potpourri.

Fragrant Companions: *Dictamnus*, the gas plant, is a good companion for many of the plants on this list. Surround the fragrance garden with scented woody plants such as perfumed roses, viburnums, clematis, *Osmanthus*, *Elaeagnus commutata*, and *Nerium oleander*. Include some aromatic herbs, particularly lavender (English, French, or Spanish) and mints, in the garden, too.

ACIDANTHERA bicolor var. **murieliae**, Peacock Orchid. Tall, elegant, long-lasting, very fragrant flower for cutting gardens, containers, or bedding. The stem grows from swordlike foliage and bears 4 to 6 or more gladiolus-like flowers, creamy white blotched with purple-crimson. In most regions, the corms must be lifted and stored for winter. Also called Abyssinian or fragrant gladiolus. See list 4, Summer-into-fall Bulbs.

AMARYLLIS belladonna (syn. *Brunsvigia rosea*), Belladonna Lily, Naked Ladies. A magnificent fragrant flower from 24 to 36 inches tall, resembling the large-flowered amaryllis *(Hippeastrum)*. This one is grown outdoors to Zone 5, as well as indoors. The fragrance is fine, spicy, and sweet. Long blue-green leaves develop in spring; after they subside, in late summer and fall, a tall, naked stem rises bearing 2 to 4 fragrant rose pink blossoms. Plant with mums or hostas to mask the bare stems. In Zone 8 and south, it is an essential element of the fall garden. See list 5, Fall and Winter Bulbs. In colder regions, grow these indoors like *Hippeastrum* on list 7, Exotic Bulbs.

CHEIRANTHUS (kye-*ranth*-us) **cheiri**
Wallflower   Tender Perennial
The scent is of clove and lilies, and the 12- to 18-inch-tall flowers resemble stocks in bright shades of yellow, orange, pink, white, and clear red to mahogany. In the North, these are early spring bloomers. If planted in the lee of a wall where summers are moderate, they'll flower in late winter through spring and perennialize. Recommended are 'Blood Red', an early, deep velvety red; 'Cloth of Gold', with large golden flowers; 'Eastern Queen', a salmon-red; 'Fire King', a brilliant orange–scarlet. Doubles such as 'Fair Lady', which includes pastels in its color range, tend to be more fragrant than singles and bloom longer, but may be hard to find. *Erysimum asperum (C. allionii)*, which grows wild in California, is similar, a scented winter annual. There are annual forms but the seeds are notoriously untrue.

Culture: In the moist Pacific Northwest, the wallflower is perennial. Where summers are hot, handle as an annual or biennial. Plant seeds in summer for next spring bloom in a semi-sunny location, in ordinary well-drained, rather alkaline soil.

CONVALLARIA (kon-val-*lay*-ree-uh) **majalis**
Lily-of-the-valley   Zones 2-7
Creamy little white bells with a unique and exquisite perfume bloom in mid-spring on 4- to 8-inch stems rising from furled green leaves. Lily-of-the-valley is loved for its fragrance and is delightful in bouquets. In shady corners of light woodlands and wild gardens it naturalizes easily and becomes a spreading ground cover. Recommended are 'Fortin's Giant', 10 to 12 inches tall, a full-flowered white, and 'Rosea', to 8 inches high, a less fragrant lavender-pink. In catalogs, lily-of-the-valley may be grouped with bulbs for forcing and/or with perennials.

Culture: In mid-fall or very early spring, bury the roots so the pointed tips ("pips") are near the surface in well-drained, humusy, somewhat acid soil with a pH of 5.0 to 6.0. It is most successful in the dappled light under trees or tall shrubs, and may be forced into early bloom indoors.

Three of nature's remarkable perfumes:
TOP Lily-of-the-valley, *Convallaria majalis*, the fragrance of Joy perfume. (Viette)
ABOVE 'Sweet Harmony', *Dianthus*. The little pinks have a rich spicy clove scent. (Viette)
RIGHT Tuberose, *Polianthes tuberosa*, as fragrant as lily-of-the-valley. (American Horticultural Society)

DIANTHUS (dye-*an*-thus)
Pink

Annuals, biennials, and perennials of varying heights and bloom periods. The spicy clove scent of the genus is strong in both the large florist's carnations and the little grass or cottage pinks, and the flowers have been used since the Middle Ages as both flavoring and scent. The old species and the whites tend to have the most fragrance, but many modern pinks are also well perfumed. Pink is just one of its several clear colors—others are red, rose, salmon, white, yellow (*D. knappii*), and bicolors. Late spring or early summer is the usual flowering time, and some little pinks repeat sporadically if deadheaded or sheared. The slender gray-green foliage tufts or mounds of the smaller types is usually evergreen, fine for edging and as ground cover. All the pinks are long-lasting as cut flowers. The short-lived flower called Sweet William is described on list 71, The Cutting Garden.

Culture: Sow seeds or plant seedlings or root divisions in early fall (warm climates) or spring in full sun, in well-drained, neutral, sandy soil that includes humus. Withstands high heat and some drought. The mounds increase quickly. The little pinks are easily multiplied by division in spring.

D. × allwoodii Allwood Pink   Zones 3/4-8
Midsize, hardy, very fragrant fluffy carnations 2 to 2½ inches across, from 8 to 15 inches high, in blends of pink, red, and white. Two flowers per stem appear in early summer. Tolerates heat and drought. 'Doris' is a very fragrant salmon-pink with a red eye. The slightly taller 'Sweet Wivelsfield' has single or double flowers.

D. caryophyllus Carnation, Clove Pink
Zones 8-9
This is the tall, usually leggy 14-inch fragrant carnation raised in hot, dry climates for florists and perfumeries. It needs lots of sun, and staking; it is challenging to grow, but it is a superb flower for cutting. Ask local nurseries for varieties hardy in your area. The elegant 'Black Knight' and 'White Queen' are well perfumed. Whites and pinks tend to be most fragrant, yellows the least.

D. chinensis 'Magic Charms' Rainbow Pink
Annual/Biennial/Perennial
An All-America Selections Winner, 7 inches high with large, fringed, single blooms in salmon-pink, white, coral, scarlet, or crimson, some speckled. Though the species is said to be fragrant, the wild garden varieties are chosen more for their performances as edging and ground cover. Spring-sown seeds bloom throughout the summer and may return a second year. Not reliably perennial.

D. gratianopolitanus Cheddar Pink Zones 3-9
Pretty, wonderfully fragrant 1-inch miniature, single carnations in rose or pink that bloom all summer, 2 or 3 flowers to a stem, in grassy mounds about 6 to 9 or 12 inches high. Charming in rock gardens, edging walks, and almost indestructible even in the hot South. Recommended are: 'Tiny Rubies', 4 inches high, a very floriferous double-flowered deep pink; 'La Bourbille', 3 inches high, a single clear pink on compact, evergreen tufts

perfect for nooks and rock gardens to Zone 4; 'Warbonnet', 10 inches high, double deep red flowers. Cheddar refers to the species' native habitat, the Cheddar Gorge in southwest England, according to Allan M. Armitage in *Herbaceous Perennial Plants* (Athens, Ga.: Varsity Press Inc., 1989).

D. plumarius Cottage Pink, Grass Pink
Zones 3-9

This is as strongly scented as the Cheddar Pink, has grassy foliage, and in spring and early summer bears charming 1½-inch single or double flowers, 2 or 3 per stem. The color range includes shades of salmon, rose, white, and red. 'Mrs. Sinkins', an old-fashioned, fully double ruffled white, has a powerful fragrance. Seeds are hard to get and it is rarely offered as a seedling, but this probably is the most fragrant.

D. superbus
Zones 4-9

So fragrant it can be detected 60 yards away. The white, cool pink, or lavender-pink flowers are exquisitely lacy, borne from July to frosts on branching stems 12 to 16 inches high, with 2 to 12 flowers per stem. It is evergreen in warm climates but usually grown as a biennial. 'White Lace' is superb in August. The Rainbow Loveliness strain has feathered and eyed pastel flowers that are exceptionally clove-scented.

GALTONIA candicans, Summer Hyacinth. Excellent. This South African bulb resembles a tall hyacinth, and in late summer bears spikes of slightly fragrant, green-tinged white flowers on stalks to 36 inches tall. The strap-shaped leaves are 2 inches wide and 3 to 4 feet long. Good cut flower. Lovely massed at the back of the border or grouped in large containers. See list 4, Summer-into-fall Bulbs.

HELIOTROPIUM (hee-lee-oh-*troh*-pee-um) arborescens
Heliotrope, Cherry Pie   Zones 10-11

A tender perennial 15 inches tall that from spring to early fall fills the garden with a sweet scent rather like vanilla—or cherry pie. The flowers are flat clusters of florets in deep purple, pale lavender, or white, attractive in arrangements, fresh or dried. Buy only container plants whose fragrance you can verify. Heliotrope is attractive trained to standard or tree form. Valerian, *Valeriana officinalis*, is similarly scented and also is known as Garden Heliotrope.

Culture: In the North, this plant is often container-grown and wintered indoors, or is grown as an annual. Set out potted plants in full sun, in well-drained, humusy soil. Sustain moisture. Pinch back branch tips to encourage bushiness and bloom.

HESPERIS (hess-per-iss) matronalis
Dame's Rocket, Sweet Rocket, Dame's Violet, Rogue's Gillyflower   Zones 3-9

Delicious fragrance especially in the evening. Tiny florets arranged loosely on terminal racemes make a showy flowerhead 24 to 36 inches above a basal rosette of narrow, hairy leaves. Blooms in mid- to late spring. More fragrant double-flowered forms are sold as container plants; singles may be purchased as seed.

Culture: Perennial in the South, annual or biennial in cool regions. In the North, sow fresh seed in early spring in full sun; in the South, sow seeds in autumn and provide

afternoon shade. Prefers well-drained, humusy, alkaline soil but is adaptable. Self-sows generously. Renew the beds with fresh seed every few years. Deadheading encourages a second round of flowering.

HOSTA plantaginea, Fragrant Plantain Lily. The hostas are vigorous foliage plants with gleaming, lush green leaves. In late summer, this 18-inch-tall species lifts a stem covered with compact flower buds like pearls set in a spiral of pale bracts. They open beginning at the bottom and have the scent of Madonna lilies. Handsome enough to feature as specimens. The stem lengthens as the flowers open. 'Aphrodite' is a beautiful double with fragrant white flowers. 'Grandiflora' is also fragrant, the ancestor of many modern hybrids. 'Summer Fragrance' has large lavender-blue flowers in midsummer. See list 54, *Hosta*.

HYACINTHUS. Unique, and the most powerful fragrance of spring both indoors (it forces very well) and outdoors. The starry, outward-facing flowers cluster thickly on straight spikes 8 to 12 inches high.

Plant early, midseason, and late types in groups of 2 or 3 along paths, and in pockets near patios and entrances. Generally, the whites are the most fragrant, then the pastels, but some deeply colored hyacinths are perfumed, too. Among very fragrant whites are 'L'Innocence', 'Edel-weiss', and 'Carnegie'. 'Pink Pearl' is very sweet smelling. 'King of Blues' and 'Ostara' are tall, fragrant deep blues. The light blue 'Cote d'Azur' is unsurpassed for perfume. Among the notably scented large doubles are the white 'Mme. Sophie' and 'Ben Nevis', and the luscious pink 'Chestnut Flower'. For culture, see list 3, Spring, Large-flowered Bulbs.

LATHYRUS odoratus, Sweet Pea. Sweet peas and mignonette are the most fragrant annuals. The old-fashioned sweet pea is a fresh, sweetly scented, crisp little flower that blooms on a long, slender stem growing on a vine, like its cousin the edible pea. Mixed colors make delightful bouquets. The flowers appear in early to mid-spring, masses of blooms from purple to pale lavender, ruby red to pale pink, and white, and there are bicolors. 'Penine Floss', 'Rosy Frills', 'Maggie May', 'Hunters Moon', 'Royal Wedding', and 'Snowdonia Park' are among those recommended for fragrance. An antique strain with outstanding perfume is 'Antique Fantasy'. For a long season of bloom, especially in warm climates, choose heat-resistant strains such as 'Burpee's Galaxy' and 'Giant Late Heat Resistant'. For small gardens, choose self-supporting 6- to 10-inch-high dwarfs and 8-inch-high bush types, such as Burpee's 'Bijou', 'Super Snoop', and 'Snoopea'. See also list 71, The Cutting Garden.

LILIUM Lily
List 11 describes modern hybrid lilies that last and are a superb addition to the back of any flowering border. The focus here is on species lilies whose famous fragrances modern lilies are heir to, and the most fragrant modern strains. They are regal beauties for the back of the border and will scent the garden in evening as no other flower can.

Culture: For general information on culture, see list 11, Lily.

L. auratum Gold-banded Lily, Golden-rayed Lily, Mountain Lily   Zones 4-8
Each blossom may be 8 to 10 inches across, fragrant, and good for cutting. The color range includes white to pink and yellow, and the scent recalls narcissus and nicotiana. 'Black Dragon', 5 to 7 feet, white with a purple reverse; intensely fragrant; up to 20 blooms on each stem. Early and midseason.
'Damson', 32 inches, rich maroon; fragrant. Midseason.
'Gold Eagle', 5 to 6 feet, golden yellow; very fragrant. Midseason.
'Golden Temple', 36 inches, yellow with a dark reverse; fragrant. Midseason.
'Lady Ann', 36 inches, white with gold center; fragrant. Midseason.
'White Henryi', 6 feet, superb white flowers with yellow spotted centers; fragrant; virus-resistant. Midseason.
'Anaconda', 38 inches, apricot; fragrant. Late.

L. candidum Madonna Lily   Zones 4-8
The species is still sold in catalogs, a 4-foot tall, lovely, very fragrant, pure white, one of few lilies that thrives in soil sweetened by calcium or wood ashes (many require acid-range soils). The fragrance is unique, as sweet as violets. Plant in early fall; to bloom, it must produce a tuft of leaves before frost. Set bulbs so their tops are covered by an inch of soil and maintain moisture until the ground is frozen.

L. longiflorum Trumpet Lily, White Trumpet Lily
Zones 6-8
Our Easter lily. Usually fragrant florist's plants to 36 inches tall with 1 to 6 outward-facing flowers, these are forced into early bloom and sold for Easter giving. Planted out, they'll bloom again in midseason, especially in warm regions. Some are hardy enough to survive in gardens in southern Canada, especially in places with lots of snow cover. 'Nellie White', 28 inches, is one of the fragrant selections.

Oriental Lilies   Zones 4-8
The flowers are highly fragrant, spectacular—up to 10 inches in diameter—and either bowl-shaped, flat-faced, or with sharply recurved petals. There usually are 8 to 10 flowers on stems 28 to 38 inches tall. These are the last lilies to bloom.
'American Eagle', 36 inches, white with lavender spots. Early.
'Blushing Pink', 4 to 5 feet, unspotted, with a wonderful fragrance. Early to midseason.
'Imperial Silver' strain, 6-foot huge white flowers with maroon spots; fragrant. Midseason.
'Journey's End', 36 inches, rose with a red band; very, very fragrant. Midseason.
'Everest', 38 inches, white with spots. Late.

LOBULARIA maritima, Sweet Alyssum. This is a very sweet-scented and dainty flowering edger from 4 to 8 inches high that grows into a low mound 12 to 18 inches across. In summer and fall, it covers itself with tiny, sparkling white, rosy violet or purple florets. A midsummer slump in flowering can occur in extreme heat, but flowering resumes when cooler weather returns. Self-sows. Recommended are: 'Little Sorrit', 'New Carpet of Snow', 'Noel Sutton', 'Elizabeth Taylor', 'Royal Wedding', 'Creme Beauty', and 'Geranium Pink'. 'Cloth of Snow' is a dwarf form. For culture, see list 43, Flowers for Edging.

BELOW, LEFT Evening stock, *Matthiola incana*, is called "perfume".
(McDonald)

RIGHT Mignonette, *Reseda odorata*, smells of sweet pea/rasp-
berry/tangerine. (McDonald)

BOTTOM Heliotrope, *Heliotropium arborescens*, called "cherry pie"
for its sweetness. (Viette)

MATTHIOLA Stock

Almost as beautiful as delphinium, a highly prized, erect bushy plant whose multipetaled blossoms cluster along sturdy flower spikes to 30 inches tall. The remarkable scent blends lilies and spices. Blooms over a long period in summer in pink, white, pale blue, or red. Fast-growing and excellent cutting flowers.

Culture: Generally grown as annuals or biennials, and will flower from seed the first season. For summer bloom in cool regions, sow the very fine seeds indoors in early spring, in a sterile growing mix. Transplant where they are to bloom. Space the plants 10 to 15 inches apart in an airy location and avoid excessive or night watering. In mild regions, sow the seeds outdoors in late summer where they are to bloom, and provide winter mulch. Prefers full sun or bright shade and well-drained, fertile soil that is in the neutral range. Do not grow where mildew is a severe problem.

M. 'Giant Imperial' Annual/biennial

Stately, very attractive bushy biennial grown as an annual. The colors are white, pink, pale blue, and red.

M. incana Stock, Gillyflower, Brampton Stock, Imperial Stock Annual/Biennial/Tender Perennial

A rich, spicy perfume comes from this gray-leaved species 18 to 24 inches tall. The flowers may be old rose, sapphire, lavender, pale pink, soft yellow, or lilac. The flowerheads are heavy and need support. The perennials are grown as biennials. True annuals, such as the many-branched, old-fashioned 'Beauty of Nice' and the 18-inch-high Ten-Week strains, bloom 10 to 12 weeks after seeding. The many-branched Dwarf Double Ten-Week stocks are prolific bearers about 12 inches tall. 'Brompton' blooms in late summer or early fall from seed started indoors.

M. longipetala Evening Stock, Perfume Plant
Annual

Perfumes the whole garden most of the summer. It is a night bloomer with broad-petaled, pale lilac flowers that open as the light fades, releasing a far-reaching, heady fragrance that blends lily and honey. About 12 inches tall, straggly in daylight (grow it in out-of-sight places) but glorious at night. Hardy; requires 5 or 6 hours of full sun a day.

MIRABILIS (mihr-*rab*-il-iss) **jalapa**
Four-o'clock, Marvel-of-Peru, Beauty-of-the-night
Tender Perennial/Zones 10-11

A leafy, bushy, durable old-fashioned plant 18 to 30 inches high that opens in the late afternoon and has a lemony scent that grows sweeter in the cool evening. The showy rose-red (most fragrant), bright yellow, white or striped, veined, or spotted flowers resemble small petunias. Group the plants in the middle of the border, or plant as a low hedge. Blooms in mid- to late summer and on until frosts.

Culture: Started from seed in early spring, four o'clocks grow up quickly and, in mild regions, self-sow extravagantly. Sow seeds in spring in full sun, in well-drained, rich soil. Tolerates poor soil, partial sun, and drought. The tuber can be dug in fall, stored as dahlias are stored, and replanted in mid-spring, but the little black seeds are far easier to handle. Drought-resistant, care-free, very easy to grow.

MUSCARI, Grape Hyacinth. Like miniature unopened hyacinths with tiny blue, sterile flowers thickly clustered on stems to 8 inches high. Grassy leaves rise in fall. There's a spice-and-grape fragrance, especially in *M. macrocarpum,* a rare yellow species. See list 1, Early Spring, Specialty Bulbs.

NARCISSUS, Daffodil. Many large-flowered daffodils, for instance 'King Alfred', have a sweet, distinctive scent when held, but there are 4 general types of daffodils for fragrance: The richly perfumed, cold-tender Paperwhites, good for winter forcing; Tazettas, or Poetaz and Polyanthus daffodils, particularly the fruity 'Soleil d'Or' and 'Yellow Cheerfulness'; spicily fragrant Poeticus or Pheasant's Eye narcissus; and distinctive Jonquilla hybrids which bear clusters of 2 to 6, usually very fragrant, yellow flowers on each stem, for instance 'Baby Moon' and 'Trevithian'. See list 9, Daffodil.

NICOTIANA alata, Jasmine Tobacco, Flowering Tobacco. Tender perennial grown as an annual, large-leaved, lush, 15 to 24 inches tall. It blooms lavishly in summer to early frosts, sending up clusters of dainty, tubular white flowers that open and release a lilylike fragrance late in the day. The hybrids and red types are less scented. The colorful Sensation strain stays open all day, but the white flowers of the species plants are more fragrant. Other scented species include *N. suavolens* and *N. sylvestris,* but this one is the easiest to find. For culture, see list 31, Annuals for Sun.

PETUNIA. Trumpet-shaped flowers on droopy stems that bloom boldly all summer in dozens of colors and combinations. Flowering stems last rather well when cut. Some white and purple petunias release a sweet, spicy fragrance in cool evening air, among them the Double Grandifloras. But a search of seed catalog fine print is required to locate them; generally in their background is the night-scented *Petunia axillaris,* Large White Petunia. See list 40, *Petunia.*

PHLOX paniculata, Summer Perennial Phlox, Fall Phlox. In July and August the sweetly fragrant, purplish-pink, 24- to 48-inch-tall flowers of the species bloom in the wild. For the home garden there are durable, sparkling phloxes from 6 to 36 inches tall with big, lush panicles of flowers in a range of colors—white, pink, salmon, scarlet, and purple, many with a contrasting eye. The perfume of this species is the most pervasive, but *P. maculata,* Wild Sweet William, is also fragrant; *P. drummondii,* the annual, has a meadowy scent; *P. bifida* (list 66, The Rock Garden) and *P. subulata* recall honey, and *P. divaricata* is similar to scented irises. For culture, see list 27, *Phlox.*

POLIANTHES tuberosa, Tuberose. Source of commercial perfume, these dainty flowers are exquisitely scented of orange blossoms or hyacinths. Waxy and white, they are borne from July to fall in loose spikes on wandlike stems from 18 to 36 inches tall. Stocky doubles such as the 24-inch-high 'The Pearl' are best for flower borders. Plant near porches or entrances where the heady scent can be enjoyed, especially in the evening when it is most intense. For culture, see list 4, Summer-into-fall Bulbs.

RESEDA (res-*seed*-uh) **odorata**
Mignonette Annual

This plain little cone-shaped flowerhead has a refined sweet-pea/raspberry/tangerine scent that carries, especially when it is growing in moist, limy soil. Long lasting, it blooms in all summer on sprawling, leafy branches 12 to 14 inches high. 'Grandiflora' flowers are cream-white with orange anthers. Plant it in window boxes and containers near patios and entrances.

Culture: Self-sows, so let only the most fragrant plants set seed. Sow seeds outdoors in full sun or bright shade in poor, alkaline soil where plants are to bloom (they transplant badly) and mark the place—the seeds may be slow to sprout. Thin to 8 inches apart. Attractive to butterflies, and gophers consider them a real delicacy.

TULIPA, Tulip. A few tulips are very fragrant. Among the easiest and best are the single, clear yellow, orange-blossom-scented 'Bellona'; big, scarlet 'Dr. Plesman', with a fragrance like lily-of-the-valley; the double, honey-scented 'Fred Moore'; orange streaked with scarlet 'General De Wet'; yellow 'Golden Melody'; orange-red 'High Society'; the double, golden yellow 'Hoangho'; and the lily-flowered 'Ballerina'. The Single Early Division is also known for fragrance. See list 12, Tulip.

VALERIANA (vall-eer-ee-*ay*-nuh) **officinalis**
Valerian, Garden Heliotrope Zones 4-9/10

In flower from late spring through summer, the fragrant white, pinkish, or lavender flowers are sweetly scented of heliotrope and bloom in 2- to 4-inch-wide, rounded clusters on stems 2 to 4 feet high above rather weedy foliage. The scent is stronger at night. The roots are used in making perfume. 'Marine', from 16 to 20 inches high, and its 8-inch dwarf have large, deep purple flowerheads.

Culture: Sow seeds in early spring or plant root divisions in early fall, in full sun, in well-drained soil, and maintain moisture. Self-sows and often is invasive. Its attraction for cats can be a nuisance.

VIOLA (vye-oh-luh) **odorata**
Sweet Violet Zones 6-9

A perfume comes from this sweetly fragrant woodland violet whose flowers still are candied and used as bonbons and pastry garnishes. The flowers look like tiny white or blue-purple, sometimes pink, pansies, and flower in late spring and often again in the cool autumn. The lasting heart-shaped foliage grows in bouquets 8 inches high that are attractive as ground cover but flower well only in full sun. The old purple species flowers are the most fragrant, but the most famous for fragrance are the large-flowered, lavender-violet double Parma violets 'Duchesse de Parme' and 'Lady Hume Campbell'. See list 30, Violet—Pansy. If possible, buy from specialists in fragrant plants.

SOURCES: RAYFORD CLAYTON REDDEL, FOUNDER AND CO-OWNER OF GARDEN VALLEY RANCH, PETALUMA, CALIFORNIA. THE NURSERY IS DEVOTED EXCLUSIVELY TO FRAGRANT PLANTS AND ROSES. RAY IS THE AUTHOR OF *GROWING GOOD ROSES,* AND COAUTHOR WITH ROBERT GALYEAN OF *GROWING FRAGRANT PLANTS.* AND ED R. RASMUSSEN, FOUNDER OF THE FRAGRANT PATH, A NURSERY SPECIALIZING IN SEEDS FOR PERFUMED FLOWERS, P.O. BOX 328, FORT CALHOUN, NEBRASKA 68023.

71. THE CUTTING GARDEN

■ The dream of many gardeners is to walk into the garden all a-blooming, cut masses of flowers, and spend the rest of the day arranging them. The fact is, I've never met a flower that couldn't charm a container and brighten a corner of my house. Astilbes, asters, marigolds, even impatiens—all summer's major flowers can be harvested. And spring's first bulbs are thrilling if rather short-lived in bouquets, especially the narcissus. The sinuosity of tulips inspired Colette, and they do seem to last longer with pennies in the water. (Caution: before combining just-cut daffodils with tulips, place the daffodil stems in water overnight.)

Flowers for cutting are grown in a garden where the flowers taken won't be missed, or with vegetables. If their foliage adds grace notes even with the flowers gone, like that of peonies, for example, flowers for cutting can be grown in flowering borders.

There are two lists in this section, one of perennials and the other of annuals. Some of the plants are traditional cutting flowers—baby's-breath, gladiolus, and zinnias, for example. A few are flowers rarely found at reasonable prices in florists' shops—like fragile sweet peas and peonies. Yet others are for bold effects and to extend the arranger's creativity.

Harvesting Flowers: Take flowers just before their peak of bloom, in early morning or at sunset. Cut the stems only to the place where the next bud is rising, so that as many flowers as possible mature from each plant. Taking flowers then becomes a form of pinching, which encourages branching and continued flower production.

Have a bucket of warm water in the garden with you and the moment each stem is cut, place it in deep water. Stems seal themselves when exposed to air, and that makes it difficult for them to take up water afterward and harder to stay fresh. Cut the stems at a very long angle.

To help woody-stemmed flowers such as chrysanthemums absorb water, crush or split a 2- or 3-inch segment of the stem starting at the bottom. Seal the hollow stems of flowers that exude milk—such as euphorbias and poppies—by searing the end over a flame, or by dipping them quickly into boiling water. This stops the milky flow and prevents clogging of water-conducting cells.

Stand just-cut flowers overnight in a big bucket of water in a cool place to condition them. Sun and heat are enemies.

Everything associated with cut flowers must be clean—shears, knife, container, and water. A few drops of liquid chlorine bleach (great for cleaning glass vases) and ¼ teaspoon of granulated sugar added to the water helps the flowers last. Strip all foliage from stems that will be below the water level. Top up the vase with fresh water daily, or change the water; recut the stems often, and remove at once any fading flowers or greens.

Companion Plants: Flowers in blue and lots of fillers are companions for the flowers on this list: *Centaurea, Felicia dubia*, the little blue daisy, *Trachymene caerulea* (Blue Lace Flower), *Lobelia erinus* (Edging Lobelia); the many blue *Gentiana* species. Or, try sprays of fluffy pink asters, even wild blue asters. Include for filler to touch and taste the very fragrant herbs, especially mints, oregano, lavender, and the big 'Purple Ruffles' basil in flower (exquisite with pale pink dahlias). Other good companions include many of the flowers for drying on list 72, especially statice; ferns, ferny asparagus foliage, *Senecio cineraria* (Dusty-miller); Queen-Anne's-lace, and most of the perennials on lists 20 to 30.

PERENNIALS FOR THE CUTTING GARDEN

ALSTROEMERIA (al-strem-*meer*-ee-uh)
Lily-of-the-Incas, Peruvian Lily   Zones 7/8-11
Familiar florist's filler. A tuberous-rooted perennial from 12 to 18 inches tall, it bears its flowers in summer on slender erect stems branched like lily or freesia. The flowers are upright clusters of blossoms, rather like azalea florets, up to 2 inches long, daintily etched or blotched with black, and often bicolored in pink, rosy salmon, red, mauve, lavender, cream, or white.

Culture: The tubers look like bunches of slender fingers and require careful handling. Plant in spring in sun or bright shade 12 inches apart. Spread each tuber over a mound of well-drained, moderately rich, humusy soil in a hole at least 6 inches deep or deep enough so there are 2 inches of dirt over the top. Requires sustained moisture. With protection the species recommended should be hardy in Zones 6 and 7. In frost-free areas they perennialize.

A. aurantiaca   Zones 6/7-11
The hardiest species grown, 24 to 36 inches tall with clear orange or yellow flowers tipped with brown. The variety *lutea* is bright yellow and 30 inches tall. In Zone 6 it needs a winter mulch. Thrives on the dry West Coast.

Barry Ferguson's arrangement of annuals includes the annual sunflower, *Helianthus annuua*. (McDonald)

BELOW Snapdragons, *Antirrhinum majus*—the more you cut, the more they branch and bloom. (McDonald)
RIGHT *Alstroemeria auriantica*, the florist's filler. (McDonald)
BOTTOM, LEFT Peony 'Moonstone', spring's most elegant bouquet. (Klehm)
BOTTOM, RIGHT Elvin McDonald's twin arrangements of lemon yellow day-lilies, daisies, ferns, roses, annuals, Queen-Anne's-lace, and lythrum. (McDonald)

A. ligtu   Zones 6/7-11

The colors are pale pink, lilac, or off-white, and the plant reaches 4 feet in good conditions. The strain called Ligtu hybrids are choice for bedding and bloom in lovely shades of pink, salmon, flame, orange, and yellow.

ANEMONE hupehensis var. japonica, Japanese Anemone. Beautiful for several weeks in summer and early fall. Airy flowerheads 2 to 3 inches in diameter, white through pink and deep rose, flower on open plants 24 to 30 inches high, with multibranched stems and ferny foliage. Best varieties for cutting: 'Alba' (syn. 'Honorine Jobert'), single, white; 'Whirlwind', a favorite late bloomer, white, double; 'Margarete' and 'Queen Charlotte', semi-double or double, deep pink. For culture, see list 17, Summer-into-fall Perennials.

ASTILBE, Spiraea, Perennial Spiraea. These are 6 inches to 6 feet tall with feathery flowerheads in late spring or summer that stand well above deeply cut green or bronzed foliage. The colors are from palest pink and coral to bright red and cream white. Outstanding fillers for flower arrangements. Cultivars of A. × arendsii offer a range of colors and bloom periods: 'Deutschland', to 24 inches, creamy white, early; 'Snowdrift', similar, to 30 inches, whiter; 'Federsee', early, intense salmon-pink panicles to 24 inches tall, good for dry situations; 'Fanal', late spring, 24 inches high, 12-inch-long, garnet-red panicles, bronzy foliage; 'Cattleya', 36 inches tall, orchid-pink, blooms later with 'Peach Blossom' (A. × rosea), which is 36 to 48 inches tall, salmon-pink. The vigorous 'Superba', from 2 to 4 feet, a lilac (A. taquettii), blooms in late summer and fall. Allow astilbes to mature fully before harvesting the flowers. For culture, see list 21, Astilbe.

DAHLIA. Excellent. Lush tuberous perennials that from midsummer to frost bear many-petaled, luminous flowers in pastels, strong colors, and bicolors. Wonderful with sprays of asters, wild or garden varieties, and purple basil. Show-caliber blooms can measure 6 to 7 or even 10 to 12 inches across, and come in many sizes and forms. Modern hybrids are 3 to 6 feet tall, and are often grown just for cutting. For flower arrangements, the daintier long-stemmed cactus-flowered types are choice, in shades of peach, salmon, white, cream, lemon, soft pink, heliotrope mauve, and red—a vivid quality indispensable to the flower arranger. See list 10, Dahlia.

Among the best dahlias for arranging are: cactus-flowered 'Orchid Lace', 6-inch flowers, glowing white with orchid-edged petals, 5-foot bush; 'Juanita Bella', 6-inch flowers, velvety ruby red, 4-foot bush; 'Estralita', 7-inch cream white cactus type brushed lightly with lavender, 4-foot bush; and 'Tequila Sunrise', 7-inch flowers in an unusual shade of caramel orange with golden highlights, 5-foot bush. A superb old favorite in the formal decorative class is 'Gerry Hoek', a 4-foot plant which bears 5-inch shell pink blossoms with a silver reverse.

Place cut dahlia stems in 2 to 3 inches of hot (150° to 160° F) or boiling water and allow to cool for a couple of hours or overnight. Stems may then be recut to any length for arranging.

DIGITALIS, Foxglove. Blooms in spring and early summer, 2 to 6 feet tall. Foxgloves bear tall spikes of pendulous thimble- or finger-shaped cream, rose, and magenta blooms, usually with dark spots. There are annuals, biennials, and perennials. Among the best for cutting are 'Alba', 4- to 5-foot-tall white cultivar of the biennial D. purpurea; D. ferruginea Rusty Foxglove, a striking, lanky 6-foot biennial, with coppery yellow flowers with a furry lower lip; D. grandiflora (syn. D. ambigua), Yellow Foxglove, 24 inches tall, tidy creamy yellow clumping perennial, delicate and refined; and D. lutea, 36 inches tall, small green-lemon flowers, excellent in woodlands and arrangements. See list 60, The Cottage Garden.

EUPHORBIA, Spurge. In spring, the species recommended for cutting bear clusters of big round or oval flowerheads composed of greenish yellow bracts surrounding inconspicuous brownish flowers—long lasting above attractive foliage. Sear the flower stems over a flame or in boiling water before putting them into an arrangement. Recommended are E. characias subsp. wulfenii, 4 to 5 feet tall with tremendous heads of greenish yellow flowers, hardy in Zones 8 to 10 and grown as an annual in the North; E. griffithii, 24 to 36 inches tall, with brick red bracts above lance-shaped green leaves with pink midribs, hardy in Zones 4 to 8; and E. myrsinites, trailing rockery plant with intense yellow-green flowers and evergreen blue-gray-green leaves on woody 8- to 10-inch stems, hardy in Zones 5 to 9. Be cautious—the milky juice can cause skin irritation, especially on hot days. For culture, see list 57, Seashore and Sandy Soils.

GYPSOPHILA (jip-soff-ill-uh)
Baby's-breath

Excellent. Airy, many-branched, spangled with tiny, dainty, roselike flowers in summer; a popular filler for summery floral arrangements. In the garden it spreads like a cloud over spaces left empty by, for instance, the big Oriental poppies, and ties everything together as it does in bouquets both fresh and dried. The taller sorts belong in the back of the border or in the center of island beds. Grouped or massed, Baby's-breath is enchanting with herbs, blue salvia, and roses.

Culture: In spring, set out root divisions in full or partial sun in well-drained, rather dry, neutral to alkaline soil, and allow lots of space. Maintain moisture. In south Florida, replant yearly.

G. paniculata Baby's-breath   Zones 3-9
The traditional baby's-breath for bouquets; 24 to 36 inches tall and blooms all summer. The more you cut, the more the flowers come. In the warm South it is treated as an annual or biennial and replanted every autumn. 'Bristol Fairy' is the favorite double-flowered white. 'Pink Fairy' is similar, about 18 inches tall, an almost-white pink. 'Red Sea', from 3 to 4 feet high, bears double rose pink flowers.

G. repens   Zones 3-8
A creeping, mat-forming baby's-breath 8 to 12 inches high, delightful in rock gardens and as ground cover. Gray-leaved and white flowered, it blooms from summer into early fall. Manages in slightly acid soils but must be very well drained.

HELLEBORUS, Hellebore. Evergreen plants with distinctive, deeply divided foliage that is interesting in winter. In the warm South, the unique nodding flowers appear in early winter—December and January—in light shade, in damp, humusy woodland soil. Left undisturbed, handsome colonies form and self-sow. The following are recommended for cutting: H. foetidus, 18 to 24 inches, bears panicles of drooping, bell-like pale green flowers edged red, and has blackish green leaves. Allow the flowers to mature before cutting—they can last weeks. H. lividus subsp. corsicus, to 18 inches, shrubby with gray-green, holly-like foliage and clusters of pale lichen green flowers suffused underneath with purple. H. niger, Christmas Rose, 12 to 18 inches, bears large, porcelain-white nodding flowers with yellow stamens from December through February. It will bloom in the snow during the lengthening days of early spring.

H. orientalis, Lenten Rose, 15 to 18 inches, is one of the finest low-growing very early flowers. Nodding, long-lasting blooms 3 to 4 inches wide, pale green, creamy white, pink-crimson, or maroon-purple can be harvested after the flowers have matured, and even when the stamens droop. Make a vertical 1-inch cut up the center of each stem and stand it in hot water 1 or 2 minutes before placing in cold water to cure for a time before arranging. The leathery, nearly evergreen foliage is especially valuable in winter. See list 14, Spring Perennials for Shade.

LIATRIS spicata, Spike Gay-feather. Flowers in mid- to late summer and fall, 24 to 36 inches tall. Excellent in a wild garden and quick to perennialize near water, dense tufts of grasslike foliage are topped by decorative, ragged-edged pink-purple florets on narrow spikes. The flowers open from the top down and are lasting when cut. 'Kobold', a compact well-established hybrid 18 inches high, is lilac-mauve, attractive with pale yellows and greens, and blooms earlier than other liatris. 'Floristan White' is 36 inches tall and perennializes well. For culture, see list 4, Summer-into-fall Bulbs.

LILIUM, Lily. Excellent. Outstanding as a cut flower is 'Green Dragon', with 5 foot stems and soft lime or green-cream flowers with cinnamon stamens. But the old species lilies have great charm, for instance the spotted orange tiger lily, L. lancifolium, which blooms in summer and fall.

Recommended for cool regions are the 5- to 6-foot-tall early Martagon (Turk's-cap) lilies which bear small, nodding flowers, and the fragrant Easter lily, L. longiflorum. Replanted in the garden after its indoor flowering period, it will flower again in summer and for another season or 2. The Asiatic and Oriental hybrids are the most likely to succeed in warm regions, but not below Zone 8. See list 11, Lily.

The lilies most widely grown as garden plants and for cutting are the colorful Asiatic hybrids, which bloom the earliest in June and early July in my Washington, D.C., garden. They come in every color but blue, including bicolors. Some outstanding Asiatic hybrids are: 'Enchantment', classic orange; 'Connecticut Beauty', cream to vivid yellow; 'Monte Negro', dark red; 'Pirate', dark red; 'Queen Juliana', almost white; 'Starfire', cream; 'Cote d'Azur', pink rose.

The Trumpets flower in midseason, from mid-July to mid-August. Vigorous plants 5 to 6 and 8 feet tall, with up to 12 large trumpet-shaped blooms on a stem. The color range is white, gold, and pink. For cutting, plant 'Golden Splendor'; 'Pink Perfection', a deep pink shade; and 'Thunderbolt', apricot with a flaring trumpet tinged green outside, up to 5 feet tall.

Among the last to bloom—from July into September—are the spectacular Oriental lilies. The flowers are fragrant, up to 10 inches in diameter, with 8 to 10 flowers on stems 28 to 38 inches tall. For cutting, plant: 'Black Beauty', dark red; 'Casablanca', an immaculate white with huge, reflexed blooms; 'Journey's End', rose with a red band; or the very fragrant, upward-facing, 4-foot crimson 'Star Gazer'.

Some interesting species lilies are recommended on list 70, The Fragrance Garden. See also list 11, Lily, and note the effect of cutting on next year's blooms.

TOP Sweet peas, *Lathyrus odoratus*, delicate, sweetly-scented cutting flowers, are cousins to eating peas. (Viette)
ABOVE Baby's-breath, *Gypsophila* 'Bristol Fairy', an airy filler for borders and bouquets that ties everything together. In the background, *Knophovia* and *Achillea*. (Viette)
RIGHT A bouquet of *Aquilegia* 'Songbird'. (Pan American Seed)

PAEONIA, Peony. Excellent. Blooms in spring, 3 to 4 feet tall. The whole tribe are superb cut flowers, but especially the reliable herbaceous peony (common garden peony) hybrids. Recommended cultivars for arrangements include: 'Festiva Maxima', a double white with crimson flecks; 'Venus', sensual pink; 'Baroness Schroeder', a full double cream-blush on good stems; 'Sarah Bernhardt', a vigorous strawberry-cream variable pink with darker details; 'Kelways Brilliant' or 'Nippon Gold', anemone-centered brilliant cerise-red single with gold staminoids. Other peonies for cutting are recommended on list 26, Peony.

PHLOX. Excellent. The big upright phloxes bloom in summer to fall on plants 2 to 4 feet tall. The big silky-soft flowerheads are preferred fillers for sunny summer borders and for cutting. For bouquets, grow the hardy, long-lasting, mildew-resistant, pure white, 'Miss Lingard', 24 inches high. It blooms early, doesn't set seed and so never goes wild and reverts to magenta, as do many phloxes. It may rebloom in autumn. The backbone of summer borders is *P. paniculata*, Summer Perennial Phlox, Fall Phlox, which has the unmistakable phlox scent. The colors range from white and pale pink to red, orange, crimson and purple, many with a contrasting eye. Favorites for cutting are 'Bright Eyes', a pretty pink with a crimson eye; 'Blue Ice', a vigorous, hardy white with a lavender eye; 'Prime Minister', white with a crimson eye; 'Fujiyama', a strong, vigorous white with a golden eye; and 'Orange Perfection', an almost luminous standout, especially when combined with 'Starfire', an equally luminous red. For culture, see list 27, *Phlox.*

SEDUM 'Autumn Joy', Stonecrop. Colorful flowers from late summer through autumn, 20 to 24 inches high. One of the most valuable flowers for fall; the nice spring show of gray-green foliage 18 to 24 inches tall is followed by fresh apple green flowerheads in early summer, which slowly change to rich pink, through rose to salmon-bronze and then finally with the cold to rosy russet. Also recommended is *S.* 'Vera Jameson', 9 to 12 inches tall, with maroon foliage and pink flowers in autumn. This is one of the best sedums for sunny gardens and may be dried. Plant them among early-flowering bulbs, including tulips and fritillaria, or fall-flowering colchicum to extend the color. For culture, see list 56, Dry, Hot Conditions.

ANNUALS FOR THE CUTTING GARDEN

. . . .

ANTIRRHINUM (an-tihr-**rye**-num) **majus**
Snapdragon   Tender Perennial
Excellent. A tender perennial grown as an annual; in spring through fall spires of dainty leaves are covered with fat, bright flowers in many colors and bicolors. These are lasting and generous bloomers, staples of any cutting garden. For big bouquets choose 'Double Supreme' hybrids, 36 inches tall, in clear, solid shades of red, pink, rose and yellow. 'Wedding Bells' and 'Madame Butterfly' are 30-inch-high doubles in soft pastels; 'Monarch Mixed' is 16 to 18 inches high, an in-between size. The Princess strain, 12 to 15 inches high, white with a purple eye, is a luscious

bicolor and one of the most useful cut flowers over a long season. For low arrangements choose dwarfs such as 'Tahiti', the smallest and earliest, whose compact, bushy plants are 7 to 8 inches high; charming, but not as colorful as the bigger types.

Culture: Choose resistant strains where rust is a problem. In Washington, D.C., my snapdragons usually winter over (with protection) and flower a second season. Sow seeds outdoors in early spring, or plant seedlings after danger of frost in well-drained, rich, humusy soil in the neutral range. Maintain even moisture. Pinch out leaders early to encourage bushiness, and deadhead all season to keep the snapdragons coming. Also self-sows.

BUPLEURUM rotundifolium
Thoroughwax   Annual
Blooms all summer; from 12 to 18 inches high, with greenish yellow flowers that resemble euphorbia. They are prettily arranged against eucalyptus-like leaves. The striking, lightly branched flowerheads animate a summer bouquet.

Culture: Sow seeds where the plants are to grow, in sun or even fairly shaded areas in well-drained soil. Grows quicky.

CENTAUREA cyanus, Cornflower, Bachelor's-button, Bluebottle. Has shaggy or fluffy little flowerheads 1½ inches across, in an unmistakable deep blue (sometimes purple, pink, or even white) intensified by a dark brown eye; 12 to 24 inches. Blooms all summer and into early fall if successive sowings are made. A fast-growing, gray-leaved standard of the cutting garden. See list 34, Annuals That Self-sow.

COSMOS bipinnatus. Excellent. Blooms from summer until frost; 3 to 4 feet high. These tall, delicate but tough plants bear 2- to 4-inch wide-petaled flowers with a central yellow disk in white, pink, or burgundy red on willowy stems. Long lasting in arrangements; cutting encourages new growth. Sow all the colors in one grand patch; they are wonderful in mixed bouquets. Especially good for cutting are 'Sea Shells', 3 to 3½ feet tall, with yellow, buttonlike centers and creamy white or shell pink or crimson and pink interiors; 'Psyche Mixed', to 36 inches tall, semidouble and single, large upright flowers; and the variegated white and pink 'Candy Stripe'. For culture see list 33, Annuals for Fall.

DIANTHUS, Pink. Excellent. Annuals, biennials and perennials of varying heights and bloom periods. The spicy clove scent of the genus is strong in both the large florist's carnations and the little grass or cottage pinks—all long lasting as cut flowers. The 3 species described here are grown for cutting. *D. barbatus*, Sweet William, is a short-lived, charming, old-fashioned plant, 18 inches high, that for a brief period in spring bears flat-topped flowerheads of small toothed or fringed carnation-type florets, often with a distinct crimson eye. There are reds, pinks, and bicolors with flashes of white. *D. caryophyllus*, Carnation, Clove Pink, Divine Flower, is perennial, the tall,

large-flowered, fragrant florist's carnation that blooms in late spring and summer, according to region. Leggy and in need of staking, it is challenging to grow, but bears superb, fragrant, very long-lasting flowers. For small bouquets, grow the annual *D. chinensis*, Rainbow Pink, a small pink from 6 to 10 inches tall. See list 70, The Fragrance Garden.

GLADIOLUS (glad-ee-**oh**-lus)
Corn Flag, Sword Lily
Excellent. The long, tapering gladiolus stem studded with big, bright blossoms is one of the most elegant and long-lasting summer flowers for cutting. The blossoms open starting at the bottom and in some forms look like perched butterflies. It comes in every color but blue and many breathtaking bicolors. Bloom time is according to type. There are 2 major groups—the big 36-inch modern plants that flower in summer, and the 18-inch, small-flowered types that flower in late spring and perennialize in warm climates. Both tall and smaller gladioli are long-lasting if cut when the first flower colors. Attractive sword-like foliage develops before the flower stem.

Culture: In Zones 3 through 7, the big florist's gladiolus is treated as an annual and planted in spring. In Zones 7 through 9, it may be grown through winter in the garden with a mulch. Corms flower 60 days after planting. The big gladioli for cutting usually are set out in the cutting or vegetable garden. In the North, plant gladiolus in mid-spring; after the foliage dies down, dig and store the corms for winter at 50° F with good air circulation—place on wire trays or in mesh bags. In the South, plant in spring or fall for spring flowers. Set the corms 5 inches deep, 4 inches apart in well-drained, moderately rich soil with lots of peat moss. Maintain moisture.

For magnificent bouquets, plant groups of a dozen corms in full sun every 10 days from mid-spring to midsummer.

G. byzantinus   Zones 7-10
An excellent small historic gladiolus recommended for restoration landscapes and collections, this violet-red species is 18 to 20 inches tall with narrow leaves.

G. × colvillei   Zones 5-11
A modern miniature 18 inches tall that blooms in early summer in white, salmon-pink, red, and in bicolors. Hardy above − 20° F. Plant in fall or early spring, 3 inches deep.

G. × hortulanus   Zones 7-10
The name covers the hundreds of beautiful, big, modern hybrids borne on tapering stems to 36 inches inches tall and more, grown as annuals in the North. Large-flowered types may be 4 to 7 inches across; butterfly-flowered hybrids with striking throat markings are smaller. There are many colors and bicolors.

HELIANTHUS, Sunflower. Blooms in late summer. The annual species, *H. annuus*, may be 12 feet tall and the flowerheads 12 inches across with a central disk surrounded by yellow rays. But the best sunflowers for arrangements are smaller: 'Autumn Beauty' produces 6-inch blossoms in gold, lemon, bronze, and mahogany with a darker zone, on 6-foot plants; 'Sunburst Mixed' seed produces 4-inch flowers in deep crimson, lemon, bronze, and gold on strong, branching stems to 4 feet high. These susceptible flowers are best cut in evening or early morning. Remove the leaves and plunge the stems into boiling water for 1½ to 2 minutes, then condition the stems in cool water in a tall container overnight. Once hardened, the stems can usually be recut and used without further treatment. Perennial sunflowers are discussed on list 17, Summer-into-fall Perennials.

LATHYRUS odoratus, Sweet Pea. Excellent. The old-fashioned sweet pea is a fresh, delicately scented little flower that blooms on a long, slender stem borne on a leafy vine that grows to 4 to 6 feet in a season, like its cousin the edible pea. It can bloom all summer if given shade for the hottest part of the day. Cultivars include nonclimbing dwarfs suitable for small gardens and containers. For the South look for heat-resistant sweet peas. May self-sow. Mixed colors make delightful bouquets. The flowers appear in early to mid-spring, masses of blooms from purple to pale lavender, ruby red, pale pink, and white, and there are bicolors. An antique strain with outstanding perfume is 'Antique Fantasy'. For a long season of bloom, especially in warm climates, the best choices are the heat-resistant strains such as 'Burpee's Galaxy' and 'Giant Late Heat Resistant'. For small gardens, choose self-supporting 6- to 10-inch dwarfs and 8-inch-high bush types, such as 'Burpee's Bijou', 'Super Snoop', and 'Snoopea'. For culture, see list 47, Climbers.

NIGELLA damascena, Love-in-a-mist. The flowers are spidery, 1 to 2 inches wide, on fast-growing plants from 18 to 24 inches tall; then bloom all summer in blue, purple, pink, or white if successive plantings are made. Small horned bracts that surround the petals add a fascinating texture to small bouquets, and toward midsummer the seedpods swell to fill the bracts and turn gold or mauve, a great addition to dried flower groups. The finely divided bright green foliage is a good filler for hanging baskets and boxes of mixed flowers. 'Miss Jekyll' is blue; 'Persian Jewels', 12 to 18 inches tall, has white, pink, red and purple flowers. There are also dwarfs, such as 'Blue Midget', 8 to 10 inches tall. For culture, see list 72, To Dry for Winter Bouquets.

SALVIA farinacea, Mealycup Sage. For cutting, choose this blue sage, a perennial grown as an annual in the North, which bears slim wands of florets in whorled spikes. A good filler. It blooms towards late summer and lasts until and even beyond the first frosts on leafy plants 18 to 24 inches tall. The more you cut, the more the flowers come. If the stems grow woody, bruise or scald them before putting them into water. Cultivars of *S. viridis* (syn. *horminum*), an 18-inch annual, are topped by spires of substantial bracts in white, brilliant pink, purple, or rich violet-blue that combine well with summer bouquets. They dry well. See also the Blue Sages on list 41, *Salvia*.

ZINNIA elegans. Excellent. Loved for its color and free-blooming habit and bred to a mind-staggering number of vibrant colors, shapes, heights, and forms. There is a beauty for every garden use and they are unbeatable for cutting flowers. Some of the slightly smaller forms are more attractive and versatile than the giants. Recommended for cutting are the tall green 'Envy'; 'Border

Beauty' hybrids, 20-inch-high, dahlia-type semidouble flowers on bushy plants; 'Bouquet' hybrids, 22 inches high, large, semi-ruffled, fully double blooms 3½ inches across with long strong stems on sturdy branching plants; and 'Candy Cane' mix, 17-inch plants, semidouble and double flowers with bright pink, rose, and cerise stripes on white. See also list 42, *Zinnia*.

MORE PERENNIALS FOR CUTTING

The following perennials, all of which are listed elsewhere in this book, are also good for cutting.

ACHILLEA 'Moonshine', see list 15, Summer Perennials for Sun.

ALCHEMILLA mollis, Lady's-mantle, see list 75, Herbs with Showy Flowers.

AQUILEGIA vulgaris 'Nora Barlow', European Crowfoot, Garden Columbine, see list 13, Spring Perennials for Sun.

ARUNCUS dioicus, see list 50, Foliage for Form and Texture.

ASTER lateriflorus 'Horizontalis', tataricus, Tartarian Aster, see list 20, *Aster*.

CHRYSOPSIS 'Golden Sunshine', Golden Aster, see list 64, Seashore and Sandy Soils.

ECHINACEA purpurea 'Bright Star' and 'Magnus', Purple Coneflower, see list 64, The Meadow Garden.

ERYNGIUM 'Amethyst', 'Blue Star', and 'Miss Wilmott's Ghost', see list 56, Dry, Hot Conditions.

LAVANDULA angustifolia 'Hidcote', English Lavender, see list 76, Fragrant Herbs for Drying and Potpourri.

NEPETA 'Blue Wonder', see list 74, Herbs with Fragrant Foliage.

PEROVSKIA atriplicifolia, see list 57, Seashore and Sandy Soils.

PLATYCODON grandiflorus var. mariesii, Dwarf Balloon Flower, see list 15, Summer Perennials for Sun.

RUDBECKIA fulgida var. sullivantii 'Goldsturm', see list 15, Summer Perennials for Sun.

SOURCE: J. BARRY FERGUSON, A BOTANIST, FLORAL DESIGNER, AND LECTURER, DESIGNS THE FLORAL ARRANGEMENTS FOR MAJOR SOCIAL EVENTS IN MANHATTAN AND HOLDS THE AMERICAN HORTICULTURAL SOCIETY FRANCES JONES POETKER AWARD FOR CREATIVE FLORAL DESIGNS. HE IS THE AUTHOR OF *LIVING WITH FLOWERS*.

72. TO DRY FOR WINTER BOUQUETS

■ Another fantasy of flower gardeners is a cozy hearth where the spirit of summer lives on in great dried bouquets, all buff, blue, gold, apricot, and carmine, rich in fruits and seeds. The American colonists harvested their gardens and fields in the last drowsy days of Indian summer and bundled the plants into airy, rich arrangements in stillrooms, or used them as fragrant strewing herbs.

This list includes both traditional flowers for drying and innovative plants that invite the imagination. Your garden offers many more subjects than those described below—zinnias large and small, roses, hollyhocks, dahlias, the various salvias, and red anemones. Dried arrangements can also include herbs for fragrance. The fields are full of fillers already halfdry; milkweed, Queen-Anne's-lace, and goldenrod, for example. You will need lots of them.

Harvesting: Cut flowers for drying just before the peak of bloom in a hot, dry hour of the day. Pure colors are retained more accurately than subtle shades. Orange-reds dry redder than pink-reds.

Dry-textured plants such as baby's-breath, heather, broom, everlastings, goldenrod, herbs, and grasses dry quickly when tied into small bunches and hung head down in an airy, dry, dark room. Left upright in a waterless jar, they'll dry into interesting forms.

Simple flowers such as cosmos, zinnias, and daisies once were dried in fine, clean sand or a half-and-half mix of laundry borax and white cornmeal. Chemical drying agents and the microwave oven are faster.

Companion Plants: Attractive companion plants that provide interesting drying materials are plumy ornamental grasses such as *Briza*, Quaking Grass, and *Stipa*, Feather Grass; flowers that are followed by pods, such as Siberian iris, single peonies, yucca, and hibiscus; and the cone-forming echinacaeas. Other possibilities are echinops, rudbeckia (with its dark seedheads), banksia, hydrangeas, and the artichoke *(Cynara scolymus)* and its relative the cardoon *(C. cardunculus)*.

ACHILLEA, Yarrow. Deep gold or dusky pink flowers to 5 inches across in late spring combine with deeply divided, ferny foliage and exuberant growth in heights from 8 to 36 inches to make this a superb flower for most regions. The florets are borne in branching flat-topped heads (corymbs) several inches across that last well cut. The golds are among the best of all flowers for drying and combine well with the other materials favored for dried arrangements and wreaths. See list 15, Summer Perennials for Sun.

ALLIUM, Onion. Excellent for drying. The ornamental onion flowerheads are composed of many blue-purplish or white-pink florets and stand on leafless stalks well above tufts of dark green, strap-shaped foliage that gives off an onion scent when crushed. The most distinctive have strikingly round tops. Some are very tall. The following are recommended: *A. christophii* (syn. *albopilosum*), Stars-of-Persia, is the largest flower in cultiva-

Statice, *Limonium sinuata*, superb cutting and drying flowers, with salvia 'Blue Bedder'. (McDonald)

Among the best for drying:

TOP, LEFT Pincushion flower, *Scabiosa caucasica*, a perennial with grayish ferny foliage and pale blue, white or lavender flowers. (McDonald)

TOP, RIGHT Chinese lanterns, the fruit of *Physalis alkekengi*, follows small nodding starshaped white flowers. (Harper)

ABOVE Stars-of-Persia, *Allium christophii*, is one of the largest flowers in cultivation and excellent for drying. (McDonald)

RIGHT Dainty globe amaranth, *Gomphrena globosa*, dries easily and makes a good filler for dried arrangements. (Viette)

tion and one of the best for drying; summer bloomer from 10 to 20 inches tall with a huge, airy round head, 8 to 10 inches in diameter, composed of 50 or more star-shaped, silvery purple florets. *A. giganteum*, Giant Onion, in late spring and early summer, bears round reddish purple flowerheads about 6 inches in diameter on stems 35 to 45 inches tall; 'Rosy Giant' is a pinkish mauve, extraordinary in fresh arrangements with branches of weeping flowering trees such as dogwood and cherry. *A. sphaerocephalum*, Round-headed Garlic, is excellent as a cut flower and for drying; small, perfectly round reddish lavender flowerheads bloom in late spring on stalks 20 inches tall. Combines well with dried Aurelian lilies. The foliage is pungent, like wild garlic. *A. tuberosum*, Chinese Chives, Garlic Chives, Oriental Garlic, in late summer produces spreading clusters of fragrant white flowers with a green midriff, on 18-inch stems. For culture, see list 3, Spring, Large-flowered Bulbs.

ARTEMISIA ludoviciana, Western Mugwort, Cudwort, White Sage.

Grown for the silver or gray foliage—exquisite next to shades of pink, purple, and light blue. This species is 24 to 36 inches tall, airy, with delicately divided gray leaves, white-woolly underneath on white, branching stems. In late summer there are panicles of gray florets useful with the foliage in dried arrangements. Beautiful cultivars of the variety *albula* are 'Silver King', a fragrant, frosty compact that has a hint of red in autumn, and the slightly shorter 'Silver Queen'. See list 73, Herbs with Colorful Foliage.

CELOSIA cristata, Cockscomb hybrids.

The velvety flowerheads of the showiest resemble a rooster's crested comb from 12 to 24 inches high. The colors are dazzling—red, magenta, yellow, orange, apricot, and pink. The Plumosa Group (Feathered Amaranth) are just as brilliant but have feathery flowerheads, like bright-colored goldenrod. The dwarf Fairy Fountains series develop 4- to 6-inch plumes on plants only 12 inches tall. Mass closely to hide the somewhat weedy leaves. Air-dries well if cut at the peak of bloom. For culture, see list 31, Annuals for Sun.

ERYNGIUM amethystinum, Amethyst Sea-holly.

In summer this very cold-hardy, sea green thistlelike plant with colorful stems produces round heads of small blue flowers surrounded by long, spiky, darker blue bracts. About 18 to 24 inches tall and handsome in groups of 3 to 5 in a big border. Dries well and keeps its color. See list 56, Dry, Hot Conditions.

GNAPHALIUM (naf-*fay*-lee-um) 'Fairy Gold'

Wood Cudweed   Annual/Biennial

Grouped with the everlastings, this is a favorite florist's filler for fresh or dried arrangements. The woolly foliage is silver-gray, a perfect background for the clusters of tiny disk-shaped, double yellow or orange flowers. For drying, cut the flowers just before the peak of bloom.

Culture: Every year in early spring sow seeds or plant root divisions in sun, in very well-drained or sandy soil.

GOMPHRENA (gom-*free*-nuh) globosa

Globe Amaranth   Annual

This is a colorful little annual whose long-lasting flowers look like fat clover heads in white, mauve, purples, pink, and orange. About 12 to 18 inches tall, it blooms in late summer and autumn. Good edger for containers. Provides bright buttons of color for dried arrangements if picked just before maturity.

Culture: Sow seeds indoors in late winter, and in late spring set the seedlings out in full sun 8 to 12 inches apart in well-drained soil. Or, in mid-spring, sow seeds where the plants are to bloom. Tolerates drought, wind and searing sun.

HELIPTERUM (hee-*lip*-ter-um)

Everlasting

Soft, silky everlasting daisies, 18 to 24 inches tall, in white and rosy colors with spiky petals and woolly whitish leaves. Usually grown for drying, but pretty and long lasting in the border. The flowers close at night and do not open fully on dull days. For drying, pick before they are quite open.

Culture: Blooms in 3 months from seed sown in early spring. Sow seeds when the soil is workable, in full sun in well-drained, somewhat dry soil that is not particularly fertile.

H. humboldtianum   Annual

The small, golden, faintly fragrant flowers bloom in clusters of 3 above silvery foliage.

H. manglesii Swan River Everlasting   Annual

Bears masses of little single or double silver-white, rose, and carmine flowers with golden centers. Nice in rock gardens and borders, and dried in mixed colors.

H. roseum (syn. acroclinium)   Annual

The flowers are larger, the colors white, rose, and carmine. Good, strong stems.

LAVANDULA, English Lavender.

Since classical times the dried flower buds—harvested just before they open—have been a staple in dry perfumes and pot-pourris. The evergreen shrubs or subshrubs are 24 to 36 inches tall, with needlelike gray leaves; every part of the plant is sweetly fragrant. In late spring leafless shoots bear the tightly packed, small tubular flowers which, according to species, range from deep purple and blue to lavender, pink, white, and gray-blue. For drying, pick just before the buds open. Two species are recommended for drying: *L. angustifolia*, English Lavender, is a modest, sprawling lavender grown for fragrance, whose florets bloom on upright stems; 'Hidcote', 'Hidcote Giant', and 'Munstead' have better color than the species. *L. latifolia* is hardy only to Zone 6 but is very fragrant, and has brighter, fuller lavender flowers throughout summer and pretty silver-green foliage. See list 76, Fragrant Herbs for Drying and Potpourri.

LIMONIUM Sea Lavendar, Marsh Rosemary, Statice

Colorful, airy fillers that bear many small, tubular, rather dry florets in open flowerheads on well-branched stems—a staple of dried and fresh floral arrangements. The purple form is the most popular, but the range is from white and yellow to lavender and pink. For drying, cut the flowers as soon as they show good color.

Culture: For early bloom, in late winter or early spring sow seeds indoors, and when the soil has warmed transplant to the place where the plants will grow. Or, sow seeds directly outdoors. In the North, plant in full sun; in the South, partial shade is preferred. Best in well-drained, porous soil that is slightly acid and not too rich. Very successful at the seashore.

L. bonduelli   Biennial

Grown as an annual, 18 to 24 inches tall, this form bears many clusters of small yellow blooms that stand above light green foliages. Blooms from late summer to frosts.

L. dumosum   Zones 4-8

The statice sold under this name is a hardy perennial that bears clouds of small silvery blooms on curvy tangles of slender branches. Blooms in mid- to late summer.

L. latifolium 'Blue Cloud'   Zones 5-9

Large, open, diffuse sprays of airy blue and white florets bloom above big leathery oval leaves on plants 12 inches tall. Blooms in summer.

L. sinuatum   Tender Perennial/Biennial

A popular statice grown as an annual. The typical tubular flowers may be purple, white, yellow, or pink with a white spot. Winged stems. Blooms from August to frosts.

L. suworowii (syn. Psylliostachys suworowii)
                                                                      Annual

Known as rat-tail or Russian statice, these handsome lavender and green florets bloom in midsummer on rounded spikes 10 to 20 inches long.

LUNARIA (loo-*nay*-ree-uh)

Honesty, Money Plant, Moonwart, Satin Flower

An old-fashioned favorite for drying. The very flat seed-pod's satiny white central wafer is revealed when the grayish white parchmentlike cover is peeled off. Harvest as seedheads begin to dry; light-catching in a bouquet alone or an arrangement.

Culture: In early spring or fall sow seeds where the plants are to grow, in full sun and well-drained, humusy soil. Or, set out container plants in spring. Tolerates drought.

L. annua Honesty, Bolbonac, Silver-dollar, Penny Flower   Annual

Slightly fragrant flower spikes from 18 to 36 inches tall in white or crimson are borne in spring, followed by roundish disks 1½ to 2 inches across. Self-sows readily.

L. rediviva Perennial Honesty   Zones 4-8

Less colorful, the perennial species bears oval disks on plants 3 to 4 feet tall. Requires sustained moisture; most successful when seed is sown in the fall.

NIGELLA (nye-*jell*-uh) damascena

Love-in-a-mist, Wild Fennel   Annual

Charming 18- to 24-inch-high blue, purple, pink, or white spidery, spurred, many-petaled flowers 1 to 2 inches across. Excellent for cutting, and the light, interesting seedpods are favorites for dried arrangements. The finely divided bright green foliage is a good filler for hanging baskets and boxes of mixed flowers. 'Miss Jekyll' is a lovely blue; 'Persian Jewels', 12 to 18 inches tall, bears white, pink, red, and purple flowers. There are also dwarfs, such as 'Blue Midget', 8 to 10 inches tall.

Culture: For a long season of bloom, in early spring make successive sowings of seeds where the flowers are to grow, in full sun, in well-drained soil. Tolerant of drought.

PHYSALIS (*fye*-sal-iss) **alkekengi 'Gigantea'**
Alkekengi, Winter Cherry, Chinese-lantern, Japanese-lantern, Strawberry Tomato   Zones 3-9
Grown for the delightful little bright red-orange "fruits", which look like Chinese lanterns 2 inches wide. The plant is 24 to 36 inches high and in summer bears small, nodding, star-shaped white flowers which in fall inflate and color brightly as the berry inside enlarges. Pick after the lanterns mature. Makes a pretty, rustic dried arrangement.

Culture: Sow seeds indoors in late winter and plant out when the weather warms. Or, set out root divisions in late spring. Site in full sun in well-drained, humusy soil. Tolerant of drought. Invasive—restrict to its own space.

SCABIOSA (skay-bee-*oh*-suh)
Sturdy, hardy flowers grown primarily for arrangements. They bloom in summer on willowy stems in good shades of white, pink, yellow, blue and very dark reds and purples.

Culture: In early spring, sow seeds of the annual or set out root divisions of the perennials in full sun, in well-drained soil in the neutral range. Maintain moisture. Provide a light, dry winter mulch.

S. caucasica   Zones 4-8
Known as the pincushion flower and grown for cutting, this is a large, showy perennial with grayish ferny foliage and pale blue, white, or lavender flowers from summer to frost.

S. stellata 'Drumstick'   Annual
Known as paper moon and grown for the seedheads. Each plant produces from 20 to 30, 6- to 12-inch stems bearing pale blue flowers which develop into bronzy, globe-shaped seedheads. The ferny foliage is grayish.

STACHYS byzantina (syn. *lanata*), Woolly Betony, Lamb's-ears. The big, semievergreen, gray leaves 12 to 15 inches high are almost luminous in moonlight and so woolly they invite stroking—a wonderful contrast in color, outstanding texture, and charming in tussie-mussies and wreaths. From midsummer until frost they are topped by small, usually violet or white flowers—although some gardeners prefer to remove them to keep the focus on the leaves. Great dried in low arrangements, nosegays, and tussie-mussies. For culture see list 50, Foliage for Form and Texture.

SOURCE: J. BARRY FERGUSON, A BOTANIST, FLORAL DESIGNER, AND LECTURER, DESIGNS THE FLORAL ARRANGEMENTS FOR MAJOR SOCIAL EVENTS IN MANHATTAN AND HOLDS THE AMERICAN HORTICULTURAL SOCIETY FRANCES JONES POETKER AWARD FOR CREATIVE FLORAL DESIGNS. HE IS THE AUTHOR OF *LIVING WITH FLOWERS*.

73. HERBS WITH COLORFUL FOLIAGE

■ **The great historical herbs are generally weedy plants—tufts, clumps, and fountains of green. These striking exceptions add the essential element of color. One or more of the silvery *Artemisia* species will brighten early spring borders and bring a white light to fall's green doldrums. Combined with white flowers the silvery sages and santolinas make magic at noon and in the moonlight. Silver tones are exquisite with pinks and blues, arresting with collections of all-yellow or all-orange flowers. The big silver-veined, white-variegated, and mottled foliage of tall herbs lends character to the usual solid greens in the back of the border.**

A different value occurs with plantings of the variegated tiny-leaved herbs such as thyme; at a distance, these plants appear as light green or grayish. They're attractive as edgers alternating with clumps of green herbs and pink begonias or bright French marigolds.

Many other popular herbs have been bred to variegated or colored-leaved forms, for instance, the purple basils, *Ocimum basilicum*, notably 'Purple Ruffles'; use them in the garden with joy, and thoughtfulness.

Companion Plants: See individual herbs.

ARTEMISIA (art-em-*miz*-ee-uh)
Sagebrush, Wormwood
These plants, along with the gray lavenders, are among the most important herbs for foliage color and texture, and are recommended here and on many other lists in this book. All season to frost the silver- and gray-leaved species have the impact of cool white flowers; they are exquisite next to shades of pink, purple, and light blue. Their small yellow or white flowers are endearing, but not a factor. Some are used for color accents, others are ground covers, others are highly scented, still others are tall, textured plants for the back of the border. Some interesting species not recommended here are *A. abrotanum*, Southernwood, which has weedy foliage and a fruity scent; and *A. pontica*, a filigree of pale green leaves. See also list 77, Popular Culinary Herbs.

Culture: Plant or transplant root divisions or divide established artemisias in early spring or late summer (except for the woody 'Lambrook Silver' and 'Powis Castle', which are always propagated from cuttings). Best in moderately fertile, very well-drained soil in full sun or, in the South, bright shade. Artemisias are heat- and drought-resistant; water sparingly. Invasive species are restrained by planting in heavier clay soils or in 3- to 5-gallon containers buried in soil up to the rim. In hot, humid areas, the foliage may die back in midsummer; prune plants to promote new growth.

A. absinthium Absinthe, Wormwood Zones 3-8
Semievergreen, from 24 to 36 inches tall, with satiny, feathery gray-green foliage that smells of ether and anise and bears attractive yellow, buttonlike flowers in summer that are excellent for drying. Foliage and flowers are made into wreaths and used to discourage moth larvae; to flavor liqueurs, ice cream, and candy; and medicinally. Trim back after blooming. Especially attractive growing with foxgloves, monkshood, Russian sage, and lavender, in sheaths of iris, and sweet rocket. 'Lambrook Silver' is the choice for the North.

A. lactiflora White Mugwort   Zones 5-8
A tall, textural plant 4 to 5 feet high for the back of the border, it bears magnificent creamy white plumy flowers that last into fall. The dark green leaves are paler underneath. Evergreen in milder regions, must have moist soil, and usually needs staking.

A. ludoviciana Western Mugwort, Cudwort, White Sage   Zones 5-9
About 24 to 36 inches tall, airy, with delicately divided gray leaves, white-woolly underneath, on white, branching stems. In late summer there are panicles of gray florets. Good for massing. Scented, invasive, and succeeds in southern gardens. Beautiful plants of the variety *albula*, Silver-king Artemisia, are 'Silver King', a fragrant, frosty compact hardy to Zone 3 that has a hint of red in autumn, and the slightly shorter 'Silver Queen'.

A. 'Powis Castle'   Zones 5-8
Silky soft, feathery, it makes a rounded clump 18 to 24 inches high.

A. schmidtiana 'Silver Mound'   Zones 3-7
For the front of the border and edging paths. It makes a mound 12 inches high by 18 to 20 inches wide of soft, feathery, silver-gray leaves with a bluish green undertone. Don't encourage with overly rich soil. If the clump opens at the center and flops over by midsummer, cut the stems back to the ground; recovery is quick and the foliage remains in good condition till frost. Choice for dry, sandy places.

ASARUM canadense, Wild Ginger, Snakeroot. Handsome heart-shaped leaves up to 5 inches across make this one of the preferred deciduous foliage plants for a wild garden in shade. The 1-inch purplish brown flowers are near the ground. It is a delightful, easy ground cover. The aromatic rhizomatous root is used as a substitute for ginger. In Zones 4 to 7 several species are evergreen in mild winters; recommended are: *A. europaeum* and *A. shuttleworthii*, which is wonderfully mottled. In the West, grow *A. caudatum* and *A. hartwegii*. For culture, see list 48, Wildflowers to Naturalize.

CHRYSANTHEMUM parthenium, Feverfew. Charming old-fashioned mum 12 to 36 inches tall that bears masses of little 1-inch daisylike white or yellow button flowers with yellow centers in late summer. Dwarf forms are used for edging but not in the warm South. 'Aureum', Golden-feather, from 8 to 12 inches tall, has yellow foliage that turns green when the plant blooms. For culture see list 23, Mum—Daisy.

TOP, LEFT Knot garden of herbs and flowers includes: Lamb's-ears, *Stachys*, chives, green and gray *Santolina*, shasta daisies, peonies, coral bells, and bellflowers. This is in the George Vance Gardens, Mt. Solon, VA. In the background, a cypress gazebo. (Viette)

TOP, RIGHT Rue, *Ruta graveolens*, a haze of yellow-green. (Harper)

ABOVE *Santolina virens*, aromatic edger and choice hedge for rose beds. (Viette)

LEFT *Teucrium chamaedrys*, used for hedging in formal herb gardens and as a substitute for boxwood. (Harper)

IRIS pseudacorus 'Variegata', Yellow Iris, Yellow Flag, Water Flag. This is a magnificent variegated form of the biggest of the water irises, lovely in pools and ponds or in a humusy, flowering border where it can be kept evenly moist. In late spring or early summer there are bright yellow canna-like flowers that may be blotched or veined with violet or brown. For culture see list 25, *Iris*.

MENTHA suaveolens, Pineapple Mint. A very decorative, vigorous but fine upright mint with fresh, bright, smallish white-splotched leaves. Completely white leaves sometimes occur, and white flower spikes in summer double the effect. Ten to 18 inches high, the plant fairly sparkles along path edges and that's where the fragrance can best be experienced. Must be appreciated close-up. Delightful in a strawberry jar, hanging basket, or other small container on porch or patio. Grow it with small white petunias and with dark green foliage plants, or combine it with single petunias in solid red, purple, or magenta. Not good with yellow. The tips of young shoots smell of pineapple and the overall scent is of a good mint, charming in fresh bouquets, tussie-mussies, and potpourris. For culture, see list 74, Herbs with Fragrant Foliage.

ORIGANUM vulgare, Marjoram, Pot Marjoram, Wild Marjoram, Oregano, Organy. There are many decorative types of this useful culinary herb. The 8- to 12-inch-high clumps sprawl but individual branches lift panicles of faintly scented, edible, tiny whitish, pink or lavender florets in summer. The dainty leaves are slightly hairy and the biting flavor, reminiscent of thyme, enhances other herbs and fresh bouquets. It is used in Italian cooking, with tomatoes, in salads, and in potpourris. For color plant 'Aureum', which has golden leaves that in midsummer turn green. 'Dr. Ietswaart' is a more ornamental form but not reliably hardy in Zone 7 and north. *O. × majoricum* 'Well Sweep' is streaked with yellow. For culture, see list 77, Popular Culinary Herbs.

RUTA (**rew**-tuh) graveolens
Rue, Herb-of-grace   Zones 6-10
Dense, nearly evergreen subshrub from 12 to 24 or 36 inches tall with flattish, delicately cut blue-green leaves. 'Variegata' is edged with white. Attractive seedpods. In summer, modest blooms make a haze of yellow-green; pleasantly impressive and an excellent foil for gray in the garden. The leaves have a bitter taste and a strong odor repellent to fleas, but in water the aroma becomes a sweet scent. Used with salad burnet, lavender cotton, sage, germander, and lavender, in tussie-mussies and flower arrangements, and for bonsai. 'Jackman's Blue', 18 to 24 inches tall, is a more intense blue, lovely in fall. The leaves of *R. chalapensis*, Fringed Rue, have the shape of a teardrop, but the plant is slightly less hardy and scarce.

  Culture: Set out container plants in early spring or fall, in full sun in well-drained, humusy soil. Mulch well in winter and in spring prune back to old wood.

SALVIA argentea, Silver Sage. To 24 inches tall, the basal rosette of low-growing, 6-inch-long hairy, silvery gray-white leaves glows in the midst of the garden's usual greens. The flowers are white with a pink or yellow tint. This is a perennial usually grown as a biennial and started from seed. Several types of *S. officinalis*, the culinary sage, are colorful. Particularly pretty is the little *S. o.* 'Tricolor', 6 to 10 inches high, whose leaves are red, pink, gray, cream, and purple. The gray leaves of the often-seen 'Icterina' are variegated with gold and lend fragrance and beauty to flower arrangements fresh or dried. See list 41, *Salvia*.

SANTOLINA (san-toh-**lye**-nuh)
The species here are gray or gray-green evergreen shrubs and subshrubs 12 to 30 inches high, with aromatic leaves and in late spring and summer, inconspicuous buttonlike flowers. The cool, gray foliage brings a silvery softness to rock gardens, mixed flower borders, and rose beds. Useful as edging, a low hedge, or specimens in formal borders, parterres, and knot gardens, and as screening for tall, leggy plants. May be sheared. Attractive in containers.

  Culture: In early spring set out container-grown plants in light, sandy or gravelly soil with very good drainage. The species here prefer full sun and withstand drought but do poorly in hot, humid climates; water only in the morning. Cut back old flowerheads in fall. Mulch where temperatures go below zero.

S. chamaecyparissus Lavender Cotton
                                                      Zones 6-9
A highly valued dense, pine-scented evergreen perennial from 18 to 30 inches high and as multibranched as coral with needlelike foliage. Leaves are white-woolly underneath, silvery in moonlight, and whiter when growing in dry conditions, sandy soil, and full sun. Spectacular background for its summer crop of bright yellow button flowers. When flowers and foliage are dried, the sharp aroma lasts; lavender cotton is used as a moth repellent, in wreaths, arrangements, and sachets. Take branches liberally after flowering in late summer or early fall for drying and to control sprawling and woodiness of the plant. 'Nana' is a dwarf to 14 inches tall.

S. neapolitana   Zones 9-10
Smaller, rounded, bushy shrub about 24 inches high with conspicuous yellow flowers in summer, wonderful with lady's-mantle and purple basil.

S. virens Green Santolina   Zones 6/7-8
Smaller yet, this 15-inch species with yellowish white flowers has brilliant green leaves and is perfect with brooms, heathers, thymes, sedum, and sempervivum. Nice as a clipped hedge. Thrives in poor, sandy soil in the neutral range and by the sea.

SYMPHYTUM (**sim**-fit-um)
Big herbs grown for historical interest, with thick rootstocks and large soft, dark green basal leaves. In summer, blue to pink flower clusters appear on one side of stems that curve under their weight. Nice in wild gardens or at the back of a large border. Shows off to good advantage with poppies, elecampane, lovage, iris, and fennel.

  Culture: In early spring, set out container-grown plants in sun or dappled shade, in moist, well-drained, humusy soil. Divide and replant the fleshy roots in spring. Maintain moisture.

S. grandiflorum   Zones 4-8
Twelve to 18 inches high, it is called ground-cover comfrey and may also be listed as *Pulmonaria lutea*. The leaves are very dark green, crinkled, and have a rough, bristly texture. Cream and white flowers in late spring are a bonus. There are few weeds that will find their way through massed plantings. An excellent plant for dry sites, but it spreads faster in moist soils.

S. officinale Comfrey, Healing Herb, Boneset
                                                      Zones 2-10
A big, tropical-looking plant 2 to 4 feet tall for low spots and near water, well-branched, dense, and rather coarse. The tiny bell-like flowers may be rose, purple, red, or yellow. The leaves of 'Variegatum' are irregularly edged with white. Once widely used in folk medicine.

S. × uplandicum 'Variegatum' Zones 3/4-7/8
A variety to 16 inches high of this unbranched species, it has cream-white margins and lilac-blue flowers. Hardy in Zone 4 and possibly 3, but the southern limits are not certain.

TEUCRIUM (**tewk**-ree-um) chamaedrys
Wall Germander   Zones 3-8
Small evergreen subshrub from 10 to 12 inches high, often used as a substitute for boxwood and as a clipped hedge. Attractive when allowed to develop naturally and show off the rosy flowers distributed in late summer along the stem tips. It has dense, finely textured oaklike leaves, dark green and glossy, whose aroma attracts cats. Nice clumped in a rock garden, or clipped and used as edging in a knot garden. Recommended for low edging is the dwarf *T. c.* var. *prostratus*, 6 to 10 inches high; nice with thyme, lavender cotton, and artemisia. Once used medicinally, its herbal role now is largely flavoring liqueurs and vermouths. Two other species, much less hardy, are worth noting for their gray foliage effects: *T. fruticans*, Tree Germander, and *T. marum*, called cat thyme.

  Culture: In spring set out root divisions in full sun in light, very well-drained soil with enough humus to keep the roots moist. Tolerates partial shade but must not be allowed to dry out. Divide in spring. Mulch for winter in harsh climates.

THYMUS Thyme
The thymes are mostly low, attractive, evergreen herbs with trailing branches and tiny leaves that release a "clean" aromatic scent when crushed. They are related to mints; 6 to 10 inches high, durable, often fast-spreading, charming when surging over walls, edging containers, between stepping-stones, and as specimens in rock gardens. In summer there are small clusters of tiny flowers in pale pink, white, or lilac. The variegated types add valuable color accents. See list 74, Herbs with Fragrant Foliage.

SOURCE: JANET WALKER IS CURATOR OF THE NATIONAL HERB GARDEN AT THE U.S. NATIONAL ARBORETUM, AND LECTURES AND WRITES ON HORTICULTURAL SUBJECTS.

74. HERBS WITH FRAGRANT FOLIAGE

■ These are popular herbs, including two of the great culinary plants, that serve the garden in many ways. But their greatest gift is their intensely aromatic foliage—fragrance for hot summer noons and the cool moments after rain.

Plant the big hyssops and the low-growing silvery lavenders in working areas of the mixed garden where they will be brushed against often. Set the vigorous mints so stems will spill onto paths and be walked on; trips through such a garden are memorable experiences and these plants can stand the abuse.

The low-growing thymes are the best herbs for greening the spaces between stones and flagstones since they can be trodden repeatedly with little ill effect. For really long paths, choose thymes without too much aroma—the smell of crushed thyme can be overwhelming.

If you love birds, beware of the fatal attraction a couple of these herbs have for cats!

Companion Plants: See individual herbs.

AGASTACHE (ah-gas-*tah*-chee) **foeniculum**
Anise Hyssop, Blue Giant Hyssop, Fennel Giant Hyssop, Fragrant Giant Hyssop   Zones 4-9
Also known as licorice mint, this is an upright herb 3 to 4 feet tall with 4- to 5-inch-long clusters of blossoms at branch tips—all redolent of anise. The flowers bloom from early summer to mid-fall, cornucopias of nectar coveted by bees who process it into a light, fragrant honey. The coarsely toothed, oval leaves are dark green with whitish undersides. Native Americans steeped the leaves to make tea and they still are used fresh or dried as culinary seasoning and in potpourri. Birds prize the seeds. For the back of the border.

Culture: Blooms the same year from seed. Sow seeds in early spring where the plants are to grow or set out container plants in moderately full sun in well-drained, light, sandy soil. Cut back after flowering. Divide the roots in spring or autumn. Maintain moisture. It will self-sow and can be a slight pest.

Nepeta mussinii, massed catmint, becomes a sea of lavender. It is a sprawling plant with aromatic foliage that blooms from late spring to late summer. (Viette)

GALIUM   odoratum, Woodruff, Sweet Woodruff. The shiny star-shaped leaves are fragrant when dry and, in spring, dainty white flowers are arranged in layers along the stems. A neat plant about 6 to 12 inches high and a fine decorative ground cover under woodland shrubs and roses, charming with forget-me-nots. Longtime favorite of herbalists for flavoring May wine, liqueurs, and for garnishing pastry and desserts. Dried, it acts as a fixative for dried perfumes and potpourris—the aroma invokes vanilla. For culture, see list 76, Fragrant Herbs for Drying and Potpourri.

HYSSOPUS (*hi*-suh-puss) **officinalis**
Hyssop   Zones 2-10
Nearly evergreen, pretty subshrub 8 to 16 inches tall that has a mass of small, hairy, elongated, dark green leaves and, in late summer, blue, white, or pink flowers in whorls around the flower stems. Its pungent, rather bitter aroma

of camphor-mint still is valued in perfumery and as a flavoring agent in bitters and liqueurs. Clippings are used as fragrant strewing herbs, and the leaves and flowers are placed in potpourri. Hyssop can be sheared to make a low hedge for knot gardens, parterres, and topiary. Attractive with thymes such as 'Orange Balsam' and 'Argenteus'.

Culture: In early spring, set out container plants or sow seeds where they are to grow in full sun, in well-drained, ordinary garden soil with lime added. Dry, rocky soil is best. Replace the plants every 4 or 5 years.

LAVANDULA   angustifolia 'Hidcote',
'Munstead', English Lavender. Two colorful fragrant lavenders from a modest, sprawling, silver-leaved woody species whose every part is perfumed. Pretty in containers and delightful as low foundation plants for flower borders and herb gardens in dry, sunny places. North of Zone 5 they'll need winter protection. There should be at least one in every garden! See list 76, Fragrant Herbs for Drying and Potpourri.

MENTHA (*menth*-uh) Mint
The mints are upright or sprawling herbs 12 to 36 inches tall with extremely aromatic, crinkly green leaves (hairy in some species) that are pungent when brushed against, in bouquets, and even when dried. In summer, fuzzy, mint-scented, purplish, white, pink, mauve, or lilac flower spikes appear. The dried leaves have medicinal value, are steeped for *digestif* teas, and are used to decorate and flavor desserts and confections; they are also used in Middle Eastern and Indian foods, and in potpourris. Allowed to fall on garden walks, straggly branches become a carpet of magical fragrance. Bees graze them diligently.

Culture: Hybrid mints such as peppermint do not come true from seed; preserve the best plants by rooting cuttings in spring or planting root divisions in early spring or late summer. The big-leaved mints need watering when planted but later are fairly drought-resistant and hardy. All flourish in full sun or bright shade in well-drained soil

preferably in the slightly acid range. Unless ground cover is the goal, grow invasive species in containers or poor or clayey soil. Replant every 4 years with a topdressing of composted manure, and mulch.

M. aquatica Water Mint, Bergamot Mint
Zones 4-9
Aromatic lavender-scented mint, 36 inches tall, with hairy leaves, purple flowers, and a mild aroma of bergamot. Used in perfumes and sachets, potpourris and scented pillows. 'Crispa' is a curly leaved variety found naturally on wet soils, streambanks, drainage ditches.

M. arvensis var. **piperescens** Japanese Mint
Zones 4-9
Fast-spreading mint about 24 inches high with a strong smell of menthol. Thrives in moisture and bears small purplish flowers in whorls around the stems. Used to spice drinks and in commerce.

M. × piperita Peppermint   Zones 4-9
Spreading perennial from 12 to 24 inches tall, with a peppery mint flavor, a dark purple or chocolate tinge and purple flowers, usually in summer. Widely used in candies, gums, soft drinks, desserts, liqueurs, and for herbal teas and potpourri. Cut back often.

Herb foliage and flowers provide fragrant fillers for bouquets.
TOP Hyssop, *Hyssopus officinalis*. (Harper)
ABOVE Luxuriant foliage of fern-leaf tansy, *Tanacetum vulgare* variety *crispum*. The species is used to scent potpourris. In flower is *Ballota nigra*, Black Horehound; in the lower right corner, decorative foliage of Bear's-breech, *Acanthus balcanicus*. (McDonald)
RIGHT Anise Hyssop, *Agastache foeniculum*, attracts bees and butterflies. (Harper)

M. requienii Menthella, Corsican Mint, Creme-de-menthe Plant   Zones 8-9
A semievergreen, creeping mint under 3 inches high with very tiny leaves. In the right shade and with adequate moisture it rapidly grows into a solid ground cover, but it is a bit difficult even in a greenhouse. The flowers are lavender; the odor of pennyroyal.

M. spicata Spearmint   Zones 3-9
Ten to 24 inches high with small, pointed dainty leaves and a fine sweetish mint flavor, this is the best culinary herb—choice for teas, juleps, vinaigrette, lamb sauce, desserts (use tiny tips), jellies, soups, and Indian and Middle Eastern foods. If you grow only one mint, choose this.

M. suaveolens Pineapple Mint   Zones 3-9
Vigorous but fine upright mint with fresh-looking small-ish, white-splotched leaves. Completely white leaves occur and white flower spikes in summer double the effect. Ten to 18 inches high, the plant fairly sparkles along path edges and that's where the fragrance can best be experienced. Not invasive. See also list 73, Herbs with Colorful Foliage.

MONARDA didyma, Bee Balm, Oswego Tea.
Attractive whorls of shaggy scarlet petals surrounded by red-tinted bracts bloom through summer on stiff stems above neat plants 3 to 4 feet tall, with mint-bergamot scented, pointed bright green leaves. Tips of young shoots are used as garnishes for drinks and salads, and tea is made of the fresh or dried leaves. Attractive to hummingbirds, butterflies, and bees. See list 75, Herbs with Showy Flowers.

NEPETA (nep-et-uh)
Catmint
Aromatic herbs usually 12 to 24 inches tall with attractive, aromatic gray foliage beloved of cats. Some are handsome ornamentals. The small, tubular flowers are yellow, blue, lavender, or white, borne in summer at the tips of leafy branches. Good for edging, as ground cover, as filler for big planters, to underpin bare-legged shrubs such as roses, and in the wild garden.
   Culture: Plant root divisions any time or in spring sow seeds in well-drained soil, in full sun in cool regions, semi-sun farther south. Tolerates drought. Shear back after flowering to encourage repeat bloom. Under good conditions it self-sows profusely.

N. 'Blue Wonder'   Zones 3-9
Twelve to 18 inches high, when massed in the garden this is a sea of blue in spring and early summer. Shear after the first round of blooms to encourage new flowers.

N. cataria 'Citriodora' Lemon-scented Catnip   Zones 3-10
Somewhat straggly, 30-inch plant with aromatic silvery foliage and slender spikes of violet-spotted white florets. It is lemon-scented and more appealing than the species, which is the one cats love best.

N. × faassenii Persian Ground Ivy   Zones 4-8
Lovely upright, gray-green herb from 12 to 15 inches tall, with strongly aromatic foliage and fuzzy spikes of deep or pale lavender-blue flowers all summer. Cut back after flowering for a second season of bloom.

N. mussinii   Zones 3-9
Sprawling plant with aromatic foliage and lavender-blue spires of flowers from late spring to late summer.

ROSMARINUS officinalis, Rosemary.
Shrubby, from 2 to 4 feet tall, strongly scented of pine and nutmeg with needlelike, glossy evergreen leaves usually dark green with white undersides and sometimes yellow-striped. Rather like a heather, the foliage shows off the mostly blue, white, or pink florets along the stems. The warm, piny, somewhat bitter taste is used in Italian and Mediterranean cooking, and the dried needles often appear in potpourris. An age-old symbol of remembrance, and beloved of bees, rosemary is a good bonsai, pot plant, or specimen to place near entrances, windows, and garden seats where the fragrance will be experienced. Fine as a small hedge and with heathers, lavender, rue, savory, and oregano. R. o. 'Arp' is hardy to New Jersey; R. o. 'Prostratus' in southern California; this rosemary prefers neutral-range soil. For culture see list 77, Popular Culinary Herbs.

SALVIA elegans, Pineapple-scented Sage.
Shrubby, branching plant from 3 to 4 feet tall, with light green leaves deliciously scented of pineapple. Slender, velvety red flowers about an inch long and beloved of hummingbirds emerge just before frost. Pruning forces bushiness. Nice with bee balm, anise, hyssop, catnip, ferverfew, horehound, tansy, yarrow, and other sages. Also fragrant is the scarce S. dorisiana, peach-scented sage, which bears attractive spikes of pink flowers and has thick, fuzzy, heart-shaped leaves. For culture, see list 41, Salvia.

SANTOLINA chamaecyparissus 'Nana', Lavender Cotton. Dwarf to 14 inches, of the multibranched evergreen, shrubby species. The foliage is white-woolly underneath and silvery in moonlight; whiter in dry conditions, sandy soil, and full sun. The small, bright yellow flowers stand well above the foliage in late spring and summer. Dried, the sharp scent lasts (it doesn't smell of lavender); a valuable herb for moth bags and wreaths. For culture, see also list 73, Herbs with Colorful Foliage.

SATUREJA hortensis, Summer Savory, a slender annual 12 to 18 inches high, is more pungent than the perennial winter savory, though less desirable as a landscape plant. The tiny leaves are narrow and the flowers are pink, lavender, or white, borne in spikes with just a few widely spaced flowers. S. montana, Winter Savory, is crisp and fresh when it is in full bloom, with whitish flowers arrayed against a mass of fine, shiny dark green leaves. Many varieties and subspecies are available. See list 77, Popular Culinary Herbs.

TANACETUM (tan-uh-seet-um) vulgare 'Crispum' (syn. Chrysanthemum vulgare 'Crispum')
Fern-leaf Tansy   Zones 3-9
The colonists established the species by their front doors so the strong, sharp aroma could repel insects; it also served their medicinal purposes (the leaves and stems are toxic). It is used today to scent potpourris and winter arrangements. 'Crispum', 24 to 36 inches tall, has very lacy leaves and buttonlike, bright yellow flowers in flat-topped clusters in summer.

Culture: Plant root divisions in spring in full sun or semishade, in ordinary well-drained soil. Tolerates drought.

THYMUS (tye-muss)
Thyme
The thymes recommended are low, attractive, evergreen herbs with trailing branches and tiny leaves that release a "clean" aromatic scent when crushed. They are related to mints; prostrate or 6 to 10 inches high, durable, often fast-spreadingl delightful when surging over rock walls, edging containers, between stepping-stones, and as specimens in rock gardens. These species are tough enough to thrive in crevices in stone walks and walls and to carpet rocky slopes. In summer there are clusters of a few florets each in pale pink, white, and lilac. Most thymes have some aroma to impart but the best for cooking is T. vulgaris and its varieties.
   Culture: Set out root divisions in early spring in full sun, in very well-drained, ordinary soil. Semi-sun is suitable, particularly in the South. Tolerates considerable drought and abuse. The stems of old thyme plants eventually get dry and wiry; shear mercilessly in early spring.

T. 'Argenteus'   Zones 3-9
Has silver-variegated leaves and is the more colorful from a distance. The leaves are less scented but very decorative.

T. × citriodorus Lemon Thyme   Zones 3-9
Ornamental little plant to 8 inches high, with shiny leaves and wiry stems, that smells of lemon-mint-thyme. 'Aureus' has gold-variegated leaves.

T. herba-barona Caraway Thyme   Zones 4-9
The fragrance of the crushed leaves is wonderfully rich in caraway. A hardy ornamental with small dark green leaves in a low trailing mat that covers itself with broad clusters of lavender-purple flowers in summer. Fast spreading.

T. praecox subsp. **arcticus** Mother-of-thyme   Zones 3-9
A creeping thyme to 4 inches high that stands a lot of abuse, choice for walkways. 'Albus' is white-flowered, 'Coccineus' is a good-looking crimson, and 'Splendens' is red. 'Lanuginosus' is a dainty, mat-forming creeper barely ½ inch high that bears a few pale pink-white flowers in the leaf axils and is perfect for between flagstones. 'Mayfair' and 'Pink Chintz' are similar.

T. vulgaris Garden Thyme, Common Thyme   Zones 4-9
This is the delicious, strongly scented cooking thyme, a small upright bush that is slender when young, but gradually billows out and over walls and containers. 'Orange Balsam' has a hint of orange. The best cooking thymes smell rather like dried thyme, not quite lemony or balsamic. Choose by smell, carefully, and keep the plantings of a good thyme renewed.

T. 'Wedgwood English'   Zones 4-9
An excellent taller thyme.

SOURCE: JANET WALKER IS CURATOR OF THE NATIONAL HERB GARDEN AT THE U.S. NATIONAL ARBORETUM, AND LECTURES AND WRITES ON HORTICULTURAL SUBJECTS.

75. *HERBS WITH SHOWY FLOWERS*

■ The great herbal gardens of the past were devoted to plants that seemed to have healing properties and to aromatic and scented species with flavor and fragrance. The showiness of flowers was very secondary. Recommended below are plants that combine the sharp scents and useful properties of herbs along with flowers colorful enough to brighten the whole herb border.

At the end of this section there's a list of herbs most of us think of as flowers but which are classified as herbs by horticulturists. Because of their herbal properties they belong in herb gardens, where they add great splashes of color to the sea of green.

Follow-on and companion plants: Roses and more roses are the best companions. See also individual herbs.

ACHILLEA millefolium, Yarrow, Millfoil. Large compact flat-topped clusters of yellow, white, pink, or red flowers above excellent ferny, long-lasting foliage. At its height in July, yarrow forms large clumps to 18 inches tall. Nice with valerian, foxglove, tansy, and elecampane. Showy plants include the red-rose 'Crimson Beauty', 'Fire King', and 'Red Beauty'; pink 'Cerise Queen', 'Rosea' 'Rubra'; 'Paprika', a superb German cultivar that is a spicy rose-red; 'Hoffmuny' has pale yellow flowers with pinkish overtones. See list 15, Perennials for Summer Sun.

ALCHEMILLA (al-kem-*mill*-uh)
Lady's-mantle
Mounds of scalloped gray-green leaves with sprays of tiny yellowish green flowers that stand above the leaves in late spring or early summer. Very effective foliage accent plant in a border, and a favorite old-fashioned herb believed to possess magical power. Nice companion to fennel, rue, sage, grasses such as blue fescue, and boxwood.

Culture: Optimum growth occurs where summers are cool and moist, but it also succeeds in hotter, drier regions. Sow fresh seeds in late summer in well-drained, humusy soil with some protection from hot afternoon sun. Maintain even moisture. Early spring is the time to divide and replant clumps.

A. alpina Alpine Lady's-mantle   Zones 3-7
Low, neat plant to 8 inches high, used in borders and rock gardens for the handsome, deeply divided silver-edged leaves. In spring there are sprays of small yellow-green flowers.

A. erythropoda Dwarf Lady's-mantle Zones 4-7
A choice low-growing, shade-tolerant plant for edging small borders or to tuck at the base of steps. Like *A. mollis* but in miniature, it is just 6 inches high. Especially attractive after rain, when drops of water are held on the edges of the leaf pleats.

A. mollis Lady's-mantle   Zones 4-7
A woodsy plant 12 inches high or taller for edging and massing in shaded gardens and under trees. This low-growing, wonderfully durable species has scalloped, silvery foliage that hold shimmering drops of rain after a shower. In spring, it bears sprays of tiny, chartreuse-yellow star-shaped flowers. Attractive edger or massed as ground cover.

A. vulgaris   Zones 3-8
The showy yellow flowers appear over a long season above a low clump of light green leaves 12 to 18 inches high.

ANGELICA (an-*jell*-ik-uh)   **archangelica**
      Zones 4-8
A stout and architectural herb 4 to 6 feet tall with dense, fist-sized, green-white flowers. The large green leaves are coarse and thin and have cut-edged leaflets. All parts of the plant are aromatic, with a flavor of anise. Leaf midribs are eaten like celery, and the leaf and flower stalk can be candied. Seeds, root, and stems are used to flavor desserts, syrups, and liqueurs and to scent potpourris. Nice backdrop for lavender, bee balm, iris, and perilla.

Culture: Set out root divisions or sow seeds in fall as soon as they have ripened, in sun or part shade, in well-drained, moist soil. Maintain moisture and remove the too-numerous volunteers.

CHRYSANTHEMUM   **parthenium**, Feverfew. Wonderful old-fashioned mum from 12 to 36 inches tall that bears masses of little 1-inch, daisylike, white or yellow button-type flowers with yellow centers in late summer. Dwarf forms are used for edging in the North, but not in the warm South. *C. coccineum*, Pyrethrum, Painted Daisy, has showy 3-inch red, pink, or white single or double daisylike flowers with yellow centers and rich green foliage. Choose dwarfs that need no support. Recommended are the pink 'Eileen May Robinson' and the double 'Pink Bouquet', and 'Crimson Giant', a cerise single-flowered type. For culture see list 23, Mum—Daisy.

FILIPENDULA (fil-i-*pen*-dew-luh)
Meadowsweet
Often sold as false spiraea, these are big architectural plants with bold foliage and in summer, soaring sprays of showy, sweetly scented small flowers that toss in the wind. For the back of the border or to group as specimens. Good in wet places and wild gardens. Nice in the border with fennel, Russian sage, foxglove, tansy, valerian, yarrow, or bee balm.

Culture: In spring or fall sow seeds or set out root divisions in full sun or partial shade in well-drained, alkaline, definitely moist soil. Maintain moisture. Cut to the ground in early spring.

F. palmata   Zones 3-8
Best garden species and smallish, to 36 inches. The pink flowers come up in early summer, last 2 or 3 weeks, and turn toward white as they mature. The foliage is bold and textural, and lasts all season if moisture is maintained.

F. rubra Queen-of-the-prairie   Zones 3-9
Very tall—6 to 8 feet or taller—with pink-peach flowers. 'Venusta' has deep pink flowers.

F. ulmaria Queen-of-the-meadow   Zones 2-9
Dense, showy sprays of sweetly scented, small white or cream flowers in summer above compound leaves that are coarse, thin, and dark green with white undersides on plants from 2 to 4 feet tall. The cut-edged leaflets resemble tiny elm leaves. Honey-sweet tea is made from the dried plant and the leaves are used as sweeteners. 'Aurea' has golden yellow foliage. Remove volunteer seedlings—they revert to green. 'Flore Plena' is a creamy double-flowered white from 3 to 4 feet tall.

HYSSOPUS   officinalis, Hyssop. Nearly evergreen, this pretty subshrub 8 to 16 inches tall has a mass of small, hairy, elongated, dark green leaves and, in late summer, blue, white, or pink flowers in whorls around the flower stems. Clippings with their pungent, rather bitter aroma of camphor-mint have been used as fragrant strewing herbs, and the leaves and flowers in potpourris. It can be sheared to make a low hedge for knot gardens, parterres, and topiary. Good with thymes such as 'Orange Balsam' and 'Argenteus'. For culture, see list 74, Herbs with Fragrant Foliage.

LAVANDULA   stoechas, Spanish Lavender, French Lavender. Tender evergreen lavender cultivated for perfumery whose flowers are showier than English lavender; deep purple backed by rosy bracts on stems that stand well above the silver-gray foliage. Pretty as a pot plant. See list 76, Fragrant Herbs for Drying and Potpourri.

MONARDA (mon-*nard*-uh)   **didyma**
Bee Balm, Oswego Tea   Zones 4-9
Attractive whorls of shaggy scarlet petals surrounded by red-tinted bracts bloom through summer on stiff stems above neat plants from 3 to 4 feet tall, with mint-bergamot scented, pointed bright green leaves. Tips of young shoots are used as garnishes for drinks and salads, and tea is made of fresh or dried leaves. Nice with chamomile and lemon balm; attractive to hummingbirds, butterflies, and bees. Among bee balms ranging through shades of cerise to red, white, and violet, 'Croftway Pink' is notable. Also recommended are 'Adam', clear red; 'Cambridge Scarlet', red-crimson; 'Mahogany', deep Indian red; and 'Snow White', a creamy white.

Culture: Set out container plants or root divisions in spring or autumn in well-drained, humusy soil with a pH of 5.0 to 6.5. In moist, slightly shaded situations, bee balm spreads and may need restraining, but it blooms well in direct sun, especially in cooler regions. Deadheading lengthens bloom time.

NEPETA   × faassenii, Persian Ground Ivy. Lovely, upright, gray-green herb from 12 to 15 inches tall with strongly aromatic foliage and fuzzy spikes of deep or pale lavender-blue flowers all summer. Cut back after flowering for a second season of bloom. Recommended is 'Six Hills Giant', 36 inches tall, which has gray foliage under a haze of blue flowers. The flowers of *N. mussinii*, a sprawling species, are lavender-blue from late spring to late summer. For culture, see list 74, Herbs with Fragrant Foliage.

Fragrant white Chinese Chives, *Allium tuberosum*, brighten the herbal greens of a knot garden. (McDonald)

Herbs with very showy flowers:

ABOVE Chives, *Allium schoenoprasm*, blooms all season. (Viette)

TOP, RIGHT Queen-of-the-prairie, *Filipendula rubra* 'Venusta'. (Viette)

RIGHT Bee balm, *Monarda didyma* 'Mrs. Perry'. The pointed bright green leaves are mint-bergamot scented. (Viette)

FACING PAGE 'Coronation Gold' Yarrow, *Achillea millefolium*. At its height in July, it is shown growing with *Artemisia* 'Silver King.' (Viette)

ORIGANUM 'Kent Beauty', Oregano. Grow this oregano for its very pretty summer blooms, short spikes of pale pink flowers backed by dark pink bracts. The leaves are aromatic. For culture see list 77, Popular Culinary Herbs.

SALVIA leucantha, Mexican Bush Sage. A robust tender perennial from 3 to 4 feet tall with fragrant velvety leaves, it is grown as an annual in the North for its sheer beauty and regal stature. In late summer through frosts, it covers itself with lavender flowers that have white corollas. For culture, see list 41. *Salvia.*

SYMPHYTUM × uplandicum. This is an un-branched species of this big herb, from 2 to 4 feet tall, with thick rootstocks and large, soft, handsome, dark green basal leaves; grown for historical interest. In summer, lilac-blue flower clusters appear on one side of stems that curve under their weight. Nice in wild gardens or at the back of a large border. *S.* × *rubrum* is known for its showy flowers. For culture, see list 73, Herbs with Colorful Foliage.

THYMUS praecox subsp. arcticus, Mother-of-thyme. The thymes are mostly low, attractive, evergreen herbs with trailing branches and tiny leaves that release an intense "clean" aromatic scent when crushed. This is a creeping thyme to 4 inches high that stands a lot of abuse; it is choice for walkways. 'Coccineus' is a good-looking crimson. For culture, see list 74, Herbs with Fragrant Foliage.

MORE HERBS WITH SHOWY FLOWERS

The following herb garden plants also have pretty flowers.

ALLIUM tuberosum, Chinese Chives, Garlic Chives, Oriental Garlic, see list 3, Spring, Large-flowered Bulbs.

ARMERIA maritima, 'Alba', 'Bloodstone', 'Brilliant', 'Corsica,' 'Dusseldorf Pride', 'Laucheana', and 'Vindictive'; see list 13, Spring Perennials for Sun.

CALENDULA officinalis, Pot Marigold, 'Bon Bon', 'Fiesta Gitana', 'Geisha Girl', 'Indian Song', 'Kablouna', 'Mandarin', and 'Pacific Beauty'; see list 33, Annuals for Fall.

CATHARANTHUS roseus, Rose-Periwinkle, Madagascar Periwinkle, Carpet series, Little series, 'Morning Mist', 'Pink Carousel', 'Polka Dot', and 'Snowflakes'; see list 60, Urban Conditions.

CENTAUREA cyanus, Cornflower, Bachelor's-button, Bluebottle, 'Blue Boy', 'Blue Diadem', 'Pinkie', 'Polka Dot Mixed', and 'Snowman'; see list 34, Annuals That Self-sow.

CENTRANTHUS ruber, Red Valerian, Jupiter's-beard, Fox's-brush, 'Alba', 'Atrococcineus', and 'Roseus'; see list 18, Perennials for the South.

COLCHICUM autumnale, Autumn Crocus, Fall Crocus, Meadow Saffron, Mysteria, Wonder Bulb, var. **album**, var. **atrorubens**, 'Lilac Wonder', 'The Giant', 'Waterlily'; see list 5, Fall and Winter Bulbs.

CROCUS sativus, see list 5, Fall and Winter Bulbs.

DIANTHUS caryophyllus, Carnation, Clove Pink, Divine Flower, **plumarius**, Cottage Pink, Grass Pink; see list 70, The Fragrance Garden.

DIGITALIS purpurea, Foxglove, Excelsior Hybrids, 'Foxy', Shirley Hybrids, × **mertonensis**; see list 60, The Cottage Garden.

GOMPHRENA globosa, Globe Amaranth, 'Buddy', 'Tall Mixture', var. **rubra**, see list 72, To Dry for Winter Bouquets.

HEMEROCALLIS fulva, Orange Daylily, Tawny Daylily, Fulvous Daylily, **minor**, Dwarf Yellow Daylily; see list 24, Daylily.

PULMONARIA angustifolia, 'Azurea', 'Munstead Blue', 'Rubra', 'Salmon Glory'; see list 44, Flowering Ground Covers.

SOLIDAGO odora, Sweet Goldenrod; see list 64, The Meadow Garden.

STACHYS officinalis, Betony; see list 50, Foliage for Form and Texture.

TAGETES, Marigold; see list 39, Marigold.

TROPAEOLUM majus, Garden Nasturtium, Tall Nasturtium, Indian Cress, Jewel Mixed, 'Whirlybird'; see list 63, The Container Garden.

VIOLA odorata, Sweet Violet, 'Red Giant', 'Royal Robe', 'White Czar'; tricolor, Johnny-jump-up; see list 30, Violet—Pansy.

ZINNIA elegans, Zinnia, Youth-and-old-age; see list 42, Zinnia.

SOURCE: JANET WALKER IS CURATOR OF THE NATIONAL HERB GARDEN AT THE U.S. NATIONAL ARBORETUM, AND LECTURES AND WRITES ON HORTICULTURAL SUBJECTS.

76. FRAGRANT HERBS FOR DRYING AND POTPOURRIS

■ In long ago and far away times, homes were perfumed by grasses, flowers, and roots from the fields, woodlands, and herb garden. All through autumn and winter great bundles of fragrant herbs were brought indoors and hung from rafters to dry—in cottages as in the stillrooms of the great houses.

Drying herbs and flowers by hanging them upside down from rafters, and other airy places out of direct sun, remains a fine way to ready them for winter use. The method works especially well for tall plants being dried for winter arrangements. There are short cuts, of course—microwave drying and chemical processes—which may, or may not, be better. But the fragrant plants are the same as the ones our ancestors dried, and lavender is the best.

This list contains aromatic plants for dry perfumes as well as fragrant winter arrangments, wreaths, tussie-mussies, and nosegays.

Companion Plants: See individual herbs for suggestions, and list 72, To Dry for Winter Bouquets.

Lavender, rosemary, and dusty-miller in a garden of herbs with asters and verbena in bloom. (McDonald)

ACORUS (*ak*-or-us) calamus
Sweet Flag, Myrtle Flag, Calamus, Flagroot

Zones 4-10

The green, grassy, swordlike leaves to 36 inches tall are spicy and once were woven into fragrant dormats, wreaths, and baskets. Sweet flag is a good filler for low, poorly drained spots. When it grows in water, it bears small brown-green conelike flowers. The dried and ground rhizome is a fixative for potpourris and other dry perfumes and, candied, is considered a substituted for gingerroot. 'Variegatus' has rather striking vertical off-white stripes.

Culture: In early spring, set out root divisions in up to 6 inches of water in full or partial sun. Or, plant in the back of a mixed border in soil that is humusy and moist.

ALOYSIA (al-*loy*-see-uh) triphylla
Lemon Verbena   Zones 8-10

Finely textured, tender shrub from 4 to 5 feet tall, with lemon-scented, bright green leaves, indispensable in the herb garden. It blooms infrequently and late; the flowers are white, cream, or pinkish. Dried leaves are used in cooking and herbal teas, sachets, and potpourris. Where hardy, plant it as a centerpiece for a small garden or courtyard in a position where it can be brushed against to release the fragrance. Nice with geraniums, basils, and sages.

Culture: In warm regions, set the plant in full sun in well-drained, humusy soil and maintain moisture at the roots. Prune seasonal growth to keep the plant compact, especially when pot grown. In cool climates, grow it in a pot that can winter indoors in a cool room. Prune back pot-grown plants in mid-winter to 6 or 8 inches.

ARTEMISIA, Sagebrush, Wormwood.
This is the best group of perennials for silver or gray foliage. The small yellow or white flowers are nice when dried. Some species are good ground covers, others are strongly scented herbs. See list 73, Herbs with Colorful Foliage.

BALSAMITA (bal-sah-*mee*-tuh) major (syn. *Chrysanthemum majus*)
Costmary, Bible Leaf, Alecost   Zones 3-10

A clean, warm balsamlike scent of camphor, lemon, and mint comes from this dense, sprawling herb, 24 to 36 inches tall with coarse green leaves and insignificant flowers. Tips of branches are used to flavor food and for fragrance. The dried larger leaves are placed in linen closets and traditionally between the pages of Bibles and hymnals. Nice with bugleweed, sage, nasturtiums, borage, scented geraniums, lamb's-ear, and mints.

Culture: In early spring (fall in the South) set out root divisions in full sun or partial shade, in well-drained soil that is somewhat dry and very slightly acid, with a pH of 6.5.

GALIUM (*gay*-lee-um) odoratum
Woodruff, Sweet Woodruff   Zones 4-9

The shiny star-shaped leaves are fragrant when dry and in spring, dainty white flowers are arranged in layers along the stems. A neat plant about 6 to 12 inches high, it makes a fine decorative ground cover under woodland shrubs and roses, and is lovely with forget-me-nots. It is a longtime favorite of herbalists, and the leaves flavor May wine and liqueurs, and garnish pastries and desserts. Dried, it acts as a fixative for dried perfumes and potpourris—the aroma invokes vanilla. Sometimes still listed as *Asperula odorata*, its old name.

Culture: In early spring plant root divisions or seeds in semishade, in well drained, moist, humusy soil. Best in acid-range soil but adapts to moderately alkaline situations. Naturalizes readily (or rampantly) in light woodlands.

TOP, LEFT Woodruff, *Galium odoratum*, is used dried and as a flavoring. (Viette)

TOP, RIGHT Catmint, *Nepeta mussinii*, attracts cats, though not so irresistibly as catnip. (Viette)

ABOVE Woodruff in bloom. (Viette)

BOTTOM, RIGHT 'Hidcote', a showy English lavender, *Lavandula angustifolia*, is often planted with French lavender, (not shown), a less colorful species best for dried fragrance. (McDonald)

LAVANDULA (lav-*van*-dew-luh)
Lavender

Since classical times lavender has been a staple in perfumes and cosmetics; the dried flower buds, harvested just before they open, are still the best home garden source of fragrance for dry perfumes and potpourris. These evergreen shrubs or subshrubs are 24 to 36 inches tall with needlelike gray leaves, and every part of the plant is sweetly fragrant. In late spring, leafless shoots bear small spikes of tightly packed, small tubular flowers which. according to species and variety, range from deep purple and blue to lavender, pink, white, and gray-blue. Lavenders also are used in herbal cooking mixes and to flavor sweets. They are beautiful fillers for borders, knot gardens, and rock gardens, and especially enhance plantings of roses.

Culture: In spring, set out container plants in full sun in well-drained, somewhat dry soil, with a pH above 6 (they are very sensitive to pH). Does best on a gravelly slope; withstands heat and drought. Prune 1 to 2 inches from branch tips in early spring to encourage new growth, and mulch with sand.

L. angustifolia English Lavender   Zones 3-10
This is the best lavender for fragrance, either fresh or dried; a modest, sprawling plant whose florets bloom on upright stems. Suited for the front of the border or as a clipped hedge. Recommended are vivid ornamentals usually more tender to frost than the species and often less fragrant—try the scent before you buy. Dark lavender-blue 'Hidcote', (hardy to Zone 5) is 18 inches tall with deep purple flowers; 'Munstead' (hardy to Zone 5) is 12 inches tall and blooms early. Some other cultivars are: 'Rosea', 'Loddon Blue', 'Mitcham Gray', 'Summerland Supreme', 'Backhouse Purple', 'Bowles Early', 'Folgate', 'Gwendolyn Anley', 'Irene Doyle', and 'Twickel Purple'.

L. latifolia   Zones 6-9
Fully fragrant, has brighter, fuller lavender flowers through summer and pretty silver green foliage.

L. stoechas Spanish Lavender, French Lavender
Zones 7-10
Tender evergreen lavender cultivated for perfumery whose flowers are showier than those of English lavender—deep purple backed by rosy bracts on stems that stand well above the silver-gray foliage. Pretty as a pot plant.

MENTHA, Mint. The mints are upright or sprawling herbs 12 to 36 inches tall with extremely aromatic, crinkly green leaves (hairy in some species), pungent when brushed against, in bouquets, and even when dried. In summer, fuzzy mint-scented flower spikes appear—purplish, white, pink, mauve, or lilac. The dried leaves have medicinal value, are steeped for *digestif* teas, and used to decorate and flavor desserts and confections; they also appear in Middle Eastern and Indian foods, and in potpourris. Allowed to fall on garden walks, straggly branches become a carpet of magical fragrance. Bees graze them diligently. See list 74, Herbs with Fragrant Foliage, and list 77, Popular Culinary Herbs.

NEPETA **mussinii.** This is a sprawling catmint with aromatic foliage and lavender-blue spires of flowers from late spring to late summer. The dried leaves attract cats, though not so irresistibly as catnip. Also recommended is 'Blue Wonder', from 12 to 18 inches high, which is a sea of blue in spring and early summer. See list 74, Herbs with Fragrant Foliage.

ORIGANUM **vulgare** subsp. **hirtum,** Italian Oregano. Pretty and pungent fresh or dried herb for flavoring food and scenting potpourris. The 8- to 12-inch-high clumps sprawl, but individual branches lift panicles of faintly scented, more-or-less edible, whitish, pink, or lavender florets in summer. The golden leaves of *O. v.* 'Aureum' turn green in midsummer. 'Dr. Ietswaart' is a more ornamental form. For culture, see list 77, Popular Culinary Herbs.

PELARGONIUM, Geranium, scented-leaved types. Several species of geraniums have crinkly, sweet or spicily scented leaves. These plants flower sparsely compared to the big house geraniums but are treasured for foliage that has a strong aroma of nutmeg, mint, rose, lemon, or other fruits or flowers when brushed or crushed. The long-lasting fragrant oils win a place in potpourris, and in the past were used in jams, jellies, and sweets. Tender perennials, in cool regions they are grown as pot plants and wintered indoors. See the scented herbal geraniums on list 37, Geranium—Ivy Geranium.

ROSMARINUS **officinalis,** Rosemary. An evergreen, shrubby herb from 2 to 4 feet tall and strongly scented of pine and nutmeg. The foliage is needlelike and glossy, usually dark green with white undersides, sometimes yellow-striped. Rather like a heather, the leaves show off the mostly blue, white, or pink florets along the stems. Their warm, piny, somewhat bitter taste is used in Italian and Mediterranean dishes and the leaves are included dried in potpourris. An age-old symbol of remembrance and beloved of bees, rosemary is a good bonsai and pot plant and specimen to place near entrances, windows, and garden seats, where its fragrance will be experienced. Fine as a small hedge and with heathers, lavender, rue, savory, and oregano. R. o. 'Arp' is hardy to New Jersey; R. o. 'Prostratus' in southern California. For culture, see list 77, Popular Culinary Herbs.

THYMUS **vulgaris,** Garden Thyme, Common Thyme. The thymes are mostly low, attractive, evergreen herbs with trailing branches and tiny leaves that release an intense "clean" aroma when crushed. This species is the very fragrant cooking thyme, pungent when dried and choice for potpourri. 'Orange Balsam' has a hint of orange. Also recommended for drying is 'Wedgewood English', an excellent tall thyme. For culture, see list 74, Herbs for Fragrant Foliage.

SOURCE: JANET WALKER IS CURATOR OF THE NATIONAL HERB GARDEN AT THE U.S. NATIONAL ARBORETUM, AND LECTURES AND WRITES ON HORTICULTURAL SUBJECTS.

77. *POPULAR CULINARY HERBS*

■ **These dozen herbs are treasured for flavoring foods. They are low-growing, mostly green, and small enough to fit nicely into window boxes, container gardens, or flowering borders. Three of the best—parsley, thyme, and summer sage—develop attractive clumps that look at home with flowers, especially when edging walks or spilling over walls. The green basils, large or small, freshen any mixed flowering border, and the flowers and leaves of big purple basils like 'Purple Ruffles' are extremely fragrant, as wonderful in flower arrangements as in pesto sauce.**

If I had room for only a few herbs, I'd grow parsley, basil, some thymes, and a good mint. And lavender, *Lavandula:* it's the mystery ingredient in my favorite herbal mix for salad dressings, *Herbes de Provence,* and delightful in salads made with violet buds.

Companion Plants: Zonal geraniums, petunias, verbena, marigolds, and dwarf zinnias are good companions for these herbs. See also the individual herbs.**

ALLIUM (*al*-lee-um) **schoenoprasum**
Chives   Zones 3-10
Tufts of 10- to 12-inch-high thin, tubular, hollow leaves grow upright from this onion bulb; the leaves look like round grass, adding pretty linears to a rock garden, small container, or border. The patch is sprinkled liberally with fluffy little lavender balls ¾ to 1 inch in diameter. The flowers are edible if picked young. The onion-scented leaves may be harvested at will by taking some leaves down to the base, but don't shear the tops like grass. Chives are used chopped as an onion flavoring and garnish for salads, soups, and stews. Nice with thymes, pinks, sage, lavender, salad burnet, winter savory, yarrow, and lavender cotton. Ornamental onions are described on List 3, Spring, Large-flowered Bulbs.

Culture: Sow seeds, divide established clumps, or set out container plants in early spring in well-drained, rich, slightly acid soil; maintain moisture. Fertilize early and every month during the growing season.

ANETHUM (an-*neeth*-um) **graveolens**
Dill   Annual
A pretty plant 12 to 36 inches tall with hair-fine, ferny leaves resembling *Foeniculum,* with a strong taste of—dill (the flavor is hard to describe, perhaps like caraway plus anise?) Dill weed, as the foliage is called, is a major flavoring in northern European cuisine, excellent with potatoes, green beans, salads, soups, preserves, and pickles. The flowerheads are like fine green Queen-Anne's-lace, and are edible. Seeds are harvested and dried for winter seasoning. Dill is handsome toward the middle of any flowering border, or in containers with petunias and geraniums.

Culture: In early spring sow seeds where the plants are to grow, and repeat in 10 days to keep young dill coming. Transplants poorly and tends to be short-lived, especially in warm climates. If you buy container-grown seedlings, choose those one in individual containers and disturb the roots as little as possible during transplanting. Prefers soil in the somewhat acid range and full sun (partial shade in the warm South); maintain moisture.

A cook's herb garden with curly and flat parsley, dill, oregano, and chives. In the background, pot marigolds, *Calendula officinalis*. (McDonald)

ARTEMISIA **dracunculus 'Sativa'**, French Tarragon. This plain green artemisia is related to the silvery ornamental species but it is grown only as an herb. The flavor-scent is unique—sweet and haunting, employed to flavor good vinegars, dressings, French and southern European cuisines, and potpourris. About 24 inches tall, hardy only in Zones 5 to 9. For culture, see list 73, Herbs with Colorful Foliage.

FOENICULUM (fee-*nik*-yew-lum) **vulgare**
Fennel   Zones 4-9
This anise-scented perennial, from 4 to 6 feet tall, is grown as an annual, has a cloud of very fine leaves softer even than those of dill, and develops a bluish stem in rich soil. The yellow flowers resemble Queen-Anne's-lace. The warm, sweet flavor enhances fish, salads, and soups. The seeds are used in cheeses, meat and vegetable dishes, sweets and pastries, and have medicinal uses as well. Pretty screening for the back of the border. Nice with sage, tansy, foxglove, rue, and southernwood. The variety *azoricum*, Florence Fennel or Finocchio, is 24 inches tall and develops a thick, celery-like swelling at the base which is eaten raw or cooked.

Culture: Sow seeds where plants are to grow, in midspring, in full sun, in well-drained soil with a pH above 6.0. Maintain moisture. Cut back if the plant becomes unkempt.

MENTHA **spicata**. Spearmint. If you grow only one mint, choose this. It grows to 10 to 24 inches high and has small, dainty, pointed leaves and a fine sweetish mint flavor and aroma. This is the best culinary mint, choice for teas, juleps, vinaigrette, lamb sauce, desserts (use tiny stem tips), jellies, soups, and Indian and Middle Eastern foods. See 74, Herbs with Fragrant Foliage.

OCIMUM (**oss**-im-um) **basilicum**
Basil, Sweet Basil   Zones 9-10
Well-branched plants from 12 to 24 inches tall, with somewhat puckered fresh green leaves whose fragrance and flavor combine anise and hot cloves. The pinkish green flower spikes are insignificant and best removed. Basil is an essential herb with fresh tomatoes, in salads and Italian and Mediterranean dishes, and that famous sauce called pesto uses it by the cupful. The best flavors are found in forms with bright green leaves, but there are interesting ornamentals and flavor variations, including 'Camphor', 'Lemon', 'Cinnamon', and the purple-flowered 'Licorice'.

Dark 'Opal Basil' is a purple form with fair flavor. 'Purple Ruffles' is an 18-inch-high, very dark purple with pinkish flowers and a heady aroma. It is wonderful in flower arrangements toward the end of the summer when it has grown big, especially pretty with pink dahlias and cosmos. 'Silver Fox' is variegated.

'Crispum' is the very pungent lettuce-leaf basil and 'Minimum' is a somewhat sweeter, smaller-leaved bush basil. The very compact green forms have excellent flavor; 'Bush' and 'Spicy Globe', 8 inches high, are charming in window boxes and small parterres and may be sheared for topiary and edging in knot gardens.

Standard basils are attractive with oregano, sage, thyme, feverfew, and santolinas—the smaller forms are pretty tucked in among pink fibrous begonias.

Culture: Sow seeds in early spring and/or set out seedlings in late spring in well-drained, humusy, rich, somewhat acid soil and maintain moisture at all times. In spring, bunches of fresh cut green basil will root in water and may be planted. Pinch out branch tips and the edible flowers early and often to encourage branching and leaf production.

ORIGANUM (o-*rig*-an-um)
Marjoram, Oregano
Several forms are popularly called oregano. The plants form graceful arching or upright mats or clumps from 6 to 24 inches tall with small, bright green, sometimes woolly wedge-shaped leaves. These are Mediterranean herbs whose pungent aroma and flavor enhances salads, sliced tomatoes, tomato sauces, ratatouille, and potpourris. They are good basket plants, as ground cover, and edging beds, between rocks, and in retaining walls. Nice companions to basil, winter savory, sage, and thyme. The branches and flower spikes are charming as garnishes and in small bouquets and centerpieces.

Culture: Set out root divisions in early spring or fall, in full sun, in well-drained and slightly alkaline soil. Also succeeds in partial sun, especially in the South. Very durable and drought-resistant once established. Cut back in mid-spring.

O. 'Kent Beauty'   Zones 5-7
Purely ornamental. Must have good winter drainage. This is an oregano to grow for its summer bloom—short spikes of pale pink flowers backed by dark pink bracts. The leaves are aromatic. Very pretty.

O. majorana Sweet Marjoram,
Annual Marjoram   Tender Perennial
This 8-inch-high, delicious, indispensable herb is grown as an annual. It is the finest oregano for cooking. The tiny leaves are an attractive green, and more tender than *O. vulgare*, which is hardy. The flavor is more delicate. Sow seeds in early spring or set out seedlings.

O. vulgare subsp. **hirtum** Italian Oregano
                                                          Zones 6-10
Durable, decorative culinary herb. The 8- to 12-inch-high clumps sprawl, but individual branches lift panicles of faintly scented, edible, tiny, whitish, pink, or lavender florets in summer—fragrant in bouquets. The dainty, slightly hairy leaves have a biting flavor reminiscent of thyme that enhances the flavors and fragrances of other herbs and potpourris, Italian dishes, tomatoes, and salads. The golden leaves of *O. v.* 'Aureum' turn green in midsummer. 'Dr. Ietswaart' is a more ornamental form, but it is less vigorous and not reliably hardy in Zone 7 and north.

Outstanding herb combinations:
ABOVE Oregano, *Origanum vulgare* with rue, *Ruta grave-olens*. (Harper)
TOP, RIGHT Green and dark purple basil with parsley, marigolds and blue salvia. (Viette)
RIGHT Fennel, *Foeniculum vulgare* and purple basil. (McDonald)

PETROSELINUM (pet-roh-sel-*lye*-num)
crispum var. **crispum**
Parsley   Biennial, Zones 3-8

Primary green herb and garnish used in French and international cuisine, 8 to 18 inches tall, with many branches ending in curly or flat and divided, dark green leaves. Chopping releases the pungent and unique flavor for fresh use with tomatoes and salads; sprigs added to simmering stews, soups, baking fish, and sauteed meats tie together and enhance other flavors and give character. Small, crisp, edible green-yellow flowers appear the second year; keep them pinched out and the plant may last a second season. Harvest, mince, and freeze leaves before frost. This species is curly and easy to chop fine: the variety *neapolitanum* is the flatleaf pungent parsley of Italian cooking, preferred by some for flavor but not as attractive in the garden. Parsley is pretty with red or pink geraniums and in window boxes.

Culture: Sow seeds early every spring in full sun—or a bit less—in well-drained, humusy, somewhat neutral soil. Often found green and well under deep snow cover, but it is a biennial, and goes to seed rapidly the second year. Tolerant of some drought.

ROSMARINUS (ross-muh-*rye*-nus)
officinalis
Rosemary   Zones 7-9

An evergreen, shrubby herb from 2 to 4 feet tall, strongly scented of mint, pine, and nutmeg. The foliage is needle-like and glossy, usually dark green with white undersides, sometimes yellow-striped. Rather like a heather, the leaves show off the mostly blue, white, or pink florets along the stems. Their warm, minty-piny, somewhat bitter taste flavors Italian and Mediterranean cooking and the needles are dried and added to potpourris. An age-old symbol of remembrance and beloved of bees, it is a good bonsai and pot plant and specimen to place near entrances, windows, and garden seats where its fragrance will be enjoyed. Fine as a small hedge and with heathers, lavender, rue, savory, and oregano. *R. o.* 'Arp' is hardy to New Jersey; *R. o.* 'Prostratus' in southern California.

Other recommendations include: var. *angustifolius* 'Benenden Blue', with handsome blue flowers; low-growing 'Prostratus' in Zone 8 and southern California, which roots readily and is used as ground cover, is veiled in winter with ethereal light blue blooms; 'Lockwood de Forest' has brighter leaves and bluer flowers; 'Kenneth Prostrate' and 'Huntington Carpet' are superior; 'Golden Prostrate' is variegated; the upright *rigidus* 'Tuscan Blue' has bright green leaves and violet-blue flowers. Pink-flowered forms are 'Majorca Pink' and 'Pinkie'.

Culture: Plant rooted cuttings in early spring in full sun. In the North, rosemary is grown as a pot plant, summered outdoors, wintered indoors on a bright, cool windowsill. Like many familiar herbs, it is a Mediterranean native that thrives in very well drained, neutral, sandy, somewhat dry soils and withstands considerable heat. But be sure to water when it is dry.

SALVIA officinalis, Sage.
This is the best-known culinary sage, an erect subshrub to 24 inches tall with violet, blue, or white flower spikes in summer and downy, sharply aromatic gray-green foliage. It should not be banished to the herb garden for it is attractive with perennials, and a good edger and ground cover. Look for new types with variegated leaves. Particularly pretty is the little *S. o.* 'Tricolor', from 6 to 10 inches high, whose leaves are red, pink, gray, cream, and purple. The gray leaves of the often-seen 'Icterina' are variegated with gold. These are less hardy than the species. In warm California a handsome gray plant, *S. clevelandii,* Blue Salvia, is often used as a substitute for *S. officinalis* in cooking. For culture, see list 41, *Salvia.*

SATUREJA (sat-yew-*reej*-uh)
Savory

These very fragrant herbs are grown for seasoning, but they are decorative enough to use as edgers and as specimens in rock gardens and containers. The compact plants have dark green, glossy foliage covered with dainty pink to white flowers in summer. Variously described as spicy, peppery, oregano-like, resinous, or like camphored honey—the aroma, no doubt, is a paradox to moths. Used to flavor liqueurs, salami, sausages, and bean dishes, to soothe bee stings, and medicinally. Nice with hyssop, germander, boxwood, bayberry, and miniature roses.

Culture: Set out root divisions or seedlings in early spring in full sun in limy, well-drained, rocky soil. Tolerates considerable drought.

S. hortensis Summer Savory   Annual
Slender annual to 12 inches high and superior for culinary purposes to the perennial winter savory, though less desirable as a landscape plant. The tiny leaves are narrow and the flowers are pink, lavender, or white, borne in spikes with just a few widely spaced flowers. In early spring seeds can be sown where the plants are to grow, but germination is slow; seedlings started indoors are easier to establish.

S. montana Winter Savory   Zones 4-9
Delightful in full bloom with its whitish flowers arrayed against a mass of fine, shiny dark green leaves. Many varieties and subspecies are available. Benefits from heavy pruning in early spring and a lighter once-over after flowering.

THYMUS vulgaris, Garden Thyme, Common
Thyme. The thymes are mostly low, attractive, evergreen herbs with trailing branches and tiny leaves that release an intense "clean" aromatic scent when crushed. They are related to mints; durable, often fast-spreading little plants rarely more than 6 to 10 inches high, delightful surging over walls, as edging in containers, between stepping-stones, and as specimens in rock gardens. This is the delicious cooking thyme, a small upright bush that is slender when young but gradually billows out and over walls and containers. 'Orange Balsam' has a hint of orange. Some excellent thymes are sold as *T. v.* 'English' and *T. v.* 'French'. The best cooking thymes smell rather like good commercial dried thyme, neither lemony nor balsamic. Once you find one just to your taste, never let it go! For culture see, list 74, Herbs with Fragrant Foliage.

SOURCE: JANET WALKER IS CURATOR OF THE NATIONAL HERB GARDEN AT THE U.S. NATIONAL ARBORETUM, AND LECTURES AND WRITES ON HORTICULTURAL SUBJECTS.

78. FLOWERS WITH VEGETABLES

. . . .

■ Here are colorful annual flowers to combine with vegetables in landscapes that rival flower gardens. These annuals and vegetables look good together and succeed in the same somewhat acid soil, full sun, and sustained moisture. The airy nature of one contrasts with the solid structures of the other to create dynamic balances that delight the eye and excite the palate.

Vegetables develop many different forms and foliage shapes and colors. To prevent a jumbled look, limit the range of flower colors in one bed. Some flowers reseed so well that they become weeds in some climates; examples are alyssum, forget-me-nots, cosmos, and calendulas. Avoid these in vegetable beds used for plants that need heavy thinning, such as carrots and beets.

For mixed gardens, choose colorful food plants. For instance, red-stemmed rhubarb chard is brilliant interplanted with 'Empress of India' nasturtiums, which are deep red and twine in around the bottoms of the plants. The edible nasturtium flowers and leaves may be harvested along with the chard. Tomatoes and peppers also have colorful fruit.

Plant cool-weather vegetables for late summer and fall—baby white and purple eggplant, variegated flowering cabbages, and kales.

When available, opt for the extraordinary; red rather than green romaine, Bibb, or oakleaf lettuce; red scallions instead of white ones; yellow and orange sweet peppers instead of red and green; scarlet or purple runner beans; violet broccoli. For summer squash, zucchini, choose the round 'Gourmet Globe' or yellow 'Gold Rush', 'Butterstick', and pattypan 'Sunburst', which all have controlled form and striking foliage—and are prettier with flowers than the standard squashes.

For containers, small and miniature vegetables are the best choices. For example, the beautiful radicchio is small; 'Tom Thumb' is a 4- to 6-inch heading lettuce; and there are baby cantaloupes and watermelons, dwarf peas and beans. A few bright radishes can be dropped into the garden almost anywhere in early spring and will be ready to harvest in 22 to 25 days.

Rapid growers like eggplants, tomatoes, and summer squash need 24 to 36 inches between plants. Plant spreading flowers such as *Lobelia erinus* (Edging Lobelia), alyssum, nasturtium, and multiflora petunias less than 12 inches from such vegetables. As the flowers spread they cover the soil with a living mulch and are most attractive spilling out from under or near the leaves of big plants. However, this cuts down air circulation and isn't a good technique where there are fungus problems.

Culture: Most vegetables need full sun all day. Position vegetables so they are not shaded by tall background flowers. Tall flowers are placed to the north in the bed, and shorter vegetables and flowers are placed to the south.

For root vegetables, sow both vegetable and flower seeds in drifts in a row no more than 36 inches wide. When the seedlings are thriving, transplant the flowers to the edges of the bed and tuck them into any holes left by seeds that didn't germinate. As the root vegetables are harvested they will leave holes, but nearby flowers will fill in.

Don't combine edibles with poisonous plants—children can make mistakes. Larkspur and foxgloves are toxic, and so are the fragrant old-fashioned flowers called sweet peas, *Lathyrus odoratus.*

. . . .

Outstanding vegetable and flower combinations:
TOP, LEFT Corn with a border of zinnias and marigolds.
(Creasy)
TOP, RIGHT Verbenas, begonias, tithonias, with corn,
squash, beans, peppers. (Creasy)
ABOVE Lettuce and nasturtiums. (Creasy)
RIGHT Peppers with marigolds. (Creasy)

Sorrel and zucchini with begonias, impatiens, dahlias, and nasturtiums. (Creasy)

VEGETABLES AND COMPANION FLOWERS

. . . .

Artichoke

In back, plant cleome and pink cosmos (Sensation strain 'Pinkie').

In front, grow eggplant and purple alyssum.

Beans, Bush Type

In back, plant tall red zinnias, ruby chard, and annual coreopsis (calliopsis).

In front, plant dwarf white, yellow, and red zinnias and sweet peppers or small yellow French marigolds.

Or, for a pink and blue theme, plant pink, lavender, and blue 'Crego' or Powder Puff series asters in back of the beans, and in front, ageratum or dwarf purple gomphrena and purple basil.

Beans, Pole Type

Intertwine red or white runner beans with cardinal vine. In front of the beans, grow tall red salvia, dwarf white dahlias, and red chard.

Or, intertwine snap beans with a few plants of morning-glories—but not in regions where it becomes a pest. In front plant blue salvia, white cosmos (Sensation strain 'Purity'), and ageratum.

Cabbage, Early

Pink and lavender 'Giant Imperial' stocks are nice behind early cabbage. Interplant flowering kale among the cabbage. In front, plant blue or white violets or a mixture of pastel pansies. For a warm color scheme, plant mixed calendulas in back of the cabbage; in front, grow orange, yellow, and red nasturtiums, or yellow and apricot pansies.

Cabbage, Summer and Fall

In back, plant pink cosmos (Sensation strain 'Pinkie').

In front, use blue, lavender, or white lobelia.

Another option: back the cabbage with tall 'Bonfire' red salvia, or mixed, tall cutting, or State Fair mixture zinnias. In front of the cabbage, plant white ivy geraniums or white lobelia.

Carrots

Interplant summer carrots with blue lobelia, low-spreading Gem series marigolds, or *Sanvitalia*.

Corn

In front, plant yellow and orange tithonias and sunflowers in mixed colors. In front of these, annual coreopsis (calliopsis) and gloriosa daisies can be interplanted with sweet and chili peppers.

For a red, white, and green garden, plant magenta *Amaranthus caudatus* and multicolored *A. tricolor* 'Joseph's Coat' or crimson 'Illumination' in front of the corn, and in front of these, a short border of white cosmos 'Purity' or shasta daisies and green chard.

Eggplant

Pink cosmos 'Pinkie' or purple, pink, and white tall zinnias and borage are pretty behind eggplant. Interplant purple basil among the eggplant. In front, plant purple alyssum, pink, or lavender single multiflora petunias, or ageratum.

Lettuces, Spring

Plant all colors of lettuce, and in back grow champagne-colored Bubbles series Iceland poppies, or nemesia. In front of spring lettuce, plant 'Pacific Giant' primroses, pansies, English daisies, or inexpensive spring-flowering specialty bulbs that will be discarded after flowering. See list 1, Early Spring, Specialty Bulbs.

In back of bronze spring lettuce, plant white stocks, or orange and yellow calendulas. In front, grow white candelabra-type primroses and white, blue, or copper-colored pansies.

Lettuce, Summer

Plant the green summer lettuces in semi-sun, and plant low-growing impatiens behind them. In front, plant lavender or white lobelia.

Low-growing red, white or coral impatiens are pretty behind bronze summer lettuce. Plant white or blue lobelias or orange Gem series marigolds in front.

Lettuce, Fall

Potted chrysanthemums are nice behind green fall lettuce. In front, plant small solid-color pansies in assorted colors.

Place white or copper chrysanthemums in back of bronze fall lettuce, with creamy white dwarf nasturtiums in front.

Peas, Bush Type

In back, grow stocks. In front, try white alyssum or pastel pansies.

Peppers

In back of peppers, you can plant Mexican zinnias and French marigolds in the Nugget or First Lady series. In front of the peppers, plant yellow or orange Gem series marigolds and dwarf bush basil.

Another very colorful combination is coreopsis in back of the peppers with red dianthus 'Bravo', or a mix of dianthus from the Charm series, or red verbena in front.

Yet another option is to back the peppers with dwarf feathered amaranth (*Celosia*) in mixed colors, and plant portulaca in mixed colors in front.

Swiss Chard, White

Tall red salvia and white cosmos 'Purity' are pretty behind red-stemmed Swiss chard. Nasturtiums in mixed colors are pretty in front.

Swiss Chard, Red

Another scheme places red and orange cosmos behind red-stemmed Swiss chard, and in front, Jewel or Gleam series mixed nasturtiums, or Thumbelina or Peter Pan series mixed dwarf zinnias.

Squash, Summer

Tall yellow or orange marigolds and blue salvia are handsome planted behind summer squash. In front, grow single blue multiflora petunias or white alyssum.

Or, plant pink cosmos 'Pinkie' in back of the squash and pink wax begonias in front.

Tomatoes, Intermediate

In back of tomatoes, plant cleome, or salmon, pink, and white hollyhocks. In front, grow red geraniums or red gomphrena, with single red multiflora petunias.

SOURCE: ROSALIND CREASY, A CALIFORNIA LANDSCAPE DESIGNER, IS THE AUTHOR OF THE COMPLETE BOOK OF EDIBLE LANDSCAPING AND COOKING FOR THE GARDEN.

APPENDIX

COMMON NAMES—A SMALL GLOSSARY

Names commonly used for plants are rarely common the world over, or even in a single country. Because they can vary from region to region, they are not as much help in locating plants as the scientific botanical names. These are given in Latin—genus, species, subspecies, variety, and form. You know more of them than you suppose—impatiens, begonia, petunia, salvia, zinnia, aster, astilbe, phlox, and iris, for example. With time, gardeners acquire the scientific names of the plants that interest them most. It's not an effort. It just happens.

The common names given in this book are often antiques inherited from England, and not all that many are used today. Here are some that we all still do use often.

The index that follows gives the scientific names for the plants: check the glossary of common names below to find the genus name, then turn to the index to find the genus and page(s) where the plant is discussed.

Aaron's Beard, *HYPERICUM calycinum*
Absinthe, *ARTEMISIA absinthium*
Adam's-needle, *YUCCA filamentosa*
African Marigold, *TAGETES erecta*
Anise Hyssop, *AGASTACHE foeniculum*
Annual Delphinium, *CONSOLIDA ambigua*
Annual Phlox, *PHLOX drummondii*
Autumn Crocus, *COLCHICUM autumnale*
Aztec Lily, *SPREKELIA formosissima*
Baby's-breath, *GYPSOPHILA paniculata*
Bachelor's-button, *CENTAUREA cyanus*
Balloon Flower, *PLATYCODON grandiflorus*
Balsam, *IMPATIENS balsimina*
Basil, *OCIMUM basilicum*
Basket-of-gold, *AURINIA saxatilis*
Bee Balm, *MONARDA didyma*
Belladonna Lily, *AMARYLLIS belladonna*
Bellflower, *CAMPANULA*
Bergamot, *MONARDA*
Betony, *STACHYS officinalis*
Bible Leaf, *BALSAMITA major* (syn. *Chrysanthemum majus*)
Black-eyed Susan, *RUDBECKIA hirta*
Black-eyed Susan Vine, *THUNBERGIA elata*
Blanket Flower, *GAILLARDIA*
Bleeding-heart, *DICENTRA spectabilis*
Bloodroot, *SANGUINARIA canadensis*
Bluebell, *CAMPANULA rotundifolia; Endymion; Mertensia; Pushkinia scilloides; Scilla*
Bluebottle, *CENTAUREA cyanus*
Blue False Indigo, *BAPTISIA australis*
Blue Flag, *IRIS versicolor*
Bluewings, *TORENIA fournieri*
Boston Fern, *NEPHROLEPIS exaltata* 'Bostoniensis'
Bugbane, *CIMICIFUGA*

Buttercup, *RANUNCULUS*
Butterfly Weed, *ASCLEPIAS tuberosa*
Calamus, *ACORUS calamus*
California Poppy, *ESCHSCHOLZIA californica*
Calla Lily, *ZANTEDESCHIA*
Candytuft, Perennial, *IBERIS sempervirens*
Canterbury-bells, *CAMPANULA medium*
Cardinal Flower, *LOBELIA cardinalis*
Carnation, *DIANTHUS caryophyllus*
Carnation, *DIANTHUS*
Carpet Bugle, *AJUGA repens*
Catmint, *NEPETA*
Catnip, *NEPETA cataria*
Checkered Lily, *FRITILLARIA meleagris*
Cheddar Pink, *DIANTHUS gratianopolitanus*
China Aster, *CALLISTEPHUS chinensis*
Chinese Chives, *ALLIUM tuberosum*
Chinese Lantern, *PHYSALIS alkekengi*
Chives, *ALLIUM schoenoprasum*
Christmas Rose, *HELLEBORUS niger*
Cigar Flower, *CUPHEA ignea*
Clove Pink, *DIANTHUS caryophyllus*
Columbine, *AQUILEGIA*
Coneflower, *RUDBECKIA; ECHINACEA*
Cornflower, *CENTAUREA cyanus*
Costmary, *BALSAMITA major* (syn. *Chrysanthemum majus*)
Cottage Pink, *DIANTHUS plumarius*
Coxcomb, *CELOSIA cristata*
Cranesbill, *GERANIUM*
Creeping Zinnia, *SANVITALIA procumbens*
Crown Imperial, *FRITILLARIA imperialis*
Daffodil Garlic, *ALLIUM neapolitanum*
Daisy, *CHRYSANTHEMUM* species
Daylily, *HEMEROCALLIS*

Dill, *ANETHUM graveolens*
Dusty-miller, *ARTEMISIA stellerana; Centauria cineraria; Lychnis coronaria*
Dutchman's-breeches, *DICENTRA cucullaria*
English Daisy, *BELLIS perennis*
Everlasting, *HELICHRYSUM*
Fall Crocus, *COLCHICUM autumnale*
Feather Reed Grass, *CALAMAGROSTIS × acutiflora*
Fennel, *FOENICULUM vulgare*
Fescue, *FESTUCA*
Feverfew, *CHRYSANTHEMUM parthenium*
Flax, *LINUM*
Flossflower, *AGERATUM*
Forget-me-not, *MYOSOTIS*
Four-o'clock, *MIRABILIS jalapa*
Foxglove, *DIGITALIS*
Foxtail Lily, *EREMURUS*
French Marigold, *TAGETES patula*
French Tarragon, *ARTEMISIA dracunculus*
Funkia, *HOSTA*
Garden Nasturtium, *TROPAEOLUM majus*
Garlic Chives, *ALLIUM tuberosum*
Gay-feather, *LIATRIS*
Geranium, *PELARGONIUM*
Germander, *TEUCRIUM*
Giant Feather Grass, *STIPA gigantea*
Giant Reed, *ARUNDO donax*
Globe Amaranth, *GOMPHRENA globosa*
Globe Thistle, *ECHINOPS*
Globeflower, *TROLLIUS chinensis*
Glory-of-the-snow, *CHIONODOXA*
Golden Marguerite, *ANTHEMIS tinctoria*
Goldenrod, *SOLIDAGO*
Grape Hyacinth, *MUSCARI*
Grass Pink, *DIANTHUS plumarius*
Hens-and-chickens, *SEMPERVIVUM*
Herb-of-grace, *RUTA graveolens*
Holly Fern, *CYRTOMIUM falcatum*
Honesty, *LUNARIA annua*
Hyssop, *HYSSOPUS officinalis*
Iceland Poppy, *PAPAVER nudicaule*
Indian Cress, *TROPAEOLUM majus*
Italian Oregano, *ORIGANUM vulgare* subsp. *hirtum*
Jack-in-the-pulpit, *ARISAEMA triphyllum*
Jacob's-ladder, *POLEMONIUM*
Japanese Holly Fern, *CYRTOMIUM falcatum*
Jerusalem Artichoke, *HELIANTHUS tuberosus*
Johnny-jump-up, *VIOLA tricolor*
Jonquil, *NARCISSUS*
Jupiter's-beard, *CENTRANTHUS ruber*
Kaffir Lily, *CLIVIA miniata*
Lady's-mantle, *ALCHEMILLA mollis*
Lady's-slipper, *CYPRIPEDIUM*
Lamb's-ears, *STACHYS byzantina*

Larkspur, *DELPHINIUM*
Lavender, *LAVANDULA*
Lavender Cotton, *SANTOLINA chamaecyparissus*
Lemon Verbena, *ALOYSIA triphylla*
Lenten Rose, *HELLEBORUS orientalis*
Lily Leek, *ALLIUM moly*
Lily-of-the-Nile, *AGAPANTHUS africanus*
Lily-of-the-valley, *CONVALLARIA*
Lilyturf, *LIRIOPE*
Love-in-a-mist, *NIGELLA damascena*
Madagascar Periwinkle, *CATHARANTHUS roseus*
Maidenhair Fern, *ADIANTUM pedatum*
Marguerite, *CHRYSANTHEMUM leucanthemum*
Marigold, *TAGETES*
Marjoram, *ORIGANUM vulgare*
Marjoram, *ORIGANUM*
Marsh Marigold, *CALTHA palustris*
Meadow Rue, *THALICTRUM*
Meadow Saffron, *COLCHICUM autumnale*
Meadowsweet, *FILIPENDULA*
Mexican Bush Sage, *SALVIA leucantha*
Michaelmas Daisy, *ASTER*
Mignonette, *RESEDA odorata*
Milkweed, Money Plant, *LUNARIA*
Mint, *MENTHA*
Morning-glory, *IPOMOEA*
Moss Rose, *PORTULACA grandiflora*
Mother-of-thyme, *THYMUS praeecox* subsp. *arcticus*
Mugwort, *ARTEMISIA*
Naked-lady Lily, *AMARYLLIS belladonna*
Nasturtium, *TROPAEOLUM*
Orange Daylily, *HEMEROCALLIS fulva*
Oregano, *ORIGANUM vulgare*
Organy, *ORIGANUM vulgare*
Origano, *ORIGANUM vulgare*
Ornamental Onion, *ALLIUM*
Ornamental Pepper, *CAPSICUM annuum*
Oswego Tea, *MONARDA didyma*
Oxeye Daisy, *CHRYSANTHEMUM leucanthemum*
Pampas Grass, *CORTADERIA selloana*
Pansy, *VIOLA × wittrockiana*
Parsley, *PETROSELINUM crispum* var. *crispum*
Passionflower, *PASSIFLORA*
Peppermint, *MENTHA × piperita*
Persian Ground Ivy, *NEPETA × faassenii*
Pineapple Mint, *MENTHA suavolens*
Pineapple Sage, *SALVIA elegans*
Pink, *DIANTHUS*
Pink Vinca, *CATHARANTHUS roseus*
Plantain Lily, *HOSTA*
Plumbago, *CERATOSTIGMA plumbaginoides*
Plume Poppy, *MACLEAYA cordata*
Pot Marigold, *CALENDULA officinalis*
Pot Marjoram, *ORIGANUM vulgare*

Primrose, *PRIMULA*
Pyrethrum, *CHRYSANTHEMUM coccineum*
Quaking Grass, *BRIZA media*
Quamash, *CAMASSIA quamash*
Queen-of-the-meadow, *FILIPENDULA ulmaria*
Queen-of-the-prairie, *FILIPENDULA rubra*
Rain Lily, *ZEPHYRANTHES*
Red-hot-poker, *KNIPHOFIA*
Red Valerian, *CENTRANTHUS ruber*
Rock Rose, *CISTUS*
Rose Periwinkle, *CATHARANTHUS roseus*
Rosemary, *ROSMARINUS officinalis*
Rue, *RUTA graveolens*
Sage, *ARTEMISIA*
Sage, *SALVIA*
Savory, *SATUREJA*
Sea-holly, *ERYNGIUM amethystinum*
Sea Lavender, *LIMONIUM*
Sedge, *CAREX*
Shasta Daisy, *CHRYSANTHEMUM* × *superbum*
Shield Fern, *POLYSTICHUM*
Shirley Poppy, *PAPAVER rhoeas* Shirley series
Signet Marigold, *TAGETES tenuifolia*
Silver Grass, *MISCANTHUS*
Silver Sage, *SALVIA argentea*
Snakeroot, *ASARUM canadense*
Snapdragon, *ANTIRRHINUM majus*
Snow-in-summer, *CERASTIUM tomentosum*
Snowdrop, *GALANTHUS*
Snowflake, *LEUCOJUM*
Solomon's-seal, *POLYGONATUM*
Southernwood, *ARTEMISIA abrotanum*
Spider Flower, *CLEOME hasslerana*
Spider Lily, *LYCORIS radiata*
Squill, *SCILLA*

Stock, *MATTHIOLA incana*
Stonecrop, *SEDUM*
Strawflower, *HELICHRYSUM bracteatum*
Striped Squill, *PUSCHKINIA scilloides* (syn. *libanotica*)
Summer Hyacinth, *GALTONIA candicans*
Sunflower, *HELIANTHUS*
Sweet Basil, *OCIMUM basilicum*
Sweet Flag, *ACORUS calamus*
Sweet Goldenrod, *SOLIDAGO odora*
Sweet Pea, *LATHYRUS odoratus*
Sweet Violet, *VIOLA odorata*
Sweet William, *DIANTHUS barbatus*
Sweet Woodruff, *GALIUM odoratum*
Switch Grass, *PANICUM virgatum*
Sword Fern, *NEPHROLEPIS*
Tarragon, *ARTEMISIA dracunculus*
Tawny Daylily, *HEMEROCALLIS fulva*
Tickseed, *COREOPSIS*
Thrift, *ARMERIA maritima*
Thyme, *THYMUS*
Tuberose, *POLIANTHES tuberosa*
Tufted Hair Grass, *DESCHAMPSIA caespitosa*
Tulip, *TULIPA*
Violet, *VIOLA*
Wallflower, *CHEIRANTHUS cheiri*
Water Flag, *IRIS pseudacorus* 'Variegata'
Wild Ginger, *ASARUM canadense*
Wild Marjoram, *ORIGANUM vulgare*
Windflower, *ANEMONE*
Winter Aconite, *ERANTHIS*
Woodruff, *GALIUM odoratum*
Wormwood, *ARTEMISIA*
Yarrow, *ACHILLEA millefolium*
Yellow Flag, *IRIS pseudacorus*
Yellow Iris, *IRIS pseudacorus*

SOURCES OF SEEDS AND PLANTS

There are hundreds of nurseries, large and small, that specialize in uncommon flowers. Hard-to-find plants also may be located through the American Horticultural Society's Gardener's Information Service. Mail-order sources also advertise in the Society's monthly publications, *The American Horticulturist*, both the color magazine and the news edition. And every few years, the Society publishes the *North American Horticulture Reference Guide*. The publications mentioned are member benefits, but the Society responds to requests from nonmembers.

You can track down uncommon flowers with the help of plant societies. Many maintain memberships in the Society and can be reached through AHS. Agents of the USDA Agricultural Extension Service offices located in state universities usually are familiar with the local nurseries specializing in uncommon plants.

The nurseries that follow are keyed to list 67, Rare and Choice, and are here at the request of Mary Ann and Fred McGourty, sources for that list.

1. Canyon Creek
   3527 Dry Creek Road
   Oroville, CA 95965

2. Carrol Gardens
   444 East Main Street
   P.O. Box 310
   Westminster, MD 21157

3. Crownsville Nursery
   P.O. Box 797
   Crownsville, MD 21032

4. Holbrook Farm & Nursery
   115 Lance Road
   P.O. Box 368
   Fletcher, NC 28732

4a. Hillside Gardens
   P.O. Box 614
   Norfolk, CT 06058
   (no mail order)

5. Viette Farm and Nursery
   Route 1, Box 16
   Fishersville, VA 22939

6. Wayside Gardens
   1 Garden Lane
   Hodges, SC 29695

7. Charles Klehm & Son Nursery
   Route 5, Box 197
   Penny Road
   South Barrington, IL 60010

8. Woodlanders Inc.
   1128 Calleton Avenue
   Aikin, SC 29801

9. Kurt Bluemel Inc.
   2740 Greene Lane
   Baldwin, MD 21013

10. Siskiyou Rare Plant Nursery
   2825 Cummings Road
   Medford, OR 97501

11. Rice Creek Nurseries
   1315 66 Avenue NE
   Minneapolis, MN 55432

12. We-Du Nurseries
   Route 5 Box 724
   Marion, NC 28752

The U.S.D.A. Plant Hardiness Zone Map

This map from the United States Department of Agriculture represents 11 different zones in North America and the annual minimum temperature for each zone. It is based on extensive research and reports from more than 14,000 meteorological stations over a 10-year period. It replaces the 1965 map from the United States Department of Agriculture and can be used in conjunction with the zone numbers given in the Flower Finder lists.

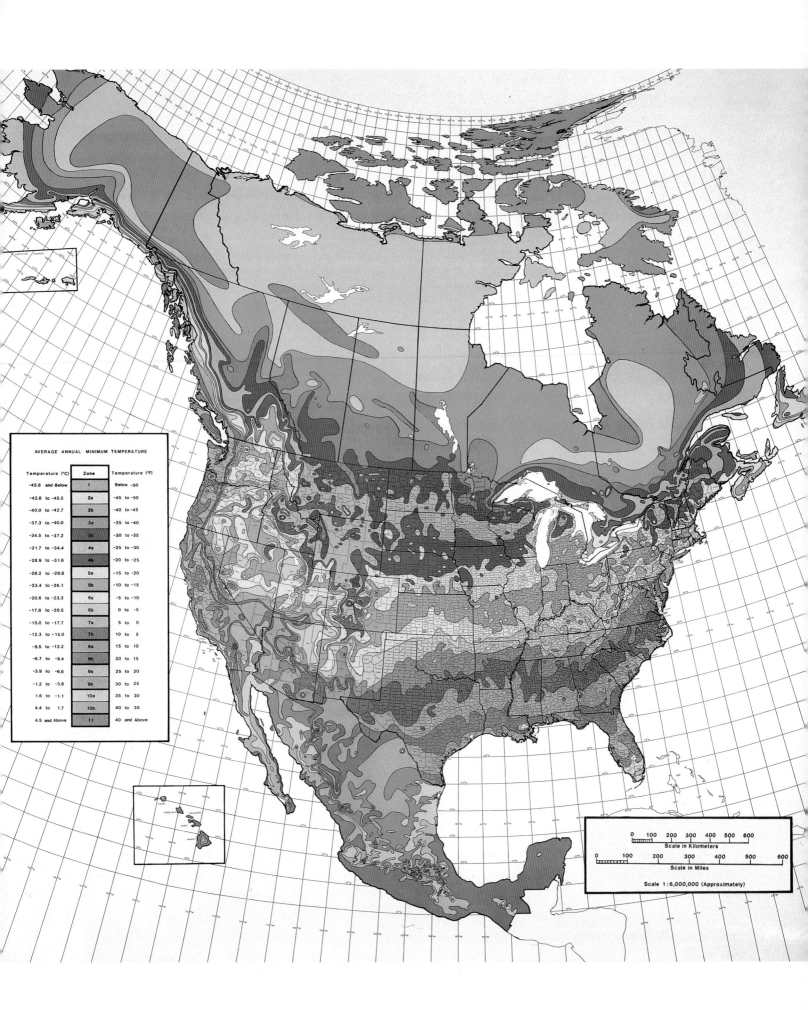

AVERAGE ANNUAL MINIMUM TEMPERATURE

Temperature (°C)	Zone	Temperature (°F)
-45.6 and Below	1	Below -50
-42.8 to -45.5	2a	-45 to -50
-40.0 to -42.7	2b	-40 to -45
-37.3 to -40.0	3a	-35 to -40
-34.5 to -37.2	3b	-30 to -35
-31.7 to -34.4	4a	-25 to -30
-28.9 to -31.6	4b	-20 to -25
-26.2 to -28.8	5a	-15 to -20
-23.4 to -26.1	5b	-10 to -15
-20.6 to -23.3	6a	-5 to -10
-17.8 to -20.5	6b	0 to -5
-15.0 to -17.7	7a	5 to 0
-12.3 to -15.0	7b	10 to 5
-9.5 to -12.2	8a	15 to 10
-6.7 to -9.4	8b	20 to 15
-3.9 to -6.6	9a	25 to 20
-1.2 to -3.8	9b	30 to 25
1.6 to -1.1	10a	35 to 30
4.4 to 1.7	10b	40 to 35
4.5 and Above	11	40 and Above

ALEUTIAN ISLANDS

KAUAI
HONOLULU
OAHU
KALAND
MAUI
HAWAII

0 100 200 300 400 500 600
Scale in Kilometers

0 100 200 300 400 500 600
Scale in Miles

Scale 1:6,000,000 (Approximately)

INDEX

This index contains all references found in the main heading and subheadings of the Flower Finder lists. It also includes the coding system developed by the American Association of Nurserymen. If readers use these codes when purchasing flowers at suppliers using them, they can be certain of getting the flowers described in the text. Codes appear in capital letters between parentheses.